Never Despair

Never Despair

SIXTY YEARS IN THE SERVICE OF THE JEWISH PEOPLE
AND THE CAUSE OF HUMAN RIGHTS

GERHART M. RIEGNER

Translated from the French by William Sayers

Ivan R. Dee

CHICAGO 2006

Published in Association with the United States Holocaust Memorial Museum

NEVER DESPAIR. Copyright © 1998 by Les Éditions du Cerf. English-language translation copyright © 2006 by Ivan R. Dee. All rights reserved, including the right to reproduce this book or portions thereof in any form. For information, address: Ivan R. Dee, Publisher, 1332 North Halsted Street, Chicago 60622. Manufactured in the United States of America and printed on acid-free paper.

www.ivanrdee.com

Published in association with the United States Holocaust Memorial Museum, 100 Raoul Wallenberg Place, S.W., Washington, D.C. 20024.

The assertions, arguments, and conclusions herein are those of the author. They do not necessarily reflect the opinions of the United States Holocaust Memorial Council or of the United States Holocaust Memorial Museum.

Library of Congress Cataloging-in-Publication Data:
Riegner, Gerhart
  [Ne jamais désespérer. English]
  Never despair : sixty years in the service of the Jewish people and the cause of human rights / Gerhart M. Riegner ; translated from the French by William Sayers.
     p. cm.
  "Published in association with the United States Holocaust Memorial Museum."
  Includes index.
  ISBN-13: 978-1-56663-696-4 (cloth : alk. paper)
  ISBN-10: 1-56663-696-5 (cloth : alk. paper)
  1. Riegner, Gerhart. 2. Jews—Germany—Biography. 3. World Jewish Congress—Officials and employees—Biography. 4. Jews—Social conditions—20th century. 5. Jews—Politics and government—20th century. 6. World War, 1939–1945—Jews—Rescue. 7. Holocaust, Jewish (1939–1945) 8. Jews—History—1945– 9. Judaism—Relations—Catholic Church. 10. Catholic Church—Relations—Judaism. I. United States Holocaust Memorial Museum. II. Title.
  DS135.G5R47613 2006
  305.892'40092—dc22   2006003855

Contents

	Acknowledgments	vii
	Preface	ix
1	Background and Family Origins	3
2	The Time of the Shoah and the "Riegner Telegram"	35
3	The Struggle for Human Rights	164
4	Our Relations with Christian Churches	234
5	Working for North African Jewry	354
6	Other International Activities	366
7	The Jewish Student Movement and International University Organizations	400
8	The World Jewish Congress	417
9	Into the New Millennium	434
	Index	443

Acknowledgments

THANKS ARE DUE the following individuals and institutions for their assistance in the preparation of the English-language edition of this work: Central Zionist Archives, Jerusalem; Mr. Benton M. Arnovitz, United States Holocaust Memorial Museum, Washington, D.C.; Dr. Brewster S. Chamberlin, Key West; Dr. Michael Fichter, Free University Berlin; Dr. Yaacov Lozowick, Yad Vashem, Jerusalem; Ms. Linda Mittel, New York City; Dr. Marion Neiss, Zentrum für Antisemitismus Forschung, Berlin; Dr. Gero Neugebauer, Free University Berlin; Dr. Kevin Profitt, American Jewish Archives, Cincinnati; Dr. Robert Rozett, Yad Vashem, Jerusalem; Ms. Barbara Tzoukermann, Jerusalem; Ms. Christine Watkins, Chicago; Dr. Gary Zola, American Jewish Archives, Cincinnati.

Preface

IN THESE MEMOIRS I have tried to give an account of my most important activities in the service of the Jewish people and of human rights. This book also
constitutes a personal history of the World Jewish Congress, with which I have
been associated for more than sixty years. At a time when the organization occupies a vital public position on the political scene, it seems that a presentation of its ideological foundation, its objectives, and its accomplishments will
be of benefit to the reader.

I have focused my account on objective problems and their development.
This approach, in keeping with my character, has perhaps led me at times to
give insufficient emphasis to the contribution of my collaborators and partners
to these tasks. I have always had the good fortune to be able to count on devoted collaborators and colleagues, inspired by idealism and faith in our cause.
Although I cannot name them all, my gratitude toward them is immense.

These memoirs began with a series of far-ranging, sustained conversations
with Léon Abramowicz, a Parisian journalist of Polish origin. He possessed a
great knowledge of Jewish history and the Shoah, and was deeply engaged in
Jewish cultural life. Over the course of several years I worked three days a
month with him, my other activities in practical terms preventing me from
devoting more time to this undertaking. In this fashion we drafted the greater
part of the first version of this work together.

Unfortunately Léon Abramowicz had serious health problems and finally
succumbed to illness. This delayed the editing of the work for a year and a
half. I can never sufficiently express the great debt of gratitude that I owe him.
His contribution to the elaboration of my work was an essential one and was
always made in harmonious and fruitful understanding. This comprehension

was sustained with his son, Emmanuel Abramowicz, who had the kindness to oversee the delicate work of transferring to Geneva all the manuscripts that had been keyed into the computer in Paris.

After the passing of Léon Abramowicz, I was happy to find an extremely efficient and collegial collaborator in the person of the Geneva journalist Jean-Paul Darmsteter, with whom I completed the entire text and who contributed a great deal to making it more accessible and lively. I express my deepest thanks for his attentive interest in and support of my work.

It remains for me to state the great debt of gratitude that I owe my two principal secretaries, Myra Becker and Ruthy Alcheh. Both of these close collaborators have provided incomparable support over decades. I honor their great competence, their faithfulness, their devotion that was never affected by my impatience, and their constant readiness and willingness—all qualities that have made my activity possible and without which this book too would not exist.

G. M. R.

Never Despair

[ONE]

Background and
Family Origins

I COME FROM a cultivated, middle-class Jewish family, of which there were so many in the German Empire before World War I, and in particular in the Weimar Republic. I belong to what is conventionally called the post-assimilationist generation. Our acculturation to German life had been a *fait accompli* for a long time. If we were conscious of our Jewishness, this was the result of a deliberate choice.

Let me speak first of my mother Agnes's family. My grandfather, Max Arnheim, was born in Magdeburg, my grandmother in Halle. Both came from profoundly German backgrounds in that their ancestors had been established there for several generations.

I had particularly close ties to my grandfather. A businessman of great personal modesty and absolute integrity, he had a deep sense of justice. Born in 1911, I was the first boy in the family. He had three daughters, and the elder two had both given birth to girls. My birth made him very proud, very happy. He spoiled me, played with me. Throughout his life he gave evidence of his love for me in numerous ways.

My grandmother was a Lewandowski. She was the daughter of a *hazzan*, a cantor, Jacob Lewandowski, and the niece of the famous Louis Lewandowski, who as choirmaster of the great Oranienburgerstrasse Synagogue in Berlin, had reformed the music played in synagogues in the nineteenth century. Thus I was related to the famous composer who had revolutionized modern Jewish liturgical music. This revolution was peaceful in every way, realized with

3

splendid melodies and sumptuous song. A variety of Lewandowski's compositions are still being performed today.

On my father Heinrich's side, family culture was even more thoroughly German. My paternal grandmother had been born in Neu-Brandenburg, my grandfather in Lower Silesia, in Namslau. For decades one of my great-uncles had a Jewish hotel in Breslau (now Wrocław); generations of Jews stayed there. While still a young man, my grandfather went to Berlin. His father had given him a few ducats and advised him to make a life for himself in the great city.

I heard Namslau spoken of only once in my life. One day, when arranging to have some purchases delivered, my mother gave her name to the saleswoman at one of a chain of food stores, Kaiser's Kaffee Geschäft: "Riegner? Are you from Namslau?" Astonished, my mother asked why. "I'm from Namslau myself, in Lower Silesia. In my town everyone is named Riegner." I never tried to learn anything more about it, even though this revelation made a strong impression on me. It must mean that in Namslau, whether Jews or not, many of the residents also bore my name.

Thus my family was soundly anchored in Jewish tradition, a situation to which my great-uncle Louis Lewandowski made a great contribution. In addition, his daughter Martha married Hermann Cohen (1842–1918), the neo-Kantian Jewish philosopher who created the so-called Marburg School of philosophy.

Cohen was one of the glories of the German Jewry of the era. He was also a Jewish thinker, celebrated for the work since published in English as *The Religion of Reason Out of the Sources of Judaism*. The book is also available in a French version, and a study of Cohen's Jewish philosophy has been published in the United States and in France. Cohen was a highly respected voice of German Jewry well beyond national borders, especially after the *Antisemitenstreit*, the Berlin quarrel over the movement against the Jews, a controversy born of the vehement article by Heinrich von Treitschke, published in 1879 in the *Preussische Jahrbücher*. This was an important journal, and Heinrich von Treitschke enjoyed the prestige of an eminent historian. The article in question violently attacked Jews. Here one first reads the terrible slogan "*Die Juden sind unser Unglück*" ("The Jews are our misfortune"), one that would later be regularly found in the Nazi weekly *Der Stürmer*, the fearsome anti-Semitic newspaper of sinister memory published by Julius Streicher. Thus, in reaction to these accusations, Hermann Cohen was one of the first and most ardent defenders of the Jews, the veritable spokesman of German Jewry.

Cohen had begun his studies in the rabbinical seminary in Breslau. His father had been a *melammed*, a teacher in a Jewish religious school. All this took place in central Germany. From this branch of my family I inherited a very developed sense of Judaism. On the philosophical level, my father was a neo-Kantian and very close to Cohen's ideas. Always cordial and close, our family relations were strengthened even more after 1912, the year Cohen left Marburg for Berlin. He taught courses at the School for Advanced Jewish Studies, the first institution to study Judaism from an academic perspective and one I would describe as influenced by positivism. This prestigious school, which also trained rabbis, was under the direction of exponents of what was then called the "science of Judaism."

Every Sunday we would go to dinner with my grandparents. With a subtle mixture of infinite kindness and great firmness, my grandmother presided over these family meals, which continued even after the death of her husband. Her cooking was marvelous. I still remember some of the dishes such as roast goose with red cabbage, or her deep dish apple pie. My mother and my younger sister, Marianne, in turn continued to use "Grandmother's recipes." The aromas still awaken innumerable memories in me.

After dinner we would go to the Cohens' for tea or coffee. There we met a great variety of persons, among whom were Russian Jews, disciples of Cohen who had come to study in Berlin. Thus there could be ten or twenty people surrounding Hermann Cohen, wanting to discuss all kinds of problems with him. I can still see him in his rocking chair, one of numerous such pieces of furniture spread around the house. Much later I was struck by the parallel with John F. Kennedy's chair.

Cohen was short, with a huge head surrounded by silvery hair. He had poor eyesight and wore large, blue-tinted glasses. He was extremely kindly disposed toward us children and liked to take part in our games. I still remember the evening when I saw him for the last time. It was in 1917 in the autumn, during the *Simhas Torah* (Rejoicing in the Law) holiday, at the synagogue in Fasanenstrasse. I was then a little boy of six. On this holiday there was a procession in the synagogue; all the Torah scrolls were carried about. Just behind the rabbi came Hermann Cohen, bearing a small Torah set in a wooden case. Seventy-six years old and visibly frail, he walked in the steps of the rabbi, with great dignity and the air of a biblical patriarch. In my eyes he personified the Jewish spirit. On the child that I was then, the impression was profound; it lived on within me and still does. The influence thus exerted on me went far beyond that of simple family relations; rich and fruitful as these were, they were as if transcended.

We were rarely alone at my grandparents'. Almost every Sunday we found the Goldschmidts there, the family of my mother's youngest sister. My aunt was the wife of a highly cultivated lawyer who was later called to important functions in the Prussian Ministry of Justice. They had a son and a daughter.

These meetings of the extended family contributed to the establishment of excellent relations between generations and to friendly ties within the younger generation, stimulating a real comradeship. It is worth noting that my uncle, while exercising his profession as lawyer, was associated—as was my father— with a socialist member of the Reichstag, Oskar Cohn, who was elected to parliament in 1912, during the reign of Wilhelm II. Toward the end of the 1920s, Oskar Cohn gave up his career as a German politician in order to devote himself entirely to Jewish affairs. He became increasingly sought after as a legal counsel for refugees from the countries of Eastern Europe. He was particularly engaged in relief activity on their behalf, which made him a natural candidate to become the leader of the Socialist Zionists (Poale Zion) on the Jewish community council in Berlin. After leaving Germany in 1933, he was a member of the Committee of Jewish Delegations (Comité des délégations juives, CDJ) in Paris, a predecessor of the World Jewish Congress, established in 1919 to represent the Jewish people at the Versailles peace conference. In this capacity he collaborated closely with Leon Motzkin and Nahum Goldmann, Zionist leaders and among the founders of the World Jewish Congress, which replaced the CDJ in 1936, both within the framework of the committee's work and in preparations for the first World Jewish Congress. Oskar Cohn would become co-author, with Motzkin, of the celebrated *Black Book* (*Das Schwarzbuch— Tatsachen und Dokumente: Die Lage der Juden in Deutschland 1933*) on the anti-Jewish policy of the Third Reich, published by the CDJ in 1934.

In general it is the children who distance themselves from the religious traditions of their parents. In our case, however, it was the children who brought their parents back toward the practice of Judaism. One day my older sister prompted my father to attend synagogue again by asking him, "How is it that unlike Mother you don't go?"

There we have an important phenomenon, and I remain very conscious of it today. It was we, the children, who insisted on celebrating the Jewish holidays, on having a *Seder*. I don't wish to claim that we were Orthodox, but we reintroduced a certain Jewishness into the family.

The German Judaism in which I grew up was then in a stage of evolution. In the main it retained a deep attachment to tradition and to family practices that were linked to religion. The relaxation of rules inherited from the past— as much by "Reform" Judaism as by "Neo-Orthodoxy"—certainly contributed to the reinvigoration of the communities. When some liberal Germans suggested to Jews that they give up their religion and their traditions if they wished to enjoy emancipation, the latter vigorously refused. They fought for their full civic rights along with the right to retain their Jewish identity, which was founded to a great extent on socio-historical and religious bases.

Nonetheless the communities experienced substantial losses—on the one hand through indifference, for many Jews had abandoned all religious practice; and on the other hand because a law had abolished all automatic affiliation with a religious community, consequently leaving numerous people outside formal religion. But there was yet another important reason: the increasing number of mixed marriages. In these unions it was most often the Jewish partner who assimilated to the Christian majority. Paradoxically, the fall of the barrier between Jews and non-Jews sometimes led to quite an amount of anti-Semitism.

As if to compensate for this diminution, the progressive influx of Jews from Eastern Europe reinforced the communities, even if the newcomers, often viewed as "primitives," were not always favorably received by German Jews of "old stock." Whatever the case, strong in its lofty spirituality, German Judaism exerted an immense influence on Jewish communities around the world.

This period was essentially characterized by the confrontation between Judaism and modernity. This clash also entailed an encounter with German culture, the culture of Lessing and Schiller, which left a deep mark. It has scarcely any equivalent in the meetings between Judaism and other European peoples or cultures. A Jewish-German symbiosis has often been posited. Even if the events that I experienced prompt me to view such a process with caution, we cannot claim that the tendency was completely absent. The existence of a certain mutual influence has been the bearer of a number of elements of great value, the basis for ongoing enrichment in myriad domains. An eminent critic of this evolution, the Jewish historian and philosopher Gershom Scholem, noted that this symbiosis existed only in the minds of Jews. He nonetheless recognized the importance of the phenomenon. The concepts of Kant and Schiller, in particular on human liberty, were informed by the notion of universal fraternity, and Kant's critical philosophy offered a system of thought that permitted emancipated Jews to inscribe their own religious convictions in a philosophical conception that was universal and—or so they hoped—universally accepted. The passionate attachment of cultivated Jews to classical literature and to German idealism led them to construct an idealized image of the German, an image that was increasingly distant from reality. On the other hand, Germans at this time, for the most part, knew only a caricature of the Jew.

Among my memories from this time I recall a certain evening in the 1920s when my father told us that he had received in his lawyer's office a Jewish

National Fund delegate who had come to Europe to raise money to buy land in Palestine. At that time Jewish pioneers in Palestine were accomplishing wonders. My father told us at length the wonderful stories of these settlers who were making the desert fertile and were draining the unhealthy swamps. Yet he was no Zionist. In fact, in his family people were even more assimilated than in my mother's. My father was one of nine children in a very patriarchal Berlin family. I never knew my paternal grandfather, who died the year I was born. From origins in Lower Silesia, he was a self-made man and had created his own business.

A grain wholesaler, he was associated with a certain Herr Preuss. The corporate name of the firm was quite naturally Preuss and Riegner. The association was to last for some thirty years, and the business flourished. Herr Preuss was the father of Hugo Preuss, who would go on to become a famous professor of constitutional law and later minister of the interior and the drafter of the Weimar constitution. Our families were very close because my father formed close ties with Hugo Preuss and shared his democratic and progressive political views. Like many Germans of the time, the elder Preuss had a great desire to experience the beauties of Italy before dying (did the expression "See Naples and die" originate in Germany?). As he was rather elderly, he expressed a wish to have a young traveling companion and chose my father, knowing that he was knowledgeable about the history of art. This trip through Italy, from north to south, was the great adventure of my father's youth. Some sixty years later and with great emotion he showed me the sites he had first seen in the company of Herr Preuss.

On his death, my grandfather left his family a million and a half gold marks, a fortune before World War I. Later, inflation would cause it to melt away entirely, but initially our financial situation was comfortable. It is doubtless for this reason that in our family we never had an exaggerated concern for money. Psychologically it was important; we knew what it was, that one could have it and that one could also lose it.

My father was an intellectual who had become a lawyer rather in spite of himself. He would rather have been an art historian, something that his father would not allow. At the time that kind of vocation did not inspire confidence. One of his brothers was studying medicine; my grandfather decided that one intellectual in the family was enough.

Thus my father had to force his parents to allow him to pursue university studies. In exchange he had to accept a kind of compromise by choosing law, then considered a practical matter. Yet in the years that followed he became profoundly attached to his profession of jurist. Notwithstanding, my father was a man of broad culture, as much at home in modern philosophy as in German literature, economics, history—and in particular in art history. He was a typical example of the German Jewish bourgeoisie, profoundly attached to universal education and culture. The climate of openness that characterized my family left a deep imprint on me. What was lavished on me around the family dinner table would have been a hard apprenticeship for many other young persons. In fact, all my schoolmates used to come to our house to consult books when they had various assignments. All the essentials were there in my parents' library.

After being admitted to the bar, my father quickly became associated with another German Jewish lawyer, Kurt Rosenfeld, a political activist and, even under the monarchy, one of the most prominent political defense lawyers of the time. A co-founder of the Unabhängige Sozialdemokratischepartei Deutschlands (USPD, Independent Social Democratic party) in 1917, he served in the Reichstag for the entire period of the Weimar Republic where he campaigned against capital punishment, and as Prussian minister of justice during the revolutionary period of November 1918 through January 1919. When the USPD dissolved in 1922, some of its members went to the Communists, but Rosenfeld joined the left wing of the mainstream Sozialdemokratische Partei Deutschlands (SPD, Social Democratic party), so often at odds with the majority that he was thrown out of the party in September 1931. Shortly thereafter he co-founded the Sozialistische Arbeiterpartei as a left alternative to the SPD. An extremely courageous man, he led the defense in numerous political trials involving right-wing violence against leftist organizations and individuals. In one of these cases before the Reichsgericht (Supreme Court), he called a certain Adolf Hitler as a witness. Rosenfeld deliberately baited the witness, and at one point Hitler shouted that he would answer no more questions "from this Jewish lawyer" (*"Ich gebe dem jüdischen Rechtanwalt überhaupt keine Antwort mehr!"*). The defense lawyers vigorously protested this insulting behavior, and the court thereupon fined Hitler 800 marks for refusal to testify while under oath and 200 marks for improper behavior in court. This occurred in June 1932; Hitler would not forget it.

As for my mother, in her youth she taught in an elementary school, then gave courses at vocational schools for girls, in particular classes in civics, explaining the rights and responsibilities of women in society. In this fashion she hoped to give German girls a sense of citizenship.

My mother was deeply engaged in women's movements. This is why, during World War I, she undertook studies of political economy, studies that remained incomplete because she was expecting her third child. This condition did not, however, prevent her from later actively committing herself to politics and activism within the Democratic party. During the Weimar Republic she was even a member of the party's central committee. This was an opportunity for her to organize for elections, to campaign, to speak out at public meetings.

My father was also keenly interested in political life, but without participating directly in it. He was, in fact, a left-leaning democrat with a deep social conscience. As his actions were wedded to his ideas, he often defended people without charge. My father was to publish numerous articles promoting the ideal of social justice and to stigmatize the attitudes of justice officials working solely on behalf of important private interests. Thus, at a certain point, he ran as the youth candidate in the election to the advisory board of the bar association, and received the greatest number of votes in Berlin. This was astonishing for a person so modest in his behavior. He was particularly respected for his honesty and his heightened sense of social responsibility.

It was then normal that my family should follow the political events of the Weimar Republic with passionate interest. In our house, politics was a principal concern and occupied a dominant position. Every day we ardently discussed the good and bad fortunes of our democracy.

My father was rather reflective by nature, my mother more inclined toward action. These two elements are both represented in me. On the one hand I have a theoretical bent for logic, analysis, a systematic, methodical, and philosophical approach to things; on the other hand I have always felt the necessity of drawing the practical consequences of my reflections, that is, of passing from thought to action. I have always been aware of my need to come to grips with situations, to engage myself in them.

These, then, are the two principal sources of my calling. From the one comes my passion for political action, from the other my profound attachment to Jewish tradition, to the Jewish people. My character is the reflection of these influences, intimately merged in me, like the waters of a river.

From the War of 1914–1918 to the Weimar Republic

My father was called to service in the second year of the war. He had not done military service in his youth. He was nonetheless drafted to fight in the German army, seeing action on one front and then on the other. He was first in the East, in Russia, then in the West, in France. The experience he gained would mark his life profoundly—and ours as well.

During the war on the Eastern Front, my father encountered the Jews of Eastern Europe. As for many German Jews, this was a revelation to him. When he was not at the front, he got to know them, to know them at home. Being invited to share their life, to celebrate the eve and beginning of the Sabbath was a very special experience for him. This reception into the family exposed him to the rich culture of Eastern European Judaism, profoundly rooted in the ideas and beliefs that sprang from a deep knowledge of the Bible, the Talmud, and the rabbinical commentaries, and tradition. As for most of his fellow Jews in the army, this was an unhoped for, gratifying discovery. A whole generation of writers evoked this marvelous experience. The painter Hermann Struck illustrated a text by Arnold Zweig, *Das ostjüdische Anlitz* (*Faces of Eastern Jews).* Sammy Gronemann wrote *Hawdoloh und Zapfenstreich* (*Hawdoloh and the Taps*), and Zweig his famous *Der Streit um den Sergeanten Grischa (The Argument About Sergeant Grischa*), which tells the fantastic and tragic story of the trial of a brave soldier and of the dispute over his fate.

Later, with the war behind him, my father would speak to us with gratitude and emotion of the Jewish families who had welcomed him to their homes in Thorn, Kovno, and Aleksandrovo. My family never displayed toward Eastern Jews the frequent arrogance of other German Jews.

World War I was a long time of anguish for our family, with grave difficulties to be overcome. When my father was at the front, we might go months without news, with a mute anxiety anchored inside us. The winter of 1917 was particularly severe. Boiled cabbage and turnips were the staples of our diet. Turnips, in particular, became our pet dislike: the bread was made from turnip flour; there were turnips in the soup that was the main dish; even the desserts contained turnips. In any case, what else was there to eat? At times I saw my mother get up at night to look for a piece of sugar. She did not wish to deprive the children of their ration of food, and tried to assuage her own hunger in that fashion. There were three of us children, me and my two sisters. The elder, Helene, was almost three years my senior. A dreamer and romantic, she often gave the impression of lacking any sense of reality. She was passionately interested in German, French, and Spanish literature. Before World War II she went off alone to the United States, where her life would then follow its own course. During the war she earned a doctorate in literature at Radcliffe and then taught at various American universities. She married and had two children.

As for my little sister, Marianne, ten years younger, she was the baby of the family; all of us had to look after her. As a child she saw in me, already a grown lad, her brotherly protector. Unfortunately I did not get to see her grow up at close hand, since I had to leave Germany in 1933. I did not witness her early development or her maturing. Much later she left with our parents for the United States, to make her life in Boston. Then she married and had four children in New York City. But, again, distance was no obstacle to our mutual love.

Unfortunately, my younger sister passed on a few years ago. This was one of the great losses in my life. Shortly afterward her husband died as well, after a ravaging illness. In a way, the children of my younger sister adopted me as I adopted them. They are my little family, to which I am united with strong ties. I see them quite often. Also a member of this little family is the son of my Dutch cousin who, having lost his parents at an early age, became very attached to me. He has had a brilliant academic career in Britain. Similarly, several members of my Dutch family are very close to me. In all, we are a family that is both American and European.

School Years and Family Life

I now return to my youth and to the awakening and deepening of my consciousness of being Jewish. It is as if the world planned that from my youngest years I should be increasingly aware of being a Jew. As a young man I accumulated the experiences and trials that would mark me forever.

The first demonstration by which the external world made me aware of this status was through insult. It was during my first days at school. When I went by, a youngster called out "Dirty little Jew." I was scarcely five and a half years old, very proud of going to school with my school bag, on my own. This aggression, completely unexpected, shook me deeply. I felt that I had to react. I insulted him in turn, stupidly saying, "Dirty little Christian." This was really idiotic. But you have to understand that it was only an expression of my rejection of the insult. I could not accept being treated in that fashion.

Incidents of the same kind would not, unfortunately, be absent in my gradual discovery of anti-Semitism. I see no point in listing them all, but I must describe my first encounter with social anti-Semitism, a typical aspect of which was that we were not invited into Christian families' homes. Thus for three years I lived out a real drama because of a classmate, who was also a lawyer's son. Friendship was expressed in natural, spontaneous fashion by mutual invitations, for example on birthdays. But I was never invited to his home. In my child's mind I found all kinds of excuses for him while waiting for the next time, which never came. Perhaps, I told myself confusedly, there was something that prevented invitations, some family impediment that forbade the presence of a friend—a friend who was not related—at the celebration of a first communion, or even at the funeral of a brother. This occurred when I was about ten and marked me for life. This behavior could not fail to

astonish me: our school was located in a residential area in the western part of
Berlin, where many Jews lived. Jews were so numerous, in fact, that they made
up about one-third of my own class, and in others sometimes even more. And
thus I became aware of our differences, and of our exclusion.

We were at the beginning of the 1920s, in the Weimar Republic. I was a
very lively child, curious, interested in politics. I read the newspapers; the anti-
Semitic incidents, far from escaping my attention, seized all my interest. In
this respect, the frequent discussions that we had at home helped me understand what was going on. I knew which were the anti-Jewish parties, who their
leaders were, what their activities were. Yet my life at school, in the main, pro-
gressed harmoniously. Despite the anti-Semitic events, which were certainly
annoying though few in number and relatively minor, these school years have
left me with a positive memory.

Some of the friendships established during this period have lasted my
whole life. I think particularly of that schoolmate Walter Alkan, with whom I
shared the same bench for twelve years, from our entrance in 1917 until we
graduated in 1929. My ties to him extended to his whole family. He remained
a faithful friend who became a celebrated physician in Israel.

As elsewhere, there were several nationalistic teachers in our school. But,
for obvious reasons, they hardly revealed whether they were—or were not—
anti-Semites. When they advanced monarchist ideas, we were shocked. It was
unsettling because we were well integrated into the republic, which had rejected the empire.

Some of the teachers were excellent, introducing new teaching methods in
all disciplines, including physical education. It was the great era of innovative
ideas that promoted an active pedagogy. Thus it was judged insufficient simply to learn things by rote: knowledge must come through understanding.
Students could finally express their knowledge, things they knew personally.
Raised in an environment where intellectual curiosity and respect for learning
were veritable hymns to knowledge, I felt like a fish in water in this liberated
educational environment.

In the spirit of this new pedagogy we undertook various trips in the south
of Germany. The teachers had us visit ancient cities famous for their monuments and works of art, cities such as Regensburg, Passau, and Nuremberg.
These cultural excursions bore witness to the change that had been effected:
passive learning had given way to a participatory educational method. In this
case the pedagogy was also based in teaching that addressed art and the beautiful. The same was true of sports outings, organized by the physical education
teacher. Skiing had always been my favorite sport. By the age of twelve I was a

good skier and I very much enjoyed our trips to the Riesengebirge. What fine memories I have of that time!

Three events left a special stamp on my childhood. The first was the assassination of Weimar's German Jewish foreign minister Walther Rathenau; the second, the funeral of the Social Democrat President Ebert; the third, the election of Marshal Paul von Hindenburg to the presidency of Germany.

The first event, then, the assassination of Walther Rathenau. I was only ten years old at the time he was killed, in 1922. Fanatical young nationalists had just murdered the only Jewish minister in the government, an exceptional man with multiple talents. He had been an excellent executive, gifted with a broad sense of corporate organization (particularly evident on the national level). His interest in politics proved fatal. He was a man of great vision, and everyone knew that he was profoundly attached to peace. Minister of foreign affairs, he was convinced that, in the eyes of the Western powers, the recovery of Germany must occur in the context of a reconciliation with the Soviet Union, which, moreover, had been the first country to sign a peace treaty with Germany. He had given himself this goal by signing the Treaty of Rapallo, which put an end to the disputes that were the heritage of World War I. My family, and indeed the entire left-liberal community, were overwhelmed by his assassination. This murder revealed to us the depth of anti-Semitism on the German extreme right. For the child that I then was, the effect was profound.

Upon President Ebert's funeral in 1925, I participated in the silent mass demonstration in homage to his memory on the great square of the Lustgarten. On that square, black with the huge crowd, I intuited that the republic itself was being buried. This premonition was charged with singular foreboding: what dark tomorrows would befall that world still committed to democracy?

The third event was the election of Field Marshal Hindenburg. I remember very well that the great weekly, the *Berliner Illustrierte Zeitung*, devoted a special issue to the election. Two photographs on the cover presented the candidates. The portraits were of the republican candidate, the former Center party chancellor Wilhelm Marx, and the candidate of the right, the celebrated Hindenburg. It would be difficult to find a greater difference, a greater contrast between two men. On the one side there was Marx in a dark suit, in all his simplicity, the civilian *par excellence*. On the other, in full uniform under his gleaming pointed helmet, Field Marshal Hindenburg, with all his decorations, the symbol of the German militarism of the past. Only of the past? The juxtaposition of the two images was a shock to me.

Admittedly I was very young, scarcely an adolescent. A nice boy, they probably said. But I was a precociously mature child. This explained why, even at that age, the uniform did not impress me, at least not favorably. And then my father was not very proud of what he had had to do during the war. He confided to me on several occasions: "It's true, I was a soldier, but I have no one's death on my conscience." This brings me to recall a telling incident that occurred during the war. On one of my birthdays, my mother gave me some tin soldiers and other war toys, like those typically given to boys at the time. I remember that a little quarrel erupted that day between my mother and Rosenfeld, my father's partner, who had come by to give me his birthday wishes. Rosenfeld reproached my mother for the choice of toys. Need I emphasize that despite the tin soldiers I never became a militarist?

The great inflation of the years 1922–1924 was another difficult period for my family. Our fortune and all our savings evaporated. How could you earn the money a family needed when galloping inflation reached astronomical figures, for example 100 million marks for a postage stamp? How could one support a family? Most often my father's fees were paid months after he sent his bills. What remained of the value of the invoiced amounts? Often practically nothing. When he did succeed in getting immediate payment, and received his fee in the morning, he would only get a portion of it when he cashed the check at the bank that same afternoon. As a consequence we had to take exceptional measures. Imagination came to my parents' rescue: they opened a little art business. My mother ran it but my father, with his great knowledge of art, was the real driving force. This went on for several years, as long as it proved necessary. Although it had been imposed on us by the terribly difficult situation, this activity gave us enormous satisfaction. For it not only sufficed to meet the family's needs but the business also decorated the walls of our apartment with a succession of the works of great artists. Thus we learned an enormous amount about art and artists. Our home was open to numerous painters, engravers, and sculptors, who in turn received us in their studios. I often went along with my parents. I particularly remember visits that we made to Lesser Ury, a German Jewish artist with whom we had very cordial relations. One day he tried to persuade me to sit as a model for one of his huge biblical canvases. But because he wanted to paint me naked, my modesty was offended, and I refused.

We tried, in those troubled times, to maintain family cohesion as much as possible. Sunday morning we generally went for a walk in the Tiergarten, the great park in the center of Berlin. Our encounters there were not without their surprises. Thus on one outing we met the philosopher Ernst Cassirer, out

walking with his wife. My parents often met them at the Cohens. We chatted
together for quite a while. Another time we walked along with Theodor Heuss
and his family. My father had known him since his youth. They had both been
followers of Eugen Richter, the leader of the Progressive party, the
Fortschrittspartei. They also met from time to time at the Democratic Club or
at the homes of mutual friends.

More than thirty years later, leaving the Hôtel Baur au Lac in Zurich in the
company of Nahum Goldmann, I suddenly found myself face to face with
Theodor Heuss, who was then president of the Federal Republic of Germany,
with his entourage. Heuss and Goldmann greeted one another cordially, and
Goldmann introduced me to the president. As my name is a bit uncommon,
Heuss at once remembered my father and asked me for news of him. I gave
him this information and reminded him of our encounter in the Tiergarten,
noting that as a little boy I had had a good time playing with his son. He
smiled and with a gesture said, "Here is the son you played with."

My parents occasionally visited an old couple, Theodor and Paula Rosenstock, whose children were part of their circle of friends. All of them had gone
on to professional careers, and the best known among them was the philosopher and theologian Eugene Rosenstock-Huessy. It was precisely on the occasion of one of these visits that we met the great Jewish philosopher Franz
Rosenzweig, whose fascinating and fertile work I would later discover with
such admiration. Rosenzweig was extremely kind to children. He would even
play hide-and-seek with us. I can still see him hiding behind the long drapes
in the Rosenstock salon.

I was not aware that he was engaged to Edith Hahn, who was my teacher
of religion at school in 1917. This was long before the terrible illness that was
to befall him.

Every year our family would take long trips together, which are among my
finest memories of this period. These occurred during the summer holidays,
the only time of the year when for four whole weeks we had our parents all to
ourselves. We truly lived together during those times, without the external
world and its cares troubling us. These exceptional moments made a great
contribution toward forging the ties of affection that bound us together. It
also permitted us youngsters to become familiar with the cultural heritage of
our parents. We spent these vacations in Bavaria or in the Tyrol, later in
Switzerland. I learned to love the high peaks and, more generally, the mountain environment, for which I have had a true passion all my life.

Theater and music played an important role in my personal development.
Berlin was then a world capital for culture, and artistic life there was extremely

lively and creative, with an incredible number of actors and musicians of very high quality. We were fully engaged in this artistic life, going to as many performances and concerts as possible.

Let me open here a musical parenthesis, one that I think will explain my deep attachment to music. From my childhood on I played the cello and took lessons with a series of remarkable teachers. I was also a member of the small orchestra at school. My passion for the instrument has lasted until today, and I have a collection of recordings by all the great cellists. To my great regret, however, I left my cello behind when I was forced to leave Germany with two suitcases in my hands.

At the close of the 1920s and in the early '30s, during which the city celebrated the centenary (1927) of the death of Beethoven, and that of Schubert the following year, Berlin offered, as I have said, a cultural life of extraordinary intensity, which granted me a series of dazzling "musical moments." In my family, as well, we had a number of excellent musicians. When I was still quite young, my parents had introduced me to chamber music. Thus we frequently went to the home of Martha Cohen, the wife of Hermann Cohen and daughter of Louis Lewandowski. Martha Cohen was herself a remarkable pianist. I remember with great emotion her playing, especially when she surprised us with her interpretations, in particular of Jewish melodies, on the occasion of my bar mitzvah. Martha Cohen often hosted the quartet directed by Albert Einstein. The second violin was Professor Alfred Lewandowski, Martha Cohen's brother. People used to tell of his amusing sally at the expense of the famous mathematician, whom he accused of "not being able to count up to three."

I would not, however, wish to give the impression of a fully harmonious family, with no conflicts. Differences of character and temperament affected our appreciation of situations and our judgments, which were often far from unanimous. But surely it was normal that disputes arose here and there, and that some of them were followed by longer or shorter periods of grumbling. Moreover, this gave a very special flavor to the reconciliations that did not fail to follow. Perhaps these eruptions and tensions added to the depth of feeling that created a solid, unified family, the family to which I owe so much.

After my secondary schooling, in 1929 I spent two months in Dijon where the university had organized summer courses. The capital of the dukedom of Burgundy permitted me to appreciate many treasures: the beauty and richness of the French language, architecture, art in general, without forgetting the attractions of the regional cuisine, one of the tastiest in a country oh so spoiled with gastronomy. This multiple discovery of France was not just that of a single proud province. I also took advantage of my time there to spend a few days in Paris. Today that first visit to the capital seems to me a previously unimagined experience, made up of innumerable discoveries: avenues, squares, monuments, museums. I still have very emotional memories of that time.

University Studies and a First Meeting with Nazism

My sense of the onrushing threat of Nazism only became stronger with the years. Naturally I read a great deal. We used to get two or three Jewish newspapers at home. They often enraged me, because I understood instinctively what I would much later deduce rationally. I increasingly felt that faced with pre-Nazi and Nazi anti-Semitism, the fight should not be fueled by rational arguments that were destined to failure. We were facing prejudices, reactions, and passionate arguments that issued from the depths of the German soul. The anti-Semitic harassment gave expression to irrational forces and assumptions. It seemed clear to me that they could not be countered with rational arguments. To win on the level of logic was surely to lose everything.

But there still existed a policy of debate based in logic, inspired by a blind faith in reason. This was the way the Centralverein deutscher Staatsbürger jüdischen Glaubens (Central Union of German Citizens of the Jewish Faith) worked. It united all the Jewish movements, from the assimilationists to the Orthodox. The real splinter group was represented by the Zionists, a small minority lost in the majority. The Union was engaged in fighting anti-Semitism. All of us had long supported it, perhaps too long. Although it was a slow evolution, we concluded that its methods were absurd when confronted by the true nature of Nazism, which refused Jews the most elementary human rights.

After graduation from secondary school came university studies. I first spent a summer term at Freiburg-im-Bresgau. The second term was spent at the University of Berlin, then a third at Heidelberg. I completed my studies in Berlin.

I began with law and political science, with an especially marked interest in public law and the philosophy of law. Faithful to family tradition, I did not limit myself to the sphere of the law alone. I also took courses in history, philosophy, literature, sociology, and art history. I thus pursued my father's vision to attempt to win access to a truly universal culture.

Freiburg also represented for me the discovery of nature. Born and raised in a large city, for the first time I lived several months in the countryside, in the Black Forest region. It was a wonderful experience.

I began my legal studies in Freiburg and, contrary to custom, I did not begin with Roman law but with the civil law then in force. This was no doubt a result of my pragmatism, which would explain my impatience to engage myself in the concrete problems of life rather than the history of law. So in my first term I enrolled in "practical studies," where real cases had to be adjudicated either in class or at home. I was quite successful and was very proud to be invited by my professor to a collegial excursion with a small group of his best students. This gave me confidence in my ability as a jurist and was a great encouragement for the future.

In order to complete my legal knowledge and gain some familiarity with the business world, during the holidays and between university terms I took a voluntary internship with a large private bank in Berlin.

My time in Heidelberg—and here I must pause for an instant—marked me for life. At that time, in 1930, it was truly a prestigious university. On the intellectual level, studying there gave me a great deal of pleasure. The spirit of Max Weber still infused the place. His brother, the sociologist Alfred Weber; the philosopher Karl Jaspers; and some eminent jurists such as Gerhard Anschütz and Gustav Radbruch maintained the tradition. Radbruch was also minister of justice for several years. Another one of the glories of the University of Heidelberg was Friedrich Gundolf, who taught literature. All of them formed part of the best that the German intelligentsia had to offer. It would hardly be exaggerating to say that in Heidelberg we lived in a sort of permanent intellectual force field. It was undeniably a great center of knowledge. In this rewarding climate I took flight, in a spirit that literally enriched my training and development for ever. Retrospectively I can see how my studies in Germany, then in Paris, Geneva, and The Hague (at the Academy of International Law) gave me one of the most complete educations a jurist could dream of. This privilege no doubt partially explains the success I had with my professors, to judge by the way in which they showed their appreciation of me.

During my university years in Freiburg and Heidelberg I took an active part in the student democratic movement, in student rallies, and in campaigns for university elections. This was my apprenticeship, in the field, in political life. I was particularly active in the struggle against Nazi students and the terror they wielded.

From the first year of my studies I took part in the election to the student council. Such elections no longer existed except in the little state of Baden. In Prussia the Nazis had everywhere obtained such a majority that the government had suppressed all such elections. The electoral campaigns taught me about Nazi behavior, in particular about their cynicism, fanaticism, and brutality. For several terms, in 1929 and 1930, I was even the secretary of the Association of Democratic Students at the University of Berlin.

It was in the framework of these elections that I worked with Harro Schulze-Boysen who later became one of the leaders of the "Red Orchestra," the famous Communist spy network during World War II. The astonishing Schulze-Boysen began on the right. When I knew him he was a democrat. Then he joined the Communist party. It was from within the Nazi war ministry, where he found work and which was directed by Göring, that he launched his Communist sabotage activities against the Wehrmacht, the German armed forces. He was finally exposed and was executed by the Nazis.

My student years, a serious period, coincided with the world economic crisis and with the catastrophic increase in unemployment. These years also saw the victorious assault by the Nazis against the republic. I have already alluded to the terrifying demonstrations of anti-Semitism generated by Nazism, which grew in ever-increasing waves until they became a flood from which escape was impossible.

Jews were being separated out and excluded in a painful, progressive process that inexorably seized all of us. This increasingly turned the young Jew that I was proud to be back toward my roots.

I remember how the Nazi Brown Shirt commandos, the Sturmabteilung (SA), armed with sticks and clubs, came one day to drive the Jewish students and professors from the University of Berlin. This occurred in 1930 or 1931, long before the Nazi accession to power. I remember their mass arrival and their brutality. Their savagery was so great that we had to jump from the windows as our only means of escape from them. Such was the atmosphere in which I concluded my studies. Then I sat for the state examination, which I passed in early January 1933 with the highest grades, and I immediately entered what is called in Germany the "practical years of legal training." I became the assistant to a judge at the lower court in Wedding, a northern Berlin suburb. The training period normally was three years. For me it ended after three months.

It was with full legality that the Nazi party acceded to power on January 30, 1933. President Hindenburg appointed Adolf Hitler chancellor. This date marks a fracture in the life of every German Jew. As soon as they were installed in the seat of power, the Nazis launched their reign of terror.

From the outset I observed their rallies and their violence. I knew that it was the Nazis who had set fire to the Reichstag in order to be able to accuse their opponents of this crime. Very quickly I learned of the existence of concentration camps in Oranienburg and Sachsenhausen. I knew that people were being beaten and tortured on the former premises of the Communist newspaper *Die Rote Fahne* (*Red Flag*). In short, I had taken the measure of Nazi brutality.

The Day of the Jewish Boycott

April 1, 1933, was proclaimed by the Nazis a "day to boycott Jews." This was one of the most terrible days in the lives of all German Jews. On that day thousands of persons were driven from their work and attacked in their businesses and in the offices of doctors, lawyers, and architects. That first of April a Brown Shirt was stationed in front of virtually every Jewish business, shop, and office to keep non-Jews from purchasing anything from a Jew. The goal was to make all business relations with Jews impossible. They went so far as to mishandle German gentile women who had dealings with a Jew. It would be a long list to include all the hate crimes then perpetrated against Jews simply because they were Jews.

These measures also struck me personally. During the preceding three months I had gained some experience in judicial work by drafting sentences, entering the testimony of witnesses, and carrying out what constituted the daily work of a court.

The boycott affected all German Jews and thus of necessity also my family. From the first of April 1933, everything was thrown into turmoil for me and my family, an upheaval comparable to a tidal wave. After all my studies, I was let go by the court, my father was disbarred, my sister was dismissed from her teaching position in a Frankfurt secondary school, and my younger sister was expelled from elementary school. Admittedly the majority of the population was on Hitler's side in this matter, but a good share of the German intelligentsia was horrified. In complete confusion, our family was comforted by the visit of two ladies who had come to express their solidarity with Jews and their personal friendship. One was Agnes von Zahn-Harnack, the daughter of the distinguished Protestant theologian, Adolf von Harnack. The other, Illa Uth, a Catholic, was a close associate of the labor leader Anton Erkelenz.

Our situation was all the more urgent as my father was then experiencing health problems. His physician had ordered him to live outside the city in order to get a change of air and recommended that he avoid exerting himself. Thus we had moved into a house in a Berlin suburb. The evening of the infamous first of April I was alone at home with my little eleven-year-old sister. Tired from the day's events, I was going to have a bath. No sooner was I in the tub when I heard the Brown Shirts shouting, a whole chorus of them. We were the only Jewish family in the neighborhood, and they knew it. They had gathered under our windows in order to intimidate us, and for a good quarter of an hour they chanted—or rather shouted—without end, "*Juden 'raus!*" ("Jews out!"). I didn't stir from the bathtub, but this made a traumatic impression on me.

Since my father had become very weak, I didn't want him to run the risk of exposing himself to such incidents. This is why I delayed for some time my departure from Germany. But some weeks later, I left for good.

The atmosphere of the days that followed the boycott became unbearable. In order to follow developments in the situation, we had no choice but to listen to the radio. This had the result that even in our own house we were constantly being insulted by official statements; Hitler, Goebbels, Rosenberg, Streicher, and their lackeys made the air impossible for us to breathe. One day, exasperated by the flood of insults, I seized the radio and threw it to the floor, which at least gave us some peace and quiet at home.

Some people then tried to dissuade me from leaving, but in vain. I remember, with keen emotion, the last meeting I had, a little before my departure, with Professor Rudolf Smend, a conservative German nationalist. Professor of public law and among the most eminent at the University of Berlin, he wanted to convince me to stay and had asked me to meet him on the university grounds since all Jews were forbidden entry into the buildings. But Professor Smend would have none of that, and he accompanied me to his office, flouting the prohibition. In the course of a conversation of several hours he tried to get me to give up my plan to emigrate. He was persuaded that the situation could not go on forever, that it was all just an episode and would soon be a thing of the past.

The young law student saw things more clearly than the professor. I knew that the exclusion of Jews from German life was one of the principal objectives of the Nazis. I knew their fanaticism and their brutality, the savagery that would never give way. I had read *Mein Kampf* and I had understood that April 1, 1933, was the beginning of the end of German Jewry. Consequently I did not follow the advice of my professor. This conversation is all the more engraved in my memory as Rudolf Smend, among the hundreds of Germans whom I knew, was the only one to inquire about my fate after I left the country, keeping in touch with me by letter for a time. In fact, after 1933 I never received another word, not a single message, from any other non-Jewish German. None of my schoolmates, my university colleagues, my numerous acquaintances, members of the various associations to which I belonged—none of them ever again gave me the least sign. It should be remembered that I had lived in the country for more than twenty-one years. This rejection clearly proved the profound cowardice of the German intelligentsia of the time. It would haunt me for long years to come; its memory has never been totally effaced.

The ongoing correspondence with Professor Smend had a special purpose. He had been impressed by the presentation I had made as a quite young student in his seminar on the evolution of the concept of the Rechtsstaat (constitutional state). He wanted to have the text published outside Germany, since the writings of a Jew could no longer be printed in the country. So that readers will understand why my text had so impressed Professor Smend, I should here point out that after considerable research I had found in a publication from the latter eighteenth century the first German formulation of the Rechtsstaat, the state founded on a legal system, a state with constitutional guarantees. It was this that made it so fraught with symbolic value, since I was convinced that the Nazi accession to power had buried the constitutional state in Germany. Professor Smend doubtless shared this view. He was not, however, prepared to give up the fight. But the fact that there was a total rupture between the traditional conception of the state founded in law and the new Nazi state—founded in the concept of the Führer and his arbitrary omnipotence—was not yet understood in Germany, nor abroad. Nor did most German Jews apparently have any greater consciousness of it.

I remember my last evening in Berlin. On the eve of my departure I took part in the fiftieth-birthday celebration of one of my father's colleagues. I would not again see the friends who had gathered there. The whole evening I pleaded with them, tirelessly repeating, "But don't you see that this is the end of German Jewry?" I begged the older generation at least to permit those younger to leave. If I, at age twenty-one, could understand what was happening, how could the others fail to understand? Perhaps simply because they really did not wish to.

Leaving My Native Soil: France, Switzerland

Before leaving I still had to resolve a number of problems. Once my decision had been made, I had to face up to the large question of where to go. Since 1930, despairing of German politics, I had drawn progressively closer to Zionism. Having several friends in the movement, I knew what it entailed. During my studies, one of them had abandoned his law studies to enroll at an agricultural college because he planned to work the land in Palestine one day.

At that time I understood that in order to realize the Zionist ideal it would not only be necessary to settle in Palestine but to live there in a kibbutz. Well,

I knew that I was not cut out for rural collective life, and that it would not work for me. I am, and always have been, too much of an individualist for that. What else, except medicine, was there for an intellectual to do there? Consequently I did not choose to make Aliyah to Palestine. Two of my friends made the attempt but did not succeed and left after a brief period. I am tempted to say this was unfortunate for the three of us because later, had we had the patience, there would have been interesting possibilities to be passionately engaged in the conditions of life there. But it was not to be.

Because of my fascination with the problematics of law and the state, and the solid training I had acquired in this field, I decided to continue my studies. I left for Paris armed with many recommendations from professors of law. None of that would have helped much, however, without the support of my uncle in Holland, the husband of my mother's older sister, who initially gave me a small monthly allowance. This uncle was in fact providential for my entire family; he was a great help in their escape from Germany.

Once arrived in Paris in May 1933, like other young lawyers fleeing Nazism, I benefited from a favorable regulation: refugee law students from Germany were exempted from taking all their courses again. Our various German degrees and diplomas permitted us to take the French examinations at once.

Despite having passed the examinations and despite the fact that I was comfortable in France, I nonetheless left the country in November of the following year. Had I not, for the last eighteen months, immersed myself in its rich culture? I had devoured its great novels and become a fervent admirer of Balzac, Flaubert, Anatole France, Proust, Roger Martin du Gard, and Jules Romains. I was equally taken with the architecture of the cathedrals, the treasures of the museums, and the castles. In order to familiarize myself with French judicial procedure I had also worked several months as a volunteer in a large legal firm in Paris.

But in the early summer of 1934, at the request of the French bar, the parliament passed a law forbidding foreigners to exercise any judicial profession for ten years following their naturalization as French citizens. And since it would be necessary to be a resident in the country for at least five years in order to become naturalized, this was the equivalent of exclusion. This was a stupefying development. At the very most there were only about fifty of us young Jewish lawyers who had come from Germany. Admittedly we were dynamic, persevering, ambitious: we wanted to succeed in our profession. Yet it was regrettable for such a great country to treat us this way, even to have had recourse to a special law. I still had two or three months to complete the studies I had begun in France. This was not the moment to abandon them. Without yet realizing it, though, I was about to experience one of the decisive moments of my life.

At that time the Sorbonne had invited the Austrian professor Hans Kelsen to give three lectures. Since 1911 he had been teaching law in Vienna and was the founder of the famous school of "pure law." In 1929 he had left the Austrian capital, where in fact a virulent anti-Semitism, particularly at the university, poisoned the atmosphere. The Nazis played an enormous role in all this; they continually mounted demonstrations against the Jewish professors, Hans Kelsen in particular. Kurt Waldheim may still claim that the association of Nazi students was engaged in activities of a purely social nature, but no one was ignorant of the fact that it really was part of an extremely violent political movement. During this period, Konrad Adenauer, the future German chancellor, was the mayor of Cologne. To add to the luster of the city, Adenauer had created a new university, though in Bonn, just on the other side of the Rhine River, there was already an ancient university with a great reputation. To establish a great new university, Adenauer had appealed to famous professors, among them Hans Kelsen. At the end of World War I, Kelsen had been one of the most trusted counselors of Emperor Karl of Austria, having loaned the emperor his support in various peace efforts. After the war he drafted the Austrian constitution, which was abrogated by the Nazis in 1938, then reinstated after World War II. This is evidence enough of its exceptional value.

Hans Kelsen had then been invited to Paris for three public lectures at the Sorbonne. Filled with admiration but a bit casual as young students often are, I had written him on various occasions beginning during my first university term in Germany. After the second lecture, I screwed up my courage and went up to him. "Could you possibly help me, give me some advice?" I asked. "I am at the end of my rope." At the time Kelsen was teaching at the Swiss Graduate Institute of International Studies in Geneva. Some terms he also taught at the German university in Prague at the invitation of Edvard Beneš, the president of Czechoslovakia. In addition, Kelsen was associated with Professor William Rappard, of whom I shall have more to say later.

Kelsen heard me out and then said: "Come to Geneva." I felt obliged to retort: "Easier said than done; I am a refugee." Here let me say parenthetically that I had just received a French university stipendium. Therefore I was able to relieve to some extent the demands I was making on my uncle in Holland, who was helping our whole family.

At the end of our conversation, Kelsen asked me whether I could hold out for four or five months on my own in Geneva. "Theoretically, yes," was my reply. Then he repeated that I should come to Geneva, and added in order to convince me, "I know you, you are an intelligent young man, we have a magnificent institute in Geneva and an excellent director. Come and work with us. At the end of five months you will receive a one-year stipendium that we will be able to renew. For two years at least you won't have any material worries." This was the attitude of a great scholar, who truly sought out students to train and direct.

In addition, he understood the problems faced by refugee intellectuals. As soon as I had taken and passed the final examinations for my law degree in Paris, I left for Switzerland. I should say in this regard that examinations and degrees have never been particularly gratifying for me but rather a necessary step, a kind of formality. It was intellectual life itself that was interesting, important, indeed essential for me.

After five months in Geneva I did indeed receive a one-year stipendium. And then another. In addition to my studies and my research, I regularly attended a private seminar that Professor Kelsen gave in his home. He read us his manuscripts on the concept of justice in Plato, Aristotle, and so on. It was extremely stimulating and gave me immense pleasure. What fine, unforgettable evenings!

Let me now turn to William Rappard, a man of impressive stature who had invaluable contacts in the world of politics. This great liberal possessed a powerful personality. He had played a considerable role in international relations, well beyond the sphere of teaching political economy and public finance, his academic disciplines.

Before World War I, Rappard taught at Harvard University. He became friendly with Woodrow Wilson who was then at Princeton. It was Rappard who had convinced Wilson to choose Geneva as the seat of the League of Nations.

He became the first director of the League's Mandate Department of the General Secretariat. Later he himself became a member of the Mandate Commission, the agency responsible for overseeing the exercise of mandates, in particular in former German colonies and in certain territories of the former Ottoman Empire. By reason of the fact that Palestine was one of the territories placed under the mandate of Great Britain, the commission had an essential role to play in the future of the country and its Jewish and Arab populations.

Rappard was a great friend of the Jews. In 1925 he had represented the University of Geneva when the first stone was laid for the Hebrew University of Jerusalem. He was a keen admirer of Chaim Weizmann, the great Zionist leader and first president of Israel, and had excellent relations with Nahum

Goldmann, who then represented the Jewish Agency at the League. At certain difficult moments he proved his friendship toward Jews, in particular on the occasion of the great crisis provoked in 1939 by the white paper of the British government, which brutally limited the immigration of Jews to Palestine.

When I arrived in Geneva in 1934, Rappard was playing a preeminent role and exercised numerous functions. And when I joined the Institute, he served as one of its two directors. He stamped the institution with his strength of character and open-mindedness. This latter quality was, for example, evident in his custom of attracting highly esteemed professors who had been driven from their countries by dictatorships. The other director was the distinguished professor and remarkable historian of the industrial revolution, Paul Mantoux, a French Jew of very old stock. During the Versailles peace conference he had been an interpreter for the four great powers. He was a magnificent figure, as learned as he was modest, and was appreciated too for his inexhaustible treasure of political anecdotes.

Professor Kelsen, the historian Guglielmo Ferrero, the economists Wilhelm Röpke, Ludwig von Mises, and Louise Sommer all became teachers at the Institute, along with other famous professors such as the Swiss Carl J. Burckhardt, the Frenchman Georges Scelle, and the Belgian Maurice Bourquin. They all added considerably to the international prestige of the institution. The presence of these eminent teachers attracted numerous young intellectuals, among them many Jewish and non-Jewish refugees from Germany, Austria, and Italy, to all of whom the Institute provided material support.

The Swiss Graduate Institute of International Studies was one of the schools where young people extended their knowledge of international affairs and prepared for careers as diplomats or senior officers in international organizations. I had begun at the Institute in late 1934. Now the next year had run its course. In April 1936 my scholarship was renewed for the following academic year, which was to begin in September.

The Congress Arrives on the Scene

In the summer of 1936 Stephen Wise and Nahum Goldmann, after several preparatory conferences, decided to convoke the founding assembly of the World Jewish Congress in Geneva. By way of material organization, they chose to create a modest permanent office there.

The temporary office of the future Congress was in Paris, on the extensive premises of the former Committee of Jewish Delegations to the Versailles conference. Its activities had been maintained through the 1920s. Leon Motzkin, the former chairman, continued to be extremely active, in particular with regard to the Jews of the Diaspora. When he died in 1933, Nahum Goldmann succeeded him. Goldmann had been living in Geneva since 1935 as the representative of the Jewish Agency for Palestine to the League of Nations. This was an important post, especially in relation to the Commission on Mandates.

Two urgent, imperative reasons dictated the foundation of the World Jewish Congress: one was the fight against Hitler and Nazism; the other was the protection of millions of persons who made up Jewish minorities in the countries of Central and Eastern Europe. They were suffering profoundly from the political, economic, and social discrimination being exercised against them.

All these communities lived under the system of treaties and declarations for the protection of minorities that had been worked out at the Versailles peace conference—and in its aftermath, the implementation of which was under the guarantee of the League of Nations. The establishment of the offices of the future World Jewish Congress had been foreseen for Geneva because the city had become a very important center for international activities. For this reason numerous journalists were based there, and their influence extended throughout the world. The Congress had also chosen Geneva because it was the seat of the League of Nations, which was the guarantor of the treaties.

To make the little Geneva office truly operational, the Congress founders needed a young Jew who had specialized in international law, human rights, minority rights, and international procedures. With this end in view, Nahum Goldmann consulted with three professors whom he knew very well at the Institute, Rappard, Kelsen, and Paul Guggenheim, asking them to recommend a candidate to him. Without telling me, and even without consulting among themselves, the three of them spontaneously designated me as the man for the job. As I was seeing quite a lot of Kelsen and Guggenheim, this did not completely surprise me. Indeed, Kelsen and I met regularly. As chance would have it, I lived very close to his home. At one time I was even in love with his daughter.

Here I should make a little confession with regard to the fact that even though I was very attached to my family, and to the concept of the family in general, I never married. I was in love on more than one occasion, without ever drawing what I am tempted to call the normal conclusions. This for several reasons. First, the unease I experienced living in a period that was so subject to the unknown and, I confess, the difficulty in those terrible circumstances of finding the courage to set up a household, and to begin a family, a family that I would quite simply have wished to be happy, a situation to which the stress of my professional life would hardly have contributed. To these circumstances were to be added the financial problems that resulted from my support to my family, which I would not have suffered abandoning. These reasons that I now evoke were very real back then. I should, however, add another motive for my bachelorhood. If I hesitated for a long time to marry, and finally renounced the idea definitively, it is that I had acquired the habit, even the taste for independence. This independence had been acquired over the course of years and was finally so profoundly anchored in me that it was difficult to give it up. In short, right or wrong, I never started a family, and I occasionally regret it.

I also knew Guggenheim very well: he used to invite me every week to chat over a cup of tea. Rappard, on the other hand, was the real surprise, because I had much less personal contact with him. Yet he must have made an assessment of my abilities and identified my areas of interest. Whatever the case, shortly after these consultations I was approached by Goldmann, who gave me a rather vague account of his projects and asked me whether I found them of interest. I answered that I didn't really know. I still had fifteen months of scholarship support, and I had no financial worries at the time. Basically my situation was quite agreeable. I could do what I wanted and work on the topics that interested me most. All this without having to look for employment. Nonetheless Goldmann asked me to come for another conversation, so that he could provide a more detailed explanation of what he wanted. Naturally I had given matters a lot of thought in the meantime. I didn't know Goldmann, other than having heard him speak in public several times. I had always been very favorably impressed. And I knew that the people who would constitute the future World Jewish Congress—then a simple preparatory committee— were the only ones in the Jewish world who were truly fighting against Hitler, resisting Nazism by mobilizing international public opinion. This was courageous, well-reflected conduct. This became an important factor that weighed on my conscience. Yet Goldmann's proposals remained vague; in fact, he was not authorized to make a full commitment. Nothing had been decided, and no framework was in place. The job involved working *toward* the creation of the World Jewish Congress. As nothing was definite, I maintained a certain vagueness myself.

What exactly was Goldmann expecting of me? An agreement in principle? He had asked me whether the project was of interest to me, whether I was ready to collaborate. But the future was still very much in doubt. I made it clear that the matter had certainly seized my attention, but I didn't explicitly commit myself. Then Goldmann said to me, "Still, I would like to know what kind of work you can do," and he gave me a weighty file. "Could you write me a memorandum on all this?" The memorandum was fairly quickly completed, and I think he was pleased with it. This was in June. Goldmann questioned me again. "The Congress is to meet in the month of August. Where will you be spending the summer? Will I be able to get in touch with you?" All this certainly seemed very imprecise to me. I did not feel it was going to work out. For me, it was far from a certainty, it was just a possibility. A bit later I left to join my family in Holland.

For the summer of 1936, as every year at that time, my uncle had rented a house at the seashore at Noordwijk, where he would gather the family. My parents, who were still living in Berlin, came as well. This was our only opportunity during the year to meet. Ten days after my arrival, there was a telegram from Goldmann: "Come immediately; we need you. It is very important." I was very happy to have had at least those few days of vacation. I felt rested. I then hurried to Geneva to meet Goldmann—but he was in Saint Moritz. I went to the planning office of the Congress, which was to convene the next week. We had to draw up some summary reports for the delegates. It was a Sunday morning. All the previous day and night I had been traveling by train, in third class, from Amsterdam to Geneva. At the planning office they gave me a huge file. "Write a report on the problem of Jewish refugees from Germany; summarize what has happened since 1933, what has been done. Outline a program of what needs to be done." "By when?" I asked. "By last week!" And then they added, "The text will have to be translated into several languages. Hurry back, because you will have other topics to deal with."

We had only a few days to get everything done. Thus I set myself at once to studying the file. I knew the problems of the German Jews, numerous and complex, fairly well. But in order to prepare a complete report I had to have a command of all the details of the diplomatic negotiations of the preceding three years, in the course of which Chaim Weizmann had played a decisive role. These negotiations had reached their culmination in 1935 with the resignation of the League of Nations High Commissioner for Refugees James G. McDonald, who in this way lodged his protest over the negative attitude of the member states which, for the most part, were not granting visas to Jewish refugees from Germany. The report I drafted in two or three days was judged to meet the criteria that had been set for me. It sought not only to give an overview of what had happened between 1933 and 1936 but also to suggest a policy for the future. I even drew on it myself over the next few years. I imagine that Goldmann considered this memorandum a test of my abilities. As soon as I submitted the text, I was given other topics to address.

Then, a few days later, the assembly opened, on August 8, 1936, a Saturday evening. The atmosphere was that of a great international congress that had major decisions to take. For me, it was something entirely new. The opening ceremony was solemn, moving. Wise, the moral inspiration, and Goldmann, the brilliant intellectual leader, were remarkable. Indeed, Nahum Goldmann gave one of the great speeches of his career.

In the face of the skepticism of some and the cynicism of others, which only strengthened Hitler's audacity, Wise and Goldmann stated loudly and clearly the urgent necessity of fighting against the forces of evil. They had not the least illusion as to the destructive will of the dictator. Wise even quoted Hitler: "*Wir werden die Juden ausrotten*" ("We will exterminate the Jews") and added, "Just like Haman, Titus, and Pobiedonosteff, Hitler will not succeed!"*

Goldmann's analysis was more pessimistic. "The magnitude and urgency of the Jewish problem in Europe exceeds everything that has existed for centuries. It is no longer a matter of struggling for the rights of minorities, or for equality, *but for physical survival in the most elemental sense of the word*." And this was in 1936!

I found all this of passionate interest. In the middle of the meeting someone came to tell me, "You are to be the permanent secretary of the commission on German Jews," and a moment later, someone else, "You are going to be the permanent secretary of the commission on the rights of minorities." How could I take on both positions, which, moreover, were at times to be concurrent? Who cared at the time? That was to be up to me to sort out, regardless of the prevailing disorder that so characterized the organization of all the work to be done. No one was talking to me about the future. I said to myself, "Fine, that's the way it is; it's not the moment to be asking questions. I'm on their side and they need me. In addition, everything they are doing is useful, necessary, even indispensable. I am here to help out, to participate. I'll do it as well as I can."

For me the constitutive assembly of the World Jewish Congress was an experience both exalting and trying. My first function was to be the secretary of the two commissions. I had to follow their debates in order to take part in the

---

*Haman was the grand vizier of the Persian Empire under Xerxes who attempted to destroy the Jews because one of them, Esther's cousin Mordecai, refused to prostrate himself before the powerful official as Persian custom required. Titus was a Roman general who led the imperial forces against the rebellious Jews and who was responsible for the destruction of the Temple in 70 C.E. Pobiedonosteff was a vehemently anti-Semitic Slavophile and procurator of the Holy Synod who in 1882 instigated a massive pogrom against the Jews in Russia.—ED.

drafting of resolutions and then to take responsibility for the minutes, which also had to be translated and distributed. And that was not all. Given the urgency, I had to take part in all the work, respond to the calls of all those who solicited my help. I became aware that an instrument was taking shape before my eyes, an instrument to combat the injustices that were striking the Jewish people. It was self-evident that I would take part in that struggle.

The constitutive assembly of the Congress sat for a full week. I did an enormous amount of work. Some evenings I was on duty until one in the morning. At that time of the night there were no more buses or streetcars running; I had half an hour's walk on foot. I can still see myself walking through the deserted city one night. Suddenly a car stopped and someone said, "What are you doing here?" It was Goldmann, who gave me a ride home. And this was the beginning of a long relationship.

In what follows I shall return to the Congress, its work, its struggles, successes, and failures. But there in Geneva in 1936 the assembly created a structure that was unique in the vastness of its tasks and its ambitions, encompassing the problems of the entirety of the Jewish people in the whole world. The body had clearly posed the principle of the unity of the Jewish people. From this perspective, it is significant that the question of Soviet Jews was already being addressed and that the Congress supported the Zionist movement, which sought to ensure a haven and national homeland for Jews who had been persecuted and discriminated against, and whom no country wanted.

My Personal Commitment

The day after the first assembly, the executive committee held a meeting that I did not attend. In the course of that discussion Goldmann advanced the idea of opening a small office in Geneva and appointing me secretary for legal affairs. There was resistance from some members of the executive whose origins lay in Eastern Europe, people with whom I later had the best possible relations. One of them said, "But Riegner doesn't speak Yiddish!" To which Goldmann retorted, "I need him at the League of Nations. They don't speak Yiddish there, but French and English, two languages that he does know." This argument, however, did not win over the committee. Then the only German present, Professor Georg Bernhard, the undisputed leader of the German émigrés and editor-in-chief of the *Pariser Tageblatt*, stood up. Before the advent of Nazism he had been a member of the Reichstag, professor at the Berlin Higher Commercial School, manager of the union of German department store employees, and editor-in-chief of the great liberal newspaper *Vossische Zeitung*.

He was a responsible politician, very well known, with an international reputation and great authority. He had just accepted the directorship of the Congress's department of economic studies.

In the face of continuing opposition, Professor Bernhard rose and said, "But Riegner comes from a very, very good Jewish family"—which for Jews was much more important than speaking Yiddish. That can be learned, while a family is not something you can improvise. This assertion persuaded the committee to accept me.

Since then I have often asked myself why Professor Bernhard insisted that I belonged to a very good family. I knew that he and my father had known each other since their youth, and that they met from time to time at the Democratic Club in Berlin. It also happened that my father had collaborated on the legal section of the *Vossische Zeitung*. But the real reason lay elsewhere. One day I told my father the story of Professor Bernhard's intervention. At first he hesitated a bit, then he told me the following story. Professor Bernhard's father had been my grandfather's coachman. He was an imposing man who used to drive Grandfather to visit his clients in a carriage drawn by a team of fine horses. The double-yoked team had apparently made a great impression on my father in his youth. My father continued: "I have to tell you in confidence a very strange story. One fine day, this Herr Bernhard disappeared. He abandoned his wife and children without leaving a trace. And we noted later that some money was missing. We never saw Herr Bernhard or the carriage again, nor any of the money." My grandfather, who was a gentleman, never thought of getting back at the family. On the contrary, he displayed a great deal of concern for the wife and her two small children. He supported them, and even saw to the education of the children.

I then understood that I was not taken on by the World Jewish Congress for my merits, nor because of Nahum Goldmann. I was hired because my grandfather was a gentleman!

This is how I began with the Congress, renouncing for all practical purposes my career as a jurist. I had dreamed of becoming a professor of public law and of the philosophy of law. I have often thought with some sadness (but not too seriously) of the great loss that this represented for the world in the form of the books that I did not write and the courses I did not teach to admiring disciples!

In September 1936 I became an employee of the newly born World Jewish Congress, with, I believe, one hundred Swiss francs a month more than I had been getting from my stipendium at the Institute. But I had a title and was invested with weighty responsibilities and serious assignments. It is true that at the end of the month the money did not always arrive on time, while my stipendium had always been paid with Swiss punctuality. At times I even had to advance the money for stamps, for the secretary's wages, and for other office expenses. The secretary, a telephone, a typewriter . . . that's all the office of the World Jewish Congress was at its very beginnings. A month later I found a new office to rent. I chose premises in the great building of the Palais Wilson, a building that the League of Nations had just left. At the flea market I turned up some office furniture. Thus the office was not completely empty.

All this was close to improvisation and betrayed our uncertainties. I used to tell myself, "Since those who make up the Congress are the only ones to resist the Nazis, I will work for them for a few years. And afterwards, I'll see." But things did not turn out that way. More than a half-century later, I'm still there. Of course, I began modestly enough, then I became secretary-general, and ended up as co-president of the governing council. And today I am the honorary vice president of the World Jewish Congress. In sum, I have given sixty years of my life to the organization. The very fact that I stayed so long is proof that I found ample satisfaction there. Moreover, would I not have left long ago if I had regretted my choice? I was attracted by the incredible diversity and scope of the problems that unceasingly arose, and the need to address them and try to resolve them. What a challenge it was!—the most demanding but also the most enduring of passions.

Looking back, I contemplate the great course that we have run in all domains. I see the drama of the Jewish people and the immensity of their destruction. I see the rebirth of the State of Israel and of the Jewish people. I see the immense work that has made the Congress into a great, global Jewish organization. I see the renewal of Jewish communities, the emergence of a new kind of Jew, and the coming of new relations between Jews and the world.

Admittedly, huge tasks remain to be accomplished, tasks that I force myself to view with my feet on the ground, my vision ranging both high and wide. These tasks require a great deal of goodwill and beyond that a firm belief in our mission to enable us to confront them with all the vital force that hope can furnish. Without this nothing can be accomplished, but with it everything becomes possible.

TWO

The Time of the Shoah and the "Riegner Telegram"

THE MANNER in which I experienced the Shoah will form the beginning of the account of my professional activities. This was the most dramatic period of my life, which, as fate would have it, made me the first person to transmit authentic information to the Western world about Hitler's plan for the total annihilation of European Jewry. It is, then, not at all surprising that my testimony has often been called on and that there has been interest in knowing how I experienced that tragedy.

Here are the facts. The story begins on July 29, 1942. I received a telephone call from my friend Benjamin Sagalowitz, press officer with the Fédération des communautés juives de Suisse (Federation of Jewish Communities of Switzerland) in Zurich. With the utmost urgency, Sagalowitz insisted on seeing me. Our meeting took place on August 1 in Lausanne.

Sagalowitz informed me that one of his friends had been in touch with a prominent German industrialist, the head of a combine employing tens of thousands of workers and actively contributing to the war effort. This function gave him access to the highest military circles. The friend occasionally saw this powerful German corporate leader in Zurich, where he regularly came on business. Now, a few days earlier, he had come again, apparently to relieve his conscience. He had learned that at Hitler's headquarters the Nazis were discussing "a plan aimed at transferring all the Jews of Europe, from three and a half to four million people, to the countries of Eastern Europe, in order to annihilate them and thus resolve once and for all the Jewish problem in Europe."

The German manufacturer had suggested that this revelation be transmitted to the Jews and to the Allies. The message went on to say that discussion had focused on the means by which this might be done, and that there was talk of prussic acid. It was only much later that we learned that the Zyklon B used in the gas chambers of Auschwitz and other extermination centers was based on prussic acid.

When Sagalowitz shared this information with me, we discussed it for five or six hours while walking along the lake shore. Was it to be taken seriously? Was it conceivable that the Nazis would plan to kill millions of people? Wasn't it just a provocation? Was the message credible? Despite everything we already knew about what was happening in Germany itself and in occupied Europe— and we knew a great deal—this seemed extraordinary to us. Over the course of several days we asked ourselves these questions. In spite of all the information in my possession, in spite of the discussions we pursued in ever greater depth, in spite of what I had already experienced myself, I still needed another two days to convince myself that these events really were possible and, finally, to believe in them. Sagalowitz went through the same complex of questions, the same states of mind, examining this disclosure from every conceivable angle. We stayed in continual contact.

Three sets of established facts guided our deliberations, and it is appropriate that they be recalled at this point.

First, Hitler had clearly enunciated his intentions toward the Jews on several occasions. He had done so under solemn circumstances, on the occasion of celebrations of the anniversary of the January 30, 1933, assumption of power by the Nazis. On the day of the 1939 celebration Hitler had accused the Jews of inciting war, a war which, if it were to come, would conclude with the end of European Jewry and emphatically not with that of the German people. This announcement of the prospective end of European Jewry—essentially repeated on the same public occasion in 1940, 1941, and 1942—had not caught the world's attention, as few took the threat seriously. We remembered the same stance from our reading of *Mein Kampf;* even though Hitler had announced all his aggressive plans, virtually no one had found them any the more credible. Were we once again to ignore his menace, commit yet again the same error?

Second, it was early August 1942, and just two weeks earlier a massive roundup of Jews had occurred all over occupied Western Europe. On almost the very same day, August 14, large-scale arrests were carried out in the streets of various major cities: Amsterdam, Antwerp, Brussels, Paris, Lyon, Marseilles. Tens of thousands of Jews were arrested and interned in transit camps pending deportation. We were even more conscious of this as we had received reports backed up with precise figures. Among the Jews who had been arrested we also knew that a number had already been deported to the East. We immediately asked ourselves what these waves of arrests and deportations could mean. We were naturally informed of the arrests and deportations that had already taken place in Berlin, Vienna, and Prague, for which we had supporting figures. (As yet we remained ignorant about the deportations from Warsaw, which began on July 25.) Suddenly all Europe seemed engaged in a process of annihilation. The message from the German industrialist finally gave meaning to everything that was happening.

Third, we were aware of the criminal character of the Nazi regime and of the terror it exercised. I had personally experienced this, as I have already said early in this book, and I shall return to it. I had, in fact, seen the Nazis at work, had observed their brutality, unchecked by any ethic or morality. The arrest of those who opposed them, the creation of concentration camps, the torture—all were known to me. The burning of the Reichstag, an enormous provocation, afforded sharp insight into the true nature of the Nazi regime. From 1933 onward it was possible to understand that the Nazis intended to implement the Nazi party program outlined in *Mein Kampf* through the use of terror. Those who had not grasped in 1933 that they were dealing with a criminal regime ought to have understood it in 1934, a year whose most portentous event was the "Night of the Long Knives" and the murder of Sturmabteilung (SA) Chief of Staff Ernst Röhm. In a brutal act of intraparty repression, without any trial or proceedings, the Nazis killed hundreds of members of the SA, the party's street-fighting unit until that time. Once into their stride, they also assassinated a number of other political adversaries, such as former Chancellor Kurt von Schleicher. After this bloody settling of accounts, the Nazis proclaimed by a vote in the Reichstag that this action had been legal and that Hitler was "the German people's supreme magistrate" (Des deutschen Volkes oberster Gerichtsherr). At that moment, who did not understand the criminal nature of the regime?

Corresponding to the Nazi policy of terror within the country was a cynical policy of military-based actions abroad, in violation of all the rules of international law. The Nazis proclaimed in clear accord with their ideological conceptions: "What is just is what is good for the German people." The remilitarization of the Rhineland in 1936, the incorporation of Austria in 1938, blackmail over the Sudetenland and the dismemberment of Czechoslovakia in 1938–1939, and, finally, the aggression against Poland—a sequence of criminal stages leading to the Second World War.

In all our reflections we were fully conscious that hatred of the Jews constituted the central tenet of Nazi ideology and of the Nazi program. The ultimate objective of the Nazis was world conquest, domination by the German race. Their "racial superiority," the Germans claimed, conferred upon them the right to dominate all other peoples. But the primary target was the Jews.

Their powerful propaganda concentrated on hatred of Jews, who were cast as the source of all the ills of the earth, afflicted with the most contradictory characteristics: responsible for capitalism, for communism, for liberalism, for socialism, for democracy, for all miseries and all ill-gotten gains. An almost medieval demonization was the common denominator and, in a way, the psychological weapon of this destructive rage. Reason had no place here. The battle against the Jews and Judaism was at the center of the Nazi program.

As we have already seen in Hitler's pronouncements, this battle was to end in the destruction of the Jewish people. From the moment of their accession to power, the Nazis systematically pursued this policy: the day of the Jewish boycott, April 1, 1933; a bit later the first anti-Jewish legislation, which excluded Jews from public functions and from the professions; the Nuremberg laws of September 1935, which deprived Jews of their political rights and ordered their exclusion from the economic life of the country, leading to the despoiling "aryanization" of Jewish property. Innumerable Germans, from the biggest bankers to the smallest shopkeepers, threw themselves shamelessly over the plunder stolen from the Jews.

The national pogrom in November 1938, after the assassination of the third secretary at the German embassy in Paris, which was followed by the burning of 267 synagogues, the destruction and pillaging of 7,500 businesses, the internment of almost 30,000 Jews in concentration camps, a collective fine of one billion marks, and the unpunished killings of almost 100 Jews—these were the culminating points of prewar persecution and the bloody portent of much worse crimes to come.

I believe that only a German Jew who had witnessed Nazi methods was capable of understanding Hitler's designs and the mortal danger they represented. From this perspective, the German manufacturer's revelations had the decided ring of truth.

During my discussions with Sagalowitz, another memory kept recurring. For years I had struggled beside the Jews of Danzig to defend and preserve their status, which had been guaranteed by the League of Nations. One of their leaders, Walter Gerson, had come to see me at Shavous (Pentecost) in 1939. That day we took a long walk through the Geneva countryside. The moment came when we spoke of the war. We knew it was inevitable and the only means of stopping Hitler. But we also knew the war would be terrible. And we were heartbroken over it.

I have never forgotten that at one moment Gerson said to me, "Do you know what the war will mean for us? It will be a catastrophe the likes of which we have never known. The Nazis are going to kill millions of Jews and we do not have the means to stop them, because of their brutality and their determination." And with astounding prophetic imagination, Gerson described to me what was going to happen when war broke out. He expressed in concrete terms what we had only felt in confused fashion and had not dared formulate.

Some months later, after the invasion of Poland, when the first massacres of Jews took place in Poznań and Bromberg, I learned that he had been among the earliest victims to have been assassinated there by the Nazis. This memory haunts me still. My assessment of the situation owed a great deal to Gerson's apocalyptic vision.

The German industrialist's report threw a whole new light on the tragedy. On the one hand we discovered with horror that behind all the details of the persecution there existed an overall plan for annihilation that had been decided at the highest levels. On the other hand this news was of decisive importance because, contrary to most of our intelligence, it did not come from the victims but from a German source, originating in the highest councils of power.

Thus our reflections proceeded. At this stage my first duty was to determine the sources and the credibility of the messenger. Sagalowitz did not know the German industrialist personally. He had seen him in the company of the Jewish directors of a large Zurich company, whom he counted among his friends. Their chief executive officer, Jacques Rosenstein, had left Zurich for New York, where he would stay for the entire war. Rosenstein knew Dr. Nahum Goldmann and supported the policies of the World Jewish Congress. The company official to whom the message had been given by the German informant was Isidor Koppelmann.

I insisted on meeting Koppelmann and hearing from his mouth the exact message that had been communicated. The more intermediaries, the greater the risk of error. I was not keen on meeting the German informant himself— no more, apparently, than he was on seeing me. Let us not forget the atmosphere in Switzerland of intense suspicion and mistrust during the war years which in many Swiss reached the level of paranoia.

Two days later, accompanied by Sagalowitz, I had a conversation with Isidor Koppelmann in Zurich. Throughout our discussion, which went into considerable detail, the latter confirmed to me everything that Sagalowitz had transmitted. He specified that the Nazis envisaged full execution of the plan for the physical elimination of Jews by the end of 1942; there were to be no survivors. As for the means to this end, Koppelmann, too, alluded to prussic acid and added that there had been talk of giant crematoriums, in which the Jews of Europe, transferred to concentration camps in the east of the continent, were to "go up in flames." However strong the impression made on me by this expression, I must admit that I could not succeed in picturing it to myself and did not mention it in the course of the steps I subsequently took.

Koppelmann had been greatly impressed by the personality of the German manufacturer whom he had, moreover, known for some time, and who had already given him information of primary importance about the war. In particular, he had announced several weeks in advance the imminent invasion of the Soviet Union by the Germans. There could be no doubt that he had access to very highly placed figures in the Nazi regime.

The news that Koppelmann confirmed for us was not the first notification of a considerable worsening in Nazi policy toward the Jews. From the Eastern front, that is, after the attack on the USSR, terrible reports of the massacre of Jews had been reaching us continually.

We did not grasp exactly what was happening, and the notion of *Einsatzgruppen* (mobile killing units) was still not known to us. In any case, by the fall of 1941, two to three months after the invasion, we had received news of the horrifying events that were unfolding there. Without having very many details, we knew that in this place the Nazis had gunned down ten thousand Jews, that in another they had massacred thousands. Intelligence of this nature came in successively from different locations. It permitted us to realize that a massive killing of Jews had been organized at the front and in the territories to the east.

This news convinced me to write to Nahum Goldmann on October 27, 1941: "It is becoming increasingly clear that there will be no future life for Jews in Europe. What is happening at present is perhaps the final stage of the total suppression of European Jewry. Even if we do not know how many Russian Jews will escape, there will not be much left standing west of the Prut and the Vistula. I more and more fear that we cannot save more than a very few people and their property."

In March 1942, Richard Lichtheim, the Geneva representative of the Jewish Agency for Palestine, and I undertook an initial intervention through the papal nuncio in Bern, Msgr. Filippe Bernardini, in order to alert the Vatican. The nuncio was a high-ranking and highly respected figure. He had carried out important missions, and we know today that a great number of the messages from the Vatican went through him. When he received us, we said to him in essence: "Do something in the Catholic countries at least, there where you have influence, to stop the massacre." At Msgr. Bernardini's request we drafted a memorandum for him (to which I shall return below), describing, country by country, the actions involved in the liquidation of Jewish communities.

It was also during this period, at the turn of the year 1941–1942, that I received information on lethal experiments with gas and injections. The gassing experiments had been carried out in sealed trucks, and all those locked inside were asphyxiated.

Occasionally the same piece of news would reach us several times. The first time we would ask ourselves whether such things were possible. But when it was repeatedly communicated from different locations, we began to believe it. We were convinced that the situation was growing worse with each passing day.

I initially kept the news of the German industrialist to myself. I shared it with only one person, Professor Paul Gugggenheim, the legal counsel of the World Jewish Congress. Since I was a very young director of the office, Goldmann, when he left Geneva in 1940, had recommended that I consult Guggenheim on major problems. I did so and set out for him what I intended to do. I also asked that Guggenheim put in a word for me with Paul Squire, the United States consul in Geneva, whom I had met several times in his home.

A Swiss professor of law and a man of experience, Guggenheim was a cautious person. In principle he agreed with my plan. He nonetheless insisted on attenuating the text of a telegram I had drafted to be sent to the United States. Referring to these reservations, some people have asserted much later that "Riegner didn't believe it himself." But, as the testimony of the American vice consul proves, this was not true. The professor's prudence in no way altered the sense of the telegram.

I had by then decided to inform the Allies officially, in practical terms the Americans and the British. In fact the Soviet Union had no diplomatic relations with Switzerland and as a consequence had no official representation there. France, of course, was represented by the anti-Semitic Vichy government.

On August 8 I went to the United States consulate. It was during the holidays, and the consul was absent. I met the vice consul, Howard Elting, Jr. His account of our discussion is found in Arthur D. Morse's book, *While Six Million Died: A Chronicle of American Apathy* (1967).

I remember discussing matters with him for a long time in order to explain in detail the profound reasons for my conviction, which obliged me to take the German's information very seriously. Elting was quite upset. His report, drafted that same day, stated that despite the enormity of what I had reported, he judged that I was sincere and profoundly convinced of what I asserted. He was specific: "Riegner is a serious and balanced individual . . . [with] confidence in his informant's reliability."

I requested three things of Elting. I told him: "First, here is a report that I have received from a very trustworthy source." I did not give the name but I explained the situation of the informant. "I am asking you to inform your government.

"Second, you have a secret service; I do not. Have your secret service verify the accuracy of these affirmations.

"Third, send this telegram to Stephen Wise, president of the World Jewish Congress in the United States. He is a well-known public figure and a personal friend of President Roosevelt."

The Text of the Telegram

Out of prudence I had prepared two draft telegrams, one on the terrible news, and another, longer one in which I summarized everything I knew at the time concerning the deportations to Central and Eastern Europe.

I gave the consul the shorter version; this is the original text:

RECEIVED ALARMING REPORT THAT IN FÜHRERS HEADQUARTERS PLAN
DISCUSSED AND UNDER CONSIDERATION ALL JEWS IN COUNTRIES OCCUPIED
CONTROLLED GERMANY NUMBER $3^{1}/_{2}$ TO FOUR MILLION SHOULD AFTER
DEPORTATION AND CONCENTRATION IN EAST AT ONE BLOW EXTERMINATED
TO RESOLVE ONCE FOR ALL JEWISH QUESTION IN EUROPE STOP ACTION IS
REPORTED PLANNED FOR AUTUMN METHODS UNDER DISCUSSION
INCLUDING PRUSSIC ACID STOP WE TRANSMIT INFORMATION WITH ALL
NECESSARY RESERVATION AS EXACTITUDE CANNOT BE CONFIRMED STOP
INFORMANT STATED TO HAVE CLOSE CONNECTIONS WITH HIGHEST GERMAN
AUTHORITIES AND HIS REPORTS GENERALLY RELIABLE STOP

Elting probably telephoned Paul Squire. In any case, he transmitted my report to the American legation in Bern and backed up my requests. In the end it was the legation that cabled the report to the State Department in Washington.

Then I went to the British consulate. The consul, H. B. Livingstone, whom I had known for several years, was not there, and I was received by the vice consul, a Mr. Armstrong. I gave him the same report and made the same requests as to Elting, except that my message was to be transmitted to S. Sydney Silverman, a well-known member of Parliament, who at the time was chairman of the British section of the World Jewish Congress. It is of interest to note that the text of the telegram was the same as that addressed to Wise, with however one shade of difference. At the close of the text sent to Britain, I added: "INFORM AND CONSULT NEW YORK." That was self-evident. But it did reveal the doubts I had about the Americans forwarding the telegram to Wise. I told myself that the Foreign Office would not dare purely and simply to suppress a telegram sent through British diplomatic channels to a prominent member of Parliament.

I was not mistaken; things turned out exactly as I had foreseen. The message to Wise was never sent on by the State Department. We know today that it prompted extremely lively discussion. One of the senior officials, Paul Culbertson, assistant chief of the department's Division of European Affairs, even said, "If Rabbi Wise some day finds out that we kept the message and didn't forward it to him, he could start a scandal and hit us very hard."* Wise's temperament was well known.

The World's Incredulity

In a letter dated August 24, 1942, the U.S. consul informed me that the State Department had not delivered my message to Wise "because of its unsubstantiated character." Squire, who gave me this news, was kind and understanding. And he was devastated. He asked me to give him any information that would corroborate my message. Later we became very good friends.

As for my telegram to Silverman, it was sent to the Foreign Office in London by the British legation in Bern. It took a full ten days to work its way to Silverman. During the period when the House was not sitting, Silverman was not in London. The message finally reached him at his home in Liverpool.

As soon as he received the telegram, Silverman tried to inform Wise. In wartime all communications abroad required authorization. Silverman asked for permission to telephone Wise, but the War Office could not authorize his call despite his status as an MP. Finally Silverman succeeded in sending the telegram through the intermediary of the War Office. Wise received it on August 28, 1942, three weeks after my efforts— three weeks during which thousands of Jews were massacred daily.

I have often been asked, "Why did you send telegrams through the intermediary of diplomatic missions and not simply by mail?" Those who did not experience the war years cannot know that every letter, every telegram sent from Switzerland to the Allied countries was intercepted by German intelligence. And

*Culbertson's statement is quoted in Morse, *While Six Million Died*, p. 9.—ED.

from their side, the Swiss practiced a very strict military censorship. Careful not to give offense to the Germans, they would never have permitted a telegram with such content to go through. The telegraph service would quite simply have refused to send it.

When Wise received the telegram he was overcome. One can see this in the poignant terms of the letters he sent in the days following to his friends Supreme Court Justice Felix Frankfurter and the Rev. John Haynes Holmes.

As soon as he received my message, Wise got in touch with Undersecretary of State Sumner Welles, without knowing that the same message had been in the hands of the State Department for weeks. According to Wise's memoirs, Welles asked him not to make the message public before verifying its truthfulness. In order not to cut himself off from sources of information in the State Department, Wise respected this request. At the same time he sent me a message through a senior official with the Protestant churches of America, Samuel McCrea-Cavert, one of the few American visitors to Switzerland at the time. Wise asked me whether we were absolutely sure that "deportation" meant "extermination." Our confirmation was transmitted by telegram to Wise by the same individual.

For its part the State Department tried to have the news verified by the Vatican and by the International Committee of the Red Cross. The Vatican gave a vague reply: "We are aware of the bad treatment of the Jews but have no confirmation of a global plan for their extermination."

As for the International Committee of the Red Cross, its October 21 response made clear that it was informed of the deportation of Jews "under conditions of great suffering," but it could not confirm the existence of a plan for total extermination.

In Great Britain the reaction to my information was skepticism, as is shown by materials in archives that have since been opened. In my file drawers I have photocopies of notes written by various officials of the Foreign Office. During the first ten days following the receipt of my telegram, instead of trying to learn whether its contents were accurate or not, everyone was asking, "Who is Riegner?"

At that time my name was unknown in diplomatic circles. On the one hand I was still a young man; on the other, when I joined the Congress in 1936 my family was still in Germany. In order not to expose my parents to danger, I intentionally avoided, until the close of 1938, letting my name appear in public documents. Thus, until the outbreak of the war, my name had appeared nowhere.

No one believed the background to the news. A note from a senior official in the Foreign Office even claimed to know that it was a matter of "wild rumors born of Jewish fear." It is only when the news was reiterated, coming from different sources, that the British government little by little began to change its attitude. It can be seen how the flood of such news after my telegram in particular influenced the British approach to the problem of war criminals.

All this is astonishing, for we know today that the British secret service had succeeded in breaking the German code and was then well informed on the progress of the "Final Solution."

The slow Allied reaction shocked me terribly. I felt that they doubted the truthfulness of our reports. This pushed me to redouble my efforts to obtain additional testimony confirming the plan for total annihilation.

Our priority became to seek out new information and complementary proof, and to furnish the Jewish organizations of Great Britain and America with as much reliable intelligence as possible. And I succeeded.

Here is some direct testimony from among the most important that I collected, confirming our information on the "Final Solution."

In September 1942 two letters arrived in Switzerland from Warsaw. A Jew who was living illegally outside the ghetto had sent them to Isaac Sternbuch, the representative in Switzerland of Agudath Israel, the Orthodox Jewish religious organization. The two letters reported in thinly veiled language the daily deportation of Jews from Warsaw. They left no doubt about the fact that these people were being exterminated. Hebrew terms are found in the German text of the letters in which *gerush* (repudiation, banishment) evokes deportation and *uncle akhinu* (the uncle, our brother) the fate of the Jewish people: *uncle akhinu ist verstorben*—"our people are dead."

From other sources too information reached us on the vast deportation of the Jews of Warsaw in July 1942, which signified the approaching end of the ghetto.

In a report dated August 15, 1942, Richard Lichtheim of the Jewish Agency for Palestine, with whom I had close relations, wrote: "The Warsaw ghetto is in the process of liquidation. The same news is reaching us from Vilna and other cities. In certain provinces of eastern Europe, there is no longer a single Jew—they have all been killed."

Another report dealt with the massacre of fifty thousand Jews in Lwow (Lemberg).

Among the most important direct testimony was that of a young Latvian Jew, Gabriel Zivian. In September 1942 he reached Geneva, where he had distant relatives. Zivian told me about the fate of the Jews of Riga, the capital of Latvia. He described to me in great detail what had occurred during two

nights in November and December 1941. During those two nights the entire
Jewish population of the city had been exterminated, including the famous
Jewish historian Simon Doubnov.

Beginning with the arrival of German troops on July 1, 1941, raids had
been carried out with unconstrained brutality. Countless Jews were taken off
for various kinds of forced labor. At the same time between one and two thousand people were imprisoned. Later it was learned that on July 20 all of them
had been shot in a forest.

One day the Riga Jews were forced to leave their homes and enter a ghetto
without delay. Disorder, crowding, and misery were the common lot. Many of
them had not been able to bring with them the least personal possessions, to
say nothing of furniture, linens, or a change of clothing.

The Jews of Riga were rounded up with terrible brutality. Any attempt at
flight or even hesitation resulted in execution on the spot. When these people,
brought to nearby ravines, understood that mass murder awaited them, it was
too late. The shooting and screams could be heard all around.

Gabriel Zivian, who had experienced all this in Riga, escaped. Since he was
a medical student, he then worked for a few months under a false identity in
a hospital in Stettin.

After various close calls, he finally succeeded in obtaining a visa for
Switzerland. When he was sent to me, I interrogated him for eight hours. He
described to me in detail everything that had happened in Riga nine months
earlier and of which the rest of the world knew absolutely nothing. In the
course of two nights, 24,000 Jews had been killed with machine-gun fire by
specially trained units. This was the first time I had heard the account of an
eyewitness.

A bit later I received other testimony, even more staggering. During the
same month of September I had a telephone call from the cantonal hospital.
A Jewish woman doctor of my acquaintance, Cecile Rhein, said to me, "Come
quickly, I am going to reveal something astonishing. I can't tell you over the
telephone what it's about."

At the hospital she introduced me to a man named Isak Lieber. I have
never divulged his name before now because it was illegal to be in contact with
someone who was under police surveillance. I did not wish to create problems
for the doctor or for her patient. The doctor told me, "Listen, there is a fellow
here who is telling very strange stories. I can't understand anything, but you
will certainly have a better idea of what he's talking about."

The patient was a young Jewish man who had been seized by the Nazis in
Brussels in one of the great roundups of July–August 1942. Transferred to Ma-

lines, the Belgian transit camp near the capital city, he had then been deported to Eastern Europe. Very precisely he described to me his own arrest, the camp at Malines, and then the various stages of his deportation until he reached Rava Ruska. He was then sent close to the military front at Stalingrad, where he was put to work on fortifications. After he had been working there for some time, a young German officer asked if there were a driver among the detainees. Since he was a mechanic and knew how to drive, Lieber volunteered. The officer took him on as driver for several weeks. This Wehrmacht officer, who had lost two of his brothers in combat, was extremely tired of war. He decided to help the young Jew escape. As they were driving around, Lieber asked for information on what was happening to the Jews. Lieber asked what had happened to the people—the women, the children—who were with him. The German explained to him: "Those who were fit to work were taken for all kinds of forced labor, especially on military fortifications on the Eastern front. The others were done away with. Those who were no longer fit for work were done away with too." That was the procedure. Thus the whole tragedy was summed up in a few simple sentences.

Having decided to save Lieber, the officer hid him on a freight train that was heading west, loaded with the uniforms of German soldiers who had fallen at the Battle of Stalingrad. The officer also gave him money, occupation marks, and food for a few days. So the Jew, hidden in a car filled with uniforms, rolled westward. The train went on and on, an unimaginable trip, for days and nights. Finally it stopped on a siding, in the station of a great city. There he left the train. He immediately recognized that he was near the Gare de l'Est in Paris. Since he had some money, he was able to survive.

Lieber eventually left Paris. After crossing the demarcation line to reach the "free zone" of France, he tried to cross the border to Switzerland. There he was arrested by a soldier. Since his feet were terribly swollen, he was put into a hospital.

Lieber was a very simple man. He told me all this over five or six hours. He was yet another eyewitness.

There was also a report that I did not relay at the time. Here it is in brief: In the course of the winter of 1941–1942 a Swiss medical mission was sent to the Eastern front. It was intended to mollify German anger at the Swiss. The Germans were unhappy because Swiss public opinion did not support their cause and was severely critical of the Reich.

The Swiss sent doctors and medicine to relieve the suffering wounded and sick German troops on the Eastern front. This was a military mission, and the whole expedition was made up of representatives of the Swiss army medical corps. The president of the Swiss Red Cross also took part.

The mission returned to Switzerland in February 1942. On the Eastern front it had been able to observe terrible events. A German-speaking Swiss doctor by the name of Bucher was deeply affected by the atrocities he had seen and spoke on the subject to a closed meeting of Bern doctors. I was not able to read the text of his remarks, but people heard about it. He openly revealed the facts about the systematic annihilation of Jews in the East.

As a consequence, Dr. Bucher drew the censure of the head of the Swiss Military Department, that is, the war ministry, and received the order, "You have no right to speak of it." The Swiss government has always claimed that it did not know of the abominable things that were happening in the East when it closed its borders to Jews in August 1942. Here is proof to the contrary.

Another extremely important piece of testimony for us was that of Professor Carl J. Burckhardt, the vice president of the International Committee of the Red Cross. When we were informed of the existence of the Nazi plan for the total extermination of the Jews, we asked him whether he or the International Committee had any information on the subject. The question was put to him by Guggenheim, his colleague at the Institute of International Studies, in the faculty common room where they frequently met.

Burckhardt, whom I also knew fairly well from my years at the Institute, confirmed to us that he had received similar, corroborating intelligence from two German individuals, one working in the Ministry of Foreign Affairs, the other in the War Ministry. Their statements, made under the seal of secrecy, confirmed our own information.

Burckhardt's reply, based on the statements of these two German individuals, left no doubt as to Nazi Germany's intention to be rid of the Jews. The expression that was used was to make Europe *judenfrei*, free of Jews. But, he said, since there existed no country to receive the Jews, there could be no doubt about the significance of the term.

Burckhardt at the time was very well informed. When we read today the various reports that Heydrich, the head of the Reich Security Main Office, sent to von Ribbentrop, the minister of foreign affairs, in the autumn of 1941 and later, concerning the massacre of Jews and the progress of the "Final Solution," we see that he everywhere uses that same term, *judenfrei*.

Burckhardt also told us that an official with the German consulate in Geneva, Albrecht von Kessel, had asked him in early September no longer to intervene on behalf of certain individual cases, as such steps thereafter would be quite useless.

It seems strange that Burckhardt should never have spoken to his International Committee of the Red Cross colleagues of the information on the "Final Solution" he had obtained from German sources. According to the most recent literature, in particular the work of Professor Jean-Claude Favez (now available in English as *The Red Cross and the Holocaust* [1999]), on the role of the ICRC during World War II, no trace of such a communication from Burck-hardt is to be found in the archives of the organization.

It is no less strange that he should not have communicated this informa-tion a few weeks later to Paul Squire, the U.S. consul, when Squire approached him after my discussion with Leland Harrison, the head of the American lega-tion in Switzerland.

Meanwhile the German industrialist had returned to Switzerland. In his first version of the facts, communicated in late July, he spoke of the "Final So-lution" as a project. On his return to Zurich a few weeks later, he made it clear that it was not a question of a proposal, that an order from Hitler did exist, and that decisions taken at the highest levels were in the process of imple-mentation.

This is what we knew, and how we came to know it. We had gained intel-ligence about a whole series of highly important facts, originating from dif-ferent sources, all confirming the German industrialist's report.

Throughout this period I continued to pass on information as I received it to Squire and the others.

Somewhat later, toward mid-October 1942, I was called to Bern by Leland Harrison, the U.S. envoy. The invitation had been suggested to Sumner Welles by Wise. By telegram, Wise asked me to give Harrison the complete file of in-formation I had acquired. Wise also asked me to involve Richard Lichtheim, the Geneva representative of the Jewish Agency for Palestine, in my activities.

I was on very good terms with Lichtheim; his office and mine were on the same floor. But I had not immediately brought him up to date on the most re-cent news I had from the German source. I spoke to him of this only some-what later. We had been able to exchange a great deal of other information that had come in between August and October, and discuss it together.

Lichtheim was terribly pessimistic, much more so than I. He was consid-erably older than I and had greater political experience. As early as 1920 he was a member of the executive committee of the World Zionist Organization. During World War I he had been in Constantinople with Victor Jacobson, and served his diplomatic apprenticeship there. In the face of his pessimism, I still had some small reserves of hope.

Lichtheim thought, I believe, that everything we were doing was quite senseless. Despite the fact that I too was fundamentally pessimistic, I said, "We have to do everything, absolutely everything that we can. Even if it doesn't succeed, we must try and try again. It's our duty."

As planned, then, the U.S. legation in Bern summoned us. Both of us briefed ourselves quite thoroughly for the meeting, to which we attached the greatest importance.

The American envoy was not a career diplomat but likely a senior businessman with wide experience. In the course of the meeting we turned over to Harrison a memorandum of about thirty pages summarizing all the intelligence we had at our disposal: what we knew about the deportations, and the specific reports such as the notes from the oral testimony of Lieber and Zivian. An overview of the deportation of Jews across all Europe completed the file.

Harrison, without saying a word, began to read the thirty-page memorandum. For twenty minutes profound silence reigned in his large office. Having completed his reading, he picked up the file again and went through it page by page, asking questions about points that he wanted to have clarified. He gave no sign of sympathy or antipathy. His unchanging countenance led Lichtheim later to call him "poker face."

Here I want to emphasize two important matters. First, this meeting was the only time in my life when, in a sealed envelope, I gave the name of the German informant and his function in the German war industry. The man in question was Herr Eduard Schulte, director general of a complex of mining companies, Georg von Giesche's Erben. It was only after historians found Schulte's name in the State Department archives that I confirmed his identity. Indeed, in truth I had only learned the full identity of this man several days before the meeting with Harrison. Second, I gave an oral report of Burckhardt's confidential testimony, citing his name and his position. I felt that this meeting would be decisive: either the Americans would believe me or they would not believe me. I would have to risk everything to win everything. At the end of the meeting, Harrison asked that Zivian make an official deposition under oath, an affidavit, in confirmation of his report. Harrison also asked for an affidavit from Professor Guggenheim concerning his conversation with Burckhardt. I forewarned Harrison that Guggenheim was unlikely to mention Burckhardt's name, and the envoy made a note of it. In fact, Guggenheim spoke of an "important international figure." The sworn depositions were added to our file. We know from other sources today that Harrison asked the U.S. consul in Geneva, Paul Squire, to pay a call on Professor Burckhardt in order to verify the truthfulness of my report. The consul drafted two notes on his discussion with Burckhardt confirming my oral report. They are now preserved in the State Department files at the National Archives and Records Administration in College Park, Maryland.

These facts demonstrate the seriousness with which Harrison treated our file. From what is known today, he had been highly skeptical when I presented my first information to the American consulate in Geneva. But it seems that our documentation impressed him and led him to change his position.

All these measures took time. When the complete file finally arrived in Washington, Undersecretary of State Sumner Welles summoned Stephen Wise and said to him, "These documents confirm and justify your worst fears." As a consequence, Welles gave Wise his consent to have the reports published. Wise and Goldmann did so at once.

As soon as Wise and Goldmann published the report, Jewish organizations around the Free World began to act. As early as the first days of September, when he received my first telegram through Silverman, Stephen Wise convoked the most important American Jewish organizations to two confidential meetings. They discussed the contents of my telegram as well as a telegram received a few days later by Agudath from its representative in Switzerland, reporting the killing of 100,000 Warsaw Jews.

From that moment on, American Jews mobilized: they organized protest rallies, they collected monies, they deliberated over a coherent relief program. The Jewish press devoted its daily headlines to the terrible drama of European Jewry.

In London, Jewish organizations were equally active. Spurred by the dynamic British section of the World Jewish Congress, they pressed the British government to take action. They addressed themselves to all the governments-in-exile and informed the churches and other important figures in public life. The representative Jewish body, the Board of Deputies of British Jews, organized a large public rally at Albert Hall in London.

For Jewish groups on both sides of the Atlantic it was a matter of obtaining and publishing statements by prominent political and religious figures, of organizing press campaigns, of approaching the Allied governments in order to obtain a common declaration. Some people even envisaged threats of reprisal, such as the seizure of German property and assets, and the like. All were agreed that after the war these crimes should not go unpunished.

In London the reactions of the several governments-in-exile were extremely varied. They reflected the hesitation on the part of the Allies. The Polish government assumed a very energetic position, undertaking a whole series of actions addressed to the other Allied governments and the Vatican.

At the time all of us were a bit skeptical about the attitude of the Polish government-in-exile with regard to the Jews and the annihilation process. When today we consider what was done, what was published, I have the impression that these Poles behaved much better than we feared at the time. For example, the letters addressed by its president, Władysław Raczkiewicz, to Pope Pius XII, in particular that of January 2, 1943, are extremely moving. Curiously, the Czechoslovakian president, Edvard Beneš, who was a great friend of the Jewish people, believed that it was all a German provocation and put no faith in the report.

The only one to express any real sympathy for the actions of the World Jewish Congress in London and to accept the report as plausible and worthy of belief was Ivan Maiski, the Soviet ambassador to London. Historically this is of considerable interest. He probably knew from his own experience that such massacres could take place without the world learning about it.

Alas, everything seemed to indicate that such reasoning, simply human as it was, was hardly within the reach of career diplomats. Thus the historian Arthur Morse calls attention to the story of the president of Honduras who, during the war, spoke with the American ambassador about the tragic fate of the European Jews. The ambassador's reply: "All that comes from a Jew living in Switzerland." Unbelievable!

I have often been asked whether the news in my telegram actually found a positive reception among Jewish leaders and whether they believed in the truthfulness of my report. It will be helpful, in this regard, to share several of my personal experiences.

I asked this question in particular of Maurice Perlzweig, who was then the political director of the World Jewish Congress in New York and who had naturally taken part in all the discussions on this subject. He spontaneously replied, "We naturally believed what you were communicating. No one had any doubts about your report."

Other people have told me: "Your news was not really news." The Polish government had already published a report in May 1942 on the atrocities, persecutions, and extermination of Jews occurring in Poland.

I then took the occasion to ask this question of one of the two Jewish members of the State Council of the Polish government-in-exile, Dr. Ignace (Itzhak) Schwartzbart. Schwartzbart confirmed to me that my telegram had caused a great shock and had immediately been considered of the greatest importance. He added, "Naturally, we knew what was happening in Poland. We knew that the Nazis were persecuting and killing masses of Polish Jews. But your news was sensational because, for the first time, we learned of the existence, from the Nazis themselves, of a comprehensive plan for the extermination of all the Jews of Europe. We had not known of this."

Other testimony that profoundly struck me came from René Cassin, professor of international public law, minister of justice in the National Committee of Free France, and close collaborator of General Charles de Gaulle. I knew him very well. On the conclusion of my law studies in Paris, he had been one of my examiners. This was our first subsequent meeting.

Allow me briefly time to digress here. Years later at the United Nations, Cassin and I saw each other fairly regularly at the Commission on Human Rights, at the Economic and Social Council, and on many other occasions. One day René Cassin came up to me in the course of a meeting of the Commission on Human Rights and told me that he was in the process of writing his memoirs and that he wanted to consult me on some details of my August 1942 message about the extermination of the Jews. He told me then that he had learned of it in the course of a gathering at the home of Israel and Rebecca Sieff. The Sieffs, a well-known London Jewish family, used to have a lively political salon. Meeting there regularly were a number of Jewish and non-Jewish figures, British and foreign, among whom were members of the various governments-in-exile. Aneurin Bevan, Cassin, and Masaryk often attended.

Rebecca Sieff was herself very active in the affairs of the World Jewish Congress. Politics dominated the Sieff salon, and in this respect it was truly unique. Its goal was to strengthen contact between Jewish leaders and the heads of the different countries that were engaged in the war. Cassin then described to me in energetic fashion the reaction at the Sieffs when he and others learned of my news for the first time. He remembered exactly the discussions that had arisen and confirmed for me that it was indeed the first time that any of them had heard of a comprehensive scheme for the extermination of all the Jews of Europe.

Cassin was proposing to deal with this in his memoirs, but he died before they were completed. I do not even know whether he left any working notes in his personal archives.

A last piece of testimony may be cited. It comes from Dr. Schneier Levenberg, who was in the office of the British section of the WJC and was at the same time an active member of the London bureau of the Jewish Agency for Palestine. Present at the WJC meeting at which Sydney Silverman introduced my telegram, Levenberg later described to me the enormous shock that the news had caused everyone there. He determined to go at once to the office of the Jewish Agency in Great Russell Street to inform his Zionist colleagues of the terrible news. Berl Locker, a member of the Zionist executive, at once called a meeting of his colleagues for the next day. Among those present at that meeting were Lewis Namier, Selig Brodetsky, Joseph Linton, and Levenberg himself. The group decided to alert their colleagues in Jerusalem, and to do so by means of a coded telegram. Unfortunately I could find no trace of this message in the Zionist archives.

The Declaration of the Allied Governments

The important and concrete result of all the activity my message had stimulated was the Allied governments' December 17, 1942, declaration concerning the extermination of the Jews. Actually the very idea for such a declaration also originated with me. It appeared for the first time in a letter I sent to Nahum Goldmann in October 1941.

When the notion of such a declaration was first mooted, negotiations, often laborious, took place over several weeks, in particular between the British and American governments. The Soviet government also introduced some amendments.

It should be noted that the idea met with various kinds of opposition, both on the part of bureaucrats in the State Department and from some officials in the British Foreign Office. They were afraid lest a declaration condemning Nazi crimes encourage Jewish organizations to demand more action to combat the Nazis' "Final Solution."

A text was finally adopted as a United Nations Declaration, under the title "German Policy of Extinction of the Jewish Race."

Here is the text:

The attention of the Belgian, Czechoslovak, Greek, Luxembourg, Netherlands, Norwegian, Polish, Soviet, United Kingdom, United States and Yugoslav Governments and also of the French National Committee has been drawn to numerous reports from Europe that the German authorities, not content with denying to persons of Jewish race in all the territories over which their barbarous rule has been extended, the most elementary human rights, are now carrying into effect Hitler's oft repeated intention to exterminate the Jewish people in Europe. From all the occupied countries Jews are being transported in conditions of appalling horror and brutality to eastern Europe. In Poland, which has been made the principal Nazi slaughter house, the ghettos established by the German invader are being systematically emptied of all Jews except a few highly skilled workers required for war industries. None of those taken away are ever heard of again. The infirm are left to die of exposure and starvation or are deliberately massacred in mass executions. The number of victims of these bloody cruelties is reckoned in many hundreds of thousands of entirely innocent men, women, and children. The above mentioned governments and the French National Committee condemn in the strongest possible terms this bestial policy of cold-blooded extermination. They declare that such events can only strengthen the resolve of all freedom loving people to overthrow the barbarous Hitlerite tyranny. They reaffirm their solemn resolution to ensure that those responsible for these crimes shall not escape retribution and to press on with the necessary practical measure to this end.

The text was made public simultaneously in Washington, Moscow, and London. In London, Parliament and the government gave it the special form of a declaration in the House of Commons whereby Anthony Eden, the foreign secretary, responded to a question by Sydney Silverman. At the end of the declaration the British Parliament stood and observed two minutes of silence.

Anthony Eden notes in his memoirs: "It [the declaration] had a far greater dramatic effect than I had expected." For his part, Lloyd George, the "old man" of British statesmanship and representative of one the four great powers that had negotiated the Treaty of Versailles, later said: "I cannot recall a scene like that in all my years in Parliament."

Some historians have averred that this declaration by the Allies was poorly disseminated. I do not agree. On the contrary, I think it had considerable resonance. I remember that even in Switzerland, where people were very cautious about condemning the Axis powers, it was widely published in the press. In any case, the extermination of the Jews by the Nazis was thenceforth in the public domain. No one could ignore it any longer.

The Allied declaration fueled enormous hope, but that quickly moderated. Subsequent proposals were aimed at saving the lives of European Jews—a great number of rescue projects. I shall return to these. The Jewish proposals, formulated in precise fashion, asked for immediate actions by the Allied governments. The Jewish organizations did not succeed in having them adopted. The constant Allied response, which had several variants, was "We must first win the war."

To the comprehensive proposal of large-scale negotiations with the Germans through the intermediation of neutral countries or the Vatican, the Allies replied that you cannot treat with the enemy. Under various pretexts, practically all the specific proposals we made were rejected.

Nowhere was there to be found a country of refuge for the Jews. The restrictive legislation on immigration to the United States was considered sacrosanct and untouchable.

Great Britain refused to allow Jews to enter Mandate Palestine. The country remained closed because the British did not wish to provoke the Arabs. At the same time Jews were denied entry into Britain itself.

In South America there was no place. The countries there were afraid of spies who might infiltrate among the refugees.

Finally some of the Jewish refugees were able to find refuge on Mauritius, an island in the Indian Ocean near Madagascar.

Many special actions were attempted on behalf of children. Mrs. Roosevelt was herself personally engaged. But all of these failed. No country had room for Jewish children, even as a temporary haven. Switzerland, for example, made considerable effort to aid the victims of war and children in particular, specifically by hosting them for some time in the country. But most of the time Jewish children were excluded from such programs.*

When efforts were made to ameliorate the conditions of detention and to establish the status of Jews interned in the camps, or to obtain entry to the camps by the Red Cross, people encountered the intransigence of the Germans.

The implementation of an economic blockade of enemy countries, which prohibited sending money, food, medical supplies, or other goods, reduced to virtually nothing all efforts intended to improve the diet of Jews starved by the Nazis in the ghettos and camps.

For my part, I did not honor the blockade. I judged that from Switzerland, which was neutral, we had the right to send parcels and boxes. We sent more than 100,000 parcels to people in camps, under circumstances to which I shall refer in detail below.

Proposals for the exchange of persons, of sanctions against the Germans, of guarantees of immigration to other countries—all these were buried in one way or another. This list could be continued indefinitely.

Why We Failed

A whole series of reasons can be adduced to explain why and how our activity met insurmountable and permanent difficulties that reduced our efforts to naught for several years.

---

*The internationally governed city of Shanghai accepted approximately 20,000 Jewish refugees before the Japanese occupation. The United States accepted 982 mainly Jewish refugees in August 1944 and interned them for the duration at Fort Ontario in upstate New York.—ED.

The first reason, which seems extremely important to me, is that no one was prepared for such a situation. There was no precedent for the Shoah. This demonstrates the unique character of the "Final Solution." There had never been such a persecution, such an effort to exterminate a whole people: men, women, children, babies, the disabled, sick, elderly, everyone without exception. Those targeted were pursued by perpetrators with police files in hand, drawn up with unprecedented bureaucratic precision. Also available were the most modern techniques of mass destruction.

In their history the Jews had overcome much persecution, many misfortunes. But in one way or another they always managed to survive. They suffered enormous losses, but a great number of them were saved. But here was a unique adversary whose hatred, determination, and power were without precedent in history.

A second factor, little known but extremely damaging, was the precedent of reports on German atrocities during World War I, which after the war proved to be false. This caused us serious problems and we were always being told, "That's all made up, just like during the First War." We had to make enormous efforts to convince people of the veracity of our reports on the Shoah.

The third factor, which in my opinion played a very large role, is the secrecy deliberately imposed by the Nazis on everything related to the "Final Solution." Himmler spoke of this in his notorious speech to senior SS officers in October 1943: "[It] is a page of glory never mentioned and never to be mentioned."

Many other documents attest to this secrecy. For example, in a November 20, 1942, letter from Himmler to Heinrich Müller, one of the senior officials in the Reich Security Main Office, Himmler refers to a September 1942 memorandum that his intelligence people had secured—a document authored by Dr. Stephen Wise. We have never located this memorandum, probably written at the moment when Wise had just received the first news of the "Final Solution."

Wise's memorandum must have denounced the extermination of the Jews, since Himmler writes, "That such rumors should be spreading in the world doesn't surprise me, given the huge migratory movement of Jews. We both know that the Jews who are put to forced labor have a higher mortality rate. . . . You must guarantee me that everywhere the bodies of deceased Jews will either be burned or buried, and that nowhere will any other disposition of these bodies be made."*

*A copy of Himmler's letter to Müller is in the WJC Geneva office files currently at the Central Zionist Archives in Jerusalem and, on microfilm, at the United States Holocaust Memorial Museum Archives in Washington, D.C.—ED.

Everything was intended to conceal what actually happened and to destroy any traces that might have persisted.

In the same sense, in order to maintain the secret, a special language was devised. Instead of "deportation," officials used "evacuation"; for "killing" they used "special treatment" (*Sonderbehandlung*); "final solution" meant "total extermination." All this was intended to hide from Germans and from the world what was actually happening in the camps and elsewhere in Eastern Europe. In addition, any allusion to these matters was strictly forbidden and carried sanctions.

A fourth factor was anti-Semitism among the Allies. German propaganda in the Western countries was a great deal more effective than has been generally recognized. There were large organizations, such as the German-American Bund, under Nazi direction in the United States.

The Nazis also had *Gauleiter*, country by country, for Germans living abroad, for whom they functioned as local heads of the Nazi party. The one in the United States, who had ample means at his disposal, pursued a clear and precise policy in order to promote the ideas of Nazism among Germans abroad and to make all these Germans instruments of Nazi propaganda.

Anti-Semitic activity could even be found on American radio, which at the time was the most effective means of propaganda. The Roman Catholic priest Charles E. Coughlin and the propagandist Gerald L. K. Smith broadcast several times a week and incited their listeners against Jews.

Nazi propaganda accused the Jews of being responsible for the war "against" Germany. The Jews were accused of wanting to drag the United States into the war and of pushing President Roosevelt toward a more bellicose policy, hostile to Germany. These propagandists often called Roosevelt "Rosenfeld" and claimed that he was of Jewish origin.

This Nazi propaganda in particular sought to make Americans believe that if they wished to keep America in a state of peace, they had to fight the Jews.

Between 1940 and 1942 this propaganda was quite well received. Few in the United States wished to be "drawn into" the war. Roosevelt, who was perhaps the most farsighted of American officials in the sphere of foreign policy, could not permit himself to commit acts in direct contravention of the country's neutrality, the Lend-Lease Act of March 11, 1941, and American escort of British convoys notwithstanding.

By recognizing this constant anti-Semitic agitation we can understand why for a very long time the American press scarcely spoke of the drama of the Jews.

For their part, the American Jewish organizations, alarmed by the success of this propaganda, adopted an extremely cautious attitude toward American policy concerning the war and Nazi atrocities.

This anti-Semitism was quite openly displayed, even in some actions by U.S. government authorities. Such tendencies were clearly discernible within the State Department. We know today that one of its most senior officials, Breckinridge Long, was hostile to the notion of reserving visas for European Jews, in particular those of German origin. The quotas, quite limited for all that, were never fully used. Some officials in the State Department tried to prevent Jewish immigration, which they judged already too substantial.

This attitude explains the reactions of the State Department to my first telegram of August 1942, which revealed the "Final Solution." As we know, the telegram was never forwarded to Dr. Wise. On February 10, 1943, the American legation in Bern was advised, over Sumner Welles's initials for Secretary Cordell Hull, no longer to send through diplomatic channels messages or reports that originated with private persons or organizations in the United States unless extraordinary circumstances suggested otherwise. This State Department message, contained in telegram 354, was clearly aimed at me. By way of proof, we have its reference to the legation telegram 482 of January 21 that transmitted my earlier report. The purpose was to eliminate the source of information and to put an end to agitation in Jewish circles to exert pressure on the authorities.

The same negative attitude was assumed by the State Department in April 1943 when I submitted a number of proposals to New York concerning the rescue of Jews from various European countries. This long telegram, sent through the American legation, dealt in particular with what might be done at that time in Romania. It was based on reports that had reached us from Romanian Jewish leaders through the International Committee of the Red Cross. We were alerted to changes that had taken place in the attitude of Marshal Ion Antonescu; in response, an evacuation plan with Palestine as its destination was proposed for the Romanian Jews deported to Transnistria, if funding could be obtained. The Romanian sources also identified new methods for such financing.

This telegram also contained a number of other proposals, in particular regarding the rescue of Jewish youngsters and children from Western Europe—Belgium, the Netherlands, and France. More specifically, I was proposing the dispatch of convoys toward Spain and Switzerland.

The essential point underlying these proposals was that the financial blockade prevented us from sending money to enemy countries. This regulation, normal in times of war, was aimed at reducing the adversary's resources. As I have already stated, the blockade was creating enormous difficulties for us. It clearly did not take into account the dramatic situation that had been created by the Nazis' decision to annihilate all European Jews.

Thus in order to take the blockade into consideration, my telegram made it clear that for these operations it was not necessary to send money into enemy countries. It would be sufficient to deposit the agreed-on sums into a Swiss bank in an account that would be blocked until the end of the war. This would exclude its possible use in a war effort against the Allies.

I was surprised by the difficulties I encountered in trying to send these proposals by telegram. At the time I was ignorant of the State Department's desire that my telegrams not be forwarded.

When I submitted my telegram to the Americans at the legation, they behaved in a curious fashion. At bottom they seemed simply not to know what to do. They knew they should honor the advisory against forwarding private communications. But, judging the contents to be very important, they offered me the possibility of sending the telegram on the condition that I pay the cost.

This was the most costly telegram of my life. The charge amounted to one month of my salary. But, considering the consequences that it later had, it was the most profitable telegram I ever sent.

My proposals, forwarded by Wise, were accepted by Roosevelt and Secretary of the Treasury Henry Morgenthau, Jr. When Wise returned to the fray and saw Morgenthau in July 1943, asking why nothing had been done, the latter replied, "You know that I approved that rescue plan months ago." Surprised but also troubled because he knew that each day that passed increased the number of victims, Morgenthau assigned two of his staff at the Treasury Department, John Pehle and Josiah DuBois, to find out the causes for the delay. The two Treasury officials discovered that the State Department had sabotaged the relief action on behalf of Jewish victims.

The two men disclosed the situation in a thundering memorandum entitled "Report to the Secretary on the Acquiescence of This Government in the Murder of European Jews." Dated January 13, 1944, and initialed by Randolph Paul for the Foreign Funds Control Unit of the Treasury Department, it was submitted by Morgenthau to President Roosevelt after consulting the secretary of state. As we shall see, this led to the creation of the War Refugee Board, which proved to be the sole effective act intended to save Jews who remained alive.

The negative attitude of the State Department had its counterpart in that of the British government, in particular in the Foreign Office and the Colonial Office.

The very important study by the historian Bernard Wasserstein on the actions of the British government with regard to the Jews during World War II cites a great number of sources and documents now finally accessible to the public. Reading some of these reports you may well ask yourself who were Great Britain's enemies, the Jews who were trying to save a few lives or the Germans who sought to kill them? This is devastating reading!

The negative attitude of the British is particularly evident in the context of efforts to save Jews by sea. Between 1942 and 1944, ships were specially chartered to transport to Palestine several hundred Jews who had succeeded in fleeing persecution. These were often ships in very poor condition, overloaded with hundreds of additional passengers.

The *Struma*, sailing from Constanta, Romania, on December 12, 1942, reached Istanbul on the 15th with its engines out of service. During repairs the Turks did not permit the ship to enter the harbor nor the passengers to come ashore. The British, who controlled all maritime traffic in the area, behaved in very singular fashion. Contrary to the freedom-of-navigation principle that they always defended with vigor, they intervened with Turkish authorities to have them prevent the *Struma* from sailing through the Dardanelles to enter the Mediterranean. In effect the British had refused in advance to permit the Jewish passengers on the *Struma* to disembark in Palestine. The Turks allowed only nine to come ashore, quarantining the vessel under terrible conditions in Istanbul harbor for seventy days. Eventually towed back to the Black Sea with a useless engine on February 23, 1943, the ship was torpedoed the next day by a Soviet submarine. Finally, a communiqué reported that the *Struma* had gone down in the Black Sea with the loss of all but one of its more than seven hundred passengers. Among other things, the event testifies to the harshness of British officialdom.

A similar drama in 1944 cost the life of more than three hundred passengers and crew of another ship, the *Mefkure*. Only a few survived.

Numbers of other vessels, some of them hardly seaworthy, transported refugees from one port to another without ever being able to discharge their human cargo. Some did reach Palestine, some sank, and others were turned back.

In the face of these disasters, it would be vain to seek a bit of compassion on the part of senior British officials. In his work *Britain and the Jews 1939–1945* (1979), Bernard Wasserstein cites a Mr. Downie, an official with the Colonial Office, who declared in a report that these ships were a Gestapo ruse to destabilize the British Empire!

When the United States legation in Bern issued me the first extraordinary "license," authorizing me to contact enemy nations in an attempt to help the Jews there, in December 1943, the British legation, at the insistence of the British minister responsible for the blockade, tried until the very last minute to stop this humanitarian gesture. The British succeeded in delaying the delivery of the American license to me for several weeks. This was one of the last manifestations of the bureaucratic sabotage of my initiatives.

Later, when Roosevelt set up the War Refugee Board, senior officials in the Foreign Office observed that the president was doing it purely for electoral reasons as he would be seeking a new term the following year, in 1944. Virtually no one among a set of senior British officials seemed to think that a great statesman could hold compassion for people who were suffering and for a people who were in danger of extinction. Nor, it seems, could they imagine that he possessed a genuine sense of human responsibility.

A Matter of Moral Indifference

The anti-Semitic attitudes of national administrations were not the only obstacles in our path. Even more important—and this is my fifth point—was the moral indifference of civil servants and military leaders who refused any action that departed from daily routine.

At times I was deeply struck by the total insensitivity of these officials that prevented them from taking the indispensable and urgent measures that we were proposing to them. They did not understand that the tragic situation of the Jewish communities, destined for total destruction, dictated extraordinary efforts beyond the routine.

When we insisted that one of the objectives of the war was also to save millions of human lives, they tirelessly repeated to us that first they had to win the war. They did not take a moment's time to reflect whether some exceptional rescue actions might be undertaken without jeopardizing military operations.

This moral indifference had deadly effects. How, in fact, was it possible, despite our insistent and repeated demands, for military leaders to refuse to bomb the gas chambers at Auschwitz when they were dropping bombs some few miles away?

How was it possible to permit the huge ships that brought hundreds of thousands of American soldiers to Europe to return home empty while assuring us that there was no transport to evacuate the Jewish refugees of Europe?

How was it possible consistently to assert to us that immigration quotas to the United States had been filled, when we discovered after the war that this was far from the truth?

During that tragic period, no one wanted us.

Let us return momentarily to the problem of bombing Auschwitz, concerning which Professor David Wyman and some others have published very detailed studies. In 1944, in the course of the rescue action to save Hungarian Jews, we especially insisted on the necessity of bombing the cremation ovens in Auschwitz as well as the railroad network that brought thousands of victims there from all over Europe every day.

I myself pleaded on several occasions for such an action at the United States legation in Bern. I even went to the archives of the League of Nations to get the most detailed geographical maps of the region. They had been prepared for the 1922 plebiscite on Upper Silesia. I placed them at the disposal of the American authorities.

Even Professor Chaim Weizmann, who in general intervened only in matters that concerned Palestine, argued vigorously with Churchill on this matter. Impressed with Weizmann's pleadings, Churchill supported his request and Anthony Eden, impressed in turn by Churchill's memo, backed up the initiative.

It is stupefying to follow the course of this proposed measure. The proposal went from the Foreign Office to the Air Ministry, from there to the high command of the armed forces, finally to return to the Foreign Office. And nothing was done.

At the United Nations, Nahum Goldmann was in direct contact with one of General Dwight Eisenhower's immediate subordinates; Eisenhower was then Supreme Commander, Allied Expeditionary Forces in Europe. The American Jewish Congress had lobbied U.S. Army Chief of Staff General George C. Marshall. Results were no better.

Those who controlled the military told us that the action was too difficult and that the distance was beyond the point of no return for the bombers. We know today that during 1944 Allied domination of the air space of all Europe was virtually absolute. We know that the air forces had many aerial photographs of the region of Auschwitz and the camp, which today still exist at a special center in London and at the National Archives in Washington. Dino Brugioni and Robert Poirier's postwar analysis employing great magnification shows the Auschwitz II (Birkenau) extermination camp in great detail.

We also know—and this is even more surprising—that the bomber pilots of the era made various raids on Auschwitz III (Monowitz), where the chemical factories of I. G. Farben stood, some three miles east of the Auschwitz main camp. In light of this, let no one claim the insufficient range of bombers then in service! Why did they lie to us? Why did they not pair up the targets of Monowitz and Birkenau if they did not wish to devote a raid to the extermination camp alone? Why did they not mount a commando operation to blow up the cremation ovens with the aid of a detailed plan? Admittedly, losses probably would have been very high, but would volunteers have been lacking, Jews in particular, to make up the commando forces? Without doubt, had the bombing taken place the number of victims would have been high among the prisoners, but should the risk have stymied the project when the crematoria each day were exterminating some six thousand people? All these questions have remained without what I and many others consider a satisfactory answer.

A sixth substantial factor played an important role in the failure of rescue attempts: a great lack of imagination.

In truth, for a long time, neither the major Jewish organizations nor the senior politicians, military officials, and diplomats were capable of breaking their respective routines to devise solutions that went beyond the ordinary, that were on the scale—or the lack of scale—of the extraordinary challenge that extermination posed.

The governments, philanthropic organizations, and humanitarian associations did not succeed in shaking off the yoke of their routines in order to generate new ideas. They all knew, however, that in the face of such a cataclysm it was not possible to remain within traditional limits of welfare and relief work. But their capacity for any sort of adaptation was at best slow in revealing itself.

At least once, however, imagination did come into play. One day, toward the end of the war, a ship carrying one thousand Yugoslav refugees approached the United States' East Coast. As immigration laws did not permit them to disembark, Wise obtained permission for those souls to come ashore in the United States by having the harbor where the ship docked declared a free port for the duration of the war. Thus, without violating the quota legislation, it proved possible to offer asylum to a number of persons during the war. Why was the same thing not done at fifty different coastal sites?

Continuing this enumeration of the reasons for our lack of success, I believe that one of the decisive factors was our total powerlessness, our absolute lack of political influence. I believe that never in our history have Jews been so bereft of power as during that period of our greatest need.

We had no political weight. Our actions had no effect, and we had nowhere to turn. We could not say to the Allies, "If you do not intervene on our behalf, we'll go over to Hitler's side." We had no influence. An American journalist could write: "The Jews were expendable."

This is a situation that many members of a younger generation, born after the war, simply cannot understand. Today there is the State of Israel, whose power on the international scene cannot be ignored. Today American Jews have considerable influence in the political arena. Virtually none of that existed during World War II.

Yet one more observation: the facts that were reported told of such brutality and such violence that a normal human being could not imagine them. People knew the truth and yet refused to believe it. They could not bear to confront absolute evil or live with such a reality. Although on one level they were aware of the tragedy, everyone hoped in their inner being that it was simply not true.

Let me give some examples from my own experience. One of the most desperate incidents occurred in 1943; I received a huge parcel that had been sent to me by the Union of Polish Jews in the United States. The package contained thirty thousand addresses. I was asked to send food parcels to all those addresses in the various cities of Poland.

After receiving it I could not sleep for several nights. I asked myself whether the American Jews had still not understood what was happening. The Union of Polish Jews of the United States had its offices in the same building and on the same floor as the World Jewish Congress. Its leaders were familiar with all my reports.

Everything pointed to the fact that none of these addresses was any longer valid. Everyone knew that all these Jews were no longer in their former residences. Many were in concentration camps; others, perhaps the majority, were already dead. But no one could accept that tragedy could strike so close, that the addresses of family members no longer had any meaning, and that almost all of them had disappeared. They thought they must do something; they could not remain inactive. So, with a kind of irrational defiance and to ease their conscience, they collected these addresses and sent them to me.

We were faced with a case eliciting a schizophrenic reaction: one might "know" but not accept what one knew. In the end, after some time, virtually everyone knew. And almost everyone refused to accept the reality of it. It was simply unimaginable.

Another example: In November 1942 the Polish Home Army sent one of its officers, Jan Karski, to the West to explain to the rest of the world the fate of the Polish Jews. Karski was one of the finest figures of the resistance. Before that he had been secretly introduced into the Warsaw Ghetto. For two days he accompanied Jewish leaders there (a Bundist socialist and a Zionist) and could see with his own eyes how people lived and died in the ghetto. He was even taken, still under cover, to or close to where he witnessed the extermination of Jews. Although the exact identity of this camp is in doubt, Karski reported it to be

Belzec. There people explained to him over the course of several hours what actually occurred at that facility. However this was managed, he had very precise knowledge of what was going on in the camp.

On his arrival in the West, Karski met a number of political leaders. In accordance with his mission, he gave them an account of what was happening in Poland and transmitted to them proposals for measures to counter Nazi activity.

Among others, Karski met the minister of foreign affairs of the Polish government-in-exile, Edward Raczynski, and British Foreign Secretary Eden. In the United States he met President Roosevelt, Secretary of State Hull, Secretary of War Henry Stimson, and many others. But almost always he encountered incredulity in his listeners.

Subsequently Karski told how he came to meet a justice of the U.S. Supreme Court, Felix Frankfurter, one of the most respected Jewish figures in America. At the end of the conversation, Frankfurter said to Karski, "I can't believe it." To which Karski responded, "Do you think I'm lying?" "I didn't say that you were lying," replied Frankfurter, "I said that I couldn't believe it."*

In November 1943, almost one year after the declaration by the Allied governments, the prime minister of the Dutch government-in-exile, P. S. Gerbrandy, was still not completely convinced of the truthfulness of reports on the Shoah, as we learn from the German historian Eberhard Jäckel.

Louis de Jong, then working for the Dutch radio-in-exile, confronted the prime minister with some of my reports describing with precision the extermination of European Jews. The prime minister, completely stupefied, turned to the young man and said, "De Jong, do you believe that is true?"

De Jong, who had just learned that his parents and sister had been deported, replied, "Yes." The broadcaster would go on to become a specialist in the history of the Shoah, but up to this day he is not sure that he convinced the prime minister.

Here is another telling illustration of this state of mind. John J. McCloy, U.S. assistant secretary of war, in December 1944 received a World Jewish Congress delegation that had come to inform him of decisions taken at a great conference in Atlantic City.

After the meeting he found himself alone with A. Leon Kubowitzki, who was then secretary-general of the WJC. McCloy asked him, "Now that we are alone, tell me, do you really believe the terrible stories that you are spreading about?" This means that toward the end of 1944, senior Allied officials still

---

*Karski became a professor of history at Georgetown University and died only in 2000.—ED.

doubted the truth of the mass exterminations, and this five months before the end of the conflict.

People refused to accept what was happening because it outstripped human understanding. We deny what is incredible and inadmissible. This refusal to accept reality is in part responsible for the tragedy.

And this is the great paradox of such behavior. For the refusal itself proves that human beings do not accept absolute evil and cannot live face to face with it. It also signifies that *human beings cannot live without hope.* The rejection of absolute evil helps us not to despair of the future, and in a sense restores our faith in humankind.

The Jewish Rescue Program and the
Failure of the Bermuda Conference

As soon as they learned of the information available about the "Final Solution," Jewish organizations became feverishly active. They mobilized all the Jewish communities of the Free World. The organizations met and debated rescue tactics. They lobbied governments and organized huge rallies in the United States, Britain, and other free countries to incite these governments to action. They appealed to churches and public opinion; they organized relief committees. At the beginning all this yielded few results other than expressions of sympathy.

Finally, under this concentrated pressure, the British and American governments announced they would meet to draft a plan to address the urgent situation. The conference would discuss the means of coming to the aid of Jews in the hands of the Nazis, and of saving the greatest possible number of those in Europe.

Thus an immense hope was born. American Jewish organizations agreed on an ambitious program, which they submitted to the U.S. government. They also asked to send a delegation to participate in the conference. But the Allied governments decided that the meeting, at a location in the Caribbean, would not be open to the public. This is what came to be called the Bermuda Conference.

The Jewish proposals made public in April 1943, at the time of the Bermuda Conference, were numerous and diverse. As the situation had evolved over the course of the preceding tragic years, a wide variety of possibilities took shape, and many of these found reflection in the discussion agenda.

The principal projects submitted to conference organizers confirm that, far from being inactive and following the drama without initiative, the Jewish representatives explored a whole range of ideas in an attempt to save those who might still be saved.

One idea was that of negotiating with Germany through the intermediation of neutral countries or the Vatican, in order to secure authorization for the total evacuation of European Jews and the agreement of the Free World to receive them. This was clearly an extremely bold proposal on an extraordinary scale.

The other ideas were of more limited scope. Yet each corresponded to a particular need and offered possibilities of realization. A second suggestion was to obtain asylum sites in a number of countries where Jews might be taken in. It would first be necessary to determine which countries had room for such an immigration, and whether it should be definitive or temporary. Beyond the great Allied countries, the plan envisaged exploring immigration possibilities in some countries of North Africa, Latin America, the British Empire, and the Caribbean. With this in mind, it would also be necessary to assure transit through intervening countries such as Spain and Turkey.

A third proposal, clearly with the United States in mind, was to obtain an exceptional modification of immigration policy and legislation in order to make such a rescue operation possible. This would entail that the rigid system of quotas by nationality would have to be suspended in the face of the urgent necessity of rescue.

In order to make some of these proposals practicable, a fourth request foresaw the United States exerting pressure on the countries of Latin America in order to have their immigration policies modified and to obtain a set number of visas.

A fifth point had Great Britain receiving a reasonable number of refugees from the occupied countries.

A sixth point was of particular importance: it was a call for the gateways to Palestine to be opened. They had been practically closed as a consequence of the British white paper of 1939. It was advanced that, despite the opposition of the Arabs, the Mandate power ought to make a contribution to the rescue effort.

Yet another proposal, the seventh, was to explore the idea of exchanging German civilians living in the Allied countries, some as internees, for Jews in the occupied countries.

An eighth point concerned the creation of a food-relief plan for Nazi victims who were starving in the camps and ghettos. This would entail an exceptional relaxation of the food, financial, and economic blockade that the Allies had mounted against Germany.

A ninth important idea was to offer guarantees to neutral countries that would be ready to receive Jews fleeing Nazi-dominated lands. These countries would be provided finances for the support of these people during the war, and political and financial guarantees of their departure after the war.

Tenth, the organizations envisaged specific actions on behalf of children.

An eleventh proposal suggested the establishment of an international commission for the punishment of war criminals. This would make it clear that the Allies intended to pursue and punish those who had participated in the extermination of the Jews.

Finally, the establishment of an appropriate international agency was proposed. It would be provided with the necessary means and would be charged with the execution of all these projects and would, through the exercise of this function, be the body responsible for the implementation of the rescue of the Jews of Europe, where extermination continued implacably and systematically.

Everyone hoped that the Bermuda Conference would bring precise and constructive responses to these encompassing proposals that were the culmination of myriad studies, suggestions, and debates.

Finally, the long-awaited moment arrived. The Anglo-American conference that was to decide how to come to the aid of the victims of Nazism met in Bermuda in April 1943. The choice of this small island, with easy control over access, was intended to ensure secrecy and to exclude the public and the press. Nor did the conference permit the Jewish organizations or other humanitarian institutions to present their proposals directly to the delegates.

All this only heightened public anticipation. While American and British Jewish organizations waited, no one communicated to them the decisions that had been taken. Only a bit later, after the conclusion of the conference, did we learn what had taken place. And to general stupefaction, we discovered that the great secret of the conference was that they had decided to do practically nothing at all.

For many Jews this was one of the most dramatic moments of the war. Until then, people had been able to hope. They had anticipated that for the duration of the war rescue actions would be constrained. But to learn that this fine assembly, specially gathered in Bermuda, had decided to do nothing was more than a horrible disappointment. It was a terrible shock for us. To all these requests, the constant reply of the Allies was yet again: "We can divert neither our attention nor our forces from the primary objective, which is to win the war."

Sometime after the war, voices were raised among Jews harshly criticizing the Jewish leaders of the Free World at the time of the Shoah. Some have blamed Zionist leaders for not having done enough to attempt rescue, suggesting that they were devoting themselves entirely to the creation of a Jewish state. Those who argue this commit a profound error. They designate as cause what actually was effect.

The failure of the Bermuda Conference led Jewish leaders to conclude that if our best friends would not help us in such a catastrophe, if no one were ready to receive at least some significant number of the otherwise doomed Jews, we had no option but to take our destiny into our own hands and forge our own state. However small it might be, a state was necessary. And it was absolutely necessary so that we could act on our own and not depend on others.

The idea that the creation of a Jewish commonwealth ought to be the principal Jewish objective of the war already had been proclaimed by David Ben-Gurion at the Biltmore Conference in New York in May 1942. But nearly a year was needed before action in this direction became a central focus of many Jews.

The wider adoption of this view was a direct consequence of the great disappointment of Bermuda. The great Zionist leader Chaim Greenberg would later express this feeling well in a text entitled "Bankrupt!", published in the February 1943 issue of *Yiddische Kemfer* and later in *Midstream* (March 1964).

Much later, after the war, Jewish leaders were reproached for not having acted with sufficient energy, for not having exerted influence on world statesmen. This criticism said, in effect, "You did not do all that was necessary and thus you failed in your duty."

In my opinion these reproaches are to a great extent unjust. Of course, faced with the death of six million Jews, no one could ever claim that he had done enough, that he did or attempted all that was possible. Of course, each of us ought to have done more. But it is absolutely false to aver that little or nothing was attempted.

Once again we should not compare our present situation with that of wartime, however often this is done. The world is different, the methods are different, the protests are different, the results are different. For example, let us not forget that during the war even the democratic states did not permit public expressions of protest. When people tell us today, "You ought to have staged a mass sit-in in front of the White House," you have to recall that in wartime the police would quickly have dispersed the protesters. In any case, we had not yet learned to think in such terms.

Some more pointed criticism faults Stephen Wise for having been politically naive and for having renounced, under the effects of Roosevelt's charm, the energetic defense of Jewish interests.

This is not true. Wise worked his entire life in the political world. He was certainly not naive. And, in fact, he changed his attitude toward Roosevelt several times.

A letter sent by Wise to Nahum Goldmann on April 22, 1943, while the Bermuda Conference was in progress behind a wall of secrecy, illustrates very clearly that he was following American politics with the greatest clear-sightedness and with no illusions:

> Of course the thing is going very badly, but no worse than we anticipated from the start. The thing that I am most fearful of is that any strong complaint against FDR, at this time, will simply mean that we will hand him a gift of Congressional support for the first time in this Congress, because Congress will certain approve of what is not being done for the refugees. It is very easy to hold press conferences and to call meetings, but we must in advance consider what it will lead to—that it will shut every door and leave us utterly without hope of relief as far as FDR is concerned. He is still our friend, even though he does not move as expeditiously as we would wish. But he moves as fast as he can, in view of the Congress on his hands, a bitterly hostile and in a very real sense partially antisemitic Congress.

Admittedly the Jewish communities made many mistakes. The greatest error of the Jewish communities, however, was not committed during the war but before it: not having understood early on the danger posed by Hitler; not having supported Wise; and not having supported the policies of the one man who was the symbol of the struggle against Nazi Germany.

I remember that when I was still in Germany, *Rabbiner Wise* already appeared in many of the Nazi newspapers such as the *Völkischer Beobachter* and Goebbels's *Der Angriff.* For them, Wise was the symbol of the Jews' struggle against the Nazis and was their most formidable enemy. From the rise of Nazism in 1930 and especially after 1932 Wise had denounced to the American and international public the mortal danger that Hitler constituted. He demonstrated that Hitler threatened Jews first, then other peoples as well.

Among the Jewish masses, particularly in America, there was a true will to combat Nazism, and Wise was their preeminent spokesman. In March 1933, he, Bernhard Deutsch, and other leaders of the American Jewish Congress organized the great New York City public demonstration against the boycott of Jews in Germany. A million and a half people took to the streets. I believe that, in all our history, there has never been a demonstration on such a scale, not even today. Alas, virtually no one remembers those measures today.

There was, then, a popular will to oppose Nazism. But some Jewish organizations and leaders of the American Jewish establishment did not follow
through. On the contrary, they denounced Wise. They even sent an American
rabbi to Berlin to warn German Jews and the American ambassador not to
take this "crazy rabbi" and his initiatives seriously.*

In particular the establishment did not like Wise's populist methods. He
unified and represented the Jewish masses. He was the spokesman of the
great majority of Jews of Eastern European origin. He did not back off from
a confrontation with those who supported the Nazis and their friends. But
the "respectable" Jewish organizations did not follow him. In America they
were cautious at that time. In Britain and France the official Jewish organizations followed their governments' policy of appeasement toward Germany.

In my opinion our prewar failure to unify Jews and to impress upon them
the gravity of the situation is serious; had we done so perhaps we could have
changed things. If American Jewry and its most powerful organizations, and
with them the other great Jewish communities, had followed Wise during the
years when Hitler might still have been stopped, if they had unanimously supported Wise's policy instead of denouncing it as irresponsible, the course of
history might have been different.

Whatever the case, as soon as he was alerted by my telegram, Wise did not
cease shuttling between New York and Washington, where he met in turn a
great number of members of the administration, of Congress, and senior civil
servants. He desperately attempted to convince each of them of the horrible
reality of extermination and of the urgent need for action. He continued to do
this until the end of the war.

The attitude of Nahum Goldmann, the other great leader of the World Jewish
Congress, with regard to the annihilation was more complex. He was among
the first to understand the mortal danger of Nazism, not only for Jews but also
for other peoples. It is sufficient to read his great address to the founding assembly of the World Jewish Congress in 1936 to be convinced of this.

---

*The story of the "crazy rabbi" may be apocryphal (there is no mention of this in Melvin
I. Urofsky's exhaustive biography of Wise, *A Voice That Spoke for Justice* [Albany, N.Y.,
1982], nor does Wise mention it in his memoirs, *Challenging Years: The Autobiography of
Stephen S. Wise* [New York, 1949], but it does encapsulate the opinion of many American
Jewish leaders at the time. There is some irony in the fact that, at the request of Assistant
Secretary of State Sumner Welles, Wise agreed to withhold from the public the contents of
the Riegner telegram until State could "confirm" them (ibid., pp. 319–320).—ED.

When the "Final Solution" began to be implemented, he was among the first to understand the extent of the catastrophe. His impressive report at the Biltmore Conference in May 1942 on the fate of European Jews offers moving testimony to this. But at the same time he understood that in the face of an enemy like Hitler there was very little chance of success.

During the tragedy, Nahum Goldmann concentrated on simple but large-scale schemes. He advanced the idea of negotiating with the German government for the evacuation of the Jews of Europe, suggesting that it be done through the intermediation of neutral countries or the Vatican. He understood that in the face of such a catastrophe only an extraordinary scheme, one without precedent, could be effective.

American Jewish leaders accepted this idea. But it met fierce opposition from the Allied powers, in particular Great Britain, which repeated the same refrain: "We do not negotiate with the enemy."

In 1943 Goldmann took the initiative to mount a rescue operation for a second time. Again it was a grand but simple idea that he advanced: the creation of a huge fund for relief and rescue. He suggested that the governments of the United States and Great Britain each contribute $5 million and that the Jewish organizations add $2 million.

This idea of a large rescue fund, which naturally would have required the financial participation of the Allied governments, came up against the narrow-mindedness of the Jewish philanthropic organizations. These organizations had still not understood that an extraordinary situation demanded extraordinary political action, and that in confronting the destruction of European Jews emphasis had to be placed on the responsibilities of governments. These organizations considered that philanthropic activity was *their* responsibility and that no funding should be requested of government. In particular this was the operating principle of the American Jewish Joint Distribution Committee, familiarly known as the "Joint."

Only much later, toward the end of the war, was the United Nations Relief and Rehabilitation Administration (UNRRA), originally called the International Organization for Refugees, established. Only then did most come to understand that the problems associated with the rescue of millions of people and their relief were the responsibility of governments and could not be resolved without their participation and financial aid.

Similarly, toward the end of the war the Allies gained a better understanding of the urgency and exceptional character of the situation. Thus in 1944 the principle of not negotiating with the enemy did not prevent them from establishing contact with a government with which they were at war, when the deportation and extermination of the Hungarian Jews was in progress. At that moment President Roosevelt addressed a note to the Hungarian regent, Miklos Horthy, to warn him and demand that he halt the deportations.

Once again later events validated ideas advanced by Goldmann. But he too, despite his brilliant analyses that went to the heart of reality, could not live in permanent confrontation with this tragedy. His profoundly optimistic, life-affirming character did not permit him to do so. But when he was approached concerning individual cases, he did everything in his power to assist or save people. He was very sorely tried by the failure of his effort to save Robert Stricker, one of the leaders of the Viennese Jewish community, and other European Jewish leaders.

It should be noted that after the war Goldmann was the first and practically the only Jewish leader to admit openly and publicly that his generation bore a heavy responsibility for what had happened, that it had failed to act as it should have acted, and that it had not risen to the unprecedented challenge posed by the mass murder.

For a very long time he questioned the rightness of some of the principled positions he had adopted in the face of the horrific bloodletting. On several occasions he spoke to me of his 1934 meeting with Mussolini on dealing with the problem of the Jews of the Saarland.

Approximately a year before this meeting, Mussolini had asked the chief rabbi of Italy, Angelo Sacerdoti, to contact Nahum Goldmann. Mussolini proposed to intervene between the Jews and Hitler so that world Jewry would not adopt a hostile position toward Hitler. He suggested that in order to come to an arrangement, the Jews ought to accept legal limitations on their rights. Mussolini wanted to know the Jews' minimal demands with regard to Hitler. Goldmann rejected the idea and did not take advantage of the proposed audience.

When he finally did meet with Mussolini on November 13, 1934, Goldmann communicated his position: for the Jews of Germany nothing less than complete equality of rights was acceptable. The very notion of equality made it an indivisible entity. Either you have it or you don't. You can't have 50 or 80 percent equality. Moreover, anything less than full equality in Germany would be tantamount to a renunciation of equal rights for Jews in all other countries as well, in the present and in the future.

Yet after the Shoah, after the loss of six million lives, Nahum Goldmann questioned whether he had been right to take this principled stand. Each time he raised the issue with me, I always told him that all speculation on that subject was vain, and that he could not have adopted any other position, nor could he have renounced the principle of equality of rights for Jews around the world.

For, in the end, no confidence could be placed in Hitler's promises. Acceptance by Jews of a status of inferiority would have been no binding Nazi guarantee of any Jewish rights; indeed, no concessions to the Germans would even have assured the Jews an escape from destruction.

The World Jewish Congress Geneva Office

Before offering an account of the political dimensions of the large-scale rescue projects in which I was involved, I want to describe our daily activity—what we did in our office and what my role was.

When war broke out in September 1939, at the World Jewish Congress in Geneva we created a special relief agency or committee for Jewish war victims. This committee afforded us a venue through which we could stay in touch with communities in the occupied countries. Naturally, as a political organization, the parent World Jewish Congress could not be active in the countries dominated by the Nazis.

Through the intermediary of the committee we tried to provide the maximum possible aid to Jewish victims of the war. In addition, we had immediately informed the International Committee of the Red Cross of the creation of this body, and we collaborated with the ICRC throughout the war. The committee was known as "Relico," an abbreviation of its English name, Relief Committee for the War-Stricken Jewish Population.

In the course of this period we became a true little "Jewish Red Cross," dealing with practically all aspects of philanthropic and humanitarian aid.

One of our first initiatives in 1940 was to collect medical supplies from all the Jewish pharmacists in Switzerland and send them to the Jewish community of Warsaw.

In the years 1939 to 1941 thousands of people were in touch with us to maintain or reestablish contact with members of their families from whom they had been separated, to search out those relatives' addresses, to assist them, to send them money, and to provide all sorts of other services. During these years we made tens of thousands of personal research inquiries, sent tens of thousands of messages. In thousands of cases we also sent small sums of money on their behalf to help out and provide relief.

In my May 1941 letter to the World Jewish Congress in New York I observed that between January 1940 and May 1941 alone we had sent eighteen thousand letters, seven thousand of these between January and April 1941. During the same period we responded to fifteen hundred search inquiries.

Perhaps not all this activity was entirely legal under international law, but it provided immediate aid to large numbers of persons who were suffering from the consequences of the war.

We also established a service to send food parcels, initially to countries where people were suffering from malnutrition, and later to the camps. At the beginning we dispatched a large number of parcels from Yugoslavia. When that country was occupied by the Germans in 1941, we established a similar service in neutral Portugal, doing so with the help of the small Jewish community in Lisbon. During the war years we sent several hundreds of thousands of small parcels from Lisbon to the occupied countries, especially to the camps.

We put these services at the disposal of the general public. Individuals could order a shipment or mailing for family members or friends. We added a small surcharge for these deliveries and used that money to pay for parcels to people who had neither family nor friends and whose addresses we had. We took systematic pains to see that prominent Jewish figures, in particular worthy former leaders, should benefit from this assistance.

Every Friday, when we toted up the number of possible free parcels, there was a small dispute among my volunteer co-workers of different nationalities, each wishing to benefit the greatest number of Jews in his or her country of origin. I then had to play the arbiter in order to effect a distribution that was as fair as possible.

This distribution was not particularly favored by the authorities of the World Jewish Congress in New York. Several members of the executive board intervened on several occasions to put a stop to the activity, since it was deemed to be in contravention of the Allies' economic blockade. I, on the other hand, believed that on neutral territory we were not obliged to conform to these rules, which did not take into account the tragic situation of the Jews under the Nazi occupation.

For greater effectiveness, at the beginning of the war in 1939–1940 the International Committee of the Red Cross along with many national Red Cross societies created a joint aid commission that was charged with the transport of material aid to the needy in countries at war. The cooperation of this commission was invaluable to us, in particular for sending food relief to communities and camps.

Our shipments to Jewish organizations for distribution to individuals consisted above all of fortifying foodstuffs: condensed milk, sugar, fats, cooking oil. On several occasions we benefited from gifts from large chemical firms in Basel, who placed at our disposal large quantities of medicine and stimulants. These actions have been completely forgotten, and I am pleased to have the opportunity to note them here.

The Czechoslovak minister in Geneva cooperated with our work and obtained a financial contribution from his government-in-exile in London for shipments to the camp-ghetto in Theresienstadt.

The Jewish Agency also took part in financing shipments of food and medicaments. We sometimes made shipments to Cracow to the Unterstützungsstelle, the Jewish relief agency, which distributed the aid among the communities that still existed on the Polish territory designated by the Germans as the "General Government."

These shipments were in principle not authorized at their point of reception. The joint aid commission of the Red Cross had to negotiate an agreement for each location. As a consequence, we obtained permission for shipments only to the Unterstützungsstelle of Cracow and to Theresienstadt.

We have often been asked how we could risk such shipments if we were not sure they would arrive at their intended destinations. I was frankly very far from certain that each successive shipment would arrive, though official receipts reached me regularly. But I took risks because I knew the terrible misery of the recipients. To my great surprise, I learned after the war from eyewitnesses that everything had been shipped and that all the shipments had been delivered. An official who had been with the Jewish relief organization in Cracow and who later worked in the office of the World Jewish Congress in Stockholm gave me very precise details in this regard.

The personal shipments also allowed us to draw up a file of tens of thousands of persons who were detained in the camps. In each dispatched parcel we included a reply card. People regularly sent back their cards to indicate that they had received the package. Despite a prohibition, they often added messages to these forms. We learned a great deal from these semi-clandestine messages. The file thus assembled later served as the basis of a dedicated family search service. At the end of the war we were able to compile an extensive file for that purpose.

The shipment of food and medication parcels was greatly extended after the financial, food, and economic blockade was lifted, that is, in January 1944 after the creation of the War Refugee Board. From that moment on, the shipment of parcels was organized on a very large scale and they were routed through the International Committee of the Red Cross.

Obviously we did not limit our efforts to sending parcels to the civilian population. We always kept in mind the Jewish prisoners of war from the various

armies who were in the hands of the Germans. And our special service systematically collected personal data cards that made it possible for us to send them
parcels or mail. These shipments were organized through the intermediation of
the ICRC.

More often than not the families of the Jewish prisoners of war had been
scattered or even deported. As a result, and unlike all the other prisoners, the
POWs were deprived of all support. It was then particularly important to assist them. For years I maintained contacts with a number of camps.

I especially remember the camp for Jewish Yugoslav officers who, after the
war, made up the leadership of the small Yugoslav community that survived.

Through the offices of the YMCA, which was particularly responsible for
such services, we also sent prisoners of war various religious objects: phylac-
teries, prayer books, and prayer shawls as well as nonreligious books and other
items. The recipients appreciated them.

Although we were a very small team, we accomplished an enormous
amount of work from this office. Because we needed a lot of help, we brought
in a number of volunteers, among whom were locally resident Jewish refugees
of various nationalities.

Many dreamed only of emigration. We gave them advice, and aid too when
we were in a position to offer it. This was not our principal task, of course, but
we wanted to help them find haven elsewhere, and we often were best able to
do that by putting them in touch with Jewish organizations overseas.

Among these refugees were some exceptional figures, such as Pierre
Mendès-France, a member of the French parliament who had served in Léon
Blum's second Popular Front government in 1938, and after the war served as
French prime minister from 1954 to 1955. As soon as Pétain was in place, on
June 17, 1940, the Marshal declared, "Fighting must cease." Mendès-France,
then an air force officer, was determined to continue the fight. He and a number of other members of parliament left Marseilles aboard the *Massilia* to sail
to North Africa. Government minister Georges Mandel, who also sailed on the
Massilia, was assassinated as he disembarked. Forced to return along with others from Casablanca, Mendès-France was arrested in France where he was
condemned as a deserter to a long prison term. Some months later he escaped
and fled to Switzerland where his friend, the socialist deputy and president of
the Swiss parliament, Rosselet, hid him. But Rosselet also informed the Swiss
police. Then, suddenly, Mendès-France appeared in the WJC office. Initially
he refused to divulge his identity, but later he confided it to us.

Adolf Silberschein, a former member of the Polish Sejm, advised us on
Eastern European matters. Mendès-France had heard that Silberschein could

help him get to London, where he wanted to join de Gaulle and continue the fight. Silberschein was not up to date on French politics, but when I learned Mendès-France's identity we assured him of our complete support.

Organizing a trip to London was not an easy matter. A passport had to be obtained, a false identity created, an overseas visa secured for Lisbon, whence he would be able to take a plane for London. Transit visas were needed for Spain and Portugal. The only overseas visas that could be obtained at that time were for Cuba, which required a $500 deposit. And we had to get him accepted into a convoy of refugees through unoccupied France accompanied by Swiss officials.

We took care of all that. Silberschein, thanks to his good relations with the Polish ambassador in Bern, got him a passport in the name of Jan Lemberg. I provided the money for the Cuban visa. We attended to all the arrangements and organized his passage through France. It was a dangerous, roundabout business. Mendès-France showed great courage in daring to undertake it. Fear of being identified had driven him to begin to grow a huge mustache, to part his abundant hair in the middle, and to wear large glasses. Fortunately everything worked out well; he arrived safely in Lisbon and finally was able to join the Free French.

Mendès-France always showed us the greatest gratitude. I remember with great emotion his visits to Geneva as General de Gaulle's minister in 1945 and then again as prime minister in 1954–1955 when the end of the conflict in Indochina was negotiated. When he saw me in the crowd as he was on the way out of an important meeting, he pushed everyone aside in order to come up and shake my hand, and shortly after that he telephoned Silberschein's widow.

I later had the privilege of discussing matters with him, sometimes at great length. To our benefit this was particularly the case when as a member of the United Nations Economic and Social Council he provided us with invaluable support in our struggle against the persecution of Jews in the Arab countries. But that is another story.

All these activities clearly fell outside the traditional framework of the activities of the World Jewish Congress, which was fundamentally a political organization. But we were aware that it was absolutely essential to provide these services to the thousands and thousands of people who needed them. At the time, no other Jewish organization was so engaged.

We had enormous difficulties in persuading our colleagues in New York of the necessity of maintaining these services. This was all the more true after the defeat and collapse of France, when Nahum Goldmann and his colleagues in New York wanted to close the Geneva office. I fiercely resisted this initiative.

The situation in Switzerland was indeed difficult. At times we didn't know whether the Germans would invade the country. In these uncertain times I kept a knapsack filled with the essentials I would need to hide out in the mountains. I was also equipped with a Bolivian passport that Nahum Goldmann had acquired for me when he left Geneva. Fortunately I never needed to use either the backpack or the passport.

In August 1940 I was among the first persons to whom Stephen Wise sent an American emergency visa. These visas for the United States had been created for a limited number of Jewish intellectuals and leaders from European countries. I had the visa entered in my passport, but at the same time I decided that I had to stay at my post. For as long as any of us could do some work and provide some services, our position could not be abandoned. This decision was not an easy one because my closest family had succeeded in leaving Holland and had emigrated to the United States.

In the great confusion that reigned in 1940 among Jewish and non-Jewish organizations in Geneva, I was thus able to preserve the office of the World Jewish Congress in continental Europe and maintain its full capacity for effective action. This is perhaps the greatest personal contribution I made: to stay on the scene to continue the work of intelligence, relief, and rescue that we were able to accomplish throughout the war. This seemed essential to me.

The principal and permanent function of the Geneva office was to provide the World Jewish Congress and Jewish organizations of the Free World with serious, well-founded, and adequate intelligence. I regularly sent to New York and London highly detailed reports on the evolving situation. Often, urgent reports had to be sent about particular events. Organizing this information became increasingly difficult.

By this time we already knew a great deal about what was happening in the East. In fact we monitored the developing situation from one day to the next. Beginning in 1940 we were informed of the ghettoization of the Jews in Poland. We knew of the inadequate food rationing imposed by the Germans. Isolated from the rest of the world, the millions of Jews in the ghettos were condemned to die of hunger. We also knew of the terrible sanitary conditions, the diseases and epidemics that ravaged the ghetto population. During the single month of October 1941, two thousand cases of typhus were reported in the Warsaw Ghetto alone.

We also received information about the horrifying situation in the concentration camps. I remember, for example, that shortly after the occupation of Yugoslavia, and thus before the invasion of the Soviet Union, terrible news reached us concerning the camps of Jasenovac and Zemun (Sajmište). Thirty thousand Jews were deported to the islands off the coast of Yugoslavia, without resources, and were locked up in concentration camps there.

We had multiple sources of information: first, the surviving Jewish communities and their leaders in a number of places. We knew them and we knew that we could trust them. If these communities ceased to function, surviving Jewish leaders continued to send us information privately. We also had other informants, Jews and anti-Nazis from various countries. Some of them could travel; otherwise they sent us visitors with messages.

Consequently we were extremely well informed in Geneva. Our archives hold copies of the letters, reviews, and innumerable memoranda that reached us from all over Europe. Beginning in June–July 1942 I sent the World Jewish Congress in New York a summary report each month on the principal events affecting the Jews in occupied Europe, broken down country by country. The first element of these reports dealt with anti-Semitic measures taken by the Nazis and various local authorities.

Once a year and jointly with Richard Lichtheim of the Jewish Agency for Palestine I sent a telegram with an overview of the situation at that moment, as we understood it. The continuous flow of our communications, often reporting on one event at a time, by the end of the war amounted to a staggering total.

The reports show that we were indeed well briefed and show too how we viewed the unfolding and worsening situation. The volume of intelligence is still impressive, even today when many people claim that nothing was known.

But to be truly effective we had to find other sources of information as well. Among these, one obvious source was the Jewish press. We tried to receive as many Jewish newspapers as possible from the various occupied countries. They published pieces of local interest, regulations and ordinances imposed on Jews by the Nazis and their collaborators, and a great deal of information on the ever-increasing discrimination and persecution in the various countries.

In addition, we systematically subscribed to the official publications of all the occupied countries. We kept up on them and translated portions into all the major Western languages. I received these subscriptions through a Geneva bookstore where my customer name was "Mondial" (Worldwide). What I could not obtain directly by subscription, I received though the library of the League of Nations. The librarian was very understanding. He permitted us to consult and to photostat some official publications that were otherwise inaccessible— published by the military administrations, for example, in the Baltic countries, Alsace-Lorraine, and other areas.

I systematically selected material from these sources and set up files that were continually updated, and I collected all sorts of published texts relating to Jews. Some fifteen volumes of documentation were thus established, country by country. We communicated this information as it was gathered to the Institute of Jewish Affairs* and to the World Jewish Congress in New York, where officials reviewed and studied it for their own purposes. Some of these volumes contain up to three hundred specific documents (laws, decrees, orders) from a single country. All this documentation, which was absolutely indispensable at the time, is today housed in the archives of the Yad Vashem memorial in Jerusalem.

But institutions, newspapers, and documents were not our sole sources of intelligence. We tried by all means possible to establish personal contacts and maintain them as long as possible. The extraordinary times also produced extraordinary individuals. We shared some exceptional experiences with many, including some courageous young people who, in spite of restrictions, traveled illegally. They showed up at our offices asking for support, funding, advice. At the same time they brought in a wealth of information on local situations.

I particularly remember a young Dutch Jew who was living in Belgium. He was in charge of a whole network of young people who tried to arrange the departure of as many Jews as possible to Spain, Portugal, Switzerland, and the rest of the Free World. He was of remarkable intellectual and moral purity and had immense reserves of courage. Unfortunately the Germans later captured and executed him.

One rather enigmatic figure, a Jewish businessman from Denmark, Hugo Rothenberg, mysteriously traveled under the protection of the German War Ministry. He would show up all of a sudden, no one knew from where. Then just as mysteriously he would disappear. But on each visit he proved an extremely useful source of information.

One day he showed us documents proving that the Reichsbahn, the German state railroad company, had submitted invoices to the Berlin Jewish community. These were *bills* for the deportation of Berlin Jews to the East—to Łódź, Riga, and other localities—the height of *chutzpah* and cynicism. A young Danish Jewish historian, Bert Blüdnikov, has since discovered Rothen-

*In 1941 the WJC and the AJC established the IJA in New York as the research and fact-gathering agency to investigate the past and present of World Jewry and make recommendations for Jewish claims in a postwar settlement. After the war the IJA continued its activities, moving to London in 1965. In 1997 it became the Institute for Jewish Policy Research.—ED.

berg's relationship with Hermann Göring, to whom this Jewish businessman had rendered great services at the end of World War I.

Certain officials from the various Swiss consulates, in particular those from Prague, would visit us at important moments to transmit messages from leaders of the Jewish communities in their cities. These messages, which were memorized, gave us detailed information on major developments on the situation of Jews there.

My office also assumed responsibility for editing a number of brochures and booklets on the situation of the Jews of Europe and on the evolution of the catastrophe. Dealing with the situation of the Jews during the ongoing Hungarian crisis, five booklets that I had mimeographed in French, German, and English in several hundred copies each became major references in political circles and for the Swiss press.

I later collaborated in the publication of accounts of the first trials of war criminals in Russia, in particular that of Kharkov. The volume that contained the account of this trial also had reports on the camps at Buchenwald, Auschwitz, and Majdanek, and on the martyrdom of Jews in various regions of Eastern Europe. I myself published a French translation of the report of two Slovak Jews who had escaped from Auschwitz, which reached us in June 1944. Known now as the Vrba-Wetzler report, it had a print run of five thousand copies and appeared under a title borrowed from Dostoyevsky, *Memories from the House of the Dead*. I was also responsible for another brochure on the struggle of the Jews against the Nazis: it dealt with the Jewish resistance in Poland, Russia, France, and Belgium.

These last-named texts were printed clandestinely with the aid of a pro-Communist group. I can admit this today. I am also proud to have had the courage to produce them. I was convinced that the largest public possible ought to be made aware of the atrocities committed against Jews, atrocities that were summarized in these documents.

We were also in touch with the Jewish resistance in France and in Italy. The leaders of the Jewish resisters in France regularly sent us reports. Myra Becker, my secretary of many long years, was wakened from time to time at six in the morning by French railroad workers who came into the Eaux-Vives station in Geneva to bring her messages reporting on the situation—the financial accounts and the actions of the various units. Our contacts with the armed resistance were also not limited to the Jewish resistance.

We responded as best we could to the requests that reached us, from both the Jewish and non-Jewish resistance. Obviously Jews found their way to our door more readily. My colleague Marc Jarblum was in touch with Jewish leaders in France. They were in charge of groups of young people who smuggled individuals out of the country illegally. These youngsters needed money and weapons to protect the convoys. We attempted to get them what they needed for their operations. At times resistance groups would contact us directly.

For example, one fine day in the course of the second year of the war a Catholic priest came to see me, accompanied by a man whom I knew. It was the former president of the Jewish community of Turin, an engineer who had worked for Fiat before the war. The priest told me more or less the following: "I have come on behalf of the resistance committee and the leaders of a partisan group in the South Tyrol, in Bolzano, Merano, and the surrounding mountains. We have about ten thousand Jewish refugees in our region, hidden in the mountains. We are ready to protect them. But we lack weapons, boots, and all kinds of things that are absolutely essential for our defense. Can you help us?"

When he finished, he held out to me a little piece of badly crumpled paper. On one side was the stamp of their unit and on the other a kind of list, a homemade order form.

I took this "document," which I have preserved all these years, to a British friend who worked for the British military attaché in Bern. The matter was of extreme interest to the British military staff. My friend made me wait at least fifteen minutes. Finally he came back and said, "It's true, we know the group and we know where it is. You can count on us; we will do what is necessary."

Thus not too long afterward these Italian resistance fighters received weapons and equipment by parachute.

I was later approached by Raffaele Cantoni who, after the liberation, became president of the Union of Jewish Communities of Italy. I knew Cantoni, a well-known anti-fascist who had been arrested and interned for a long period in a prison on a small Mediterranean island. I had met him for the first time when he came under cover to Switzerland, after the promulgation of anti-Jewish legislation in Italy, in order to give us a detailed report on the situation of the Italian Jews. Cantoni asked me for financial support for the Italian resistance. I at once got in touch with the representative committee of Italian Jews in New York, which organized a collection. This resulted in a substantial sum, which I forwarded to the resistance.

These activities were clearly out of the ordinary. But in the course of that terrible war, we had learned that we had to use every available resource. Those of us on the scene had learned long before that in the occupied countries the "legal regulations" were contrary to justice; "illegal" measures were imperative. But it took a long time for many Jewish and non-Jewish leaders to understand this, just as so many of the potential victims too long remained blind to what they must do to save themselves.

One of the victims' great weaknesses was that they continued to respect the normative notions of everyday life. Neither the organizations nor the individuals were capable of quickly breaking with their respective routines. For years the lack of boldness, on both the national and international levels, was an obstacle to innovations that might have saved lives. At that time what was needed was the play of imagination and a readiness to invent measures that in more normal times would have been considered extraordinary.

In our everyday activities we often had to improvise solutions. Thus one day, probably in 1943, I received a telegram from Itzhak Grünbaum, the head of Va'ad Hahatzala in Jerusalem. This council, which functioned from within the Jewish Agency for Palestine, was trying to save Jews everywhere it was possible, just as we were doing at the WJC.

I had come to know Grünbaum well at the WJC. Before the war he had been one of the great defenders of equal rights for Jews, doing so in the Polish parliament, where he had distinguished himself by his courage and combativeness. We all liked him. Grünbaum telegraphed me to ask me to try to find his son, who was in Poland. I asked myself, "How can he send me such a telegram; he knows very well what is going on in Poland." But I couldn't ignore Grünbaum. At first this request prevented me from sleeping for several nights. I readdressed the questions: "How can he ask me to do such a crazy thing? How could you find a person in that world of millions of persons in perdition?" Then I had an extravagant idea. I sent ten food parcels to *Monsieur Grünbaum fils* (son of Mr. Grünbaum) to ten different camps. And I found him in one of the camps. It was a kind of miracle. One of the parcels arrived and was turned over to him. He returned the form to acknowledge receipt. This is one illustration of the need for imagination and for knowing how to abandon ordinary bureaucratic paths. Each case, of necessity specific, required its own inventive solution.

Another time I suddenly found myself involved in a rescue action on behalf of a whole group of young Jews being held in the main camp at Auschwitz. There too I had to improvise and use my wits.

One day, around June 10, 1944, the Slovak resistance succeeded in getting to the Czechoslovak minister at the League of Nations, Dr. Jaromir Kopecky, a twenty-seven-page report on the Auschwitz II (Birkenau) camp. This report, which has since become famous, was the work of two Slovak Jews who had miraculously escaped from the camp. It was the first of its kind. The report not only gave an overview of the terrible conditions of life in Birkenau but also tried to reconstruct the chronology of arrivals and the composition of the various shipments of the deported from all the corners of Europe.

Kopecky, who maintained good relations with us, called my colleague Fritz Ullmann at the Jewish Agency, who was responsible for relations with Czechoslovak Jews. Kopecky asked Ullmann to forward the file to me so that I could prepare a summary that he could then send by code to his government.

While analyzing the file I discovered that at a certain moment the report mentioned the arrival in Auschwitz of a group of young Czechoslovak Jews who were members of the Jewish athletic club, the Maccabees, coming from Theresienstadt "to undergo a six-month quarantine." We had never heard of a quarantine at Auschwitz.

A little later on, the report pointed out that the quarantined group had been exterminated. And still again, a little later on, the report mentioned the arrival of another group from Theresienstadt, also being "quarantined" for six months.

I then looked at the calendar and noted that the second group's six-month period would be up in five days. I immediately jumped into a taxi and went to Kopecky's. I showed him the report and said, "Let's try to save these people." During the taxi ride I drafted a telegram for the Czech government in London, asking that the BBC at regular intervals during the next few days broadcast a precise warning to alert the group to its danger. Kopecky turned directly to the BBC representative in Bern—she worked at the British legation—and she passed along the message, which the BBC broadcast several times. During the war I never knew if this desperate attempt to warn the deportees had been heard in Auschwitz. More than twenty years later, when I was going through Prague, I met a survivor from Auschwitz, Erich Kulka. He confirmed for me that there were secret radio sets within the camp and that the message had been heard. He assured me that the camp underground had then cleared the group out of the barracks in which they had been placed. He could not, however, tell me whether the group had finally been saved. I fear that this intervention may have had no long-term consequences. But this too illustrates how much imagination and initiative were needed to break free of the daily routine.

WJC Activities and the Creation of the War Refugee Board

The creation of the War Refugee Board was a consequence of the discovery by the U.S. Treasury Department of the State Department's sabotage of the urgent measures I had proposed in my telegram of April 1943.

Before going to President Roosevelt with a full report on the situation drafted by two trusted subordinates, Treasury Secretary Morgenthau turned to Cordell Hull, the secretary of state, to complain of the delays in the implementation of the rescue proposals I had submitted and, as I later learned, had been approved by the president. After Morgenthau's intervention the State Department finally reacted positively and gave instructions to the U.S. legation in Bern.

Suddenly, on December 23, 1943, I was urgently called to the American legation in Bern where they asked me in stupefaction, "What have you done? How did you do it?" I myself was ignorant of what had happened in Washington. At a single blow the whole policy of the financial and food blockade, the whole policy of indifference with regard to the victims of Nazism, had changed.

On the spot I was given a document, a "license" of four or five pages, drafted in complicated legal language, by which the President of the United States authorized me to establish contact with enemy countries in order to aid the Jewish victims of Nazism. At the same time the American government authorized the World Jewish Congress to send me $25,000 for this purpose.

This was the first time such authorization had been given. I was also invited to present my views on the text of the license. After my remarks, the license, which I still found much too restrictive, was amended. The Americans also told me it was an experiment. "If the project works, we'll get you more money and more resources."

Finally on January 16, 1944, Morgenthau met with Roosevelt and gave him the report, now entitled "Report to the President of the United States." The president understood that it was explosive and that he must make a rapid response.

Morgenthau had anticipated the president's reaction. Consequently he did not simply submit the report. Drawing conclusions from the situation, he now presented to Roosevelt a proposal the president could use as his response: the creation of the War Refugee Board.

The idea for the establishment of such an agency, intended to save and assist Nazi victims, came from Professor Milton Handler of Columbia University in New York. For two years he had unsuccessfully promoted his idea before the relevant American government authorities.

Now taken up again by officials in the Treasury Department and fine-tuned by Professor Handler, the project was approved by Professor Oscar Cox, an excellent lawyer and undersecretary in the Department of Justice, and one of Roosevelt's closest advisers. This was the plan Morgenthau took to the president.

In the terms of the proposal, the administration of the agency would be drawn from three departments, State, Treasury, and War. Thanks to Morgenthau's energy and in spite of difficulties of all kinds, the board was established on January 22, 1944. It was ultimately to this board that responsibility was given to pursue and support efforts to save Jews until the war ended.

The next day, January 23, 1944, my license was amended for the third time. The new text, more liberal, made rescue work a great deal easier. Immediately the efforts of all the Jewish organizations, such as the Joint, were able to benefit from the new resources.

Finally a step of great importance had been taken, the only consquential one that was intended to assist us. But it was already very late. Since my first telegram, eighteen months had passed, during which the inexorable massacre had continued: millions of Jews had been murdered.

Here let me quote a passage from the letter that Milton Handler wrote me well after the end of the war: "I know how important your work was and without it there would never have been any action on the part of the United States government." Coming from a figure so well informed concerning his government's conduct in this matter, his message touched me deeply.

To guarantee the effectiveness of the new body, representatives of the War Refugee Board were appointed in the capitals of all the neutral countries, at the American embassies and legations in Stockholm, Madrid, Lisbon, Ankara, and Bern. They were charged with leading and supporting the rescue efforts and with coming to the aid of victims in every possible manner.

In Switzerland the American government appointed Roswell McClelland, until then the representative of the Quakers in Geneva, a man whom I knew well and valued.

When the U.S. legation in Bern issued me the first license in December 1943, the British legation, on the instructions of Hugh Dalton, the British minister of economic warfare, attempted until the very last minute to halt this humanitarian gesture and did succeed in delaying the issuance of the license for several weeks. This was one of the last attempts at bureaucratic sabotage.

Other than prosecuting the war itself, the establishment of the War Refugee Board was the single real contribution of any of the Allies to the fight against the Nazi extermination of the Jews. It fundamentally changed the situation, finally making possible a vast effort to rescue and provide relief. During the fifteen or sixteen months of its operation until the end of the European war, no less than $20 million passed through the War Refugee Board. All this funding came from Jewish organizations. It was exclusively intended to save and assist Jews in the European countries overrun by the Nazis.

It is impossible to list all the activities and actions in which the WRB participated, at times under very difficult circumstances. Some were extremely dangerous, some even fantastic.

Unfortunately, when my rescue plan was finally accepted and the War Refugee Board had been created, it was no longer possible to evacuate the Jews who had been deported to Transnistria, even though, in Romania, the political situation had changed. On the other hand, a number of other important rescue and aid projects could be carried out with the assistance of the WRB. The World Jewish Congress was the initiator of, or was associated with, a large number of these projects. Among the WRB's most important undertakings, the following merit special mention:

—the very substantial food-parcel distribution program, sent through the International Committee of the Red Cross, financed by the Joint;

—support for underground resistance movements in the various countries, with financial backing that was indispensable for the rescue action;

—the single *political* action to save Jews, which affected Hungary;

—various activities to bribe high Nazi officials in order to free several thousand Jews;

—encouragement and support for the Bulgarian government in its refusal to turn over to the Nazis the fifty thousand native Jews of that country; and

—preservation of survivors in the concentration camps during the last phase of the war.

I personally took part in three large-scale rescue actions: the rescue and evacuation to Switzerland and Spain of children and young Jews from Western European countries; political action on behalf of Hungarian Jews; and the action that sought to prevent the massacre of survivors in the camps in the course of the last phase of the war.

Saving Children and Young People

Thanks to our contacts with the Jewish resistance in France, we had been able to transmit millions of French francs (using French Jewish money in France and buying French francs on the market under the supervision of the American legation) into the country in order to organize a vast rescue effort for small children and young people and to create false identity papers for them. Countless false documents were made up in specialized underground printing shops: identity papers, work permits, baptismal certificates, food ration cards, and even passes, which had to be periodically renewed. Equipped with these, numerous convoys left for Switzerland and Spain.

Here is the message that Marc Jarblum and I sent to the U.S. legation in Bern on August 28, forwarded to the New York WJC on September 2, 1944:

> Replying yours 22/8 informing you that thanks funds put at our disposal by [World Jewish] Congress and thanks funds put at disposal Jarblum by [Jewish Agency for] Palestine and by Joint following achievements were made in France: 1,350 children have been brought to Switzerland; 70 children to Spain. 700 are hidden at the top [= still in France]. Furthermore 700 youngsters have been brought to Spain. 200 parents accompanying their children were evacuated. Finally 4,000 to 5,000 adults are hidden thanks action our people. The whole rescue action was necessarily intimately linked with illegal work of all kind notably procuration of monthly about 5,000 identity, rationing and worker's cards birth and baptism certificates etc. as well as with appropriate equipment of armed convoys to frontiers. At present moment it is impossible to separate rescue children adults according various funds utilised as whole action was organised by our people with all available means. Our own participation amounted to more than eighteen million French francs. Our merit is to have initiated the whole action. Ourselves awaiting details from France which shall communicate as soon as possible.

The necessary funds were collected by the Representative Committee of the Jews of France (Comité représentatif des Juifs de France) in New York, under the chairmanship of Edouard de Rothschild. In a memo of August 28, 1944, which I sent by diplomatic channels to the Representative Committee, one reads the following:

> The activity of the World Jewish Congress in the rescue of children in France was directed by Monsieur Jarblum. The work was carried out by a group of young Zionist Jews centered in Lyon, and who work in other French cities including Nice, Toulouse, etc.
>
> This team worked with tireless devotion, despite the fact that it was being relentlessly hunted by the Gestapo. A heartfelt tribute must go to Ernest Lambert, shot by the Germans in Montluc, who was one of the souls of the Resistance devoted to this task.
>
> The Congress has had the privilege of being the first to put important sums at the disposal of this rescue action and, as in many other cases, has cleared the way for other organizations by putting in place a body capable of accomplishing this great undertaking.

This text reflects our effective participation in the rescue activity. In our cross-checking of the figures we found that in this action alone between 8,300 and 9,300 persons were saved from extermination.

Saving the Hungarian Jews

The War Refugee Board also made possible the one large-scale political action undertaken during the war: the effort to save the very large Jewish community of Hungary.

During the first three years of the war, most Hungarian Jews had been spared even while suffering under increasingly repressive anti-Semitic legislation. But their situation took a tragic turn in the spring of 1944.

Even before the occupation of Hungary by German troops, which occurred on March 19, 1944, I had sent telegrams to London and New York to alert the WJC to the new dangers that threatened the 800,000 Jews then residing in Hungary. In consideration of what had happened in Poland and elsewhere, I asked that everything possible be done to mobilize the Free World against this threat of additional exterminations.

In particular I suggested that eminent figures—Jewish or otherwise—of the English-speaking world, including church dignitaries and prominent Americans of Hungarian origin, should appeal to the Hungarian people to oppose the German extermination projects and to help Jews escape. I requested that this declaration make explicit that the attitude of the Hungarian people toward the Jews would be an important test of its conduct, which would be taken into account in future peace arrangements. I asked that this message be systematically broadcast in Hungarian.

My telegrams suggested that after the wanted public declarations of the British and American governments, such a statement should similarly be obtained directly from the Soviet government. A declaration warning the Hungarians against anti-Jewish measures could have a definite effect, given that Soviet troops were not too far distant from the Hungarian border. I suggested that American, British, and Soviet radio stations broadcast appeals to the Hungarians and encourage all segments of Hungarian society to help save the Jews.

Declarations and encouragement of this sort would have to be broadcast repeatedly, in Hungarian but also in German and the various Slavic languages. I suggested at the same time that the anti-Jewish broadcasts by Hungarian radio be met with adequate explanations and counterarguments, broadcast in these same languages, so that the peoples of Hungary and territories occupied by Hungarian forces would be told the truth and be given an explanation of the objectives of their own government's anti-Jewish campaigns. Leaflets bearing the official declarations of the Allied governments should be dropped over Hungary by Allied aircraft.

The respective Allied governments were to be ready to save as many Hungarian Jewish children as possible by granting them visas. The Allied countries were to approach neutral countries such as Sweden, Switzerland, and Turkey with a view to encouraging them to provide temporary asylum for these children. The necessary means had to be found, through official or other channels, to enable the Hungarian children to leave the country.

Given the desperate situation of Hungarian Jewry, while still bearing in mind that no sacrifice was to be spared to save at least a portion of what remained of European Jewry, an extraordinary effort had to be undertaken by the Allies and by all civilized nations to save the Jews of Hungary by granting them special protection.

Thus we had to determine if some countries might employ their representatives in Hungary to grant Jews citizenship and a passport. The relief organizations and the associations of Jews of Hungarian origin in the United States and Great Britain had to be informed of the urgent need for substantial sums of money that would be indispensable to the Hungarian Jews. These had been progressively pauperized; they needed this money in order to seek asylum in other countries or to hide with non-Jews.

On March 23, only a few days after the occupation of Hungary by German troops, I gave the following message to the American consul in Geneva with the request that it be transmitted to Silverman in London and to Dr. Wise in New York:

OWING TO RECENT POLITICAL DEVELOPMENTS IN HUNGARY BEING MOST
ANXIOUS ABOUT DESTINY HUNGARIAN JEWRY ONLY IMPORTANT SECTION
EUROPEAN JEWRY STILL IN EXISTENCE AND NUMBERING ABOUT 800,000
STOP SUGGESTING WORLD WIDE APPEAL OF ANGLO-SAXON PERSONALITIES
NON-JEWISH AND JEWISH INCLUDING LEADERS OF PROTESTANT AND
CATHOLIC CHURCHES AND OUTSTANDING AMERICANS OF HUNGARIAN
ORIGIN TO HUNGARIAN PEOPLE WARNING THEM NOT TO ADMIT
APPLICATION OF POLICY OF EXTERMINATION OF JEWS BY GERMAN BUTCHERS
OR HUNGARIAN QUISLINGS AND TO HELP JEWS BY ALL POSSIBLE MEANS IN
ORDER TO PREVENT THEIR FALLING INTO HANDS OF GERMANS STOP
WARNING SHOULD PARTICULARLY INSIST UPON FACT THAT ATTITUDE
HUNGARIAN PEOPLE TOWARDS JEWS WILL BE ONE OF THE MOST IMPORTANT

TESTS OF BEHAVIOR WHICH UNITED NATIONS WILL REMEMBER IN PEACE
SETTLEMENT AFTER WAR STOP SIMILAR BROADCASTS SHOULD BE MADE
EVERY NIGHT IN HUNGARIAN LANGUAGE DURING THE NEXT WEEKS STOP

On April 14 I sent the details of the German extermination plan, indicating what could be done to warn the Jews of Hungary in order to prevent them from falling into German hands. They must be publicly advised to disobey orders to be registered, to refuse to wear the yellow star, and to disregard summonses. They had to be urged to hide and to seek protection from their non-Jewish neighbors and Christian religious institutions.

In Geneva, day after day, we followed the events with anguish. For reasons as yet unexplained, however, the Nazis succeeded in imposing an information blackout for several months. Today we know that a number of alarming reports from the Jewish community in Hungary had reached the International Committee of the Red Cross. But, contrary to the wishes of the Jewish community of Budapest, the ICRC did not forward them to us.

When, finally, around June 15 we were able to receive the first direct news from the Jewish institutions of Budapest, we learned, stupefied, that during the three months that had passed since the entry of German troops into Hungary, most of the Jews in the Hungarian provinces had been deported en masse and sent to their deaths in Auschwitz. Already the victims totaled 335,000.

It was about this time that we in Geneva received the report of the two Slovak Jews who had miraculously escaped from Auschwitz, the so-called Vrba-Wetzler report. It consisted of an extremely detailed report on the Nazi methodology for the mass extermination of Jews there and on the various shipments of deportees that reached the camp. Now it was imperative to act as quickly as possible to save the Jews of the capital city, Budapest, as well as all those who were still alive in the forced labor battalions and camps in Hungary.

A large-scale political action was then undertaken in which the World Jewish Congress played a preponderant role. The New York office lobbied the American government in particular, and the London office the British government. The two were also in continual contact with the Vatican and the Church of England. The Stockholm office took the initiative to mobilize the Swedish government.

It was our responsibility in Geneva to get the International Committee of the Red Cross to act and to influence the World Council of Churches to make a strong statement.

Meanwhile we also had to mobilize public opinion. We did this in Geneva with the publication of the aforementioned five brochures, each in French, English, and German. They provided a detailed account of the tragic situation of the Hungarian Jews and described their progressive persecution and deportation.

The War Refugee Board representative in Switzerland helped us disseminate these reports, which were turned over to Swiss journalists and to hundreds of public and political figures who could influence public opinion.

The king of Sweden, Gustav V, was the first head of state to send a telegram, in June 1944, to Regent Horthy urging him to cease the deportations immediately. On June 25, 1944, Pope Pius XII, in one of his rare interventions on behalf of the Jews, addressed himself to Horthy in the same terms. But the most spectacular action, which contravened all the customs of war, was undeniably the *verbal note* that the United States addressed through Switzerland to Regent Horthy on June 26, 1944. Written in the firmest of terms, the note was accompanied by President Roosevelt's demand for an immediate cessation of deportations.

Backed by Professor Guggenheim, I exerted strong pressure on the International Committee of the Red Cross, in particular on one of its top officials, Professor Carl J. Burckhardt, to get the president of the ICRC to take similar action. We did not fail to point out the meager effort made until then by the ICRC to protect Jews, nor to remind Burckhardt that after the war the ICRC would be called to give an account of its actions. Acting on my request, though without making explicit reference to it, the World Council of Churches undertook similar interventions with the ICRC president.

As a consequence, on July 5, ICRC President Huber addressed a handwritten letter to Horthy in which he informed him of the reports that had come from the entire world to the ICRC concerning the harsh measures that were reputed to have been taken against Jews of Hungarian nationality. He strongly recommended that the regent issue orders that would permit the ICRC to answer the content of these reports in a way that would reflect well on Hungary.

All these actions made a profound impression on Horthy. The regent responded to all the appeals and stopped the deportations. This was a considerable success: the head of a state allied with Germany had halted deportations and communicated his decision to the foreign public figures who had contacted him. Alas, Horthy was no match for the actions undertaken directly by Adolf Eichmann, assisted by Edmund Veesenmayer, the Nazi ambassador to Hungary.

In the final instance, Eichmann made the decisions concerning Jews. Thus, despite Horthy's orders, deportations resumed a few months later in different forms. Significant numbers of Jews were deported, beginning with those of the Budapest suburbs. Tens of thousands of others were forcibly conscripted into formations for "labor in the Reich."

The principal events of this action were the death marches begun in late November 1944, in the course of which tens of thousands of Jewish men and women (some sources speak of fifty and even sixty thousand) were forced to walk, in the rain and without food, via Hegyeshalom toward a camp in Austria 125 miles distant. Several thousand died on the way of hunger, cold, and exhaustion. The soldiers guarding them gunned down numerous Jews who could march no farther.

The situation within Hungary had worsened in October 1944 when the Horthy government was replaced by the brutal and profoundly anti-Semitic regime of Ferenc Szálasi's Arrow Cross party. The seizure of power was accompanied by the slaughter of six hundred Jews.

All summer and autumn we continually struggled against these various developments by warning the ICRC and the American and Swiss governments. I unceasingly and fiercely protested the slowness that characterized every position taken by the ICRC.

The archives of the World Jewish Congress and the ICRC bear witness to my own actions continued during this whole period. In his work devoted to the day-to-day activities of the WJC and ICRC with reference to the Jews of Hungary, *Facing the Holocaust in Budapest: The International Committee of the Red Cross and the Jews in Hungary 1943–1945* (1988), Arieh Ben-Tov frequently refers to my views, to their accuracy, and to the quality of the many initiatives and tireless work accomplished by the WJC office in Geneva.

I undertook all this activity in close collaboration with Roswell McClelland, the WRB representative in Bern, who often supported my initiatives through his own channels.

In the face of the new Szálasi regime, we had to redouble our efforts to prevent new deportations, to protect the occupants of the designated "Jewish houses," and to get at least minimum guarantees for individual Jews.

Fortunately, as we shall see a bit later, Robert Schirmer and Friedrich Born, the representatives of the ICRC in Budapest, had more courage and more imagination than the administrators at the central office in Geneva.

During this whole period the problem of drawing up individual certificates of protection for the Jews played a central role. We know that Raoul Wallenberg of the Swedish delegation and Carl Lutz, the Swiss consul, issued thousands of certificates to the Jews of Budapest, which saved tens of thousands of them.

The ICRC representatives also issued such documents. In this connection Professor Burckhardt consulted me to determine whether the ICRC representatives should increase the number of protection certificates that they were giving to Jews in Budapest. Burckhardt feared that multiplying their number might call the very value of such certificates into question.

I replied that we must not view matters as if these events were happening in Switzerland in a normal, orderly atmosphere. Budapest was chaotic; life-and-death decisions were being made arbitrarily. The fate of a Jew arrested by a policeman or a member of the Arrow Cross would depend on the good humor of that functionary, depending on whether he had slept well, quarreled with his wife, or enjoyed a good lunch. According to his mood, he could rip up the certificate or recognize its validity. Every instance when the Jew had no paper to show him meant arrest and deportation. Increasing the number of these certificates gave the Jews a chance of surviving. I convinced Burckhardt, and the ICRC agent in Budapest continued to issue protection certificates to Jews. Other categories of protection documents were certificates of nationality or the passports of certain Central American countries, which were sent to Budapest, as they were to some other locations and occasionally even to internment camps. The validity of these documents was challenged on various occasions. Here too the WRB accomplished valuable work by asking the Central American governments not to challenge the validity of these documents until after the war.

Finally, several thousand Jews, a portion of whom were lodged in the protected houses of the ICRC, were spared because they had departure certificates for Palestine.

My relations with the ICRC also permitted me to establish contact with some of its representatives in Hungary, with whom we were able to discuss actions to be undertaken.

The activity of the ICRC in Budapest was described to me in detail by Dr. Robert Schirmer, the ICRC representative in the Hungarian capital. I met him in Geneva on November 9, 1944. Dr. Schirmer gave me an account of all the actions he and his colleague, Friedrich Born, had undertaken in order to protect the Jews of Budapest. His report pointed out in particular that the ICRC representatives had extended the organization's protection to houses, hospitals, and soup kitchens, thus covering tens of thousands of persons, while also assuring them of the minimum means of survival. When they had regular and adequate incoming supplies, the soup kitchens typically distributed eighteen to twenty thousand meals twice a day.

To ensure the proper functioning of the entire operation, the ICRC had set up an elaborate organization of appointed personnel: approximately 150 persons undertook this work, the majority of them Hungarian Jews, who thus also found a place to work.

Two thousand children, some accompanied by their mothers, found shelter in five or six houses, protected by the "official" nameplates of the Red Cross.

At this time, in late October 1944, between 160,000 and 170,000 Jews still remained in Budapest. Jewish institutions resumed their activity under the protection of the ICRC.

Then Dr. Schirmer gave us an account, lively and colorful, of his rather bizarre meetings with the minister of foreign affairs and the minister of the interior of the Szálasi government. The "head of Hungarian diplomacy," clearly a crude and ignorant man, accepted at face value everything the ICRC representatives wanted to have him believe. Seeing that they were dealing with an ignoramus, the ICRC personnel bluffed all the way. In particular they made the diplomat believe that all the arrangements that had been taken to protect Jews were part of the Geneva Conventions. They also led him to believe that similar measures had been taken in other countries.

The minister eventually came to call the ICRC people "comrades," which only added to the grotesque dimension of the situation. For his part, Dr. Schirmer thought that when dealing with a gangster one should use the language and methods of gangsters. And so they won the day.

I was very impressed with Dr. Schirmer. It was the first time I had seen an ICRC representative who was anything out of the ordinary, who disregarded diplomatic form, who set aside the customary prudence of his superiors in Geneva, and who, going straight at the goal, obtained a number of remarkable successes. My assessment of Dr. Schirmer is equally valid for his colleague Friedrich Born.

Since deportations from Hungary had now slowed, we lobbied various organizations in order to assure the Budapest Jews supplies of food and clothing. Through my contacts with Schirmer and the WRB, it was even possible to create a special fund to assist eighteen thousand Jews in the Vienna region, among whom were conscripted workers from Hungary, Poland, and Czechoslovakia.

In late 1944 deportations from Hungary ceased. The actions on behalf of Hungarian Jews were a relative success, especially when measured against Nazi goals. Everyone agreed that this effort, heavily supported by the War Refugee Board, had saved a considerable proportion of the Jews of Budapest.

Negotiate with the Nazis? The Role of the Jewish Councils

In the course of the rescue of Hungarian Jews, direct negotiations took place between Jews and high-ranking German officials. The creation of the War Refugee Board had made this possible. With the knowledge of the WRB, with its authorization to act, and because these steps were virtually under its control, it was possible to make a number of deals. In the course of these multi-faceted negotiations, attempts were made to bribe some senior Nazi officials so that victims would be allowed to leave.

The best known of these dealings was that between Reszo Kasztner and Joint official Saly Mayer on the Jewish side, and Kurt Becher, responsible for the operational office of the anti-Jewish action in Hungary. Initially it was a matter of saving several thousand Hungarian Jews. This then led to large-scale negotiations concerning all of the remaining Jews under German control.

Another example: Elie Sternbuch of Agudath Israel, with the help of Jean-Marie Musy, a former Swiss federal councillor, sought to save twelve hundred Jews from the ghetto-camp of Theresienstadt by negotiating with German officials.

Negotiations were also initiated between Hillel Storch with the WJC Stockholm office, and Felix Kersten, a Finnish physician who cared for senior German officials, including Heinrich Himmler himself. At stake initially was permission for some thousands of deportees to leave for Sweden and then to prevent the annihilation of the survivors of the camps.

Thanks to the evolution of the military situation, which was becoming increasingly unfavorable to the Germans, Jewish leaders succeeded in making contact and beginning negotiations with high-level Nazis, who tried thereby to save themselves.

For my part, I was informed of some of these deals. Kasztner paid me undercover visits in Geneva several times and kept me informed, against the wishes of Saly Mayer.

I was also in telephone contact with Storch in Stockholm. Conscious that German intelligence was listening to us, we communicated in a language invented for the circumstances. I brought Storch up to date on what I knew of Kasztner's doings.

As for the large-scale transactions, the goal of which was to stop deportations in return for the delivery of transportation resources and war materiel, they were encouraged by Rabbi Michael Dov Weissmandel, who lived in hiding in the Slovakian mountains. I never saw any trace of Weissmandel's project in Geneva and learned of it only after the war. His later reproaches regarding my alleged failure to support it are quite unjustified. At the time they were talking about an exchange project involving ten thousand trucks for one million Jews. When I learned of these ideas, they seemed to me completely out of touch with the reality we had been confronting.

I cannot imagine how either side could have embraced such a deal. On the one hand, it was unlikely that the Germans would completely stop the deportation of Jews. On the other, it was unthinkable that the Western Allies would give in to demands that called for the delivery of military materiel that the Germans could use to continue the war against the Soviets. Everyone who understood the situation at all knew that for the Americans and the British, the alliance with the Soviets took priority.

Moreover, when we reflect on the fierce opposition the British displayed to my first American "license" to transfer $25,000, a grandiose project such as the truck proposal clearly was a fantasy.

In my opinion, the sole positive feature of these discussions was that they slowed down deportation operations. For that to happen it was necessary to adopt a delaying posture and prolong the discussions as long as possible—in short, to win time. But I find it impossible to believe that they could actually have resulted in saving and liberating all the Jews. The Nazis' plans for full-scale annihilation were already too far advanced and their determination too well proven to permit me to conclude otherwise.

I knew the men who conducted negotiations with the Nazis: Dr. Reszo Kasztner as well as Saly Mayer. In my opinion the latter was not the great hero that some, after the war, claimed him to be. Mayer had the best intentions, but his intellectual and political abilities were not equal to the dramatic needs of those apocalyptic times. He had instructions to drag out the negotiations. He carried out these instructions as best he could.

For his part, Kasztner was certainly not the monster some people tried to make of him after the war. He too was animated by the best of intentions. He wanted to save those people. But the circumstance that he himself was to select the people whom he was to save placed him in a dramatically untenable position. Choosing who would live and who would die was tantamount to playing God. No human being is well suited to such a role. He undertook the task as well as he could, applying a formula of his own devising for selecting among the various Jewish religious and political groups. He was blamed for having included his own family. Anyone who presumes to judge Kasztner's behavior should be prepared to answer the question, What would you have done in his place? Undeniably his actions furthered the rescue of several thousand Hungarian Jews, among whom were accomplished and prominent people. Kasztner was a great charmer and given to bluffing. On occasion he would boast of his activity while embellishing reality a bit. These contradictions finally were his undoing. At the postwar trial of SS-Standartenführer Kurt Becher, Kasztner testified in the German's favor, as expected, but he added an emphasis to which many reacted vehemently.

Hillel Storch was an extraordinary personality. A native of Riga, the capital of Latvia, he escaped to Stockholm at the beginning of the war. As soon as he arrived he undertook a rescue operation on behalf of the Jews of the Baltic countries. He put a great deal of energy and boundless enthusiasm into this enterprise, attributes that collided with the much more reserved character of the Scandinavian Jews.

Storch creatively sought all sorts of channels to enter into negotiations with senior Germans. He eventually established contact with Himmler, in large measure through the offices of the Finnish physician Felix Kersten, who, as we already have noted, cared for the Reichsführer-SS.

When Kersten arranged for him to meet Himmler, Storch's wife told him not to go: "We have already lost thirty-six members of our family; that's enough!" Storch never forgave Norbert Masur for having taken his place in these negotiations at the last minute, negotiations that Count Folke Bernadotte, then vice president of the Swedish Red Cross, actively supported. These contacts led to the liberation of several thousand people before the cease-fire and to saving an even larger number immediately afterward.

The relations and deals with the Nazis posed a more general problem for the Jewish councils, the *Judenräte*. Of course these Jewish councils were hardly normal phenomena. Some of them, especially in Poland, were able to recognize Hitler's policy with surprising lucidity. They analyzed the situation and played for time. At any cost they wished to maintain their fellow Jews as a labor resource useful to the Germans. It was the sole possibility that might save even some of the Jews.

Others were much less clairvoyant. Among them were people extremely devoted to the Jewish cause. I knew several of them. Some of them had even participated in the prewar struggle against the Nazis. But face to face with the Nazis, their response was both inappropriate and inadequate. Many chose to cooperate with the occupiers because they believed that otherwise things would take an even more ferocious turn. They chose the wrong option. They prevented nothing, and their cooperation made the execution of the Nazi plan that much easier. Without their cooperation a certain amount of disorder probably would have developed, which might have permitted a great number of people to escape.

As I have said, all this is terribly difficult to judge in retrospect because one cannot put oneself into the position of the leaders of the time, each one of whom experienced the pressures of specific conditions. It was also a matter of personal conduct. Some people were honest to the end, others were not.

At the end of the war I was personally quite reserved toward everyone. Not all those who survived were angels. The dehumanization of those deported to the camps was a policy systematically pursued by the Nazis; a great many people were victims of this process. In many circumstances the only people who survived were those who were strongest and who had the fewest scruples. Of course, many people were of perfect integrity. I know that a journalist one day said to Simone Weil, "You survived, therefore you were a Kapo." This was and remains an intolerable insult.

I remember very well that during the first years after the war I never interrogated survivors about their past—first, because I didn't know with whom I was dealing, and second, because I was not sure that they would tell me the whole truth. In any case I believed and still believe that those who lived sheltered lives had no right to judge what happened in the world of camps and ghettos where the rules of humanity did not exist.

But an unwillingness to judge does not prevent recurrence of memory and of emotion that cannot be compared to any other. One day, looking for a document in my archives, I found in the file for 1945 a report on my first meeting with survivors from a camp in that part of Germany near the Swiss border that had been occupied by the French. That event occurred three or four days after the end of hostilities. A French officer had arranged for us to visit the camp. I cannot recount that entire report here, but it reflected one of the most moving experiences of my life. In the intervening years I had forgotten that first encounter with survivors. Finding the report again, I was overcome with emotion, as if the events had occurred only the day before. Reading it, I heard myself asking again the question, Why did they suffer so much, why they and not I? I could not live with that recurring self-interrogation, and thus I suppressed the report in my memory. It revealed limitations that were my own, but not mine alone.

In all the complex situations we have to face, one's sense of responsibility, sense of individual conduct, always plays an important role. Since the war a number of questions have been raised as to what the Jewish agencies and their officials actually did. There were, of course, the Judenräte, often appointed by the Germans even without the consent of their council members, and there were all sorts of other institutions.

In France, for example, the Vichy government imposed the creation of the General Union of Israelites of France (Union Général des Israélites de France [UGIF]), a central body that was a form of *Judenrat* on a national scale. The UGIF was intended to replace all Jewish organizations in France. But all sorts of other organizations—this youth movement or that—continued their activity, to a great extent outside the intended controls. Some, like the Federation of Jewish Societies of France (FSJF), the Union of Jewish Societies of France (USJF), the Jewish Boy Scouts of France (EIF), and the Zionist youth movements, deliberately tried to maintain their distance from "official" circles and the UGIF. They understood that this allowed them to act much more effectively and to organize illegal activities of rescue and resistance. These organizations probably hid the greatest number of people, fabricated and distributed the greatest volume of counterfeit papers. We helped fund them and helped them in other ways.

The UGIF was and remains highly controversial. As a consequence of our work together I came to know very well the Warsaw-born Marc Jarblum, one of the great prewar leaders of the socialist Zionist movement in France. He was the president of the Federation of Jewish Societies of France, which united the majority of the Jews who had immigrated to France from Eastern Europe. In this capacity Jarblum was also on the executive of the WJC. But he was also picked to be one of the members of the UGIF. Not wishing to be part of a body controlled by the Germans, he refused. Going underground in spring 1943, he succeeded in reaching Geneva, where he spent the duration of the war.

There were other very clear-sighted people, such as Professor William Oualid, whom I had known at the Sorbonne, who also refused to become part of the UGIF. In addition, many prominent figures were opposed to the disappearance or subordination of all the community structures that the UGIF was designed to replace.

On the whole these structures created by the Nazis did more harm than good. And this despite the fact that some clear-minded local leaders tried to use them to keep a greater number of Jews alive. But very few succeeded. We must, however, refrain from generalizing or assuming too rigid a stance.

Saving Jewish Survivors in the Nazi Camps

The third significant rescue action that I initiated was an attempt to save the survivors of the camps. From October 1944 onward, when victory was approaching, I became obsessed with a single idea. I was terribly afraid that in order to wipe out the traces of their crimes and do away with witnesses, the

Nazis, just before the end of the war, would murder all those who were still being held in the camps. Hundreds of thousands of lives were at stake, and we had to find a course of action to avoid such a slaughter.

At the time I was haunted by the infernal Wagnerian image from the *Twilight of the Gods* where, at the last minute and before disappearing, the gods vow the total annihilation of those who are in their power. Everything the Nazis did at that time, such as mobilizing the elderly and youngsters in order to continue to the last breath a fight that could end in only one way, made us fear the worst. It seemed likely that these suicidal individuals would attempt to include all the victims in their power in their own destruction.

Haunted by this image, I was driven to undertake a desperate action in conjunction with some of the continental Allies, some of them recent Axis adherents. In the face of this danger we were all in the same situation: each of the parties had its prisoners, its political detainees, forced laborers, deported Jews—all in the same boat.

What drove me was not a fantasy. It was based on threats that had been made on several occasions by Himmler himself. To carry out this action I chose Dr. Jaromir Kopecky, the Czechoslovak government permanent delegate in Geneva: he seemed to me best positioned to unite the greatest number of government representatives and national Red Cross societies.

It was paradoxical that it should be I, a stateless Jew, who took the initiative to organize the actions of nations and their governments. But the urgency of the situation dictated that.

Kopecky shared my fears, and he promptly convoked a first meeting of representatives of Allied, exile, and other governments in Geneva for November 17, 1944. Ten countries were represented, either by government delegates or by those of their national Red Cross organizations—Belgium, France, Greece, the Netherlands, Italy, Norway, Poland, Romania, Yugoslavia, and Czechoslovakia.

I explained to the meeting the gravity of the situation and suggested a coordinated action by all these governments, directed either to the neutral countries or to the Vatican, or even to the International Committee of the Red Cross, in order to obtain from Nazi Germany a promise to extend to all categories of the interned, deported, and detained, foreign workers or other persons who had been deprived of their freedom, the minimal guarantees enjoyed by prisoners of war.

All those present greeted Dr. Kopecky's initiative with enthusiasm. The delegates unanimously recognized the value of the initiative and of backing the proposed action. I now had the full support of these representatives of the various countries for my urgent lobbying of the ICRC. We also decided to advise the Americans and the British of our plan.

Furthermore I raised before the group the extremely pressing problem of the separation of Jewish prisoners of war from other prisoners. I shall discuss this in greater detail in a later section dealing with the Red Cross.

On December 7, Dr. Kopecky sent all participants the minutes of the first meeting as well as a request to submit to their respective governments my suggestion for a collective approach to the ICRC, with a view to improving the lot of the interned or deported populations in territories controlled by Germany. His communication laid out the various options available for such an action and enumerated the concrete guarantees that must be exacted.

Reactions from these governments were some time in coming. Meanwhile I had also suggested to our colleagues in London that they organize a similar meeting of all the affected governments that were represented in the British capital. But this proved impossible to arrange.

We continued our efforts in Geneva, and a second meeting took place at Dr. Kopecky's office on February 17, 1945. We were then truly into the final stage of the war: effective intervention was imperative, as quickly as possible.

The meeting, in which representatives of the same countries participated with the addition of Mr. McClelland as the WRB representative, decided that all Red Cross representatives of the various countries should individually and simultaneously send memoranda to the president of the ICRC, urging him to make a supreme effort to have the civilian detainees in Germany and in the occupied countries liberated.

This note was to be submitted to the president's office on Wednesday morning, February 28, 1945, between nine and ten o'clock. It was similarly decided to send a copy of all these undertakings to Mr. McClelland, in order to have them backed up by the United States government. The British minister in Bern was informed as well with a similar objective. The diplomatic personnel of the various countries were to take analogous steps with the Swiss Federal Political Department and its Division of Foreign Affairs, in order to win support from those quarters.

I drafted the text of the note to the ICRC, which served as a basis for all these measures. It referred to intelligence from very credible sources which affirmed that "as a consequence of the evolution of the political situation, for various reasons, Reich authorities, desired to divest themselves of civilian detainees whether in Germany or in the occupied territories." The note asked the president of the ICRC "to approach the authorities of the Reich with a view to obtaining from them the liberation of civilian detainees, that is, persons detained by reason of political opinion, religion, or race."

It asked for "the dispatch with the briefest of delays of a delegation with the authority necessary to initiate such negotiations with the relevant authorities of the Reich."

The collective undertaking that had been decided on was executed as agreed. Meanwhile the secretary-general of the WJC, Leon Kubowitzki, had joined me in Geneva. We had personal meetings with Carl J. Burckhardt, ICRC president from January 1, 1945, to demonstrate and support the urgent need for action.

This collective undertaking made a great impression on the ICRC. It prompted the president to ask for a personal meeting with the relevant high officials of the Reich who had jurisdiction over the ghettos and camps. In a letter dated March 5, 1945, President Burckhardt informed me that he had taken this step. He added by hand that he hoped to leave "in the next few days, perhaps tomorrow."

On March 12, President Burckhardt personally met Ernst Kaltenbrunner, Heydrich's successor as head of the Reich Security Main Office, and who represented Reichsführer-SS Himmler, chief of all security and police forces in Nazi Germany. Another meeting took place between Burckhardt and German Foreign Ministry officials at Kreuzlingen, on the German-Swiss border.

At a special meeting convoked on March 26, Burckhardt gave a report of his discussions with German authorities. All the Red Cross officials who had participated in the meetings with Kopecky as well as representatives of the British and the American Red Cross attended.

The most important result of these discussions with the Germans was their acceptance of the presence of ICRC representatives in all the camps with civilian detainees. This changed the situation fundamentally: the presence of observers could prevent mass killings. Burckhardt spoke among other things of Red Cross observers who would be admitted to the camps on the condition that they not leave before the end of the war.

As might be expected, there were few volunteers for an assignment of this kind. The Red Cross undertook to recruit volunteers from the Swiss army and among Swiss firefighters.

Burckhardt also reported on the German intention to regroup camp inmates by nationality, as well as plans for evacuation. When I asked whether these national groupings would not once again exclude the Jews, Burckhardt answered that there had been no reservation of this sort from the German side and that the agreement affected all civilian detainees without distinction.

The president of the ICRC also spoke of the possibility of getting food relief to the prisoners and civilian detainees.

On leaving the meeting Burckhardt took me aside and told me that he had discussed the question of the Jews for a considerable time with the German representatives, and that officers of the German political police had assured him that the International Red Cross would have ample opportunities to see to the needs of Jewish detainees.

Without doubt the steps taken by Burckhardt in the name of twelve nations, their respective Red Cross organizations, and the International Committee made the Germans understand the importance of this problem and the need for them to take it seriously. In addition, the fate of hundreds of thousands of German prisoners of war held by the Allies, over whose treatment the ICRC exerted a certain beneficial influence, made the German negotiators more flexible and attentive.

Acceptance of Red Cross delegates in all the camps holding nonmilitary prisoners constituted a substantial concession. All the other arrangements discussed with the Germans concerning evacuation, exchanges, or food relief to the detained were in practical terms overtaken by the rapid evolution of the military situation, except for the evacuation to Sweden of a number of women from the Ravensbrück concentration camp. Sweden now opened its doors more widely than before to accept refugees and liberated inmates of the camps.

As for the establishment of national groupings, the Germans found good reason not to follow through on the promise made to the ICRC: the deported were deemed to know "military secrets," which somehow precluded their being moved from one camp to another. Consequently, while ICRC representatives entered some of the camps, the Germans released no large numbers of inmates, most of whom remained where they had been, except for the Jews forced on death marches.

On his side, Hillel Storch in Stockholm was prompted by the same fears for the camp prisoners. During this whole period we were in continual communication, sharing the same anxieties and convictions: we must at all costs prevent the massacre of the survivors.

Through various channels Storch sought contact with high-ranking Germans. He succeeded in establishing relations with senior officials in the German Foreign Ministry. Acting on the instructions of von Ribbentrop and with a green light from Himmler, they were trying to establish a channel to the Allies and, with hoped-for assistance from desperate Jews, to explore possibilities of a separate peace on the Western front. Hitler finally stopped these initiatives.

Storch remained constantly in touch with Count Bernadotte of the Swedish Red Cross. His most fruitful relations were those he forged with Felix Kersten, the Finnish physician who had Himmler, among others, in his care. Together they drew up a relief program for the camps, to include guarantees for the preservation of Jewish internees and the evacuation of certain groups to Sweden and Switzerland. Kersten saw Himmler during the first days of March 1945 and found the Reichsführer-SS favorably disposed. Himmler was looking for a way to protect himself and reportedly promised to turn over all the concentration camps to the Allies. This discussion took place on almost the same day as the meeting between Burckhardt and Kaltenbrunner. At the suggestion of Kersten, Himmler said he was ready to meet a representative of the World Jewish Congress and to discuss with him the situation of the surviving Jews, promising safe conduct for the emissary. The idea of such a meeting was clearly an extraordinary development. Himmler did receive the WJC emissary, Norbert Masur, on April 21, 1945, in Harzfeld, near Berlin, and promised the liberation of one thousand Jewish women from Ravensbrück and a number of French women and Norwegian Jews who had been interned. A few hours later, Count Bernadotte, who maintained continual communication with the Swedish section of the WJC, also met Himmler and obtained a considerable increase in the number of Jewish internees to be freed.

Bernadotte's negotiations with Himmler had the same goal: to free the maximum number of deportees and keep the detainees alive. Our activities were fully coordinated.

Meetings at Dr. Kopecky's continued regularly until the end of the war. Extremely concerned with the fate of the people liberated from the camps, the delegates made coordinated appeals to Allied military authorities to obtain the necessary materials, in particular to provide food for former detainees and then to see to their repatriation.

In retrospect, the gathering of representatives of the twelve Allied countries led to very important results that no individual lobbying would have been able to obtain. The WRB representatives who collaborated in our efforts lent us their full support at every stage of this activity. Even if the assurances given to the ICRC were not fully realized—in part because of the rapid deterioration of the German military situation—I remain convinced that this action undertaken in the closing hours in the name of the great Western powers and another ten Allied countries, as well as the parallel activity of the Swedes, contributed to preventing an even worse outcome. It is true that in one or two camps fanatical Nazis did not honor the agreement and were killing prisoners right up to the last minute. But these were exceptional cases.

I am surprised that the success of this great rescue undertaking is scarcely ever mentioned by those writing on the Shoah. For my part, I viewed the preservation of camp survivors—and we are speaking of hundreds of thousands—as an extremely important accomplishment.

My Meeting with Henry Morgenthau

Henry Morgenthau had been the driving force behind the creation of the War Refugee Board, an agency whose positive role can hardly be overestimated.

Among all the wartime personalities, Morgenthau remains my personal hero. And not because of his attitude toward Germany. It has been claimed that after the war he wanted to turn it into an agrarian state, totally devoid of industry; this was a gross exaggeration and came from Goebbels's propaganda kitchen. I have great respect for Morgenthau's role during the war. In the first instance, along with Harry Hopkins, he decisively influenced the course of the war by forcefully supporting the idea that led to the U.S. Lend-Lease legislation.

This law, passed on March 11, 1941, probably saved the Free World from defeat. It permitted Britain, then at war, to secure its overseas communications lines, and made it possible to pursue the urgent resupply of food to populations and troops, and to import the raw materials necessary for the war industry.

The fact that American warships accompanied these convoys, despite the systematic and destructive attacks of the Nazi submarine fleet, permitted the British to prevail against the German navy, whose U-boats had caused them terrible losses.

These maritime convoys probably decided the outcome of the war. Without them the Germans very probably would have succeeded in their blockade and invaded Britain.

America's passage and implementation of Lend-Lease legislation were bold acts, testifying to great courage, and it would be hard to find historical precedent. They certainly went well beyond the normal conditions of neutrality. The ingenious law created extraordinary opportunities. It is difficult to imagine what the world would be like had Britain fallen. It is even more difficult to contemplate the fate of the world's Jews.

With Britain defeated, there would have been no forces to defend Egypt and Palestine. This is why I frequently remind others that if Roosevelt is accused—with some justification—of having witnessed the destruction of millions of Jews without much reaction, one must recall that through his policies he also saved at least one million, more precisely those of Britain and Palestine, who were directly threatened by a German invasion. Of the total $40 to $50 billion in Lend-Lease aid, Britain received approximately $30 billion. And I have not yet touched upon the vital effect of the $11 billion in Lend-Lease aid that went to the Soviet Union.

In my opinion, Morgenthau, through his participation in drafting the Lend-Lease Act, had a determining influence on the course of the war. It is perhaps not surprising that the same person should have been primarily responsible for the creation of the War Refugee Board, the sole substantial contribution to the rescue of European Jewry. This is an additional reason to admire him.

In November 1947 I was in New York just at the moment when Morgenthau's memoirs appeared in installments in *Collier's* magazine. In the issue of December 1947 he dealt with the problem of the persecution of the Jews in Europe and his resolve to do something about it. It was then that he disclosed to the general public that I was the first to have informed the Free World of the "Final Solution." He described in detail all the difficulties I had encountered with the Roosevelt administration, my efforts to inform American Jewish leaders of what was happening in Europe and to bring aid to the victims of Nazism. This article had an enormous impact.

Since I was in New York at the time, Wise suggested that I meet Morgenthau. The rabbi said, "He would certainly like to make your acquaintance." And Wise said he would arrange the meeting.

At that time I was still a shy young man. When the day came, I entered his office and greeted him. He was truly impressive. His stature was imposing. But this great statesman was also extremely kind in his personal relations. He looked me over from head to foot, with his head tipped to one side, and said to me with a teasing smile, "So, this is the fellow who changed my life!" Then he asked me questions about the various activities in which I had been engaged during the war. He asked me about the various American figures with whom I had been in contact in Bern and Geneva. Morgenthau had left public office and could discuss these things quite openly.

Morgenthau belonged to a highly assimilated Jewish family and was at heart very American. Fully engaged in the platform and activities of the Democratic party, he was a committed supporter of Roosevelt's policies. His father had been the U.S. ambassador to Ottoman Turkey during World War I and had saved the Jewish colony in Palestine from the dangers that threatened it in the Ottoman Empire. He also helped illuminate the horrors that befell the Armenians during that period.

The Morgenthaus did not participate actively in Jewish life. In an address given on the occasion of the seventieth birthday of Stephen Wise, Henry Morgenthau told how he could never forget the moment when Wise, accompanied by his son, came to see him in Washington to show him my telegram of August 1942. It was at that moment that he became active in Jewish life. You will understand why I cherish that memory.

Approaching the Christian Churches

The role of the churches during the Shoah must be examined on two levels: the international and the national. Let us begin with the Roman Catholic church. On the international level and during the first years of the war, we did not approach the Catholic church to ask for its assistance.

A number of circumstances militated against gaining support from the Roman Catholic church. Among these were the attitude of German bishops after Hitler's rise to power; the appeasement policy of the Vatican with regard to the Nazi government during the first period of its rule, which led to the concordat of 1933; the increasing difficulties to which the Catholic church in Germany found itself exposed, leading to the encyclical *Mit brennender Sorge* (With Burning Sorrow); and the powerlessness of the Vatican in the face of more and more brutal anti-Catholic measures. Additionally at play was the traditionally anti-Semitic stance of large segments of the Catholic church in Poland, where the greatest tragedy occurred. The atmosphere clearly was not favorable for help from those quarters.

Moreover the Vatican was an enclave in fascist Italy and was not easily accessible to us.

For all these reasons we did not think to exploit this avenue in the first instance. It was only in 1942, when events were moving with tumultuous speed and the worst was in view, that we thought of trying to mobilize the Catholic church.

This action was undertaken on my initiative, first in Geneva and then in London and New York. In Geneva we worked principally with the papal nuncio, Msgr. Filippe Bernardini, one of the Vatican's most respected diplomats. Documentation published by the Vatican testifies to his great influence and demonstrates his important intermediary role in numerous communications with the Free World, particularly with the United States.

The World Jewish Congress in London, and principally its political secretary, Alec Easterman, established excellent relations with Archbishop of Westminster Arthur Cardinal Hinsley and later with the papal delegate, Msgr. William Godfrey.

The WJC office in New York coordinated its work with that of Myron Taylor, President Roosevelt's personal representative to the pope, and with Taylor's deputy, Harold H. Tittmann. During the last years of the war, frequent communications passed through the apostolic delegate in Washington, Msgr. Amleto Cicognani.

Our first step, then, was to approach the papal nuncio in Bern. In March 1942 Richard Lichtheim, the representative of the Jewish Agency for Palestine, and I, on behalf of the WJC, decided to pay a visit to Msgr. Bernardini. We brought him up to date on the situation of the Jews in the countries controlled by the Nazis, a situation that became more heart-wrenching from one day to the next.

At this time—six weeks after the infamous Wannsee Conference—we still did not know of the Nazi decision to implement the "Final Solution." But on the basis of the considerable intelligence in our hands, we informed him of the deportations and of the mass elimination of Jews in all the countries of Europe. Concluding, we asked the Vatican to help us to restrain these waves of persecution, at least in Catholic countries or those under Catholic influence.

After our presentation, Msgr. Bernardini asked us to prepare a memorandum that he would transmit to the Vatican. Our memorandum gave an account of the catastrophic situation of the Jews in a number of Catholic countries or countries with a large Catholic population, such as France, Romania, Poland, the protectorate of Bohemia-Moravia, Slovakia, and Croatia. We set out the situation country by country. Repeatedly we emphasized that the Nazis' measures gave ample evidence of being aimed at the total liquidation of the Jewish population.

Copies of this memorandum have been preserved in various archives. But curiously it is not to be found in the eleven volumes of diplomatic documents that the Vatican published on its activity during the war. Only Msgr. Bernardini's covering letter is found there. There is also our letter of thanks for the Vatican's intervention in Slovakia.

The omission of the memorandum in the Vatican's publications is all the more regrettable since the text demonstrates that detailed information on the scope of anti-Jewish persecution was in the hands of the Vatican relatively early, barely some six weeks after the Wannsee Conference, which mobilized all Germany's ministries and agencies in the service of total extermination.

In our memorandum we had emphasized the fact that some of these states had Catholic leaders and in one case even a clergyman as head of state who could be expected to be sensitive to any initiative by the Vatican.

Following this request, the Holy See intervened in Slovakia and informed us of its action. For a while there was some relaxation in persecution in that country, and deportations ceased. The Vatican had pressured Abbé Tiso, president of the Slovakian state, to moderate his policy. Tiso and his ministers were obliged to explain their actions.

But this did not last for very long. The Germans were no doubt furious, and deportations began again less than a year later. This led us to undertake a fresh round of lobbying on behalf of the Slovakian Jews during 1942 and 1943, in particular through the intermediary of the WJC offices in London and New York.

But while the Vatican acted in Bratislava following our request, the documents published by the Holy See disclose no evidence that such an intervention was attempted in other countries such as Croatia. What occurred in Romania seems to have been as a consequence of local initiatives. In this regard the humane attitude of the papal nuncio in Romania, Msgr. Andrea Cassulo, who was solicited by Chief Rabbi Alexandre Safran, relieved a great deal of suffering and even permitted a temporary stay in deportations.

The Vatican was approached again concerning the persecution of the Jews of Europe, this time after my August 1942 telegram revealing the "Final Solution."

Recall that when this telegram was finally forwarded to Rabbi Stephen Wise, Undersecretary of State Sumner Welles forbade its being made public. At the same time the State Department decided to approach the Vatican through Ambassador Myron Taylor, Roosevelt's personal representative to the Holy See. Welles requested that Taylor use his contacts at the Vatican to ask whether its officials could confirm intelligence concerning the extermination of the Jews.

On September 26, 1942, Myron Taylor delivered to Vatican Secretary of State Luigi Cardinal Maglione the contents of a letter from my colleague Richard Lichtheim of the Jewish Agency in Geneva. This letter of August 30, some weeks after my telegram had been sent to Wise, contained detailed information on the liquidation of the Jews of the Warsaw Ghetto and of all the Polish provinces. Taylor also requested that measures be suggested that would put an end to these atrocities.

During Taylor's absence from Rome, representation was assumed by his deputy, Tittmann, who asked for a special audience with the pope. After twice having insisted on a response, on October 10 Tittmann received from Vatican officials an unsigned note according to which "reports coming from other sources concerning the harsh measures against non-Aryans have also reached the Vatican. But until now, it has not been possible to verify their accuracy."

It is interesting to follow in detail how the matter was handled by the Vatican. We can do this by reading through the volumes of published Vatican documents.* Cardinal Maglione noted, "I do not believe that we have a confirmation of these very serious reports."

The cardinal suggested consulting Pirelli G. Malvezzi of the Institute for Industrial Reconstruction.† I gather than Malvezzi was part of the Vatican secret service.

Shortly thereafter, Msgr. Battista Montini (who would become Pope Paul VI in 1963), one of Maglione's deputies, noted after a discussion with Malvezzi that the latter had alerted him to new developments in Poland, "the bombing of cities by the Russians and the systematic massacre of the Jews."

Malvezzi reported that "the massacres have taken on enormous proportions and occur on a daily basis."

The Vatican's October 10, 1942, response is all the more curious in light of the fact that the nuncios had correctly reported on the deportation of Jews from Bukovina and Bessarabia (Romania) in December 1941, from Bratislava (Slovakia) in March 1942, from Zagreb (Croatia) in July 1942, and from Paris in that same month.

It is also apparent from the documents published by the Vatican that reports originating with Father Pirro Scavizzi, the chaplain of a health transport service operated by the Order of Malta, had come to the attention of the Vatican. Father Scavizzi was fully informed of the Jewish tragedy that was being played out in Poland and on the Eastern front. He was apparently serving as intermediary between some Polish bishops and the Vatican. In May 1942 he wrote in a report destined for Pius XII: "The anti-Jewish assault continues inexorably and becomes worse with deportations and mass executions. The massacre of Jews in Ukraine is now complete. In Poland and in Germany preparations are under way to conclude matters with systematic mass killings."

On October 17, 1942, only a few days after the dilatory response of the Vatican, Scavizzi reported: "The elimination of the Jews through mass killings

*Many of these documents are printed in Pierre Blet, et al., eds., *Actes et documents au Saint Siége relatifs à la Seconde Guerre Mondiale* (11 vols., 1975), esp. vol. 8, pp. 665–666 and 755–756.—ED.

†Created by the fascist Italian state to mediate among economic interest groups and allow the corporate state to control economic development.—ED.

is almost complete. We have heard that another two million Jews have been killed."*

For his part, Archbishop Cesare Orsenigo, the papal nuncio in Berlin, wrote to Cardinal Maglione on October 19: "When reference is made to non-Aryans, the reply is 'nothing can be done.'"

If we today survey the activities of the Roman Catholic church during the war, we must conclude that its actions to a great degree depended on the local situation. The personality of the papal nuncio and local clergy also played a great role. But initiatives from higher up could also be of great importance. For example, in 1944, after the pope's appeal to Horthy, the nuncio in Budapest, Msgr. Angelo Rotta, undertook a number of lobbying efforts with the government, mobilizing representatives of the neutral nations and the Hungarian episcopate.

The Vatican was very well informed—as concerns the extermination of the Jews, probably better informed than we were. Hundreds of priests, monks, and other active Catholics continually carried all sorts of information to Rome, arriving there on pilgrimage or for other reasons.

Among other sources, the remarkable book by a journalist and former priest, Carlo Falconi, speaks in detail of the large number of such individual reports that reached Rome.[†] He comments on the enormous volume of intelligence material that travelers from all over Europe brought to the Holy See. As we have seen, the Vatican's publications themselves reflect this to a degree.

In consideration of all these facts, I cannot see why church officials have insisted they were ignorant of what was happening. Everything demonstrates that the Holy See cannot justifiably claim not to have been truly informed of the tragedy that was occurring in the death camps. The problem was not a lack of information; the question is whether they wished to use it and, in particular, whether they were prepared to draw the inescapable conclusions.

Yet a third important appeal was made to the Vatican when news of the "Final Solution" had become a certainty, leading the Free World to react. At the same time the December 17, 1942, action solicited the Allied governments' declaration denouncing the extermination of the Jews, specific efforts were made to induce the Vatican to take a public position. My colleagues at the World Jewish Congress in London, who were in constant touch with the

*See Blet, et al., vol. 8, pp. 669–670, fn 4.—ED.
†*The Silence of Pius XII* (1970).—ED.

British government and the governments-in-exile that had been established in the British capital, multiplied their efforts to encourage concerted, effective action by all political, social, and spiritual parties.

Several governments too attempted to get a public declaration from the pope. The initiative here was taken by the Polish government in London, joined by other governments-in-exile as well as those of Great Britain, the United States, Brazil, and Uruguay.

All these efforts finally led to the pope's radio address on Christmas 1942. For the first time he expressed an opinion on the subject. But, directly, he said nothing of the Jews. The word "Jew" was not even uttered. In his address, Pius XII spoke nonetheless of "hundreds of thousands of persons . . . who without any fault on their own part, sometimes only because of their nationality or race, have been consigned to death or to a slow decline."*

In his address to the Sacred College of Cardinals on June 2 of the following year, Pope Pius XII reiterated word for word his Christmas message.

The church is proud of this message which, in its eyes, proves that contrary to some accusations Pope Pius XII did not remain silent. I must recognize that at the time the papal declaration also seemed to me to be very important. It was, in fact, the first time that the pontiff personally alluded to the massacre of the Jews. But when we read his speech again in hindsight, it appears especially timid.

Even at that time critical voices were soon heard. The pope had not spoken of what was really happening: the extermination of a whole people. He was surprised when some Allied diplomats remarked to him that his declaration had been too cautious and could not be judged satisfactory. His message was criticized for, among other things, the absence of the word "Nazi," an absence that the pope explained by saying that when he spoke of atrocities he could not name the Nazis without at the same time mentioning the Bolsheviks. This point is made formally in Harold Tittmann's report on his meeting with Pius XII on December 30, 1942.

Among the reactions, we are struck by the moving and insistent appeals addressed to the pope by the Polish president-in-exile, Władysław

---

*Since there has been some confusion over various translations of this radio message, "Con sempre nuova freschezza" (December 24, 1942), the relevant passage is given here in the original Italian: "Questo voto l'umanità lo deve alle centinaia di migliaia di persone, le quali, senza veruna colpa propia, talora solo per ragione di nazionalità o di stirpe, sono destinate alla morte o ad un progressive deperimento." Cassell's Italian Dictionary (1958) gives "stirpe" in English as "stock, race; descent, lineage, extraction." The meaning of the Pope's sentence is clear, at least in retrospect.—ED.

Raczkiewicz, who hoped for a clear and energetic condemnation of Nazi persecution.

It is also significant that the bishop of Berlin, Konrad von Preysing, one of the most courageous opponents of the Nazi regime, addressed the pope on January 17, 1943 (after the Christmas radio broadcast), asking whether the Holy See could not do something for the Jews of Germany and the bordering countries, and suggesting a public appeal on behalf of the unfortunate. This indicates that at that time in Berlin the pope's declaration was still not known. Three months later, Konrad von Preysing—now referring to the pope's Christmas message—wrote again to the Holy Father, asking him whether it might not be possible "to try once again to raise his voice for these unfortunate and innocent people," adding that this was "the final hope and urgent prayer of all right-thinking people."

In a long letter dated April 30, 1943, Pius XII replied to the bishop of Berlin. The letter contains some moving phrases on the suffering borne by the Jews; it praises the Catholics of Berlin for their attitude toward the Jews; it praises the prelate Bernard Lichtenberg for his actions on behalf of the Jews and expresses deep sympathy for the imprisoned cleric.* Here the pope speaks quite openly of the "inhuman acts that have come to our knowledge over a long period." "Acts," he continues, "that are in no way the product of the necessities of waging war and that are now having a paralyzing and terrifying effect." These very strong words were never published nor uttered publicly. "In the tragic conflicts between the powers of this world," continues Pius XII, "the Popes have shown the most honest will to face them all with total impartiality, while scrupulously attending to the interests of the Holy Church, which has rarely experienced a challenge such as that it must face today." The pope adds that "this is one of the reasons that oblige us to moderation in our messages." Here his motives are clearly evident: the general interests of the church and the fear of reprisals and of all forms of coercion.

Thus the Holy See failed to express itself forcefully in humane terms on the situation of the Jews threatened with annihilation. The pope even "left to the national bishops"—and he says this explicitly—"the responsibility of judging how far in this regard they should go," acting on their own analysis of the situation. The Vatican, for its part, did not wish to expose itself to the

---

*Lichtenberg (1875–1943) was a Catholic priest in Berlin who in 1941 protested against the euthanasia program and publicly prayed in his church for Jews deported to the East. Denounced in 1942, he was sentenced to two years in prison; released in October 1943, the Gestapo sent him to Dachau. The seventy-eight-year-old priest died en route. In 1996 Pope John Paul II took steps toward Lichtenberg's beatification.—ED.

slightest risk by publicly taking a clear stand in support of the victims. It believed that speaking out strongly would make matters worse. We know that the Vatican maintained this attitude of extreme restraint, which is still defended by some spokesmen in Rome. But I am convinced that a clear and open condemnation by the pope would have motivated a large number of Catholics to aid and protect victims, and thus would have contributed to saving many of them. Perhaps some reprisals might have followed, but the overall result would have been positive and in accord with the moral imperative.

The only time the Holy See took a vigorous stand in favor of the Jews during World War II was, as we have seen, on the occasion of the action taken to save Hungarian Jews in the summer of 1944. The pope telegraphed Regent Horthy on June 25, 1944, and received a reply on July 2. Five days later President Roosevelt took the same step, as had somewhat earlier the King of Sweden. And we must recall the energetic action of the papal nuncio in Budapest, Msgr. Angelo Rotta. For its part, the Hungarian Conference of Bishops also protested, encouraged in its stand by the gesture of the pontiff.

Throughout the summer and autumn of 1944 a series of dramatic appeals were addressed to the pope by my colleagues in the World Jewish Congress from London and New York; and contacts continued between the WJC and papal delegates in Britain and the United States. The latter transmitted to WJC leaders the responses, on occasion very moving, of Cardinal Maglione and Msgr. Domenico Tardini, who also provided information on the initiatives taken in the field and on reports from Msgr. Rotta in Budapest. The energetic action of the church in Hungary undeniably saved many Jewish lives. Our own efforts find reflection in Volume 10 of the documents published by the Vatican. Twenty-four communications refer to the World Jewish Congress in the materials dealing with this period.

The effectiveness of the Vatican generally depended on the positions taken and energy spent by its representatives on site. The nuncio in Bucharest, Msgr. Andrea Cassulo, and that in Bratislava, Msgr. Giuseppe Burzio, undertook numerous measures to assist the rescue of Jews.

On the other hand, the apostolic nuncio in Berlin, Cesare Orsenigo, reacted hardly at all. Presumably he was afraid. The Nazis may well have threatened him and informed him that any such efforts on his part would be in vain. I am not sure, but this speculation seems reasonable under the circumstances.

In Vichy France, the nuncio Msgr. Valerio Valeri took an intermediate position. At the moment when the French government promulgated its anti-Jewish legislation, Vichy's ambassador to the Holy See, Léon Berard, was charged with sounding out the Vatican on the subject of the discriminatory laws. After consultation, Berard replied that the Vatican would raise no objections except as concerned mixed marriages and converted Jews. Subsequently Msgr. Valeri, who appeared to disagree with the anti-Jewish legislation, stated his reservations in public. But the Vatican never took a stand on this subject.

This should not surprise us when we consider that none of the anti-Jewish legislation of Nazi Germany from 1933 on, nor all that followed it in the occupied countries, ever provoked an open protest from the Vatican.

As we have noted, the situation of the Jews differed from country to country, according to local circumstances and personalities. This was equally true of the national churches and their bishops, priests, monks, nuns, and congregations. In France, Emmanuel Cardinal Suhard, profoundly committed to the Vichy regime, was content to send to Marshal Pétain a protest—never made public—from the French episcopate against the harsh conditions of the raids of 1942. In this context, the attitude of Pierre-Marie Cardinal Gerlier, the Primate of Gaul, was clearly of prime importance. Very cautious at the beginning, this loyal admirer of Pétain was content to wait and see. But he hardened his stance over time and during the final stages of the war even carried out courageous public acts on behalf of the persecuted Jews.

We witnessed in France other magnificent examples of courage and character, such as that of Jules-Gérard Cardinal Saliège, archbishop of Toulouse, who as a sign of protest went to the railroad station when the Jews of his city were being obliged to board the deportation train and who had a remarkable pastoral letter read in all the churches of his diocese. We must also mention Msgr. Pierre-Marie Théas, bishop of Montauban, who adopted a similar position.

We may legitimately ask, what would have happened if the Bishop of Rome (or one of his deputies) had acted in the same fashion when the Jews were deported from the Eternal City?

Pietro Cardinal Boetto, the archbishop of Genoa, despite all the obstacles to providing relief to Jewish refugees, took over the activities of DELASEM, the Delegation for Assistance to Jewish Emigrants from Italy. Cardinal Boetto commissioned a priest from his diocese to see to the distribution of financial aid to the needy. He even succeeded in having funds from the United States pass through the Vatican, thereby continuing to support relief activities.

In Italy a great many priests, heads of convents and monasteries, and lay people came to the aid of Jews and thus helped save lives. In most cases these Italian men and women had been raised in a secular tradition of humanitarianism before entering the priesthood and nunneries.

The Dutch episcopate acted courageously when Jews were deported from the Netherlands, as did numerous priests, monks, and nuns in Holland, Poland, France, Belgium, and Italy. Many of these individuals tried to help save Jews, often at the risk of their own lives. This did not occur on an order from the Vatican. Christians, motivated by their faith that demands respect for human life, acted spontaneously. These people, whether they were lay or religious, had a sound conception of their own Christianity. A number of them have been honored as "Righteous Among the Nations" at the Yad Vashem memorial in Jerusalem.

It is also appropriate to mention here Msgr. Angelo Roncalli, the papal nuncio in Sofia and later in Ankara. This cleric, who later would become Pope John XXIII, was in continual contact with Jewish organizations in Istanbul. Full of sympathy and understanding, he constantly strove to aid the victims of Nazism.

In the Allied countries the attitude of Catholics was quite clear. Britain's Cardinal Hinsley, for example, delivered a whole series of supportive speeches and declarations. In New York's Madison Square Garden, during a rally against Hitler's policies toward Jews, the organizers received a message of support from the seriously ill Cardinal Hinsley. More than 25,000 people stood and prayed for his health—one of the most moving events of that period. One might cite analogous examples of support from individual Catholic leaders.

On the other side of the coin, how can we understand why the Roman Catholic church of Germany never publicly condemned the first anti-Jewish laws of 1933, nor the Nuremberg legislation of 1935, nor the pogrom of 1938, nor the deportations and extermination policy during the tragic years of the war?

In autumn 1941 German bishops, encouraged by the success of their public action against the "euthanasia" of the mentally and incurably ill, did prepare a pastoral letter to defend human rights in general, personal liberty, and the right to life. But this project met the determined opposition of Adolf Cardinal Bertram, president of the Conference of Catholic Bishops of Germany, who caused it to be dropped. Bertram did send the Führer birthday greetings every year.

Should we then be surprised that in May 1945, three days after Hitler's suicide and five days before the end of the war, this same Cardinal Bertram gave instructions to all the parishes in his archbishopric to celebrate a solemn requiem to the memory of the Führer? I do not know whether these instructions were followed. By this time the majority of his colleagues probably ignored his instructions.

Bertram's text, written in a castle in Silesia where he had taken refuge, is the most pathetic evidence of the mentality of the German Catholic church, symbolized by the man who presided over it during the Nazi period.*

Let me add that it took thirty years for the Conference of German Bishops to acknowledge, in a public declaration, the failings of its members under the Nazi regime.

I believe that in general it took the Vatican a very long time to truly understand what was happening. During the first years of the war, officials who were responsible for Jewish matters were concerned almost exclusively with converts from Judaism. The activity of the *Raphaelsverein*, created especially for matters relating to Catholics of Jewish origin, occupies a large place in the documentation published by the Vatican.

The first to understand the extreme gravity of the situation was probably Msgr. Tardini. After the death of the secretary of state, Cardinal Maglione, Pius XII split this position's functions. His two assistants, or deputies, who were in a sense co-secretaries, were the Monsignors Montini and Tardini. Montini later became Pope Paul VI. According to some testimony, Tardini began to grasp the true immensity of the disaster in the spring of 1943.

In general, however, senior Catholic dignitaries understood only very late the whole scope of the drama of the extermination of the Jews and thus did not consider the Jewish tragedy a matter of priority.

The traditional theology of the church with regard to Jews and Judaism contributed to this attitude. Clearly Nazism was a pagan aberration, in essence as anti-Christian as it was anti-Jewish. Yet had it not been able to avail itself of the church's centuries-old teaching of contempt for the Jew, Nazism never would have been able to implement its anti-Jewish program.

The racial anti-Semites, despite their antagonism to traditional Christianity, learned a great deal from it. They appropriated many anti-Jewish concepts that the church had developed over the centuries. They thus succeeded in creating a systematic ideology with its own logic, transforming and adapting to their needs the traditional forms of religious anti-Judaism.

That the tragedy of Judaism was not a priority for the Holy See is particularly evident in two events. First, in 1945, at the end of the war, the secretary-general of the World Jewish Congress at the time, Leon Kubowitzki, went to Rome where he had audiences with both Msgr. Montini and Pope Pius XII.

*Adolf Cardinal Bertram (1859–July 16, 1945) served as Archbishop of Breslau (now Wrocław) from 1930 until his death.—ED.

Kubowitzki suggested to the pope that he issue an encyclical on the Jewish question. He stated his opinion that after the unprecedented tragedy that had struck us, the church had to make a solemn declaration of its attitude toward the Jews. Kubowitzki's initiative was prepared and supported by a number of eminent Catholic theologians, including Jacques Maritain and Father Charles Journet (who would later become cardinals), Father Jean-Pierre de Menasce, and others. Despite the weight of this support, Kubowitzki received no response.

If there was a moment when the head of the Catholic church ought to have shown that it understood the full scale of the tragedy, it was indeed then. But apparently the time was still not ripe. Another twenty years would have to pass before the church made a clear pronouncement. It was only in 1965 at the Vatican II Council, and at the prompting of Pope John XXIII, that the Catholic church took the opportunity to publish a text, the celebrated declaration *Nostra aetate*, which dealt in its fourth section with the church's relations with Jews.

A second circumstance confirms my conviction that the Catholic church did not fully comprehend the enormity of what had happened and that it had therefore accorded no priority to this problem: my conversation in November 1945 with Msgr. Montini.

I was then in Rome for the first congress of the 25,000 displaced Jews who had taken refuge in Italy. I brought to the congress the greetings of the WJC. The organization of the congress was in the hands of Lithuanian Jews.

Kubowitzki had asked me to take the opportunity to meet Msgr. Montini and to request his help in locating Jewish children who had been saved by Catholics. The president of the Union of Jewish Communities in Italy, our friend Raffaele Cantoni, accompanied me on this call.

The problem of the children was of great concern to us. We were desperate over the enormous loss of Jewish children in the course of the Shoah. We viewed it as a sacred duty to seek out the children who had been hidden.

This was one of the most dramatic and unhappy undertakings of my life. In presenting my request for assistance, I said to the deputy: "We, the Jewish people, have lost a million and a half children. We cannot allow ourselves to lose one more. We are very grateful to the institutions and to the Catholic faithful for what they have done to save Jewish children and to help them survive. But we now judge that the danger is past, and they should be restored to us. Since we do not know where they are, we are asking you to help us find them."

We had a twenty-minute discussion that was extremely painful for me. Montini contested my attestation that a million and a half children had been lost. He was not at all convinced that this figure was accurate, and considered it inflated.

I had briefed myself in order to explain the number to him. In Poland before the war, approximately 60,000 Jewish children were born each year. Reliable statistics are available to prove it. Multiplied by sixteen, this gives 960,000 children under the age of sixteen. Thus in Poland alone we ought to have been able to find almost a million children after the war. Do you know how many we found? 3,648!

Before the catastrophe about 800,000 Jews lived in Hungary and the territories annexed to it by Hitler. Approximately 400,000 of these lived in the provinces. Taking the prevailing birthrate into account, this should have given about 100,000 children. In all the Hungarian provinces we found eight! And so on.

After listening to me, Msgr. Montini replied: "That is not possible. They probably emigrated." I replied, "Where would they be and how did they get there? Emigration was forbidden all over Europe. Where could they go? To Romania, through the mountains, perhaps two or three hundred. A thousand at most."

For the remainder of that first twenty minutes I argued with Msgr. Montini, finally realizing that he had become greatly upset. Only at that moment, I believe, did he grasp for the first time the extent of our catastrophe: that six million Jews had been murdered, including a million and a half children lost.

I remember that this seemed to have made a great impression on him. But that did not mean he was ready to help us. In substance he said the following to me: "Point out to me where these children are and I will assist you in recovering them." I replied in essence, "If I knew that, I wouldn't need you."

What did it all mean? I do not question Msgr. Montini's good faith. But his reaction showed that during the entire war neither he nor the senior bureaucracy of the Catholic Church understood what had happened. Even after the war, ignorance of the scope of the tragedy persisted. That is a simple fact.

I had maintained relations with the World Council of Churches since 1939. At that time this Protestant organization still was in the process of formation, and its general secretariat was in Geneva. The Council had members and correspondents in various countries around the world. Its executive had seats in three locations: in Britain, Switzerland, and the United States.

The secretary-general, Willem A. Visser 't Hooft, lived in Geneva. A Dutch Calvinist clergyman, he was strongly committed to his role in the World Council of Churches; he was, in short, the very soul of the movement. After the German conquest he also functioned as liaison between the resistance in Holland and the Dutch government-in-exile in London. Numerous messages of all kinds passed through him, and his underground activity was extensive.

I was in frequent contact with him and with one of his assistants, the Rev. Adolf Freudenberg, a German who had earlier been a lawyer in the Foreign Ministry. Because he was married to a woman of Jewish origin, he resigned his government position in 1935, even before he would have been dismissed. He decided then to undertake theological studies and become a clergyman. Quite soon he became an important member of the German Protestant church, which united the Protestant opposition in the stand against the Nazi concept of the role of churches. Obey God more than the state—such was their basic principle.

On the eve of the war, almost at the last minute, seeing that he could not work in his country, the German church sent him abroad. At the beginning of the conflict he was transferred to Geneva in order to administer the department for Protestant refugees within the framework of the World Council of Churches.*

Both Visser 't Hooft and Freudenberg devote moving passages in their memoirs to relations with our office during the war. Visser 't Hooft was impressed with the quality of the intelligence we were able to assemble concerning the situation of Jews in all the European countries. He said after the war that he had not had much more success than I in convincing the world of what was happening.

Freudenberg describes our relations in rather more detail. Among other things, he notes that he used to like to come to my office: it was so much more pleasant than his own. I had, and still have, a very large office. He was also a sensitive individual: he felt that it was not appropriate at that time to ask a Jew in an official position to come to see a German.

Our cooperation was quite close; he came to my office to share and obtain information on the situation of the Jews in various countries. Since we had amassed a great deal, he made good use of it, especially by disseminating it in quarters to which I did not have access. At times I judged it preferable to have this information pass through the World Council. He also arranged the contribution of funds to some of the relief activities that we organized.

For its part, the World Council undertook a number of important initiatives. One of our most serious concerns was to obtain reliable information

---

*In 1941–1942 the World Council of Churches established an ecumenical council and under it a refugee aid agency, of which Freudenberg became the secretary.—ED.

on the situation in the occupied countries and to send there credible people who could bring us objective reports. I must have spoken of this to our friends at the World Council for Dr. Visser 't Hooft sent a significant letter to the International Committee of the Red Cross asking it to send an observer to Poland.

The following passage from Visser 't Hooft's October 29, 1941, letter to the ICRC, is characteristic of his stance:

> The Jewish organizations are in general no longer in a position to undertake effective steps on behalf of their coreligionists. The Jewish question is at the heart of the Christian message. Here a failure of the Church to raise its voice in warning and protection and to do everything that is in its power to assist would be to disobey its God. For this reason it is the duty of the Christian Churches and in particular their ecumenical representative, the World Council of Churches, to intervene in the name of the persecuted.

Throughout 1942 the clergyman approached the Red Cross on several occasions. In his last missive, dated December 3, Visser 't Hooft requested that the ICRC send observers to Theresienstadt and to Poland. His request now included a new argument: "There are reasons to believe that such steps, even if they do not lead to the desired end, will encourage certain circles in Germany to fight more energetically against the mass executions."

Visser 't Hooft revealed later that he was here alluding to members of the *Kreisauerkreis*, an important German opposition movement, as well as to Dietrich Bonhoeffer and his friends, with whom the WCC was in contact.

The World Council was extremely effective in its relations with the Swiss government. I among others used its contacts to transmit to the federal government practically all the reports I possessed. The Rev. Alphons Koechlin, who headed the Swiss Federation of Evangelical Churches, also was one of the officers of the World Council of Churches. He was close to Visser 't Hooft and a member of the small executive committee of the WCC. On several occasions he intervened with the Swiss minister of justice, Eduard von Steiger. In particular Koechlin intervened in favor of the admission of Jewish refugees when the borders were closed in the summer of 1942, and he shared with von Steiger the reports on the "Final Solution" that I had put at their disposal. The executive of the WCC was highly useful and effective in a number of other instances, as well.

I also cooperated closely with the Rev. Henri-Louis Henriod, who was in charge of the Protestant office for aid to refugees in the French-speaking part of Switzerland.

Henriod held the rank of colonel in the Swiss army and was a prominent figure in the ecumenical movement. He assumed responsibility for communicating my reports to senior Swiss military authorities. This was important in light of the role the army was playing in the country at that time.

Visser 't Hooft and I undertook one political intervention together, perhaps a unique case in the history of Jewish-Christian relations. On March 22, 1943, we submitted to the governments of Great Britain and the United States a joint memorandum putting forward a number of suggestions for saving European Jews, which we also communicated to the Vatican and to the Intergovernmental Committee on Refugees in London.

After a brief preamble explaining why the situation of the Jews in Nazi-occupied territories was particularly and acutely in need of immediate attention by the Allied governments, the memorandum called for "the absolute necessity of organizing without delay a rescue action for the persecuted Jewish communities on the following lines:

"1. Measures of immediate rescue should have priority over the study of post-war arrangements.

"2. The rescue action should enable the neutral States to grant temporary asylum to the Jews who could reach their frontiers."

To meet the expected resistance of the neutral countries to this idea, we noted that "Only explicit and comprehensive guarantees of remigration of the refugees, given by the Anglo-Saxon Powers as a reinforcement of any assurances of repatriation which may be given by the Allied Governments in exile, can lead the neutral countries to adopt a more liberal and understanding attitude toward the Jewish refugees." We further noted that "These guarantees should provide for the granting of facilities concerning the supply of food and funds for the maintenance of refugees during their stay in the supply countries."

Our third point recommended that a "scheme for the exchange of Jews in Germany and the territories under German control for German civilians in North and South America, Palestine, and other Allied countries, should be pressed forward by all possible means.

"In view of the immediate urgency of the situation, the admission of Jews to the scheme of exchange should be granted en bloc to the greatest possible number, as conditions no longer allow of time-wasting and in many cases fruitless individual investigations. This scheme might include war-time security measures."

Finally, we suggested that the International Committee of the Red Cross could also be approached and asked for assistance in the project.

Later Visser 't Hooft was attacked for this move. Some people blamed him for having fallen into the trap of dangerous Zionists. He ought never to have intervened on behalf of the Jews alone, said others.

This criticism highlights the significance and novelty of our joint efforts, and also reveals that the authors of this criticism remained the prisoners of old prejudices and had understood little or nothing of the scope of the catastrophe. But the Rev. Visser 't Hooft defended his actions with conviction. I believe that today the World Council of Churches is proud to have taken up the defense of the Jews during those difficult times. We can only regret that it was not more effective. But through its actions, through its will to act, it was extremely helpful to us.

This fruitful collaboration lasted throughout the war. At times we were in almost daily contact. During the tragedy of Hungarian Jewry, in the summer of 1944, our relations were closest.

The WCC's refugee aid agency raised a public protest against the deportation of forty thousand Hungarian Jews to Auschwitz. Another similar appeal was signed by Visser 't Hooft, Karl Barth, Emil Brunner, and many other leaders of the Reformed Church. At my suggestion the Archbishop of Canterbury again addressed the British prime minister and—in a BBC broadcast—exhorted the Hungarian people to do everything in their power to save the threatened Jews, if necessary taking risks themselves.

We established cooperation between the British churches and the World Jewish Congress in London. Jointly and individually we sent telegrams to London. The churches mobilized around Dr. George Bell, bishop of Chichester, who was particularly active in the refugee question. William Temple, Archbishop of Canterbury, made a series of vigorous efforts, particularly from 1942 on. The Archbishop and other dignitaries of the Anglican church pressed Churchill and the British government to act on behalf of the Jews.

Here, for example, is an excerpt of the archbishop's March 23, 1943, speech:

> We are confronted . . . with an evil the magnitude and horror of which it is impossible to describe in words. There has been a concentration of this fury against the Jews. We should give special attention to what is being carried through. We know that Hitler near the beginning of the war declared that this war must lead to the extermination of either the Jewish or the German people, and it should not be the Germans. He is now putting that into effect, and no doubt we are to a very large extent powerless to stop him. . . . My whole plea on behalf of those for whom I am speaking is that whether what we do be large or little it should at least be all we can do.

My chief protest is against procrastination of any kind. . . . It took five weeks from December 17 [the date of the UN declaration on the "German policy of extinction of the Jewish race"] for our government to approach the United States, and then six weeks for the government of the United States to reply, and when they did reply they suggested . . . a meeting for preliminary exploration. The Jews are being slaughtered at the rate of tens of thousands a day on many days, but there is a proposal for a preliminary exploration to be made with a view to referring the whole matter after that to the Intergovernmental Committee on Refugees.

We at this moment have upon us a tremendous responsibility. We stand at the bar of history, of humanity, and of God.

Never had I so strongly felt the sense of abandonment, of powerlessness and solitude as when I sent the Free World those messages of disaster and horror, when no one believed me, and I waited for a reaction and help from the Allies. We know that, in relation to the immensity of the Shoah, in the end little was done.

During those terrible days and months, the humane comprehension, friendship, and helping hand of some of our Christian friends was the sole point of light in the darkness into which we had plunged. I hold them in my memory with infinite gratitude.

The International Committee of the Red Cross

The International Committee of the Red Cross is a Swiss legal entity. It is not to be confused with the League of Societies of the Red Cross and Red Crescent, which groups the Red Cross and Red Crescent of the various countries.

The mandate and jurisdiction of the International Committee of the Red Cross have been defined and recognized by the international conventions that govern the conduct of war. This movement began in 1859 at the Battle of Solferino where its founder, Henri Dunant, had seen the suffering of soldiers and the wounded on the field of battle. At that moment Dunant conceived of the need to alleviate this suffering and to study how the spirit of humanity and charity could be preserved in the midst of the hostilities of belligerents. He wished, for example, that the wounded, whatever their origin, should be cared for by the first medical personnel to encounter them.

We should not forget that even on the battlefield these were human beings, and that even in war certain fundamental rules of humanity must be observed. From this innovative concept was born the Red Cross movement, which has made considerable progress from its beginning in the last quarter of the nineteenth century.

Since then similar progress had also been achieved by the great international conferences on the law of war as well as by more circumscribed conferences devoted to specific problems. A great many rules applicable to belligerents and neutrals have been adopted. Some, for example, deal with the utilization or prohibition of certain weapons; others deal with the treatment of the wounded, of prisoners of war, and of all those who find themselves otherwise involved in a war.

In order to propose, implement, and oversee the application of these rules, it was necessary to create a responsible body capable of observing strict neutrality. The International Committee of the Red Cross was the product of that need; it was founded by a group of Swiss citizens and headquartered in Geneva.

From the beginning of World War II the World Jewish Congress recognized that the ICRC would play an important role during hostilities. We immediately approached that body to establish permanent relations with it.

This was not the first time we had had recourse to the ICRC. In 1936, during my first year of service with the WJC, we encountered serious problems during the Spanish Civil War. Reports reached us on the particularly delicate situation of a number of Jews, especially those of German origin. On the one hand, the Spanish Popular Front, which was the legal government of Spain, considered them Germans and thus potential enemies. On the other hand, Franco's armies, aided by Germany, treated them, most often correctly, as anti-Nazis, as people in whom they could have no confidence.

For the first time, then, I appealed to Professor Burckhardt, already an active member of the International Committee. I asked the ICRC to concern itself with this question and to exert a moderating influence on the two opposing Spanish sides in their actions toward Jews. Documents in our archives attest that Burckhardt lobbied his colleagues on the ICRC with this objective.

When World War II began we informed the ICRC leadership that we had created our own special committee to intervene on behalf of Jewish populations adversely affected by the war. We sought to utilize the ICRC apparatus and structures to aid and protect the Jews at risk.

An early matter of concern was securing traditional protection for Jewish soldiers called up to serve in the armies. We wished to ensure that wounded or captured soldiers of Jewish origin would be accorded the same humanitarian rules that had been internationally established for all combatants under such circumstances. We also sought assurances that other rules under ICRC oversight would be scrupulously observed as well.

An additional aspect of the conflict, the sphere of intelligence, also prompted us to cooperate with the ICRC. Verified information was certainly extremely important to us; we could hardly make plans for effective action without knowing what was happening in the field.

During the first months of the war, we were still able to take some initiatives in this regard. One of our colleagues, the director of the Palestine Office in Geneva, Dr. Samuel Scheps, traveled to Germany in October 1939 to gather firsthand information for us on conditions there. This reconnaissance trip was followed by several others. Scheps was Swiss, and at that time it was still possible to travel in Germany with a Swiss passport, though one ran certain risks.

But that became more and more difficult. Some months later we turned to two non-Jewish Swiss citizens with the suggestion that they go to Poland to study firsthand the situation of Polish Jews under the occupation and report to us. The men had worked for the Red Cross and already had some experience in analogous matters. One was Sydney Brown, who had been active on what one might call the humanitarian front during the Ethiopian War. The other was Kurt Höppli, of the celebrated Swiss-origin family of publishers and booksellers in northern Italy. Both went to Poland purportedly as journalists. Their report to us was extremely useful, especially the explanation as to why the Jews there welcomed the Russian occupation forces so warmly and so feared the Germans when these two governments divided Poland according to the secret provisions of the Russo-German Treaty of August 1939.

Initiatives like these became progressively more difficult and eventually impossible for us to mount on our own. The ICRC, though, could help us learn more about the true situation in the occupied countries. From the occupation of Poland by Nazi troops, we saw the problem that was to concern us throughout the duration of hostilities. Unfortunately there were very few if any rules and no conventions dealing with the treatment of civilian populations.

Although the ICRC had taken the initiative in 1934 to propose a special convention to protect civilian populations in times of war, this Tokyo Draft Convention was never adopted or ratified. As a consequence, its provisions never came into force.

Nonetheless, when war broke out a special arrangement was made. Thanks to negotiations led by the Red Cross it was agreed among the belligerents that foreign civilians who were in enemy countries at the beginning of the war should be treated according to the rules of the Tokyo Draft, as if this convention had been ratified. Later, the number of such persons was deter-mined to be between forty and fifty thousand.

I knew many of the leaders and the staff of the ICRC, but I was in particularly close contact, as I've mentioned before, with Carl Burckhardt, the reflective political head of the International Committee, and with its president, Max Huber. The latter, a great jurist, had for years been president of the Permanent Court of International Justice at The Hague. For long periods of time he was also the Swiss government's legal counsel for international affairs. For many years he held the prestigious chair of international law at the University of Zurich. Huber was undeniably the most respected specialist in international law in Switzerland.

At the beginning of the war he was already well on in years. As a conse-quence, he did not attend every ICRC meeting. But he dominated the Red Cross not least by his rigorous jurist's attitude. He was attentive to the rules of in-ternational law, prudent, opposed to all extraordinary or even slightly bold undertakings, and careful in the first instance that the ICRC in no way trans-gress the strict framework of its rules. This attitude was to create enormous problems for us.

Burckhardt was a highly cultivated man, a diplomat, writer, and historian, and animated by great artistic inspiration. I had known him at the Institute for International Studies. In his youth he had formed ties in Vienna with the great poet and dramatist Hugo von Hofmannsthal. One day Burckhardt in-vited me to his home to have me meet von Hofmannsthal's widow; nothing in her recalled her husband's spirituality.

Burckhardt enjoyed a great reputation in German circles, even after Hitler's accession to power. I don't know if the reports were true, but people said that his book on Richelieu was on the Führer's night table. Like a good number of German-speaking Swiss intellectuals, Burckhardt suffered a great deal from the interruption, during the Nazi dictatorship, of traditional rela-tions with colleagues and friends in Germany.

Appointed in 1938 the League of Nations high commissioner for the Free City of Danzig, he was given the mission to appease the Germans and reach a *modus vivendi* with all the important elements in that troubled city. This broke with the openly anti-Nazi attitude of his predecessor, the Irishman Sean Lester.

It was in this context that I, as representative of the World Jewish Congress, met him on several occasions. Very rapidly the situation became confronta-tional. Our position, in fact, was much more combative, more aggressive with regard to the violation of rights committed by the Nazi leaders of the "Free City." We could not accept the introduction of anti-Semitic and discriminatory Nazi legislation in a city that had been placed under the guardianship of the League of Nations and ought, as a consequence, to serve as a model for the entire world.

Among a number of Red Cross figures with whom I often had dealings were two women for whom I have the greatest regard. One was Mlle. Suzanne Ferrière, who headed the entire ICRC Prisoners Agency. Her department carried out all the personal searches in the countries at war, the occupied countries, and the prisoner-of-war camps. Mlle. Ferrière was the daughter of a highly regarded Swiss physician. Later she was placed at the head of a philanthropic organization. To the end of her days she was driven by her humanitarian ideals, always ready to devote herself to their realization.

Another such woman was Mlle. Lucy Odier. Mlle. Odier came from a school of nursing and was concerned with the medical aid being given to those who suffered. Also a very important member of the ICRC, she too was from a great Geneva family. Until 1933 practically all the members of the ICRC were from Geneva, were Protestant and, *ipso facto*, members of the very conservative National Democratic party. Even members of the Swiss Radical party did not reach leadership positions in the ICRC.

It was then initially a very restricted circle, a kind of upper-middle-class, conservative, right-thinking environment. Later, during the war, it became less restrictive. A member of the Socialist party even became a member of the Committee. In fact this change had already begun somewhat earlier when Max Huber, a German Swiss, was appointed president of the ICRC. Carl Burckhardt was also a German Swiss.

I knew a number of other ICRC people less well but met with them from time to time. Here I am speaking of the members of the International Committee and not of the staff. The writer Jacques Chenevière was one of these and a friend of our cause. Col. Edouard Chapuisat of the Swiss army brought his military experience to bear, and Mlle. Renée-Marguerite Frick-Cramer did a great deal to move the ICRC toward a more liberal stance.

On another level, some important figures who assumed responsibilities for ICRC services were not members of the Committee. Among these were Prince Jean-Étienne Schwarzenberg. At one point Prince Schwarzenberg was made responsible by the ICRC for the *Judenreferat*,* the section responsible for

---

*One wonders if G. Riegner is playing with a subtext here. The word *Judenreferat* is usually used to describe Eichmann's unit in the SS hierarchy.—ED.

Jewish matters. As a consequence, he was one person at the ICRC who was specially authorized to deal with the Jews.

Schwarzenberg was descended from the famous Austrian family of that name, and, like many aristocrats, had several nationalities. He was also a Swiss citizen. His family had extensive properties in the canton of Neuchatel. Later he became the Austrian ambassador to Great Britain and to the Vatican.

Since he was the ICRC official with whom I was expected to be in frequent contact, I knew him quite well. I still remember the day when he was appointed, around mid-December 1942. He received me quite often and cordially. Numerous Jews tried to establish relations with him on an individual basis or within the context of their organization. He told me that he made a great distinction between the World Jewish Congress and the Joint, on the one hand, and the other Jewish organizations. He considered Saly Mayer and me "permanent clients," and he kept us informed of his contacts and activities.

Prince Schwarzenberg was much younger than the other officials of the ICRC, about forty years of age. He was of average height and very Austrian in his manners. On the whole, I believe he could have done much more. In view of the scope of the calamity, he was too reluctant to act; his caution could and ought to have been overcome.

The first time he received me in his office he insisted on showing me a large number of telegrams he had received from the Red Cross societies of Latin America—messages concerning German conduct toward the Jews. These telegrams urged the ICRC to intervene. When he had shown me everything, I smiled to myself. He could not know that I had instigated all this lobbying activity. I had, in fact, asked Mr. Yaacov Hellmann, the WJC representative in Latin America, to approach the South American Red Cross organizations in order to press the International Committee for more effective action on behalf of persecuted Jews.

One ICRC figure whom I liked a great deal was Hans Bachmann, an assistant to Professor Burckhardt who later had a career as one of the leaders of the city of Winterthur. Bachmann was then still quite young. I met him fairly often when I could not get to see Burckhardt himself. Bachmann appeared to be filled with sympathy and understanding for our situation and our cause.

André de Pilar's real name was Ritter Piller von Pillersdorf. He was of the Baltic gentry and through his connections with the international European aristocracy, also held Swiss nationality. Motivated by genuine concern for our problems, he seemed attracted to Jewish spirituality. He came from Riga, the capital of Latvia, which at the time had a fine and large Jewish community. He had personal connections with a number of the leaders of that community.

De Pilar worked at the Joint Relief Commission of the ICRC, about which I shall report more below. At one of our first meetings, de Pilar asked me if we had a representative in Stockholm. If this were the case, de Pilar wanted to involve him in some common activities. And when I mentioned that our representative in Sweden was Hillel Storch, he said, "He's from Riga; I know his family." I immediately understood that he had a great deal of respect for the Storch family. He told me: "Hillel Storch is a man very different from you. He is a Jew of the people and you are an intellectual." In any case, de Pilar understood our needs and our resources.

I bear de Pilar a profound debt of gratitude. For example, each time the German Red Cross sent a delegation to Geneva, which happened occasionally, he called me in to tell me what they had reported. That information was often of great interest. In my reports to New York and London, traces of his information echo, naturally without my revealing their source. De Pilar displayed friendship, comprehension, and a genuine desire to help us. It was, for example, he who advised me on several occasions to insist to the Allies that they exert more pressure on the International Committee of the Red Cross.

If de Pilar was one of the most attractive personalities of the team, his opposite was Schwarzenberg. But it was certainly part of Burckhardt's strategy to have at his side both sorts of men. There was even a Jew on the Joint Relief Commission, a pharmacist from Basel, a Dr. Feinstein, with whom I had dealings when shipping medical and pharmaceutical supplies. He too made great efforts to help us.

These, then, were some of the Red Cross people with whom I cooperated in our efforts. I endeavored to maintain very correct relations with all of them.

As we have seen, from the very beginning of the war the German occupation created very serious problems in the large Jewish population centers in Poland. We promptly took the first urgent initiatives: sending medical supplies to Warsaw. But this could not be done through the postal service. German authorization was needed, and we had to turn to the ICRC as intermediary to arrange for these shipments. To permit the transport of shipments by the Red Cross, the ICRC established a special body in cooperation with the League of Red Cross Societies. This was the Joint Relief Commission, which in time became a relatively autonomous organization. On the one hand the commission was charged with buying all sorts of things—food, pharmaceuticals, dietary supplements—for philanthropic shipments to various countries. On the other hand it had to take complete responsibility for purchasing as well as for all the formalities associated with shipping such goods to the occupied countries. These efforts, under extremely difficult and closely controlled transportation conditions, have no parallel today. For each shipment, for each destination, authorization had to be obtained from the warring parties.

Of course many others followed these initiatives. The great problem was to move materials for which people had the greatest need, especially in the ghettos of the East where brutal rationing had been imposed. Jews were allowed only starvation rations, clearly inferior to those supplied the rest of the population. The situation in the large Jewish centers became increasingly desperate as the Germans more and more restricted the possibility of their receiving substantial aid.

Our relations with the ICRC were multifaceted: individual and collective shipments of food and medications were only one element; we also sought their help in the search for missing persons and in regard to Jewish prisoners of war. Our greatest concern was to protect Jewish populations in the occupied countries. We followed with anguish the ghettoization of Jewish communities in Poland, the progressive evacuation of the large Jewish centers—first from Central Europe and then from Western and Eastern Europe—through deportation to annihilation. We constantly asked ourselves what we could do to bring an end to the deportations, what we could do to improve the lot of the deported, what we could do to protect the great mass of the deportees.

In this desperate situation we turned repeatedly to the ICRC, the sole neutral body internationally recognized as such. It was imperative that we enlist its unquestioned moral authority in the struggle for the survival of communities in distress.

In this spirit we sought three fundamental requirements of the ICRC:

First, we wanted Red Cross delegates to be sent to all the areas where ghettoization, deportation, and extermination were taking place. The presence of impartial and independent external witnesses, we hoped, might at least limit the persecution and the atrocities.

Second, we wanted the Red Cross to find a way to confer upon civilian internees in the camps a legal status similar to that of prisoners of war, accompanied by minimum guarantees.

Third, we proposed the organization of a large-scale material aid program under ICRC auspices in order to help the starving masses survive in the ghettos and camps.

The ICRC reacted to these proposals with extreme reluctance and long-term temporizing. I believe it was particularly under the influence of Max Huber that the ICRC repeatedly insisted that it had a clear mandate with regard to prisoners of war: responsibility for four million of them. In this domain, said the ICRC, we are within our rights, for the rules have been ratified by international conventions. We cannot go beyond this framework, because if we do we will be jeopardizing our activity on behalf of the millions of persons who have been placed in our care.

The argument was a strong one but, in my eyes, hardly persuasive. Moreover, if at one moment the ICRC was indeed responsible for four million prisoners of war, that number was greatly reduced after the liberation of a great number of French prisoners. But the ICRC position posed an obstacle. ICRC officials said to us at the same time, "It is not we, the Red Cross, who are responsible for the fact that the Tokyo Draft, intended to protect civilian populations in time of war, is not in force. We made proposals, but the countries we approached did not follow our lead. This is not our responsibility. We cannot run the risk of taking initiatives that go beyond our legal position."

Throughout virtually the entire war we attempted to convince the ICRC to modify its rigid position. At times, I believe, we somewhat attenuated its severity. But in practical terms it scarcely changed. This is the fundamental reason for the wartime tension between the WJC and the ICRC. We did not resign ourselves to the limits to which they adhered; we returned to this matter numerous times. Notwithstanding its strict legal position, there was an implied mandate for humanitarian initiatives beyond the prisoners of war that had been recognized by ICRC actions in the past; unfortunately it made little use of this mandate during the war.

For a time I asked myself what good it was to visit them so frequently, to try to push them. I would ask for passes to gain access to the occupied countries, passes to visit the ghettos and camps, for efforts to take care of those who needed aid. I eventually became so disappointed and pessimistic that for several months I did not set foot in the ICRC building. But as the situation became more desperate I told myself that I must make further attempts. So I returned to the struggle. But, as I have said, all this generated only the most limited results.

We especially concentrated our efforts in the summer of 1942 when we received news from the German informant of plans for the "Final Solution." We again approached the ICRC to try to counter the German plans, to try to convince the Red Cross to raise a general moral protest that might find some echo in public opinion. I already have given an account of how Professor Burckhardt confirmed to us that his information on the situation in Germany was consistent with what we had learned. But for me it remains a mystery to this day why Burckhardt apparently never shared this intelligence with his ICRC colleagues.

Today we know that some members of the ICRC nevertheless came to know enough that they believed a public protest should be raised against the way the war was being waged and the violation of elementary human rights, especially those of civilian populations.

Favez's *The Red Cross and the Holocaust* provides a detailed account of the efforts that were made in this direction.

By the autumn of 1942 we were persuaded that we were running into a brick wall of refusal from the Germans and that the ICRC could win no direct concessions from them, even had the Red Cross made all the efforts we might wish. This is why we thought the only possibly effective course would be a protest, a proclamation in which the ICRC condemned Nazi crimes against the Jews. It seemed to us that a public statement from the most important international humanitarian organization of the time was absolutely necessary. No other body had the prestige of the Red Cross. On several occasions I pleaded this case to ICRC administrators.

And indeed the Committee eventually did ask its members whether they believed that a protest or an appeal in regard to the treatment of Jews and other violations of humanitarian rules was called for. The great majority of ICRC members responded positively, but they were divided as to the form such an action should take. At an October 1942 meeting of the Committee the initiative was abandoned.

But that is not the whole story. At this decisive meeting the federal councillor in charge of the Department of Interior, Philippe Etter, who was a member of the Committee but generally did not attend its meetings, voiced his opposition to such a public protest. He was supported by Professor Burckhardt himself and by Colonel Chapuisat, who in the absence of Max Huber chaired the meeting. The Swiss government delegate responsible for humanitarian affairs, Edouard de Haller, and Pierre Bonna, the most senior official of the Political Department (the Swiss Ministry of Foreign Affairs), had taken care to brief the members of the Committee before the meeting. These officials explained to their Committee colleagues that the Swiss government did not wish such a declaration. In the event of its adoption the Swiss government expected repercussions from the Germans. The majority of ICRC members fell into line. Thus it is important to note that the responsibility for the failure of this initiative rests with the Swiss government.

Some have defended this stance by saying that such an appeal would certainly not have succeeded in modifying Nazi plans. In their view, nothing would have been changed, for the Nazis' attitude was such that no one could in any way influence their fanaticism and resolution. Even if it were true, I cannot condone this silence. I have never accepted the ICRC position on this issue.

In the life of large international humanitarian organizations there are times when the fundamental principles of their actions are called into question, when a stand must be taken without regard to the success or failure of the initiative. I believe that in 1942 such a moment had come for the ICRC. It ought to have followed its conscience and embraced a higher morality by publicly reaffirming its humanitarian principles and condemning one of the most atrocious crimes in the history of humanity.

Henri Dunant and the founders of the Red Cross had understood very well that appeals to public opinion were indispensable to their activity and that, without such support, humanitarian law would never be defined or applied.

Some weeks later, at our meeting of November 17, 1942, Carl Burckhardt gave me a personal account of what had happened at the ICRC meeting in October. Fortunately, he said, the Committee had turned down the idea of a protest. He added that two women on the Committee had vigorously supported my point of view. He asked me what, in my opinion, the ICRC ought to undertake in the future.

He informed me at the same time that in September 1942 the International Committee had sent to its delegation in Berlin the draft of a diplomatic note in which guarantees were requested for civilian internees in concentration camps. These guarantees were to be similar to the minimum guarantees granted to prisoners of war.

Responsibility had been left with the Berlin delegation of the ICRC to decide whether or not the note was to be transmitted to the German Ministry of Foreign Affairs. Burckhardt said the note had in fact been transmitted and that he was awaiting a response. He was quite proud that this had been sent. I believe I can say that the transmission of this note was the result of Guggenheim's and my insistence that Burckhardt and the other members of the Committee undertake some effective action in response to news concerning the "Final Solution."

When, during that November 17 meeting, Burckhardt asked me what I thought the Red Cross ought to do in the future, I told him that in the summer, when we received information on the "Final Solution," it had seemed to us that there was nothing else left but to publicly protest. If today, I said, you and the ICRC believe that some action is again possible and that there is some chance of obtaining improvements in the situation in the field, I will not push you to protest. But I will tell you: doing nothing and still not protesting is not acceptable. If you do not protest, you must act. Burckhardt then assured me that he would continue the action that had been begun September 24—that is, to call for a response from the Germans to the ICRC note.

We should not forget that at the close of 1942 the political situation had begun to change profoundly. We were then at a decisive moment, a turning point in the war. Soviet resistance at Stalingrad would bring about Germany's greatest defeat. Montgomery's operations in North Africa were leading to one of the major victories of the Western armies. I knew that Burckhardt had great political sense and that these developments would strengthen the ICRC position with the Germans.

For a long time I was given to believe that support for this note and the principles it enunciated continued to exist. In fact, we know today that from the delivery of the note on September 24, 1942, until the 1944 tragedy in Hungary, no steps in this direction were taken by the ICRC.

In fact, Professor Favez informs us in his book that at the end of December 1942, at a sitting of the coordinating commission in the absence of Burckhardt, who was ill, the members of the Committee decided to give up trying to obtain a written reply from the German government to the September 24 note, and decided not to relaunch the initiative. We were never informed of this. Nor were we informed that until October 1944 the ICRC took no further steps, leaving us to believe all this time that the Committee was pursuing the matter of its September 24 note.

This decision of late December 1942 was typical of the policy that the ICRC pursued during the entire war with regard to Nazi Germany: a timid and deferential attitude aimed at avoiding any action that could be interpreted as an offense or as criticism of the German government. But this attitude was based on an erroneous evaluation of the political reality. The ICRC position was actually stronger than its own leaders believed.

The Swiss historian and diplomat Paul Stauffer, in a study devoted to the notorious Katyn massacre of Polish army officers, called attention to this aspect of ICRC policy.* After the discovery of the enormous charnel pit at Katyn in April 1943, the Polish government-in-exile and the German government, each on its own side, requested that the ICRC make an inquiry and urgently send a delegation to Katyn. The ICRC refused this request, given that the third power that was implicated, the Soviet Union, had not given its consent. Ac-

*Paul Stauffer, "Die Schweiz und die Tragödie von Katyn," in *Schweizer Monatshefte*, Heft 11 (1989), pp. 899–918.—ED.

cording to its established rules, the ICRC could not act without the consent of all the affected governments. The Germans were naturally "furious" at the ICRC position. Goebbels, who was behind this action, which had been undertaken for Nazi propaganda purposes, was particularly dissatisfied. But, at all events, he judged that they must avoid a confrontation with the ICRC.

Stauffer quotes Goebbels's reaction as expressed in his diary:

> Nevertheless I don't deem it good policy to attack the Red Cross. We are so dependent on it in the matter of prisoners of war that it does not seem opportune to start a fight.*

Goebbels's attitude indicates that the ICRC could have adopted much bolder positions without serious reprisal from the Germans.

The World Jewish Congress did not cease to exert pressure on the ICRC to pursue a response from the German government. In this regard the WJC central office in New York undertook a whole series of lobbying activities and prepared a number of memoranda that were communicated to the ICRC. Eventually this lobbying resulted in President Huber drafting a comprehensive text agreeing with our requests. But it was only during the last phase of the war, in 1944, that the ICRC again undertook such representation.

In evaluating the activities of the ICRC in their entirety and in particular with regard to the Jewish victims of the war and of persecution, latter-day publications, such as the work of Professor Favez, disclose negative Red Cross attitudes that were even more pervasive than I had suspected during the period.

In certain respects the attitude of the ICRC even fell short of the legal stipulations of the convention under which the organization operated. Red Cross people, among others, were ready to adapt themselves in broad terms to the reality of the Nazi domination of Europe. Many even accepted Nazi racist doctrine as established fact.

When the German Red Cross asked the ICRC in late 1943 to indicate on search requests for people who had disappeared in the occupied territories whether the person being sought was or was not "Aryan," the central agency acquiesced in this demand.

Dr. Jean Rudolf von Salis, head of the ICRC delegation in Italy, asked his local representatives to concern themselves with the fate of Jews who had just been removed from the Rome region to camps in northern Italy. When these delegates addressed themselves to the SS troop command, the Geneva ICRC

---

*Entry of April 24, 1943. *The Goebbels Diaries 1942–1943*, ed. and trans. by Louis P. Lochner (New York, 1948), p. 205.—ED.

sent them a harsh reprimand. The ICRC delegates in Italy replied: "We thank you for your clear exposition of the question, and we assure you that in the absence of special orders from the Committee we will concern ourselves in the future only with questions related to prisoners of war or civilian internees who are of the Aryan race." This was written in May 1944.

One can see in other documents too that the Committee was somewhat embarrassed to expose itself on behalf of the Jews. Thus we read January 27, 1943, instructions given to the ICRC representative in Bucharest, Vladimir de Steiger, concerning the Transnistrian Jews: "We would, however, ask you to proceed with all possible caution and discretion. At all costs, we wish to avoid alerting public opinion or the authorities and encouraging speculations about a major action to be undertaken by the ICRC on behalf of Jews. Such a speculation would have very adverse consequences and would be liable to jeopardize our intention, which is simply the inclusion of the Jews in the activities organized by the Joint Relief Commission."*

The International Committee also abstained from supporting some of our initiatives that, in good conscience, it should have. Thus ICRC officials refused to subscribe to the appeal to neutral countries and to the national societies of the Red Cross in neutral countries that they open their borders more widely to those who might still escape.

Similarly the ICRC refused to support our proposal for an appeal to Roosevelt, Churchill, and Stalin for the creation of a large fund, to be administered by the ICRC, to assist the populations of occupied Europe. I am not persuaded that such a supportive action would have violated its obligation to neutrality.

I was later informed on several occasions that some in ICRC circles viewed the World Jewish Congress as too political an organization to be considered a partner in its sphere of activity. This may explain, for example, that at a crucial moment it did not transmit to us—as it should have—the reports it received from leaders of the Jewish community in Hungary during the summer of 1944, and which reached us much too late for action.

In short, our humanitarian efforts were not well received by some ICRC officials because they demanded continuous political pressure and constant appeals to public opinion. Evidently they would have preferred the purely philanthropic, much more moderate, reverent, and discreet attitude of the Joint Distribution Committee, which could offer them large sums of money for material aid, leaving aside the political dimension. Yet the true solutions to problems ultimately lay in the political arena.

---

*The instructions to de Steiger are printed in Favez, pp. 201–202.—ED.

It has often been asked if the ICRC was really informed of what was happening in the occupied countries and, in particular, if its members were aware of the atrocities that accompanied the process of persecution and extermination. The evidence shows that ICRC delegations had very effectively kept abreast of events. The Berlin delegation and those in Budapest and other localities submitted highly detailed reports on the situation. No one in authority could have been unaware of them. On the other hand, I myself transmitted to several members of the Committee all the reports of substantial interest that reached us, bringing them up to date as these reports were received. Thus there simply can be no doubt that the administrative circles of the ICRC were very well informed.

Their attitude becomes clearer when one takes into account that despite the reports we regularly and continually furnished them, they apparently never tried to contact the known eyewitnesses. Nor is there any valid explanation for the fact that the ICRC did not try to approach the senior political authorities of the Reich during all these years. As I was informed then by various ICRC sources, proposals to this effect were made several times by its own delegates or by certain members of the Committee. But until the final phase of the war, the ICRC made no real attempt to contact Himmler or other highly placed figures. The sole exception was the Burckhardt-Kaltenbrunner meeting to which I have referred above.

The problem of Jewish prisoners of war was of enormous concern to us during the final stage of the hostilities.

In principle the rules of war, on both sides, were the same everywhere and for everyone. But as early as 1940 and 1941 our attention was called to irregularities in the treatment of Jewish POWs. The complaints that reached me dealt in particular with the separation of captured Jews from other imprisoned military personnel. At the outset this occurred only in some localities, but it particularly affected Jewish prisoners from the Yugoslav army. It seemed then as if these were only isolated, provisional incidents and that on the whole the Jewish POWs would be treated according to the Geneva Conventions. During 1943–1944, however, we received growing reports of a more systematic separation of Jews in prisoner-of-war camps.

The situation became progressively worse, especially toward the end of the war. In 1944 especially alarming complaints reached us from various communities, from prisoners themselves, and from still other sources. They all stated clearly that Jewish prisoners of war had been separated from the others, especially in the POW camps the Germans operated in Poland. In some camps the

Jewish prisoners were housed in barracks separated from the others by
barbed-wire fences.

On March 13, 1945, we renewed our protest to the ICRC on the subject of
the separation of Jewish prisoners of war from other captured soldiers. We
added a written brief to our oral presentation in which I pointed out specific
situations and named *Stalags* (camps for enlisted men and officers), and
Oflags (officer camps). We were promised immediate intervention by the ICRC
delegation in Germany.

On March 23 the ICRC confirmed to us that its German delegation had informed it

> that as a consequence of a recent measure, Jewish prisoners of war have been
> separated from others in all the Oflags and that a similar measure has been
> taken some time ago in the Stalags. Nonetheless, it would seem that this
> separation has not in general entailed unfavorable treatment of the Jewish
> prisoners of war.

We vehemently opposed this opinion and demanded that the ICRC not
countenance it. In a March 29 letter to President Burckhardt we maintained
that the International Convention of 1929 concerning the treatment of prisoners of war accepted differences in treatment only on the basis of military
rank, the state of physical and psychological health, and the sex of the prisoners. All other discrimination was prohibited. We continued:

> In the light of the extermination policy systematically implemented by Ger-
> many against the totality of the Jewish population detained by it, the separa-
> tion of Jewish prisoners of war from other prisoners can only be considered
> an act preparatory to measures identical to those carried out on other cate-
> gories of Jews.

The ICRC did not seem persuaded by our arguments. President Burckhardt's
letter of April 5, 1945, contends that if Jewish prisoners of war received the same
treatment as others, the separation in and of itself did not constitute a violation
of the rules of the conventions. In other words, as long as the Jewish prisoners
received the same soup ration as the others, the ICRC saw no violation.

We sent a letter to Burckhardt on April 27, 1945, in which we made our
point explicit:

> We have expressed our amazement at seeing the ICRC adopt a legal position
> that seems to oblige it to wait to intervene until the prejudicial effects resulting
> from this separation have been actually produced. At the moment the material

damage occurs, the situation is generally irreparable. To avoid such situations, it is appropriate to react, to refuse all discriminatory measures.

This correspondence, initiated from our office by Professor Guggenheim and me, reflects our firmness in the matter. We would not accept the Committee's position, which nevertheless remained inflexible.

Such correspondence continued until the end of the war. It concluded with our request to be consulted in efforts aimed at revising the humanitarian conventions of the Red Cross in the light of the World War II experience.

Important developments of this sort did occur after the war. In 1946, for example, we were invited, along with other charitable organizations, to a preparatory meeting for the revision of the Geneva Convention. President Huber and the principal directors of the ICRC gathered with representatives of forty relevant organizations. Since the Joint representative did not attend, I was the only Jew there.

The ICRC proposed that the revised convention incorporate an article on cooperation with other charitable organizations. For my part, I had come especially to raise certain basic questions, particularly concerning the protection of civilian populations. Wartime abuses, I thought, had made such changes imperative. My request to have this matter placed on the agenda was refused, but I was authorized to make a presentation on the problem at the end of deliberations.

The end of the meeting was marked by a significant event. One delegate moved that the International Committee of the Red Cross be thanked for all that it had done during World War II for prisoners of war and civilian internees. For various reasons, in particular to strengthen its position vis-à-vis the Soviet Union, which continued to hold hundreds of thousands of POWs, the ICRC judged that it needed such a declaration from all the philanthropic organizations.

I found myself in an extremely delicate position. It seemed difficult for me to be impolite by refusing. But I felt that inviting us to their own premises for a vote of confidence and thanks was overreaching. After thinking it over, I requested the floor and simply said, "I propose striking from the motion the four words 'and the civilian internees.'" And I sat down.

The meeting erupted in turmoil. The nonratification of the Tokyo Draft came up again, and I no longer recall what other arguments arose.

I then replied:

I, too, have a public opinion to be concerned with. When civilian internees are mentioned, it recalls those who were deported to the concentration camps and death camps. You were not able to protect them; we were not able to protect them. This is not the place to say whether more could have been done or not. Therefore, I have no right to express any satisfaction at all with what was done.

The debate again became heated until someone finally suggested the phrasing "prisoners of war and assimilated persons" (*"personnes assimilées"*). They asked me whether I could accept that. I replied, "That doesn't make any sense. No one will understand it. But if that will do . . ."

Some time later Professor Guggenheim told me that Max Huber had been greatly impressed by my intervention at the meeting. Huber reportedly also told Guggenheim that he had passed several sleepless nights wondering whether the Red Cross truly had done everything possible during the war.

Manifestations of such an attitude were, however, rare. This question was never raised in any of the Red Cross publications. For many years I always told senior officials of the ICRC that theirs was a mistaken policy uncritically defending everything that had been done or not done by their predecessors during World War II—as if the world had not evolved in the course of the last decades, as if our concepts and our system of values had not been affected by the events, as if the ICRC could invoke some kind of infallibility for all its actions. Even with regard to the work of Professor Jean-Claude Favez, to whom the ICRC opened all its archives, the Committee had somewhat distanced itself from and expressed a series of reservations about his conclusions.

In the end it took fifty years for a president of the International Committee of the Red Cross, in the person of Cornelio Sommaruga, to admit for the first time, in an address that caused a great stir, the "moral failure" of the institution. It would require, in late May 1995, the atmosphere of the fiftieth anniversary of the end of World War II for an ICRC president to openly acknowledge:

> . . . our share of responsibility in this general failure of a civilization that was not able to prevent systematic genocide against a people and against certain minorities. . . . I recall this moral failure of our institution, which was not capable of going beyond the legal framework that the states had set for it. Today the ICRC can only regret the omissions and errors of the past! . . . Fifty years ago, some explained their passivity by affirming that they had no knowledge of the horrific scale of the acts committed by the Nazi regime. . . . Today, no one—neither simple citizens, nor particularly the representatives of states, nor those responsible for humanitarian action—can take refuge in real or feigned ignorance. . . . Today, the

international community ignores nothing of the massive, most serious violations of the Geneva Conventions.*

Our Position in Switzerland During the War

The fact that our office was in Switzerland, the only WJC office in Central Europe, allowed us to maintain contacts with nearly all the European countries. This had manifest implications for our work, and consequences for the conditions under which I worked.

The problem was not evident at the beginning of the war, but it appeared clearly in the summer of 1940, after the defeat of France. Significant changes then occurred. Since I was an employee of the WJC I had a residence and work permit that had been issued by the authorities. I had to renew it each year. Around August 1, 1940, I applied to the Swiss authorities to have my permit renewed. In reply the federal police sent me a message that as I was a refugee, I should prepare to leave the country. I turned to a reputable lawyer to protest this order, citing the utility of the work I was doing. The Department of Justice and Police consulted the president of the Jewish community in Geneva, whose opinion was judged competent to determine the need for my activities. His judgment, which was positive, emphasized that our office assisted the emigration of refugees *from* Switzerland. On this basis, Bern withdrew the order obliging me to leave the country.

Yet, to my great surprise, there was no other reply to my application to have my residence and work permit extended. As it turned out, I was allowed to work quietly without restrictions on my activities. Thus there was gradually established between me and the government a kind of gentleman's agreement, a tacit accord: the Swiss government would allow me to continue my work; for my part, I would try not to create difficulties for the government and would carry out my tasks with discretion; I would abstain from all public action—press releases or the like—that might have political repercussions. This did not prevent me from giving lectures in various Jewish communities, in camps for internees, and in labor camps that took in Jews. In any case, it was not the role of the World Jewish Congress to make public statements. Its principal task consisted of informing New York and London, that is, the Free World, of what was happening in occupied Europe.

---

*It should be noted that the United States Holocaust Memorial Museum played a not insignificant role in convincing the ICRC to achieve this position and in opening its archives for the war period to scholarly research.—ED.

Thus the Swiss authorities permitted me to work but did not wish to be bound to me in any way at all. They actually did not officially renew my permit until late 1943. During the intervening three years I had to have my old card stamped each month as proof of the fact that I had requested the authorities to renew my permit. In this way I had the indispensable piece of paper that proved I was "legal." And since we all lived under rationing, each month I was also obliged to renew the card that authorized me to draw food coupons. None of this was very convenient. But because my Swiss colleagues in the office took care of some of these things, I was not greatly inconvenienced by them.

The Swiss authorities probably had some apprehensions. This was quite clear even though they never told me so directly. They likely feared that at some moment the Germans would demand the suppression and closure of the WJC office, which had such a solidly anti-Nazi reputation. Were that to occur, the Swiss would not have wished to be obligated to us by any permit they might then have been obliged to rescind. Moreover I am convinced that the authorities monitored my activities quite closely.

Thus, little by little, this tacit agreement was established and lasted until relatively late in the war. When, in 1943, the Swiss saw that the Allies were likely to be victorious, and only at that moment, they responded to my request for the renewal of my residence and work permit from 1940. The authorities did not hesitate to have me pay the fees and charges for the intervening years—a typically bureaucratic touch that amused me.

It was only much later, and without my requesting it, that I was issued a permanent residence permit, which allowed me to stay on in Switzerland and work there.

A few recollections will illuminate the wartime situation in Geneva and the singular atmosphere that prevailed there. At the beginning of the conflict I was on very good terms with the vice consul of one of the great European powers represented in Geneva. This was in the first days of the war. His wife had not yet returned from summer holidays, and we dined together every evening. He used to come by and fetch me at the office with his little car, and we would drive somewhere, generally out into the countryside. On September 2, 1939, the second day of the war, he came looking for me and said, "We're going to such and such a place for dinner, but first I have to run two errands and you can come with me." He drove me to a residential building, stopped in the entryway, took a key out of his pocket, opened a letterbox, removed all the contents, took out a satchel, pulled another packet of letters from it, and put them into the box. At another location he repeated the operation.

All this activity had to do with two journalists or Nazi officials who were working in Geneva and who he suspected were working as spies for German intelligence. For me, on the second day of the war, this was a lesson in how countries at war behaved on neutral territory. I have never forgotten it, nor did I ever discover what was in those letters.

The police never caused me any worries personally, with one exception. It was an interesting case. In 1942 the Jewish Anti-Fascist Committee was created in Kuiybyshev in the Soviet Union. After its founding meeting, the committee sent to the Jews of the entire world a grand manifesto, in which they were asked to support the Soviet war effort. Our office in Geneva received a copy. It was a twenty-page telegram, and we could see how important it was. Two days later the Swiss political police summoned me to their office and interrogated me about my relations with Soviet Russia. I should point out that the Swiss had not formally recognized the new Soviet government in 1918 but had allowed a Soviet mission to operate in the country until November of that year when the Swiss political police expelled the mission for its Bolshevik agitation and propaganda activities. Throughout the 1920s and 1930s informal Swiss-Soviet relations went through many ups and downs, but diplomatic relations were not initiated until after the Second World War.

Consequently the Swiss were particularly sensitive to anything having to do with the Soviet Union, which explains why the police officers insisted: "How do you happen to have relations with the Soviet Union? How do they know your address?"

I believe I received the telegram because on several earlier occasions I had made search requests of the Soviet Red Cross. I never received a reply. But, apparently, the Soviets had kept my address. This led to a rather amusing discussion with the policemen, who asked me whether I was a Communist. I answered them rather coolly.

I was more concerned about the Germans. I was certain that I was under German surveillance. I had been to the German consulate once or twice before the war to have my passport extended, but I did not have ongoing relations with them. I am sure I was on one of their special lists. I later learned that the German consul, Wolfgang Krauel, was not a Nazi. He was an individual who had experienced the whole Stresemann era and he was not a particularly zealous proponent of German policies with regard to Jews or to others out of favor with his government. It is quite possible that he spared me a good deal of trouble.

Switzerland's position with regard to Germany was quite clear: it was firmly determined to maintain its neutrality. Ongoing German propaganda tried to sway the Swiss. In many countries there were Nazi party regional officials responsible for Germans living abroad, with propaganda resources for local use. The official in Switzerland was Wilhelm Gustloff; the authorities let him operate, but he was assassinated by a Yugoslavian Jewish medical student, David Frankfurter, on February 4, 1936.*

German propaganda favored the emergence of a pro-Nazi movement in German-speaking Switzerland. These "Frontists" called for the incorporation of Switzerland into the German Reich. In French-speaking Switzerland, a fascist movement sprang up, led by Georges Oltramare. But he looked rather toward Italian fascism. Yet all of them, pro-Nazis and pro-Fascists together, never made up more than 10 percent of the population.

The great majority of the Swiss were horrified by what was happening in Germany. Switzerland was certainly highly critical of the German government's methods and remained all the more attached to the country's democratic traditions of legal guarantees for individuals.

To simplify, we could say that during World War I sympathies in Switzerland were divided along ethnic lines: the German Swiss looked to Germany, those in the Suisse Romande toward France, those in Ticino toward Italy. This led to considerable tension in Switzerland at the time.

What happened during World War II was, in much of the country, just the opposite. The closer one came to the German border, the more the German Swiss were anti-Nazi. The closer one went to the Italian border, the more anti-Fascist the population became. For its part, French-speaking Switzerland played its own rather curious game. On the whole the French-speaking Swiss always had a tendency to look toward the example of France. The Swiss Radical party was greatly influenced by the ideas of the Radical party in the France of the Third Republic.

---

*Frankfurter served nine years of an eighteen-year sentence; after the war the Swiss pardoned him and he moved to Israel where he spent the remainder of his life. The Nazis named a party passenger ship after Gustloff. A Soviet submarine sank the ship on January 30, 1945, as it transported almost eight thousand women and children refugees and wounded soldiers from Gdynia to Germany. More than six thousand people died, making this the worst maritime disaster in history. The event is the pivotal point in Günter Grass's controversial novel *Im Krebsgang* (*Crabwalk*, 2002). The novel itself is an element in the recent debate about atrocities committed against Germany during the war.—ED.

Suddenly, in the Suisse Romande all this disappeared. Instead of the Third Republic there was Marshal Henri Philippe Pétain. Very curiously, French-speaking Switzerland followed this move and made a hero of Pétain. From then on you could see in many restaurants a photograph of Marshal Pétain beside that of General Henri Guisan, the commander-in-chief of the Swiss army.

It was only gradually that the photos of Pétain disappeared and that the Free French movement gained in popularity as people came to appreciate the role played by Charles de Gaulle. In Bern the representative of the Vichy government continued to represent France.

None of this was simple or easy. There can be no doubt that public opinion in general was critical of Germany. The newspapers constituted one of the large bones of contention between Switzerland and Nazi Germany, which continually complained of the critical attitude of Swiss journalists.

Officially the Swiss government observed an attitude of absolute neutrality. This neutrality was recognized and guaranteed by the European powers in the 1815 Treaty of Vienna; it had been confirmed by the Treaty of Versailles in 1919. At the same time its recognized status obliged Switzerland to defend its neutrality. Thus this determination to remain neutral relied on the Swiss army and its fighting capacity. The Swiss were immediately mobilized to defend their borders when hostilities broke out. And since Switzerland had a popular army based on conscription, the whole country was involved, in one way or another, in military service.

After the fall of France the traditional attitude of Switzerland became extremely delicate and difficult to maintain. Switzerland, which had been surrounded by four great powers, Germany, France, the Austro-Hungarian Empire, and Italy, suddenly, after the *Anschluss* of 1938, lost its opening toward Austria. Also in 1938, the creation of the Berlin-Rome Axis resulted in Switzerland being closed in on three sides.

In 1940 the defeat and occupation of France again transformed the nature of the borders. Switzerland was practically surrounded by the armed forces of the Reich. Only a small opening toward unoccupied France existed, which Hitler had not succeeded in closing. And we know today that the Germans, pushed by Hitler himself, made efforts to do this, even after the 1940 armistice with France. According to contemporary historians, this was probably Switzerland's most dangerous moment.

Switzerland feared not only invasion. Its difficult situation was complicated by the fact that it could not live off its own means and production. Practically without raw materials, it had to feed itself to a great extent through imports. This presupposed open borders and a corresponding export capacity. And Switzerland had neither ports nor navigable rivers.

On the other hand, Switzerland had to keep its population at work. It lived to a great extent from the export of its industrial production. For all these reasons, it depended completely on German goodwill.

Basically, Switzerland had a choice: it would work for Germany, or it would refuse. In the event of a refusal, its factories would close, leading to massive unemployment and doubtless to a radicalization of the population. Such a situation predictably would have enhanced the popularity of the Frontist movement, which promoted annexation by Germany. Under these constraints, Switzerland chose to let its economy work for Germany, with all the risks that this entailed for its neutrality.

Fortunately, before the war Switzerland had a minister of economic affairs of superior intelligence. This was Wilhelm Oprecht. Against the possibility of war, over several years he had built up enormous stocks of food in the interior of the country, as Joseph had done in Egypt. Thanks to these reserves and to rationing, which was introduced from the beginning of the war, Switzerland was able to assure its food supply. The food stocks, which were drawn on throughout the war, were complemented by imports that had been astutely negotiated. Imported material came through Marseilles or Genoa under very specific conditions and brought in food and raw materials in quantities sufficient to keep the country alive.

There was, however, a considerable risk. In fact the Swiss were never sure that the Germans would not be tempted to occupy the country. The situation was then extremely delicate, especially after the French defeat in June 1940. At that moment even some of the federal councillors fell victim to a measure of panic. In particular, the head of the Political Department, Max Petitpierre, made a speech in which he foresaw the adaptation of Switzerland to the new conditions of Europe, which manifestly meant submitting to German domination.

This was Switzerland's most difficult and most dramatic moment. Petitpierre's speech was counterbalanced some weeks later by a very firm statement by General Henri Guisan, commander-in-chief of the army, who—from the historic plateau of Grütli near Geneva—called his fellow citizens to the unconditional defense of the homeland, its independence and their freedoms. This opinion did not always prevail; there were also moments of weakness. Yet the great mass of the people and most of their leaders had the will to preserve the country's independence.

We know today that Switzerland did not maintain its official neutrality solely by virtue of its will to defend itself. The constant pressure of the Reich resulted in a large measure of cooperation with its neighbor, especially in the economic domain. This cooperation certainly went beyond the limits of strict neutrality. The recent great debate about Switzerland's conduct during World War II has revealed features that were not then known to large sectors of the population, but for which the leaders of the time bear full responsibility. The Federal Council itself has recognized that "it was particularly in the economic and financial domains that concessions were made to the Axis powers, concessions which, in the light of the profoundly held convictions of the populace and even in consideration of the necessity of the times, are difficult to conceive of today."

In 1933 the Swiss confederation had adopted a very strict policy with regard to Jewish refugees who were trying to reach and remain in the country. This policy was in complete contradiction to what Swiss historians are pleased to call the "great tradition of Swiss asylum." But only recently has it been discovered that the application of this policy was not as consistent as has been believed.

After 1933, access for refugees became more and more limited. In the past one could simply show up at the Swiss border with a German passport. With my German passport, I was also able to enroll in the Institute for International Studies. But even then acquiring refugee status was extremely difficult. Before the war about seven thousand Jewish émigrés of German origin had obtained the right to asylum.

The great crisis in this matter came after the *Anschluss* in 1938. It is a notorious fact that at that time, after negotiations between Switzerland and Germany, it was agreed that the passports of Jews would be stamped with a large "J" in order to distinguish them from "ordinary" German passports. Only the Jewish passports were required to carry an entry visa. The objective of this initiative clearly was to limit the access of German and Austrian Jews who were seeking refuge in Switzerland. We know today that this idea originated with the head of the Swiss police for foreigners, Heinrich Rothmund, and that the Germans accepted it willingly. This is one of the sorriest episodes in the history of Swiss policy toward refugees.

The introduction of the "J" stamp inside the passports of German Jews did not only prevent them from entering Switzerland. It was also detrimental to German Jews who sought refuge in other countries as well, in particular to Latin American states, which increasingly denied visas to holders of such passports.

It became more and more evident that foreign Jews were simply not wanted in Switzerland. This attitude was motivated by the perceived need to prevent an

Überfremdungsgefahr (literally, the overalienization danger), the threat of loss of
the Swiss national character. It was also presented as being in the interest of the
Jewish community in Switzerland, in order to protect it from the anti-Semitism
that might result from too great a Jewish immigration.

In fact these attitudes were based in anti-Semitic feelings that were profoundly anchored in large segments of the population. All this led to the fatal
distinction between "political refugees" and "racial refugees" during the war,
which paved the way for refusing asylum to the latter. Subsequently this practice was introduced even in the treatment of military refugees. This is clearly
evident in a July 1942 government circular that provided for the following interpretation of Article 13 of the Hague Convention of 1907: "General rules for
admission cannot be established. Each individual case must be determined according to the circumstances. As a general rule, however, undesirable elements
(Jews, political extremists, persons suspected of espionage) should be kept
out."

Once war had broken out, the Swiss passed new regulations for refugees,
stricter than the earlier ones. On October 17, 1939, the Federal Council passed
a decree, Article 9 of which stipulated that foreigners entering Switzerland illegally could be expelled from the country without due process. This clause
was not, however, rigorously applied. Up to July 1942, twelve hundred new
Jewish refugees were nonetheless admitted. But as the situation of Jews in Germany deteriorated with deportations, especially from the countries of Central
Europe, increasing in 1941, and massive roundups and deportations occurring in France, Belgium, the Netherlands, and the Eastern European countries
in the summer of 1942, thousands of Jews tried to save their lives by entering
Switzerland.

Then came a most dramatic moment. On August 13, 1942, the head of the
federal Department of Police published a directive by which he practically
closed the border to all Jewish refugees. As stated, clear and decisive distinction was made between "political refugees" and "racial refugees," that is, Jews,
and asylum was denied the latter.

This wholly arbitrary distinction was clearly in complete contradiction to
Swiss traditions of the right of asylum. The Jews who had been driven from
their countries were victims of the Nazi "policy" that proclaimed them enemies of the German people. Who more than they could lay claim to the title
of political refugee?

Closing the borders to Jewish refugees had catastrophic consequences.
Tens of thousands of Jews were turned away from Switzerland and to a great
extent returned to the hands of the Gestapo. It is known today that at least

thirty to forty thousand Jews were turned away. Several thousand others had intended to seek refuge in Switzerland but gave up their plans when they learned of the fate of those who had been denied entry.

This inhumane decision occurred at a time when the deportations and massacres were reaching a high level. The responsible Swiss authorities knew what awaited those who were turned away. They were well aware of the fate of the deportees but nevertheless sent them to a certain death.

This very harsh regulation provoked an enormous reaction, not only on the part of the Jewish community but also from many other Swiss. Fundamentally it was one of the finest moments that I experienced in Switzerland. From the moderate right to the left there was a veritable intellectual revolution against these measures. I knew the spokesman for the moderate right, *Basler Nachrichten* editor-in-chief Dr. Albert Oeri. Also a federal councillor, he was a political figure cut on grand lines. The whole spectrum, from the right to the socialists, expressed profound opposition to Nazi methods and supported the moral imperative of not closing the Swiss door to all those who were knocking to be let in.

I should add that many of the churches also played an important role in opposing this government policy. Here, too a broad spectrum criticized the government. The voice of Zurich pastor Paul Vogt was particularly prominent. On his initiative Swiss Protestants financed housing for approximately eleven hundred Jewish refugees.

The popular reaction took numerous forms. In particular it found expression in a whole series of measures undertaken by the Jewish community as well as by a central office for refugees, which united all the organizations, Jewish and non-Jewish, political and religious, that were concerned with refugees. Gunzberg banker Paul Dreyfus, vice president of the Gemeindebund, the Swiss Federation of Jewish Communities, played an important role, as did the Protestant Gertrud Kurtz, who took in refugees during the entire war, deservedly earning the appellation "mother of the refugees." Both intervened with the minister of justice and police, Federal Councillor Eduard von Steiger, even interrupting his summer vacation at Mont Pélérin.

As a consequence of these interventions, the government announced relaxation of the regulations. Most important, Switzerland henceforth accepted an unlimited number of children up to sixteen years of age. It also accepted parents who accompanied them, which made it possible to organize the transportation of refugees.

Although the new instructions introduced exceptions, softening some of the measures, they maintained the distinction between political refugees and "racial" refugees. Now, however, it became possible to admit particularly pressing cases: the seriously ill, pregnant women, and refugees older than sixty-five.

These rules were further modified from time to time. As the eventual outcome of the war became clear, in particular after the fall of Mussolini's regime in 1943, Switzerland opened its door quite wide to Italian and Yugoslavian Jews coming from Italy.

When the war came to an end in 1945, the number of Jewish refugees in Switzerland totalled 28,500, of whom 7,000 had received asylum before the war. So Switzerland did, after all, save some Jews during the war. And few countries can claim to have saved so many.

But this does not mean that Switzerland could not have saved more. I am convinced that it could saved two or three times as many more Jews without serious consequences for the Swiss population, its food situation, the country's labor market, or its security concerns.

I cannot forget that while the Swiss pursued a generally harsh policy toward the Jews, they also opened the door wide for long periods, if not throughout the war, to other people. Among these were the so-called military refugees, who, according to the Hague Convention, had right of access to neutral countries. No fewer than 100,000 persons categorized as internees, escaped prisoners, deserters, and hospitalized persons were present in Switzerland at the end of the war. There was never any discussion over deciding whether these persons should be admitted. And if Switzerland was capable of accommodating them, it could have absorbed at least an equivalent number of Jews.

Many Jews who enjoyed the right of asylum in Switzerland complained of the roughness with which they were treated, sometimes even brutal, and of a lack of basic respect due fellow human beings. These claims certainly were true and applied in particular to the behavior of some surveillance personnel. The Swiss were not prepared to receive such a wave of refugees. They had to improvise reception and other services with personnel resources that were not up to the task. Often they did this as hotel keepers would have. When they interned people in a camp, they opened a "current account," just as in a hotel. They charged refugees 3.50 Swiss francs a night and billed them an additional amount for food and for other supplies and services. They forced refugees to turn over the money they had with them, and from this they deducted the costs of room and board. They then submitted to the Dutch, Belgian, and other governments bills for the living costs of those refugees who had not the means to pay. In the refugees' circumstances, this approach often displayed little grace.

This having been said, and despite the fact that I often sympathized with the internees in the camps and hotels, I always said that gaining a haven for more refugees was the most important concern, even if we had to accept often unpleasant treatment. And I directed my efforts to that goal.

I have already noted that I consistently abstained from meddling in purely Swiss politics. But I did support the activity of Swiss Jewish organizations. And I exploited my contacts with the Protestant churches in Switzerland in favor of the admission of new refugees. As I have indicated, I forwarded virtually all my significant intelligence to them and to the World Council of Churches, one of whose officers, the Rev. Alphons Koechlin, president of the Swiss League of Evangelical Churches (SEK), was in touch with the minister of justice. I also shared information with the head of the office for Protestant refugees in Suisse Romande, Col. Henri-Louis Henriod, who had relations with General Guisan and his associates. Both of these men intervened with the federal authorities on several occasions.

I utilized these channels in particular to try to push the government attitude in a more liberal and receptive direction. Occasionally we achieved moments of success. For example, when the borders were completely closed, authorities granted the churches the right to submit lists of particularly meritorious persons who ought to be admitted to Swiss territory in the event they appeared at the border.

Building on this precedent, we also obtained permission to draw up similar lists based upon other characteristics, and we submitted these. I detested proceeding in this way. Making and submitting lists was too much like playing God. It was clear that all those whom we did not recall, who had not stamped themselves on our memories, would be excluded. In addition, this method made us dependent on the goodwill of authorities and deprived us of much of our freedom of action.

Some additional steps I took during this period are likely to be of interest to numbers of readers.

First, on behalf of refugees I maintained ongoing relations with the representatives of the various governments. Second, I cultivated no less close relations with Jewish refugees in Switzerland, of these various nationalities. Among them were many former community leaders, often with a great deal of experience. This gave me an opportunity to consult these knowledgeable people both on the situation in their respective communities and on actions that might be undertaken on behalf of the latter, and to meet the needs of their Jewish refugee nationals in Switzerland.

Among these former leaders were figures of the first order from Austria, Belgium, France, the Netherlands, Hungary, Italy, Romania, Czechoslovakia, and Yugoslavia. On one occasion, toward the end of the war, I formed a small consultative committee at the WJC with representatives of these communities. The views of these leaders were of great help to me in understanding and interpreting the situation in their own countries. At the same time such contacts also prompted them to maintain and enhance communication with their home countries, which resulted in our obtaining considerable amounts of complementary intelligence.

My relations with Italian Jewish leaders are worth separate mention. When in 1943, after Mussolini's first fall from power and the subsequent creation of the German-sponsored Italian Social (or Salò) Republic in northern Italy, a large number of Jews arrived in Switzerland, I obtained from the Representative Council of Italian Jews in New York substantial amounts of aid. Together with representatives of Italian Jews in Switzerland, we decided to use these funds to create a Jewish school. It operated in Weggis on Lake Lucerne. This initiative permitted one hundred children, formerly students at the Jewish secondary school in Milan, to continue their studies for a year under the direction of their own teachers, who also had taken refuge in Switzerland. At the end of the school year, external examinations were organized under the supervision of royal Italian education authorities.

In Switzerland the Jewish community had always been a small minority of the population. During much of the first half of the century it amounted to about twenty thousand persons. This number had been fairly stable since 1910, and constituted less than 0.5 percent of the total population. Today this proportion is even smaller because the general population has increased.

During the period under consideration here, about half of these Jews did not have Swiss nationality. In 1930, 45.5 percent of Jews were aliens; in 1941, 47.1 percent. In 1950 this figure fell to less than 40 percent. For this reason the Jews of Switzerland have had very little influence, playing a restricted role in politics, publishing, journalism, and the economy. Parliament had one or two Jewish members from the Socialist party, sitting most of the time on the opposition benches. These were people of great character.

In the press world there were no Jewish journalists. At the head of the great financial and industrial institutions Jews were scarcely represented. Jews made up an active element in business and the professions. They founded some well-regarded private banks, clothing stores, and a number of small watch-making factories. But, even taking this into account, they could not be said to be represented in the senior administration of the banks, insurance companies, or the metallurgical and chemical industries, or the world-famous watchmaking firms that were the force behind the Swiss economy.

Clearly the Swiss Federation of Jewish Communities could not remain indifferent to the numerous events that at times affected the very foundation of the legal rights of Jews. For example, the Federation intervened vigorously in February 1941 when the official military publication *Armeé et Patrie* (*Army and Fatherland*) published a virulently anti-Semitic article that singled out Jews as inassimilable, going so far as to call for special status for them. As a consequence of the protest, the minister of defense expressed his regrets and promised sanctions against those responsible.

On another occasion it was a matter of reacting against the confiscation of Swiss Jews' property in occupied France. In response to a written question in the Swiss parliament, the government replied in part that insofar as Jews in France were subject to particular regulations, these were questions of public order, which then also applied to foreign nationals. This risked creating a very dangerous precedent. On the one hand it was contrary to the provisions of French-Swiss international treaties guaranteeing equal treatment of each other's citizens. On the other hand this was equivalent to a Swiss government admission that foreign powers could discriminate at will against any Swiss citizen.

At the insistence of Professor Paul Guggenheim of the postgraduate Institute of International Studies in Geneva, the Federation of Jewish Communities of Switzerland intervened with the Swiss government. The government finally effected an elegant retreat tactic, denying to all the right to discriminate among Swiss citizens. But the government also pointed out that in actual circumstances the protection of Swiss Jewish interests was, in fact, impossible.

Moreover Swiss Jews were arrested in occupied France simply because they were Jews. The Federation of Jewish Communities had to intervene with the government on behalf of thirty Jewish Swiss citizens who had been arrested in this fashion. Switzerland did finally call for their return, demanding that no discrimination be made among its citizens. The Jews were released.

General military censorship was imposed in Switzerland during the war. The fashion in which this censorship was implemented made it evident on several occasions that those who experienced it had no particular sympathy for Jews. Censorship was exercised in particular in order to maintain neutrality and, relatedly, to preclude published attacks on the German Reich. The censors did not look favorably on reports about the fate of German Jews and of Jews in other countries. Occasional incidents revealed a significant measure of anti-Semitism. The constraints of censorship even prevented the Jewish newspapers from publishing accounts of and testimony on the anti-Jewish atrocities in Hungary and Poland.

We understood that the military authorities' principal motivation was to avoid trouble with Germany, but we were obliged to be extremely critical of that policy.

My relations with the Jewish community of Switzerland were quite normal at the beginning of the war. The Federation of Jewish Communities of Switzerland was a member of the World Jewish Congress, and it represented Swiss Jews at the first congress of the WJC in 1936. Federation delegates attended all our meetings, and we enjoyed quite close relations with them. During the first year of the war, the president of the Federation, Saly Mayer, came to Geneva more than once to visit our offices and discuss matters with us.

Things changed somewhat after the defeat of France, though it is difficult to date this development precisely. I had the impression that the moment the central office of the WJC was to be transferred from Paris to New York and, to a large extent, to London, President Saly Mayer distanced himself from us in order not to violate what in his mind constituted Swiss neutrality. I believe our relations had absolutely nothing to do with Swiss neutrality, which was the position of the government with regard to other governments. But when the United States entered the war in December 1941, the Swiss government demonstrated that it too sought to establish more distance between itself and an organization with its vital centers in Allied countries.

I was not happy with the Federation's policy toward the Swiss government, especially on the issue of the admission of refugees. I judged that Mayer, as president of the Federation, instead of being the representative of the Jews to the authorities, was more and more becoming the government's representative to the Jews. He was confident in his good relations with the authorities. He believed that there lay the guarantee of the security of Swiss Jewry.

At the WJC we did not share this opinion. Many of my friends, in particular Erwin Haymann, Veit Wyler, and Benjamin Sagalowitz, were of like mind. We believed that at the time we ought to rely much more on public opinion and find support among the powerful elements of the country, among the popular forces of democracy. By these I mean political parties, trade unions, and professional associations, bodies of the sort that would also have to be mobilized to defend the rights of the Jewish community.

The reserved attitude of the president of the Federation did not prevent me from having cordial relations with many of its leaders and with the presidents of the local communities. They shared my opinion and together tried to influence the Federation's policy toward a more resolute and effective stand.

This conflict eventually led to a change in the presidency of the Jewish community. The new president, Saly Braunschweig, adopted a more courageous stance. The new executive closed the distance between itself and the World Jewish Congress in the last year of the war. I was then invited to be part of a Federation-sponsored special commission, charged with responsibility to make proposals on Jewish problems in the postwar period. I even became the editor of the commission's report, which the Federation published.

During the last phase of the war, most of us involved in this struggle took a few more liberties. Along with Professor Guggenheim I lobbied the Political Department several times, encouraging it to act with greater determination in its efforts to save the Hungarian Jews. We also discussed with senior officials of the Political Department a number of general problems that affected the Jewish situation. For quite a long time I was in touch with officials in the section that was in charge of the representation of foreign interests. This section was particularly well informed on what was happening in the various countries, including the situation of the Jews. We had cooperated with these officials for a sufficiently long period that together we tried to alleviate the situation to the extent that this was possible.

More than a decade after the end of the war, the Swiss government asked Professor Carl Ludwig, state councillor for Basel, to prepare a comprehensive report on Swiss refugee policy from 1933 to 1955. Professor Ludwig consulted both Sagalowitz and me at great length. Sagalowitz himself submitted a great deal of documentation in the name of the Federation. Professor Ludwig's 1957 report is extremely honest. Concealing nothing, he exposes the sad reality of the period. And this is to Switzerland's credit. Ludwig's report led to a revision in all the regulations affecting refugees.

Some other historical works that deal with this dramatic period in Switzerland also are honest and frankly expose the facts and errors that were committed. This is true of Professor Edgar Bonjour's monumental nine-volume work on Swiss neutrality. In the course of its preparation he had access to all the civil and military archives. Another important work is Jean-Claude Favez's study of the position of the International Committee of the Red Cross during the war, a work that deals with the Nazi concentration camps.

After the war I drew some rather odd satisfaction from one aspect of dealing with Swiss policy toward refugees. One fine day in December 1946, Saly

Mayer, who previously had several contacts with me because the Joint, which he represented, had forbidden cooperation with the WJC, came up to me during the Zionist congress in Basel. He asked for an urgent meeting at the hotel where both of us were staying. It seemed that he wanted to discuss something critical, and so I accepted the invitation despite the late hour. It was a quarter to midnight when we began our "discussion."

Mayer kept me for about two hours in order to get me to understand, in his rather convoluted language and without giving me a chance to speak, that, in the end, he had not been so ill-disposed and that he had a great deal of respect for what I had done during the war. Despite our difference of opinion, he implied, he understood my position.

Saly Mayer was a rather curious man. He did not speak in simple sentences. Part of what he wanted to express always remained obscure. Often he purposely let some doubt about his statements remain. When I think of him, I always think of Mynheer Peeperkorn in Thomas Mann's novel *The Magic Mountain.* That enigmatic character rarely completed a sentence, and his discourse was rather muddled. But everyone respected him greatly. He managed to prevail by force of personality. The same was essentially true of Mayer.

I also drew a measure of satisfaction from a meeting requested by Heinrich Rothmund. For many years the head of the federal police, he was certainly one of several officials primarily responsible for the Swiss policy on refugees. The positions that Rothmund advocated and defended were shared and supported by a number of senior officials; these were the successive ministers of the Department of Justice and Police, initially Councillor Johannes Baumann and later Councillor von Steiger. Moreover the Swiss government was a collegial body and as such took collective responsibility for its policies.

The federal councillors defended their political programs before the Swiss parliament in the name of the Federal Council. And that legislature, which over the course of the years held a series of important debates on the refugee question, regularly supported and approved the very cautious and hence restrictive executive policy.

On several occasions the Jewish community of Switzerland was in touch with federal councillors in order to inform them of the true situation and to try to persuade them to adopt more liberal policies. My friend Sagalowitz was specially assigned to this work, which he performed energetically. He certainly influenced several speeches in parliament on the situation as it actually was. But this brought practically no change in government policy. In fact, in each instance parliament reaffirmed its position.

Some time before we met, Rothmund had stepped down as police chief. He had taken leave and was working in Geneva as the representative of the Intergovernmental Committee for Refugees. It was in 1947, I believe, that he telephoned to ask that we meet.

Rothmund came to my office where for several hours he explained to me his policy and his motives during the entire war period. He tried to convince me that fundamentally his behavior toward would-be Jewish refugees was decent, and that he had wanted to do his best. I concluded from this exchange that he wanted now to go down in history with a reputation omitting what appeared to be questionable actions on his part. I had never had any relations or any discussion with him before, and I had never met him when he was exercising his authority. This effort at *ex post facto* justification of past activities on the part of the all-powerful head of the federal police before an official of the World Jewish Congress, himself a stateless refugee and without papers, was not lacking in irony.

When the Ludwig report was published, the former federal councillor and head of the Department of Justice and Police, Eduard von Steiger, was invited by federal authorities to comment on the report as concerned the period during which he was president of the department (1941–1951). In his response, von Steiger cited those Ludwig report passages that referred to my own wartime intelligence on the situation of Jews in various countries, as well as that which Sagalowitz had furnished Ludwig.

In his statement von Steiger said that he had had no connection with me or with Sagalowitz and that the information to which the report referred had not been known to him. I had never had direct communications with the senior officials of the Swiss confederation. Nevertheless I had communicated most of my reports to the World Council of Churches; it was through this channel that the principal content of the intelligence that I had at my disposal was made known to the head of the Department of Justice and Police. Moreover, today no one any longer contends that the Swiss government was truly unaware of the dramatic situation of the Jews in Europe during the war.

Concluding this chapter, I will add my voice to that of Professor Edgar Bonjour, in his celebrated *Histoire de la neutralité suisse* (*History of Swiss Neutrality*), which well expresses my own thoughts:

> The Swiss ship was not overloaded, nor even filled. Even in an era when
> political waves were running high, she could, without capsizing, have taken
> on a very much greater number of refugees. It is certain that compared to
> that of earlier eras, more recent Swiss asylum policy appears more complex,

more problematic. It required the deployment of a far larger number of administrative personnel than previously. But the judgment to be delivered on the last period of war is much less favorable as concerns the spirit of sacrifice on the part of authorities and individuals than that due earlier periods. The pitiless measures of those charged with implementing asylum policy and the insufficiently evident private will to assist can be explained by an international situation that was at times very disturbing and by the precariousness of food supplies.

But these are not at all considerations that oblige us to excuse this official policy of restraint toward these asylum-seekers, who had death at their heels, this lack of understanding for Switzerland's humanitarian mission. Our status as human beings and citizens gives all of us the right to refuse our approbation, after having retrospectively judged the facts.

In the end it took fifty years for the highest Swiss authorities to feel the obligation to recognize the wrongs their predecessors had done to the Jews. At an extraordinary meeting of the federal chambers, commemorating the fiftieth anniversary of the end of World War II, Kaspar Villiger, the president of the Swiss Federation, made a solemn declaration in the name of the Federal Council:

> There is a subject that the "external circumstances" prevailing during that period do not permit us to justify. This is, in effect, the matter of the numerous Jews who awaited certain death after they were turned away from the Swiss border. Was the ship truly full? Would Switzerland have risked sinking if it had engaged itself more fully than it did on behalf of the persecuted? Did antisemitic feeling in our country play a role in this matter? Did we always do everything that was possible on behalf of the persecuted and the exiled?
>
> For me it is beyond doubt that the policy practiced by the people and by the parliament with respect to Jews obliges us to carry a great share of responsibility. Germany was frightening. We feared that mass immigration would feed an overpopulation of foreigners. We sensed the political thrust of an antisemitism that existed in our country as well. All these concerns at times weighed much heavier in the balance than our tradition of asylum and our humanitarian principles. Painful conflicts of interest, in the wake of inordinate fear, were also resolved to humanity's loss. The stamp "Jew" was a concession, a concession contrary to its own objectives, that Switzerland made to Germany.

This stamp was approved by Switzerland in 1938. At other times too we have made the worse choice in the name of a national interest taken in its narrowest sense.

The Federal Council profoundly regrets this wrong, while remaining conscious that such an aberration is in the final instance inexcusable. . . . We can only bow our heads silently before those whom we led into suffering and captivity, even into death. We can only bow our heads before the members of their families and their descendants.

This same shift of public opinion gave rise to the November 1995 posthumous legal reinstatement of Paul Grüninger, the former head of the St. Gall police, twenty-three years after his death and fifty-five years after his condemnation and dismissal for violation of his official duties. After the *Anschluss* of Austria, Paul Grüninger had admitted to Swiss territory hundreds of Austrian Jewish refugees in violation of federal instructions. The reopening of criminal proceedings and the annulment of his conviction, leading to acquittal, constitute an extremely rare, if not unique, case in the history of Swiss jurisprudence. Recognition of strictly humanitarian motives underlay this reversal. These motives had been completely ignored in the 1940 judgment, a condemnation after Grüninger was found guilty of falsifying documents. This act of rehabilitation testifies to the new consciousness of a generation that was not implicated in the horrors of war and the grave mistakes that were committed at that time. This new consciousness allowed the St. Gall court not only to transform the infamous condemnation into acquittal but also to pay grateful homage to a man who saved Jews.

[THREE]

The Struggle for Human Rights

THE STRUGGLE to win respect for human rights has always been a central task of the World Jewish Congress. The two great objectives of the Congress, as defined and adopted by the founding assembly of the WJC in 1936, were: first, the struggle against Hitler and Nazism and, second, the protection of the large Jewish minorities in Central and Eastern Europe. This second mandate was given to me when I joined the WJC.

If defense of human rights has always been at the heart of our concerns, the WJC clearly had as its primary goal the protection of Jews and Jewish communities. In any case, we never considered that the rights we claimed for Jews were exclusive privileges. On the contrary, we have always believed that enjoyment of such rights ought to be guaranteed to all human beings. From this derives a concept of universal respect for human rights, an approach that strives for the protection not only of the rights of the individual but also those of linguistic, religious, and ethnic groups and communities. Through its constant activity, the Congress became one of the great protagonists in the struggle for human rights throughout the world, and we have often been in the vanguard of that fight.

This movement began long before the creation of the WJC. In some respects it is even possible to describe the history of the Jews in the modern era as that of their struggle for human rights. This began with the efforts for the emancipation of the Jews at the end of the eighteenth century, the commencement of the modern movement for human rights for all. The struggle for equal rights for Jews at the same time constituted a step on the way toward recognition of human and civil rights in all their importance.

Before moving to the modern period, let me say a little about Hebrew law. I am convinced that it is not by chance that the Jews are the champions of human rights in modern times. In this they are following in the great biblical tradition, where the concepts of the unity of the human family and the equality of races are sacred. The belief that all humankind is descended from Adam and not from different fathers of different colors reflects this notion of human equality as a foundation of Jewish tradition. The Ten Commandments and biblical law that demand respect for other people—foreigners and even slaves—are cornerstones of this conception that Jews have observed throughout their long history, just as it is the position of the modern Jewish community. Our traditional sources do not directly expound the concept of rights, but rather that of duties—duties toward God and toward one's fellows, and this is but a different way of expressing the same basic idea.

The modern conception of human rights has two principal sources. In the New World the constitutions of Massachusetts, Pennsylvania, and several other American states led to the principles of the U.S. Constitution in 1787. In Europe the decisive tradition sprang from the French Revolution, which after struggles to overcome many obstacles led to the adoption in 1789 of the Declaration of the Rights of Man and of the Citizen and, two years later, recognition of full rights of citizenship for Jews.

We know the important contribution of the great actors of the French Revolution to this maturation of outlook, of which the emancipation of the Jews was one consequence: Mirabeau, Robespierre, Condorcet, Adrien Du Port, Clermont-Tonnerre.*

The flaw in their conception was "to refuse everything to the Jews as a nation and to grant them everything as individuals" (Clermont-Tonnerre to the National Assembly on December 23, 1789). This concept of the French Revolution found its corrective and complement in the twentieth century with the recognition of the rights of minorities and the victory of Zionism.

This struggle for equal rights played a role in all the great European political congresses of the nineteenth and twentieth centuries. The Congress of Vienna in 1815, which fundamentally influenced the destiny of Europe, dealt

---

*These men were leaders of the Revolution at various stages. Adrien Du Port and Abbé Grégoire proposed in 1791 that the Jews be considered "free and equal" citizens.—ED.

with the equality of German Jews without resolving the problem. The Berlin Congress of 1878 marked an important new stage in this process. Disraeli and Bismarck obliged Romania officially to respect religious freedom and the equal rights of Jews. Nineteenth-century international conferences also secured the rights of Christians in certain Muslim countries.

The Versailles peace conference of 1919 was of particular importance for Jews. There a system for the protection of minorities was instituted. In Versailles, representatives of the Jewish communities of Central and Eastern Europe, including those of Russia, Ukraine, Poland, Romania, and Lithuania, joined delegates of the American and Canadian Jewish Congresses in order to present their claims jointly.

At the peace conference they formed the Committee of Jewish Delegations—the precursor of the World Jewish Congress. As one group they presented the great powers with their demands for the recognition of individual and collective rights for religious, ethnic, cultural, and linguistic minorities.

Leon Motzkin was the central figure of the committee. The most important American spokesmen were Stephen Wise, Julian Mack, and Louis Marshall. Thanks to their work and their lobbying, it proved possible to erect a system for the protection of minorities, guaranteed by the League of Nations, either in peace treaties or in treaties and declarations that had been specifically formulated to that end.

The system established in Versailles foresaw for the first time rules according to which protection would not be limited to the rights of individuals. Protection would be extended equally to the recognition of the collective rights the committee espoused.

The representatives of the Committee of Jewish Delegations also called for the establishment of a national Jewish homeland in Palestine, as had been foreseen in the Balfour Declaration of November 1917. But it was the Zionist delegation, led by Chaim Weizmann, that determined and directed lobbying action on behalf of the national homeland.

These treaties and declarations in principle guaranteed the protection of the life, liberty, property, and equality of rights of all, without distinction, whatever their language, race, or religion. The texts also sought to guarantee the complete freedom of religious practice for all creeds. Equality before the law was enhanced by opening to all citizens access to state employment of all kinds.

A vitally important clause for the Jews of the Eastern European countries guaranteed freedom of use of their respective languages by all the affected minorities, in both public and private life, which entailed recognition of the cultural identity of minorities.

Other clauses of the treaties on minorities guaranteed to citizens belonging to a minority the right to create, administer, and control, at their own cost,
charitable, religious, and social institutions, schools and educational estab-
lishments, and to benefit in equitable fashion from public funds designated
for such areas. Here there was much more than simple equality; there was veritable cultural and religious autonomy.

This legal framework for the protection of minorities was placed under the
guarantee of the League of Nations. The League set up a system to supervise the
implementation of the clauses of the treaties on minorities and determined pro-
cedural rules for communications and appeals in the event of infractions. The
regulations in particular foresaw the creation of a "Committee of Three," composed of the president ex officio and two members of the council of the League
of Nations appointed by him to examine such complaints. This system functioned fairly well until 1934 when Poland renounced the treaty it had signed.

The weakness of the system lay in the fact that it was not generalized and
did not apply to all states. The countries on which the treaties or declarations
for the protection of minorities had been imposed considered themselves discriminated against; they experienced a measure of humiliation at having to
guarantee freedoms that other states were not obliged to observe. This was the
principal reason offered by Poland for repudiating its obligations, which led
to the progressive dislocation of the overall system of protection.

The other vital error made in Versailles was that Germany was not subject
to the same rules for the protection of minorities. Consequently, when the
Nazis took power and began to implement anti-Jewish measures of a violently
discriminatory nature, the League of Nations, without a legal basis, felt it
could not intervene.

One exception did, however, exist. It concerned the Jews of Upper Silesia and
became famous as the Bernheim Petition. After the plebiscite on Upper Silesia that had been foreseen in the Versailles treaty, and the following division of
the territory between Germany and Poland in 1922, these two countries
signed a special treaty concerning the inhabitants of this region.

This treaty introduced, for a fifteen-year period, provisions for the protection of minorities that had been accepted by Poland in the Versailles treaty
as they pertained to German and Polish nationals living on either side of the
new border. This treaty was also placed under the guarantee of the League of
Nations.

When the Nazis' anti-Jewish measures were introduced in 1933, a German
Jewish citizen who was a native of Upper Silesia, a man named Franz Bernheim,

who had been dismissed from his position as a consequence of racial discrimination, challenged this legislation before the League of Nations.

One of the members of the Committee of Jewish Delegations (the WJC, which would succeed it, at the time existed only in embryonic form), the Czech lawyer Emile Margulies, pleaded this case. The evidence was clear and irrefutable. Nazi Germany gave in, and we won.

This was a considerable victory. For more than four years Nazi laws were not applicable in that part of Upper Silesia subject to the Polish-German treaty of 1922. Jewish public officials continued to exercise their functions there. Jewish doctors and lawyers worked normally at their professions. While throughout Germany terror and anti-Jewish discrimination reigned, none of it existed in this German region protected by an international treaty. Several thousands of Jews could calmly prepare for and carry out their emigration plans without interference from Nazi authorities, which thus saved their lives.

The Polish-German treaty was scheduled to expire in 1937. The World Jewish Congress made great efforts to have the agreement extended. In fact this was one of my first tasks at the Congress. Backed up with memoranda and the expertise of eminent jurists, we appealed to the great democratic powers to help us and support this undertaking. But our efforts were in vain, for neither Germany nor Poland was interested in prolonging the terms of the agreement.

A place where action by the Committee of Jewish Delegations (and of the future WJC) led to a resounding success, despite the fact that Germany was not subject to the obligations of the treaty on minorities, was the Saar.

In 1934 political action was undertaken with regard to the plebiscite to be held in January 1935 in the territory of the Saar. As it was foreseen that the plebiscite would lead to a German victory and that as a consequence the Saar would return to Germany, a great effort was made to guarantee the rights of the Jews who were living there.

These efforts, undertaken before the Council of the League of Nations, finally led to a declaration by the German government committing itself before the Council—in the event the territory should return to Germany—for one year to take no measures against its inhabitants prompted by religion, race, or language and to permit residents of the Saar to emigrate, taking all their goods with them.

This agreement was reached as a consequence of negotiations conducted at the Council of the League of Nations, in which Italy played an important role. The efforts of Nahum Goldmann and his direct contacts with Mussolini were particularly evident in brokering this agreement, which permitted the

Jews of the Saar to emigrate without constraint after the plebiscite. All of this occurred before I joined the WJC.

My first great battle in the struggle for the rights of Jewish minorities—my trial by fire—was waged against policies of the government of Romania. At the end of 1937 that country formed the first fascist and openly anti-Semitic government in Eastern Europe. Its leader, Octavian Goga, was an experienced politician. His theorist and inspiration was Alexander Cuza, an academic who was well known as the titular leader of anti-Semitic extremists. From the outset their government adopted a program that was openly anti-Jewish.

The Goga-Cuza administration proclaimed the elimination of Jews from Romanian life as its central goal and took as its model the anti-Semitic legislation of the Third Reich. The government declared that its policy was aimed at establishing a regime based on the dominance of the Romanian "race" and that it considered people belonging to other races as alien to the state.

It announced its intention to strip between 250,000 and 500,000 Jews of their citizenship, as well as of their rights of settlement and residence. These individuals, claimed the government, had no legitimate claim to Romanian nationality. The government began to dismiss Jews from public office; it announced that certain professions and activities would be closed to Jews; it began the expropriation of Jewish agricultural businesses; it excluded Jews from commercial activity in rural communities; it prohibited them from employing non-Jewish servants; and it warned Jewish lawyers, doctors, and members of other professions, as well as artists and journalists, that they would be denied the right to work. And so on. The whole range of Nazi prohibitions and exclusions was imposed in this country which, under the terms of treaties on the protection of minorities, was bound to respect the equality of all its citizens and minorities.

We reacted immediately. I was commissioned to prepare a petition through which we would demand that the League of Nations adopt urgent procedures as foreseen in the Council resolution of June 27, 1921.

We resubmitted our petition on January 13, 1938, a day when the Council of the League of Nations was in session. A whole team had worked with me day and night for more than a week to prepare the document. With its appendices, including a long memorandum of statistical data concerning the Jewish population of Romania, and clippings from the Romanian and foreign press, the petition made a document of about a hundred pages.

At the last minute the meeting of the Council of the League of Nations adjourned because of the fall of the French government. While we waited for the next session, the Romanian government pursued its anti-Jewish activities. The culminating point was the decree of January 22, 1938, which ordered a revision of the citizenship status of all Jews in the country and prohibited local authorities from issuing Jews the documents they needed to prove their rights as citizens.

This placed Romanian Jews in an extremely critical situation. I had already been confronted on several occasions in the course of the years 1936–1937 with cases where the Romanian nationality of Jews individually or in groups had been challenged, particularly in the country's new provinces.

Since 1919 successive Romanian governments had refused to grant Romanian citizenship to Jews from the provinces that had been turned over to Romania by virtue of the Versailles treaty. This affected Jews in Transylvania, Dobruja, and Bessarabia, where half of the 800,000 Romanian Jews lived. Attempts were made, through bureaucratic and police quibbles over their citizenship, to prevent hundreds of thousands of these Jews from earning their living. In the face of the disastrous situation of these people, we fought for their integration as citizens of the Romanian state.

I was familiar with this sort of problem. The January 1938 decree from the Romanian authorities, however, gave the issue a new and dramatic dimension. It was clearly aimed at the expulsion of Jews from all Romanian life and created a life-and-death problem for all the Jews in the country.

The Council of the League of Nations finally met two weeks later, on January 26, 1938. We had used the time to prepare a supplementary petition of about fifty pages, which confronted the defamatory accusations and declarations of the Romanian government and which noted all the anti-Semitic measures that had been promulgated by the Romanians in the meantime.

A few days before the opening of the Council meeting, the Romanian minister of foreign affairs, Istrate Micescu, arrived in Geneva to try to create a climate that would be favorable to Romania and to establish contact with the League of Nations secretariat, the various delegations, and above all the press.

In the face of this Romanian action, several members of the WJC executive, in particular Marc Jarblum (Paris), Rabbi Maurice Perlzweig (London), and Rabbi Mordechai Nurock (Riga), joined Dr. Goldmann in Geneva to reinforce our action. A press conference in our offices drew some fifty journalists from around the world and allowed us to explain the objectives of our petition.

A lively public debate ensued with Micescu, who did not shy away from employing tricks and lies. We responded blow for blow to his cynical declarations. I was constantly in the thick of it, communicating by telephone to the chief correspondents of the world press our responses to his phony allegations.

Let me here cite a personal event. During this period my parents, who were still living in Berlin, came to Geneva to celebrate with me my father's sixtieth birthday. The celebration was to take place on January 26, 1938. But this was the very day that the Council meeting was to begin and that we were to hold our large press conference. We had worked until six o'clock in the morning to complete updates to the file. My parents arrived while this work was in progress. There was no question of my taking time off, so a friend went to meet them at the station. On the 26th the entire Jewish delegation met at noon in the restaurant La Perle du Lac. My parents and I had lunch at a separate table. We had agreed to meet for dinner at the station restaurant. Then I went to the WJC offices. When I arrived at the station restaurant at about eight in the evening, I heard that Micescu had issued a new statement. I had to draft a reply and telephone it to eight press services. This unexpected development brought the entire Geneva WJC staff into action, and me first of all.

Completely seized by the urgency of the Romanian problem, I had to leave the dinner with my parents to make telephone calls. It was only toward 10:30 that I was able to rejoin them. All I could do was to buy a bottle of champagne at the station bar to celebrate my father's birthday in its last hour.

Our delegation was in nearly continuous contact with the League of Nations secretariat and with the principal representatives of the states on the Council. I was personally in constant touch with the director of the section for minorities at the general secretariat of the League, the Norwegian Skylstadt.

We met, among others, the French minister of foreign affairs, Yvon Delbos; the British undersecretary for foreign affairs, Lord Cranborne; the Belgian minister of foreign affairs, Paul-Henri Spaak; and that of Sweden, Richard Sandler; as well as the Soviet ambassador, Yakov Suritz, and we obtained their support for our initiative.

After our briefing of the British, Anthony Eden, the foreign secretary, and Lord Cranborne immediately met Micescu and exerted a great deal of pressure on him. Meanwhile Stephen Wise had sought out President Roosevelt in Washington and had obtained from him a public statement in which he expressed his distaste at the persecution of racial and religious minorities and his indignation at the new repression, as well as at the exclusions from which the Jewish populations of Central and Eastern Europe were suffering.

Pressure from the great Western powers on Romania was intense. The League of Nations meeting concluded with a decision to turn down our request that the urgency clause be invoked. They did, however, de facto concede this status by immediately appointing a Committee of Three, made up of the president of the Council of the League of Nations ex officio, who was Iranian, and the foreign ministers of France and Great Britain. The committee was charged with dealing with the problems raised by our petition before the next session.

The president of the Council reserved the right immediately to consult his French and British colleagues to consider which nonofficial measures might be taken in the current situation. He viewed these results as a real success. In particular, people noted our innovative procedures to meet the situation. This was our first great battle as the World Jewish Congress, and we had fought well.

Pressure from the great Western powers continued in the weeks that followed, and on several occasions our representatives in Paris and London were called to the Quai d'Orsay and to the Foreign Office.

Finally, on February 10, 1938, when the Congress executive was meeting in Paris, the resignation of the Goga government was announced. I still remember the words with which Goga accompanied his resignation, "*Juda, du hast gesiegt*" ("Judah, you have won").

This arduous effort constituted one of our great political actions. We won because we succeeded in convincing the Western powers that their interests coincided with ours. Foreign policy is an art. You succeed when you finally convince your partners that their interests are identical, similar, or parallel, to your own.

Western powers such as Great Britain and France had substantial economic interests in Romania. Just as we, they feared that a long-lasting fascist, extremist regime in that country would have constituted a threat to their investments and to the stability of Europe. This is why they exploited our cause to oppose the Goga regime.

Unfortunately the benefits of this success did not last. One month later Hitler entered Austria. This disrupted the entire European equilibrium and made irrelevant the results of our political work. Nevertheless our action proved that under certain conditions and through systematic efforts, international agreements for the protection of minorities could be made to work and bar the ambitions of hate-motivated regimes.

After the Anschluss

The events that followed were tragic. The drama began with the March 1938 incorporation of Austria by the Reich and continued with the brutal action of the Nazi government against Czechoslovakia. This latter tragedy was played out at two distinct times: in September 1938, ending in Hitler's ultimatum to Czech President Edvard Beneš and in the Munich conference, and in March 1939 when Hitler's army invaded Czechoslovakia and transformed the western half of the country into the German protectorate of Bohemia and Moravia while the eastern half became the puppet Slovakia.

We were quite active during this whole crisis. But despite the protests we raised at the League of Nations and with the governments of the great powers, we could not achieve important results. After these events we concentrated our efforts on bringing relief by any means possible to the vast numbers of Jewish refugees from Austria and Czechoslovakia.

The time that followed the *Anschluss*, during which the carving up of Czechoslovakia was being prepared, was one of the most feverish activity that we experienced in Geneva. It was particularly in September–October 1938, at a time when Germany was exerting pressure on Czechoslovakia and when the Western powers gave in to Hitler's blackmail in Munich, that we in Geneva felt that the fate of the League of Nations, the fate of peace itself was being definitively played out. We were fully conscious that we were at a turning point in history, especially after the failure of the League of Nations sanctions against Fascist Italy as a consequence of its aggression against Ethiopia (then Abyssinia). This was the decisive moment when the destiny of the world was at stake. I shall never forget the torment we experienced during these events.

I was then part of a small group of young diplomats, officials from the consulates of various countries or from the secretariat of the League of Nations, and correspondents of the foreign press in Geneva. I don't know how this group came together. Perhaps I was included because I made myself useful to them by serving as interpreter. Each time the radio broadcast a speech by Hitler I made a simultaneous translation for the journalists and officials who didn't understand German well. This allowed them to prepare their commentaries almost immediately. In this way I formed ties of friendship with a number of them.

Our little group of young men used to meet every evening during those tragic months of September and October 1938 at the famous Bavaria restaurant, which was then popular with the best-known figures who worked at the League of Nations. The restaurant had long been a key locale for the exchange of information. The walls of the restaurant that was now serving as our headquarters were covered with superb caricatures, often quite humorous, of the upper crust of the League of Nations.

There was another reason, a very specific one, for these daily meetings at the Bavaria. During this entire period communications with Czechoslovakia were extremely poor, and the outside world was largely ignorant of what was happening there. The official representative of the Czech government in Geneva had the privilege of an hour's telephone conversation each evening with his minister. The Geneva correspondent of the *Prager Tagblatt*, the great German-language newspaper of Prague, had succeeded in persuading the Czech minister to give him ten minutes of this communication time each evening for his colleagues in Prague. After these phone calls, of course, all the correspondents of the foreign press threw themselves all over him to find out what he had learned so that they could in turn inform their own newspapers. Thus this journalist, taking advantage of the situation, succeeded in joining our circle, where he would otherwise never have been admitted. In fact this individual, who was also a novelist and who even described us in one of his novels, was not considered a very serious journalist. But this didn't prevent him from making a great career for himself in later years.*

The rest of the evening was given over to dancing in nightclubs. We tried to escape from reality in order to drive away our anxieties, our fear of the war, our deep troubles over what the next day held in store for us. We would dance until four in the morning to the "Lambeth Walk" and other juvenile tunes that were fashionable then. These corresponded well enough to the feeling of uncertainty that gripped us all.

The Jews of Danzig

The second great lobbying action that the WJC brought to the League of Nations during this period concerned the Jews of Danzig. A small Jewish community lived in that municipality that after World War I had been accorded the status of an autonomous "free city," with its existence and constitution guaranteed by the Council of the League of Nations.

When the Nazis won the elections in the Free City and began to introduce their anti-Semitic legislation and policies, we concluded that we ought to protest to the League of Nations against these violations of the Danzig constitution. We saw that the problem was much more than the violation of a small state; since this was a model state, existing under international guarantee, the introduction of anti-Semitic legislation there jeopardized the equal rights of Jews in all countries. If the League of Nations accepted state anti-Semitism in Danzig, it risked accepting it everywhere else.

---

*The person referred to is Janos Bekessy (1911–1977), better known as Hans Habe, who made a successful career after the war as a popular novelist.—ED.

So we brought the question before the responsible bodies of the League. In acting to defend the situation of the Jews of Danzig we also indirectly attacked the discriminatory legislation in the Reich as well. We did not have the means to combat Germany directly for not subscribing to the obligations of nondiscrimination with regard to minorities. Thus we exploited the case of Danzig, modeled as it was on the Third Reich example, in order to attack German anti-Semitic policies on the whole. We appealed unceasingly at all the relevant meetings of the League of Nations and its agencies, denouncing the increasing persecution of Jews in the Free City.

Until 1936 the League of Nations was represented in Danzig by a high commissioner who held the same fundamental principles as we did. This was the Irishman Sean Lester. But, inspired by the policy of appeasing Germany, practiced first by the British and then by the other countries, the League pursued a deliberate policy of compromise and abandonment.

It was then, in February 1937, that Carl Burckhardt of the International Committee of the Red Cross was appointed high commissioner to Danzig, on the recommendation of the British diplomatic corps. We know today that the idea came from Ernst von Weizsäcker, then the German ambassador in Bern. I have related earlier how I knew Burckhardt at the Institute. I greatly admired his writing, his books, his historical analyses, his cultivation; from time to time I had been invited to his beautiful home in Geneva.

The appointment of Burckhardt was the beginning of a period of additional tension for us. We knew very well what had led to his appointment, and we could not subscribe to a policy of appeasement. We were one of the groups most committed to maintaining resistance to the Nazi regime; our entire policy was oriented to that end.

We had reason to believe that Burckhardt would particularly try to help a number of individual Danzig Jews emigrate, and we were not opposed to such efforts. But we were obliged to maintain our principled position in regard to the treatment of *all* the Jews; we could not back away from our continuing denunciation of violations of the principles on which the League of Nations was founded.

Numerous WJC and League documents reflect our initiative in raising this issue on every appropriate occasion. At one time we submitted to the League of Nations a long memorandum in which we compared, article for article, the anti-Semitic legislation of the Third Reich with the introduction of the same measures in the Free City of Danzig. The only result we registered was the postponement of some of these measures.

For example, in 1937 the introduction of the "Aryan paragraph" in the Danzig bylaws was delayed for about a year. But it quickly became clear that the grim determination of the Nazis would make it impossible for our principles to prevail. We know the fate of Danzig, occupied by the Germans on the first day of World War II.

In our actions on behalf of the Free City we forcibly denounced the anti-Semitic policy of the Third Reich to world public opinion. If resonance with public opinion in democratic countries had any value, we did achieve that.

From the Protection of Minorities to the Defense of Human Rights

When war broke out in 1939, the system of collective security that had been established by the League of Nations, as well the framework for the protection of minorities that it had developed, disappeared.

We then addressed the question of how to erect a new security system and by what means we could assure the protection of Jewish communities in the future. The idea of establishing an Institute of Jewish Affairs, charged with studying postwar Jewish problems, developed out of our discussions. The original notion was to establish this institute in Geneva. Dr. Goldmann had invited Dr. Jacob Robinson of Kaunas, Lithuania, an international jurist with an encyclopedic knowledge of Jewish culture, to direct the institute.

The collapse of France in the summer of 1940 forced the modification of this project. The executive secretariat of the Congress, located in Paris, moved to New York, where Dr. Goldmann took up residence. In the end the executive also established the Institute for Jewish Affairs there.

During the first phase of the war many Jewish leaders attempted to forecast the problems that Jewry would have to face after the war, but these were posed in rather superficial fashion, based on the World War I experience. But the further evolution of the war, with its catastrophic consequences for the Jewish people, eventually dictated a different approach.

Among the first problems addressed by the Institute of Jewish Affairs was the protection of minorities, as those concerns had been envisaged at Versailles. Thus in 1943 a major study was published under the title *Were the Minorities Treaties a Failure?*, written by Jacob Robinson and several other eminent specialists in international law.

At the same time, however, the most terrible catastrophe that ever befell the Jewish people, the extermination of the vast majority of the Jews of Europe, was being carried out. Could one really return to the notion of minorities treaties for communities that had been completely annihilated, that in many cases represented only the remnants of the nine million European Jews who had lived just before the war? We believed that it would be difficult to request specific treaties for mere handfuls of survivors in countries where hundreds of thousands of Jews only recently had lived.

While the Institute of Jewish Affairs pursued the study of postwar problems, we were not the only ones wrestling with these questions. In that regard, it is especially appropriate to mention President Roosevelt's forward-looking "Four Freedoms" declaration to the U.S. Congress in January 1941. With Churchill, Roosevelt restated this declaration in August of the same year, and it became known as the Atlantic Charter. It had great resonance. It proposed, as the goals of the war, these same four freedoms:

Freedom of opinion,

Freedom of religion,

Freedom from want,

Freedom from fear.

The Institute of Jewish Affairs prepared a program for the postwar period, a proposal that would be debated at the extraordinary November 1944 conference of the WJC in Atlantic City. This important meeting came out in favor of a system of universal protection of human rights, and emphatically renounced special protection for minorities. It drew conclusions from the annihilation of most of European Jewry and from the experience of the League of Nations: a number of countries rebelled against a system that imposed obligations on some but left other countries free to act as they saw fit. What had to be devised was a global, universal regime of equality. The WJC pronounced itself in favor of universal protection of human rights, as did most who were working to improve the human condition.

For some time now we have seen a change in the very concept of the protection of minorities. After the collapse of the Soviet Union and the Communist regimes of Eastern Europe, nationalist movements making claims for cultural, linguistic, and ethnic freedoms have spread through all the countries of that part of the world, and we are again facing the notion of protecting minorities in order to solve these problems. I observe, not without a certain irony, how this issue is circling back around to its point of departure.

I suggested that the modern history of the Jews can be traced through their struggles for their rights. These efforts can be followed at the Congress of Vienna, the Congress of Berlin, the Versailles conference, and, at the last stage, the San Francisco Conference, which gave birth to the United Nations, the successor to the League of Nations.

In conformity with the decisions adopted in Atlantic City, the Jewish representatives in San Francisco actively sought to establish within the United Nations framework a system for the protection of human rights. It was intended that this system should be as complete and effective as possible. Consequently the Jewish organizations lobbied for the modification of the first draft of the United Nations Charter; in this they worked together with other humanitarian organizations, particularly those in the United States. I can affirm that the Jewish delegates played a leading role in the formulation of certain provisions of the draft charter.

The results of this work can be seen in the text of the San Francisco charter. Not limiting their efforts to the Preamble and to Article 1, which mention human rights among the objectives of the future United Nations organization, these delegates introduced the principle of respect for human rights in four or five other articles. In addition, they succeeded in securing the adoption of a charter provision that the human rights body would be the only such permanent commission.

Initially, the Jewish delegates wanted a universal bill of rights to be adopted in San Francisco. But that meeting afforded insufficient time to draft it. Once the United Nations had been established, its secretariat went to work to prepare the bill of rights. It turned to several jurists and asked, among others, the director of the Institute of Jewish Affairs of the WJC, Dr. Jacob Robinson, to write a draft.

When the new Commission for Human Rights met to begin its work, it was agreed that the undertaking would be divided into three parts: a universal declaration defining fundamental rights; an international pact with a constraining legal character, which would transform the rights so proclaimed into international obligations (in the end there would be two pacts); and measures to apply and implement them.

While work on the declaration and the convention advanced fairly well, substantial difficulties were encountered in the implementation procedures, which extended the negotiations for several years. It was there, in fact, that the member states, concerned for their sovereignty, raised the greatest number of obstacles.

Some countries believed that such measures would constitute interference in their internal affairs. The World Jewish Congress, however, insisted on the decisive importance of implementation rules and constantly applied itself to strengthen them.

The Commission on Human Rights accomplished work of remarkable quality. It was inspired by an international team of eminent representatives from the various governments, among whom the leading figures were Eleanor Roosevelt, who chaired the Commission for several years; Professor René Cassin, the French statesman and professor of international law; Professor Fernand Dehousse, the outstanding Belgian jurist; Charles Malik, a Lebanese philosopher and preeminent theologian, who would later become president of the General Assembly of the United Nations; and Mahmud Azmi, the celebrated Egyptian journalist and writer, who chaired the Commission some years later. Agda Rossel of Sweden, Hope E. Whitlam of Australia, Hernan Santa Cruz of Chile, and Hansu Mehta of India all contributed to the universal nature of the deliberations.

For more than forty years from 1946, I participated in the work of the UN Commission on Human Rights, where I had a place as an observer by virtue of the consultative status of the World Jewish Congress. This advisory capacity gave us the right to attend meetings, to submit written briefs, and to address the Commission orally. On the Commission there were generally two WJC representatives, at times even three of us.

I should particularly mention here my colleague Dr. Franz-Rudolf Bienenfeld, the eminent Austrian jurist and at that time director of the legal department of the WJC in London. I collaborated closely with him and backed him fully in his efforts to innovate, in opposition to some of our colleagues in New York who were much more conservative. Bienenfeld had a rich legal imagination and was an original thinker. There is a general tendency among jurists to want to maintain order and the status quo. For my part, I have always been on the side of those who understand that the law evolves and can be changed. I had learned from the eminent jurist Kelsen that each judicial act is creative and that the techniques of law must be utilized to generate innovation.

One of my friends, Professor Alexander Pekelis, who came from Odessa and who later taught law in Florence and New York, told me one day: "Conservative jurists are the greatest enemies of the Jewish people and the obstacle to all progress." He urged me to convince Nahum Goldmann of this truth. Pekelis was a revolutionary jurist who had considerable influence on the evolution of jurisprudence in the United States in the area of the court's examination of the constitutionality of laws and acts of government.

Bienenfeld was a jurist of the same stripe. He understood that if you want to change the world, you have to have new ideas and you must try to incorporate them in the new judicial order to be created.

This was not always easy. Before every Commission on Human Rights meeting, usually held in Geneva, we received a memorandum from the central office in New York telling us that we had to present and defend the WJC view-point at the Commission. On his side, Bienenfeld would arrive from London with his own memorandum, much more constructive and filled with new ideas. At that point a number of telephone calls or telegrams commonly were exchanged with New York, with Bienenfeld and the central office maintaining their respective positions. Then it was up to me to try to resolve the matter. I would set to work in Geneva to draft a third text that tried to reconcile the different points of view. But I must say that I definitely leaned toward Bienenfeld's innovative ideas, which I found promising and productive, while still trying not to offend our colleagues in New York. Thus I had considerable influence on the political line of the Congress in this area. Bienenfeld and I worked quite smoothly together and were not content merely to submit written communications to the Commission; we also intervened orally to defend our positions.

As our consultative status authorized, we also established permanent contacts with some members of the Commission, to whom we set out our points of view in order to win their agreement and their support for our proposals. In this we succeeded fairly well. In fact, even though the positions of the major powers' representatives were generally strictly fixed by instructions from their governments, those of the middle-sized and smaller countries were much more flexible. Thanks to them, on several occasions we obtained an affirmative vote from the Commission against the resistance of the major powers.

Indeed, on the whole we obtained stunning results. At least five articles of the Universal Declaration of Human Rights bear the mark of the World Jewish Congress. That is, without our participation they would never have been drafted or would have had a very different tenor.

It was then easier to work at the United Nations and to influence its decisions than is the case today. At that time the UN had only some fifty members; now this number has more than tripled. The purely technical work there was much simpler. And this, in part, may explain our achievements.

Two or three examples will illustrate our successes. Article 26 of the Universal Declaration of Human Rights states: "Everyone has the right to education." The article then goes on to specify primary, secondary, and higher education, but no one questioned in what spirit this education should be provided. Bienenfeld put this in extremely convincing fashion: "The Germans had the best educational system in the world. Introduced by Bismarck, it was continued by the Nazis. Look at the results it achieved under the Nazis!"

We then made efforts to introduce into the text a paragraph about the spirit in which education should be provided. To our great surprise, we met enormous difficulties. In the beginning no one wished to follow our lead—not the French, or the British, or the Americans—and the Soviets even less so. To overcome this difficulty we formed alliances with representatives from a number of other states, including Lebanon and Egypt, which was rather surprising for a Jewish organization. With their support and against the will of the larger countries, we obtained the passage of the following paragraph of Article 26:

> Education shall be directed to the full development of the human personality and to the strengthening of respect for human rights and fundamental freedoms. It shall promote understanding, tolerance and friendship among all nations, racial or religious groups, and shall further the activities of the United Nations for the maintenance of peace.

Without us this paragraph would not exist. I believe that it is an extremely valuable parameter for the future activity of educators. Today no one any longer challenges the importance of this paragraph which, moreover, in part expresses the goals of the UN Educational, Scientific and Cultural Organization, UNESCO.

Let's consider a second example. Article 30 of the Declaration states:

> Nothing in this Declaration may be interpreted as implying for any State, group or person any right to engage in any activity or to perform any act aimed at the destruction of any of the rights and freedoms set forth herein.

This article too was introduced on our initiative. We had learned the lessons from the Nazis, who had abused freedoms and fundamental rights in order to abolish democracy by what were claimed legal means.

A third significant example is Article 29. The draft of the Declaration envisaged that the exercise of human rights could be limited by law. We made the case that this was exactly what Hitler had done. The Nazi government had restricted by law—in actual fact, annulled—each human right, in particular the rights of victims of persecution. In this fashion the law, instead of offering them protection, was abused to deprive them of fundamental freedoms, going so far as the assassination of six million Jews and countless other victims in Germany and the remainder of Europe.

We then suggested that every national law that restricted human rights should not be considered valid from the perspective of international law unless it conformed to the principles and objectives of the United Nations. We had complete success, and Article 29 finally took the following form:

1. Everyone has duties to the community in which alone the free and full development of his personality is possible.

2. In the exercise of his rights and freedoms, everyone shall be subject only to such limitations as are determined by law solely for the purpose of securing due recognition and respect for the rights and freedoms of others and of meeting the just requirements of morality, public order and the general welfare in a democratic society.

3. These rights and freedoms may in no case be exercised contrary to the purposes and principles of the United Nations.

Another article, number 14, also concerned us. It dealt with the right of asylum. In this sphere we did not get everything we wished, but the text was improved: "Everyone has the right to seek and to enjoy in other countries asylum from persecution." The words "and to enjoy" were added at our request. In the earlier text, a persecuted person had the right to seek asylum but did not automatically benefit from a right to asylum in the country where he or she had taken refuge. The effort to introduce a true right of asylum was energetically opposed by a majority of the great powers. The formula "and to enjoy asylum" at least precluded the extradition of the refugee back to the country where persecution had been suffered.*

Other successful lobbying by the WJC made it possible to improve Article 7, which proscribed inciting discrimination, and Article 11, which barred the retroactive application of penal laws.

When the text of the Universal Declaration was passed by the Commission on Human Rights, it was forwarded to the UN General Assembly for final passage. This debate took place at the General Assembly meeting in Paris in 1948, where Bienenfeld and I were present. Despite the fact that we did not enjoy the same rights and resources at the General Assembly as were available through our consultative status with the Commission on Human Rights, we maintained contacts with a considerable number of delegates. Since a number of them were not very familiar with the problems posed by the various articles of the declaration, we decided to draft a separate commentary for each of the ten articles that were of particular concern to us. We sent these commentaries

*The second and final clause in Article 14 reads, "This right may not be invoked in the case of prosecutions genuinely arising from non-political crimes or from acts contrary to the purposes and principles of the United Nations."—ED.

by personal letter to all the members of the UN Commission charged with responsibility of preparing the final text. We learned that these commentaries had been greatly appreciated by those who had received them and had influenced a number of votes.

The Universal Declaration of Human Rights was passed by the General Assembly of the United Nations and proclaimed on December 10, 1948, at the Palais de Chaillot in Paris. At this writing the passage of the Universal Declaration is seen as an historic event in the protection of human rights. Its anniversary is celebrated in many countries around the world as International Human Rights Day.

The declaration, which was formally a recommendation from the General Assembly of the United Nations to its member states as a common ideal to be realized by all peoples and all nations, with the passage of time acquired increasing importance, and its influence has grown ever since its adoption. At this writing the declaration has been at least theoretically accepted by all 185 member states of the United Nations. Even the countries that originally abstained later adopted it at the Helsinki Conference on European Security and Cooperation in 1975.

The declaration has inspired many national constitutions and laws in numerous states. It is constantly cited by courts of justice and other judicial bodies. At this writing many authors maintain that the Universal Declaration has become an integral part of international common law or is in the course of so becoming.

Criticism has been raised from time to time, charging the declaration with being a product of Western civilization and not being truly representative of all the cultural and social traditions of the contemporary world. This accusation, in my opinion, is unfair, not only because members of various cultures participated in its drafting—including Egyptians, Indians, and Pakistanis, people from cultures very different from those of the West—but especially because all of us sought a true meeting of minds in order to find formulas that were universally acceptable. I believe that the vast majority of those of good faith agree on these principles and that, by that fact, the Universal Declaration represents a maximum consensus on fundamental rights.

Propaganda against the declaration, invoking the specific nature of various cultures, continues even today. We may, however, note that in general the countries that invoke this argument are simply trying to evade the obligations that the declaration imposes on them.

There is all the more reason to welcome the decision of the World Conference on Human Rights convoked by the United Nations in 1993. Through its consensus adoption of the Vienna Declaration and Program of Action, the international community reasserted explicitly the universal nature of these rights and freedoms.

It is often alleged as well that in the eyes of its authors, the civil and political rights enumerated in the declaration took precedence over all other rights and that the declaration did not accord the same importance to social and economic rights. A new generation of defenders of human rights has proclaimed also the right to solidarity, referring to goals as broadly conceived as the environment, development, and peace, affirming that attention to these rights is lacking in the declaration.

In this regard it should be noted that economic and social rights are not a recent invention, and I have always shared that belief that all human rights are to a degree indivisible and interdependent. Civil and political rights are complementary to economic and social rights. There is very limited benefit to be had from civil and political rights without the material means to assure one's life. And one cannot really benefit from material well-being if at the same time fundamental civil rights and freedoms are not assured.

Therefore I believe that these allegations are not well founded. The drafters of the Universal Declaration, among whom were representatives of cultures from the Third World and in particular from the Middle and Far East, understood perfectly well the importance of social, economic, and cultural rights. In actual fact, the declaration proclaims that economic, social, and cultural rights are indispensable to the dignity and free development of the human personality. The right to work, to fair pay for one's work, to social security, to rest and leisure, to a certain standard of living, as well as the right to education are all noted in the declaration.

It is quite natural that greater emphasis should be placed today on these last-named rights, precisely thanks to the influence of Third World states. It is obvious that the application and implementation of these rights is slow, for they require the engagement of immense economic and social resources by governments. But all right-thinking people view with sympathy the impatience of many countries and many populations in this sphere.

Much more time and effort are needed to make the international community fully understand and accept the notion of cultural rights, despite the praiseworthy work accomplished in this area by UNESCO. In this domain, minority groups are particularly and deeply engaged and affected. The preservation of the identity and culture of minorities, and the need to afford minorities the indispensable means of preserving and developing their cultural heritage are tasks to which the bodies of the United Nations have thus far not paid sufficient attention. Today this remains one of the principal concerns of the World Jewish Congress.

As for the human rights claimed under the heading of the "third generation," the right to solidarity, I agree that our better understanding of the demands and also of the needs of development and the environment should encourage us rapidly to adopt possible measures that preceding generations did not fully imagine and hence did not find expression in documents drawn up in those earlier times.

Finally, I have some doubts about our ability to make true progress toward peace and development while we remain content largely to proclaim these postulates and dress them up with the sacred mantle of human rights. In order to give full significance to the rights of peoples in various stages of their development, I personally feel that we should substantially increase our efforts to transfer part of the economic and technological wealth of the affluent countries to countries that are having difficulties getting started. Any such course of action should be arranged so as to give the recipients the capacity to compete with countries that have had a more fortunate past and to permit them progressively to acquire that share of the world economy that is their due. I am not sure that in limiting ourselves to proclaiming the right to development we are making any real progress in this extremely important area.

Human Rights Treaties

The Universal Declaration was the first phase of the long process to define human rights in an internationally acceptable form. The second consisted of transforming the principles of this declaration into binding obligations for the states. During this phase, two international pacts were worked out: the International Covenant on Civil and Political Rights, and the International Covenant on Economic, Social and Cultural Rights. It proved necessary to divide the approach to the human rights issue in this way because the implementation of civil and political rights could be introduced with little delay by state powers, but even the gradual application of cultural, social, and economic rights required a considerable financial effort.

The two pacts entailed very different implementation procedures. Both carried clear and precise obligations for the states that ratified them.

Working out international pacts relative to human rights was a long and difficult process. Over the course of time we encountered many more obstacles than in preparing the Universal Declaration. It was clearly more difficult to agree on the formulation of specific rights that would entail concrete obligations for states than to draft and proclaim general principles.

The prolongation of this debate brought us into the Cold War period, where all discussion of human rights ended in a sometimes violent confrontation between East and West, often additionally marked by a discourse of aggressively partisan propaganda. Today we sometimes forget that all of this occurred during a period of constant tension, when many feared an imminent Third World War and when positions on both sides constantly hardened. From the early 1950s the United States could more and more be seen to assume distancing attitudes in regard to efforts to codify human rights. And other countries did not take this work very seriously at all.

Occasionally we even despaired of ever bringing this work to a successful conclusion, and we sensed that the relevant international pacts would never see the light of day. This was the period of witch hunts, characterized in the United States by the activities of Senator Joseph McCarthy. These events left profound imprints on the conduct of foreign affairs in the affected states.

I remember that at one moment at the WJC we were so pessimistic about the fate of these efforts that we considered abandoning the entire project. In a July 1954 brief to the UN Commission on Human Rights, I suggested that instead of drawing up two pacts that would encompass all human rights, we might perhaps make more rapid and systematic progress by drafting a set of international legal instruments, each limited to the codification of a specific right or two related rights. Work of this kind could then be spread out over a number of years.

Discussion continued nonetheless on the projects that were in progress. All this explains why the codification of these two pacts within the Commission on Human Rights, and then at the Third Committee of the General Assembly of the UN, took so long. One then understands why the states did not adopt the texts until December 1966, and that they did not come into force until 1976—in all, eighteen years of preparation and another ten years to achieve implementation.

Seeing how the evolution of international jurisprudence can be influenced and molded was one of the great experiences of my life. I am happy to be able to say that we at the WJC played a positive role in this process.

But why is this so important? Aware that the most atrocious persecution was carried out under the cover of the last world war, the World Jewish Congress asserted that no convention should permit a state of war or any other state of emergency to be abusively invoked as a reason for suppressing or reducing human rights beyond the limits that are strictly necessary in such circumstances. As a consequence, the WJC tried to modify the terms of Article 4 of the proposal on this subject. As early as its April 28, 1948, memorandum, the WJC explained that human rights and fundamental freedoms should not be suspended in times of war, that in fact they demanded special protection in such a context. Therefore a convention that did not contain a precise definition of the limits to be observed in the abrogation or curtailment of the enjoyment of human rights during such a period would allow very serious regression in regard to those rights.

As a consequence, the WJC proposed a total ban on the abrogation of the most important rights, such as the rights to life and to personal safety. We also insisted on the proscription of slavery, the right of everyone to be a legal person, and freedom of religion and of conscience.

Our organization insisted in particular that the fundamental principle of nondiscrimination be respected in all circumstances. There is no situation in the world, even in times of war or emergency, that justifies a state, a government, or any other public authority to have recourse to discrimination for reasons of race, color, sex, religion, language, or social origin. The WJC likewise suggested that if a state abrogated certain other rights, it ought to report to an international authority specially designated for this purpose, and that the abrogated rights ought to be reestablished if this authority condemned the actions undertaken.

The text finally adopted incorporated most of the WJC suggestions and in particular restricted the provisions of Article 4, which allowed states to "take measures derogating from their obligations under the present Covenant" in a time when "a public emergency threatens the life of the nation and the existence of which is officially proclaimed." This proclamation and its justification was to be reported to the other signatories of the convention through the UN secretary-general. We should recall that the original draft referred uniquely to "times of war or other public emergencies."

In addition, the adopted text prohibited the abrogation and suspension of a variety of rights: there are articles guaranteeing the right to life; forbidding torture, slavery, and servitude; excluding *ex post facto* legislation (against crimes and infractions defined as such after they were committed); guaranteeing everyone status as a person before the law; prohibiting imprisonment for the nonfulfillment of contractual obligations; and assuring the right to freedom of thought,* conscience, and religion.

---

*UN International Covenant on Civil and Political Rights.

Article 4 of the United Nations International Covenant on Civil and Political Rights also prohibited all states from exempting themselves from obligations that the agreement enjoined as discriminatory, based uniquely on race, color, sex, language, religion, or social origin.

We were inspired in presenting our proposals in part by existing humanitarian conventions and in particular by the IXth Convention of The Hague and the humanitarian conventions of 1949, which in particular proclaimed the principle of nondiscrimination, even in times of war. If it were forbidden during wars, how could it be accepted in times of peace under the pretext of a "state of emergency"?

The amendments we introduced into the texts are extremely important. We transformed what traditionally has been called natural law into positive law. This was an extraordinary experience. We obtained clear and precise limitations on emergency situations.

The prohibition against suspension or abrogation of certain human rights, even during states of emergency, signified in fact the imposition of respect for these fundamental rights in all circumstances. At the time, such a concept constituted a revolutionary action. Its introduction sparked a great deal of opposition, not only from small dictatorships but also from the great democracies. And I am astonished today, when I read commentary that refers to it, that virtually no one any longer seriously challenges these principles.

This was certainly not the only contribution we made to the formulation of the texts of the two pacts. We followed the deliberations with a great deal of attention and we sought, wherever we could, to bring improvements to the texts. And naturally we also took care that the ideas we had defended when the Universal Declaration was being drawn up were also incorporated into the texts of the pacts that followed it. Thus the right to education at all levels is now an integral part of the International Covenant on Economic, Social, and Cultural Rights (Article 13) and has become legally binding.

The system for implementation is clearly different for each of the two pacts. The reason for this, as I have already observed, is that carrying out the provisions of the Covenant on Economic, Social and Cultural Rights can be achieved only gradually, for they demand a considerable financial effort on the part of each state. Everything must be done to help accelerate this process.

We concentrated on the goal of setting up an effective system to implement the Covenant on Civil and Political Rights. It involved the assurance that each person or each organization or group defending the interests of the individual could bring a complaint before an independent body of a judicial nature in the event of a violation of rights, and could count on the measures needed to bring the violation to an end and to correct its effects.

Despite the enormous efforts we made in cooperation with other nongovernmental organizations, we never achieved this goal. Today it remains the major objective to be met. The ideal would be to institute within the United Nations the procedure that had been established within the framework of the Council of Europe by the European Convention on Human Rights and its additional protocols.

The draft text on civil and political rights foresaw regular reports on the measures that the signatory governments had passed into law in order to activate the rights recognized in the covenant. There were also to be reports on the progress realized in the enjoyment of these rights. Additionally, the draft foresaw a system within which each contracting country could register a complaint in the event another state failed to acquit itself of its obligations.

On the other hand, following certain procedures like those at the International Court of Justice at The Hague, this right was conditioned in the final formulation of the text by an express declaration by the other state that it accepted the procedure. But the institution of a complaint by one state against another before an international committee or tribunal is a rare occurrence. In itself it is an essentially hostile act and typically initiates a serious conflict. This is why we insisted that such recourse be available to individuals, groups, and NGOs.

As a nongovernmental organization, we mounted considerable pressure in this matter, and the representatives of the states finally accepted many of our ideas. But they did not introduce these regulations into the covenant itself; they formulated them in a separate optional protocol, which the states were to ratify and sign in addition to the pact. Obviously we were not pleased with this solution, because it allowed the states to evade these obligations and set back for many years the implementation of the regulations among the signatory countries. But in this connection it should be noted that our fears were perhaps exaggerated. In actual fact, little by little, a large number of states have ratified the protocol even if some important states remain absent from the roll call.

A veritable body of jurisprudence has been developed since the protocol took effect. And although the pronouncements of the committee that examines the submissions of the individual and the implicated state do not have the quality of a judgment, they are generally accepted by the state and are carried out. This represents considerable progress.

The procedure for committee supervision of periodic reports from the states, as foreseen in the pact, has not been very satisfactory, even if it has

improved over time. The NGOs have not always been granted an official position in this procedure, though in practice NGO-submitted reports on state
violations of human rights have become an important element in the examination of these situations. Their reports are distributed even to the delegations. But the enormous delays that arise after the submission of the states'
own reports have had a negative effect and have been a real obstacle to action on the periodic reports.

We are still far from true judicial procedures that are accessible to everyone. The fact that the General Assembly of the United Nations has recently
created the position of High Commissioner for Human Rights, an idea that
we had vigorously advanced for several decades, may make a considerable
contribution to progress in the cause of human rights.

Against Anti-Semitism and Racism

The World Jewish Congress has not ceased to take initiatives to advance the
cause of human rights with the UN framework. The profanation of the
Cologne synagogue in December 1959 was shocking, as was a wave of swastikas
smeared on walls and other Nazi demonstrations throughout Europe, in
America, and in Australia. These events shook public opinion, which had long
been lulled by the idea that anti-Semitism of the Nazi type had lost its viru-
lence. These disgusting events gave us the opportunity to undertake an action
that had far-reaching consequences.

I was one of the first to speak out on the gravity of the situation, doing so
at the January 1960 meeting of the UN subcommittee for the prevention of
discrimination and the protection of minorities. I called for the intervention
of the international community and an inquiry into recent events, and I demanded that the problem of incitement to prejudice and hatred be a priority
for examination.

The deliberations that followed at the subcommittee and at the Commission for Human Rights and the Economic and Social Council envisaged as response to these dramatic events a Declaration and a Convention on the Elimination of All Forms of Racial Discrimination as well as a Declaration and
Convention on the Elimination of All Forms of Intolerance and Discrimination Based on Religion or Belief.

The World Jewish Congress actively participated in the drafting of these
legal instruments and submitted written briefs to the Commission on Human
Rights and to the Economic and Social Council in addition to making oral
presentations.

On November 20, 1963, the General Assembly adopted a Declaration on the Elimination of All Forms of Racial Discrimination. It affirms:

Discrimination between human beings on the ground of race, colour or ethnic origin is an offence to human dignity and shall be condemned as a denial of the principles of the Charter of the United Nations, as a violation of the human rights and fundamental freedoms proclaimed in the Universal Declaration of Human Rights, as an obstacle to friendly and peaceful relations among nations and as a fact capable of disturbing peace and security among peoples. . . . No state shall encourage, advocate or lend its support, through police action or otherwise, to any discrimination based on race, color or ethnic origin by any group, institution or individual. . . . All States shall take effective measures to revise governmental and other public policies . . . which have the effect of creating and perpetuating racial discrimination wherever it still exists.

In addition, the declaration states that effective educational measures must be taken without delay with a view to eliminating racial discrimination.

The declaration strongly condemns propaganda and the organizations that find their inspiration in theories of racial superiority; organizations that incite racial discrimination or advocate it are to be prosecuted and declared illegal.

The International Convention on the Elimination of All Forms of Racial Discrimination unanimously adopted on December 21, 1965, by the UN General Assembly deals with the same matters as the declaration and transforms its regulations into binding obligations. In addition, it contains application clauses that in part follow those of the International Covenant on Civil and Political Rights. It even foresees petitions from individuals or groups of individuals in the event of violations of the provisions of the covenant, this process to be established by a state's simple declaration that it accepts the procedure.

The International Convention on the Elimination of All Forms of Racial Discrimination has become one of the most popular of all the conventions reached under the auspices of the UN. It has gained one of the greatest numbers of ratifications.

While the declaration and the convention against racism were drawn up in a fairly reasonable length of time by the UN bodies and entered into force fairly promptly, the decision to draft a declaration and a convention on intolerance and discrimination based on religion or belief met with enormous difficulties. If the Convention on the Elimination of Racial Discrimination benefited from a wave of support, coming in particular from Third World countries, the two other instruments dealing with religious intolerance were vigorously opposed by the Soviet bloc and by the Arab and most Muslim states.

The atmosphere of the Cold War and the efforts undertaken by these states to exclude the State of Israel from the company of nations explains to a great extent their policy of delay and obstructionism. This battle lasted almost fifteen years.

It was then that I undertook a fresh initiative: I approached the Holy See, suggesting close cooperation in order to reach the goal. The Vatican, since John XXIII but especially under the influence of John Paul II, had made the cause of human rights one of the central objectives of its political activity. We had similar interests in this matter and encountered comparable difficulties in achieving the exercise of religious freedom in the countries of Eastern Europe and in some Muslim countries. I therefore suggested to the Holy See that we coordinate our efforts with a view first to concluding the draft of the Declaration on the Elimination of All Forms of Intolerance and Discrimination Based on Religion and Belief.

I then went to Rome where, with the help of our friends on the commission of the Holy See for religious relations with Jews, I had a long conversation with Msgr. Audrys J. Bačkis, undersecretary of the Council for the Public Affairs of the Church, within the Vatican's Secretariat of State. (This is the equivalent of the position of undersecretary of state for foreign affairs.) Msgr. Bačkis received me in cordial fashion. He was of Lithuanian origin and understood our concerns perfectly. It seemed to me that he understood them all the better since among Lithuanians, as among Jews, national feelings and religious feelings are intimately tied.

We agreed on close cooperation. From that moment on, my colleague Daniel Lack, who at that time represented the WJC at the Commission for Human Rights at the United Nations, enjoyed a close and fruitful relationship with the Holy See's observer at the UN in Geneva. He was greatly assisted by the new chairman of the working group, Abdoulaye Dieye from Senegal, charged by the Commission on Human Rights to prepare the definitive text of the declaration.

Matters advanced well and quickly enough to permit the UN General Assembly to adopt the text definitively on November 25, 1981, with a broad consensus.

The adoption of this declaration after so many years of tribulation was a great success. Today it is the basic document that should guide the struggle against intolerance and religious discrimination.

The adoption of a convention on this same subject, which was to follow, still has not taken place. We must continue our efforts to bring this project to a successful conclusion. Nevertheless we learned that cooperation with the Holy See in this sphere could be effective and fruitful.

We did not limit our efforts to fighting discrimination in general. We also continued our efforts in specific areas in which discrimination had had particularly negative effects on the Jewish population. Thus we participated actively in drawing up the convention against discrimination relative to employment and the exercise of professions, which was adopted by the International Labor Organization on June 25, 1958, and in drafting the convention against discrimination in the sphere of education, which was approved by the General Conference of UNESCO on December 14, 1960.

In both cases the WJC was among those entities that took the initiative in urging the adoption of these conventions. In both cases the WJC cultural representative, Dr. Aaron Steinberg, the British deputy Maurice Orbach, a specialist in workplace discrimination, and I participated actively in the work of the specialized commissions that were preparing these texts, and we made oral and written presentations on the specific concerns and proposals of the WJC in this area.

Combating Genocide

I should mention another path that we followed within the UN framework immediately after the end of the war, in order to draw lessons from the catastrophe. This effort, undertaken in parallel to that of drafting the Universal Declaration and the covenants on human rights, was aimed at preventing and punishing the crime of genocide.

The idea of a convention against genocide was conceived by a Polish Jewish jurist, Raphael Lemkin, who worked for several years with extraordinary energy toward its realization. The WJC and I gave him our full support. I met him several times in Geneva and at Lake Success, New York, the initial location of the UN. We discussed at length his draft text, the tactics to be adopted, and the political action we needed to bring the project to fruition.

Since 1946 the WJC had submitted a series of written briefs to different UN bodies, in which we had not only supported the fundamental ideas of this initiative but had also made suggestions as to the definition of the crime of genocide, the sphere of its application, and the means of its implementation. At the same time the WJC repeatedly mobilized all the communities and affiliated organizations to persuade their respective governments to support the initiative at the United Nations. These efforts finally led to the adoption of the

Convention on the Prevention and Punishment of the Crime of Genocide by the General Assembly of the United Nations on December 9, 1948.

Here is a summary of the most important provisions of the convention:

> Having considered the declaration made by the General Assembly of the United Nations in its resolution 96 (I) dated 11 December 1946 that genocide is a crime under international law, contrary to the spirit and aims of the United Nations and condemned by the civilized world;
>
> Recognizing that at all periods of history genocide has inflicted great losses on humanity;
>
> The convention stipulates that genocide, whether it be committed in times of peace or war, is a crime against human rights.
>
> The contracting states engaged themselves to prevent it and punish it.
>
> The Convention defines genocide as one of the following acts committed with intent to destroy, in whole or in part, a national, ethnic, racial or religious group, as such:
>
> Killing members of the group;
>
> Causing serious bodily or mental harm to members of the group;
>
> Deliberately inflicting on the group conditions of life calculated to bring about its physical destruction in whole or in part;
>
> Imposing measures intended to prevent births within the group;
>
> Forcibly transferring children of the group to another group.
>
> The Convention declares that the following acts shall be punishable:
>
> Genocide;
>
> conspiracy to commit genocide;
>
> direct and public incitement to commit genocide;
>
> attempt to commit genocide; and
>
> complicity in genocide.

The great weakness of the convention, however, was that it did not establish an international tribunal to punish the perpetrators of genocide. It left prosecution to the relevant tribunals of the state on whose territory the act had been committed. The General Assembly did, however, invite the Commission on International Law to study the question, as well as the possibility of establishing a tribunal to try persons accused of this crime.

The weakness of the judicial mechanism of the convention against genocide made a number of states reluctant to ratify it. I was always of the opinion that despite all our efforts we failed to reach our objective in this matter.

Nonetheless the adoption by the United Nations of the convention against genocide became a powerful symbol and rallying point for the Jewish public.

As a consequence, Jewish communities made considerable efforts in persuading their governments to ratify the convention, despite its flaws. This led to its ratification by numerous countries, including the United States. Repeatedly put off, U.S. ratification finally took place during the presidency of George H. W. Bush in 1991, almost fifty years after its initial adoption.

I should, finally, offer some account of another initiative that I took to combat anti-Semitism. Although it was not within the framework of the United Nations, it nonetheless occurred on the international level.

As I have already stated, anti-Semitism did not disappear after World War II. From time to time there were fresh flare-ups. I have mentioned those that occurred in late 1959 and 1960. The same phenomenon appeared after the disappearance of the Soviet Union as the second world power. The collapse of the Communist regime and the partial dislocation of the former Soviet empire resulted in, among other things, the emergence of extremist and nationalist movements in almost all the states of the former Soviet Union. The collapse also made it possible to grant new freedoms to each citizen of the former Soviet Union and of the countries of Central Europe, and was greeted with joy in all of Western Europe.

But these freedoms were also granted to opponents of democracy, to those who upheld extremist doctrines and promoted chauvinism and ultranationalist, racist, and anti-Semitic theories. All of a sudden we saw dozens of extremist groups surface in the former Soviet Union. These developments caused anxiety in large sectors of the Jewish community in Russia, and this led to a substantial emigration of former Soviet Jews. While tension was not as high in the other countries of Eastern Europe, at the WJC we observed that anti-Semitic slogans played an important role in several elections in Hungary, and in Romania the old anti-Semitic demons once again raised their ugly heads. In Poland, ultranationalist circles succeeded in playing a far from negligible role in the conflict surrounding the Carmelite convent in Auschwitz, in opposition to the wishes of the government and the higher authorities of the church in Rome.*

Even though these extreme right-wing, chauvinistic organizations, vehicles of xenophobia and racism and promoters of a virulent anti-Semitism, did

---

*The function of this convent within the landscape of the camp caused contention among Jewish organizations, the Roman Catholic prelates in Poland, the Polish government, and the Vatican. In 1993 the convent was moved to a different location, resolving that particular problem. See below for a detailed discussion of the matter.—ED.

not succeed in electing many of their representatives to important political positions, they had terrifying propaganda networks at their disposal. We began to wonder whether the world had forgotten what had happened in the 1930s and whether everything was about to begin all over again.

In this picture we should not forget the effect that the reunification of Germany had on Jewish populations. On the one hand, the fall of the Berlin wall was greeted with joy everywhere, because symbolically it represented the end of the division of Europe and the conclusion of the Cold War. But on the other hand this evolution also awakened feelings of doubt and concern in many quarters.

These sentiments found expression in almost all the countries neighboring on Germany, among its partners in the European community, and, last but not least, among the major powers. Everywhere people asked what the real consequences of this reunification would be.

The same reactions were to be witnessed in the Jewish community. Jews expected that the unification treaty, signed by the two Germanys in November 1990, would contain a special clause referring to particular obligations that history imposed on the new German state regarding the victims of Nazi Germany. The president of the Jewish Community of Germany, acting on behalf of the Jewish communities of the entire world, insisted on this principle and had obtained assurances from Chancellor Helmut Kohl, who reiterated his support at the 1990 meeting of the WJC executive committee in Berlin. The fact that these promises were not fulfilled occasioned serious disappointment among Jews, despite some reassuring statements. The xenophobic and extremist manifestations which followed in Eastern Germany added to the unease felt not only by the Jews.

I spoke of this problem in October 1990 on the occasion of my visit to Belgrade, where I represented the WJC at the inauguration of the monument to the Jewish dead erected by the city on one of its great squares. This event preceded the tragic dismemberment of Yugoslavia.

My speech caught the attention of Yugoslavian and Serbian government circles, and I was received the next day by the vice minister for foreign affairs of Yugoslavia, then by the Serbian minister of foreign affairs. I was accompanied by my old friend Dr. Lavoslav Kadelburg, president of the Federation of Jewish Communities of Yugoslavia.

I took advantage of this meeting to communicate to my hosts our anxiety over the reappearance of virulent anti-Semitic movements in Eastern European countries, and I asked the Yugoslavian vice minister of foreign affairs whether his country, which had always remained independent of the East-

West power blocs and which had always been favorably disposed toward us, could not take an initiative to condemn anti-Semitism. It seemed to me at the time that the meeting of heads of state from the Conference on Security and Cooperation in Europe, which was to take place in Paris a few weeks later, could serve as a foundation for such a declaration.

The Yugoslavian minister, a man extremely well informed on the matters of concern to us, reacted very positively to my suggestion. I did not know that he had been one of the political counselors to President Tito and that he was aware of our relations with the marshal and of our long-standing cooperation with Yugoslavian authorities. He promised me that he would take such an initiative but must first consult with his government colleagues. In the afternoon of that same day he sent me a message through the intermediary of the president of the Jewish Community of Belgrade to tell me that he had obtained his colleagues' agreement and that he would act as we had discussed.

Some ten days later I learned from Swiss friends that the Yugoslav government had indeed sent proposals to the commission charged with the preparation of the Paris conference. I then informed the secretary-general of the WJC in New York and got in touch with a number of Jewish communities in Europe, asking them to lobby their respective governments to enlist their support for the Yugoslav government's initiative. In particular I approached the communities of Great Britain, Belgium, France, Spain, and Switzerland. Some time later I was informed that the Yugoslav initiative had been unanimously accepted. It was entered in the Paris Charter for a New Europe, signed in Paris by thirty-five heads of state and government on November 21, 1990.

The clause I had inspired figures in the section "Guidelines for the Future" under the title "Human Dimension" (paragraph 4):

> We express our determination to combat all forms of racial and ethnic hatred, antisemitism, xenophobia and discrimination against anyone as well as persecution on religious and ideological grounds.

This was the first time in history that so many heads of state and government had signed such a clear and precise condemnation of anti-Semitism, and I am quite proud to have proposed it.

For a New Humanitarian Law

To this point I have described our efforts to codify human rights in the context of the United Nations and other international bodies. I also undertook efforts in the realm of humanitarian law.

In this sphere, too, World War II and its catastrophic consequences for civilian populations called for a new departure and a new codification that would draw on the lessons of the recent past. We participated in this effort with great determination, considering that it was our duty toward all those whom we had not been able to save during the Shoah.

I have mentioned that at the end of the war I asked to be consulted by the International Committee of the Red Cross when it moved to revise humanitarian conventions in the light of experience gained during hostilities. By that time I had already raised the necessity of protecting civilian populations, arguing that the absence of such rules during the previous conflict had provoked the catastrophe of which we were the victims. We had submitted this request in order to be associated with the reformulation of humanitarian law. To this end, I kept up my contacts with the ICRC. This led to our being represented by an observer at the XVIIth International Conference of the Red Cross, held in Stockholm in August 1948 with the goal of revising and expanding the so-called Geneva Conventions on the conduct of states in times of war. Since then the ICRC has always invited the WJC to its international conferences.

It was at the Stockholm conference that the ICRC submitted the four-conventions proposal. Among these, the most important projects for us were those that concerned the treatment of prisoners of war and the protection of civilian populations in times of war.

This last project was the source of great satisfaction for us since it directly addressed a problem that we judged most urgent. We submitted to the conference a detailed memorandum on the protection of civilian populations in times of war, and I was able to present it in person to the legal commission, which reviewed the various projects. I made several statements, and the commission voted on one of my suggestions.

This suggestion embodied an interesting idea. It dealt with cases similar to the situation that arose on the night of the pogrom of November 1938 and was aimed at extending the mandate of the ICRC to internal conflict situations where one party lacked the resources to resist the all-powerful state.

Fortunately it proved possible to discuss the proposal under highly favorable conditions. The conference was chaired by the Swedish Judge Emil Sandström, who knew me because he was a member of the celebrated UN Special Committee on Palestine (UNSCOP), which proposed the establishment of two states on the territory there.

This review by the International Committee of the Red Cross constituted a kind of general rehearsal for the diplomatic conference that was to be convened by the Swiss government the following year in Geneva and which would rule definitively on the contents of these conventions.

The Stockholm conference has stayed in my memory all the more as it was the first international meeting in which a delegation from the Israeli government and also from Magen David Adom, led by Abracha Katznelson, participated. The government delegate was Dr. M. Steinberg, a diplomat who was also a physician, and we cooperated intimately. Most of all, however, we were very proud of their presence there.

The decisive action came in 1949 in Geneva when the diplomatic conference convoked by the Swiss government with a view to drafting and adopting the definitive text on the humanitarian conventions took place. I approached the Swiss government to request that the WJC be invited to participate in the conference as an observer provided with all the resources for active participation. In this respect no precedent existed, and I negotiated directly with the secretary-general of the conference, a senior official of the Swiss ministry of foreign affairs. The privileges we requested entailed a right to be present at the sessions, the right to take the floor in committees, and the right to submit written briefs that would be distributed to all the delegations.

On behalf of the WJC we presented a detailed memorandum by which we sought to improve and make more precise the draft texts. One of the points we made returned to our dispute with the ICRC during the final phase of the war on the question of discrimination between Jewish and non-Jewish prisoners of war.

Another point we made demanded the interdiction on religious grounds of the cremation of deceased internees' remains (except in the case of absolute hygienic necessity). This point was successfully covered by Article 130 of the convention on the protection of civilians.

On several occasions I took the floor at committee meetings in order to win support for our positions. We were fairly satisfied with the work of codification, which took account of the objectives that we worked to achieve.

All went smoothly, then, except for one issue, which would play a great role in our future relations with the ICRC. The distinctive symbol of the Red Cross as protected by international convention is the emblem of a red cross on a white field. But in the course of history and in particular at the insistence of Turkey and Persia, later conventions also recognized the distinctive sign of the Red Crescent and the Lion or the Rising Sun on a white field. During the Geneva conference, the Israeli delegation tried to introduce the red Star of David (Magen David Adom) as an officially recognized emblem.

Unfortunately this proposal was defeated by a single vote. Since then, count-less efforts have been made to rectify this situation. This is not easy, because when a distinctive symbol is approved as part of the convention it cannot be changed except by vote of the convention signatories. This did not prevent the Jewish communities, the WJC, and some national societies of the Red Cross, in particular the American Red Cross, from frequently returning to the fray to condemn the egalitarian disparity and to look for solutions that would be acceptable to all.

The fact of the nonrecognition of the Magen David Adom as a distinctive emblem did not, however, prevent us from submitting to the ICRC our ideas on certain specific situations, especially in the context of the conflict in the Mid-dle East. From the perspective of peace negotiations among the Israelis, Pales-tinians, and Arab countries, one might reasonably hope that the problem of the emblem would finally find its solution.*

The four international conventions that resulted from the 1949 meetings constituted enormous progress compared to what had gone before. We were happy to have been associated with this effort and to have been able to make our contribution to this important cause.†

In the 1970s a new effort was undertaken to reexamine and adapt hu-manitarian law in the light of experience from the period after the war. The experience of World War II, the analyses and critiques formulated by military historians, in particular with respect to the waging of total war, the new con-flicts that came on the heels of decolonialization, the emergence of move-ments of national liberation—all these posed new problems to which the ICRC sought to respond by drawing up additional protocols to the Geneva Conven-tions of 1949. The International Conference of the Red Cross and the UN Conference on Human Rights in Vienna in 1965 and in Teheran in 1968 took the initiative in this work.

A conference of governmental experts on the reaffirmation and develop-ment of international humanitarian law applicable to armed conflicts was con-voked in 1971, and forty governments were invited to be represented. These ex-

---

*In early 2006, the ICRC seemed on the verge of admitting the Magen David Adom to full membership, but at what some consider a discriminatory price. In missions outside Israel, the Star of David must be placed within a new "neutral" diamond-shaped Red Crystal sym-bol, and may not stand alone—a requirement not imposed on either cross or crescent.—ED.
†The four documents adopted on August 12, 1949, are: (1) Convention for the Ameliora-tion of the Condition of the Wounded and Sick in Armed Forces in the Field; (2) Conven-tion for the Amelioration of the Condition of Wounded, Sick, and Shipwrecked Members of Armed Forces at Sea; (3) Convention Relative to the Treatment of Prisoners of War, and (4) Convention Relative to the Protection of Civilian Persons in Time of War.—ED.

perts held a second session in June 1972 in Geneva with the participation of more than four hundred experts delegated by seventy-seven governments.

Consultations were also undertaken with representatives of the NGOs. All this finally led to the drafting of two additional protocols to the Geneva Conventions. These were submitted to the diplomatic conferences that were held between 1974 and 1977.

The WJC and other nongovernmental organizations followed this work very closely. The NGOs decided to set up a working group of fourteen international organizations that were particularly interested in these problems. Representatives of a wide variety of organizations, opinions, and interests debated in order to work out common positions.

Since I was one of those who had the longest experience with these issues, the group appointed me to preside over its sessions. That a Jew should be chosen to guide this committee at a time when no representative of the State of Israel had yet been elected to a similar position with the UN or any other international organization or conference proved that within the NGO sector there was nevertheless a certain liberal atmosphere and spirit of independence. At the same time it was a tribute to my abilities and to the spirit of openness and cooperation that I had always displayed in my relations with nongovernmental circles.

We worked on these problems for several months to draw up a memorandum, which dealt with many of the general principles we believed should animate international law in the future as well as with the individual articles of the two draft texts. When we had agreed on the content of the memorandum formulating our proposals in fifty points, we presented it for signature by all the interested NGOs. I am proud that this document, drawn up under my leadership, should finally have been signed by some fifty NGOs of all political, religious, ethnic, professional, and social persuasions. Trade union federations of all tendencies, associations of former servicemen and resisters, feminist organizations, peace movements, organizations of jurists of different schools, including Arab jurists, representative Catholic, Protestant, and Muslim religious organizations, associations for child welfare—all were represented. To have succeeded in bringing everyone to agreement in a universe as divided as ours was at that time a veritable miracle. It was in particular thanks to certain veterans of the world of NGOs, such as Niall McDermot, Sean McBride, Alice Arnold, Tadeusz Szmitkowski, and Serge Wourgaft, that I was able to succeed in this undertaking.

The document entitled "Memorandum by Non-Governmental Organizations on the Two Draft Additional Protocols to the Geneva Conventions, 1949," which we submitted in 1973, contained a certain number of fundamental principles, which we set out at the head of the text. It seems useful to recall them here since they incarnate the spirit in which we acted:

1. Guarantees for an effective application of the provisions of the humanitarian conventions, and a system for their implementation, should be established.

2. The fundamental humanitarian principles should be applied in all armed conflicts, internal as well as international.

3. The parties to conflicts and the members of their armed forces do not have an unlimited right of choice of the means and methods of combat and of targets for attack.

4. The civilian population should enjoy a special protection respecting their non-combatant status and ensuring the indispensable conditions for their survival in all armed conflicts.

5. The use of weapons, means and methods of combat which strike or affect indiscriminately the civilian population and combatants, or which are of a particularly cruel character or cause particularly cruel suffering, should be forbidden. These weapons, means and methods of combat should be specified by name in the Protocols.

A detailed analysis of the entire memorandum would be out of place here, but I will summarize our principal propositions (the whole document ran to eleven pages).

For example, we addressed ourselves to the diplomatic conference particularly to proscribe certain weapons that were among the most cruel and that caused the greatest suffering, and we made provisions for signatory states to review periodically the list of prohibited weapons. We believed the protocol should contain specific prohibitions against napalm and other incendiary bombs, certain fragmentation bombs, certain mines, and high-velocity small arms. We believed that members of liberation movements ought to benefit from the same conditions and rights as official armies.

We hailed the proposition set out in one article of the protocol in which it was forbidden

To attack without distinction, as one single objective, by bombardment or any other method, a zone containing several military objectives, which are situated in populated areas and are at some distance from each other.

This was an explicit prohibition against what was then known as "area bombing."

We also strongly supported the "proposed prohibitions concerning goods and equipment indispensable to the survival of civilian populations."

You can see the spirit in which we drafted our proposals; those ideas can be found in the definitive formulation of the protocols. On the other hand, we were clearly not satisfied with all the protocols concerning liberation movements. But in the perspective of peace in the Middle East we may hope that these problems will find a solution.*

When discussing these negotiations, I remember in particular the exchanges that occurred outside the official meetings and that at times were fascinating. For example, I recall my extremely interesting discussions with the legal counselors of the American and Canadian armed forces on certain clauses of the draft protocol. They were clearly trying not to limit the freedom of action of their respective military forces while I made appeals to their conscience. Allusion was made to certain military actions of World War II which had had catastrophic consequences but remained quite without effect on the battles that were being waged.

I continued these discussions on the occasion of several colloquiums on the development of humanitarian law in San Remo. We spoke of these problems with great frankness and great mutual respect. I was often extremely impressed by the competence of these experts, and I am convinced that this work was not in vain.

When we read, at some distance in time, the clauses of the protocol, for example, which prescribe that a distinction must be made at all times between the civilian population and combatants, as well as between property of a civilian nature and military objectives; when we examine the clauses that stipulate that "indiscriminate attacks" are forbidden, and which define in detail what is to be understood by this; when we note the prohibition against "destroying, seizing and rendering useless objects indispensable to the survival of civilian populations," we must conclude that all this new codification constitutes considerable progress in humanitarian law.

I think here in particular of the Gulf War against Iraq. I saw American flyers bomb and destroy with extraordinary precision a huge bridge in Baghdad. I then remembered in what pitiful state I had discovered the Ponte Vecchio, the magnificent historical monument of Florence, in late 1945 after the bombing it had suffered during that war. Bombing had destroyed the bridge and the historical quarter around it. And I wondered whether the manufacture of such

*The original (French) edition of Gerhart Riegner's memoirs was published in 1998.—ED.

precise instrumentation to direct bombs did not derive, at least in part, from our drafting of the Geneva protocols.

Defending Imperiled Jewish Communities

Thus far I have described the systematic struggles of the WJC to establish international rules that would guarantee security and the enforcement of human rights in the everyday life of people everywhere in the world. This activity, intended to assure the full exercise of guarantees of fundamental rights, to prevent all violation of these rights, and to provide for sanctions in the event these rights were not respected, was of course of great importance.

But clearly we could not limit ourselves to this global action. Everywhere that Jews were exposed to acts of discrimination, intimidation, persecution, despoliation, and violation of fundamental rights, we were called on for help. We were asked to act either by direct intervention or indirectly with the assistance of favorably disposed governments, to rectify the situation. It is impossible to list here all the occasions on which we had to intervene on behalf of small communities, which were often exposed to the arbitrary action of authorities. Very often we were able to alleviate the situation by means of direct representation to the relevant parties.

There were, however, two situations of exceptional seriousness that required sustained political activity on our part and that forced us to intervene over several long years. One was the situation of Jewish communities in the Arab countries of the Middle East, following the November 29, 1947, decision to partition Palestine and the establishment of the State of Israel on May 15, 1948. The other was the situation of the Jews in the Soviet Union, where the Jewish community had suffered ever since the establishment of Communist rule. This situation worsened steadily after 1945. I participated in these two great battles, and I shall narrate here some particularly noteworthy moments.

Anti-Jewish measures and pogroms in various countries of the Arab world immediately followed the decision to divide Palestine, voted on in the United Nations at the end of November 1947, and the Middle Eastern Arab states' rejection of this decision. The WJC felt itself obliged as early as January 1948 to address the president of the UN Economic and Social Council in a memorandum noting that Jews living in the Near and Middle Eastern countries were exposed to imminent and extremely grave danger.

The memorandum condemned the premeditated malice of Arab authorities: "By virtue of the challenge thrown down by the Arab states as a consequence of the decision to partition, the Political Committee of the Arab League has drawn up a law that transforms the Jews of these countries into the hostages of their own states." The memorandum also called attention to anti-Jewish incidents, as well as to very troubling acts of discrimination and violence in Aleppo, in certain cities in Iran, Aden, and Bahrein, leading to the loss of many Jewish lives and damage to synagogues as well as Jewish homes and businesses.

The WJC memorandum, coming from a consultative nongovernmental organization, was transmitted to the NGO Committee of the UN Economic and Social Council. This body reviewed it on February 13, 1948, and decided to receive a WJC representative. As early as February 16 we presented our complaint orally and urged the Council to establish a commission of inquiry charged with preparing a report on the situation for its next meeting. At the request of the NGO Committee, this recommendation was submitted to the Economic and Social Council. We submitted the recommendation in written form the same day, hoping to prevent further attacks against Jews.

In another letter, sent on February 26 to the president of the Economic and Social Council, the WJC forwarded supplementary information on the acts of violence, the measures of economic discrimination, and many other anti-Jewish excesses that had occurred in Syria, Lebanon, Iraq, and Egypt, jeopardizing the existence of the Jewish communities there. The Committee of NGOs submitted all these documents to the Economic and Social Council without recommendation and the Council, in a parliamentary move, concluded the debate without taking action.

Representatives of the WJC reacted vigorously against these maneuvers and created an atmosphere of discomfort among members of the Council as to how they had sidestepped the discussion. In a series of personal contacts with members of the Council we tried to rectify the situation. In particular we approached the Polish representative, Juliusz Katz-Suchy, and the French representative, our old friend, Pierre Mendès-France. Katz-Suchy, backed by Mendès-France and by representatives of the Soviet Union and Belorussia, demanded that the situation be reconsidered. On a motion by Mendès-France, the Council adopted by 15 to 1 the decision to transmit the summary account of the NGO Committee and invited it to submit recommendations that might prove useful at its next session.

The outcome of deliberations in the NGO Committee was astonishing. While conditions in the Arab states continually worsened, we pursued our lobbying without letup. On August 20, 1948, we submitted a document that stated:

> Since the middle of May, 800–1000 Jews have been arrested by the Egyptian authorities, and have been imprisoned in concentration camps, chiefly that of Huckersterp, 12 km. from Heliopolis. No charges have been made against these people, except that they are suspected of Zionist sympathies. Most of these Jews have, however, never taken part in Jewish or Zionist organizations, and they have been arrested through denunciation. Their property has been confiscated, causing the greatest hardships to their families. They are confined in extremely bad conditions and no opportunity of hearing or defense has been given to any of them by the Egyptian authorities.
>
> Property and funds of great value, belonging to Jews, have been arbitrarily "sequestered" by the Egyptian Government without explanation or legal process. Jews, both of Egyptian and other nationality, are similarly refused permits to leave Egypt and are thus forcibly detained to endure the harassments of legal and physical persecution and discrimination.
>
> On June 19, Egyptian Arabs laid and exploded bombs in the Jewish houses in the Jewish quarter of Cairo, according to reliable reports, causing the death of 55 Jews and serious injury to 50 others, as well as considerable damage to property. The Egyptian authorities took no action to bring to justice the perpetrators of this outrage but instead accused the Jews themselves of being responsible for it.
>
> During June and July, two pogroms against Jews in Cairo took place. 150 Jews were murdered or "disappeared" and of the hundreds of Jews wounded, 120 were brought to the Jewish hospital and to private places. Jews living in the vicinity of the Royal Palace were forced to evacuate their homes within 48 hours and scores of Jews were removed to concentration camps and Jewish houses were searched.

On June 22, 1948, the NGO Committee again granted a hearing to WJC representatives so that they could present the views of the Congress on the situation. Representatives of the Arab states also attended, and after the WJC made its presentation they presented their defense. This was a unique case in the history of the United Nations: representatives of governments had to respond to charges about the treatment of their own citizens, that is, the Jews of their countries, before a UN body, in the face of accusations raised by an NGO with consultative status.

The Egyptian delegate declared that Egypt had never shown any discrimination with regard to members of another race or religion and had always shown its goodwill and a spirit of broad hospitality toward the different communities with which it had dealings, and would continue to do so. The other Arab delegates made similar declarations.

Finally the NGO Committee adopted a resolution in which it affirmed that the Economic and Social Council had no authority to adjudicate the matter and consequently could not make recommendations concerning the subject of the WJC declaration. The committee recognized that the troubled conditions in Palestine could affect the exercise of fundamental rights in Palestine and in other countries of the region, and expressed the hope that the interested governments would safeguard the rights of persons and different religious groups.

Because this resolution was far from satisfactory, the WJC continued its activities through other channels. On the one hand, it addressed the General Assembly of the UN. On the other, it published and widely circulated a white paper on the situation of Jews in the Arab countries.

The WJC continued to pursue its objectives with the Economic and Social Council through a series of personal lobbying efforts directed toward the president and members of the Council, undertaken by myself and my colleagues Alec Easterman and F. R. Bienenfeld. We insisted on energetic action by the Council to put an end to persecutions.

In February 1949 the draft resolution of the NGO Committee was discussed at two plenary sessions. The representatives of New Zealand, Denmark, Australia, France, and the USSR, who declared that the Council ought not to tolerate human rights violations as contrary to the UN Charter, supported the WJC position. In the resolution that was finally adopted by a vote of 10 to 0 with seven abstentions, the Council asked the UN secretary-general to transmit the minutes of its deliberations to the Security Council. It should be noted that in its text the Council deleted the sentence the NGO Committee had proposed, which stated that the Economic and Social Council had no jurisdiction in the matter.

Forwarding the file to the Security Council of the UN was an act of great importance. It thereby recognized the seriousness of the situation of the Jewish communities that prevailed in the Arab countries. The Economic and Social Council thus addressed itself to the only UN body that could take binding action.

The resolution remains to this day the only action to have been adopted by the Economic and Social Council in an instance of violation of human rights addressed on the initiative of a nongovernmental organization.

The WJC precedent did not remain without consequences. Many countries recognized the danger that such a procedure could pose for them in the future, and they acted to ensure the elimination of this danger. By a resolution of July 20, 1952, communications coming from NGOs with consultative status that contained complaints against governments were excluded from the normal procedure and subjected to the special procedure of resolution 75/V, which was quite simply a first-class burial for any complaints against states.

The situation of Jews in the Arab countries remained extremely delicate throughout all the years that followed the creation of the State of Israel. It worsened each time the general political situation in the Near East passed through periods of tension and crisis. For example, after the Sinai Campaign between October 29 and November 2, 1956, the situation of the Jews of Egypt deteriorated dramatically.

As a consequence, the WJC was prompted to undertake vigorous action with the UN secretary-general, Dag Hammarskjöld, as well as with the High Commissioner for Refugees, the International Committee of the Red Cross, and the governments of France, Italy, Great Britain, Canada, the United States, the countries of Latin America, India, Sweden, Switzerland, Yugoslavia, New Zealand, and Australia.

I was personally active in dealing with the High Commissioner for Refugees and with the International Committee of the Red Cross. In this cause I also mobilized some Jewish communities with which I was especially close. Our efforts concentrated on liberating people who had been arrested and on facilitating emigration.

We particularly talked with the governments of Yugoslavia and India, whose leaders were closely allied on the political level with President Nasser and the movement of the nonaligned countries. Dr. Nahum Goldmann drew on his personal relations with the UN secretary-general as well as those with President Tito and President Nehru in order to move Egypt toward greater moderation.

The brutal measures that were meanwhile taken by the Egyptian government against the Jewish community included the arrest of numerous persons, in particular community leaders, wealthy persons, and those who ran important companies. The Egyptians seized a large number of Jewish businesses under various ludicrous pretexts—for example that their owners could not be trusted for reasons of national security. Other companies were expropriated because they were working for national defense. The Islamization of companies also constituted a pretext for such appropriations.

New negotiations blocked the bank accounts of these companies and of many of their owners and officers, and this led to the employees being dismissed.

The authorities published a general expulsion order for all Jews whose nationality was not recognized by Egyptian authorities; this affected about fifteen thousand persons. The expulsions were carried out by individual orders but on a massive scale.

Finally, on November 22, 1956, the government instituted a new law defining Egyptian nationality and permitting Egyptian authorities to deprive almost all the Jews of Egypt of their Egyptian nationality under the pretext that they were Zionists or that they might be carrying out Zionist activities. This affected more than 35,000 persons who could thereafter be treated as stateless Jews, despite the fact that their families had in some cases been living in Egypt for centuries.

The favorable representations undertaken by both President Tito and President Nehru finally contributed to calm the agitation and anti-Jewish excesses in Egypt and led the leaders of that country to a somewhat greater degree of moderation.

For years our concern was whether it would be possible to save the property of Egyptian Jews. This question has still not been resolved.

After the Six-Day War in June 1967, a new wave of persecution struck the Jewish communities in the Arab countries. In Egypt, authorities imprisoned and tortured five hundred Jews. In Libya, frenzied mobs attacked Jews in the streets and in their homes, murdering some twenty. Riots, sometimes with fatal results, broke out in Syria and Lebanon. In Iraq, authorities arrested and imprisoned some fifty Jews. The Jewish population was placed under police surveillance and deprived of all freedom of movement. Jews lost their jobs, and new regulations denied them all commercial activity.

In all the Arab countries, the situation of the Jews who remained became more and more precarious. News we received periodically gave us great cause for concern.

In the case of Egypt, however, the repeated efforts of the WJC and other organizations finally led to the liberation in July 1970 of all those detained and the right to leave the country with their families. This late but successful outcome was achieved thanks to the support of numerous governments with whom WJC leaders maintained constant contact.

An Italian colony since 1912, Libya became independent in 1951 thanks to a UN resolution. During World War II the Italian administration applied racist laws, forcing Jews to register and drawing up a complete inventory of their property and business and cultural activities. In 1943, after defeating the Afrika Korps and the Italian army, British forces assumed power in the country and held it until independence. Jewish volunteers from Palestine took part in the fighting as members of the British army.

After independence, official Libyan propaganda incited the population against Jews and against Israel. Our continual lobbying greatly contributed to Libyan Jews being allowed to leave the country. Indeed, it is worth recalling that as early as 1949 the WJC submitted to the UN a detailed memorandum on the situation of Jews in Tripolitania and Cyrenaica, strongly urging the secretary-general to take all appropriate measures to safeguard these communities.

When in November 1949 the UN General Assembly finally adopted resolutions concerning the disposition of the former Italian colonies, a decision was taken to appoint a UN commissioner for Libya. He was to be assisted by a council with ten members, among whom were six representatives of governments as well as representatives from minorities. The commissioner's mandate was to assure the transformation of the Italian colony into an independent state.

The director of the WJC Department of International Affairs in New York, Rabbi Maurice Perlzweig, was appointed by the Jewish Community of Libya to represent it before the General Assembly. On four occasions he was given an opportunity to present his views to the sixty nations that were members of the Political Commission. This was not only the first time the representative of a minority was heard by the Assembly, it was also the first time such a representative had come before the Political Commission, then chaired by Lester B. Pearson, the Canadian minister of foreign affairs and 1957 Nobel Peace Prize recipient. The UN commissioner, Adrien Pelt, continued throughout this period to consult with the WJC in Geneva and in New York concerning the status of minorities and the relevant clauses of the future Libyan constitution. As a result, Commissioner Pelt maintained close relations with the Jewish community of Libya. I myself actively participated in the discussions between the WJC and the UN through the many conversations I had with Pelt, whom I knew well from the time of the League of Nations, and on two occasions the WJC executive visited the Libyan community.

Additionally, WJC representatives had discussions with delegates from various countries at the 1952 UN General Assembly meeting in Paris, in the course of which the prime minister of Libya solemnly declared (I cite below a particularly significant passage from his address):

> We would like on this occasion to announce that the Libyan people, which has so long aspired toward liberty and independence, supports and shares the principles of the Charter of the United Nations. . . . Our constitution

adopts, in spirit and in letter, the fundamental principles of the Universal Declaration promulgated by the General Assembly of the United Nations in 1948.

Toward the end of 1958 the WJC department of foreign affairs learned that the administration in Tripoli had dismissed the leaders of the Jewish community there and placed the organization in the hands of a Muslim high commissioner. This situation represented an innovation in the long history of this community, which had been established in Libya in the third century B.C.E.

The explanation for this step, published in the Arab and Italian press in Libya, was that the 1930s law under which the Jewish community of Tripoli functioned had been established by the colonial Italian regime and was no longer applicable to the conditions of life in an independent country. Our own inquiries, conducted with the help of a certain number of friendly governments and through the efforts of representatives whom we had been able to send to Libya, revealed that the government's decision had been motivated not only by the desire to follow the lead of other Muslim governments in the region but also with a view to confiscating the Jewish community's files, hoping to discover proof of underground and illegal participation in the emigration to Israel. The Libyans did conduct such an inquiry, without prior notice, but this did not produce the anticipated results, and the honesty of the community leaders could not legitimately be doubted.

It is, however, fair to note that the formal dissolution of the community leadership was not accompanied by any interference in the daily lives of Jewish citizens and residents. In addition, not only did the organized religious life of the community continue without interruption, but the Muslim high commissioner did everything to assure that services at the synagogues were celebrated regularly and punctually.

Nonetheless this was the first act in a process of discrimination that would end with the disappearance of the Jewish community of Libya. The concatenation of these dire events (pogroms, despoliation, attacks by excited mobs, the destruction of homes and stores) forced the great majority of Libyan Jews to emigrate, largely to Israel, via Marseilles or Italian ports.

These anti-Jewish excesses, often fatal, occurred with particular intensity during the various battles and wars between Israel and the Arab countries, mainly in 1948, 1956, and 1967.

In 1969 King Idris I of Libya was overthrown by Muammar Gadhafi, whose government swept aside the country's constitution. The dictator hastened to expel those Jews who still lived there. Brutally evicted, they were received by Italy, thanks to the energetic and effective action of Raffaele Cantoni, president of the Union of Jewish Communities of Italy and a tireless member of the executive of the WJC. Thus came to an end the existence of a Jewish community more than twenty-three centuries old.

Meanwhile thousands of Syrian Jews chose to remain in their country after 1948, but their confidence in the Syrian authorities was cruelly disappointed. They were harshly discriminated against and suffered the loss of rights and a variety of hostile acts. In the Jewish quarters of Damascus, Aleppo, and Al-Qamishli, the houses of Jews who escaped abroad were confiscated, then given by the Syrians to Palestinian refugees, who satisfied their desire for vengeance on the few Jews who remained.

We struggled for years on behalf of Syrian Jews trying to recover the most elementary rights such as owning a telephone or—even more important—a legal signature, without which they could not even sell what belonged to them. We had to find new ways to furnish these Jews with material aid and to permit them at least some security in their daily lives.

After the Syrian border police killed some young Jews trying to leave the country, and after the protests that followed, the situation very slowly improved, without however achieving much with regard to human rights, something that non-Jewish Syrians did not enjoy either.

I took part in all these battles and in lobbying the governments of countries that could help us as well as the international organizations. For decades we had to intervene frequently in order to have the most elementary rights of Jews respected in the Arab and Muslim countries, from Aden to Afghanistan, and from Saudi Arabia to Sudan, where the governments subjected them to discriminatory and exceptional treatment.

The WJC's second great battle on behalf of a large Jewish community was aimed at safeguarding the rights of the Jews in the Soviet Union. This large-scale undertaking was in response to a gravely troubling situation that forced us into an engagement lasting more than four decades.

During this time the problem assumed the most diverse forms. At certain times the situation gave rise to the greatest hopes, at others it caused terrible disappointments and provoked enormous fears. The entire period was marked by continual contradictions on the part of the upper reaches of the Soviet ruling hierarchy. Even today, after the collapse of the Soviet system, we still must deal with new facets of anti-Semitism and threats that endanger the Jews of the former Soviet Union.

The revolution of February 1917 that overthrew the tsarist regime emancipated the Jews of Russia and for the first time gave them full equality of rights. The Bolshevik revolution of the following October fully incorporated this important action. Jews would thenceforth be considered as constituting a nationality and enjoying the same rights as the numerous other nationalities that made up the recently formed Union of Soviet Socialist Republics (USSR).

This period inaugurated an era of great freedom for Soviet Jews in art, literature, theater, journalism, and publishing. A radically new educational system was set up with hundreds of schools at all levels where there had previously been none. In short, this first phase of bolshevism, after the brutal repression of the tsars and despite the suffering of the civil war that followed the October Revolution, allowed at least the partial integration of millions of Jews into the new Soviet society.

This period of relative freedom for Jews did, however, involve two negative aspects. One was the fact that the state maintained an intense hostility toward their religion, against which its organs waged—as against all religions—open and relentless war. This placed religious liberty again in question and prevented the establishment of a representative central body for the faith. The second negative aspect involved the fact that the freedoms the Soviet Jews enjoyed at this time were checked by the war that the Soviet regime, for ideological reasons, had declared against Zionism. Police arrested hundreds of Zionists or suspected Zionists and sent many of them to concentration camps in the Gulag archipelago. Hebrew language and literature were practically banned, and emigration to Palestine was forbidden. The regime was even ready to create an alternative to Zionism, establishing in 1928 a "Jewish Autonomous Region" in Birobidzhan on the border with China, far from the centers of power and culture. In the belief that it could artificially create homelands for nationalities, the Soviets made efforts to encourage "colonization" there. But since the region had no roots in Jewish history and tradition, the attempt was destined to failure from the very start, though JAR exists to this day.

The period of relative freedom for Jews lasted as long as Lenin held the reins of power. The following phase was characterized by Stalin's struggle to consolidate his power and his efforts to dislodge Trotsky from government and influence. Stalin waged his battle against Trotskyism with a fanatical will to eliminate Lenin's former companions as well, a large number of whom were Jews. This power struggle rapidly took on clearly anti-Semitic features, as evidenced by the large proportion of Jews among those condemned in the great Stalinist purge trials of the 1930s.

Despite all this, with the rise of Nazism in Germany, the Soviet Union appeared to many to be the only solid bastion capable of opposing Nazi barbarism. Thus it attracted considerable sympathy both in bourgeois political circles and among the younger generation of Jews.

When the WJC met at its founding assembly in 1936 it already had to deal with this situation. At that time no one really dared to raise publicly the problem of imprisoned Zionists. We knew that we were facing a totalitarian and brutal regime that would not hesitate to use force when it wished. Nonetheless the WJC leaders courageously decided to raise the issue openly and adopted the following sober resolution:

> I. The World Jewish Congress instructs its Executive Committee to approach the authorities of Soviet Russia with a view to obtaining the following:
>
> 1. That freedom be allowed for learning the Hebrew language and for the development of Hebrew literature.
>
> 2. That the repression of Zionism and of the work of the Haluz be discontinued, and that the Jews who have been arrested and banished for their activities on behalf of Zionism be released and enabled to emigrate to Palestine.
>
> 3. That facilities be provided for Jewish emigration, especially to Palestine.
>
> 4. That religious freedom be allowed to the Jews.
>
> II. The World Jewish Congress records its regret that the Jewish population of Russia, which has always been in the forefront of the work of Jewry, has been unable to be represented at the First World Jewish Congress. It expresses the hope that relations between the Jews of Soviet Russia and World Jewry may be re-established in the near future, and that the Jews of Russia may be represented at future World Congresses.

In the years that followed, Dr. Nahum Goldmann took advantage of every opportunity to discuss with Soviet diplomats both the problem of the imprisoned Zionists and, more generally, the world situation and the dangers it entailed. He insisted that the threats that Nazism represented were applicable to all parties, not only to the Jews.

At that time Soviet Russia did not lack for professional diplomats. It recruited its representatives among educated Jews who had a knowledge of foreign languages. Almost the entire Soviet diplomatic corps consisted of Jews, including the minister of foreign affairs, Maxim Litvinov, and ambassadors such as Boris Stein, Yacov Suritz, Vladimir Sokolin, Ivan Maiski, and Marcel Rosenberg. The only important non-Jewish Soviet diplomat at that time was

Ambassador Vladimir Potemkin. Nahum Goldmann had numerous discussions with him, but these never led to concrete results.

World War II broke out after Berlin and Moscow signed the German-Soviet nonaggression pact at the end of August 1939, by which Germany sought to protect itself against the Soviet armies during its conquest of Poland, to be followed by the invasion of Western Europe. For its part, Soviet Russia wished to protect itself against the German armies, delay its involvement in the war, and take control of a substantial part of Poland. The Ribbentrop-Molotov pact dismayed and horrified the Jews of the USSR, as it did Jews and others in the rest of the world.

Germany's attack on the USSR on June 22, 1941, changed this situation completely. On the entire Eastern Front the Jews en masse fell victims to the *Einsatzgruppen*, the Nazi mobile killing units. Soviet military forces were at first incapable of checking the German advance, and Soviet casualties numbered in the hundreds of thousands.

In hundreds of localities the Nazi killing units carried out mass murder, the most notorious of which was that in the ravine at Babi Yar, near the Ukrainian city of Kiev, where the Germans and their collaborators machine-gunned nearly 100,000 Jewish men, women, and children.

Between 1941 and 1943 Nazi Germany occupied half the territory of European Russia. During the massive flow of populations toward the east, a great number of Jews, 200,000 to 300,000, sought refuge in distant Soviet republics such as Kazakhstan and Uzbekistan. Neither the Soviet authorities nor the resident populations practiced discrimination against them, but their fate as refugees was often dramatic. The lack of employment and housing, the inability to adapt to the often primitive conditions of life and the climate brought on epidemics and even deadly famines. Local Soviet authorities employed a certain number of these refugees in strenuous forced labor, building roads, cutting turf, and the like.

It should also be noted that in the territories occupied by the Nazis, most of the population did not participate in the hunt for Jews.

In this desperate situation, Stalin played the national card. He mobilized all the peoples of the Soviet Union in a sacred union to save the motherland. The Communist party and the government propaganda organs provisionally shelved the ideological struggles. For a while they adopted a moderate line intended to calm the population and motivate it in this merciless struggle. In particular they made great concessions to the Orthodox church, which until then they had viciously attacked. The Jews as well temporarily benefited from the new political line. In 1942 the Soviet government created

the Jewish Anti-Fascist Committee in order to help assure the support of Soviet Jews and the sympathy of Jews around the world for the struggle of the
Soviet Union against Nazi Germany. A large number of Jewish intellectuals,
among whom the best known were the writer Ilya Ehrenburg, the actor and
director Solomon Mikhoels, the writer and poet Itzik Fefer, and the poet
Peretz Markish, served in the organization. The Anti-Fascist Committee addressed urgent appeals to the Jews of the entire world to support the Soviet
Jews and their country in this deadly struggle for freedom.

I myself received such an appeal in the form of a telegram from Kuybyshev,
the city where the Soviet government had taken refuge. More than thirty pages
long, the telegram was addressed to our relief committee for Jewish populations
struck by the war, in whose name we were conducting our philanthropic activity. I have already referred to the reaction of the Swiss when this message arrived.

After the contacts had been established between the Anti-Fascist Committee and the WJC in the United States, the WJC invited a delegation to visit the
United States and Great Britain to support the Soviet war effort. The journey
of the committee delegates, Solomon Mikhoels and Itzik Fefer, took place in
the second half of 1943 and was a veritable triumph. Local groups organized
mass rallies, and we even agreed jointly to draft a Black Book on Nazi atrocities. We hoped to have set the foundation for genuine cooperation with the
Soviet Jews, but this proved to be a grand illusion. Permission to publish the
book was withdrawn by Soviet authorities.*

In the postwar years neither Soviet government spokesmen nor the press
wished to admit the gravity and extent of the slaughter of the Jews ascribed to
the Nazis. All public Soviet reports made no distinction between Jews and the
other nationalities that had suffered during the war.

After the war Soviet authorities refused to recognize the particular situation of Russian Jewry, and a veil of silence fell over the persecutions and their
memory. Consequently, while thousands of localities raised monuments to
commemorate their martyrs, the responsible government organ regularly refused every proposal for a collective cenotaph consecrated to the memory of
the murdered Jews. Voices were raised in protest even in the Soviet Union, the
most famous of which was that of the poet Yevgeny Yevtushenko, who composed a memorable poem on Babi Yar.

Indeed, Babi Yar soon became a symbol for Soviet Jews who tried every
year to gather at the site of the massacre. On several occasions the partici-

---

*See the first English-language publication, Ilya Ehrenburg and Vassily Grossman, eds., *The
Black Book* (New York, 1981).—ED.

pants, who had to overcome various obstacles to get there, were arrested and even prosecuted. The ravine of Babi Yar, along with the surrounding land, was turned over to the housing administration of the city of Kiev, which built apartment buildings there. An official stone placed there does not even mention that the victims were Jews.

All the members of the Jewish Anti-Fascist Committee were fervent Communists, many veterans of the October Revolution. In the immediate postwar period, between 1948 and 1952, the security organs arrested all members of the committee—Markish, Fefer, Bergelson, Hofstein, and many others, with the exception of Ilya Ehrenburg. In July 1952 a Stalinist court ordered the execution of all except Lina Shtern, who was to be imprisoned. Only after Stalin's death were the sentences annulled and the cases terminated. But this November 1955 action was too late to save those executed.*

But after the Allied victory against Nazi Germany, when the fate of Jewish "displaced persons" and the future of Palestine were discussed in international circles, the Soviet Union, through its spokesmen Semjon Tsarapkin and Andrei Gromyko, adopted a prudent, constructive attitude toward Jewish claims. As a leader of the World Jewish Congress who for many long years had not ceased to cultivate ongoing relations with the Soviet diplomats, and as a delegate of the Jewish Agency for Palestine to the General Assembly of the United Nations, Dr. Goldmann exerted a great deal of influence on the positions they adopted. The Soviets probably considered the desire of Palestinian Jews for independence as an act of liberation from British colonial rule and thus gave a rather favorable reception to the Jewish position on the question.

They probably also realized that it was impossible to require hundreds of thousands of Jewish survivors from the Nazi camps, who had become "displaced persons," to return to their former countries, and that the new state would be the natural haven to receive them. Nevertheless they emphasized that such considerations could not apply to Soviet Jews. They voted for the resolution to divide Palestine and were among the first to recognize the new state after its creation in May 1948. They even went so far in their favorable attitude as to support the efforts of the new state to procure arms in order to defend itself against the attacks by Arab countries that the British had armed.

But when the Soviet Union established diplomatic relations with the State of Israel, it noted with concern the triumphant reception that Soviet Jewish masses displayed for Golda Meir as the first Israeli ambassador to Moscow. In

*See Joshua Rubenstein and Vladimir Naumov, eds., *Stalin's Secret Pogrom: The Postwar Inquisition of the Jewish Anti-Fascist Committee* (New Haven, Conn., 2001).—ED.

the end, the Soviets dashed the hopes raised by some of their actions and statements.

At almost the same moment when the Soviet Union officially supported the State of Israel, Andrei A. Zhdanov, Stalin's designated "crown prince" and the head of the Central Committee's International Department, launched his huge campaign against "cosmopolitanism," which sought to liquidate the remains of the "decadent bourgeois culture of the West" in the USSR and to replace it with healthy Soviet proletarian culture. In fact this campaign was aimed at Jews, who were presented as elements without deep roots in Soviet society. Under this pretext the campaign sought to erase the last remnants of a specifically Jewish culture in the Soviet Union. This policy led to the successive arrest and execution of many Yiddish-language writers and poets. It has been rightly said that through cultural genocide Stalin concluded the murder of the Jews begun by the Nazis.

In addition, supported by new legislation, Soviet authorities overwhelmed Soviet Jews with all kinds of accusations. They arrested many Jews and sentenced them on charges of embezzlement and acts of sabotage. Senior Jewish officials began to be eliminated from government, followed by those of lesser importance.

The culminating point of this action against Soviet Jewry was Stalin's January 1953 accusation of a group of Jewish physicians. They were charged with being in touch with the "bourgeois and nationalist" American Jewish Joint Distribution Committee and of having received orders to eliminate the Soviet leaders. The Soviets then initiated the notorious "white coat trial" in which six of the nine doctors charged were Jews.

Added to this alarming news, very serious reports reached us that Stalin was also secretly preparing for a massive deportation of urban Jews to Siberia. According to some sources, Stalin was to have made this proposal at a special meeting of the Politburo. Israeli and WJC leaders received these reports with great anxiety. They decided that in the face of such a threat a dramatic counteraction was imperative, and by common agreement they decided to convoke a large international meeting to protest Stalin's project.

Along with Eran Laor of the Geneva office of the Jewish Agency, I was put in charge of organizing this conference in Zurich in March 1953. We had just welcomed the first delegation to that city when, like a bolt from the blue, Moscow announced Stalin's death. We immediately canceled the conference. Almost immediately, the new Soviet leadership halted the trials of the Kremlin doctors, and promptly freed them.

After the death of Stalin, persecution of the Jews passed into a generally more relaxed phase. The new leadership released several victims of the anti-

Semitic campaign and allowed others to be rehabilitated. No one spoke any longer about deporting Jews to Siberia. Relations between the USSR and Israel improved, and there was a general return to legality.

The dramatic situation of 1953 was somewhat attenuated in the years that followed, but conditions in the Soviet Union remained far from satisfactory. Even if we feared less for the lives of Soviet Jews, discriminatory and exclusionary measures continued to be applied. Jews, in particular young people, had lost all confidence in Soviet emancipation and the possibilities of equality.

The Khrushchev era that followed made claims to "liberalism," but this scarcely benefited the Jews. It must be observed that the Khrushchev speech exposing the crimes of the Stalinist era does not even mention those perpetrated against Jews and their culture.*

Soviet authorities deployed great efforts to make Jews forget their history and culture and to isolate them from Jewish communities abroad. The official explanation that was given for this state of affairs was that the Jews, now fully assimilated, in no way wanted a culture of their own. And yet all the facts proved the contrary. Numerous visitors from the USSR testified to the vitality of Russian Jews, their aspirations to live within their culture, and their desire to establish ties with other communities in the world. Khrushchev affirmed that the Jews could not benefit from cultural institutions similar to those enjoyed by other minorities within their own regions because the Jews were dispersed across the entire USSR, but his statements were only a bureaucratic pretext. Other less numerous minorities benefited from such institutions in Soviet regions that were not their own.

This situation and the anxieties to which it gave rise led to long-term concerted efforts by the leaders of the WJC, the Jewish Agency, and Israeli government. They believed with increasing conviction that they could not accept the current situation of millions of Soviet Jews. They agreed to raise this question openly before world public opinion, and they chose the meeting of the WJC executive in London at the end of April 1957 as the occasion to expose the situation to public scrutiny. Dr. Goldmann personally took responsibility to do this in an address that was widely reported at the time.

Here, paraphrased, are the principal points he made:

Dr. Goldmann affirmed that the Communist regime of the Soviet Union had not resolved the Jewish problem. Even if senior leaders did not admit it, he said, they were profoundly aware of this continued injustice.

*Nikita Khrushchev (1894–1971), then first secretary of the Soviet Communist party, gave a now famous speech to a closed session of the party's Twentieth Congress on February 25, 1956, in which he discussed Stalinist crimes for the first time.—ED.

The action on behalf of Soviet Jews was not a battle against their country. We asked of the USSR what we asked for Jews of all countries of the world, whatever their government or social system: to enjoy fully equal rights and for the Jewish community to maintain its identity. As long as these demands were not met, we considered that the Soviet Union was acting wrongly with regard to the Jewish people.

We would succeed one day, Goldmann said, despite all the difficulties. The lot of the Jews of the USSR and Eastern Europe constituted one of the major problems for Jews in the years to come. The World Jewish Congress was interested only in the survival, security, and equality of rights of the Jewish people. We were convinced that Jews could live within the framework of any social system.

We had never accused the Communists of having instituted in principle a system that made life impossible for Jews. Communism had always proclaimed the right of national minorities to maintain their identity. The Soviet constitution gave this right to national minorities and, officially, Jews were also recognized as a national minority. Various Communist governments had permitted Jewish minorities in their countries to live their own lives. In Poland, Hungary, Romania, and Bulgaria, not to mention Yugoslavia, Jewish communities and community organizations existed, as did rabbinical institutions and Jewish theaters and newspapers.

Until this time the World Jewish Congress had not dealt publicly with the problem of the three and a half million Jews of the Soviet Union and Eastern Europe. It hoped that contacts with Soviet leaders could bring about a solution. In recent years the Iron Curtain had become somewhat more flexible; some delegations of rabbis had obtained permission to travel to the Soviet Union. Many young Jews showed they were more attached to Judaism than their parents had been. The younger generation did not have its parents' illusion that communism would eliminate discrimination against Jews. This generation had encountered discrimination at the universities and in certain professions.

One of the major problems of the Jewish minority in the Soviet Union was the right of its members to emigrate to Israel. Numerous Communist countries had shown in the past their understanding of the Jews' desire to be reunited with their families and to live a full Jewish life in Israel. The Soviet Union ought to have had more understanding of the desire of Jews to live in Israel.

Taking this desire into account would make a major contribution to resolving the Jewish problem in the USSR. Dr. Goldmann noted that he firmly believed that our generation would see the day when a great number of Soviet Jews would be able to emigrate to Israel. Indeed, he said: "One day the doors will open."

Expressing the deep disappointment of world Jewry in light of the spectacular deterioration in the Soviet attitude toward the State of Israel, Dr. Goldmann recalled that the Soviet Union was partly responsible for the creation of that state. Its representative, Andrei Gromyko, at that time the USSR minister of foreign affairs, had presented with more conviction than any other statesman the moral case of the Jewish people in its claim for a state of its own. Were the arguments that he had advanced just ten years earlier now false? Even if the Soviet Union disagreed with certain aspects of Israeli policy, threatening the existence of Israel and at times denying its right to survive would not help solve the problem. If peace were a dominant element of Soviet policy, as its leaders continually proclaimed, they should equally well apply this principle to the Middle East.

From this moment on, the question of Soviet Jews became a priority on the WJC agenda and all the Jewish organizations in numerous countries that followed its lead. To orient the actions to come, a coordinating committee under the chairmanship of Dr. Goldmann was established with the participation of the relevant services of Israel and the World Zionist Organization. Clearly the Jews of the entire world were to be mobilized in support of the freedom of Soviet Jewry. This was the beginning of a massive campaign that would last for several decades and conclude in the Gorbachev era. It ended with freedom for Jews to emigrate and in the former USSR itself with the reestablishment of conditions necessary for the renewal of Jewish cultural and religious life.

Dr. Goldmann's speech defined the WJC policy for years to come. It was clear that we could not possibly force a great power such as the Soviet Union to change its policies. This is why we tried to convince its leaders with rational arguments and to make them understand the profound reasons for our action. We were particularly concerned to persuade the Soviet leadership that action on behalf of Soviet Jews was not a hostile act against the USSR and its government, nor was it part of the Cold War, but resulted rather from the need to maintain the existence and identity of this great community.

Not all Jewish circles comprehended or agreed with the WJC program and its political approach. Some people criticized us for being too timid and for not leading the fight with greater energy and aggression. The bellicosity of some of these critics poorly masked their lack of faith in the chances for success in the struggle against an empire that had triumphed over many other adversaries and their anxiety that the Soviet government would impose sanctions against its Jewish citizens. In actual fact, despite our precautions, the first reactions of the Soviets and their allies showed that they considered us instruments in the Cold War. After fluctuating for some time, this attitude fortunately changed for the better. But at that time the situation appeared difficult to us all and to some of us even desperate.

In the absence of any Soviet reaction to our requests, the argument was increasingly adopted in Israel that the problem of Soviet Jews could only be solved by massive emigration to Israel. For our part we continued to hold the position that it was necessary to fight simultaneously both for the right to emigrate and to assure the opportunities that would permit Soviet Jews to lead a truly Jewish life in their country.

Given that we were dealing with a community of several million persons, it was clear that emigration, if it were ever allowed, would take many long years. In the meantime there had to be educational and cultural resources to sustain the Jewish sprit of the community still in the country. Without that, no future emigration could be envisaged. The divergence among various points of view at certain times was sharp, regrettably dividing the international Jewish community.

Only when Soviet Jews roused themselves and began to react against the oppression of their authorities, at first in small groups, then in mass movements, did the situation begin to change—first with acts of severe repression, then, finally, with concessions.

On the occasion of its Fourth Plenary Assembly, held in Stockholm August 2–12, 1959, the World Jewish Congress expressed formal regret at the absence of its brethren from the Soviet Union. The assembly recalled forcefully the inalienable right—independent of any political or social regime—to organize representative bodies and religious, cultural, and social institutions; to maintain the identity, traditions, and spiritual values of Jewish life; to bring the distinctive contribution of their Jewish citizens to the life of the countries of which they were citizens. The Jews of the Soviet Union should enjoy the same opportunities as those offered other nationalities and ethnic groups, and thus be capable of developing their spiritual heritage in Hebrew and in Yiddish, in particular in the fields of publishing, the theater, and institutions devoted to culture and education. The WJC deplored the fact that the enjoyment of these legitimate rights was so often stymied by all kinds of obstacles raised against them.

Additionally, the Congress expressed its keen apprehension for all the communities following the closures of synagogues and sanctuaries by local Soviet authorities. Finally, the WJC appealed to the Soviet government to authorize those who so desired to rejoin their families in Israel. "May . . . the Soviet Union," the WJC resolution concluded, "translate the ideals of human rights into a living reality for all humanity."

We were not content just to adopt a resolution. During the months that followed the Fourth Assembly, the Congress continued numerous lobbying actions with Soviet authorities as well as international political and cultural circles in order to orient world public opinion about the problem. We saw the need to exert constant pressure without breaking off contacts and negotiations with the Soviets.

To this end, Dr. Goldmann, in concert with the great Jewish philosopher Martin Buber, in 1960 convoked in Paris the first international conference on the situation of Jews in the Soviet Union. Prominent non-Jewish figures participated in the meetings.

During the period that followed, no immediate benefits to Jews in the Soviet Union accrued from this meeting, but the gathering succeeded in keeping the question before the world public and maintained pressure on the Soviet government. The plenary assembly in Stockholm and the Paris conference's occasional rays of light did little to mitigate the increasingly dark horizon. The process of closing synagogues continued to spread. According to Soviet sources, 450 functioning synagogues existed in 1956 while the number open for services in 1963 was 96. The number fell considerably after that date.

Other Soviet religious communities also saw a decline in the number of religious buildings, but not in the same proportion as the Jewish community. In 1962 the preparation of matzoh, unleavened bread for Passover, was forbidden in public bakeries, a prohibition that was later moderated by the announcement that a special bakery would be opened in Moscow and that a certain quantity of matzoh could be imported from abroad. Unfortunately it was not long before authorities closed the bakery for "public health reasons," and substantial quantities of matzoh shipped from the United States, Britain, Israel, and other countries were not turned over to the Jews or to Jewish communities. For a long time this problem remained at the center of the struggle for the Soviet Jews. Later these restrictions were somewhat relaxed so that matzoh could be baked in Moscow, Leningrad, and other large cities. But the volume of production was quite low and could not satisfy the needs of even a small portion of the Jewish community.

The yeshiva established in Moscow in 1957 for the training of rabbis did not meet the expectations of the community. In 1958 thirteen students were enrolled. In 1962 the majority of students did not receive authorization to continue their studies after the summer holidays, this under the pretext that a housing shortage in Moscow precluded their finding places to live. At that point the yeshiva enrollment consisted of three students.

In 1961 authorities dismissed the presidents of the six synagogues situated in the large provincial cities and followed this measure with the arrest of several Jewish lay leaders in Moscow and Leningrad. Some of them were taken before secret tribunals and sentenced to lengthy prison terms.

Another troublesome element was the publication of a number of anti-Jewish propaganda works. For example, in 1962 the state publishing house for political works published and widely distributed the Russian translation of a book by Paul-Henri Thiry, Baron d'Holbach entitled *A Gallery of Saints*, written in the mid-eighteenth century and crammed with vicious attacks not only against the Jewish religion but also against the Jewish people.* Yet the most striking example of anti-Semitic propaganda remains Trofim Kichko's Soviet-era work entitled *Judaism Without Embellishment*, printed by the state publishing house in Kiev. A book of virulent anti-Semitism with ugly satirical cartoons, it caused cries of protest in the Jewish world as well as in some progressive non-Jewish circles and even in Communist circles outside the USSR. As a consequence, the ideological committee of the Soviet Communist party was obliged to condemn the work, which was subsequently withdrawn from circulation and destroyed.

After Kichko's book had been pulled, however, new publications appeared, such as *Judaism and Zionism Today* by Mayatsky, published in 1964 in Moldavia, and *The Decline of the Judaic Religion* by Mikhail Iosifovich Shakhnovich.

Despite these troubling occurrences, we saw evidence of some relaxation in restrictive measures toward Jews and a certain improvement in the overall situation. The publication of the Yiddish-language newspaper, *Sovietisch Heimland*, first a bimonthly and then a monthly paper, was by its very existence a memorable phenomenon for many years, despite its detestable ideological stance.

A number of additional publications appeared, among them an excellent Hebrew-Russian dictionary, an anthology of modern Israeli poetry, translated into Russian from Hebrew, Yiddish, and Arabic, and two Yiddish works, reportedly the first of many more. The editors of *Sovietisch Heimland* organized cultural conferences in several cities; Jewish writers and readers of the paper participated. There were a number of cultural exchanges between the Soviet

---

*A highly influential radical materialist philosopher, d'Holbach (1723–1789) also wrote virulent attacks on Christianity.—ED.

Union and Israel, including concerts given by well-known orchestras and musicians. Similar events were announced for the future.

Aleksei Kosygin, the Soviet prime minister, and *Pravda*, the official organ of the Soviet Communist party, both made references to anti-Semitism. In a speech given in Riga, Kosygin denounced anti-Semitism as an attitude "alien to the principles and doctrine of Communism."

But these promising swallows were not followed by a spring of Jewish cultural renewal in the USSR. Bertrand Russell noted in a message published at that time that although an improvement in the situation had been promised in 1956 and 1957, only some symbolic cultural activity had been authorized—a handful of books in Yiddish, published by small presses and exploited for propaganda purposes, a monthly magazine in Yiddish, one or two amateur theater troupes, and a few tours by Jewish singers.

A new phenomenon aided efforts to obtain some relief for the lot of the Russian Jewish community: knowledge of the difficulties encountered by the Soviet community had spread beyond the limits of Jewish public opinion. The general press around the world began to publish news about Jewish protest meetings and the resolutions they adopted.

Through its committees and associated organizations the WJC undertook a vast global lobbying program in order to mobilize intellectuals and politicians who were not engaged in the Cold War and who understood that the struggle for Soviet Jewry should be conducted beyond the limits of that country.

Beginning in 1960, world figures of great moral standing such as Bertrand Russell, Willy Brandt, Vincent Auriol, Olaf Palme, Pierre Mendès-France, Martin Luther King, Eleanor Roosevelt, Vladimir Rabi, Vercors, and many others, made resounding statements and asked their governments to intercede with the Soviet Union. Rare were the meetings between Soviet representatives and those of the West at which the problem of Soviet Jews was not raised.

We extended this lobbying action to the leaders of the Western communities and to those of national associations having cordial relations with the USSR. I participated in meetings with the leader of the French Communist party, Waldeck Rochet, and the secretary-general of the labor union, Confédération Générale du Travail, and with André Blumel, leader of the France-USSR Association, as well as with Umberto Terracini and Enzo Sereni of the Italian Communist party.

All these meetings and public statements had a certain impact. Intellectuals, philosophers, academics, and eminent internationally recognized representatives of a wide spectrum of political positions and opinions, most of them non-Jews, organized conferences in Paris, London, Washington, Rome, Rio de Janeiro, Buenos Aires, and Mexico City. Friends of the Soviet Union and politicians from numerous countries raised their voices to make direct appeals to the Soviet leadership.

The United Nations and the Council of Europe formally discussed the situation of Soviet Jews. On several occasions the Council of Europe voted in favor of statements that emphasized the unacceptable discrimination against our Soviet brethren. The matter was the object of reports published by the International Group for Socialist Studies, which included representatives from Great Britain, Denmark, the Netherlands, Norway, Sweden, and the International Commission of Jurists. In 1962 the World Council of Churches sent a delegation to the USSR to study the problem of Soviet Jews. The delegation's report spoke of the "harsh persecution" of the Jewish minority.

The attitude then adopted by the Communists and by the left in a number of countries such as Italy, France, Great Britain, the United States, Canada, the Scandinavian countries, and Australia, which expressed their concern over the discrimination being practiced on the Soviet Jewish community, constituted a particularly important factor in our campaign. The world clearly saw that the two most influential Communist parties after those of the Soviet bloc, the French and Italian parties, displayed a lively interest in the issue.

The first positive and important measure on the part of the Soviet government was the declaration in December 1966 by Soviet Premier Kosygin, who affirmed that Soviet authorities would raise no objection to the reunification of families that had been separated by the war. Meeting in Paris shortly thereafter, the WJC executive committee noted this statement with satisfaction and expressed the hope that resources would be made available in the shortest possible time in order to permit families separated for years to be reunited.

Unfortunately this slight improvement in the Soviet attitude toward emigration was brief. After the Six-Day War in 1967 the USSR did not content itself with adopting a hostile attitude toward Israel but denounced "Zionism" with increasing vigor, which meant that Jewish emigration suffered a radical setback.

It should be noted that in 1968 the WJC's Institute of Jewish Affairs in London launched a new publication called *Soviet Jewry*, which subsequently accomplished much positive work and published studies of great value.

Meeting in Rome in January 1969 the executive committee approved a proposition by Armand Kaplan, director of the WJC Department of International Affairs, to hold a conference of experts to closely examine recent developments in the Soviet Union, in particular the resurgence of a national Jewish consciousness among Soviet Jews, as well as the increased militancy shown by numerous Jews in their efforts to obtain authorization to emigrate to Israel. The Congress's future policy on this issue would be based on the conclusions reached by this conference, which met in December 1969 at the Institute for Jewish Affairs.

In the course of the spring of 1970 the movement in support of freedom to emigrate to Israel increased substantially among Soviet Jews. Around the world, communities affiliated with the WJC took part in activities intended to reinforce these demands. The movement continued to gain strength. In June 1970 several desperate Jews (and reportedly at least a couple of non-Jews) planned to hijack a Soviet airliner in Leningrad, hoping to fly first to Sweden and then to Israel. The Leningrad trial and its echo around the world led to the creation of a new organization, the Conference on Soviet Jewry, of which the Congress was one of the founding members.

Faced with these developments, we all understood that we had to mobilize both the Jewish and the non-Jewish worlds on behalf of the Soviet Jews. As a result we planned to convoke a large world congress in Brussels on the issue. I participated actively in these activities and in the preparations for mobilizing all the communities and organizations around the world.

The conference took place in February 1970. The WJC sent a large delegation, of which I was a part.

As WJC secretary-general, before the conference I sent a communiqué to the communities and organizations that were members of the WJC, requesting their full support. Seven hundred sixty delegates, representing thirty-eight countries, attended. The Conference received messages of support from the most prominent moral, political, and academic authorities throughout the world. And the meeting demonstrated in impressive fashion the solidarity of world Jewry with Jews in the Soviet Union, reaching its culminating point in the ceremonial appeal from Brussels, which found a large audience around the world.

These agitations and the constant pressure on the Soviet government were sure to have consequences. The period that followed was characterized on the one hand by the continual harassment of Soviet Jews who expressed a desire to emigrate, and on the other by the beginning of a trend to grant exit visas.

Those who wished to leave and applied for a visa lost their employment and their means of subsistence. Action continued against the volunteers who taught Hebrew and those who learned it in preparation for emigration. At a certain moment Jews who had university degrees and who wished to leave the country found themselves forced to pay a heavy "exit" tax as a condition. A large group of prestigious academics from around the world mounted an international campaign to force the Soviets to repeal the tax regulation.

Numerous Soviet "activists" who lobbied on behalf of emigration and who had been denied an exit visa were imprisoned. They were called—as many will remember—*refusniks*.

The WJC and Jewish organizations consistently raised protests against these arbitrary and inhumane practices. It was probably thanks to this pressure that from 1972 on, the government granted an increasing number of exit visas to Soviet Jews. This action took such a positive turn that by 1974 almost 100,000 Jews had obtained visas. Then the flow progressively diminished. Furthermore Soviet authorities would not consent to any reestablishment of the right of Soviet Jews to maintain their community, that is, their religious and cultural identity.

A new phase in the struggle on behalf of Soviet Jews began when leaders of the American Jewish community succeeded in convincing their government and the leaders of the two parties in Congress of the need to obtain assurances from the Soviet government that a more liberal emigration policy would be adopted. It soon became clear that congressional agreement to include the "most favored nation" clause in an important trade agreement then being negotiated between the United States and the Soviet Union would depend on a liberalization of Soviet emigration practices and an end to the harassment of Soviet Jews.

The energetic action of the American administration and Congress may have found its inspiration in a resounding precedent: between 1907 and 1909, during the negotiation of a far-reaching commercial agreement, the United States exerted pressure on tsarist authorities by making the concession to Russia of "most favored nation" status subject to the termination of the severe persecution Russian Jews were then suffering.

In any event, the American government's political activities and diplomatic exchanges reached a culminating point in the exchange of letters between the secretary of state, Henry Kissinger, and Senator Henry Jackson in October 1974. Known as the Jackson-Vanik Amendment, after its congressional sponsors, Senator Jackson and Representative Charles Vanik, this legislation contributed to reinforce substantially the emigration of Jews from the USSR. The amendment prohibited the extension of trade benefits to countries that limited or made emigration excessively difficult. This success had the positive effect of mobilizing support for the cause of Soviet Jews, with many other governments acting along similar lines.

The Riegner family in 1934. Clockwise from top, Gerhart, his mother Agnes, his father Heinrich, his sisters Helene and Marianne. *(Linda Mittel)*

Gerhart on a skiing outing with his parents in Switzerland, January 1938, celebrating his father's sixtieth birthday. *(Linda Mittel)*

Riegner in 1939.

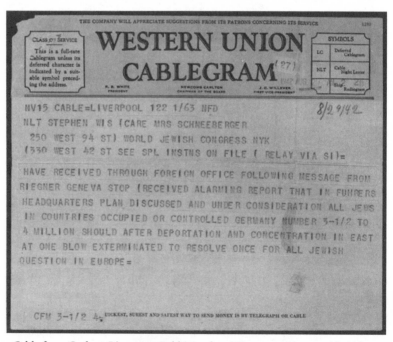

Cable from Gerhart Riegner to Rabbi Stephen Wise, reporting on a Nazi plan to exterminate European Jewry, August 29, 1942. *(USHMM, courtesy of the Jacob Rader Marcus Center of the American Jewish Archive)*

Jewish leaders attend a meeting of the World Jewish Congress in Montreux, Switzerland, 1948. Rabbi Stephen Wise is at left, Sidney Silverman in foreground. *(Linda Mittel)*

Riegner, second from right, at a gathering of Jewish leaders at the Montreux meeting of the World Jewish Congress, 1948. *(Linda Mittel)*

Riegner, left, after his election as president of the Conference of Non-Governmental Organizations in consultative status at the United Nations, with Dag Hammarskjöld, center, UN secretary-general, and Gerald Meade of Great Britain, 1953.

Riegner, second from right, greeting Zalman Shazar, president of Israel, in Tel Aviv, 1970. Nahum Goldmann is at left.

Riegner, second from right, at the first meeting of the International Committee for Liaison Between Jews and Roman Catholics, in Paris, 1971. From left, Chief Rabbi Jacob Kaplan, Fritz Becker, Arthur Hertzberg, Msgr. Roger Etchegaray, Rabbi Marc Tanenbaum, Riegner, Joseph Lichten.

Riegner, center, with Philip Klutznick, left, Henry Kissinger, and Nahum Goldmann, right, in Washington, 1977.

Riegner at
Auschwitz, 1983.

Riegner at the consultation between Jews and African Christians organized by
the World Council of Churches, the African Council of Churches, and the
Jewish International Committee for Interfaith Consultation, in Nairobi, 1986.

French president François Mitterand awarding the Legion of Honor to Riegner in Paris, 1987.

Riegner with Pope John Paul II in Rome, 1990.

The signing of the fundamental agreement between the Holy See and the State of Israel, in Jerusalem, 1993. Left, Msgr. Claudio Maria Celli, the Vatican's undersecretary for foreign affairs; right, Yossi Beilin, deputy minister of foreign affairs for Israel; center, Riegner.

Gerhart Riegner in 1997.

At the same time the WJC attentively followed the course of the preparations being made for the 1973 Conference on Security and Cooperation in Europe (CSCE) in Helsinki. Initiated by the USSR, its objective was the promotion of European security and cooperation as well as a lessening of tensions between East and West.

The inclusion of humanitarian questions on the agenda of the future conference considerably increased our interest. The WJC saw the possibility of alleviating the acuity of some of the most anguished problems faced by the Jewish communities of the Soviet Union and Eastern Europe. Consequently we arranged to be represented at the various sessions of the CSCE and in February 1974 circulated a memorandum to the delegations of the participating countries outlining our position on the emigration of Soviet Jews and related matters.

These appeals and the efforts undertaken directly by the WJC or the Conference on Soviet Jewry resulted in a small increase in emigration, but even this situation did not last. Increasing tensions between the East and West, culminating in the Soviet intervention in Afghanistan in 1979 and the crisis that followed, coincided with a noticeable decline in emigration.

The final accords of the Helsinki conference, signed between July 30 and August 1, 1975, stated the desire of participating nations to further regular meetings that would contribute to the reunification of families; to promote a freedom to travel, whether for personal or professional reasons; and to expand contacts, including those among nongovernmental organizations. The final accords also foresaw the continuation of the conference and of procedures designed to simplify and stimulate exchanges and meetings. The first of these meetings would be held in Belgrade in 1977 and would review how the decisions reached in Helsinki had been implemented.

These decisions marked the beginning of a trend toward greater flexibility in the attitude of Soviet authorities, which we then hoped to exploit for our cause. But events soon dashed those hopes.

Conscious of the parallel between the adoption of the final accords of the Helsinki conference and the deterioration in the situation of Soviet Jews, the presidents of the World Jewish Congress and the World Zionist Organization called their leaders together at a special meeting in Paris in September 1975. They noted the worsening of the situation and the substantial reduction in emigration, and judged it necessary to convoke a second international conference on Soviet Jewry in Brussels in February 1976. Again the World Jewish Congress joined other organizations as a sponsor.

The second world conference on the Jews of the Soviet Union, called "Brussels 2," convened in that city on February 17–19, 1976. It was a powerful and impressive manifestation of the concern of world Jewry and of many prominent non-Jewish figures to encourage and support the struggle of Soviet Jews. Philip Klutznick, president of the WJC executive council, was one of the great personalities behind the conference. It culminated with the adoption of a formal and ceremonial declaration that called on all the men and women of the conference and all governments concerned with humanitarian ideals to voice their support for the Jews of the Soviet Union. The declaration reaffirmed the engagement of Jewish communities and Jewish organizations to continue to assist the legitimate demands of Soviet Jewry.

The WJC executive charged me with the direction of a special commission, grouping together the representatives of the Christian churches and other religious dignitaries, with a mandate to examine the roles that non-Jewish institutions and religious figures could play in this struggle.

In November 1976 the WJC executive committee met in Geneva and again expressed its concern over the harassment of Soviet Jews who wished to leave the country, as well as the failure of the Soviets to apply the human rights clauses agreed to in the Helsinki final accords and in other international agreements. The committee expressed its alarm at the anti-Zionist and anti-Semitic tones in the Soviet media and noted with regret that the Jewish community of the Soviet Union was still not authorized to have a central organization. It pleaded for clemency for those who were being called the "prisoners of Zion," and for other persons who wished to leave the Soviet Union for Israel.

The committee again took up and expanded on these subjects at a Geneva meeting in March 1977. It emphasized the anxiety caused by the dangerous and ludicrous Soviet statements accusing the Jews of "working for the CIA."

The second Brussels conference on Soviet Jewry had created a special commission to monitor the Soviet authorities' application of the clauses of the Helsinki final accords as concerned Soviet Jews. This commission was to draw up a report and prepare an action plan, following which thirteen Jewish communities in Europe, the United States, and Canada would lobby their governments to have the question raised at the Belgrade meeting of the Conference on Security and Cooperation in Europe scheduled for 1977. This conference was intended to provide an updated perspective on the situation and to assure the implementation and observance of the Helsinki agreements. During the course of this gathering, the WJC delegation contacted a large number of delegates from various governments to press our cause.

We achieved, I think, some success in this effort. Meeting in London in September 1978, the Brussels monitoring action commission noted with satisfaction the remarkable increase in the number of Soviet Jews who had obtained authorization to join their families outside the USSR. But the members expressed great concern with the Soviet refusal to allow numerous would-be emigrants to leave. The commission also expressed its alarm at the increase in anti-Semitic propaganda in the Soviet Union and the effects of an anti-Jewish campaign that restricted admission to universities and discriminated in employment and in practically all aspects of Soviet life.

The Belgrade CSCE planned a further meeting in November 1980 to yet again review the application of the Helsinki final accords. In September 1978 the European branch of the WJC met in Brussels to make its own plans for the Madrid meeting and decided to create in the Western countries committees on the issue of Soviet Jewry. Additionally, the Brussels monitoring commission of Jewish groups met in Montreal on November 16, 1979, to draw up the political line to be followed at the Madrid conference, and the presidium of the Brussels conference met in Paris to consider the declining emigration of Soviet Jews. The eventual boycott of the Olympic Games in Moscow, strongly supported by many organizations throughout the world, was a particular object of discussion; the presidium's consensus was that the Jewish communities should not support the boycott.

One of the major WJC objectives was to obtain a relaxation in the rules for the reunification of families, which the Soviets interpreted as being limited to immediate kinship. In addition, the Soviets required the agreement of all members of a family, even of those who did not wish to leave, before it would approve any exit visas. This appeared to be in flagrant contradiction with that part of the final accords devoted to human rights. We distributed a substantial file on the subject to the delegations.

By maintaining close contact with the nongovernmental delegations, my colleague Dr. Stephen Roth, of the Institute of Jewish Affairs, to his great credit greatly influenced the formulations that were finally adopted by the Madrid conference. The resolutions guaranteed freedom in human relations, freedom to use postal and telephone services, the free shipment of parcels and presents, freedom for tourist activity, and freedom of written and electronic information. Other points stipulated that the signatory countries would respect and protect religious freedom, the cultural freedom of minorities, and the exchange of books and educational material.

The WJC persevered in pursuing the priorities established by Dr. Goldmann. The situation of the Soviet Jews remained at the top of our list, preceded only by the security of the State of Israel. Edgar Bronfman, who became president of the WJC, in 1981 continued his predecessor's efforts to establish and maintain direct contacts with Soviet leaders, in the first instance through the Soviet ambassador in Washington, Anatoly Dobrynin, with whom Dr. Goldmann had maintained ongoing relations for many years. The new WJC secretary-general (as of 1981), Israel Singer, provided constant support of Bronfman's work.

Eventually, stimulated by the new climate of *glasnost* and *perestroika*, WJC leaders sustained these relations through repeated visits to the Soviet Union. The former Soviet ambassador to Canada, Alexandr Yakovlev, who had come to know the leaders of the Canadian Jewish Congress, was of great help in initially establishing contacts in the USSR.

These efforts led finally to meetings with Edouard Shevardnadze, the Soviet minister of foreign affairs, and later in 1991 with Mikhail Gorbachev, then president of the USSR, and thereafter with his successor, Boris Yeltsin. The combined effect of these meetings, discussions, and lobbying activities finally led to a complete reversal of Russian policy with regard to Jews and the State of Israel.

We can view with pride the results of our incessant struggle on behalf of the large Jewish community in the former Soviet Union. Today the Jews there who so wish can emigrate to Israel or elsewhere—many to Germany, curiously enough. They are free to organize on religious, cultural, and educational levels. Some two hundred Jewish institutions are currently grouped in a cultural union, which has created a regional section of the World Jewish Congress and has since participated in our activities.

Since I was no longer secretary-general of the WJC I did not participate in these agreements. But I followed them passionately from my office in Geneva, rejoicing at the success of Edgar Bronfman and Israel Singer, a success that crowned a work of more than fifty years.

Given this positive and happy development, one major concern engaged and troubled us: organizations with nationalistic, xenophobic, and racist tendencies were now free to act in the new atmosphere of Russia. Yet despite the noise they generate, they remain marginal on the Russian political scene.

At the Ninth Plenary Assembly of the WJC in Jerusalem in 1991 a large delegation of Russian Jews made its ceremonial entry into full participation in the World Jewish Congress on behalf of all Russian Jewry. Emotions ran high at this event. In the welcoming words I addressed to the Russian delegation, I evoked the major episodes of the struggle for their rights: the founding assembly of the WJC in 1936; preparations for the great conference of 1953, when confronted with the threat of Jewish deportations to Siberia; the renewal of our initiative in 1957 to place the problem of Soviet Jewry before public opinion as well as to keep the public informed of all subsequent struggles. I recalled as well that Dr. Goldmann and the rest of us at the WJC had never doubted that one day Russian Jewry in all its greatness would join us. Our common dream had become reality.

FOUR

Our Relations with Christian Churches

DURING THE TERRIBLE YEARS of the Shoah, when almost the entire world abandoned the Jews, I realized that we ought never in the future to be left in such an isolated position. I concluded that after the war we would have to establish relations with the great movements and organizations in the non-Jewish worlds, including the churches. Since then I have worked to build bridges to these other worlds, in particular with the Christian world and the so-called Third World. This has also played a certain role in my relations with university organizations. Having been in turn a member of the executive, treasurer, and president of Entraide universitaire internationale, the International Student Service, I had set up and maintained contacts with the great global movements of Protestant and Catholic students and intellectuals. I created bonds of friendship with these young academics, many of whom conducted themselves magnificently during the war. I maintained these contacts, which proved very useful for me later on, especially at the time of the Vatican II Council.

I pursued the same objective in my work with the various bodies of the United Nations, the International Organization of Refugees, and UNESCO, where I represented the World Jewish Congress for many years.

Within the framework of these activities I always endeavored to create links with other international groups. Earlier I referred to my activity as president of the Conference of Non-Governmental Organizations with consultative status at the UN. At that time the conference included a number of Protestant organizations and about fifteen Catholic organizations. We met regularly and cooperated smoothly. Needless to say, this activity became much more concrete and systematic by the time of the Second Vatican Council (1962–1965).

When we Jews learned that the Second Vatican Council would be held, some of us saw in this a unique opportunity to put the Jewish question to this great assembly. We would try to bring the church to reflect on its relations with the Jews in light of the recent past, and attempt to create a new basis for our future relations. These new relations should be unencumbered by the "teaching of contempt" and the anti-Jewish positions that had characterized the attitude of the Roman Catholic church throughout the centuries.

Pioneers of a New Christian Vision of Judaism

This development did not simply drop out of a blue sky. Relations between Jews and the Christian churches, with delays and spurts, evolved over a long period of time filled with obstacles and opened doors. Of course the Holocaust and the catastrophe of World War II greatly affected this evolution. The process had begun, albeit cautiously, with the persecution of Jews in Germany and, after the war began, across virtually all Europe.

A number of important pioneers in this process deserve to be noted here. The first of these is the British Anglican cleric James Parkes. Beginning in 1930 Parkes wrote several noteworthy books on the origins of anti-Semitism and on the conflict between the church and the synagogue, themes he continued to work on throughout his career. He began in Geneva, as the international study secretary of the Student Christian Movement, and later became the study secretary of the International Student Service (1928–1934), where I also held several responsible positions.

In 1933, after the German president appointed Hitler chancellor, Parkes personally witnessed the tragedy of the Jewish students of Germany. He convoked the first international student conferences on the problem of anti-Semitism, at one of which Nahum Goldmann spoke. After these experiences, James Parkes devoted practically his entire life to improving relations between Jews and Christians.

The story is told that when he wished to establish in Britain an institute devoted to studying the origins of and combating anti-Semitism, he solicited the aid and financial support of the great British Jewish industrialist Israel Sieff. When Sieff asked Parkes how much time he thought it would take to change the situation, the latter replied, "At least fifty years." Whereupon Sieff said, "If you had told me anything else, I would not have lent you my support." James Parkes died in 1981, having led a righteous life.

Karl Thieme was another pioneer, a thinker of German origin whom I had known at the School for Advanced Political Studies in Berlin. In his capacity as a Christian theologian, Thieme was among the very first to contribute to a deepened reflection on this problem. His book *Dreitausend Jahre Judentum* (1960) remains an important study. At the end of his life Thieme lived in Basel, where I saw him from time to time before he died in 1963.*

The third pioneer I wish to cite is Father Paul Démann of France. Hungarian in origin, he was the author of an extremely important book on catechesis and Judaism. Father Démann edited the publication *Cahiers sioniens* (*Zionist Journals*), which dealt with these problems in methodical fashion. In his activities and his writings, Father Démann must be considered one of those who led Catholic circles to reflect on the then almost taboo problem of misguided and false Christian teachings as they concerned Jews and their effects on Christian consciences.

It is also appropriate here to name the theologian Malcolm Hay, the Scottish Catholic who wrote an important early work in 1950 on Jewish-Christian rapprochement. Entitled *Europe and the Jews: The Pressure of Christendom on the People of Israel for 1900 Years*, it appeared in the United States in 1960. It is a very good book on the problem of the church's responsibility for harmful teachings about Jews and Judaism, and had great resonance around the world.

The influence of this generation of pioneers in the context of the World War II experience gave birth to a movement of major importance. In the postwar era it first took root in the Jewish-Christian friendship associations in Britain and in France, then in other countries, in particular the Federal Republic of Germany, beginning with meetings in Oxford in 1946 and in Seelisburg in 1947.

This movement did not include the official churches, however. It gathered together churchmen who understood what had happened during the war and who decided that the appropriate conclusions regarding Christian doctrine with regard to Jews and Judaism must be drawn from the tragedy. One of these consequences was the clear necessity for them to meet with Jews to start discussing the issues.

---

*The reference here is to Thieme junior, not his conservative theologian father (1862–1932), who also wrote and edited many books on Christian theology.—ED.

After the war the Catholic church itself was still not ready to confront the problem. As I noted earlier, immediately after the end of the war in 1945 the World Jewish Congress proposed to Pope Pius XII that he publish an encyclical on the Jewish question. Unfortunately we never received a reply to our submission. Professor Jacques Maritain, who later became the French ambassador to the Holy See, pursued this idea for several years, but his efforts achieved no greater success.

Meetings such as the Oxford gathering noted above involving the various Jewish-Christian friendship movements culminated in the celebrated Seelisburg Declaration. It was formulated by the Christian participants at the Emergency Conference on Antisemitism held in August 1947 in this little Swiss town on the shore of Lake Lucerne, attended by some sixty eminent Christian and Jewish figures. They included Chief Rabbi Jacob Kaplan of Paris, the French historian Jules Isaac, Abbé Charles Journet, Tadeusz Mazowiecki, Fathers Jean de Menasce and Calliste Lopinot, the Rev. Adolf Freudenberg, Neville Laski, Dr. Everet Clinchy, Dr. Pierre Visseur, Rev. Simpson, Professor Selig Brodetsky, Mme. M. Davy, Chief Rabbi Alexandre Safran, and Rabbis Vadnai and Zwi Taubes.

For the first time after the war, these notables established the basis for a new Christian theological approach to the Jews in a concise declaration. Its celebrated Ten Points constituted a veritable action program that subsequently played an important role in the modification of relations between Christians and Jews.

Here is the text:

I. Remember that One God speaks to us all through the Old and New Testaments.

II. Remember that Jesus was born of a Jewish mother of the seed of David and the people of Israel, and that His everlasting love and forgiveness embraces His own people and the whole world.

III. Remember that the first disciples, the apostles and the first martyrs were Jews.

IV. Remember that the fundamental commandment of Christianity, to love God and one's neighbor, proclaimed already in the Old Testament and confirmed by Jesus, is binding upon both Christians and Jews in all human relationships, without any exception.

V. Avoid distorting or misrepresenting biblical or post-biblical Judaism with the object of extolling Christianity.

VI. Avoid using the word "Jews" in the exclusive sense of the enemies of Jesus and the words "the enemies of Jesus" to designate the whole Jewish people.

VII. Avoid presenting the Passion in such a way as to bring the odium of the killing of Jesus upon all Jews or upon Jews alone. It was only a section of the Jews in Jerusalem who demanded the death of Jesus, and the Christian message has always been that it was the sins of mankind which were exemplified by those Jews and the sins in which all men share that brought Jesus to the Cross.

VIII. Avoid referring to the scriptural curses, or the cry of a raging mob: "His blood be upon us and our children," without remembering that this cry should not count against the infinitely more weighty words of our Lord: "Father, forgive them, for they know not what they do."

IX. Avoid promoting the superstitious notion that the Jewish people are reprobate, accursed, reserved for a destiny of suffering.

X. Avoid speaking of the Jews as if the first members of the Church had not been Jews.

Several of my colleagues from the World Jewish Congress such as Dr. Aaron Steinberg, who later led the Cultural Department of the WJC, Dr. Georg Guggenheim, president of the Jewish community of Zurich, and a number of others, attended the Seelisburg deliberations. Personally I was led to concern myself systematically with these problems during preparations for the Second Vatican Council. Jules Isaac would play the role of catalyst in the course of these developments. The Oxford and Seelisburg international conferences led to the formation of the International Council of Christians and Jews in 1948, an association that exists to this day in Geneva.

The Vatican Council

A well-known French historian and assimilated Jew, Jules Isaac had written a book known as *Mallet and Isaac,* the most widely read textbook in France. Isaac was fairly distant from Judaism and not particularly concerned with his Jewish roots until the Shoah swept over him. Vichy France and the Germans deported his wife and his daughter, and this personal tragedy led him to write a book, *Jésus et Israël* (*Jesus and Israel,* 1948), in which he examined the roots of modern anti-Semitism. In the book, written during the period when he was obliged to live underground in order to escape deportation, Isaac came to the conclusion that Christian doctrine furnished the basis for modern anti-Semitism.

Vincent Auriol, the former president of the French Republic (1947–1954), played an important role in making possible the meeting between Jules Isaac and Pope John XXIII in June 1960. In their capacity as successors to the kings, the presidents of France were considered ex officio canons of the church of St. John of Latran in Rome, where a place was reserved for them.

By virtue of this fact, the French presidents enjoyed special relations with the pope, who also serves as the Bishop of Rome. It seems that Auriol continued to maintain his relations with Rome after his seven-year term as president. This was all the more plausible since it was he who had bestowed the cardinal's red hat on Msgr. Angelo Roncalli when the latter was the papal nuncio in Paris. The nuncio would go on to be elected Pope John XXIII in 1958. Vincent Auriol then, very much the layman, arranged Jules Isaac's visit to the Vatican, a visit that would have far-reaching consequences. In passing it should be noted that Auriol, whom I knew fairly well, was a very warm man, a humanitarian filled with goodwill.

Before this audience, Jules Isaac submitted to the pope a memorandum proposing the creation of a mixed commission that would examine Jewish-Christian relations and make recommendations for improvement, particularly in the field of Christian doctrine concerning Jews.

Pope John XXIII was a charismatic person and probably unique in the history of the modern church. He was well prepared to discuss the issues. During the war he had been the papal nuncio in Sofia and Ankara and had thus been able to witness the tragedy of European Jewry at close hand. More than once he intervened to protect or save Jews. One day he received a delegation of American Jews in Rome, greeting them with the words, "I am Joseph, your brother," citing the famous phrase from the Bible by which Joseph identified himself to his brothers come to Egypt.

In 1961 the World Council of Churches (WCC), which joined together hundreds of Protestant, Anglican, and Orthodox churches from around the world, held its third assembly in New Delhi, shortly before the Vatican Council. I believe that my conversations with Willem A. Visser 't Hooft, its secretary-general, contributed to the fact that this assembly adopted a resolution of great significance concerning the attitude of Christians toward Jews and Judaism.

Here are the essentials: Noting that Christians had too often neglected the duties of Christian charity and even of justice with regard to Jews, the WCC asked all churches to denounce anti-Semitism as a phenomenon irreconcilable with Christian faith. The statement declared that anti-Semitism was both a crime against God and a crime against mankind, and in a significant passage it also rejected the notion of deicide.

This was an important text, emanating from the greatest gathering of Christian churches outside the Catholic church. The WCC's public position on these issues surely influenced the leaders of the Catholic church, especially many of those preparing the Second Vatican Council.

It should be noted in passing that relations between the Catholic church and the WCC are highly complex. These two international institutions that claim the spiritual leadership of countless millions of people at times appear in complete agreement and at other times seem to function as competitors. I must acknowledge that in exceptional circumstances I employed to good purpose this latter situation.

After the first steps taken by Jules Isaac, John XXIII charged Cardinal Béa with examining the issues in more depth. Augustin Cardinal Béa was himself an exceptional figure in the Catholic church. A Jesuit of German origin, he enjoyed immense prestige. A tall man, he gave an impression of strength and firmness. At the same time he was very calm in his ways, I would even say gentle. His manners, along with his proverbial great kindness, could give the impression that he was weak in character. Events would prove the contrary. Augustin Béa had a will of iron and overcame every obstacle in carrying out his projects. If John XXIII was the architect of the new attitude of the church toward the Jews, Cardinal Béa was the director of the construction company.

At this time Béa was already quite elderly and famous for his great wisdom. For decades he had served as president of the Bible Institute at the Vatican, one of the great papal academies. By virtue of this office he had become a great Bible expert. Not only did he speak Hebrew fairly well, but he also knew almost intimately all the figures of the Hebrew Bible and the Christian Old Testament.

Cardinal Béa had been Pius XII's confessor, a role that doubtless marked him deeply. Because of this, he also had an intimate and exact knowledge of what the church did and did not do during the Nazi period. Some people even said that this is what prompted him to lead the new formulation of Catholic theology with regard to the Jews. It was his way of working to remedy the terrible injustices of which the Jews had been victims. In addition to his great moral sense, I believe his German origins also contributed to his position.

Born in Riedböhringen, near the source of the Danube, Augustin Béa had spent a great part of his life in Rome, a man of the Curia considered to be a traditionalist. He had aided Pius XII in conceptualizing a number of important documents, one of them in fact defining the Catholic position with regard to the new movement in Bible criticism, *Divino afflante spiritu*.

To a great extent initiated by Protestant theologians, this school of criticism developed from the end of the nineteenth century through the twentieth. Béa had been strongly affected by it, and his reflections influenced the position of Catholic theology on the issue.

When Pope John XXIII made him responsible for Jewish affairs, Béa went to work with great conviction. His long experience had taught him how to get things done at the Vatican.

In autumn of 1960, at the beginning of his mission, Cardinal Béa had no relations with Jews. He asked his order whom he ought to meet to establish initial contact. As he would one day say, the question asked of the Jesuit administration was: Who is the Jewish figure who most resembles a Jewish pope? In response, his Jesuit colleagues advised him to meet Nahum Goldmann. The reason for this was that the World Jewish Congress had had fairly regular relations with the Jesuits for several years. The Jesuits were very interested in certain Jewish issues, in particular in the future of Israel. They wanted to establish contacts between Pope Pius XII and the Jews. In his autobiography Nahum Goldmann tells how his meeting with Pius XII, as envisaged by the Jesuits, finally did not occur because of the opposition of the Vatican Secretariat of State.

Nevertheless Béa followed the counsel of the Jesuits and met Nahum Goldmann in the fall of 1960, at which time Goldmann was the undisputed leader of the Diaspora. He was truly the *rosh galuta* (literally "head of the diaspora"). When Béa mentioned to Goldmann that his Jesuit colleagues had recommended him as the one who most resembled a Jewish pope, Goldmann replied with his usual humor, "I don't know whether I resemble a Jewish quasi-pope, but you should know that I don't believe in celibacy."

They then undertook what was basically the first real discussion between Catholics and Jews about the Vatican Council then being prepared. Cardinal Béa made two proposals to Dr. Goldmann.

First, he asked him whether the Jews wished to be invited to the Council as observers. The Catholic church had invited representatives of other Christian denominations—Protestant, Anglican, and Greek Orthodox churches—to the Council as observers, which was a great novelty at the time and would herald a new era of Roman Catholic ecumenism.

For exactly this reason Pope John had created the Secretariat for the Promotion of Christian Unity with Msgr. Béa at its head. And the fact that Béa was also charged with relations with Jews explains why, bizarrely, the Jews were also within the sphere of the Secretariat for Christian Unity. As things turned out, this caused us many problems. But the first question we had to address was whether the Jews wished to be invited to the Council as observers.

The second question raised by Cardinal Béa in his meeting with Goldmann was whether the Jewish organizations were prepared to submit a memorandum to the Council or to the Catholic church in which they would formulate their points of view concerning the problems affecting the two communities.

Faced with these two questions, Nahum Goldmann consulted Rabbi Dov Soloveitchik of Boston, considered the greatest authority on modern Jewish orthodoxy and a teacher at Yeshiva University in New York.

Soloveitchik responded that Jews ought not to participate in the Council, even as observers, since it was exclusively a matter for the church. Nevertheless he recommended submitting a Jewish memorandum to the Council. He noted that the memorandum ought to be formulated by "secular" Jewish organizations in order to indicate clearly that Jews would not engage in a religious dialogue.

I must say that personally I do not believe in this distinction between religious and secular Jewish organizations. The World Jewish Congress is composed for the greater part of Jewish communities, which according to their statutes are Orthodox religious communities. Could the WJC then be viewed as a secular organization?

Goldmann valued and acted on Rabbi Soloveitchik's advice. This proved to be the beginning of a long period of cooperation between the two men, especially concerning Jewish policy toward the Christian churches. At that time few understood the importance of the alliance between these two figures, one of whom was the protagonist of modern Jewish orthodoxy and the other of the modern national Jewish movement.

Shortly afterward, Nahum Goldmann instructed me to inform Cardinal Béa about the Jewish position on the question of a possible invitation to the Council and to alert him to the imminent submission of the memorandum. Meanwhile there were a fair number of consultations among the Jewish organizations regarding the content of the memorandum, who should sign it, and how it should be submitted. These preliminary discussions lasted a rather long time.

It was not until January 1962 that I met Cardinal Béa for the first time and gave him the replies to his questions. In the course of our long and cordial discussion I fulfilled my mission, and then I explained my opinion on the questions.

An invitation to the Council would have divided the Jewish community. The Orthodox wing would be opposed while the liberals or conservatives would adopt a more receptive, nuanced stance, and this would have provoked a huge polemic in the Jewish camp. This polemic would be carried on at the expense of improved relations with the church, because the discussion would bear in particular on our unfortunate history with Christendom. The result would have been a disaster leading to great bitterness, the very opposite of the desired goal.

Béa noted and accepted unreservedly our decisions. Then he shared with me a communication he had received from Chief Rabbi Jacob Kaplan in the name of the European Association of Rabbis. Kaplan affirmed that since the goal of the Council was the unity of Christians, and that Jews were not Christians, they could not participate in the Council. Not without irony, Béa expressed his surprise that the rabbis knew so well what the goal of the Council was while the majority of Christians still did not. Even if it were true that ecumenism was one of the issues of the Council, it was certainly not the only one.

The Cardinal also told me that he welcomed the submission of a Jewish memorandum to the church. He asked me to get it to him in as timely a fashion as possible.

Drafting the memorandum consumed much more time than anticipated. To lend it greater authority we had chosen to position it under the auspices of the World Conference of Jewish Organizations (COJO). The WJC created this body for ongoing collaboration with organizations that were not affiliated with the WJC at that time, including the International B'nai B'rith, the Board of Deputies of British Jews, and the Representative Council of Jewish Institutions of France (CRIF). Most of the organizations that then belonged to COJO are today members of the WJC or sit in on its meetings thanks to a special cooperative arrangement. But in 1962 they were not yet ready to join.

We then set to work drafting the memorandum. Not until the end of February 1962 were we in a position to submit it. Meanwhile Béa also gave us some good advice and we followed it. In particular he said, "Don't go into too much detail, it's not a good idea. We know better than you where the real problems lie for us."

Our memorandum was principally drafted by Maurice Perlzweig, director of the WJC New York office of the Department of International Affairs, backed

by a small committee that included Joseph Lichten of the Anti-Defamation
League of the B'nai B'rith. Perlzweig had an exceptional gift for writing texts of
this kind in a clear language of great beauty.

Here are some significant passages of the document sent to Cardinal Béa
on February 17, 1962:

> In all parts of the world men of the most varied religions and nationalities
> are reaching out, as though under a common impulse, to wider freedoms
> and a new affirmation of the rights of the human personality. We desire in
> this paper to reaffirm the immemorial faith of our tradition that the
> spiritual resources which are part of our common human heritage give us
> the means, as they impose on us the obligation, to master the evils of
> prejudice and intolerance. . . .
>
> The belief in the common origin, the common right and the common
> destiny of all mankind is of the substance of our faith. We seek to safeguard
> the rights and dignity of Jews not because they are Jews but because they are
> human. We ask for them neither privilege nor special treatment. We adhere
> without reservation to the doctrine embodied in the U.N. Universal
> Declaration of Human Rights that full enjoyment of human rights is the
> prerogative of all the children of men, irrespective of race, creed, sex or
> language. The struggle against anti-Semitism is for us part of the struggle for
> the emancipation of all mankind.
>
> If we address ourselves to the Catholic Church on the Jewish question in
> particular, it is because there are references to the Jews and their place in
> history in its liturgical literature, in the catechisms in many of their forms,
> and in certain commemorative practices, as well as in educational devotional
> manuals in wide use. It is unfortunately not to be denied that the ignorant
> or malicious may misunderstand or distort and exploit such references to
> foment hatred of others and to promote causes in patent conflict with the
> teaching of the Church on the brotherhood of man.
>
> We venture to draw particular attention to the allegations of ritual
> crimes, in churches in various parts of the world, which are perpetuated in
> inscriptions, pictorial representations and even commemorative services.
> Whether the many thousands who visit or worship at these shrines and in
> these churches are aware that accusations of this kind have been the subject
> of repeated papal condemnations, may well be doubted. It seems in our
> respectful submission to be evident that the existence of these relics of
> ancient prejudice cannot but be an obstacle in the promotion of the cause of
> human understanding and mutual respect. . . .

"Have we not all one Father? Hath not one God created us?" The challenge of the Prophet lays upon all of us the most solemn obligation. The differences which separate us are real and important; it were foolish to overlook and underrate them. But they cannot nullify the commandment to love our neighbor.

The fact that relations with the Jews concerned the initiators of the Council was clearly of great significance. It was part of the extremely interesting evolution that took place during the four years of the Council's duration. For the great problem, contrary to what the rabbis said, was not only the unity of Christians but the *aggiornamento*, the renewal and modernization of the church itself. Fresh air began to blow through the church, and experiencing this close up fascinated me. I had never seen an institution that had behaved until then like a fortress, an eternal and immutable whole completely turned in on itself—the traditional church that had emerged from the Council of Trent—now taking on new, invigorated life and opening itself to the world. With astounding suddenness the church began to reexamine its structures, its foundations, and its behavior in all its activities.

I went to Rome fairly regularly to stay abreast of developments in the discussions that affected us, and when I could not be there my colleague Fritz Becker guaranteed the continuity of our presence. For many years he had worked in international relations for the Union of Jewish Communities of Italy and had become the WJC bureau chief in Rome. His modesty, tact, discretion, and other talents had won him great respect and furthered our delicate work in this complex ecclesiastical environment.

At the Vatican I was a frequent visitor to the press room where the Council held press conferences in various languages every afternoon. We not only heard the latest reports on the Council's deliberations but also often witnessed the passionate debates organized by national groups and other interest groups. I met clerics of every origin and tendency, who often let us benefit from inside information and their personal commentary on various issues.

Of course I always went to the Secretariat for the Promotion of Christian Unity or to the convent on via Aurelia where Cardinal Béa resided. When schedule conflicts precluded me from personally seeing him, I talked to his secretary, Father Stefan Schmidt, or to one of the secretariat officials such as Father Stransky.

In Rome I also met old friends who were either representatives of lay organizations, such as Professor Ramon Sugranyes de Franch of Fribourg, whom I knew from my university activities, or consultants (*periti*) attached to the ecclesiastics at the Council, such as Msgr. Joseph Höfer, Msgr. John M. Oesterreicher, Gregory Baum, Hans Küng, and others.

With the passage of years I have had the pleasure of seeing some of these young, open-minded, and intelligent priests accede to positions of responsibility in the church: bishops, cardinals, professors of theology. At that earlier time they formed a living link between a church in full transformation and the external world, and many of them were not without sympathy for our problems.

The great voices of the Council who supported us included reputed biblical scholars such as Cardinal Béa and Achille Cardinal Liénart, or clerics who came from cities with substantial Jewish communities whose spirit and vitality they admired. In this category were men such as Richard Cardinal Cushing of Boston, Bishop Léon-Arthur Elchinger of Strasbourg, Franjo Cardinal Šeper of Zagreb, and many others. They had a profound knowledge of Jewish history and enjoyed ongoing relations with the great Jewish centers.

By November 1961, before we submitted our memorandum, Cardinal Béa had already established his own commission to draw up a document concerning relations with the Jews. This little group, composed of especially qualified persons, worked on the draft, which was then to be discussed at the Secretariat for the Promotion of Christian Unity.

One day when I was speaking of this committee to Eugène Cardinal Tisserand, who was quite candid and had a great sense of humor, he said to me, "Oh! you want to talk about that commission of Cardinal Béa's that is made up of two converted Jews, a Zionist, and an anti-Semite!"

Here was the membership: Msgr. John M. Oesterreicher of the Institute for Judeo-Christian Studies at Seton Hall University, a Catholic priest of Jewish origin born in Czechoslovakia. People claimed that in his native Slovakia he had been a member of the youth organization Hashomer Hatzair, close to the extreme left. I do not know how he came to change his religion. For years he edited the annual publication *The Bridge*, about which we had frequently voiced our reservations. We always had the impression that it was not free of a tendency toward conversion advocacy. During the Council, Msgr. Oesterreicher was counselor to Franz Cardinal König of Vienna.

A second member of the Commission, the Augustinian Gregory Baum, for whom I have always had a great deal of respect, was also of Jewish origin. He had studied in Fribourg in Switzerland, lived in Toronto, Canada, and had written a very important book on Jews and the Gospel, *Les Juifs et l'Évangile*, some of whose original theses he later amended.

Abbé Leo Rudloff, a priest serving in Jerusalem where he administered the Church of the Dormition, was likely the "Zionist" of whom Tisserand had spoken. I did not get to know him until later in Jerusalem. He may have been appointed to the commission to bring to its discussion a sense of the reality of the State of Israel.

The fourth, whose name I have forgotten, must have been the "anti-Semite" Tisserand mentioned. I never made his acquaintance.

When I began to work with the secretariat, I hesitated in establishing relations with the converted Jewish members. This may be a reaction natural among Jews, but I soon realized that it was impossible to ignore them because they carried out important work, and we needed to know what was going on. Consequently, overcoming my reticence, I finally scheduled meetings with them.

I have extremely interesting memories of my first meetings, both with Oesterreicher and with Baum, who was very cordial toward me. We got to know each other one evening in a restaurant in Rome. It was my colleague Becker, the permanent WJC representative in Rome, who organized our first meeting. To my great astonishment we observed that we were both originally from Berlin; we had gone to the same school and had had the same teachers.

Baum was twelve years younger than I. He had begun school just as I graduated. He came from a completely assimilated Jewish family; his parents were divorced, and in his family religion no longer played any role. Seated face to face, we politely asked each other questions about our pasts. Looking at each other, we wondered aloud how, given such similar backgrounds, one of us had ended up becoming a monk in the Augustinian order and the other the secretary-general of the World Jewish Congress.

Baum had been saved from the genocide by one of the transports of Jewish children to England. During the war he was then transferred with other Jewish children to Canada by ship. Fortunately for him the Germans did not sink that ship as they did so many others. I do not know how or why he converted to Catholicism nor how he entered orders. He was an extremely handsome man, and his manners were characterized by a great openness combined with exquisite politeness. Baum remained very attached to his mother, who died during the war in the Jewish old people's home, Jüdisches Altersheim, in Berlin. He even dedicated his Fribourg doctoral dissertation to her memory.

On that first evening we talked until one in the morning. Then he took me to the convent where he stayed in Rome and showed me the latest confidential (*sub secreto*) draft document on the Jews. He even translated the text from Latin for me. From that moment on he behaved with truly exceptional friendliness.

As for Msgr. Oesterreicher, I made his acquaintance the day that Cardinal Béa announced the completion of the draft text on relations with Jews that was to be submitted to the Council. As chance would have it, I was in Rome. In the afternoon, at the Vatican press center, Oesterreicher held a press conference in German at which he introduced the draft text. He then said, and here I paraphrase: "Now that the Church has taken this important step toward the Jews, it is the Jews' turn to take a step and to purge the Talmud of all the unfriendly and hostile allusions to Christianity."

I found that statement extraordinary, and I have never forgotten it. At that point, when the text had only just been prepared, before a discussion had even been joined, when nothing had been decided, Oesterreicher was already asking for concessions. In retrospect it is even more astonishing because we now know the opposition that the draft met in the Council and the fact that on several occasions it was almost discarded. Oesterreicher surely knew then what the text's reception would be.

I can still picture my first luncheon with him and Becker. He had been in touch with representatives of the American Jewish Committee but had absolutely no idea what the Geneva office and I were doing in Rome and what we knew about the preparations for the Council. He behaved toward us with a certain disdain, at least until the moment when in the middle of a very general conversation my colleague Becker slipped in some very precise phrasing quoting exactly from the draft document on the Jews. Here was a clear sign that we were very well informed, and from that moment Oesterreicher adopted a much different attitude toward us.

As it happened, Cardinal Béa's committee completed the draft before our memorandum reached the commission, and the Cardinal regretted that we had not submitted it earlier. When we reviewed the draft text we saw that the Secretariat for the Promotion of Christian Unity had already taken our principal concerns into account. The draft met with vehement opposition in the Council. Indeed it was very nearly set aside on three or four occasions. But our memorandum served as a basis for all the subsequent démarches to the Vatican and later to many bishops in numerous countries.

The fact that for the first time organized Jewry had addressed itself to the Roman Catholic church was an important event in itself. In fact, and I must stress this, we did not address our memorandum to the Council but rather to the church itself because we viewed the Council as an internal church matter.

When I told Cardinal Béa that we did not wish to be invited to the Council, I had suggested and he discussed other possible meeting grounds. In making these proposals I simply wanted to indicate that we were not hostile to the idea of meeting, but that the framework of the Council did not seem appropriate for us.

To our great surprise, the first important crisis of the Council in its relations with Jews had great effect. Here are the facts. Within the WJC we realized that we had no Jewish specialist on the problems of the church and Jewish-Christian relations. We thought that since we were all outsiders it would perhaps be a good idea to consult a real expert. At this moment such a man came forward, Dr. Chaim Vardi, then a senior official of the Israeli Ministry of Religious Affairs. As part of his duties he maintained constant contact with the Christian religions in Israel, which meant practically all the Christian denominations.

Apparently Dr. Vardi felt uncomfortable with the intensely Orthodox Jewish orientation of his government ministry, and he applied for a position at the WJC. For us this came at an opportune moment, and we quietly made the appropriate arrangements. We wished to inform Cardinal Béa and obtain his concurrence before we announced the appointment to the public. After all, if the church did not accept Vardi he could not carry out his new duties.

Consequently Nahum Goldmann flew from Israel and I from Geneva to see Béa, who gave us a long audience. We informed him that our Rome office would have a real specialist in Jewish-Christian relations, a man who would follow developments at the Council at close hand. The Cardinal even suggested that our expert might be the guest of the Secretariat, but he did not definitively determine anything.

When we left Béa's office, his secretary accompanied us down in the elevator and remarked in passing that a wire from the Italian Telegraphic Agency had announced that the World Jewish Congress had appointed Dr. Vardi as its representative-observer at the Vatican Council. We immediately published a denial, but the story caused an enormous scandal because it presented Vardi as an appointment to the Council as well as to the Vatican, which was absurd. What we had in mind, of course, was to have someone in our Rome office who could follow developments at the Council in an intelligent fashion and who could serve as liaison. We never learned who leaked this harmful and distorted story, but we determined that Vardi had not done it.

This mishap was first exploited by the Arab ambassadors, but it also furnished conservative circles within the Curia with a new pretext to oppose us. Various sources denounced the matter as an Israeli government attempt to exert influence over the Council and presented Vardi as an official of the Israeli Ministry of Foreign Affairs, which was not in the least true. In fact the Israeli government had nothing to do with this business. Nonetheless, all the Arab ambassadors immediately raised a public protest with the Vatican Secretariat of State. As a consequence, in June 1962, when the large organizing commission met to draw up the Council agenda, it removed the Jewish question from the program.

Many observers, even within conservative Jewish circles, unfairly blamed the WJC for this state of affairs. All those who opposed rapprochement with the Jews found fodder for their arguments in the incident.

Throughout the duration of the Council the Arabs, their official representatives to the Holy See, and the bishops from those countries loudly and persistently opposed the document concerning the Jews. As soon as they saw the least progress in this matter, they joined forces to counter it, saying publicly and privately that a document about the Jews would constitute an act favorable to the State of Israel.

In addition, some senior dignitaries in the most conservative circles of the Curia raised their opposition and to this end often exploited the Arab ambassadors. And this opposition found its most vehement expression in the Secretariat of State, the true center of power in the church.

Let me present an example of the Secretariat of State's attitude, which is also an example of Cardinal Béa's combative spirit. He never gave up in his attempts to see the project through. When in June 1962, after the Vardi incident, the preparatory commission struck the text on Jews from the Council's provisional agenda, Cardinal Béa was in the process of publishing an article entitled, "Are the Jews a Deicide People Cursed by God?" in the prestigious Italian Jesuit review, *La Civiltà cattolica*. This was an extremely important contribution to the discussion on relations between the church and Jewry. Béa had already corrected two sets of proofs when the Secretariat of State asked him to stop its publication "so as not to irritate the Arab countries any further."

The Cardinal agreed for the time being. But he did not abandon the struggle. He had the article translated into German and published in *Stimmen der Zeit*, the German Jesuit journal. And since it could not be published under his signature as cardinal, it appeared in October 1962 under the signature of a German professor, Ludwig von Hertling, of the Society of Jesus. This event shows clearly how political and theological considerations were being mixed. After all, it is difficult to understand how the problem of Jewish responsibility for the death of Christ concerned the Arab states or affected the political relations of the Vatican with the State of Israel.*

---

*Riegner may be read as being somewhat disingenuous here. As long as the church blamed the Jews for Christ's death, there could be no formal diplomatic relations between the Jewish state and the Vatican.—ED.

I did not believe that Alfredo Cardinal Ottaviani, who was in charge of the Holy Office, opposed our project. Ottaviani opposed Béa on other points, for example the document on divine revelation. In fact, Ottaviani was a Roman and had grown up in the Trastevere, the old Jewish quarter around the Roman Marcellus Theater (*Teatro Marcello*), and always stayed in touch with the Jewish community of Rome.

The Vardi affair had clearly created a shock and a major problem for us. The Jews had the understandable impression that with the deletion of the matter from the agenda, the entire project had been abandoned. Vardi could obviously not go to Rome, which would clearly have complicated an already difficult situation. But we of the World Jewish Congress planned to continue the campaign for the inclusion of the issue. Correspondence between the WJC and Cardinal Béa about the Vardi affair and about the principle of a declaration on the Jews continued for more than a year. In the beginning Goldmann's letters to Béa were polite, but, finally, he wrote him, "You know very well that the accusations against us in the Vardi affair are unfounded."

Of course our adversaries tried to exploit the confusion. But for our part we did not represent the State of Israel and did not wish to appear to do so. Our business concerned Christian theology, not the foreign policy of the Vatican.

To be sure, we remained in contact with Israel and its representatives in various countries, but we did not play identical roles. In Rome we maintained a close liaison with Maurice Fischer, the Israeli ambassador to Italy, a Jew of Belgian origin who had fought during the war in the French resistance. He was a man of great ability, one of the best of Israel's ambassadors, a rare individual who truly understood the Vatican. I thoroughly enjoyed working with him. Fischer, who had previously been the first Israeli ambassador to France, had moved to Rome a year earlier and was already familiar with the political ground there. I was glad to be able to consult him during some difficult moments during the Council's deliberations.

At this time I gave considerable thought to the idea of establishing a permanent mechanism to maintain continual contact between the Jews and the church. Achieving this would not be easy and would take a long time. For one thing, the competition among the different Jewish organizations during the Council deliberations many of us found embarrassing and humiliating. Some of them sought to contact the bishops and even the pope himself without coordinating their activities with anyone else. At the WJC we had made great efforts to build the widest front possible and had succeeded in certain respects.

But at the time neither the American Jewish Committee nor the Anti-Defamation League belonged to the group I represented, despite the fact that B'nai B'rith cooperated with us. The Anti-Defamation League is, of course, part of B'nai B'rith, but it had acquired considerable autonomy, and at certain times the two organizations operated separately.

Jewish groups from the United States practiced the American method of lobbying, which was completely unknown in Europe and was certainly not appreciated at the Vatican. In any case, the WJC believed that the church held the responsibility to remedy the wrongs against the Jewish people and the Jews ought not to go begging or demanding in raggle-taggle fashion. Some of these disorderly interventions severely damaged our cause because the bishops were not accustomed to such methods. We at the WJC had stated in our memorandum what we had to say; it was now up to the church to act.

In order to limit the damage, agree on common guidelines, and coordinate Jewish efforts, the WJC worked hard to establish some order, assisted by the support of Ambassador Fischer. We said to the American Jews, talk to the American bishops, they are familiar with your methods, they will listen to you and will take your demands into account. But as for the others, leave them alone. I am happy to say that before long we achieved a semblance of order and cooperation.

The first session of the Council took place on October 11, 1962. I remember the visit I paid Achille Cardinal Liénart, who at that time chaired the Conference of French Bishops. It was a week before the Council was to open. Cardinal Liénart was a good friend and had supported the Jews during the war in France with a great deal of courage and fortitude. He was an extremely cultivated man with a warm personality and was well versed in the Hebrew Bible. We consulted him several times in preparing for the Council, and I made a point of seeing him one more time before the opening of the first session. He said to me modestly, "You know, we are going to meet in Rome with 2,300 bishops who have never seen each other. What will happen? They speak all the languages in the world! You know, in such a situation only the Holy Spirit can help us."

I shall never forget how the Holy Spirit manifested itself. At the first meeting, after the solemn opening ceremony led by the pope, the Curia distributed lists of names for the various Council commissions that it had already prepared. Then the Holy Spirit arose in the person of Cardinal Liénart, the first speaker at the Council in his capacity as senior French bishop. Liénart asked that the discussion be adjourned so that the episcopal conferences of the various countries could study the lists and come to some agreement.

This maneuver was unheard of. Applause broke out in the back of the hall. And after Liénart sat down, Joseph Cardinal Frings of Cologne, who was the senior German bishop, rose in turn and supported Cardinal Liénart's proposal. Now enormous applause broke out throughout the hall. This was the crucial moment of the Council. The bishops showed they would not simply accept the Curia's dictates but demanded they be allowed to participate in these decisions. This was a new, almost miraculous phenomenon.

In all the discussions that followed—the first was on "Scripture and Tradition"—delegates expressed differing points of view in a spirit of great freedom, and they continued to do so. We believed it very important that from the first discussions the figure of Cardinal Liénart emerged as one of the great pioneers of the new spirit of the Council: one of our friends was becoming one of the prominent spokesmen of Vatican II. We also welcomed the fact that Cardinal Liénart benefited from the support of Pope John XXIII.

As for Cardinal Béa, after introducing several remarkable documents he found strong backing among the fathers of the Council. He too became one of the central figures of Vatican II. This allowed him to return to the matters of Jewish-Christian relations. In December 1962 Béa saw the pope and proposed that the draft document on the Jews be returned to the Council's agenda. John XXIII agreed at once. Since June the question had been left in abeyance, which gave some people an opportunity to calm down.

This text had had no official existence during the first session of the Council. But it should be noted that very few texts were discussed at all during this session. For lack of time and because of the great number of drafts, not all the texts were even tabled. Many Jewish leaders publicly expressed their disappointment. But after the first session, the cardinal returned to the offensive.

I saw Béa again in January 1963. He appeared very confident and said to me in German, "Our affairs are progressing very well. Several cardinals have spoken positively of them, and the pope has as well." Then he said to me, "You have to help me." He took out a list of cardinals and bishops whom he wanted me to meet. I told him that we were not very comfortable with the lobbying by some of the Jewish organizations. But when the Cardinal said, "Help me," it was an entirely different matter. He added, "Don't go into detail. Tell all these people what you are expecting from the Council. Now is the moment to do it, now or never."

For half an hour we discussed the list of prominent clerics who had to be approached. On the list were about ten cardinals from the Roman Curia. I said to him pointedly, "You know, with the members of the Curia it's a very delicate matter, for with them it's impossible to make any secret move. Everything is public knowledge in Rome." As a consequence, we reduced the list of members of the Curia considerably. Later we discussed in detail the list of bishops upon whom it would be appropriate to call in various parts of the world.

Without losing any time I turned to the leaders of the Jewish communities in different countries and during the weeks that followed organized explanatory visits to the church fathers, members of the Council in countries around the world.

Béa also recommended that I talk to the cardinals who presided over Council meetings. My friend Ernst Ludwig Ehrlich of the B'nai B'rith and I paid visits to Léon-Joseph Cardinal Suenens in Brussels and to Julius Cardinal Döpfner in Munich. An Italian friend, Astorre Mayer, president of the Jewish community of Milan, called on Giacomo Cardinal Lercaro in Bologna. We divided up the work in order to move faster and keep our project as quiet as possible.

During this time the Council began to discuss the placement of the re-admitted draft text on the Jews. Various alternatives presented themselves. Some recommended including it in the text on ecumenism. Others said it should be placed elsewhere. Still others suggested the drafting of a separate document altogether.

In the spring of 1963 it was decided to incorporate the draft text on the Jews into the text dealing with ecumenism, where it would become the fourth chapter. The declaration on religious freedom formed the fifth chapter. In July 1963 the coordinating commission for the Council approved the draft. In November, before the second session of the Council, the text was made public and distributed to the bishops who were present. Many of us hoped that at that time there would be a discussion and a first vote, but this did not happen. Introduced officially by Cardinal Béa on November 19, the text on the Jews was not considered by the delegates.

They voted "in principle" on the first three chapters of the text on ecumenism, but they left the two following chapters hanging. Of course this caused disappointment on the Jewish side.

I think it is appropriate to quote some important passages from the presentation of the text by Cardinal Béa at the plenary session of the Council: "This text does not derive from my initiative, but from the intitiative of His Holiness Pope John XXIII, who had reviewed and approved it five months before his death."* He continued, "This Declaration has no national or political

---

*John XXIII died on June 3, 1963, and was succeeded on June 21 by Paul VI, who served until his death in 1978.—ED.

character. In particular, it is not a question of having the State of Israel recognized by the Holy See."

Then the cardinal dealt in detail with the deicide accusation against the Jews:

> The Jews of our time can hardly be accused of the crimes committed against Christ, they are too far removed in time from those deeds. Even in the time of Christ, the majority of the chosen people did not cooperate with the leaders in condemning Christ. If not even all the Jews then in Palestine or in Jerusalem can be accused, how much less can the Jews dispersed throughout the Roman Empire be accused? And how much less again those who today, after nineteen centuries, live scattered throughout the whole world?

Then he explained why the Church should make a statement on the Jews:

> Some decades ago anti-Semitism was prevalent in various regions in a particularly violent and criminal form, especially in Germany under the rule of National Socialism, which because of hatred of the Jews committed frightful crimes, killing several millions of the Jewish people.

Béa continued:

> Now, it would have been almost impossible for some of this propaganda's claims not to have an unfortunate effect even on faithful Catholics, especially since the arguments advanced by that propaganda often enough bore an appearance of truth, particularly when drawn from the New Testament and from the history of the Church.

Béa denied that anti-Semitism drew any of its inspiration from Christian doctrine, a notion, he said, "which is completely false." On the contrary, "it is rather a question of eradicating from the minds of Catholics all those Nazi propaganda ideas that might still remain."

Béa's presentation in the great hall of the Council was received with a great deal of enthusiasm, evident in the warm and prolonged applause that followed.

As for the reference to John XXIII in Béa's address, this great pope died in June 1963. His charismatic personality remains alive in the memory of all Jews. It was a sign of the veneration and esteem that this powerful personality enjoyed that the largest Jewish organizations, in an event unique in history, sent a special delegation to represent the international Jewish community at his funeral ceremony. With great emotion, I sat in the delegation.

With the return of the text on the Jews to the Council agenda, the draft's opponents threw off all restraint in their attack on it. During the winter of 1963–1964 an avalanche of articles and pamphlets appeared, some of them extremely libelous, especially in the Arab press, most particularly in Egypt. At the same time a book appeared in Spanish entitled, *The Plot Against the Church*, a savage anti-Semitic attack.* Over several hundred pages the authors rose up against the Jews and deployed every possible effort to prevent the adoption of the text.

Our opponents did not hesitate to attack and defame Cardinal Béa personally. Several books and tracts against him appeared, filled with all sorts of calumnies: that his name was not Béa but Behar, that he was of Jewish origin, and much more of the same vicious slander. These attacks only strengthened his will to succeed.

I think he very often underestimated the resistance and difficulties he would meet. Fortunately, despite his advanced age, he enjoyed good health and was quite fit, and this permitted him to overcome a variety of obstacles.

In addition to the sensational statements of some Arab clerics who opposed any Council text dealing with the Jews, circles in several Arab countries organized public rallies that unfortunately made an impression on the Secretariat of State and the Sacred Oriental Congregation.

These events explain why, at the conclusion of the second session of the Council, the delegates not only rejected a vote but ordered the drafting of a new text. The Council gave its Coordinating Commission, a group that was much more conservative than the Secretariat for the Promotion of Christian Unity, the task of editing the new document.

Despite all this agitation, Cardinal Béa remained calm and optimistic, convinced that the text would be discussed and voted on at the following session and that the essence of its contents would be retained.

Following these developments, Béa's secretariat approved the text of a strengthened declaration on Judaism as part of the document on ecumenism and then submitted it to the Council's Coordinating Commission. Once again, the draft's opponents loosed a barrage of publicity against it and against its proponents. The Jews' adversaries thought it of no use and even pernicious for the church to adopt a document that raised the issue of Christian responsibility in the Shoah and placed Judaism on an equal footing with Christianity.

---

*The ultra-conservative attack on the reform being carried out at Vatican II was published under the name Maurice Pinay, but was actually written by twelve priests.—ED.

As events unfolded we began to realize with increasing clarity who it was that so vehemently opposed our project. The Church's ultra-conservative circles put up the greatest internal resistance. I have found the names of this "opposition group" in my personal notes. Msgr. Luigi Carli, Bishop of Segni, led the group. Another member of this group, unknown at the time but well known later, was the late Msgr. Marcel Lefebvre, the future schismatic archbishop of Dakar, whom the church excommunicated because he refused to accept certain of the Vatican II reforms. The opposition achieved a certain level of success. In June 1964 we learned that the commission had made substantial changes and returned the draft to Béa.

Each time the commission returned the document to Cardinal Béa, he again revised it in an attempt to retain our ideas. We found some comfort in the fact that he enjoyed the support of the pope and of several very influential cardinals. In order to win additional support we began a number of meetings with council delegates at the highest level: the moderators and the men who chaired the Council committees. And so we paid second visits to Cardinal Suenens, Cardinal Döpfner, and Cardinal Lercaro in Bologna, all of them committee moderators. We refrained from meeting a fourth, Gregory Peter XV Cardinal Agagianian.

At first it seemed as if our efforts had failed. Once again the Control Commission revised the text, considerably weakening the passage exonerating the Jews from the accusation of deicide. It also contained a clause affirming that "the union of the Jewish people with the Church is part of the Christian hope" and that "the Church awaits the entry of this people into the fullness of the people of God established by Christ"—in other words, conversion. Although at this point perhaps it should not have, this news shocked us, and we decided to do something about it.

We asked ourselves frankly how the draft had reached us. There are of necessity mechanisms by which such texts are communicated. That we reviewed this *sub secreto* draft was no accident. Most certainly some people who disagreed with the text saw to it that a copy came into our hands. As soon as we had it, we took steps to have it published, and on September 3, 1964, the *New York Herald Tribune* carried the draft text. This is probably what killed it. Need I admit that I was behind this whole operation, that I was responsible for the leak and for its consequences?

One can imagine the effect produced by its publication. Deeply shocked, Jewish organizations reacted vigorously by publishing a statement in October 1964 that reaffirmed "the fidelity of Jews to their faith, their history, and the constituent elements of their heritage." Citing the Council itself, the statement also recalled that "whatever the force of coercion, no sacrifice was too great for us to maintain our unique religious character." I thought this a very dignified response. It should be emphasized that for once all the Jewish organizations in the United States, the WJC, and B'nai B'rith agreed on the statement's wording.

The whole story is quite astonishing! It demonstrates that not only individuals but also great assemblies can be judged by the manner in which each conducts itself with regard to the Jews. The text of the Jewish protest was sent to Cardinal Béa's secretariat, and he had it read out in a plenary sitting to great effect. The secretariat then proceeded to draft a new version of the document on ecumenism.

But the struggle over the text on relations with Jews, going on now for three years, was not yet over. Our opponents made attempts to limit the document's scope and to have it revised by the Theological Commission. Finally, on September 18, 1964, a considerably modified and strengthened draft was submitted to the Council fathers. It condemned and deplored discrimination against Jews and warned against charging the Jews with deicide. It contained no reference to the conversion of Jews.

On Friday, September 25, Cardinal Béa introduced the text to the plenary Council with a request for its definitive adoption in principle. In his presentation Cardinal Béa insisted, "It is absolutely unthinkable to do what some Council Fathers have requested, that is, to remove this question from the agenda." Béa also distanced himself from the new phrasing that had been inserted by the Coordinating Commission. In short, he argued for the reestablishment of the earlier text, that is, the one he had just presented.

Then, on September 28, in the presence of all the great names of the universal church, the great debate began. Celebrated men of the church participated, including Cardinals Liénart, Josef Frings, Paul-Émile Léger, Richard Cushing, Joseph Ritter, John Heenan, and others, who strongly supported Béa's original text. On the other side, the opposition, led by Ignace Cardinal Tappouni, Archbishop Joseph Tawil, Ernesto Cardinal Ruffini, and other clerics from the Arab countries, argued vehemently against it. We all recognized the extreme importance of the debate and the vote to follow.

The debate concluded with the drafting of yet another revised version that took account of the opinions expressed in the great hall and that considerably reinforced the theses that were favorable to the Jews. Finally, the text on the Jews was separated from the declaration on ecumenism.

On November 20, 1964, at the conclusion of the Council's third session, the delegates voted in principle on the new text, which they adopted with

1,651 votes for, 242 votes for with amendment (*placet juxta modum*), and 99 votes against.

This represented a great success for Cardinal Béa and his secretariat, but the struggle was by no means over.

Between November 1964 and the presentation of the text for the definitive vote at the fourth session of the Council, in October 1965, the struggle continued. The draft text circulated under cover, now weakened, now strengthened as the revisions went on. Clerics from the Arab countries continued to agitate. Cardinal Béa sent two of his closest collaborators, Msgr. Johannes Willebrands and Father Pierre Duprey, the secretariat's secretary, on a mission to the Arab countries in an attempt to try to calm feelings there.

A new attack erupted in the form of an article signed by Msgr. Carli, the Bishop of Segni, who stigmatized the whole of the Jewish people as responsible for the death of Jesus. But Cardinal Béa did not give up; he responded to Carli point for point in the journal *La Civiltà cattolica*, and a majority of European and American bishops supported him.

It required three meetings of his secretariat to draft a text that took into account the various opposing opinions, in particular to satisfy the pope's wish to achieve the broadest possible consensus. The adversaries did not cease their campaign to defeat our program and continued to agitate, right up to the last minute. They did succeed in weakening the document at various points.

Among other things, opponents argued that it was not appropriate to single out the Jews when the church maintained relations with other religions and in particular with Muslims. This consideration led to a broadening of the text, which no longer limited itself to dealing with the relations of the church with Judaism but added a certain number of paragraphs concerning Buddhism, Hinduism, and Islam. Separate from the decree on ecumenism, the definitive text took the title "Declaration on the Relations of the Church to Non-Christian Religions."

This important last-minute change had serious flaws. The passages dealing with the other religions were grafted onto the text devoted to the Jews and did not reflect the same degree of reflection and development.

Known under the title of *Nostra aetate* ("Of Our Time"), the declaration was voted on October 14 and 15, 1965. The text on the Jews comprises the fourth chapter.

The Council initially voted on the text point by point as follows:

—Rejection of the collective responsibility of the Jews for the death of Christ: For, 1,875; against, 188; null and void, 9.

—The Jews should not be designated as cursed or rejected by God: For, 1,821; against, 245; null and void, 14.

—Rejection of anti-Semitism and the persecution of Jews: For, 1,905; against, 199; null and void, 14.

And here is the result of the vote on the declaration in its entirety: For, 1,763; against, 250; null and void, 10.

Before its promulgation by Pope Paul VI on October 28, 1965, the Council definitively adopted the declaration with 2,221 votes for, 88 against, and 3 null and void.

Here is the portion of the text that deals with relations with the Jews:

> As this sacred synod searches into the mystery of the Church, it remembers the bond that spiritually ties the people of the New Covenant to Abraham's stock.
>
> Thus the Church of Christ acknowledges that, according to God's saving design, the beginnings of her faith and her election are found already among the Patriarchs, Moses, and the prophets. She professes that all who believe in Christ—Abraham's sons according to their faith (cf *Ga* 3:7)—are included in the same Patriarch's call, and likewise that the salvation of the Church is mysteriously foreshadowed by the chosen people's exodus from the land of bondage. The Church, therefore, cannot forget that she received the revelation of the Old Testament through the people with whom God in His inexpressible mercy concluded the Ancient Covenant. Nor can she forget that she draws sustenance from the root of that well-cultivated olive tree onto which have been grafted the wild shoots, the Gentiles (cf *Rm* 11:17-24). Indeed, the Church believes that by His cross Christ, Our Peace, reconciled Jews and Gentiles, making them both one in Himself (cf *Ep* 2:14-16).
>
> The Church keeps ever in mind the words of the Apostle about his kinsmen, "theirs is the sonship and the glory and the covenants and the law and the worship and the promises; theirs are the fathers and from them is the Christ according to the flesh" (*Rm* 9:4-5), the Son of the Virgin Mary. She also recalls that the Apostles, the Church's mainstay and pillars, as well as most of the early disciples who proclaimed Christ's gospel to the world, sprang from the Jewish people.
>
> As Holy Scripture testifies, Jerusalem did not recognize the time of her visitation (cf *Lk* 19:44), nor did the Jews in large number accept the gospel; indeed, not a few opposed the spreading of it (cf *Rm* 11:28). Nevertheless, God holds the Jews most dear for the sake of their Fathers, for He does not repent of the gifts He makes nor of the calls He issues—such is the witness

of the Apostle (cf *Rm* 11:28-29). In company with the Prophets and the same Apostle, the Church awaits that day, known to God alone, on which all peoples will address the Lord in a single voice and "serve Him shoulder to shoulder" (*Soph* 3:9; cf *Is* 66:23, *Ps* 65:4, *Rm* 11:11-32).

Since the spiritual patrimony common to Christians and Jews is thus so great, this Sacred Synod wants to foster and recommend that mutual understanding and respect which is the fruit, above all, of biblical and theological studies as well as fraternal dialogues.

True, Jewish authorities and those who followed their lead pressed for the death of Christ (cf *Jn* 19:6); still, what happened in His passion cannot be charged against all the Jews, without distinction, then alive, nor against the Jews of today. Although the Church is the new People of God, the Jews should not be presented as rejected or accursed by God, as if this followed from the Holy Scriptures. All should take pains, then, lest in catechetical instruction or in the preaching of the Word of God they do not teach anything that does not conform to the truth of the Gospel and the spirit of Christ.

Furthermore, in her rejection of any persecution against any man, the Church, mindful of the patrimony she shares with the Jews and moved not by political reasons but by the Gospel's spiritual love, decries hatred, persecutions, and displays of antisemitism, directed against Jews at any time and by anyone.

Besides, as the Church has always held and continues to hold, Christ underwent His passion and death freely, because of the sins of men and out of infinite love, in order that all might attain salvation. It is, therefore, the burden of the Church's preaching to proclaim the cross of Christ as the sign of God's all-embracing love and as the fountain from which every grace flows.

The World Jewish Congress and the Jewish organizations gathered in the World Conference of Jewish Organizations (cojo) hailed the adoption of the text, and Nahum Goldmann telegraphed Cardinal Béa to congratulate him on his success. For my part, I sensed that new paths were opening up and that we should walk down them without delay.

It is true that the final modifications to the text evoked great disappointment in Jewish circles. While I shared this disappointment to some degree, I never judged that the Council had fundamentally altered the significance of the document. My approach stemmed from my conviction that the Council's declaration constituted a new departure in Jewish-Christian relations.

The most pressing question that followed was whether the church would implement these new guidelines. If it did—and I was personally convinced that this would be the case—the details in the modifications would not be very important. The text itself would introduce a new dynamic that would soon carry us beyond the points of friction and lead to new attitudes and ideological positions. If it did not, the details would hardly be of any importance at all.

But in another way I could not help regretting some of the concessions to which Cardinal Béa had consented in order to overcome opposition and calm feelings of anxiety. The results of the final vote demonstrate that the number of opponents did not vary a great deal, which would indicate that the concessions perhaps need not have been made.

There is no doubt that the great figure who developed and fought for this new theology concerning Jews and Judaism was Augustin Cardinal Béa. He was supported in his action by Pope John XXIII and by his successor, Pope Paul VI, who had the skills to bring this particular ship safely into port.

It is quite remarkable that the two most innovative texts from the Vatican Council II, those on the Jews and on religious freedom, were both the work of Cardinal Béa. This constituted one of his great contributions to the Council. He made a substantial effort to assure the Council's adoption of the Declaration on Religious Freedom. Béa understood that without a text on religious freedom, no progress toward union with other churches and Christian communities could be achieved. To this problem he devoted all his strength and energy. He had the backing of some of the great figures of the Council, such as Bishop Xavier Joseph de Smedt of Bruges, Father John Courtney Murray, S.J., and Cardinal Cushing of Boston, who affirmed that without the declaration on religious freedom the ecumenical movement would founder. It is self-evident to what degree these two declarations are mutually complementary.

In addition, Cardinal Béa rightly emphasized that of all the texts adopted by the Second Vatican Council, the one on the Jews was the only one that contained no reference to the traditional teachings of the church, whether patristic, conciliar, or pontifical. This fact clearly demonstrated the revolutionary character of the pronouncement.

As far as we were concerned, we could only share in the words of Pope John XXIII who affirmed that "finding Cardinal Béa was a gift from God." Indeed, to Cardinal Béa, who so deeply influenced our relationship with the Christian world, all Jews owe a tremendous debt of gratitude.

On the occasion of the centenary of his birth, the Secretariat for Christian Unity invited me to participate in a colloquium organized in Cardinal Béa's honor and to review the Cardinal's contribution to the Council's texts on religious freedom. It was a gesture without precedent to invite a Jew to expound to the Vatican on the church's concept of religious freedom.

At the gathering I observed that this was all the more remarkable in that only a century separated us from the notorious Mortara affair, the kidnapping, clandestine baptism, and disappearance of a little Jewish boy in the pontifical states, which was one of the most violent public conflicts that ever occurred between the Catholic church and the Jewish community on the subject of religious freedom.

After having emphasized the course we had traveled, I evoked the old Jewish tradition of *Lamed Vav tsadikim*, "the thirty-six righteous persons who live in each generation, whose names remain secret, who maintain the cohesion of the entire world through their generosity and their good action and without whom the world would founder."

I also recalled another Jewish tradition, that of the *Hassidei umot haolam*, "the righteous among the nations of the world," who merit a place in the world to come.

I concluded, "The way in which these two traditions interact with one another is not very clear. Whatever their coincidence, I am profoundly convinced that in the person of Cardinal Béa we are honoring today one of those righteous persons who maintain the cohesion of the world."

The expression of the Catholic Church's new approach to the Jewish people was not limited to the paragraphs of the *Nostra aetate*. It must be read in the context of other Council documents that contain passages dealing with Judaism. In particular we may quote the Dogmatic Constitution on the Church (*Lumen Gentium*), wherein paragraph 16 reaffirms "the election of the people of Israel, the people who received the covenant from God" and who are thereby not excluded from the plan of salvation.

The Dogmatic Constitution on Divine Revelation (*Dei Verbum*) speaks in its fourth chapter of the "Old Testament through which God revealed himself to the Jewish people" and affirms that "the holy books of the Old Testament are the true word of God."

In fact the Declaration of Religious Freedom leans in the same direction when it recognizes the right of other religions, including Judaism, to seek without constraints the paths of salvation and the truth of God as well as the free exercise of their religion.

In this context it was then natural that the non-Catholic observers at the Council should follow the tribulations of the text on religious freedom with the same passion as the Jews followed the successive versions of the document on non-Christian religions.

No one will be surprised to discover that during these moments of uncertainty and even anxiety I was in close contact with Dr. Willem A. Visser 't Hooft, secretary-general of the World Council of Churches, or that we met continually to exchange our intelligence and concerns. Each of us was eager to discover what effect the treatment of one of the texts would have on the fate of the other.

The Jews and Ecumenism

To maintain our relations with the Catholic church we had to rely on the Secretariat for Christian Unity, a situation that did not please us. The pope had asked Cardinal Béa to oversee relations with the Jews, and since Béa headed the secretariat, we were, so to speak, inserted into that structure. I reflected a good deal at that time whether we should raise an objection to this arrangement.

The Vatican also had a secretariat for non-Christian religions, where we logically should have been situated. On the other hand, we could not ignore the fact that the ties between Christians and Jews are of a very different order than those between Christians and Buddhists, for example. After all, we had a common spiritual heritage, the Hebrew Bible. And for us, being together with Buddhists, Hindus, Shintoists, and others did not seem satisfactory either. Moreover I knew that the cardinal who directed this secretariat was far from being a friend of the Jews and even had a reputation for anti-Semitic tendencies. And we knew that we had a true friend in Cardinal Béa. So I kept silent, thinking I might bring up the matter at the conclusion of the Council.

Nahum Goldmann left me quite a free hand in such matters and pays tribute in his memoirs to my handling of them. He spoke to me of the issue, clearly concerned about it. I explained the situation to him and the reason why I had done nothing to change it. Goldmann's concern impressed me since he rarely intervened in matters of this kind, and I decided to speak about it to one of Béa's close collaborators who sometimes acted as liaison between us, Msgr. Joseph Höfer, a German cleric who at that time was the ecclesiastical counselor to the German Federal Republic's legation at the Holy See. Since he was a member of Béa's secretariat, I met him fairly regularly. Höfer had behaved with honor during the Nazi era and had worked closely with the famous Clemens Cardinal August von Galen, the Bishop of Münster, who had had the courage to protest publicly against "euthanasia."

Höfer had followed all the events from 1933 to 1939 closely and was well aware of German Catholicism's relations and compromises with Hitler. Being a man of principle as well as utterly candid, he was highly critical of the con-cordat between the Vatican and Nazi Germany and of the role of Msgr. Lud-wig Kaas, the former leader of the German Center party who bore great re-sponsibility for the German church's actions.

One day we had a long discussion about all these matters, and I said to Höfer, "You ought to tell Cardinal Béa that being housed in the Secretariat for Christian Unity creates a problem for the Jews. I will speak to him about it af-ter the Council, but you could bring it up now. You must tell him that we have enormous respect for him, of course, but due to the fact that we are not Chris-tians, we are not part of the *oekumene* and we cannot belong to the Secretariat as a useful member. After the Council we will have to find a solution. A spe-cial body could be created that would also be headed by Cardinal Béa. You must tell him because he should know why we are not bringing up this ques-tion at this time."

Some time after the conclusion of the Council I returned to the question and picked up the thread of my discussion with Msgr. Höfer. I told him that the time had come to resolve this problem. In my opinion, an independent body should be created, separate from the secretariat, but chaired in a "personal union" by Cardinal Béa. Höfer asked me to put my ideas down on paper as suggestions—on white paper without letterhead, a procedure then used at the Vatican.

I realized the delicacy of the matter and the risk involved, but I had little choice if the issue were to be resolved. In the paper I prepared, I of course ad-mitted that the church could appoint its representatives as it saw fit, but I em-phasized that our presence in the secretariat created problems for us. The questions we had to discuss were difficult enough without burdening them with an additional handicap.

After having been briefed by Msgr. Höfer, Cardinal Béa went to the pope to consult him. Some time later he called me to inform me directly that my suggestions had been accepted. He told me that the Church would create an office for relations between Catholics and Jews, and that it would manage our relations in the future. He also told me that he would shortly be consulting me about the person who would be responsible for the office.

A bit later the Cardinal confidentially let me know the name of the person who had been chosen. When I checked into the background of this person, I discovered that he had written some articles of a clearly anti-Semitic character. I called the Cardinal's attention to this fact, and he immediately chose some-one else. This was a gesture of respect and deep comprehension that augured well for our future relations.

Finally Béa appointed Father Cornelius Rijk, a Dutch theologian, as director of the new Vatican Office for Catholic-Jewish relations. Nevertheless it would take several years before we found a definitive solution to this problem. Unfortunately in obtaining the consent of Pope Paul VI for his project, Béa had not played by the rules of the church: no written text documented the pope's decision.

Some time later Paul VI published the new constitution of the Curia, which regulated in detail the jurisdictional areas of the various offices. I discovered that the second paragraph of the article on the Secretariat for Christian Unity stipulated that this secretariat would also be responsible for relations with Jews.

This revelation took my breath away. Ever the optimist, I had in the meantime informed the various Jewish communities, and our non-Jewish partners in our relations with the church, of the arrangements announced by Cardinal Béa. This was the final period of Béa's life; he was then ninety-five or ninety-six years old, but he remained extraordinarily lucid. After the Council he published a book entitled *The Church and the Jewish People,* which explained the decisions of Vatican II.* But during the last months of his life he was bedridden and could no longer receive visitors. I am convinced that at that time he lost control of the problem and could no longer deal with it.

I then sought out and had long discussions with Father Rijk. I told him that the regulation set out in the Constitution of the Curia, promulgated in August 1967, was contrary to what had been agreed on.

I informed him of my discussions with Cardinal Béa and of the fact that I had announced the terms of our agreement to other Jewish organizations. Consequently it would be difficult for me to have to tell them that the church had not respected the agreement.

An exchange of correspondence followed. In a letter of November 14, 1967, I raised all the reasons for our opposition to the Curia's decision. Finally, in a letter of July 17, which took up all the terms that I had suggested to him, Father Rijk agreed to all our demands. He made it clear that the connection of this office to the Secretariat for the Promotion of Christian Unity had no dogmatic significance but was a simple administrative measure.

He reaffirmed that the secretariat recognized that Jews were not part of the Christian *oekumene* and that he respected and recognized Jews as they were and as they themselves conceived their identity. Here he was using phrasing

---

*The Church and the Jewish People: A Commentary on the Second Vatican Council's Declaration on the Relation of the Church to Non-Christian Religions (1966).—ED.

that I had myself first used in my relations with the church's representatives, phrasing on which I had strongly insisted.

Father Rijk's letter was explicit that the secretariat had no conversionist agenda. Rijk also emphasized the completely new character of this activity. Because of it, the structure was provisional, but we had to begin to work together. The definitive structure would be elaborated over time.

It took Rijk eight months to respond to my letter. This meant that he undoubtedly had obtained the agreement of higher authorities for each of the terms employed, and this strengthened the significance of his reply.

For the time being we were content with these assurances, but of course this was not the end of the story. The problem reemerged painfully in 1971 in the course of the first meeting of the International Catholic-Jewish Liaison Committee in Paris. (How we came to be involved in the creation of this committee will be discussed later.) In the course of this meeting, when the time came to review the conclusions and the lists of those in attendance, the head of the Vatican delegation, Msgr. Jérôme Hamer, suddenly declared that the title of director of the Office for Catholic-Jewish Relations and the office itself did not exist at the Vatican. This was obviously very embarrassing both for us and for Father Rijk, who understandably soon found another job in the church.

This problem being close to my heart, I took the whole matter up again in a long discussion with Msgr. Hamer in Geneva. It was only after five hours of discussion, in the course of which I gave a detailed history of the question and of all our negotiations, that I was finally able to settle the matter. I succeeded in convincing Msgr. Hamer of the vital importance of this matter to us. As a consequence he asked me to submit to the Vatican a formal memorandum on the matter in the name of the International Jewish Committee for Interreligious Consultations, which had become the Jewish partner in the Jewish-Christian dialogue. The International Jewish Committee supported the project despite the hesitation of one of its large member organizations, and drew up the requested memorandum, which Msgr. Hamer submitted to the Vatican.

As a consequence, in October 1974 Pope Paul VI established the Commission for Religious Relations with the Jews. While remaining to a certain degree attached to the Secretariat for the Promotion of Christian Unity, it constituted a separate body. In fact Cardinal Willebrands, who had succeeded Cardinal Béa, served both as president of the Secretariat for Christian Unity and president of the Commission for Religious Relations with the Jews. This was indeed the solution I had envisaged with Msgr. Höfer during and after the Council.

In its desire for symmetry, the Vatican at the same time created a Commission for Relations with Islam, which it attached to the Secretariat for Relations with Non-Christian Religions.

The Creation of a Unified Representative Jewish Organization

A second problem that concerned me was the representation of the various Jewish organizations to the Vatican. During the Vatican Council, as noted above, I felt humiliated by the fact that Jews did not speak with a single voice. As this feeling became stronger and stronger, I promised myself that after the Council I would try to change the situation.

Clearly the church was not as unified as it appeared. We know in today's world that there are no monolithic religious entities, but at least in the Roman Catholic church there exists a centralized authority and a hierarchy that directs and represents it.

I had always pursued the notion that upon the conclusion of the Council, Jews would need to establish structured and organized relations with the Catholic church, not contingent on circumstances. I thought we required a single representative organization empowered to undertake useful discussions with central Christian bodies. Up to that time no organization authorized to speak in the name of Jewish religious interests existed.

When the World Jewish Congress was created in 1936, we decided not to concern ourselves with religious problems. This proved to be a wise decision. Only on this condition did certain organizations agree to belong to the Congress, for example the Orthodox Jews. At that time we could not even deal with Jewish cultural questions because to do so would require discussing religious matters.

It was only after the catastrophe of World War II and the destruction of almost all European Jewry, and faced with the urgency of reconstruction, that in 1948 the Congress created a cultural department. Obviously the representation of all Jewish interests, including religious matters, before an institution as prestigious as the Vatican would be extremely difficult to arrange. I nonetheless considered it to be indispensable.

Here we had to bear in mind the asymmetry of the partners. The Jews are a people, even though they are a people with a religious vocation. Christians consider themselves the adherents of a religion.

Establishing a Jewish representative organ would have to take into account the wide spectrum of interests in the Jewish communities, their existing organizations, and their geographic distribution around the world. The project would also have to include personalities whose expertise in religious affairs was uncontested and indispensable. It would have to unite representatives of the various religious trends—orthodox, liberal, conservative—without whose participation real representation could not be achieved.

This new organization would have to take into account both the reluctance of Orthodox Jews to discuss theological problems with Christians and that of the Christians to address political problems with the Jews.

We needed a permanent but flexible framework, with meetings at regular intervals but also according to circumstances when necessary. The objective was to eliminate the "fireman syndrome"—intervention only after a fire had already broken out—by creating a body where all possible subjects could be discussed and crises and confrontations prevented.

The question of suppressing the divergent opinions of the Jewish partners did not arise: each of them would be able to express their respective positions. The goal was to identify to the greatest extent possible common positions that we could present to our Christian counterparts.

Understandably, the creation of a permanent framework for official and ongoing relations with the central bodies of the Christian churches and the establishment of a representative Jewish body for this purpose took a good deal of time.

I presented this conception more than once to my Catholic friends, and when I noticed that I was having difficulties moving forward with the Catholics I tried to achieve our goals with the Protestants.

I then went to see Visser 't Hooft, who in 1966 was serving his last year as secretary-general of the World Council of Churches. I shared with him my notion of an official, permanent framework for Jewish-Christian encounters. In 1965, Visser 't Hooft had made an effort in this direction, but it lacked an international character because it involved only American Jewish organizations and had not been a great success. Now he asked me, "Could you assure me that the organization you are suggesting would truly be representative of Jewry?" I promised him that it would.

The preparation of this complex structure dragged on. I continued discussions with the Rev. Eugene Carson Blake, Visser 't Hooft's successor, an American well disposed toward us. Finally in June 1968 we were able to have our first consultation in Geneva where we gathered thirteen representatives from the World Council of Churches and ten representatives from world Jewry. On the Christian side there were representatives of the WCC secretariat and some of its member churches. On the Jewish side we had leading figures from Europe, the United States, and Israel, including people of the three great religious branches of Judaism, ensuring that both religious and political interests were taken into account.

Acting for the Jewish side in my capacity as secretary-general of the World Jewish Congress, I and Eugene Blake, acting on behalf of the Christian side, convoked the meeting. I had taken care to invite representatives of the Synagogue Council of America, whose secretary, Henry Siegman, did not attend. But my friend Joachim Prinz, then president of the executive committee of the WJC, had obtained the participation of the various religious strands of American Jewry.

It had been agreed that this first meeting would be held without publicity, which is probably what assured its success. The meeting proceeded to a review of the entire range of relations between Christians and Jews since the assembly of the 1961 WCC in New Delhi, and worked to define areas of common interest such as economic and social justice, peace and international security, and human rights. Everyone agreed that such meetings ought to be scheduled periodically and that there ought to be an ongoing exchange of views. Consequently the conference appointed a small group to plan future consultations.

When Henry Siegman realized that the meeting Blake and I had arranged with the WCC had been a success, and that the different religious branches of Judaism had been well represented, he made an important step in my direction. The president of the Synagogue Council of America brought me a personal message in which he proposed a cooperative agreement. He desired that I not approach the American congregations and rabbinical organizations directly but that I do so using him as intermediary. Under this condition he was prepared to cooperate fully. And this is how we proceeded to take the first step toward a permanent representative Jewish body. Initially the accord involved the World Jewish Congress and the Synagogue Council of America.

This solution was fully satisfactory to me. We had often been told at the Vatican, "The WJC is in the first instance a political organization." Now we had a partner whose religious character could not be denied.

In this way we laid the foundation for the International Jewish Committee for Interreligious Consultations (IJCIC). After some time the American Jewish Committee and the International B'nai B'rith joined us. These two organizations had worked for years on interfaith issues. In addition, B'nai B'rith was linked to the Anti-Defamation League, which had also developed expertise in these matters.

It was not always easy to keep all these fine people and organizations together and to preclude independent action by any of them. And I must admit that sometimes it was even easier to negotiate with our Christian partners than to assure discipline among the Jews.

For example, within the Synagogue Council of America each of the three branches of American Judaism had a veto, something we did not allow in the WJC. At times this veto made our operations rather delicate. On occasion the Orthodox would be opposed to one project or another, and on several occasions Rabbi Soloveitchik, the highly respected and influential Orthodox scholar, helped us overcome these problems.

Later it also proved necessary to acquire an Israeli partner. In fact the problems affecting the State of Israel and Jewish-Arab relations increasingly arose during our deliberations.

We knew that the situation of the Chief Rabbinate of Israel did not allow it to be associated with our work. After many long discussions the following solution was finally adopted: the Jewish members of the International Catholic-Jewish Liaison Committee organized themselves as a Jewish Council for Interfaith Relations. In this way we were able to benefit from the collaboration of figures as prominent as Prof. R. J. Zwi Werblowsky, Prof. Shemaryahu Talmon, and Dr. Geoffrey Wigoder. Thus we were able to unite the Israeli representatives with four large organizations.

I succeeded with the World Council of Churches because we had agreed not to make any publicity. I believe it miraculous indeed that no real leak to the press occurred. A small Yiddish newspaper published a short notice about it, but that was of no matter, and we maintained confidentiality.

We held a second consultation with the WCC in Geneva in May 1969, again without publicity, devoted to the discussion of two matters: religious education and the problem of prejudice, and Jerusalem in the Jewish and Christian traditions. I should add that each meeting dealt with one great central problem in a general fashion while participants also exchanged views on current affairs.

At our third meeting in Geneva, in February 1970, our Christian counterparts declared, "Our meetings should not remain secret. We have to issue a statement." Of course we accepted, and from that moment on our relations with the World Council of Churches were publicly institutionalized. We jointly established a permanent coordinating and executive committee.

The fact that we announced the 1970 meeting in the press certainly affected the thinking of our Catholic partners. But in saying that I am getting a bit ahead of myself because a totally unexpected event intervened to accelerate this development while also influencing the attitude of the Catholic church toward us.

The WJC executive committee was scheduled to meet in Rome during the first week of January 1969. During the preparation of the agenda and the logistical arrangements, Nahum Goldmann consulted me on the possibility of requesting an audience with the pope. This occurred during the last days in the life of the very ill Cardinal Béa, and I hesitated about how to proceed. I decided to make soundings through the WJC representative in Rome, Fritz Becker, who had good contacts in the Vatican. But during the two months before our meeting, we received no response to his inquiries.

On another level we had foreseen meeting certain Vatican figures who were particularly concerned with human rights. The WJC was very active in this sphere, in particular at the United Nations, and my colleague Maurice Perlzweig, the political director of the WJC in New York, attached a good deal of importance to this aspect of our work.

One of the figures who played a vital role in our contacts with the Vatican and whom we often consulted was the banker Vittorio Veronese, the former president of our executive committee and former director general of UNESCO. From the first we had a trustworthy relationship with him, and he never hesitated to help us. Veronese had a particular situation at the Vatican by virtue of the fact that he was also one of the principal financial advisers to the Curia.

Three days before our executive committee meeting, Becker informed me that he had received a call from Veronese proposing an audience with Pope Paul VI for Nahum Goldmann and a small delegation for the following Saturday. We were all the more astonished by this sudden invitation as Veronese stated that he was acting at the request of Msgr. Giovanni Benelli, later Archbishop of Florence, the second most important figure at the Vatican.

Reflecting on the reasons for this invitation, we could surmise only one answer. Some days earlier the Holy See had rather precipitously condemned the Israeli bombing of the Beirut airport. The bombing raid caused no deaths or injuries but destroyed some military and civilian aircraft. After having released an indignant statement, the Vatican now seemed ready to modify its position.

I decided to consult Nahum Goldmann who was then in Jerusalem, because in my opinion the matter concerned the State of Israel, not the World Jewish Congress. Because of this, we ought to obtain the opinion of the Israeli government in order to find out whether we should try to be helpful in overcoming the crisis.

On the following morning I spoke with Goldmann on the telephone and laid out the situation for him, adding that since the invitation was for Saturday we might decline it on the pretext that we could not go to the Vatican on the Sabbath. I also pointed out that our answer had to be given that same day. Goldmann promised me a speedy response.

Two hours later I had a telephone call from the deputy director general of the Israeli Ministry of Foreign Affairs, Arthur Lourié. This senior official, whom I knew well, asked me whether I was truly convinced that the Vatican's invitation had been motivated by the desire to attenuate the effects of its statement on the Beirut airport bombing. I answered that I could see no other reason and that everyone I had consulted shared my opinion. "Under those circumstances," he said to me, "I don't see any reason not to accept the invitation." Since time was short, I immediately confirmed our acceptance to Veronese.

Two hours later another telephone call from Jerusalem transmitted a message from Goldmann asking me to cancel everything. Now I was highly embarrassed. You can't play around with the Vatican like that! That afternoon, with Perlzweig and Becker, I attended a meeting on human rights where I met Veronese. I asked to have a private word with him and told him that I had received instructions to cancel our presence at the audience. I tried to cover up by inventing plausible reasons for the abrupt change. In fact I was totally ignorant of the reasons, but I managed to carry it off fairly well. Veronese undertook to interpret our position to Msgr. Benelli, and apparently things resolved themselves without complications.

The next morning I went with Rabbi Joachim Prinz, the president of the executive committee of the WJC, to Dr. Goldmann's hotel to make preparations for the meeting that was to begin that same evening. I told Goldmann of my embarrassment and asked him for an explanation.

Goldmann then told me that after my telephone call he had tried hard to speak to the Israeli prime minister, Levi Eshkol, to the minister of foreign affairs, Abba Eban, and to Eban's director general. In the end he had to make do with the opinion of Lourié, the deputy director general. But a little later Abba Eban called Goldmann to tell him, "I don't need to give you advice; it's your responsibility to accept the audience with the pope or not." In the face of this attitude, Goldmann decided that he would not get mixed up in an affair that concerned only the Israeli government. The whole business was then buried.

But this was not the end of the story. That Saturday evening the WJC executive committee meeting was to begin in a big hotel in Rome attended by numerous delegates. Since I was responsible for organizing the event, I had to leave the conference hall at a certain moment to go to the secretariat. As I was crossing the foyer I spotted Father Cornelius Rijk sitting in an armchair. As readers know, Rijk was then responsible for the Vatican's relations with the

Jewish world. To my question, "What are you doing here?" he replied, "I'm waiting for Dr. Goldmann." "Does Dr. Goldmann know of this?" "No, he doesn't know about it, but I'm waiting for him."

I then went back into the conference hall and told Goldmann that Rijk was waiting for him in the foyer. I was surprised because the whole business of the audience with the pope had been handled by Veronese until then. But since Veronese had left Rome for a meeting in Geneva, Vatican officials had turned to Rijk, apparently the only one they could find on short notice who knew us.

Goldmann left the hall, and Rijk informed him on behalf of Msgr. Benelli that the pope was keen to receive a WJC delegation. He invited us to prepare a press release ourselves about the audience. Rijk added that the pontiff set great store by the audience and that the time could be set according to our availability.

After the session ended, Goldmann called Prinz, Perlzweig, and me together, and told us what had happened. We then decided again to consult the Israeli government. Barring a veto on its part, we determined to accept the invitation. Consequently we drafted the press release, and Rijk had it picked up the next morning. He returned it swiftly with the addition of a small amendment of no great importance.

Meanwhile we had been in touch with the Israeli prime minister, who finally approved our position. Over the course of that Sunday we briefed the Israeli ambassador in Rome on what we had planned to say to the pope.

Goldmann was in Rome only for two or three days. As a result we had no choice but to schedule the meeting for Monday, January 6, the day of Epiphany. This posed certain problems because it was a holiday and all the Vatican offices would be closed. But the pope made an exception to receive us in his private library.

The meeting was extremely interesting in several respects. The delegation, led by Dr. Goldmann in his capacity as president of the World Jewish Congress, included Joachim Prinz, as president of the executive committee, and me as secretary-general. The only Vatican official present was Msgr. Rijk. The pope received us cordially and the audience proceeded beyond the limits of Vatican protocol regulations.

Dr. Goldmann came directly to the point before the pope could formally welcome us, summarizing in three or four sentences formulated with great precision the principal subjects of the meeting, which reflected the contents of the press release.

There followed a conversation with the pope lasting about twenty minutes. As we began to stand up to leave, the pope said, "No, no, I want to read you a statement." He had prepared a text, but since Goldmann had plunged immediately into his explication, the pope had not been able to read it. He did so now at the end of the meeting, some of the phrasing also reflecting the press release.

In the course of this statement the pope regretted that a feeling of hostility toward the Jewish people could have been attributed to him when he made his statement about the Middle East. He explained that he condemned all use of violent means, whatever their provenance.

Even more important, Pope Paul VI spoke of the Jewish people, or rather of the Hebrew people—*populo ebraico* in Italian. I had introduced this notion of people into the press release intentionally to underline the fact that Jews did not simply constitute a religion.

I had not forgotten that in the text of *Nostra aetate* the term "the Jews" (*de judaeis*) had been replaced at the last moment by *de religione judaica*. This was, then, a moment to be specific and underline our position in the dialogue with the church. The acceptance of this text on the part of the Vatican was a source of deep satisfaction to me.

Then the pope astonished us with the unexpected. In pronouncing the words "Jewish people" the Pope suddenly broke off to add with some emotion, "You know, we have known each other for such a long time, but we are really only starting to reflect on our relationship." The phrase had visibly affected him. He realized all of a sudden that he had never before spoken of the "Hebrew people," that previously he had considered the Jews solely as adherents of a religion. This was an extremely moving moment, and we all saw the sincerity of the pope's reaction.

In his statement, Paul VI expressed his esteem for the Jewish people and "the hope that it will be possible to develop opportunities between the Church and the Jewish people, as with other people, in the service of the common causes of humanity."

This highly unusual papal audience permitted the dialogue to be opened between the Catholic church and world Jewry.

Following this epoch-making meeting with Pope Paul VI, we met with Msgr. Rijk some months later in London. Henry Siegman, on behalf of the Synagogue Council of America, and I, for the WJC, the two founding organizations of the International Jewish Committee for Interreligious Consultations, set out for him our views on an ongoing process of cooperation between us as well as on the mechanisms to be created to achieve this objective.

Msgr. Rijk suggested that we put our ideas in writing, and we did so in November 1969. A meeting in Rome in March 1970 offered us the opportunity officially to submit the memorandum, signed by Henry Siegman and me and to discuss it with our Roman partners.

The memorandum's goal was to "establish a cadre for an ongoing relationship on a permanent basis between authorized representatives of the Catholic and Jewish communities by providing for them a forum available at all times for confrontation and consultation on long-term concerns and policies as well as on specific situations as they may arise from time to time." At the same time it specified a certain number of principles that ought to be considered for the establishment of this framework and for our mutual cooperation.

Meanwhile a document on the implementation of the principles contained in chapter four of *Nostra aetate* had been prepared at the Vatican by a commission of the Secretariat for the Promotion of Christian Unity. The premature publication of this working document that was quite favorable to the Jewish cause and to the State of Israel, by the Archbishop of Baltimore, Lawrence Cardinal Sheehan, provoked a serious controversy that delayed the definitive adoption of this text, and then only greatly amended. It would not appear for several years.*

Our contacts with Rome continued, however, and finally led to the call for another meeting between representatives of the Catholic church and those of the Jewish organizations grouped in the International Jewish Committee for Interreligious Consultation (IJCIC).

This meeting took place in Rome, December 20–22, 1970. It was all the more important since at our suggestion all the departments of the Holy See concerned with various aspects of relations with Jews attended. These included delegates from the Secretariat for the Promotion of Christian Unity, the Vatican Office for Catholic-Jewish Relations, the Congregation for Religious Doctrine, the Congregation for Catholic Education, the Congregation for the Oriental Churches, and the Pontifical Commission on Justice and Peace. This was a significant church representation; Cardinal Willebrands chaired the meeting. Representatives of the World Jewish Congress, the Synagogue Council of America, the American Jewish Committee, the International B'nai B'rith, and the Jewish Council for Interfaith Consultation in Israel made up the IJCIC delegation.

---

*Entitled "Guidelines and Suggestions for Implementing the Conciliar Declaration Nostra Aetate (IV)," the Vatican finally published it in January 1975, nine years after the declaration itself. For a detailed discussion of this document, see pp. 283–285 below.—ED.

For the first time representatives of the Catholic church and the world Jewish community met on a footing of equality for discussions on a high official level. Thus all the questions that concerned us could be raised.

By common consent the meeting concerned itself mainly with drafting a broadly conceived memorandum of understanding. In particular the memorandum affirmed that relations between Catholics and Jews had a religious basis but extended into all domains of life. It distinguished between issues concerning mutual relations and issues of common interest.

In its introduction the memorandum declared that "relations should be organized so as to respect absolutely the integrity of our respective faiths; they have their justification in a shared responsibility, based on the biblical faith of the one with regard to the other and toward the world."

Here are the principal points we discussed that constituted the core of the memorandum:

1. Points relating to our mutual relations.

a. Expressions of antisemitism in various parts of the world. Obstacles to Jewish-Christian relations. Origins and causes of the lack of mutual confidence.

b. Elimination of antisemitism in all its forms, as required by the Vatican's *Nostra aetate*, particularly in religious and historical textbooks, in order to represent Judaism with respect, in conformity with its own conception of itself, at all levels of teaching and education. Liturgical and para-liturgical texts and phrasing would be reviewed in order to avoid all offensive references to or representations of Judaism, without compromising the legitimate differences between the Church and Judaism.

c. Promotion of mutual comprehension through a just and adequate presentation of our respective faiths in their specific identities through all educational methods and means. At a later stage, studies on the common heritage of Christians and Jews could be undertaken in order to deepen the mutual comprehension of the one by the other and of their common responsibility with regard to humanity and the world.

d. Among the problems concerning mutual understanding, particular attention should be paid to the ways by which the relations among the religious community, the people, and the land are conceived in the Jewish and Christian traditions respectively.

2. Questions of common interest.

a. The promotion of justice and peace in the world, as well as of liberty and human dignity; the struggle against poverty and racism and all forms of discrimination as well as the protection of individual and group human rights should be the ground of special collaboration between Christians and Jews. Religious freedom should be their common concern in all cases where it was threatened or denied.

b. Studies should be undertaken on the ways by which Judaism and Christianity, as communities nourished by common origins in the biblical faith in a unique God, the Creator, and concerned with the lot of this world, could face the problems that assail religion in the modern era.

c. The respective relations of Judaism and Christianity with regard to other world religions should be viewed as an important field of study. In this regard, special attention should be devoted to Islam as another great monotheistic religion.

The Catholic delegation stated that a better understanding of Jewish traditions would be of importance in the pursuit of Christian unity, particularly as concerns the roots of Christianity in biblical and postbiblical Judaism.

The December 1970 conference also agreed to establish a permanent liaison committee composed of five representatives of the church and five Jewish representatives, appointed for a period of three years. Cardinal Willebrands appointed the Catholic members, subject to the approval of Pope Paul VI, and the organizations making up the IJCIC designated the Jewish members.

The IJCIC established two secretariats, one in New York, in the Synagogue Council of America offices, and the other in Geneva, in the World Jewish Congress office. As WJC secretary-general I remained in close touch with Rome in the preparation of the liaison committee sessions and for other reasons as well, either directly or through the intermediary of our representative in Rome, Fritz Becker. We established a steering committee to organize the sessions, whose meetings usually took place in my Geneva office. As the only one to have participated in all the meetings of both the liaison committee and the steering committee, I could assure the continuity of the work as a whole.

In early 1971, less than a year after its creation, the International Catholic-Jewish Liaison Committee (ICJLC) launched the first of its regular meetings in Paris on the premises of the Central Consistory of the Jews of France, organized with the participation of the chief rabbi of France, Jacob Kaplan; the archbishop of Marseilles, Roger Etchegaray; and other senior figures. This meeting opened a new era of mutual cooperation within a framework for a permanent relationship in which we could discuss all our problems, one of which was the relations between theology and politics, a subject to which I shall return.

Following its creation, the ICJLC convened a total of sixteen meetings, in Israel, the Vatican, and Europe, in addition to one in Baltimore. Among the major topics we discussed were the concept of human rights in Christian and Jewish religious tradition; the mission and witness of the church; the image of Judaism in Christian education and the image of Christianity in Jewish education; religious freedom; secular challenges to our religious beliefs; the sanctity of life in relation to the violence of present world conditions; youth and faith; and the historical and religious dimensions of anti-Semitism and its relation to the Shoah.

This list suggests the scope of the problems we addressed, independent of topical questions of the day which we also dealt with at each session.

These then were the structures intended to institutionalize the dialogue between the Roman Catholic church and world Jewry. During this period the fundamental document for the evolution of the church's theological thought and the construction of a new Catholic theology concerning Jews and Judaism remained chapter four of the Vatican Council's *Nostra aetate*.

As Cardinal Willebrands said in one of his speeches: "It is important to emphasize that . . . the Church was not divided on the question of which position it ought to adopt with regard to Jews and Judaism. This has been and remains the solid guarantee of the new attitude within the Catholic Church with regard to Jews and Judaism. It is like a 'house . . . founded on rock' (Mt 7, 24). Nothing can ever destroy it."

An Analysis of Nostra Aetate

If we wish to analyze the progress made in our relations with the Catholic church over the course of the last thirty years, we must begin with an analysis of the church's principal documents that guided its conduct with regard to Jews. The declaration *Nostra aetate* constituted a true beginning and an unprecedented innovation.

From this document we may deduce eight major points that define the attitude of the church toward the Jewish people:

1. The declaration describes the spiritual ties between the church and the Jewish people.

2. The church recognizes that it has received the Hebrew Bible (that is, the Old Testament) through the people with whom God established the Ancient Covenant.

3. The text recognizes the Judaic roots of Christianity, beginning with the Jewish origin of Jesus, his mother Mary, and all the apostles.

4. The document states that God's gifts and appeals have not been revoked and that the Jews are still "very dear to God."

5. *Nostra aetate* declares that the responsibility for what was committed during the Passion cannot be indiscriminately imputed either to Jews living then or to the Jews of our own times.

6. The text prescribes that the Jews are not to be presented as repudiated nor as cursed by God.

7. The declaration proclaims that the church condemns all persecutions and hatred of Jews and all manifestation of anti-Semitism, at all times and by all persons.

8. Last, *Nostra aetate* encourages "understanding and mutual respect" through biblical and theological studies and fraternal dialogue.

Each point of the declaration is of great importance and should be read in light of the classic theses of Christian theology with respect to Jews. In fact the text sets out the parameters of a new theology concerning Jews and Judaism.

The last point, which speaks of understanding and mutual respect, seems the most important to me. It closes the era of friction and hostility and stands as a true milestone opening a new vision for the future.

Why is the emphasis on the words "mutual respect" so important? In effect these words abolish the discriminations of the past and even go beyond the spirit of tolerance inherited from the eighteenth-century Enlightenment. Seen at close hand, tolerance is a relationship between the empowered and the subject. One is tolerant, and thus one has power. Such tolerance represented progress in the Age of Enlightenment, when people were asked to accept one another despite their differences. Our century has experienced a profound change of attitude founded on the notion of human rights. Today we believe that individuals have both a right to equality and a right to difference.

When the church recognized that it received the Hebrew Bible from the Jewish people, when it recalled the Jewish roots of Christianity and the Jewish origins of Jesus and of the founders of Christianity, it entered new paths unknown to many Christians. While we judge that Jesus separates us from Christians, many of them believe that Jesus unites us with them.

The affirmation in the declaration that God does not take back the gifts and promises He has made to mankind is extremely important in theological language. For one who knows Christian and Paulist theology this means that the validity of what the Christians call the Ancient Covenant with the Jews has not been abolished and, with reference to Paul's Epistle to the Romans, states that the Jews "remain very dear to God."

If we take this affirmation seriously, it signifies that, contrary to its traditional teaching, the church (the so-called new Israel) can no longer claim to have replaced the Jewish people (the so-called old Israel) in the sight of God. If the Ancient Covenant is still in force, we, the Jews, retain a special status. I do not believe that all the consequences of this have yet been fully recognized. And from this stem many of our difficulties with Christians.

The point that exonerates the Jews of the accusation of deicide is no less fundamental. This accusation has played a terribly damaging role in the course of history.

The church's repudiation of all Jew-hatred and persecution, and all manifestations of anti-Semitism, is expressed in guarded, relatively weak terms. With regard to anti-Semitism, the authors of the text first wanted to use the term "condemn," but they changed it to "deplore" because many church leaders believed the contemporary church does not condemn, especially during a Vatican Council. These are meaningful shadings of expression and concessions that Béa thought had to be made. Nonetheless the text clearly rejects anti-Semitism, the first time a Council had made such a statement. And the *Guidelines* that followed some years later replaced the world "deplore" with "condemn," thus clarifying even further the true meaning of the document.

The church's position in this matter is of capital importance because it concerns the entire history of the persecutions and discriminations of which the Jews have been victims, including those inspired and motivated by Christian theologians or ecclesiastical authorities. It is a definitive denial of the theories supporting the idea that the lamentable fate of the Jews throughout the centuries has been a divine punishment for the sin of killing Jesus.

This not only profoundly modifies Christian doctrine but also undermines the justification for popular anti-Semitic customs practiced in some countries with harmful and often fatal consequences for the Jewish population, especially where popular custom often goes well beyond the strict teachings of the church.

The *Nostra aetate* declaration created its own dynamic as the starting point for a series of developments, certain of which could not even have been foreseen at the time of its creation. The document's practical effects developed slowly, and this created certain conflicts because the Jews took the matter quite seriously and were naturally impatient to see the text implemented. For example, when celebrating Easter at the basilica of Rome some months after the Council adopted the document, Pope Paul VI, who had approved and signed it, made a speech that threw the Jewish community of Rome into an uproar. Basically it was a routine talk, but apparently no one at the Vatican realized that the church could no longer repeat the old anti-Jewish shibboleths.

I don't recall the exact words, but the speech clearly gave the impression that the Jews were responsible for the death of Christ. Eventually, of course, the church learned from the incident and corrected its behavior, but this incident aroused the ire of the Jewish community of Rome, which raised loud cries of protest. The attitude of Roman Jews with regard to our negotiations with the Vatican had been one of extreme reserve. In the course of one of the first sessions of the Council, the Union of Jewish Communities of Italy had invited me to its annual meeting to discuss the significance of the Council for Jews.

The Union organized a special session for a debate on this subject between Chief Rabbi Toaff and me. By and large, the chief rabbi's opinion was that Jews from abroad understood absolutely nothing about the Catholic church. "The Church is in Rome and it is we, the Italian Jews, who really know the Church." To which I replied, "You know the Church of Rome very well. You would be right if the revolution which is currently taking place in the church were coming from Rome. But the revolution in the church is coming from outside Italy. It is French, German, and American theologians who are pushing for new ideas and reform in the church. So, don't tell me that you know it better than I." I believe that my argument convinced everyone there.

The chief rabbi then stated bluntly that the new Catholic theology was just another method to seduce our children. The Catholics, he said, no longer sought to convert them by force, they did it with kindness. I replied that if the church succeeded in attracting our young people, "it would be because you had not succeeded in your task as rabbi. If Jewish youth abandoned Judaism, it is because of our own weaknesses. It means that educators and rabbis have not made Judaism sufficiently attractive for our young people. If Jewish education was up to the mark, our children would not be attracted by Christianity. It is we, the rabbis and teachers, who must work on this problem. It is not because the church has used gentle methods that we will lose our children. Our task is to give them the best possible Jewish education. If we cannot fulfill this role, it will be our failure."

After the adoption of *Nostra aetate,* Catholic churchmen and the Secretariat for the Promotion of Christian Unity and its special commissions discussed the application of the new dispensation. This too took time. Several stumbling blocks arose, due among other factors to internal differences of opinion concerning what should or should not be said about the State of Israel.

Various documents issued by the central authorities of the church, papal declarations, and texts adopted by episcopal conferences and diocesan authorities on both the national and local levels, defined and expanded the *Nostra aetate* teachings. The *Guidelines and Suggestions for Implementing the Conciliar Declaration* Nostra aetate *(IV)* stands as the most significant of these documents; in a sense it is the culminating point of this period of negotiations.

Adopted on December 1, 1974, the Vatican published the definitive text on January 3, 1975. The *Guidelines* is the second great document published on the subject by the Vatican itself. Written by the Pontifical Commission for Religious Relations with Jews, the text reaffirms and extends the teaching of *Nostra aetate* and sets out an action program for dialogue, the liturgy, doctrine, and education as well as common social activities. I must say, however, that the document did not have the same authority as a declaration by the Council.

Personally I believe that the *Guidelines* contains four fundamental points, which went beyond *Nostra aetate*.

First, Christians should learn how Jews define themselves in the light of their religious experience. This was perhaps the most significant innovation.

I repeated tirelessly in my conversations with prelates that they could understand the Jews only if they took into account how Jews conceived of themselves and not how others thought or wanted them to be. I was happy to observe that this idea had been incorporated into the Vatican text. The substance of this concept is that Jews henceforth be considered a living reality and no longer a fossil found in biblical texts several thousand years old.

Second, dialogue required respect for the other party and particularly respect for the other's faith and religious convictions. This does not mean persuading the other party of one's superiority or that of one's religion. Here lies the fundamental difference between the so-called dialogue of the Middle Ages and the contemporary dialogue.

Third, and never before expressed in this fashion, was that the Old and New Testaments were not to be set in opposition to each other in the sense taught earlier—the New based in love and the Old in a dry legalist conception of justice. This opposition is false. The commandment to love one's neighbor is to be found in the Hebrew Bible and in the Ten Commandments, and immediately follows the commandment to respect the one true God.

Fourth, the history of Judaism did not end with the destruction of Jerusalem but continued and developed a rich and strong religious tradition. Given traditional Christian theology, this principle is truly revolutionary.

Traditional Christian teaching represents Jews as "the cursed people" and views their dispersal as punishment for the rejection of Christ. But now we hear from the Church, "The Jews are spiritually rich; Jewish history continues, and Jewish tradition continues to develop." This is an exceedingly important step forward in the Christian conception of Judaism.

I believe that the *Guidelines* is a document with great theological implications, but I and many other Jews were disappointed that the reference to the State of Israel was removed from the final text. Some of the texts emanating from episcopal conferences did contain such references, however, one of the most forceful being that of the French episcopate's "The Attitude of Christians with Regard to Judaism," published on April 16, 1973. This document dealt positively with the creation and existence of the State of Israel as well as with some of its spiritual significance for Jews and non-Jews. Worth noting is the sentence: "Universal conscience cannot refuse the Jewish people, which has suffered so many vicissitudes in the course of history, the right and means to their own political existence among the nations." Here we can recognize the pen of Father Bernard Dupuy, the excellent secretary of the French Episcopal Committee for Relations with Jews.

While the Vatican Council spoke only of religion, today, thanks in great part to the support of Jews in joint discussions, the speeches of Cardinal Willebrands and other important church figures recognize what I call the "asymmetry of our communities." The Roman Catholic church is a religion, the Jews are a people. Even though we are a people with our own religion, we and the church are very different entities.

I have always said that the extreme importance of this asymmetry must be recognized so that the proper conclusions may be drawn from it, beginning with the representation of the Jewish people in the dialogue with Christians. For us, the representatives of the Jewish people are not automatically the rabbis. In addition, the role of a rabbi is completely different from that of a priest or bishop.

A personal anecdote bears witness to these differences. The organizers of a large congress of the lay apostolate, following the Vatican's new line of conduct vis-à-vis the Jews, invited me to participate as an official observer. Wanting to avoid a refusal, before issuing the invitation they asked me whether I was prepared to accept it. At the same time they let me know that they had consulted the Chief Rabbi of Rome, who agreed with the idea. Of course I accepted the invitation and thus found myself the only Jew among three thousand Catholics.

At the congress I asked the organizers: "Why did you ask the Chief Rabbi of Rome whether he agreed or not?" They replied: "For us, this is normal.

When we have a meeting and we see a potential problem, we ask the opinion of the local bishop, the highest authority in the locality where the conference would be held." Accordingly, the local "Jewish bishop" was the Chief Rabbi of Rome.

I responded by noting, "With us the position of the rabbi is completely different. The priesthood among the Jews is not a sacrament. Rabbi means 'master, teacher.' He is a spiritual guide, someone who has studied, who guides you in your own studies. If you wanted to ask someone's advice, you should have spoken to the president of the Jewish community of Rome or the head of the Union of Jewish Communities of Italy." This example helped them understand the difference in our structures.

In order to underline this difference, I have always made a point at meetings—whether with the Vatican or with other churches—of having not only rabbis among the Jewish representation but also community lay officials. If these differences are not understood, the true functioning of the Jewish community will not be comprehended.

Nostra aetate and the *Guidelines* influenced whole series of declarations by a considerable number of national and local authorities of the church. Some of these reformulated and restated the general principles; others dealt in great detail with their practical implementation. In particular such texts were published in Germany, Australia, Austria, Brazil, Canada, the United States, France, the Netherlands, and Poland.

Additionally, the addresses of Pope Paul VI and John Paul II contained important passages. The latter who—let us not forget—experienced the Shoah in the proximity of Auschwitz, has made great contributions to the new Christian theology, in particular in his speeches in Mainz in November 1980 before the German Jewish community, and in 1982 in Rome to representatives of the various bishops' conferences, who in their respective countries had commissions for relations with the Jews.

In Mainz the pope spoke of "the need to correct a false religious vision regarding the Jewish people, a vision that was in great part responsible for erroneous judgments and persecutions over the course of history." He continued by speaking of "the meeting between the people of God of the Ancient Covenant, never repudiated by God, and that of the New Covenant, which at the same time constitutes a dialogue within the Church, in a certain sense the dialogue between the first and second parts of the Bible."

In Rome he evoked the crimes and terrible anti-Jewish persecutions during various periods of history and called for new relations based on the full identity of each community, marked by understanding, peace, and mutual respect, leading to a close collaboration in the service of our common heritage.

In a passage of the Rome speech the pope insisted on the need to introduce an objective image of Jews and Judaism, devoid of all prejudice or offense, into Christian teaching on all levels. He spoke of history but also emphasized the need for a Catholic education without hate, without discrimination, and without the prejudices of the past. He concluded: "We are in a position to go by different paths, but in the end these are converging paths to reach, with the aid of God who has never ceased to love his people, true fraternity in reconciliation, respect, and the accomplishment of God's plan in history."

This was phrasing that touched us deeply, but the third Vatican document—that of 1985 on teaching and preaching—stated that there are no parallel paths.

The new image of Judaism also appeared in the great address John Paul II delivered on the occasion of his historic visit to the Synagogue of Rome in 1986. On that occasion the pontiff evoked the memory of Pope John XXIII and "the decisions of the Council marking a decisive turn in relations between the Catholic Church and Judaism." He exhorted Catholics to draw inspiration from the recent texts, in particular the *Guidelines,* in order to assume a correct attitude toward Jews and Judaism. "The Jewish religion is not 'extrinsic' to us, but is in a certain sense 'intrinsic' to our religion. We have relations with it that we do not have with any other religion. You are our preferred brothers and in a certain sense one could say our elder brothers."

The pope also called for "a collaboration on behalf of mankind . . . its dignity, liberty, rights, and well-being in a society without hostility, but one of friendship and cordiality, where justice reigns and where . . . peace reigns, the *shalom* so desired by the lawgivers, the prophets and wise men of Israel."

In the Rome speech delivered to representatives of the episcopal conferences, the pope particularly emphasized indoctrination and the need to adopt Christian teaching to the new requirements of Catholic theology. This led to the publication in June 1985 of the document entitled "Notes on the Correct Way to Present Jews and Judaism in Preaching and Teaching in the Roman Catholic Church."

This was the second great post-conciliar document from the Pontifical Commission for Religious Relations with Jews, chaired by Cardinal Willebrands. The Holy See made it public on the eve of the commemoration of the twentieth anniversary of the Vatican Council. In certain respects this document represented substantial progress. Some of its theses were nevertheless strongly criticized by the Jewish side.

The document is excellent when it speaks positively of the Jewish origins of Christianity, similarly when it reconsiders in depth the Christian attitude toward the Pharisees. In Christian tradition the latter are generally presented as negative elements, people of little faith. This popular view is not at all correct and had in the past been denounced by serious Christian theologians. The 1985 document affirmed that Jesus and certain apostles were closer to the Pharisees than any other Jewish group of their time.

Another point of vital importance explains how the text of the Gospels is to be understood. As we know, there are numerous negative, even hostile, passages concerning the Jews in the Gospels. These passages form the basis for numerous anti-Semitic works.

On this topic the 1985 Vatican text is firm and courageous when it declares that these passages were not written in the time of Jesus but much later, in the context of the conflict between the proponents of the new religion and the Jewish communities. Thus this polemic reflects conflicts between Jews and Christians well after the time of Jesus. The church's statement is of capital importance if one wishes to extract the meaning of certain passages of the Gospels for today's Christians. The fact of having included these historical explanations in the catechism destined to guide teachers gives this text enormous weight.

But the document also contains some negative features. In several instances one has the impression that the church is falling back into the old theology of replacement, which I discussed above. I have quoted the pope's Rome statement about different but convergent paths. Here there is a clear and precise declaration to the effect that there are no parallel paths that lead to salvation.

The text on teaching and preaching contains certain affirmations concerning the State of Israel. It should be emphasized that this was the first time a document of this kind dealt with the problem. This was clearly of considerable importance and called for specific attention. I shall return to this topic in the context of a review of the attitude of the church with regard to the State of Israel.

The 1985 text also includes, among other things, an extended passage on typology. Typology is a traditional Christian theological concept according to which the Old Testament is the herald of certain foreseen events that are realized in the New Testament. In this conception the Old Testament is to be read not for itself but rather as an anticipation and prefiguration of the New

Testament, which assures the *sensus plenus.* Even though the 1985 text expresses a certain reserve regarding this theory, it still accepts its principle.

The extensive exposition devoted to this concept defining the Hebrew Bible as only important where it anticipates the New Testament came as a painful surprise to us. In my opinion it absolutely contradicts the thesis of *Nostra aetate* that affirms that the Ancient Covenant has not been abolished and still retains its full validity.

I believe this is the greatest current flaw in Christian theology with regard to the Jews. What does it mean to say "The Ancient Covenant is valid and continues to exist"? In what way are Christians to respect it? If this matter is not defined and clarified, all the rest is left hanging. I believe that church theologians must reflect on this question and find an adequate response.

Our severe criticism with regard to passages in the text on the catechism that refer to the concept of typology brought consequences. In a note drafted by the secretary of the Pontifical Commission on Religious Relations with the Jews, Msgr. Jorge Mejia, on the occasion of the document's release to the press, a lengthy passage attempts to justify the part of the document that deals with typology. He insists that the typological interpretation in no way constitutes a devaluation of the intrinsic value of the Old Testament. Clearly in an effort to correct the negative impression left by this text, Msgr. Mejia concludes his explanation by affirming that "the limitations of 'typological' interpretation are recognized and other approaches to the reading of the Old Testament with relation to the New Testament are not excluded." The argument did not persuade me.

Edward Cardinal Cassidy, who succeeded Willebrands as president of the Commission on Religious Relations with the Jews, undertook recently to clarify the question in a text that he read at the ceremony in which a papal honor was awarded to me:

> The rediscovery of spiritual bonds with the "mystery" of Israel is expressed through real people, and in this way the mutual witness to the specific values of the two great religious traditions, Jewish and Christian, can take place in a context of equal dignity and respect. Such an atmosphere makes for true reciprocity, free of false irenicism or facile syncretism, and allows the Church to bear witness to the centrality of Christ in the plan of universal salvation, without however denying the value of the Old Testament, which has never been revoked, and the extraordinary mission entrusted by God to Israel.

Pope John Paul II himself also returned to this problem and in particular tried to clarify the relationship between the Old and New Testaments. On

April 11, 1997, before the Pontifical Biblical Commission, the pope gave a speech that assumes capital importance in the evolution of the Jewish-Christian dialogue.

Here are the most striking passages:

> Centuries of reciprocal prejudice and opposition have created a deep divide which the Church is now endeavoring to bridge, spurred by the Second Vatican Council's position. . . .
>
> Actually, it is impossible fully to express the mystery of Christ without reference to the Old Testament. . . .
>
> Thus he became an authentic son of Israel, deeply rooted in his own people's long history. When he began to preach and teach, he drew abundantly from the treasure of the Scripture, enriching this treasure with new inspirations and unexpected initiatives. These—let us note—did not aim at abolishing the old revelation but, on the contrary, at bringing it to its complete fulfillment. . . .
>
> From her origins, the Church has well understood that the Incarnation is rooted in history and, consequently, she has fully accepted Christ's insertion into the history of the People of Israel. She has regarded the Hebrew Scriptures as the perennially valid Word of God adressed to herself as to the children of Israel. It is vitally important to retain and renew the Church's consciousness of the essential ties to the Old Testament.
>
> The Christian must know that by belonging to Christ he has become "Abraham's offspring" (*Gal* 3:29) and has been grafted onto a cultivated olive tree (cf *Rm* 11:17–24), that is, included among the People of Israel. . . . If he has this firm conviction, he can no longer allow for Jews as such to be despised, or worse, ill-treated.

This speech demonstrates yet again how close to the Pope's heart lie relations with Judaism and Jewry. He has not ceased in his efforts to clarify them and to modify the Christian witness of Israel.

Three Areas of Friction

In 1976, when we reviewed the work of the International Catholic-Jewish Liaison Committee and the progress accomplished in the course of the years since the promulgation of *Nostra aetate*, the Jewish delegation called attention to three areas in which major obstacles had been encountered: the Catholic mission to the Jews, our unfortunate common history, and relations between the Holy See and the State of Israel.

We know that the missionary efforts of the Church specifically directed at Jews have at all times profoundly affected them. After the catastrophe of the Shoah that swept across a Europe that was in the majority Christian, few Jews understand how the church could still pursue its efforts to convert them.

In accord with our Catholic partners, we decided to discuss the issue at the meeting of the Liaison Committee held in Venice in 1977. Father Tommaso Federici of the Pontifical Urban University prepared a report on the "Mission and Testimony of the Church." Several other persons participated in the preparation of this report, in particular the rector of the Lateran University, Msgr. Pietro Rossano.

Since published, the text affirms that the mission of the church and the mission of the Jewish people are identical: to preach the word of God to the world. Hitherto the church had never said this so bluntly.

The report noted a second consideration: proselytism is forbidden. It should be noted, however, that in the Catholic mind proselytism covers only conversion by illicit means, such as force, threat, or coercion.

Third, Father Federici's report states that efforts to create organizations of any kind "whose objective is the conversion of Jews must be repudiated."

This was a considerable change in attitude. But let us make no mistake: this is not yet church doctrine. It is the opinion of Father Federici and his colleagues on the International Liaison Committee. But their position is remarkable in the sense that the officially appointed representatives of the church expressed the ideas at a meeting between Catholics and Jews.

On several occasions I raised the question, "How can we move ahead?" They answered: "The first step is to publish Father Federici's text in various major Catholic journals and wait and see what will happen. If the protests are numerous and vocal, we'll stop. Otherwise we'll continue." This is what we did, and the trial balloon flew.

Let me add one significant detail. At the end of each of these sessions we would draft a communiqué that summarized the principal conclusions of the meeting. After the Venice meeting, in the course of which Federici presented his text, we proceeded in the same fashion. We made a fairly detailed summary of the theses he had advanced. The head of the Catholic delegation told us, "You can publish the text immediately; but we Catholics have to submit it to our authorities." We had to wait almost a week for this. The delay is proof that the text moved up to quite a high level in the church hierarchy. The authorization gave added authority to the report's contents. The publication of the document in the volume *Fifteen Years of Christian-Jewish Dialogue*, released in

1988 by the official Vatican press and the Lateran University, represents a remarkable step forward.

The second point of friction concerned our common history and the long
centuries of persecution, about which the central authorities of the church
had until then been extremely reticent.

We waited a long time for official word from the Church on this subject.
It was quite clear that if a new relationship were to be established between the
Catholic church and the Jewish communities, this problem could not be
passed over in silence. Moreover, Catholic voices were also being heard on the
same theme—for example the memorable intervention made by Cardinal
Roger Etchegaray at the Episcopal Synod in 1983, in which he spoke of the
"mission of reconciliation between the Church and the Jewish people" and of
"the Church's mission of penitence and repentance for its attitude toward the
Jewish people." This courageous initiative remained without consequence. We
must, however, recognize that it was during the pontificate of John Paul II that
the church began to stop ignoring the problem.

Meanwhile we had learned to deal with this question in pragmatic fashion. To prepare for the International Liaison Committee meeting in 1978, I
made a number of proposals and suggestions to Msgr. Ramon Torrella, vice
chairman of the Pontifical Commission for Religious Relations with the Jews,
and who represented Cardinal Willebrands during his absence.

In particular I proposed that the next session of the Liaison Committee
take place in Spain. This country had just found its way to democracy. I suggested that the first session be held in Toledo, in one of two historic synagogues, earlier converted into churches now become national monuments.

I requested that the session be opened by the cardinal-archbishop of
Toledo, the primate of Spain. The objective was to commemorate together the
presence of the Jews in the country, from which they were expelled in 1492.

I suggested that the rest of the meeting be held in Madrid and that it conclude with a religious service in the synagogue in the presence of the cardinal-
archbishop of the capital city, the president of the Episcopal Conference of
Spain. All my requests and my suggestions, I am happy to say, were well received and acted on. This was probably the first time in history, before or after
1492, that a Spanish cardinal was present at a religious service in a synagogue.

These public events had a highly symbolic significance. All the participants and the Jewish community of Spain deeply appreciated them.

The meeting of the Liaison Committee's steering committee in Trent in
1979 also had great symbolic value. One day the secretariat of the Pontifical

Commission for Religious Relations with the Jews suggested that we have a meeting of the steering committee in Trent, a request that had been made by the archbishop of that community. The day after the adoption of *Nostra aetate*, the archbishop suppressed by decree the cult of Simon of Trent, which dated from 1475. Simon was a Christian child who had been found dead and was the cause of a false accusation of ritual murder against the Jews of the city, with disastrous consequences.

The archbishop was eager to make an official communication about this act of reparation, both to the local Jewish community and to the representatives of world Jewry. In 1984 the International Liaison Committee met in Amsterdam and visited the house of Anne Frank. When we met in Prague in 1990 the members made a pilgrimage to Theresienstadt.

Although he had mentioned issues involved in Catholic-Jewish relations in other speeches, Pope John Paul II expressed his ideas with greater force in July 1987, on the occasion of his address to the Jews of Warsaw.

> I think that today the nation of Israel, perhaps more than ever before, finds itself at the center of the attention of the nations of the world, above all because of this terrible experience, through which you have become a loud warning voice for all humanity, for all nations, all the powers of this world, all systems and every person. More than anyone else, it is precisely you who have become this saving warning. I think that in this sense you continue your particular vocation, showing yourselves to be still the heirs of that election to which God is faithful. This is your mission in the contemporary world before the peoples, the nations, all of humanity.
>
> The Church and in this Church all peoples and nations feel united to you in this mission. Certainly they give great prominence to your nation and its sufferings, its Holocaust, when they wish to speak a warning to individuals and to nations; in your name, the Pope, too, lifts up his voice in this warning. The Polish Pope has a particular relationship with all this, because, along with you, he has in a certain sense lived all this here, in this land.

Let us also recall the pope's declaration when he visited Auschwitz and stood before the Hebrew inscription "Thou shalt not kill": "The very people who received from God the Commandment, 'thou shalt not kill,' itself experienced in a special measure what is meant by killing. It is not permissible for anyone to pass by this inscription with indifference."

These words, sincere, moving, and convincing, touched me deeply when they were repeated in my presence during the Jewish leaders' meeting with Pope John Paul II in Rome in October 1987.

It is in the context of our common history that we must similarly consider the problems raised by the establishment of a Carmelite convent in Auschwitz and by the pope's reception of Kurt Waldheim. The Jewish community deeply felt these two events and expressed its emotions and voiced its shock in various forms of protest.

As concerns the convent at Auschwitz, it seems to me that the responsibility for the decision to establish this nunnery must be shared by the church of Poland—Rome was not involved in the beginning—and the Communist Polish government. The Polish church should never have asked for permission to use the facilities called the "camp theater," in which the Zyklon B gas was stored, without consulting us. For its part the Communist Polish government should never have given its permission to establish a permanent religious institution on the site of the Auschwitz camp without prior consultation with Jewish circles.

The establishment of a Catholic convent on the site of a camp where the great majority of victims were Jewish was an act of incredible insensitivity and could only be perceived by the Jews as an act appropriating the Jewish dead. This could only offend the deepest feelings of Jews around the world. I am sure that such was never the intention, but the way to hell is paved with good intentions.

What happened may be partially explained by the fact that for more than forty years there were practically no contacts between Jews and the Catholic church in Poland. It was only in 1983, during the pontificate of John Paul II, that the Polish church officially participated in commemorations of the rising of the Warsaw Ghetto—commemorations that had been taking place regularly since 1948.

What happened also illustrates the policy of dejudicization of the former camps, which was long the official line of the Communist governments of Poland. Moreover the situation can be understood only if the firm opposition of the Polish church to the Communist Polish government and its policy of secularization is taken into account.

All the parties understood, if only very late, that for the Jews of the entire world Auschwitz, more than any other place, is the symbol of the Shoah and its unique character. This clearly does not affect the profound respect of Jews for victims of other nations killed in Auschwitz, in particular non-Jewish Poles.

Here is where the great misunderstanding lies. For Jews, Auschwitz remains the symbol of the Shoah. For Poles, Oswiecim is a sacred place, symbolizing the sufferings of the Polish nation and its resistance to the Nazi occupation.

A solution to the problem of the convent was found in the course of two meetings in Geneva between a Jewish delegation and a Catholic delegation. Prominent on the Catholic side were Cardinals Decourtray (Lyon), Daneels (Brussels), Lustiger (Paris), and Macharski (Cracow). European Jewish leaders under the chairmanship of Theo Klein, a lawyer and president of the European Jewish Congress, formed the Jewish side. I served as a member of the Jewish delegation at the second meeting, in February 1987, representing the World Jewish Congress and the IJCIC.

At the second meeting we reached an agreement that there would be no permanent place of prayer on the site of the Auschwitz-Birkenau camp. The Carmelite convent would find its place within the context of a new center for information, education, reunion, and prayer to be established outside the grounds of the camp within a twenty-four-month period, with the assistance of the European churches. This solution was approved by Rome. Unfortunately the promises to establish this center were not kept in the agreed-upon time period.

Very strong opposition arose in Poland, in particular in nationalist and fundamentalist circles, against the transfer of the convent to a site beyond the camp. Several unfortunate incidents and hasty declarations aggravated the situation and contributed to holding up the meetings of the International Liaison Committee for several years.

No other problem in Jewish-Catholic relations entailed so much work for me nor so many urgent negotiations and discussions.

I should express my thanks to our friends at the Pontifical Commission for Religious Relations with Jews for having constantly supported us. In the course of these long and difficult years Albert Cardinal Decourtray, archbishop of Lyon, and his colleagues all showed a firmness and loyalty that stood every test. Archbishop Henryk Muszynski, archbishop of Gniezno, who chaired the Polish Episcopal Commission for Relations with Judaism, and the Sisters of Our Lady of Zion were of great help to us.

After several years of observation and reflection, I became convinced that this problem could not be resolved without the pope taking a clear stand. He had avoided personal intervention to keep himself free of the divergences and tensions that divided the Polish episcopate. We understood that in these circumstances it was a delicate matter for a Polish pope to intervene officially in such a quarrel.

We had hoped that Cardinal Willebrands's unambiguous public declaration in September 1989 would disentangle the situation. This hope was also founded on the fact that the Cardinal had profited by the occasion to announce a gift from the Vatican of a considerable sum of money toward the construction of the center that would house the new convent, a gift that clearly had been approved by the highest Vatican authorities. But this proved to be an insufficient inducement. Hope faded again, and the conflict continued.

Before this impasse, Msgr. Pier Francesco Fumagalli, secretary of the Pontifical Commission for Religious Relations with the Jews, went with me to Poland to ask that the national episcopate take a clear position on the matter. This measure had a positive effect. The conference of leaders of the Polish episcopate decided to support the proposal of transferring the convent to the exterior of the camp. The question finally seemed to have been solved. Another illusion! Nothing of the kind. In addition to meetings held in Geneva, Paris, and Brussels, over a period of six months I still had to go to Rome three times and as many times to Poland to get things moving. All the affected parties seemed to be in agreement: Rome, the Polish episcopate, and the Order of Carmelites. But still nothing happened.

On the eve of the commemoration of the fiftieth anniversary of the uprising in the Warsaw Ghetto, the Polish government could not conceal its anxiety. A solution finally appeared in the form of a letter from the pope to the Carmelite mother superior, ordering her to carry out the relocation of the convent. She obeyed, and the church then officially desanctified the convent, thus ending the stalemate. The transfer of the convent was accompanied by the nomination of a new mother superior. But some efforts to sabotage the papal decision concerning the disposition of the old building continued. Fortunately they had little effect.

For our part, how could we not be pleased with the outcome of a struggle that had lasted more than seven years? The evolution of this affair taught us that a desire to respect our sensibilities existed at the highest levels of the church.

From the perspective of our common history, I should devote a few words to Pope John Paul II's reception of Kurt Waldheim, then president of Austria. This audience deeply shocked the Jewish world by virtue of Waldheim's participation in serious actions against civilian populations, Jews, and prisoners of war while he served in the German army. The Vatican's action is all the more incomprehensible after most states made it known that they would refuse to receive Waldheim and declared him persona non grata.

The vehemence of the Jewish reaction clearly surprised Vatican officials, as did the statement by Jews that this reception constituted a disavowal of the attitude toward the Shoah previously made public by the pope. Jewish representatives pleaded their case with great vigor, insisting on the depth of the moral problems that the audience posed for the Jewish people. The Catholics were finally won over, acknowledging that the feelings of the Jews were well founded.

The real response to our concerns came in the form of the announcement by Cardinal Willebrands that his commission was preparing a document on the Shoah and on the historical foundations of anti-Semitism and its contemporary expressions. This document would have enormous significance for the future because it dealt not only with the twelve years of insane Nazi persecution but also with the centuries of the church's old teachings on the Jews, a doctrine that so powerfully contributed to make the horrors of Nazism possible. This promise, made on the occasion of the International Liaison Committee meeting at Castelgandolfo in 1987, was then formally ratified by the pope.

Another source of friction between the church and the Jews was the beatification of Edith Stein, a Catholic nun of Jewish origin whom the Nazis deported. The beatification of the saints of the Catholic church is clearly not the business of the Jews. But numerous persons in the Jewish community were upset by this action, which they perceived as an affirmation that only if you have been baptized can you be counted among persons considered to have lived a life of sanctity. So the question was raised in which way the martyrdom of Edith Stein was different from that of the six million other Jews the Nazis murdered.

It has been clearly shown that the deportation of Edith Stein was not a sanction against the church of Holland for its courageous protest against the deportation of Jews. It is also known that this nun was deported not because she was a nun but because the Nazis considered her a Jewess despite her conversion and despite her vocation as nun. Was the proposal for beatification not yet another act of appropriation?

Obviously no one in the Jewish community follows the procedures of the Vatican Congregation of Saints and no one knew about the process of beatification, the first steps of which had begun twenty-five years earlier. We heard about it only when practically everything already had been decided.

After I raised this problem in Rome with the Jewish representatives at one of our regular Liaison Committee meetings, and following lengthy discussions with our Catholic partners, Vatican officials recognized that the proposed action deeply offended Jewish sensitivities. They had also glimpsed the consequences that this beatification would have for the future of Jewish-Christian relations.

The incident showed yet again that there exists today in the highest spheres of the Catholic Church a group of persons who are determined to take

Jewish sensitivity seriously. This consideration even led to a complete rewriting of the homily that the pope made in Cologne and demonstrated the will to go as far as possible to meet Jewish objections.

In his homily the pope spoke at several points of Edith Stein as a daughter of Israel. He said that she perished as a daughter of her tortured people. "She died," the pope said, "in a death camp as a daughter of Israel, *al Kiddush ha-Shem* [for the sanctification of the holy Name]." The pope spoke for the first time of the Shoah and not of the Holocaust, using the Hebrew term. He also used simple and moving words in reference to its victims. In closing, John Paul II quoted from the Gospel according to Saint John, "Salvation is of the Jews," a sentence we had never heard from the mouth of any pope.

Nonetheless, despite goodwill on both sides, the problem remained caught in an atmosphere of ambiguity. We must recognize that there exist situations for which there are no satisfactory solutions, in particular when the religious identity of an individual is at stake.

After several years of interruption, regular meetings of the Liaison Committee resumed in September 1990 in Prague. With a view to assisting in the preparation of the document announced by the church at Castelgandolfo in 1987, the committee decided that the religious and secular bases of anti-Semitism during the past nineteen centuries and their relation to the Shoah would be debated.

In his opening statement Cardinal Edward Cassidy, who had succeeded Cardinal Willebrands as president of the Pontifical Commission for Religious Relations with the Jews, declared: "That antisemitism has found a place in Christian thought and practice calls for an act of *teshuvah* (repentance) and reconciliation on our part as we gather here in this city which is a testimony to our failure to be authentic witnesses to our faith at times in the past." This statement made a great impression on the Jewish delegation. It was the first time that an act of *teshuva* had officially been expressed by a senior dignitary of the church concerning relations between Catholics and Jews.

At the conclusion of the meeting the Catholic delegation condemned anti-Semitism and all forms of racism as a sin against God and against humanity. It affirmed that "one cannot be authentically Christian and at the same time engage in antisemitism."

The discussion allowed the recognition that certain traditions of Catholic thought, teaching, and preaching, as well as the practices of the patristic period and the Middle Ages contributed to the birth of anti-Semitism in Western society and that in modern times numerous Catholics have lacked vigilance in affirming their opposition to anti-Semitism.

At the conference, Jewish and Catholic witnesses of the Shoah shared their experiences, offering testimony about the extent to which Christians let themselves be led to their own ruin through too weak a response to Nazi and fascist ideologies, just like the Jews and other victims.

The Catholic delegation also confirmed the preparation of a church document on the Shoah to include the historic bases of anti-Semitism and its contemporary manifestations. The Liaison Committee devoted particular attention to recent expressions of anti-Semitism, especially in Central and Eastern Europe. It drew up a practical program to combat new forms of anti-Semitism while defining the concrete tasks of churches and states in this regard.

It is particularly significant that on the occasion of the twenty-fifth anniversary of *Nostra aetate*, Pope John Paul II fully approved the decisions taken at the Prague meeting.

The concrete consequence of these decisions was a visit by a Liaison Committee delegation to Poland, Hungary, and the Czech and Slovak Republics, where the members began negotiations to implement the program on the national level. This was the first time a joint delegation had undertaken such a mission. The members discussed the concrete measures to be carried out not only with the conferences of bishops and the papal nuncios but also with the Jewish communities and the government authorities of these countries.

The discussions begun in Prague continued during the conference in Baltimore in May 1992, where the meeting noted that it had received positive reports from the delegation noted above. These discussions, however, led to the discovery of other challenges, such as new anti-Semitic actions developing across all of Europe, which underlined the urgent necessity of intensifying our cooperation.

With a view to creating a climate of cooperation, the Liaison Committee decided that the role of the executive committee would be expanded and that a more effective commitment to collaboration would be made to our efforts within existing international global and regional organizations.

The Baltimore meeting also discussed problems of education. Vatican representatives assured us of the full cooperation of the Congregation for Catholic Education, and we agreed to strengthen the cooperation between Catholics and Jewish institutions of higher education.

Thus far we have dealt with two major sources of friction between the Catholic church and the Jews: the church's missionary activity and our common history. Before dealing with the third source of friction, the relations of the Holy See with the State of Israel, I should like to emphasize that this long history (and the way in which it was read) was considered not only from the perspective of the past, as was often the case, but also from a future perspective, which constituted a completely new approach.

After the fall of the Iron Curtain and the reunification of the old continent, the pope in late 1991 convoked a special assembly of the Synod of European Bishops to discuss "the new evangelization of the continent." I felt that in light of this initiative European Judaism should react and mark its presence in Europe. I then proposed to the European Jewish Congress, which grouped all the Jewish communities of Europe, that it submit a memorandum to Carlo Maria Cardinal Martini, the archbishop of Milan, in his capacity as president of the Council of the European Episcopal Conferences. This document is in the form of a letter, written in French, to the cardinal and signed by Jean Kahn, president of the European Jewish Congress, as well as by Tullia Zevi and me as co-presidents of the Congress's Commission for Interreligious Relations. The following excerpts express our concerns and our suggestions for revisions.

We understand the reasons that prompted the convocation of this special assembly, given the considerable changes that have occurred in the course of the last several years and that resulted in the profound transformation in the political, social and spiritual situation, most particularly in Central and Eastern Europe.

If we take the liberty of addressing this memorandum to you, it is because some of the reflections presented by the General Secretariat of the Synod call for certain comment, even some reserve, on our part.

If you proceed, as suggested by the Secretary General's text, to "a general inquiry into the historic events that marked the lives of the European peoples particularly in the great areas of Central and Eastern Europe," it seems essential to us that the important Jewish contribution to European civilization be neither ignored nor underestimated. Moreover, it is indispensable to ensure that the fate of the Jews of Europe over the course of centuries be retained as a living memory in order to fight more efficiently against all forms of intolerance. This applies most particularly to that part of Europe which for centuries had been the cultural, religious and social center of Judaism, the birthplace of all modern movements of Jewish civilization.

In our opinion such an inquiry should also recognize the fact that there exists in Europe a great variety of religious, cultural and secular traditions which have contributed to the richness and singularity of European culture. In particular, this complex of traditions also includes those of national, cultural and religious minorities. All these traditions should be specifically recognized as legitimate expressions of European identity.

We welcome and support the efforts of the Catholic Church, to the extent that they aim at reaffirming the position of religions and at restoring religious freedom, particularly in Central and Eastern Europe where it has been suppressed under Communist regimes.

Such efforts, however, must respect and reaffirm the principle of religious and cultural pluralism that constitutes a fundamental principle of modern Europe. This implies the unequivocal acceptance of and unqualified respect for the limits that this legal system imposes on all of us. It seems to us that in the program for the "evangelization of Europe," announced as the principal goal of the Synod, the Catholic Church must take greater account of this pluralism and expressly recognize it.

On the other hand, we welcome the determination of the Church to act in every circumstance and without respite for the defense of human rights and fundamental liberties, including religious freedom, all the more so because the history of these last decades has tragically illustrated the dramatic consequences of the violation of these rights and freedoms.

Mrs. Zevi, who was also president of the Union of Jewish Communities of Italy, and I personally delivered the letter to Cardinal Martini, who received our communications with a great deal of warmth. He insisted on informing us that he had himself emphasized in a preparatory meeting of the Assembly of Bishops that "Jerusalem, Athens and Rome constitute the three poles of inspiration of European culture." The cardinal ensured that our memorandum was distributed to each of the participants in the assembly.

In the course of the Synod, several bishops, in particular Cardinal Cassidy, supported our stand in their public comments.

The assembly concluded with the adoption of a final text, in which we read among other statements:

European culture has grown from many roots. The spirit of Greece and Rome was passed on to the Latin, Celtic, Germanic, Slavic and Hungaro-Finnish peoples, and Jewish culture and Islamic influences contributed to the whole picture. . . .

Re-evangelizing is not a program for the so-called "restoration" of a Europe of former times, but helps to uncover its Christian roots and to build a more profound civilization clearly more Christian and therefore more richly human. . . .

An extremely important factor in the construction of a new order in Europe and in the world is interreligious dialogue, above all with our "elder brothers" the Jewish people, whose faith and culture are an element of human development in Europe.

After the terrible *Shoah* of our century, for which the Church feels a profound grief, new attempts have to be made to acknowledge Judaism more profoundly, rejecting all forms of antisemitism, which are contrary to both Gospel and natural law. . . .

Mindful of the spiritual heritage, above all Sacred Scripture, which links her with Judaism, the Church in the current situation intends to work for the blossoming of a new spring in mutual relationships.

Clearly, participants at the special assembly took seriously the message of the European Jewish Congress, and the Congress fully achieved its objectives.

It is remarkable that, at the close of the Synod of European Bishops, one of these—and not the least among them—Msgr. Karl Lehmann, president of the German Conference of Bishops, called it "the most important event since Vatican II."

The third great problem that deeply concerned us in our discussions with Catholics concerned the relations of the Holy See with the State of Israel. At most of our meetings we stressed that if knowledge of how the Jews conceived of themselves was a key to a meaningful mutual relationship, the Catholic church could not ignore the close ties that united the Jewish people to the land of Israel.

Jewish public opinion could not understand the reasons that prevented the Vatican, after more than forty years, from establishing normal diplomatic relations with the Jewish state. Most Jews considered this situation an act of discrimination, all the more serious since the Holy See had established diplomatic relations with a good number of recently created states that clearly did not possess the same importance as the Holy Land.

Many Jews effectively viewed the question as the litmus test for our relations with the Catholic church. Without denying its importance, I do not believe that in the short term this was the most important problem that we had to settle with the church. In fact I do not believe we needed a legitimation of the State of Israel by the Catholic church, just as we do not need its legitimization of the Jewish people. We have existed for thousands of years; our legitimacy is inherent in our existence, our history and holy scriptures.

As we know, the declaration *Nostra aetate* says nothing on the subject of Israel, nor do the *Guidelines* of 1975. This was one of the great disappointments for Jews. The 1985 text on preaching and teaching mentions Israel for the first time in a religious document from the Holy See. We raised this question on many occasions during our discussions with Vatican representatives, but it remained an irritant for many and deeply troubled our relations.

Since the church did not authorize its representatives on the Liaison Committee to deal with us on this problem, at the Jewish side's request the committee organized special meetings with the participation of eminent members of the Vatican Secretariat of State. In the course of these meetings we discussed in detail the problems of relations with the State of Israel and put forward some practical suggestions.

While our positions are different, and these differences probably will continue for some time—at least as long as tensions continue in the Middle East—some solid progress can be noted here. We can observe a certain evolution in the position of the Holy See on this subject. We are very far from the attitude adopted by Pope Pius X on the occasion of the notorious audience he granted in 1904 to Theodor Herzl, the father of political Zionism,* and of the equally infamous telegram from Pope Paul VI addressed to "President Shazar, Tel-Aviv," knowing full well that the Israeli president's residence was in Jerusalem.

Paul VI spent less than a day in Israel in 1964 without uttering the word "Israel," though he did briefly meet President Shazar at the Megiddo archaeological site.† Pope John Paul II's apostolic letter on the city of Jerusalem speaks with great reverence of the fact that

---

*Meeting with Pius X and other Vatican officials in an attempt to gain the church's support for the Zionist program, Herzl met with a condescending arrogance that refused to recognize the right of Jews to exist as Jews. "The Jews have not recognized our Lord, therefore we cannot recognize the Jewish people. . . . The Jewish religion was the foundation of our own; but it was superseded by the teachings of Christ, and we cannot concede it any further validity. . . . The Jews," the pontiff pontificated, ". . . had time to acknowledge [Jesus'] divinity without pressure. But they haven't done so to this day." See Raphael Patai, ed., *The Complete Diaries of Theodor Herzl*, vol. 4 (New York, 1960), pp. 1593–1594 and 1602–1603. For a recent discussion of Herzl's meeting with Pius X and Paul VI's questionable activities in condoning the church's assistance to Nazi war criminals escaping from Europe, see Daniel Jonah Goldhagen, *A Moral Reckoning: The Role of the Catholic Church in the Holocaust and Its Unfulfilled Duty of Repair* (New York, 2002), pp. 176, 238–239.—ED.

†On Passion Sunday, some months before the publication of *Nostra aetate* in October 1965, Paul VI preached a sermon accusing the Jews of killing Jesus. This has been viewed as an attempt at the very pinnacle of the church hierarchy to sabotage the reforms of the Vatican II Council. See Michael Phayer, *The Catholic Church and the Holocaust, 1980–1965* (Bloomington, Ind., 2000), p. 213.—ED.

For Jews, Jerusalem is a place much beloved and an everlasting magnet drawing them to her, rich in impressions and memories, from the time of David who chose her as his capital and Solomon who built his temple there. Since then their eyes turn to her every day, you might say, and consider her the symbol of their nation.

The text continues:

. . . For the Jewish people who live in the State of Israel and who preserve in that land there precious testaments to their history and their faith, we pray for the security they desire and a just peace that is the right of every nation and a necessary condition for life and progress in any society.

Similarly, the 1985 "Notes on the Correct Way to Present the Jews and Judaism in Preaching and Catechesis (Teaching) in the Roman Catholic Church" speaks in several paragraphs of the State of Israel. The text, which also recognizes the religious attachment of Jews to the land that preserves the memory of the country of their ancestors at the heart of their hopes, in particular affirms:

The history of Israel did not end in 70 A.D. (cf. *Guidelines*, II). It continued, especially in a numerous Diaspora which allowed Israel to carry to the whole world a witness—often heroic—of its fidelity to the one God and to "exalt Him in the presence of all the living" (*Tobit* 13:4), while preserving the memory of the land of their forefathers at the hearts of their hope (Passover *Seder*).

Christians are invited to understand this religious attachment which finds its roots in biblical tradition, without however making their own any particular religious interpretation of this relationship (Cf. *Declaration of the U.S. Conference of Catholic Bishops*, November 20, 1975).

The existence of the State of Israel and its political options should be envisaged not in a perspective which is in itself religious, but in their reference to the common principles of international law.

The permanence of Israel (while so may ancient peoples have disappeared without trace) is a historic fact and a sign to be interpreted within God's design. We must in any case rid ourselves of the traditional idea of a people *punished*, preserved as a *living argument* for Christian apologetic. It remains a chosen people. . . .

I have the impression that many Jews did not understand this text very well. They were satisfied by the recognition of their religious attachment to the land of Israel, but were rather critical of the sentence stating that relations with the State of Israel would be governed by international law. In my opinion, there was a misunderstanding here. This sentence meant that recognition of the State of Israel and relations with this state are not governed by theological conceptions but by the rules of international law. This signifies that recognition was not a theological act but a legal one, and that there were no theological reasons to oppose such recognition.

I was much more critical with regard to the phrasing of the 1985 document that spoke of the attachment of Jews to the land of Israel: it enjoined Christians to respect the feelings of the Jews but not to make them their own. How can one reconcile this injunction with the affirmation that the Ancient Covenant with Israel is still valid and must be respected? In fact, what is the central promise of this covenant? It is the promise of land, the promise of the land of Canaan. How then can one say that this does not affect Christians? We never received a response to this question.

At the conclusion of the Liaison Committee's meeting with Pope John Paul II at Castelgandolfo, the pope publicly confirmed the idea that the establishment of diplomatic relations with the State of Israel lay in the sphere of international law. At my suggestion, and for the first time, the church stated officially that no theological reasons existed in Catholic doctrine that would oppose diplomatic relations with the State of Israel.

At its meeting in Baltimore in March 1992, the International Liaison Committee, while recognizing that the question of diplomatic relations between the State of Israel and the Holy See initially and above all was a matter for the Israeli government and the Vatican's Secretariat of State, was also conscious of the importance of this question for Jewish-Catholic relations. The committee expressed the hope that significant progress in the matter could soon be made.

A new step was taken with the establishment of a joint Israel-Vatican commission to study conditions for the establishment of normal diplomatic relations. The commission, which worked during the peace negotiations in the Middle East, crowned its endeavors with the draft of a fundamental agreement between the Holy See and the State of Israel, signed on December 30, 1993, by Msgr. Claudio Maria Celli, the Vatican's undersecretary of state, and Yossi Beilin, Israel's deputy minister of foreign affairs. The fundamental agreement establishes full diplomatic relations on the level of the papal nunciature for the Holy See and the embassy of the State of Israel. The Israeli government had the courtesy to summon me to the signing of this agreement, thus recognizing my role in the establishment of the first legal act that linked the Holy See to the State of Israel.

The fundamental agreement includes a few particularly important points. In several respects it resembles no other accord. For example, the first article states the reciprocal engagement to preserve and respect "the right of everyone to freedom of religion and of conscience," and, for the Holy See, the desire to "affirm the respect of the Roman Catholic Church for other religions and their congregations." The second article relates to the "mutual engagement to cooperate in appropriate fashion to combat all forms of antisemitism and all forms of racism and religious intolerance." The same article reaffirms the Holy See's "condemnation of hatred, of persecution, and of every other expression of antisemitism directed against the Jewish people and against every Jew, wherever, under whatever circumstance and by whomsoever."

The December 1992 visit of the Israeli minister of foreign affairs, Shimon Peres, to Pope John Paul II; the official Israeli invitation to the Holy Father to come to Israel; and the exchange of "personal" representatives were so many steps—among many others—in the remarkable progress on the path toward the establishment of official relations.

The conclusion of the fundamental agreement unquestionably marked a significant stage in Jewish-Catholic relations. Israel and Jewish communities around the world received the agreement with keen satisfaction. The only problem linked to current affairs and still without solution was the promise by authorities of the Holy See, made at Castelgandolfo in 1987 and reiterated in Prague in 1990, to draft and make public a document on the Shoah, the historical foundations of anti-Semitism, and its contemporary manifestations. The Jewish world awaited this document with legitimate impatience and a certain anxiety due to a delay of more than a decade without any action.

The church finally circulated the text on March 16, 1998, in the form of a document from the Pontifical Commission on Religious Relations with the Jews, and made it public at the express wish of Pope John Paul II. In a covering letter the pope expressed his hope that the document would "indeed help to heal the wounds of past misunderstandings and injustices."

The text has considerable implications and will certainly be recognized as one of the major steps in the process of readjustment in relations between Jews and Catholics begun with the Second Vatican Council's *Nostra aetate*.

With deep emotion we took note of this act of repentance, which the church called *We Remember: A Reflection on the Shoah*. Here are several examples of the most important sections.

This century has witnessed an unspeakable tragedy, which can never be forgotten: the attempt by the Nazi regime to exterminate the Jewish people, with the consequent killing of millions of Jews. Women and men, old and young, children and infants, for the sole reason of their Jewish origin, were persecuted and deported. Some were killed immediately, while others were degraded, ill-treated, tortured and utterly robbed of their human dignity, and then murdered. Very few of those who entered the Camps survived, and those who did remained scarred for life. This was the *Shoah*. It is a major fact of the history of this century, a fact that still concerns us today.

In addressing this reflection to our brothers and sisters of the Catholic Church throughout the world, we ask all Christians to join us in meditating on the catastrophe which befell the Jewish people, and on the moral imperative to ensure that never again will selfishness and hatred grow to the point of sowing such suffering and death. Most especially we ask our Jewish friends, "whose terrible fate has become a symbol of the aberrations of which man is capable when he turns against God," (Pope John Paul II, Encyclical Letter *Centesimus Annus*, May 1, 1991), to hear us with open hearts.

Despite the Christian preaching of love for all, even for one's enemies, the prevailing mentality down the centuries penalized minorities and those who were in any way "different." Sentiments of anti-Judaism in some Christian quarters, and the gap which existed between the Church and the Jewish people, led to a generalized discrimination, which ended at times in expulsions or attempts at forced conversions. In a large part of the "Christian" world, until the end of the 18th century, those who were not Christian did not always enjoy a fully guaranteed juridical status. Despite that fact, Jews throughout Christendom held on to their religious traditions and communal customs. They were therefore looked upon with a certain suspicion and mistrust. In times of crisis such as famine, war, pestilence or social tensions, the Jewish minority was sometimes taken as scapegoat and became the victim of violence, looting, even massacres.

At the end of this Millennium the Catholic Church desires to express her deep sorrow for the failures of her sons and daughters in every age. This is an act of repentance (*teshuva*), since, as members of the Church, we are linked to the sins as well as the merits of all her children. The Church approaches with deep respect and great compassion the experience of extermination, the *Shoah*, suffered by the Jewish people during World War II. It is not a matter of mere words, but indeed of binding commitment. "We would risk causing the victims of the most atrocious deaths to die again if we do not have an ardent desire for justice, if we do not commit ourselves to ensure that evil does not prevail over good as it did for millions of the children of the Jewish people. . . . Humanity cannot permit all that to happen again" (Pope John Paul II, *Address on the Occasion of the Commemoration of the Shoah*, April 7, 1994).

We pray that our sorrow for the tragedy which the Jewish people has suffered in our century will lead to a new relationship with the Jewish people. We wish to turn awareness of past sins into a firm resolve to build a new future in which there will be no more anti-Judaism among Christians or anti-Christian sentiment among Jews, but rather a shared mutual respect, as befits those who adore the one Creator and Lord and have a common father in faith, Abraham.

Finally, we invite all men and women of goodwill to reflect deeply on the significance of the *Shoah*. The victims from their graves, and the survivors through the vivid testimony of what they have suffered, have become a loud voice calling the attention of all humanity. To remember this terrible experience is to become fully conscious of the salutary warning it entails: the spoiled seeds of anti-Judaism and antisemitism must never again be allowed to take root in any human heart.

We also noted with satisfaction that the document raises decisive historical questions; for example, it emphasizes that the Shoah took place in Europe, in countries with long-standing Christian traditions, and asks what influence the attitudes of Christians toward Jews over the course of centuries had on Nazi persecution; and whether the persecution was not made easier by anti-Jewish prejudices embedded in Christian minds and hearts. Did these anti-Jewish sentiments not make Christians less sensitive or even indifferent to Nazi persecutions?

These are vital, pertinent questions; unfortunately the document does not give clear answers and in particular avoids taking a position on the relationship between the teaching of contempt (to return to Jules Isaac's phrase) and the political and cultural climate that made the Shoah possible. Consequently we may say that the document is assuredly important for what it says but is also revealing in its silences.

Therefore the great disappointment of the Jewish world, as well as of numerous Catholic figures who expected firm and clear stands on these matters, is understandable. The fact that the document affirmed certain historical facts we considered to be inaccurate or misleading, about which we formally expressed our reservations, aggravated the situation.

Under these conditions I judged it necessary to continue the discussion of this painful and essential subject and not consider the text as the last word.

This is why at the meeting of the International Catholic-Jewish Liaison Committee on March 23–26, 1998, I proposed the establishment of a bilateral working group, with the participation of outside experts, in which we would frankly discuss the questions that separated us and try to find agreement acceptable to both parties. I am pleased that our Catholic partners accepted this proposal.

Thirty Years of Negotiations

As I noted at the beginning of this chapter, during the darkest days of our history, when the Jewish people stood totally isolated and abandoned, I became convinced of the need to build bridges to other peoples and to other religious communities, in particular to the great Christian churches. Never again would the Jewish people be exposed to such catastrophes, never again would it find itself in such isolation and such solitude. We had to work together for the construction of a new world, a world in which all peoples, including the Jews, would have the right to life and to an existence free of old prejudices and past demonologies.

In the course of these last three or four decades we have created a new relationship between the Jewish and Christian communities. Our work has resulted in a number of agreements in many spheres of common interest. Although they may still be fragile, they have radically changed our relationship. I am very pleased that we have made considerable progress due to the faith and perseverance of all those who were engaged in this effort, but due also to the methods employed.

To follow and observe at close hand the changes that have occurred since Vatican II has been an extraordinary experience for me: how was the Roman Catholic church, so rigid in its static and inviolable rules, suddenly able to liberate itself from these constraints and become a vital organism in the present-day world? It is an unparalleled event in modern history.

I am of course aware that conservative elements in the church have tried to curtail this evolution and even move backward in certain areas. I am nonetheless persuaded that *aggiornamento* (modernization) and the church's new orientation will maintain the essential spirit of the Vatican II Council. Each generation will naturally bring its own interpretations, but the fundamental gains will remain.

The Second Vatican Council was a response to a general crisis in our society and, more specifically, a crisis confronting the church. In order for the church to adapt to the contemporary conditions of life and to the multiple developments of modern societies, John XXIII opened the way to *aggiorna-mento*.

The crisis of Christianity required solutions to three essential issues:

1. The general problem of the secularization of contemporary society.

2. The problem of growing agnosticism in the Western world.

3. The challenge of the atheism that ruled in all Eastern Europe under Communist domination, and beyond.

To this is to be added the church's realization that Christians in the contemporary world formed a religious minority. They had always been a minority, but the great European and Christian powers' colonization of large regions of our globe concealed this fact and created the illusion that the church was one of these dominant powers. Moreover the demographic explosion in the Third and Fourth Worlds continuously aggravated the Catholic church's minority position.

The church proceeded to examine its conscience in regard to its doctrinal foundations and its situation in contemporary society. It seemed to me then that everything previously considered fixed and immutable could be called into question and new avenues of reform could be opened. More specifically, I was convinced that this could also apply to the rigid traditional positions of the church with regard to the Jews and Judaism.

When I began the work of approaching the Catholic church, I was above all motivated by three objectives:

1. The elimination of the church as a permanent source of anti-Semitism. The catastrophe of the Shoah taught us the terrifying consequences to which the secular teaching of contempt could lead us. It was a question of nothing less than a fundamental transformation of Christian teaching about Jews and Judaism.

2. Jerusalem. I realized that no durable solution could be found to this problem without a broad consensus, and that the Catholic church should play an important role there.

3. The situation of the Jewish communities of Latin America, constantly threatened by the political instability that prevailed in that region where the Catholic church played a major role in life. I knew that the church alone had sufficient influence to obtain measures of moderation from the various dictatorships that ruled many countries there.

For all these reasons I believed it necessary to establish a relationship of trust and to engage the Catholic church in a dialogue.

In following this line of reasoning I was conscious of the existence within the church of two developments that would further the adoption of a new attitude with regard to the Jews. The first of these was the ecumenical movement, increasingly strengthened during the immediate postwar years and reinforced when the Catholic church joined this movement with Vatican II. More and more people in all Christian circles believed the separation of the churches was a scandal and sought new methods of reconciliation.

In the effort to bridge the divides separating the churches and the Jews, we went back in history and looked for what we had in common before the various divergences. We believed that if one looked at history one would discover the Jewish origins of the Christian faith. This discovery would bring Christians closer to contemporary Judaism.

The second development concerned the new attitude of the church toward the modern world. In the face of the immensity of the problems that confronted all of us, the church could not remain passive. It opened itself to the world and felt more and more responsible for its destiny in that it no longer only consoled suffering humanity with blessings and promises for the world to come, *haolam haba*, but began to take an active part in the effort to transform this world, *haolam hazeh*.

If the church wishes to retain its credibility and play an active, positive role in modern life, it must respond to political evil, war, poverty, and social suffering. And this it began to do. We viewed this as a welcome and extremely important development.

By changing its attitudes and strengthening its orientation, the church moved closer to traditional Jewish teaching. It better understood our conception of the universe: that is, God began but did not complete creation; humanity must complete it and perfect it day after day through observance of the commandments—*mitzvoth*—and by conforming to their basic concepts in its actions and conduct.

These ideas of the perfectibility of the world and of the importance of social action founded on moral rules are now increasingly accepted by church leaders. And because these concepts are deeply rooted in Jewish thought and doctrine, their acceptance by Christian leaders has led them to a much greater comprehension of the fundamental elements of Judaism.

These new reflections have led the Church increasingly to attempt to adapt its message to contemporary circumstances. They also have stimulated a process of what one might call "self-purification." This began with the church's renunciation of what was called legalism, triumphalism, and romanism, leading to a more tolerant attitude vis-à-vis other religions. It created new structures such as the Synod of Bishops. The new watchword became "collegiality."

In the process, the Jews were existentially inserted into Christian concepts while all the while knowing that Judaism does not require this Christian point of reference for its survival. Had the Jews not lived for centuries in Babylon and Persia without knowing of the existence of Christianity?

The Jews cannot, however, be completely disinterested in Christianity, first because we live in the same world and we are very close neighbors, and second because we should recognize that Christianity spread Jewish monotheism throughout the world and that hundreds of millions of people learned of Jewish monotheism through the message of the church. No Jew, believer or nonbeliever, can ignore that.

When I began my work on human rights and interreligious relations, I believed we would have to struggle for at least two or three generations to achieve visible results. But things developed much more rapidly. It is in the spheres of doctrine, liturgy, and theological thinking that great steps have been made. This did not always occur without friction or turbulence. And we are still far from the goal, but we have made progress.

Our first objective for the future is to deepen the knowledge of revised Catholic theology about the Jews and Judaism. We must work to reach broad sectors of the public, because until now only the elite know about this teaching and our altered relations with the church.

Our second duty concerns problems of education. We must assure that the teaching of the new theology is transmitted to future generations of the faithful. This in my opinion is the most important task. The Liaison Committee recognized that we must give priority to this question, and the Congregation for Catholic Education has promised us its full support.

I have often discussed with our Catholic partners the need to teach the fundamentals of Judaism and Jewish history from biblical times to the present day at the pontifical universities and Catholic seminaries. My thoughts on this subject have been favorably received.

Such an effort clearly imposes duties on Jews as well. Cooperation with the Catholic church cannot be effected unilaterally.

Our third task is to continue and deepen our common theological thinking. For if we have made remarkable progress since *Nostra aetate*, we are still only at the first stage of our reflections on the subject. Much remains to be done.

The new world catechism of the Catholic church, published in 1993, integrates the teaching of *Nostra aetate* and speaks with a great deal of respect about the Old Testament. Although it dispenses with the rigid tone of the catechisms of the past, the new theses indicate, to me at least, that there is still a long way to go.

A fourth task we must together undertake is to intensify the struggle against anti-Semitism and for the protection of human rights. At a time when every day reveals to us more proof of the rebirth and anguishing expansion of new waves of xenophobia, racism, anti-Semitism, and extreme nationalism, the urgency of this task is self-evident.

Another fundamental point: the *Guidelines and Suggestions* of 1974 contained a section entitled "Joint Social Action," reminding us that "Jewish and Christian tradition, founded on the Word of God, is aware of the value of the human person, the image of God." The text then continues: "In the spirit of the prophets, Jews and Christians will work willingly together, seeking social justice and peace at the local, national and international levels. . . . Such collaboration can do much to foster mutual understanding and esteem."

It is curious that over the course of years this section of the *Guidelines* has been rather neglected. At our meeting in Prague we returned to these ideas. I believe that "the work that the two communities could effect together to respond to the needs of today's world" will in the future increasingly be at the center of our concerns.

Another task awaits us. Religious fundamentalism is spreading even more widely across large sectors of our society. A religious extremism that is often fanatical in expression has taken very aggressive forms, particularly within Islam. Unfortunately these tendencies have also appeared in other great religions. Such fanaticisms are mutually reinforcing.

It is imperative that we take into account the dangers that this evolution presents to all of us. In this arena, concerted cooperative action by the different religions, including the Catholic church, is an absolute necessity. Universal peace depends more and more on the harmonious coexistence of the great world religions.

Relations with Other Christians

My relations with the World Council of Churches date from World War II. Although the Council was not formally established until 1948 in Amsterdam, our close ties began even earlier. For several years what could be called a "council in the making" existed, with offices in Geneva, its seat; Britain, where several prominent members of the executive lived; and the United States. The first secretary-general was Willem Visser 't Hooft, for whom I have always had great admiration.

Visser 't Hooft began his career in the Protestant student movement where he participated in various conferences of the International Student Service.

He was the secretary of the YMCA, in Geneva, and the World Federation of Christian Students before becoming secretary-general of the World Council of Churches. There is a certain parallel over the course of our two careers.

In Geneva, Visser 't Hooft experienced the terrible period of the Nazi rise to power in Germany. He participated in the international student conference in Munich in 1933, at which the Nazis made their appearance for the first time and where he made the acquaintance of Heinrich Himmler. On that occasion he experienced Nazi fanaticism firsthand, and from that moment on he understood the importance of the Jewish problem and the brutality of Nazi anti-Semitism.

With time Visser 't Hooft became the central figure in the World Council of Churches, first assisting in its creation then in its direction. Uniting hundreds of Protestant, Anglican, and later Orthodox churches was no easy task. With him I had a relationship of absolute confidence, which permitted us to support each other and furthered common initiatives.

Physically he was a rather tall man with the air of an intellectual, but one who combined thought with action. He was deeply influenced by the teachings of Karl Barth, one of the great Christian theologians of the twentieth century. Visser 't Hooft was also a Calvinist with all the rigor of that faith, but this did not prevent him from being a warm and open personality. He understood perfectly the tragedy that had struck European Judaism, and as a Christian leader he had a well-developed sense of his responsibility toward the Jewish people.

In his *Memoirs* (1973) he speaks with great kindness of our relations, our cooperation, and my personal role, emphasizing the quality and scope of the information I had at my disposal. I shared with him a great deal of what I learned. I have already written of his courageous stand on behalf of Jews during the Shoah.

After the liberation he vigorously formulated his position in an address in which he said, "Hitlerian paganism wished to destroy God. To that end it wished to destroy the Jewish people, the people of God, because this people bears witness."

We may wonder whether Visser 't Hooft so clearly understood the Jewish catastrophe because he held such a pessimistic vision of the world derived directly from his Calvinist convictions. I asked myself this question at our last meeting some months before his death. He was not in good health, and I had gone to visit him in his large home. Our remarks quite naturally came around to our collaboration during the war. Neither one of us was very proud of his actions, which had not succeeded in stimulating among the Allies the vigorous reaction that we had hoped for in our common struggle against the execution of the "Final Solution." Together we analyzed the reasons why no one believed the monstrosities of the Shoah nor attempted to save the millions of victims. For my part I had deduced that no one could live faced with absolute evil. Despite the terrible consequences it entailed for so many human beings, this was—if I dare say so—the most positive aspect of the tragedy, namely, that people could not believe it was possible that other human beings, furnished with a supply of victims and with recourse to the most modern technologies, could kill great masses of the handicapped, babies, women, and men. That proves in a certain way—and I am conscious of the terrible paradox—that the person who does not succeed in believing it, who refuses to believe it, is good. And so I said to Visser 't Hooft: "That gives us renewed hope in man." "No, no," he replied, "man is not good." It was only at that moment that I realized I was speaking with a fervent Calvinist. I regretted my words, but that opened my eyes to the deep differences in the philosophical and theological tenets we each held.

After the war Visser 't Hooft was the first person to speak to the German churches of their responsibility for the Nazi crimes in the occupied countries and for the extermination of the Jews, as well as of the need to avow this responsibility publicly before the other churches.

In August 1948 the World Council of Churches was formally established in Amsterdam, a few months after the creation of the State of Israel. In the long declaration adopted by the WCC Constituent Assembly on "the Christian attitude toward the Jews," the Council found moving words to affirm the special solidarity that links the Christian churches with the Jewish people; to proclaim the unique position of Israel in God's plan; to denounce anti-Semitism as a crime against God and against man, absolutely incompatible with Christian faith; to recall the extermination of six million Jews; and to confess the failings of responsible Christians in these events.

Here are some of the significant passages of the declaration:

A concern for the Christian approach to the Jewish people confronts us inescapably, as we meet together to look with open and penitent eyes on man's disorder and to rediscover together God's eternal purpose for His Church. This concern is ours because it is first a concern of God made known to us in Christ. No people in His one world have suffered more bitterly from the disorder of man than the Jewish people. We cannot forget that we meet in a land from which 110,000 Jews were taken to be murdered. Nor can we forget that we meet only five years after the extermination of six million Jews. To the Jews our God has bound us in a special solidarity linking our destinies together in His design. We call upon all our churches to make this concern their own. . . .

In the design of God, Israel has a unique position. It was Israel with whom God made His covenant by the call of Abraham. It was Israel to whom God revealed His name and gave His law. . . .

We must acknowledge in all humility that too often we have failed to manifest Christian love towards our Jewish neighbors, or even a resolute will for common social justice. We have failed to fight with all our strength the age-old disorder of man which antisemitism represents. The churches in the past have helped to foster an image of the Jews as the sole enemies of Christ, which has contributed to antisemitism in the secular world. In many lands virulent antisemitism still threatens and in other lands the Jews are subjected to many indignities. . . .

We call upon all the churches we represent to denounce antisemitism, no matter what its origin, as absolutely irreconcilable with the profession and practice of the Christian faith. Antisemitism is a sin against God and man.

At the Amsterdam assembly the churches were confronted with the birth of the State of Israel and its theological significance. Some saw in this the fulfillment of the promises of the Scriptures, while others vehemently opposed this point of view.

We read in the Amsterdam declaration sentences that express the assembly's perplexity and its resulting reservations and hesitations.

Here is a striking excerpt from this part of the declaration:

The establishment of the state "Israel" adds a political dimension to the Christian approach to the Jews and threatens to complicate antisemitism with political fears and enmities.

On the political aspects of the Palestine problem and the complex conflict of "rights" involved we do not undertake to express a judgment. Nevertheless, we appeal to the nations to deal with the problem not as one of expediency—political, strategic or economic—but as a moral and spiritual question that touches a nerve center of the world's religious life.

Whatever position may be taken towards the establishment of a Jewish state and towards the "rights" and "wrongs" of Jews and Arabs, of Hebrew Christians and Arab Christians involved, the churches are in duty bound to pray and work for an order in Palestine as just as may be in the midst of our human disorder; to provide within their power for the relief of the victims of this warfare without discrimination; and to seek to influence the nations to provide a refuge for "Displaced Persons" far more generously than has yet been done.

The Amsterdam declaration included a third part as well. In it the assembly confirmed the church's traditional mission of evangelization efforts directed at the Jewish people.

This call to conversion deeply shocked the Jewish communities. How could the churches dare, after the catastrophe that had cost the life of one-third of the Jewish people, that had taken place in countries profoundly marked by Christianity, and that had demonstrated the failure of the spiritual forces that had dominated these countries for centuries—under these circumstances how could they dare to propose to us conversion to Christianity? The Jewish reaction was unanimous: the Amsterdam declaration was simply and completely ignored.

In the years that followed, my relations with the World Council were limited to our meetings on the occasion of international conferences of the United Nations, UNESCO, and other international agencies. We occasionally cooperated in certain areas such as refugees and human rights.

The representatives of the World Council were distinguished men, including the Welsh cleric Elfan Rees, easily recognizable by his huge mustache, who also often crossed my path in Geneva and elsewhere. We met for the first time in Czechoslovakia in 1946, after the pogrom at Kielce in Poland, one of the most traumatic postwar events, in which Poles killed forty-two of the two hundred Jews who had survived the Shoah and had returned to Poland in the hope of rebuilding their lives.

Rees was in Prague to assist the entry into Czechoslovakia of a large number of the Jewish refugees who were fleeing Poland after these killings. He also actively participated in conferences on the problems of the Palestinian refugees, convoked by the WCC in the Middle East, where he adopted a moderate position and worked to reconcile all the parties.

In late 1959 and early 1960 a wave of swastikas suddenly made their appearance across Europe and elsewhere. Anti-Semitic graffiti appeared on synagogues and Jewish homes and in cemeteries. More than 2,500 anti-Semitic incidents occurred in the space of a few weeks in a great many countries. It is important to note that most of them took place in reputedly Christian countries. This veritable epidemic of anti-Jewish manifestations deeply surprised and shocked us.

I called Visser 't Hooft and said to him, "The churches remained silent on the Jewish problem during the war. Now it is all beginning again. Are you going to remain silent in the face of the clear dangers this time?"

Visser 't Hooft replied, "No, for it concerns us very greatly." In the hours that followed he published a vigorous declaration in the name of the World Council against this wave of anti-Semitic incidents. I took the opportunity to propose that he go even further. After thanking him for the declaration, I said to him pointedly, "You are currently getting ready for the third general assembly of the WCC, which will take place in New Delhi. Wouldn't that promote a good opportunity to make a solemn declaration on anti-Semitism and on the Christian position on the problem?

"I know the resolution made by your Constitutive Assembly in Amsterdam. It contained a very positive and moving section, but it nonetheless foundered because you asked the Jews to become Christians. Perhaps the moment has come to correct that error. Don't speak of anything else. Speak of anti-Semitism. That is the most important matter of the moment."

We discussed it for more than an hour. Visser 't Hooft told me how the Jewish problem had been dealt with in the course of the preceding assembly of the WCC in Evanston, Illinois, in 1955 and how the churches had literally torn themselves to pieces over how to deal with the matter, from the political and not the theological perspective. The Evanston assembly finally remained silent on the matter of the Jews.

Visser 't Hooft showed me a copy of the Amsterdam text, and we reflected together on what he could propose. What he envisaged at the time was almost identical to the text that the conference in New Delhi finally adopted. He knew his organization well.

He told me that a group of French Protestants had also proposed dealing again with the problem of anti-Semitism at the assembly in New Delhi. He said he would be happy to receive a letter from the president of the World Jewish Congress suggesting that the New Delhi assembly speak out against the new wave of anti-Semitism. We sent the letter to him a few weeks later.

The New Delhi declaration represented considerable progress. For the first time there was a paragraph on the nonresponsibility of the Jews in the death of Jesus. In light of the recent outbreaks of anti-Semitism, and given the WCC declaration against anti-Semitism in 1948, the New Delhi Assembly noted that:

> The Third Assembly recalls the following words which were addressed to the churches by the First Assembly of the World Council of Churches in 1948:
>
>   "We call upon all the churches we represent to denounce anti-semitism, no matter what its origin, as absolutely irreconcilable with the profession and practice of the Christian faith. Anti-semitism is a sin against God and

man. Only as we give convincing evidence to our Jewish neighbors that we seek for them the common rights and dignities which God wills for his children, can we come to such a meeting with them as would make it possible to share with them the best which God has given us in Christ."

The Assembly renews this plea in view of the fact that situations continue to exist in which Jews are subject to discrimination and even persecution. The Assembly urges its member churches to do all in their power to resist every form of anti-semitism. "In Christian teaching the historic events which led to the Crucifixion should not be so presented as to fasten upon the Jewish people today the responsibilities which belong to our corporate humanity and not to one race or community. Jews were the first to accept Jesus and Jews are not the only ones who do not yet recognize him."

We found this text to be both positive and satisfactory.

Some time after the New Delhi assembly, I received a visit from the Rev. Anker Gjerding, a Dane who worked in the secretariat of the World Council. He asked me for certain information in some documents and books. I gave him what he asked for and in reply he sent me a very kind letter of thanks. But the letterhead read "World Council of Churches—Global Mission and Evangelization Division—Committee on the Church and the Jewish People." This agency succeeded the old International Council on Missions. I must admit this surprised me, and for a while I was at a loss as to how to react.

Several weeks later I met Visser 't Hooft by chance at the Geneva airport. It was a friendly meeting, and he told me how pleased he was to see the articles we had published on the New Delhi declaration.

In the course of our conversation I asked him whether the World Council really could not turn relations with the Jews over to a department other than Missions. Visser 't Hooft first expressed surprise at my request. Then, when I had given him an account of my dealings with the Rev. Gjerding, he answered me kindly but with great firmness, "Monsieur Riegner, for you the person to address remains the secretary-general of the WCC. Do you have any cause for complaint about this contact person? Reverend Gjerding ought not to have approached you. The rest is an internal affair of the WCC and does not concern you. But even with all the sympathy that I have for you, I cannot change Christian theology. Missionary effort is part of that theology. But be assured that the man that I have chosen to look after these relations is extremely moderate. This having been said, you ought to continue your direct relations with the secretary-general. Does this satisfy you?" I answered, "Yes." That certainly simplified things.

During the years that followed we continued regularly to consult and co-operate, especially in the political domain, and in the areas of human rights, refugees, disarmament, and UN activities in general.

Meanwhile the WCC had pursued its studies and reflections on the church and the Jewish people. Its Commission on Faith and Order, meeting in Bristol in February 1967, had published a high-quality and morally principled text on this subject in which it dealt with its historical, theological, doctrinal, and ecumenical aspects, seeking to draw conclusions from the recent past and attempting to throw new light on Judaism as well as to define a new approach to Jewish-Christian relations.

The commission openly condemned the failings and errors of the past and described with great honesty the fundamental divisions that persisted among the churches on the perceptions of the Jewish people and Judaism. The text also contained practical recommendations for implementing this new approach and advocated regular contacts with the Jews to discuss social cooperation and, on a deeper level, theological tenets.

Establishing a framework for permanent consultation between Jews and Protestants seemed fundamental to me. This concern obliged me to review our relations with the Secretariat for the Promotion of Christian Unity at the Vatican. Relations with Catholics and Protestants often followed parallel paths, but progress did not proceed simultaneously, and at any given time one would have moved beyond the other.

When our discussions with the Holy See became stalemated, particularly at the time when Cardinal Béa was no longer capable of supporting them, I turned to the World Council of Churches to try to make some progress toward the establishment of an ongoing and organized relationship.

In earlier sections devoted to the Catholic church, I have told how we organized our first three consultations with the World Council in June 1968, May 1969, and February 1970, and how we gradually institutionalized our relations with the WCC. The assembly of the World Council in Uppsala in Sweden in 1968 agreed to advance our relations, though no statement from that meeting explicitly speaks of the matter.

At the same time these first consultations had as a consequence the formation of a representative Jewish organization, the International Jewish Committee for Interreligious Consultations (IJCIC), capable of developing authoritative relations with the central bodies of the Christian churches. Rabbi Joachim Prinz and Professor Arthur Hertzberg served as its first and second presidents, and together we introduced a rotation system among representatives of the various organizations making up the IJCIC.

To make things easier, together with the WCC we created a planning and liaison committee composed in principle of ten persons to meet once or twice a year. Without broaching theological considerations, this committee more than once addressed political and existential questions, such as the problems affecting the State of Israel, the situation of Soviet Jews, and the racial policies of South Africa. The Jewish side shared the concerns of the World Council of Churches for the problems of the contemporary world, beyond the more controversial theological questions.

Over the course of the period when the Reverend Eugene Carson Blake served as secretary-general, the WCC implemented an important restructuring of the administration and organization of the Council. Our chief contact continued to be the secretary-general. The Rev. Blake had taken seriously our objections to being within the purview of the section for missions and evangelization. In the turmoil of reorganization, Blake created a new section of the WCC administration charged with "the dialogue with people of other living religions and ideologies." Within the framework of this new section, the WCC finally created a Consultation for the Church and the Jewish People. This consultative body was chaired for many years by Professor Mulder of Amsterdam, and then by Professor Krister Stendahl, a well-respected theologian who for thirty years had been the dean of the prestigious Harvard Divinity School. The author of a remarkable work on St. Paul and the Jews entitled *Paul Among the Jews and Other Essays* (1977), Stendahl crowned his career by becoming the Protestant Bishop of Stockholm.

Over the years and in various locations the subjects we discussed with our Christian partners comprised diverse themes: the fight against racism; the quest for a world community; particularity and universalism; the concept of power in Judaism and in Christianity and its application in contemporary social order; religion and the crisis of modernity; religious pluralism—its significance and its limits in today's world.

Inevitably not everything went smoothly. For example, as a result of the WCC central committee's August 1980 unilateral and hostile declaration on the September 1980 unification of Jerusalem by Israeli authorities, the following month we raised a sharp protest with the Consultation in Toronto. We submitted to our Christian partners the text of a declaration that the IJCIC had unanimously adopted. The IJCIC declaration criticized the WCC's purely political approach and insisted on the profoundly religious aspect that Jerusalem had for every Jew. This text was also formally communicated to the secretary-general of the WCC. Several Christian participants in the Consultation declared their solidarity with the position of the Jews.

The Christian members of the Consultation decided to offer their services to give the Jewish declaration the widest possible public airing and to search for other avenues that would permit the Jewish community to be heard within the WCC when problems that particularly affected it were discussed.

This long discussion threw into relief the need to look for ways by which the Jewish position on the major problems of the community could be brought before the WCC senior bodies.

The creation of the State of Israel did not pose a great problem for Protestants. It is true that their 1948 Amsterdam declaration was cautious because they did not wish to voice an opinion that could be viewed as a political act. At the same time the reestablishment of the Jews in their land of origin posed the theological question of the fulfillment of biblical promises regarding the return of the Jews to their homeland.

The WCC never contested the existence of the State of Israel. The problem facing the churches of the WCC was cast in terms simpler than those confronting the Catholics. The Council was not a state, and thus it did not have to recognize Israel on the diplomatic level.

For the Protestants the problem rested in the theological domain. They had to determine whether the creation of the State of Israel had theological significance. Opinions on the matter diverged radically. The WCC never considered the return of the Jewish people to Palestine and the establishment of the State of Israel as a fulfillment of the biblical promise. This contributed to the extreme complexity of the political problems for the WCC posed by the position of the Israeli state vis-à-vis the Third World.

The WCC had always considered the struggle against apartheid in South Africa one of its priorities. In this sphere, it found itself of necessity close to Third World groups and all the national liberation movements. The Palestine Liberation Organization (PLO) played an important role in this political alliance. All these movements evolved into a more or less pro-Palestinian and anti-Israeli position.

On the other hand, Africa played a great role in the hopes of many Christians who actively supported missionary work in the sub-Saharan part of that continent. These concerns certainly played a role as the WCC attempted to win the support of the great African masses; the WCC effectively played the apartheid card, which led it to support the PLO as well.

Obviously our criticism of WCC policies was not aimed at its struggle against apartheid. We had ourselves taken critical positions with regard to the South African racial system, as we did with all racist policies. But we judged that the WCC attitude with regard to the Palestinians and the State of Israel was profoundly unbalanced and unduly influenced by Arab propaganda.

This pro-Palestinian stance was furthered by the fact that the Protestant churches in the Arab countries, the latter generally hostile toward Israel, participated in the debates of the WCC Central Committee, while the very nature of these deliberations precluded a Jewish voice to support the Israeli cause.

In addition, within the WCC the commission for international relations often took a more radical position than the other bodies, especially with regard to its strong support of the Palestinians. Its official thesis may have been: "We are seeking peace between the two antagonists," but in reality it had taken a unilateral stand strongly opposed to Israel. Among the reasons for this lack of objectivity, the influence of the Protestant churches in the Middle East played a far from negligible role.

Without ever having openly questioned the legitimacy of the State of Israel, the Protestants progressively adopted positions increasingly favorable to the Palestinians.

I should, however, recall that in 1975 when the UN adopted the resolution that "Zionism is racism," the secretary-general of the WCC expressed vigorous opposition to this resolution at the UN General Assembly. Once the resolution had been adopted, I contacted him and suggested that the WCC take a stand with regard to this infamous text. In a public statement devoted to the resolution, Philippe Potter, the secretary-general, defended Zionism as a movement of national liberation.

In order not to stymie our relations with the WCC, I thought that if we could not make progress in the political domain we might possibly be able to move ahead in the theological sphere. Consequently I proposed to our WCC partners that we draw up a set of general guidelines on Jewish-Christian relations similar to those the Holy See had established in 1975.

This also confirmed me in the idea that it was important for us to have direct relations with the churches of the Third World, in particular with those in Africa. The guidelines would, I hoped, make a positive contribution in this direction.

The idea of drawing up a set of general guidelines was accepted and actively pursued by the Consultation on the Church and the Jewish People, which drafted several texts and communicated them to the Jewish partners. The IJCIC and its representatives had ample time to offer their comments, orally and in writing, and presented a detailed memorandum on a number of important points that were discussed at one of our regular meetings. Our representatives participated regularly in the meetings of the Consultation throughout the development of the project.

The draft of the major text circulated among the churches for review, and a number of them made proposals and suggestions for amendment. After a long period of review, the Consultation submitted the final text to the WCC executive.

Entitled "Ecumenical Considerations on Jewish-Christian Dialogue," the executive committee in Geneva adopted it on July 16, 1982, and distributed it to the church members of the Council with the recommendation that it be studied and acted on.

Comprising nine dense pages, the declaration is of the greatest importance. We warmly welcomed its adoption. It can be equated with similar statements of the Catholic church and in certain respects is even more explicit.

After a general introduction, the text outlines a Christian understanding of Jews and Judaism. It then deals with the hatred and persecution of the Jews as an ongoing concern and concludes with a section devoted to authentic Christian witness.

Following the Catholic model, the Protestant document expresses the imperative to better understand Judaism if for no other reason than the fact that historically Christianity developed out of Judaism, noting that as part of this development Christianity defined its own identity vis-à-vis Judaism, and that it is no surprise that the Jews resent the negative roles in which Christians cast them.

Indeed, the declaration stated that "there is a special urgency for Christians to listen . . . to ways in which Jews understand their history and their traditions, their faith and their obedience 'in their own terms.'" This could be accomplished through dialogue and the realization that the classic Christian tradition of the church supplanting Israel as "God's Chosen," the notion that God's covenant with the people of Israel only prepared for the coming of Christ after which it was abrogated, had "fateful consequences."

Now, the document said, through the study of Judaism and dialogue with the Jews, Christians had come to learn that Judaism was not a static, fossilized theology of no current relevance but rather that rabbinic Judaism had produced the Mishnah and Talmud and over the centuries built structures for a vibrant, strong creative life.

Here I think it is important to note specifically that the document declares: "The relationship between the two communities, both worshipping the God of Abraham, Isaac and Jacob, is a given historical fact, but how it is to be understood theologically is a matter of internal discussion among Christians, a discussion that can be enriched by dialogue with Jews."

With regard to Jerusalem and the State of Israel, the WCC declaration says that the city has always been central to the theology of Judaism and that it has always been more to the Jews than just a place of residence. Moreover, though Jews may differ in their views on the religious and secular meanings of the State of Israel, "it constitutes for them part of the long search for that survival which has always been central to Judaism through the ages."

The document also declares that the quest for statehood by Muslim and Christian Palestinians, "as part of their search for survival as a people in the Land—also calls for full attention."

"Ecumenical Considerations" speaks to the issue of the hatred and persecution of the Jews, much as the 1948 Amsterdam declarations, and emphasizes that "Christians should oppose all such religious prejudices, whereby people are made scapegoats for the failures and problems of societies and political regimes."

A portion of the fourth section is devoted to authentic Christian witness. The text rejects any type of proselytism, that is, conversion under coercion. It also explains with great frankness that the churches are deeply divided about the mission to the Jews and describes the different positions on this issue.

Even though it leaves unsettled the problem of missionary activity, this declaration represents a great contribution toward reconciliation. It can contribute to a positive evolution in the minds of the faithful.

In the course of one of the consultations between the IJCIC and the WCC we learned how Arab propaganda had been able to shift the opinions of the leaders of African churches in an anti-Israeli, even anti-Jewish direction.

An African member of the WCC delegation asked questions such as, "How does it happen that the Jews control all the banks? How does it happen that the diamond mines and diamond trade are in the hands of Jews? How does it happen that the Israeli airline El Al has regular service to South Africa? Why does South Africa seem to have a privileged relationship with Israel?"

Since then the person who asked these questions has changed a great deal and has adopted views that are closer to reality. But one can see the extent of Arab propaganda, nourished by old prejudices, deployed in Africa by the Christian churches.

I remember that many of my Christian colleagues on the Council were terribly embarrassed by these questions. For my part, I found it quite useful to be questioned in that fashion because the dialogue allowed us to clarify the issues. It was better that topics such as these be debated in our presence, because this permitted me to point out, for example, that the family of Mr. Oppenheimer, the head of the De Beers company, had been Protestant for several generations and that control of the banks by the Jews was a myth.

On the other hand, why blame Israel alone for its commercial and air links with South Africa, when all the major countries had similar relations with that country?

In addition, after the meeting I had a memorandum drawn up with detailed responses to all these accusations. We communicated it to all the participants, in particular to the African spokesman.

I attempted to draw useful lessons from this situation. It was obvious that we could not hope for a change in the WCC position on Israel in the short term, so I pursued the idea of establishing direct contacts with the churches of the Third World, especially those in Africa, and for several years I tried to establish such contacts with the Pan-African Conference of Churches. Unfortunately my efforts led nowhere.

A consultation with the WCC at Harvard University in 1984 finally permitted me to establish a warm, personal contact with Professor Kofi Opoku of Ghana. I shared with him our desire to organize a meeting with theologians from the African churches, stressing that we had undertaken a whole series of steps in that direction without achieving any success. Up to that point the African leaders had been reluctant to deal with us and avoided committing themselves.

It seemed to us particularly important to establish direct relations between Jews and Africans since in most African countries no Jewish community existed. As a consequence, a false image of the Jew was often projected in the African world, in particular through Arab propaganda. The only way to correct this situation was through direct and ongoing relations.

Professor Opoku expressed great interest in our project. He obtained support for such a meeting from the Pan-African Conference of Churches, which until then had always evaded our approaches.

Professor Opoku set to work to organize the conference in Africa with the objective of initiating a mutually beneficial relationship between Christians and Jews beyond a simple exchange of words. We finally met in Nairobi on November 10–14, 1986.

On the Christian side, thirteen African theologians from six countries—Ghana, Kenya, Ethiopia, Tanzania, Nigeria, and Sierra Leone—represented the various Protestant, Catholic, and Orthodox churches of Africa. On the Jewish side, twelve delegates from six countries and four continents represented the five large Jewish organizations that made up the IJCIC. But despite great efforts, representatives from the churches and the Jewish communities of South Africa were not authorized to participate in the gathering. The meeting took place under the joint auspices of the World Council of Churches, the IJCIC, and the Pan-African Conference of Churches.

As Professor Opoku so well stated in his summary report:

> This was not the first time that Jews and African Christians had met, but it was the first time they had met at this high level on African soil, where the agenda was an African, not a European, one. It was not dominated by memories of the Holocaust and persecution, but by the shared Jewish and African Christian concerns with tradition and its relationship with scripture. The European experience, with its unhistorical and culturally limited interpretations of scripture, could for once be bypassed. Scripture, after all, is not a European creation, though most of us have been taught to read it through a European perspective. For once, we did not start with problems associated with antisemitism or the existence of the State of Israel but from a point of mutual interest and tradition which binds African Christians to the Jewish heritage. In this domain, the participants have much in common.

Among the topics so representative of this state of mind that we discussed at the meeting, we included "Ancient Wisdom in African and Jewish Tradition and Its Relevance for Contemporary Life," "The Understanding of Scriptures," and "The Creation of the World in the Two Heritages." The conference also addressed the topic of the Ethiopian Jews, the unique Jewish community of African origin.

The Jewish community of Nairobi, led by Rabbi Zeev Amit, invited all the participants to a convivial meeting at the Nairobi synagogue.

At the close of the conference we issued a joint declaration that called for the establishment of a combined working group, mandated among other things to:

1. Plan and conduct future consultations between Jews and African Christians, including one involving French-speaking African Christians and Jews.

2. From time to time, organize seminars focusing on particular issues.

3. Ensure the full participation of women in future consultations and seminars, with particular attention to topics dealing with women's issues in the two traditions.

4. Explore, and where feasible, develop the following possibilities:

(a) Jewish scholars teaching Jewish studies in African institutions of higher learning and African scholars teaching African studies in Jewish institutions of higher learning.

(b) A program to make Hebrew scripture, commentaries and post-biblical sources available to libraries in institutions of higher learning in Africa.

(c) Bilateral agreements of cooperation between universities in Israel and universities in various African countries.

(d) Collaboration between African and Jewish scholars in joint research projects as well as the promotion of exchange programs involving faculty and students.

All the Nairobi conference participants judged it to have been a great success. But for financial reasons there was no follow-up. At my recent meetings with the WCC and the Roman Catholic church I suggested that it be revived. All parties expressed their agreement in principle for meeting in both western and eastern Africa.

This eventually led to a second African Jewish-Christian conference held in Johannesburg in June 1995. It brought together Christian theologians from Benin, Botswana, Cameroon, Eritrea, Ghana, Kenya, Mozambique, Nigeria, and South Africa, and Jewish representatives from Israel, South Africa, Switzerland, France, the United Kingdom, the United States, and Zimbabwe. The theme of the conference was "Family, Community, Tradition." For the South African leaders it was their first participation in such a meeting. It is desirable that as a consequence of this experience they themselves take the initiative for similar meetings in the future.

For its part, the WCC Consultation on the Church and the Jewish People continued its work. It met in Sigtuna, Sweden, in November 1988, and reviewed the overall development of Jewish-Christian relations in the course of the last decades. Representatives from the IJCIC also attended.

The debates addressed all subjects, even those that lent themselves to controversy. The spirit was one of a desire to know one another better, to understand one another better. Martin Stöhr, Rolf Rendtorff, and Allan Brockway made substantial contributions to this meeting. The WCC adopted an important new document which went into greater depth than its preceding declarations on relations between Christians and Jews. The document that emerged from these deliberations summarizes the fundamental teachings about Jewish-Christian relations as these were formulated in the principal texts of the WCC as well as in those of the Roman Catholic church.

The text affirms the importance of this evolution and encourages the confirmation and deepening of this relationship. The document also affirms that "the Jewish people today are directly related to biblical Israel and [we] are grateful for the vitality of Jewish faith and thought."

The text contains the following paragraphs:

> We rejoice in the continuing existence and vocation of the Jewish people, despite attempts to eradicate them, as a sign of God's love and faithfulness towards them. This fact does not call into question the uniqueness of Christ and the truth of the Christian faith. We see not one covenant displacing another, but two communities of faith, each called into existence by God, each holding to its respective gifts from God, and each accountable to God.
>
> We see Jews and Christians, together with all people of living faiths, as God's partners, working in mutual respect and cooperation for justice, peace, and reconciliation.

I must say, however, that relations with the Jews have not in recent years constituted a central theme in the concerns of the WCC. The Consultation on the Church and the Jewish People has played a rather marginal role during this time. The Sigtuna report was neither presented for consideration nor discussed at the last assembly of the WCC in Canberra.

A concern for the lot of Palestinians has taken the central place in WCC relations with Judaism in the course of these last years. In fact these relations are limited to a series of criticisms and condemnations of the Israeli government over the treatment of the Palestinians, as if there were no theological, social, humanitarian, or political questions to be discussed.

This attitude found its most virulent expression in the declaration released by the WCC assembly in Canberra in February 1991 on "The Gulf War, the Middle East and the Threat to World Peace." We Jews were not alone in considering this stance as strictly unilateral and pro-Arab. It led to a serious crisis between the WCC and the IJCIC and prompted us to ask that the WCC reexamine the bases for our cooperation.

Since then a new secretary-general, Dr. Konrad Raiser, has taken over the administration. An eminent German theologian, Dr. Raiser had served as deputy secretary-general for a long period under Philippe Potter, and we knew both his interest and his open position with regard to the Jewish-Christian dialogue. Consequently the turbulence of our relations with the WCC was calmed under his influence, and on several occasions we were able to hold quite constructive consultations with our Protestant colleagues. It should be noted, however, that relations with the Jewish community are no longer a priority for most members of the WCC secretariat. The members of the WCC Commission on International Affairs express from time to time a critical attitude toward Israel.

While we were far from the position of the WCC in 1941 when it affirmed that the question of relations with the Jews "touched the very center of the Christian message," nonetheless a clear estrangement developed. The WCC told us with increasing frequency that the problem of anti-Semitism was a European problem, that the churches of Asia and Africa were not interested in it and bore no responsibility for what occurred during World War II. The future of the WCC, on the other hand, lay in these regions, therefore opinion there had to be seriously taken into account.

This thesis did not seem well founded to me. Anti-Semitism is unfortunately not just a European problem but makes its presence felt in many regions of the world. Moreover, either the relationship with the Jewish people is a central theological problem for Christianity or it is not. If it is, the question is not tied to geographic borders. And if this problem does not seem urgent or topical to the churches of the Third World—because very few Jews are resident in these regions—then it is the duty of the Christian churches of the Western world to make their co-religionists in other parts of the world attentive to this fundamental truth. It is all the more important to make Christians who live in countries with only very small Jewish communities (or with none) conscious of the problem simply because these countries are more exposed to anti-Semitic propaganda. I judge this an important task for the WCC, and I hope it will take it into greater account in the future. Any other attitude would take us back to the old positions that rejected the creator God and the Old Testament.

At the meeting of the Administrative and Planning Committee with the WCC in Jerusalem in 1976, we understood that the Council, which grouped more than three hundred Protestant, Anglican, and Eastern Orthodox churches, was an extremely complicated body, that it took a great deal of time to reach common positions, and that its recommendations reached the churches and the faithful at the grassroots level only very slowly. I communicated our feeling that we should meet not solely with the WCC but also directly with the representative bodies of the various denominational families that made up the council, that is, Lutherans, Anglicans, Eastern Orthodox, Pentecostalists, and so on. The WCC delegation received this suggestion favorably and even actively assisted us in establishing relations with the World Lutheran Federation, the Anglican Communion, and the Orthodox churches.

As a result, at the close of 1979 we initiated our relations with the Lutherans. We know that Luther's teachings about the Jews, and particularly his pamphlet on "The Jews and Their Lies," contains radically violent statements, which the Nazis used widely in their anti-Jewish propaganda. It was clear to me that we had to try to persuade the most senior Lutheran authorities to repudiate this teaching so that it might never again be used for such purposes.

I also believed that the five-hundredth anniversary of the birth of Luther, to be celebrated in 1983, would be a particularly appropriate time to make a solemn act of repudiation. Toward this end I approached the Lutheran authorities at the end of 1978 in order to arrange preliminary discussions, and we agreed to meet in Berlin on February 22 and 23, 1979. Thirty representatives from more than fifteen countries, designated by the IJCIC and the Lutheran European Commission on the Church and the Jewish People (LEKKJ), met in order to exchange information on areas of common interest and to lay the groundwork for future collaboration. The time had come to initiate a series of Jewish-Lutheran meetings, similar to those that had been organized in earlier years with the Holy See and the World Council of Churches.

It was not easy for me to go to Berlin, the city where I had been born, and which I had been forced to leave in 1933. I had not set foot in the city since that date. I no longer had any relatives, friends, or acquaintances there. Forty-six years later it was to me a completely foreign city.

My stay required a considerable emotional effort. The prospect of seeing again the house in which I was born, the school where I was educated, the university where I had done much of my studies, and finally the cemetery at Weissensee in East Berlin where my grandparents and other members of my family were buried, produced a range of different feelings in me. But I judged that the meeting with the Lutherans justified this emotional wrench.

At the meeting we observed that the Lutheran European Commission on the Church and the Jewish People was not simply made up of representatives of the various European Lutheran churches; its members also included missionary societies from various countries. This was a source of a good deal of discomfort for us. And, while declaring that we stood ready to collaborate with the Lutheran churches, we insisted that the LEKKJ could not be our partner in future relations.

It was also interesting to note that the members of the Lutheran delegation at this meeting were divided on what attitude toward the Jews to adopt. Traditionalists followed the old teaching and envisaged the conversion of the Jews as a natural duty. But another group had drawn the necessary conclusions from the Shoah and saw that missionary activity aimed at the Jews was impossible. A third group, situated between the two and a prey to doubt, hesitated as to which choice to make.

The members of the second group begged us not to abandon them, since our presence was important to convince the third group to join their cause.

After long deliberations, all the participants reaffirmed the will to continue cooperation. In order to overcome the difficulties of organization, it was agreed that three responsible persons elected *ad personam*—and I was one of them—would assure the continuity of contacts and would find an institutional framework that was acceptable to all.

With this in mind it was foreseen that we would establish cooperation between the IJCIC and the World Lutheran Federation (WLF). But since the latter still had to deliberate on the matter, we could not formally adopt this structure. It was in this way that I entered into an ongoing and constructive collaboration with Dr. Arne Sovik, a senior official of the WLF, who took pains to determine an appropriate framework for relations between the IJCIC and his organization. Over time he became one of our best partners in Jewish-Christian relations and a true friend.

As a consequence, Dr. Sovik and I prepared the first official international conference between our two organizations. This took place in Copenhagen on July 6–8, 1981, with twenty-four participants from ten countries. The topic was "The Concept of the Human Being in the Lutheran and Jewish Traditions."

I gladly accepted this topic. I did not wish to begin our relationship with a discussion of the anti-Jewish teachings of Luther, which I had decided to attack during the Luther anniversary year. First we had to create an atmosphere of confidence and cooperation.

All the participants recognized the utility of this gathering and considered the frankness and sincerity that dominated the discussions to be one of the most positive characteristics of the meeting. And we mutually agreed they should continue.

The second meeting was organized in Stockholm and held July 11–13, 1983, on the occasion of the five-hundredth anniversary of Luther's birth. At our suggestion the topic for this conference was "Luther, Lutheranism, and the Jews." From each side about twenty people took part, among whom sat the flower of Lutheran theology. I co-chaired the meeting with Professor Magne Saebø of Oslo. Four scholars addressed the topic: the American professor Mark U. Edwards, Jr., and Professor Ingun Montgomery of Uppsala, Sweden, representing the Lutherans; and the great historian Uriel Tal of Tel Aviv University, who died suddenly at his home in Israel the following year, and Professor Ernst Ludwig Ehrlich of Basel, who spoke on behalf of the Jews.

The significance of the choice of subject in the context of the year devoted to Luther did not need to be underlined. That we found it possible to deal with a subject as difficult and existential for our future relations augured well for the prospects of our future cooperation. This was another sign of the spirit of openness and candor which from the outset had characterized our dialogue.

The Stockholm meeting concluded with the adoption of three texts. One had been prepared by the Lutheran theologians, the second by the Jewish delegation, and the third by all the participants. The preface to the texts stated that the two sides had committed themselves before God to seek together a way to build a bridge over the historical gulf of injustice and enmity that separated them.

The Lutheran theologians' declaration firmly and unanimously repudiated Luther's teachings on the Jews:

> The sins of Luther's anti-Jewish remarks, the violence of his attacks on the Jews, must be acknowledged with profound distress. And all occasions for similar sin in the present or the future must be removed from our churches.
> ... Lutherans of today refuse to be bound by Luther's utterances on the Jews. We hope we have learned from the tragedies of the recent past. We are responsible for seeing that we do not now or in the future leave any doubt about our position on racial or religious prejudice and that we afford to all the human dignity, freedom and friendship that are the right of all the Father's children.

Having clearly identified and definitively rejected that part of Luther's teachings that belonged to his medieval heritage, and having frankly recognized and denounced the terrible use that had been made of those teachings in our time is of the greatest importance for our future relations. Facing our unfortunate common history openly is one of our most urgent common tasks if we wish to overcome the past and lay the foundation for a happier future.

At the end of the meeting, I said to the Lutherans, "This is all very well, but it is a declaration by twenty people. How are you going to advance it in the field?" They replied, "We are going to bring this declaration before the next global assembly of the World Lutheran Federation."

Indeed, one year later this question was entered on the agenda for the Budapest assembly. I was even invited to speak to that conference and introduce the subject. This was unprecedented because a non-Christian had never before addressed such an assembly. At the conclusion of the debates the assembly of fifteen hundred delegates from around the world approved the Stockholm declaration and recommended it to all the churches for study and application. It was a great event, a historical moment in which an important branch of Christianity affirmed in solemn fashion its will to expiate Christian sins against the Jewish people.

We maintained regular contact with the WLF during the years that followed. The question of missionary activity among the Jews continued to play an important role in their own deliberations. These finally led to an important declaration, formally adopted by the European Lutheran Commission on the Church and the Jewish People at its annual meeting in the Netherlands on May 8, 1990.

The statement marked a fresh approach by Lutheranism toward the Jewish mission and represented a clear movement in our direction. Among other things we read in this text:

> I.4. We believe that God in his faithfulness has led His people of Israel through history and has preserved them as a people by the Jewish tradition of faith. We consider their return to the country of their fathers to be a sign of God's faithfulness to His covenant.

> II.4. We Christians need to meet our Jewish partners with humility, love, and respect. We must listen to their expression of faith concerning reconciliation and redemption and must take it seriously. The last judgment on man will be passed by God and will remain His mystery.

> III.2. The readiness of Christians to listen to the witness of Jews, to learn from their experience in faith and life, and thus to become aware of new aspects of the Biblical tradition, is an indispensable precondition of our encounter. Jews and Christians have much to say to each other in their encounter and can together rediscover God's reality.

> III.4. Any encounter between Christians and Jews must be based on the understanding that God Himself is the one who sends out—who is the missionary. This insight into the *missio dei* helps to understand one's own possibilities and tasks. God authorizes us to mutually witness to our faith, trusting in the independent working of the Holy Spirit; for it is God alone who decides what effect our witness will have; and it is His decision with regard to the eternal salvation of all mankind. He frees us from the pressure

of having to accomplish everything by oneself. This insight places Christians under the obligation to give witness and render service with due respect to the conviction and faith of their Jewish partners.

IV.3. We encourage that Christians be taught about Judaism, in order to help them gain a positive, undistorted attitude toward contemporary Judaism, and thus to overcome antisemitism based on secular motives as well as the anti-Judaism which has been handed down to us within the Churches.

IV.4. We request that the Jewish people, its salvation, and its peace be included in the prayers of intercession. We feel solidarity with all the people who see their home, their refuge, and their hope in the State of Israel.

This position is obviously of extreme importance. If conversion is the work of God, human effort—the activities of missionary societies—naturally loses much of its significance.

In a similar evolution in thinking, the Rhineland Synod had in 1980 already formulated the celebrated declaration, "The Renewal of the Relationship of Christians and Jews," that stated:

We believe that Jews and Christians, both according to their calling, are the witnesses of God before the world and each before the other; therefore we are convinced that the Church ought bear its testimony before the Jewish people in the same way as it does in its mission before the nations of the world. . . . There is a difference between our mission in the world and the witness of Israel. We do not have the right to treat it in the same manner. We must, then, renounce the conversion of the Jews.

This declaration served as an example for several other German synods. We can see that even in the very delicate area of missionary activity, some evolution could be noted.

It was similarly of great significance that the Synod of the Evangelical Church of the Rhineland, after long consultation, decided in January 1996 to revise its constitution by adding a clause in which the church "professes the faithfulness of God, who stands by the election of His people Israel." It then officially rejected the doctrine of substitution according to which Israel is blamed by God and replaced by the Christian Church.

Meanwhile we had also begun to establish contacts with the Anglican church and the whole of the Anglican communion.

The initiative to inaugurate these relations came from the Rev. Peter Schneider, who had served for many years in Israel before being named adviser for interfaith relations to the archbishops of Canterbury and York. We were assured from the outset of the cooperation of the archbishop of York, Stuart Yarworth Blanch, and of the chief rabbi of the United Hebrew Congregation of Great Britain and the Commonwealth, Lord Immanuel Jacobovits.

These contacts led to the organization of a first Jewish-Anglican conference in Andover in November 1980, organized under the joint auspices of the consultancy for interfaith relations of the archbishops of Canterbury and York and the International Jewish Committee for Interfaith Consultations. Eleven Christians and nine Jews participated in this meeting, the theme of which was "Law and Religion in Contemporary Society." Chief Rabbi Jacobovits and the Archbishop of York, responsible for relations with Jews, led the delegations and co-chaired the meeting. Rev. Schneider and I presented reflections on future relations between Anglicans and Jews in the expanded framework of contemporary Jewish-Christian relations.

Both sides considered the meeting to be successful, and we jointly decided that future conferences should be organized to continue our work. A committee made up of the two co-chairmen and the two co-secretaries—of whom I was one—were charged with assuring the continuity of these conferences. Subsequently we organized a second meeting in April 1987 in Stafford. The long illness and death of the Rev. Schneider in November 1982 affected the continuity of these contacts, but they were never broken off.

On the Jewish side Rabbi Norman Solomon, of the Center for the Study of Judaism and Jewish-Christian Relations at Selly Oak College in Birmingham, assured a generally systematic contact with the Anglican leaders. One of our goals was the adoption by the Anglican communion of a text on relations between Anglicans and Jews, such as we had negotiated with other Christian churches and congregations.

The bishops of the World-Wide Anglican Communion met every ten years in the context of a celebrated assembly known as the Lambeth Conference. In 1988 this conference met under the chairmanship of the Archbishop of Canterbury. Resolutions adopted at the Lambeth Conferences did not obligate the member churches, but they did have a great influence.

At the 1987 Singapore meeting of the Anglican Consultative Committee (ACC), which was responsible for preparing the Lambeth Conference the following year, the new secretary-general of the ACC was asked to draft recommendations on Jewish-Christian relations. These were to be based on existing texts in order to submit these to the 1988 Lambeth Conference for discussion and recommendation. The ACC invited Rabbi Solomon to be the Jewish adviser. The activity of the ACC, and later that of an additional committee, finally led to the document "Jews, Christians and Muslims: The Way of Dialogue."

This impressive text on Jewish-Christian relations constitutes the first such stand taken by the Lambeth Conference. In the years to follow the document would serve as a basis for teaching as well as preaching. Here are some of its most important passages, which show the breadth and depth of the new Anglican approach to the Jews:

> Whilst dialogue with all faiths is highly desirable, we recognize a special relationship among Christianity, Judaism and Islam. All three of these religions see themselves in a common relationship to Abraham, the father of the faithful, the friend of God. Moreover these faiths, which at times have been fiercely antagonist to one another, have a particular responsibility for bringing about a fresh, constructive relationship which can contribute to the well-being of the human family, and the peace of the world, particularly in the Middle East. . . .
>
> The essential condition of any true dialogue is a willingness to listen to the partner; to try to see with their eyes and feel with their heart. . . .
>
> In relation to Judaism this means, first of all, recognising that Judaism is still a living religion, to be respected in its own right. . . . Judaism is a living and still developing religion, which has shown spiritual and intellectual vitality throughout the medieval and modern periods despite the history of being maligned and persecuted. The Middle Ages saw great Jewish philosophers such as Maimonides, Bible commentators such as Rashi and the ibn Ezras, poets and mystics such as Moses Ibn Ezra, as well as scientists and interpreters of the law. Our modern world is inconceivable without the contribution of Jewish thinkers from Spinoza to Buber, scientists such as Freud and Einstein, as well as musicians, artists and others who have helped shape our cultural life. . . .
>
> . . . Judaism is not only a religion, as many Christians understand the word, but a people and a civilization. . . .
>
> We now have a far better appreciation than ever before of first-century Judaism, and not least of political factors which led events to take the course they did. The trial and execution of Jesus are now recognised by many scholars to have been brought about to serve the political interests of the Roman occupation forces and those Jews who collaborated with them. . . .
>
> For Christians, Judaism can never be one religion among others. It has a special bond and affinity with Christianity. Jesus, our Lord and the Christ, was a Jew and the Scriptures which informed and guided his life were the

books of the Hebrew Bible. These still form part of the Christian Scriptures. The God in whom Jesus believed, to whom he totally gave himself, and in whom we believe, is "the God of Abraham, Isaac and Jacob." A right understanding of the relationship with Judaism is, therefore, fundamental to Christianity's own self-understanding.

We firmly reject any view of Judaism which sees it as a living fossil, simply superseded by Christianity. . . .

Discrimination and persecution of the Jews led to the "teaching of contempt"; the systematic dissemination of anti-Jewish propaganda by Church leaders, teachers and preachers. . . .

Anti-Jewish prejudice promulgated by leaders of both Church and State has led to persecution, pogrom, and, finally, provided the soil in which the evil weed of Nazism was able to take root and spread its poison. The Nazis were driven by a pagan philosophy, which had as its ultimate aim the destruction of Christianity itself. . . . The systematic extermination of six million Jews and the wiping out of a whole culture must bring about in Christianity a profound and painful reexamination of its relationship with Judaism. In order to combat centuries of anti-Jewish teaching and practice, Christians must develop programmes of teaching, preaching, and common social action which eradicate prejudice and promote dialogue. . . .

[All] these approaches, however, share a common concern to be sensitive to Judaism, to reject all proselytising, that is, aggressive and manipulative attempts to convert, and, of course, any hint of anti-Semitism. Further, Jews, Muslims and Christians have a common mission. They share a mission to the world that God's name may be honoured: "Hallowed be your name." . . .

Genuine sharing requires of Christians that they correct all distorted images of Judaism and Islam, as it requires of Jews and Muslims that they correct distorted images of Christian faith. For Christians this will include careful use and explanation of biblical passages, particularly during Holy Week. . . .

There is also much in the way of common action that Jews, Christians and Muslims can join in; for example: the struggle against racism, apartheid and anti-Semitism; the work for human rights, particularly, the right of people to practise and teach their religion.

The 1988 Lambeth Conference recommended the document for study and encouraged "the Churches of the Anglican Communion to engage in dialogue with Jews and Muslims on the basis of understanding, affirmation and shared understanding illustrated in it [the declaration]."

A third Jewish-Anglican conference was held in April 1992 at Windsor Castle. Seventeen Anglican delegates and an equal number of Jewish representatives came together to discuss the theme "Israel in the Perspective of the Christian Mission." The new Archbishop of Canterbury, George Currie, and the new chief rabbi, Dr. Jonathan Sachs, participated in the meeting, which discussed a draft guideline for future Jewish-Anglican relations, to be submitted by the Council of Anglican Churches of Great Britain and Ireland to their member churches.

The principal objective of this text was not to advance official positions, which had already been done, but to make the new Christian theology concerning Jews and Judaism known to a wider public. Consultation on this text is ongoing and should soon be concluded.*

Among the contacts with various Christian denominational unions, those with the Eastern Orthodox Church were the most difficult. The Orthodox churches were the only branch of Christianity that did not take part in the general process of theological reform and renewal. I believe there is a simple reason for this. Under the Eastern European Communist regimes, which deprived them of all freedom, those churches organized themselves as fortresses under siege; their major concern was to preserve their identity and traditions intact.

In such a defensive atmosphere there was no room to let in fresh air or to align themselves with the modern theological movement that had seized minds in the Western churches and which in particular led to the *aggiornamento* in the Roman Catholic church.

The Middle East constituted the other major center of Orthodoxy. The Arab-Israeli conflict dominated the scene there and prevented any gesture that could be interpreted as favorable to Jews or to Israel. There too, the position of the Eastern Orthodox churches was fixed and defensive with regard to all Western influence.

I nevertheless tried to establish contact with the Orthodox Church, in particular with Msgr. Damaskinos Papandreou, the director of the Orthodox Center of the Ecumenical Patriarchate in Geneva. Msgr. Papandreou at the same time exercised the function of secretary for the Interorthodox Prepara-

---

*By 2001, the Church of England (one of the churches of the Anglican Communion) had published the pamphlet "Sharing Hope?: The Church of England and Christian-Jewish Relations," an internal document disclaiming that it is the final word on these questions, but reporting on areas of both emerging consensus and continuing disagreement within that church, and proposing positive ways forward.—ED.

tory Commission of the Panorthodox Synod. His duties put him in touch with Orthodox churches throughout the world.

Dr. Ernst Ludwig Ehrlich, of the B'nai B'rith, and I had the first discussions with Msgr. Papandreou in 1972. A few years later, in 1976, the WCC official who was responsible for relations with Jews, then Dr. Franz von Hammerstein, established official contact with Msgr. Papandreou.

After an important speech by Msgr. Papandreou in Zurich to the Jewish-Christian Friendship Association of Switzerland, reviewing the theme "On the Claim of Absolute Truth of the Christian and Jewish Religions and the Necessity of Their Dialogue," we began discussions in small groups in November 1976 on preparations for a first formal meeting with the Orthodox churches. The first Panorthodox Preconciliar Conference, which met in November 1976 at the Orthodox Center in Geneva, had in addition expressed the desire of the Greek Orthodox Church to cooperate, in a spirit of mutual understanding, with the various other religions. We saw this as the indispensable condition for putting an end to all fanaticism and thereby contributing to reconciliation among nations and to safeguarding peace and freedom in the world.

The first interreligious conference took place in March 1977 under the auspices of the theological faculty of Lucerne, of which Msgr. Papandreou was a member. The Greek Orthodox clerics insisted a great deal on giving this first gathering an academic character, the principal topic of which was "Law in the Christian-Orthodox and Jewish Conceptions." The Orthodox Center of the Ecumenical Patriarchate and the IJCIC organized the conference, at which ten Jewish and seven Orthodox figures, as well as three Catholic observers and one observer from the WCC participated.

The conference concluded with a decision to initiate a further series of meetings. The texts of this consultation were published in the *Greek Orthodox Theological Review,* which appears in the United States.

The Second Conference was held in Bucharest in October 1979 under the aegis of the Greek Orthodox patriarchate and the chief rabbi of Romania. The Greek Orthodox participants came from Romania, Bulgaria, Greece, Cyprus, Switzerland, and France. The Jewish participants came from Romania, Israel, Greece, Switzerland, France, and the United States. The conference theme was "Tradition and Community in Judaism and in the Greek Orthodox Church."

We continued to pursue these efforts and maintained contacts in Geneva with the Orthodox Center of the Ecumenical Patriarchate. The continuation of the dialogue proved to be extremely difficult for the political reasons already noted.

In the aftermath of the collapse of the Communist regimes and more promising new political developments in the Middle East, I reactivated our efforts and took a series of initiatives to approach the Russian Orthodox church by various routes, with a view to persuading it that the time had come to participate in the dialogue between Greek Orthodox Christianity and Judaism.

These initiatives finally led to the convocation of the third conference between Orthodox Christians and Jews in Athens in March 1993, again organized by the Orthodox Center of the Ecumenical Patriarchate and the IJCIC. It received the active support of the Greek government which, very generously, assumed all the costs of the meeting. The gathering took place in the very beautiful setting of Vouliagmeni, a famous seaside resort near Athens, where the Greek government holds its international conferences. Msgr. Papandreou and I chaired the meeting. Approximately fifty representatives, Greek Orthodox Christians and Jews from a large number of countries including Russia and other countries of Eastern Europe as well as from the Middle East, attended. Virginia Tsouderos, the Greek deputy minister of foreign affairs, welcomed the conference in the name of the Greek government.

A warm message was received from the ecumenical patriarch in Constantinople in which he declared that "Eastern Orthodoxy has never encouraged racist ideas or theories and has never experienced those negative phenomena . . . such as discrimination, marginalization, persecution, and the genocide of those who belonged to another culture or who worshipped God in a different way." And he expressed the hope that the encounter would open the way to fruitful meetings, leading to a dialogue between Judaism and Greek Orthodoxy.

Msgr. Papandreou gave the opening address, introducing the central theme, "Continuity and Renewal." He declared that the objective of the meeting was a sincere collaboration, "not only for purging the prejudices of the historical past, but also for confronting the pressing problems of people of our own time." I responded to this address on behalf of the Jewish delegation.

The theme "Continuity and Renewal" was discussed at four sessions. The first was devoted to "Tradition and Hermeneutics"; the second dealt with "Memory and Responsibility"; the third was devoted to an overall view of "Christian Orthodoxy and Judaism in the Modern World"; and the theme of the fourth was "Fidelity to Roots and Engagements for the Future." A Greek Orthodox delegate and a Jewish representative made presentations on each topic.

We devoted the last session to an evaluation of the meeting, showing the great interest with which all the participants had followed the discussions, and the desire to pursue these conferences in the future. A large number of practical suggestions were made as to how these meetings should be promoted and what topics should be addressed.

The final communiqué emphasized "the positive general evaluation of the meeting as concerns a mutual understanding that condemns the false ideas of racism, antisemitism, and xenophobia, with a view to contributing to interreligious peace." It was unanimously decided that the two sides ought to maintain permanent relations and hold a consultation every three years.

This third meeting with the Greek Orthodox churches constituted a real breakthrough in our relations. It was more representative than the two preceding consultations and gave us the opportunity to raise certain problems that concerned us, in particular the spread of extreme nationalist, xenophobic, and anti-Semitic movements in the countries of Eastern Europe, especially in Russia.

The conference allowed us to emphasize the necessity of an *aggiornamento* in the Orthodox churches as concerned their theology on the Jews and Judaism and the teachings related to it. This was and continues to be a difficult task because of the extreme conservatism of these churches. But listening to the Christian participants, I believe they understood that such an evolution must be initiated, explaining first of all to the faithful how certain sacred texts, certain liturgies and teachings are to be interpreted today. I continue to hope that this will happen before too long.

As a complement to the section on my relations with the Protestant churches, my activities in East Germany (the German Democratic Republic—GDR) were undertaken to a great extent at the request of the authorities of that country's Protestant churches. It all began in Budapest in 1984 at the commemoration of the fortieth anniversary of the deportation of the Jews of Hungary. At one of the official dinners I found myself seated opposite two East German figures whom I discovered with surprise not to be Jews. One taught the Old Testament and Hebrew at the faculty of Protestant theology at Humboldt University in Berlin. The other was a minister in a small city in northern Germany.

Dr. Stefan Schreiner, assistant professor at Humboldt University, was astonishingly well informed on Jewish life of our time. He knew immediately who I was and began to try to convince me to come to East Germany to lecture to a wide variety of audiences.

He emphasized the lack of Jewish partners in East Germany, which made a true dialogue practically impossible. His request surprised me. In general the Jewish leaders of the West were not particularly attracted to the idea of visiting the Communist nations of Europe. We made this kind of trip to sustain the Jewish spirit in the sparsely populated Jewish communities suffering under enormous pressures from their governments. We did it because we felt a sense of solidarity with these communities and never entertained any notion of abandoning them.

I told myself that this same policy could hardly be applied to the little community in East Germany, which probably did not consist of more than five to six hundred registered persons. True, you could probably add another two to three thousand persons of Jewish origin, Communist officials or their descendants who had no connection with the "official" communities.

Thus a trip to East Germany was at the very bottom of my list of priorities. But I had not counted on Dr. Schreiner's persistent energy and perseverance. He simply did not stop trying to persuade me. He was an influential member of the Protestant Church of East Germany (the Federation of Protestant Churches of the German Democratic Republic) and of the organization Aktion Sühnezeichen (Reconciliation Action) devoted to the reparation of Nazi wrongs done to those who had been declared enemies of the Reich, in particular the Jews, the Poles, and so on. Dr. Schreiner sent me a constant stream of messages to encourage me to accept his invitation.

One day in particular he sent me the director of the Evangelical Academy of Berlin-Brandenburg, who invited me to participate in a several-day seminar organized on the occasion of the fortieth anniversary of the end of World War II and dedicated to the commemoration of the Shoah, with the participation of members of the Protestant Church from throughout East Germany.

I was to be the keynote speaker at this seminar, and Dr. Schreiner would speak on theological problems associated with the Shoah, reflecting on them from the Christian and Jewish perspectives. Dr. Schreiner's envoy also transmitted an invitation for me to lecture on the development of Jewish-Christian relations over the last three decades; the audience was to be professors and students of the Department of Theology at Humboldt University.

Faced with this program and in particular with the prospect of being the keynote speaker at the Protestant churches' commemoration of the Shoah, I agreed to make the trip. I knew how few people in East Germany could speak competently of the Shoah.

A bit earlier, in 1982, I had participated in an event in West Berlin. The mayor of West Berlin, Richard von Weizsäcker, who later became president of the Federal Republic of Germany, had invited me to take part in the commemoration of the fortieth anniversary of the Wannsee Conference. On that occasion Dr. Franz von Hammerstein, with whom I had cooperated when he was responsible for Jewish affairs at the WCC in Geneva and who at that time was director of the Evangelical Academy of West Berlin, persuaded me to spend an evening with him and some of his colleagues. I discovered that he had gathered together all the directors of the evangelical seminaries of the Federal Republic. He asked me to give them an overview of my experience of the Shoah and my activities during those fateful years. This was an extraordinary opportunity. I discovered more and more, as the moments passed, that these leaders had a very limited knowledge of the Shoah. I was also aware that few of the people who had experienced the tragedy in its full dimensions were still alive.

Each of my remarks was followed by a host of new questions, and the meeting went on far into the night. At the end they thanked me with a great deal of warmth.

This convinced me that I could not refuse to speak of my unique experience to a new generation, and I then accepted Dr. Schreiner's invitation on two conditions: I asked that the Jewish community of East Germany be fully informed of my visit, and that arrangements be made for a meeting with the secretary of state for religious affairs of the GDR, Klaus Gysi. This was an extraordinary meeting, one to which I shall return.

The Protestant Church of East Germany organized all the lectures that I gave on the occasion of this commemoration at Humboldt University in Berlin, at the great church in Weissensee, as well as the talks I gave at the large theological seminary in Leipzig and in a church in Dresden. These presentations drew considerable audiences and gave me an opportunity to speak about the situation of Jews in the world and the relations between Jews and Christians, to men and women who were deeply rooted in their Christian faith and who were at that time still largely cut off from the world. I was pleased to see that a large proportion of young people were in the audiences. A long series of questions and answers followed each talk, during which the listeners raised all sorts of problems. One discussion went on for more than three hours. I could not but be deeply impressed by this thirst for knowledge of subjects they knew so little about. And frankly, I felt that my replies carried all the more weight for this public by virtue of their coming from the outside world.

I took advantage of this opportunity to establish contact with the central leaders of the Protestant church and to exchange views on the general situation in their country and in the world. I also informed the church hierarchy about the most urgent problems facing the world Jewish community. These visits also allowed me to speak with the leaders of the Jewish community, for whom I represented the interest and solidarity of Western Jews.

The lecture at Humboldt University did not attract a large public. Because it was scheduled in the early afternoon, only professors and students attended. Consequently, at the end of the day when I spoke to a Jewish-Christian Friendship group, in the presence of Dr. Gottfried Forck, the Protestant Bishop of Berlin, several persons excused themselves for not having been able to come in the afternoon and then asked me to repeat everything I had said at the university. This had its amusing side but was also exhausting. Since I didn't have my notes, I had to reconstruct from memory the whole of the lecture I had given early that afternoon.

I spoke at the Protestant theological seminary in Leipzig, which had replaced the old Protestant faculty of theology after the Communist authorities separated the seminary from the university. I arrived very late for this lecture; the driver who brought me from Berlin had only the vaguest idea of the lecture hall's location. When the midday bell sounded I had reached only the middle of my talk, so I then asked whether I ought to continue or stop. I knew how strict the Germans were about schedules, and I hesitated to prolong the session because the room was filled with dozens of people standing. I received the reply in true German student fashion, with a thunder of feet stamping on the floor. Grateful, I then continued for more than an hour. I was extremely moved by this reaction and, to tell the truth, by the passionate interest that my talk aroused.

Since we had no more time to discuss matters with the students, I invited those who were interested to come later to the Jewish community hall to pursue the dialogue. Some of them came, and we talked for two hours.

In Leipzig and Dresden, where I also lectured, in a church-run Jewish-Christian friendship circle, I was very well received by the Protestant leaders who showed me their city, accompanied me to the museum and concert hall, and did everything to make my stay agreeable. Later I remembered the reception of these people with deep emotion. As it turned out, they played important public roles in the dramatic events of 1989–1990.

In order to satisfy my own curiosity as well as indulge my personal nostalgia, I also went to Weimar. It was an extraordinary place, symbolizing the German intellectual life we had all considered a source of inspiration during the period that preceded Nazism. As an expression of his friendship, Professor Schreiner came to Berlin especially to accompany me on that visit. He took me to the Goethe House, the Schiller House, the Nietzsche House, and the art museum located in the castle.

These first contacts with the Protestant Church of East Germany gave rise to a whole series of meetings and a cooperation that continued for several years. After this I traveled to the German Democratic Republic on repeated occasions. During my visits I continued to maintain my contacts with the leaders of the Jewish community, with whom I discussed the acute problems they faced in an officially atheist state.

One occurrence seems to me significant and exemplary. Visiting the new library of the community, I noted that it consisted almost exclusively of novels. This probably corresponded to the level of Jewish knowledge of the librarian. Once back in Geneva I arranged to have shipped to East Berlin several hundred fundamental works on Judaism, which the Jewish community received with gratitude.

I should add that during my first visit to East Germany I also paid a call on the representatives of the Roman Catholic church. The cleric Paul Dissemond, secretary of the Conference of Catholic Bishops of the GDR, was responsible for relations with the government, and he enlightened me about the situation of Catholics in East Germany. We pursued this contact on the occasion of my later visits to East Germany. In particular I requested that the German Catholic community organize programs to understand the Shoah, similar to those that had been undertaken by the Protestant churches. I suggested that he establish relations with the GDR Jewish community and discuss the issue of Jewish-Catholic relations at church meetings.

I also encouraged the cleric to take an interest in the Jewish-Christian dialogue and in how our relations had developed under the aegis of the International Catholic-Jewish Liaison Committee. I urged that the church in the GDR be represented at the international meetings organized by this committee.

Having encountered a great deal of sympathy from this representative of the Catholic church, I encouraged him to pursue his efforts on behalf of the beatification of one of the Catholic martyrs of Nazism, the prelate Bernard Lichtenberg, in commemoration of whom a chapel had been established in Berlin's Hedwigskirche, where he had served as prior. This priest had displayed enormous courage by taking up the defense of Jews for which the Nazis imprisoned him; he died in the course of being transported to a concentration camp. I thought that he was one of the churchmen whose memory should be perpetuated.

After Dissemond reached retirement age, I regularly continued discussions with his successor in his function as secretary of the Conference of Catholic Bishops, Father Josef Michelfeit.

My relationship with Klaus Gysi, the GDR secretary of state for religious affairs, began with a visit when I was accompanied by the president of the Jewish community of Berlin, Dr. Peter Kirchner. I went to see Gysi without an agenda but to establish contact with a relevant government official. I knew that he had a Jewish mother and that during World War II both had sought refuge in France. I was surprised by the ease and speed with which a rapport was established between us. Klaus Gysi had enrolled in the Communist party at the age of thirteen, and I soon understood that he was an idealistic Communist of the old school and that he hated everything Stalinist. I was struck when I asked him one day what he thought of Gorbachev; he replied, "He's a European!"

At the beginning of our conversation, after I had mentioned my Jewish and German origins, I came to my experiences during the 1930s and my activities with the World Jewish Congress. For his part, he told me about his background and career in the GDR.

We discovered that we were about the same age and that both of us had been born in Berlin. While he studied in Frankfurt, I did so in Heidelberg. We had experienced the rise of Nazism and the end of the Weimar Republic with intense emotion. Both of us had been profoundly influenced by these events, about which we had made similar analyses and had reacted in similar ways. This analytical kinship certainly eased the development of our relationship and permitted me to frankly set out for him the problems I had on my mind, including the most politically delicate.

We then moved on to discuss the problems of the small Jewish community in East Germany. Gysi regretted that his country had not been able to educate the younger generation better concerning the positive aspects of Jewish identity. Later in the meeting, I summarized for him the objectives and some of the activities of the WJC, in particular the policy we had consistently advanced with regard to Eastern Europe. This led our conversation to the topic of Soviet policy with regard to Jews and to the scandalous resolution of the United Nations, "Zionism is racism."

I set out clearly the very difficult situation of the Russian and Soviet Jews and our positions and concerns about their fate. I spoke of our contacts with the Soviet Union concerning the right of Jews to emigrate and of our efforts to sensitize world public opinion to the problem. At one point Gysi's assistant noted a project in the GDR to celebrate the two-hundredth anniversary of the birth of the Jewish Enlightenment philosopher Moses Mendelssohn. He asked whether the participation of Jews from abroad could be considered.

My reply was clear: in principle "yes." Of course there were Jews who refused to travel to Germany because of the past, but this had not prevented official visits to the Federal Republic of Germany. But in the case of the GDR there were two factors that might preclude such participation.

First, the GDR had evaded its responsibilities in the matter of indemnification and reparation for Nazi crimes. I said that the GDR behaved as if what had happened in Germany under the Nazis had happened only in the Federal Republic and did not concern East Germany. The responsibility of the GDR in the vital issue of indemnification for persecution and the policy of extermination could not be ignored. Since Western Jews were fully conscious of this policy, this could have negative consequences.

Gysi then interrupted me to affirm, and I quote: "That is no longer true. The GDR no longer refuses to deal with this problem. It is a matter that must be negotiated. We are a small country and we have no money. We must find a solution."

The second obstacle I pointed out to him could come from the political position adopted by East Germany toward Israel. I strongly criticized the East German media's constant attacks on Israel and its policies. I pointed out that the Germans were the last people to have the right to pursue an aggressive policy toward Israel, a policy that also had anti-Jewish overtones.

Klaus Gysi's affirmation that East Germany no longer refused to recognize Jewish claims was a real sensation. I knew very well that the Conference on Jewish Material Claims Against Germany, popularly known as the Claims Conference, had tried to approach East Germany through the United States government and that diplomatic discussions on the subject had been going on for some time. The discussions involved a procedure that would have the United States buy certain goods from East Germany, the profit from which would in part be placed at the disposal of the Claims Conference. An analogous scheme under discussion would compensate American citizens who had suffered from the expropriation of property in the GDR. Negotiations to this end had been going on in secret for quite some time between the two governments. But the East German authorities had never publicly announced they were prepared to satisfy, even if only partially, Jewish claims. Never before had East German authorities made declarations of this kind to representatives of Jewish organizations. Beyond the material compensation, Gysi's statement meant that East Germany now accepted a share of the responsibility for the crimes of Nazi Germany. In the meeting with Gysi I then had a foretaste of a change of attitude that would break with the negative obstinacy of more than forty years.

I was fully up to date as concerned the negotiations and actions that Jewish organizations and in particular the WJC had undertaken to obtain from East Germany a share of the indemnification for Nazi crimes. Our original claim foresaw reparations amounting to $1.5 billion, of which two-thirds was to be paid by West Germany and one-third by East Germany. Before 1984 we had taken numerous steps, in particular through the East German embassy in Switzerland, but without the least echo or response. One day, however, the sum of one million dollars was transferred to me on behalf of the East German government, as if this were an act of charity! We considered this gesture an insult, completely unacceptable. Some days later I myself returned the sum to the sender. And that is where the matter rested.

My conversation with Klaus Gysi about material claims and East Germany opened a new chapter of great importance. I immediately informed my colleagues at the WJC and the Claims Conference in New York.

On the whole I found Gysi surprisingly open. Even on the points on which we disagreed—for example GDR policy toward Israel—it seemed to me that my arguments had some effect. He admitted quite honestly that some of my criticisms were fully justified. I later permitted myself the thought that after my visit Gysi would have telephoned the dean of the faculty of theology at Humboldt University to thank him for having invited me to East Germany. He seemed very satisfied to have found an interlocutor with whom he could discuss the problems and positions of the world Jewish community.

We met again on several occasions, on each of my trips to East Germany and also in Geneva. An important meeting took place on the occasion of an official visit by Gysi as state secretary to various international religious institutions in Geneva, in particular the World Council of Churches.

The program included an official meeting at the office of the World Jewish Congress, which took place on November 22, 1987. During the morning we dealt with problems of mutual interest. After the official meeting we continued our exchange of views during a small lunch we hosted for Gysi and the East German delegation that had accompanied him. For my part, I was invited to a formal dinner at the East German consulate in Geneva. It is also important to note that at his press conference Gysi mentioned his visit to the WJC. In answer to a journalist's question, he confirmed that the GDR did not refuse to participate in reparations to Jews who had been victims of Nazi crimes.

This was the first public, official declaration by a representative of the GDR government on this issue. It was widely reported in the world press and formed an important component of the ongoing negotiations.

My second visit to East Germany took place in November 1985, when the country's Federation of Jewish Communities celebrated the fortieth anniversary of liberation from Nazism. At the same time they were commemorating the forty-seventh anniversary of *Kristallnacht*, the Nazi pogrom against German Jews.

This was the first time that East Germany had invited Jewish figures from the Western world to participate in this kind of commemoration. It was even more exceptional that the floor be given to a foreigner. Hence my surprise when the organizers asked me to speak at the Dresden city hall in the presence of numerous dignitaries, government officials, representatives of the Communist party, the churches, and various mass organizations the party had organized as the National Front in order to manipulate their nonparty members to support of government policies.

Preceded by a religious service at the synagogue, the commemoration ceremony continued with a concert of Jewish religious and folk music in the great hall of the House of Culture, attended by between two and three thousand persons.

The commemoration also permitted me to continue my contacts with Klaus Gysi. In addition the trip gave me an opportunity to meet the Protestant Bishop of Dresden, who was one of the co-presidents of the World Council of Churches.

The leaders of the Protestant church in East Germany were fully satisfied with all the meetings and with all the contacts they had arranged for me. They also invited me to participate in the *Kirchentag*, the great weeklong annual meeting of the Protestant churches of East Germany. This immense gathering took place in July 1987. Participants met simultaneously in ten different churches in East Berlin, each meeting concentrating on a specific theme. On the last day, twenty thousand people attended a rally at one of the city's stadiums.

The panel discussion on Jewish-Christian relations drew the largest audience. In addition to the seven hundred who had registered, a large number of other, particularly younger people followed this debate. Rev. Johannes Hildebrandt, president of the Jewish-Christian friendship movement in Berlin, and Stefan Schreiner, one of the members of the executive committee of the International Council of Jews and Christians, co-chaired the panel discussion.

I was one of the principal speakers on this panel. I had been asked to speak on "Missed Chances for Dialogue Between Jews and Christians Before the Shoah." I also participated in other colloquiums and discussions. On two occasions, for more than two hours, I answered questions, first on theological subjects, then on problems of a political nature.

It seemed to me that my listeners were careful to formulate questions that revealed that they had no confidence in the authorities, the press, or other media. They wished to show their independence of judgment and their defiance of their government leaders.

They asked me all kinds of questions about the Jews in the Soviet Union—remarkable under a Communist regime!—about Jewish-Arab relations, the situation in Israel, and the problem of human rights in general. I tried to reply in a direct and factual way to their questions, without avoiding sensitive issues but without being aggressive. As for the theological questions, it was a matter of affirming a certain number of fundamental truths from the tradition of Judaism. I had the impression that those who asked these questions were not very well informed about Christian theology, let alone Jewish theology.

One of the symposia in which I participated dealt with Jewish postsecondary educational institutions that existed in Berlin before Nazi rule. Having no illusions as to the reestablishment of such teaching and learning in Germany, I concentrated on contemporary aspects, speaking of the education provided today in Jewish academic institutions in Israel and the United States. It seemed more useful to me to make people understand that Nazism had not halted Jewish life and that today there existed intense, vibrant intellectual life in Jewish institutions around the world.

My participation in the *Kirchentag* had been very intense. I believe this was intentional on the part of the leaders of the East German Protestant churches. Normally all problems affecting Jews in that country were passed over in silence; indeed, the government limited itself to harsh and violent verbal attacks against Israeli policies. As if they wished to correct this disinformation, the leaders of the Protestant church sought to inform their followers about the true situation and at the same time make them aware of the seriousness of anti-Jewish policies under the Nazi regime.

It should be noted that all the entry visas for the GDR were obtained for me at the official request of the Protestant churches. The Rev. Helmut Tschoerner generally came to get me in West Berlin in his little car and thus eased my entry. All of this was clear proof of a deliberate will to advance Jewish-Christian relations, and I found a great deal of personal satisfaction in being part of the creation of this broad-based understanding.

During my next visit to East Germany, in September 1987, I participated in a conference organized by the International Council of Christians and Jews in Buckow. This meeting brought ten Israelis and ten Poles to East Germany for the first time. So the gathering was of great importance simply because it was a first. At the end of the conference, Klaus Gysi held a large reception in Berlin for the participants, in the course of which he gave an extremely courageous speech on Jewish-German relations. Unfortunately, for reasons of which I am ignorant and despite a series of efforts on my part, Gysi's remarks were never published.

The visit also gave me an opportunity to pursue my relations with the secretary of state. I became increasingly convinced that one of the most important objectives of my visits to East Germany was to provide some of the political figures of that country with important information to which they otherwise had no access.

For their part, the Protestant churches did not hesitate to continue their relations with us. Thus I was invited to give a series of lectures in April 1988, both at the Department of Theology at Humboldt University and at the equivalent department at Karl-Marx University in Leipzig, to the clergy of the Protestant church in Leipzig, in the churches of Potsdam and Karl-Marx-Stadt (formerly and now again Chemnitz), as well as at the Evangelical Academy of Berlin.

It was then quite clear with what perseverance the Protestant church pursued its work of education and cooperation with us. The public lecture I gave on the topic "From the Night of the Pogrom to the 'Final Solution'" at Humboldt University, and then to various other Protestant audiences, had a considerable impact. Several journals in East and West Germany published the text, and it was later released in several other languages outside Germany.

This series of visits to East Germany culminated with ceremonies in 1988 on the occasion of the fiftieth anniversary of *Kristallnacht*. This time the East German government invited me to take part in the commemoration. The University of Berlin concurrently organized an important symposium for November 9 and 10 under the title "Remember for the Future," in which a number of theologians and historians took part, and I was asked to repeat my lecture "From the 1938 Pogrom to the 'Final Solution.'" This event took place in a large hall in the cathedral.

Shortly before my departure from Geneva, I learned that on the program for the symposium there was also to be a ceremony at Humboldt University in the course of which I was to be given an honorary doctorate of theology. I was informed quite late of this honor, probably because the authorization from senior authorities was slow in coming. It was nevertheless a very formal ceremony, in the course of which the rector and the chairman of the Department of Theology both spoke.

In the numerous audience in the Senate chamber of the university sat a number of eminent figures, including Kurt Loeffler, secretary of state for religious affairs; Gottfried Forck, the Protestant bishop of Berlin; Msgr. Paul Dissemond, the representative of the Catholic church; a large number of clergymen as well as several leaders of the Jewish communities in the GDR and Eastern Europe; and university professors.

The dean, Heinrich Finck, gave the traditional *laudatio* or words of praise, and the rector awarded me the diploma declaring that the degree was being conferred for my "scholarly work in the struggle against anti-Judaism and antisemitism, for the tireless work to save Jews persecuted by Hitler's Fascism and for [my] contribution to the interfaith dialogue and for world peace."

This ceremony at the Humboldt University in Berlin, where I had done a large part of my studies, and the fact of having chosen the date of the commemoration of the great pogrom of 1938 to honor me gave the degree a symbolic significance that went beyond my person. It was finally an act of reparation to German Jewry.

All sorts of other events took place on this same occasion, in particular a formal session at the East German parliament. The government organized a gala concert and gave the president of the Council of State, Erich Honecker, a reception. The reception was also a formal event and the source of a special experience for me.

At the moment I left the university, a representative of the state secretary for religious affairs approached me to ask whether I would accept the decoration that would be given to me the next day in the course of Honecker's formal reception. I had never heard of this plan. When I learned that Rabbi Alexander Schindler, vice president of the WJC, was also on the list of recipients, I decided it was necessary for us to agree on the attitude to be taken.

To tell the truth, I was not very keen on receiving a decoration from the German Communist government. We had to reflect on how we should react. We could not completely ignore that the commemoration of the fiftieth anniversary of the pogrom, to which Jewish figures from around the world had been invited, signaled a certain relaxation by the government in its attitude toward Jews.

So I went to the hotel where Rabbi Schindler was to host an official dinner for a delegation of Reform Jewish communities from the United States. There I learned that Schindler had fallen ill at the last minute and had not come to Berlin. At the same time I was informed that Edgar Bronfman, president of the WJC, who had been in the GDR a few weeks earlier, had received the same decoration from Erich Honecker. So I considered that if the president of the WJC had accepted, I could also do so. And I so informed the state secretary, who was at the hotel to attend the banquet.

A bit later that evening I learned that other persons were also to receive this decoration, among whom was an Eastern European Jewish community leader who had a poor political reputation and with whom I wished to have nothing in common. I also discovered that yet another figure from one of these communities, whom I did not think to be quite on my level, was also on the list.

Since the secretary of state had already left the hotel, I shared my objections with his assistant with a view to having them passed along to his superior. I added that he should not make this a matter of concern; since Mr. Bronfman had accepted the decoration, the WJC had already been well served. After that I returned to my lodgings.

The next morning I went to the palace of the president of the Council of State. Arriving a quarter of an hour before the opening of the ceremony, I spotted the secretary of state walking like a tiger in a cage in the entry hall of the building. He immediately came up and told me that I had played a fine trick on him the night before. I retorted that there were things I could not accept. He at once assured me that it had never been their intention to decorate the Jewish leader about whom I had raised objections, and that the other person would receive a much more modest decoration. This sudden turnaround amused me a good deal, and I replied smiling, "Then everything is just fine," and with that we parted.

All the same, it was an extraordinary experience to see that even under a Communist regime you could defend your honor and not accept everything that officials tried to impose. I am not particularly proud of the decoration I finally received, but I'm not unhappy to have succeeded in setting my own conditions for it.

I believe that my testimony on these events is quite important. After the collapse of the Communist regime in East Germany, and in the obsessive effort to identify the guilty parties, people often talk of the role of the Protestant church in the GDR and always emphasize the negative aspects. People disclose its relationship with the Stasi, the secret police, omitting to mention that without the church they could never have obtained any favors or any attenuation of the injustices that had been committed. It is rather easy to forget that the Protestant church was the only opposition that dared to stand up to state authorities and that its actions contributed greatly to the radical changes that occurred in that country.

In retrospect one can understand that the policy pursued by the churches toward the Jews was part of this principled stand and was in clear opposition to the GDR government's anti-Israel policy. The creation of Jewish-Christian friendship groups, with the participation of eminent clergymen such as Johannes Hildebrandt, Siegfried Theodor Arndt, and superintendent Friedrich Margerius, was a courageous defiance of the authorities. I quickly understood the meaning of the actions undertaken by these groups, even though we never discussed it.

[FIVE]

Working for
North African Jewry

UNTIL THE CONCLUSION of World War I, the Jewish world was wholly concerned with the grievous problem of the Jews of Central Europe, with their often desperate struggle for equal rights and their battles against poverty. There followed the terrifying confrontation with Nazi Germany and the struggle for the consolidation of a national homeland in British-mandate Palestine.

These matters represented the major preoccupation of Jewry. They monopolized our thoughts and pushed out other concerns. Perhaps only the terrible pogrom of early August 1934 in Constantine, Algeria, during which Muslim rioters killed twenty-five Jews and wounded many more, recalled North African Jewry to our minds.

After the loss of six million Jews, we began to rediscover some of the surviving communities, especially those throughout the Maghreb; these constituted a population of more than a half-million persons. This rediscovery led the WJC to undertake a series of political actions designed to protect the large Jewish communities in Morocco, Tunisia, and Algeria. In the face of the profound political transformation that was under way, but which all parties were far from anticipating, the WJC was resolved to follow political developments closely and assist those communities to meet the difficulties they would face. With this objective in mind, in 1949 we created the WJC North African bureau in Algiers under the competent direction of Jacques Lazarus. I was directly and deeply involved in this new task.

The world conflict from which we emerged raised far-reaching challenges to received opinion and prompted fresh reflection. Decolonization was at the heart of postwar political developments. At that time we asked ourselves a number of basic questions: Was the political situation in the Maghreb countries inexorably destined to change? Did anything justify our assuming that these changes would occur without disruption? And over what period of time? Faced with questions of this kind on the eve of the decisive turning point in this region, we convoked the WJC's first North African Congress in June 1952 in Algiers. Its purpose was to review the situation of the Tunisian, Moroccan, and Algerian communities. What was to be their likely evolution? Initially it was a matter of being in a position to prepare their leadership for inevitable change.

In a general way we noted that the measures undertaken by France to check the nationalist movements in its African colonies had only increased their intensity, and that the government had scarcely sought to promote compromise solutions. At this time the populations of North Africa felt strongly encouraged in their anti-colonial attitude by the independence that had recently been won by countries in the Middle East. Our task was then to make the Jewish communities, beginning with their leaders, familiar with the idea of not considering the status quo as fixed and immutable.

At the Algiers conference we were struck by the fact that most community leaders seemed wrapped in a feeling of security, far from imagining the profound changes that would threaten their way of life. Even though we were not able to determine the timing of these changes, we had to recognize that sooner or later they would be upon us, especially since we saw no reason why that part of the world should escape developments already evident in other regions, regions moreover that were relatively close at hand.

Our concrete action began in January 1954 with the visit of two political directors of the WJC to the Jewish communities in Morocco and Tunisia, visits in the course of which a considerable number of contacts were made in the most diverse circles.

It quickly became apparent that the situation in Tunisia, with only a moderate nationalist movement, was not serious, but that the situation was quite different in Morocco, where the nationalist movement had adopted an activist, hard-line course and where a certain number of anti-Jewish incidents had already occurred, creating a sharp sense of unease among broad segments of the Jewish population. In particular the WJC envoys noted the presence of a sense of fear that immediately found expression in a desire to emigrate. They then appealed for contacts to be established with the nationalist movements, contacts about which we thought it prudent to inform the French authorities.

The WJC had only a single option: either the Jewish populations should leave, or they should negotiate with the revolutionary movements in sufficient time that they could reach an understanding in order to preclude attacks.

Finally, the situation called for an informal cooperation with other affected Jewish parties, specifically the State of Israel and the Jewish Agency.

This policy, long the object of discussion, was approved by the WJC coordinating committee in the summer of 1954. Indeed, we were anxious to assure the North African communities of a transition that was as harmonious as possible through a period of history that so profoundly affected us all. The WJC was the only Jewish organization that foresaw the unfolding of potentially destructive political events in this region. We had no choice but to draw the appropriate dire conclusions. Other Jewish organizations, in France and the United States, openly and unreservedly supported the French government. With strong links to the French government at this time, Israeli authorities shared the same views.

Under these circumstances, it was all the more important to approach the French government and to make our views known.

In 1954 WJC president Nahum Goldmann met in Paris with the president of the French National Council, Pierre Mendès-France, to present him with WJC policy regarding North Africa. Mendès-France assured Goldmann that, in all future negotiations concerning the territories of North Africa, his government would take into account the particular situation and the rights of Jews and other minorities. This was the first of a series of meetings with French government officials, in the course of which we informed them of our position on the Jewish communities of the Maghreb. We noted that the WJC took responsibility for the future of these communities and that under prevailing circumstances we believed we had to make direct contact with the nationalist movements in these countries with a view to assuring the Jews' safety, status, and right to emigrate. We explained that such a stand was not in the least to be interpreted as hostile to France, for which we had feelings of profound respect and friendship.

We made a commitment to French authorities to keep them informed of our contacts and discussions with North African nationalist circles. In the years that followed, this attitude won us a great deal of understanding among senior officials of the French government with whom we had numerous meetings, especially with the successive ministers of Moroccan and Tunisian affairs, Christian Fouché, Pierre July, and Alain Savary, as well as with Jean Basdevant, responsible for these matters at the Ministry of Foreign Affairs. In fact they encouraged us to pursue these relations.

Tunisia

WJC relations with Tunisia were influenced to a great extent by the meeting of the WJC political director in London, A. L. Easterman, and the leader of the Neo-Destour movement (and future head of state), Habib Bourguiba. This memorable meeting took place in August 1954 in the Ferté-Montargis fortress, where Habib Bourguiba was interned. Easterman had been introduced to him by the internationally known Jewish British journalist John Kimche. In this interview, the Neo-Destour leader gave the WJC detailed assurances on the future political structure of the Tunisian state, a structure that guaranteed Tunisian Jews equality of all civic and political rights, including the right to emigrate to Israel.

Habib Bourguiba was at pains to explain to Easterman frankly and courageously that his country's support for the Arab League should in no way be interpreted as an automatic acceptance of the League's policies, in particular with regard to Israel. The interview with Bourguiba was the beginning of a relationship that lasted unbroken for many years.

The future Tunisian president was deeply moved that the Jewish official had sought him out in prison, and he never forgot this gesture. Remaining accessible to Easterman, Bourguiba drew his son, who would become minister of foreign affairs, into the relationship. This link was a decisive element of the good relations that the Tunisian authorities have always had with the WJC.

At the same time we closely followed the negotiations of the French and Tunisian governments on the convention that was intended to set the framework for their future relations. We remained in close contact with the Jewish community and were happy to learn that an eminent Jewish figure was included as an expert in the Tunisian delegation. This was the lawyer Albert Bessis, whom I knew well from earlier visits to the Tunisian community. I had the satisfaction of personally turning over to him a number of legal documents dealing with the protection of human rights. These texts, some drafted at the time of the League of Nations, others stemming from the United Nations, were most valuable to him in his work.

In addition, in November 1954 we had submitted to Christian Fouché, the French minister for Tunisian and Moroccan affairs, a memorandum in which the WJC formulated a series of suggestions for clauses to be inserted in the Franco-Tunisian convention. For their part the Tunisian Jewish communities addressed a memorandum on the same subject to the government in Tunis, an act both constructive and courageous. This example is evidence of the co-ordination in our efforts; it was of the greatest importance for us, and it functioned correctly. Indeed, the convention drafters included our suggestions in the text. Thus in the clause to Article 5, Tunisia recognizes "for all those who reside in its territory the enjoyment of the rights and guarantees of the individual as set out in the Universal Declaration of Human Rights."

In addition, Tunisia committed itself "to guarantee in conformity with its traditions complete equality among its citizens, whatever their origin or religious faith, in particular as concerns the enjoyment, in law and in fact, of civic rights, individual liberty and public, religious, professional or social freedom, and the collective rights generally recognized in modern states."

All the promises of President Bourguiba and the texts of the convention were scrupulously respected. The friendly relations between President Bourguiba and the World Jewish Congress continued for years in mutual confidence and amity.

Morocco

In the course of the years that followed, the attention of the WJC was increasingly drawn to the deterioration of the situation in Morocco, where surging nationalist movements made it ever more urgent to save the rights and freedoms of Moroccan Jews. And we anxiously followed the growing tension between these movements and the French authorities.

In order better to analyze the situation, the WJC engaged a young Israeli, Joseph Golan, who was descended from a family of Zionist officials. Born in Syria, he was profoundly interested in the Arab nationalist movements, spoke fluent Arabic, and had to the highest degree the gift of opening doors and establishing human relations under difficult conditions. Consequently the WJC gave him the mission of establishing first contacts with the principal nationalist circles in Morocco, the Istiqlal party and the Independent Democratic party (PDI). We thus gained access to their leaders and later to other officers in the independence movements. Joseph Golan did not lack charm—and he used it to good effect in making contacts—and he knew how to bluff, which helped him in his task but scarcely endeared him to my colleagues, the political directors. In his various activities he successively had as his base Paris, Geneva, and Rome.

The WJC executive met in January 1955 at UNESCO headquarters in Paris in order to review the principal political problems of the day. The press reported on certain observations in Alec Easterman's review of the situation in North Africa; in those comments he interspersed some critical remarks about Morocco. As a result, the leaders of the Istiqlal and PDI solicited a meeting with WJC political leaders. I participated in this first direct contact between Moroccan nationalist leaders and representatives of an international Jewish organization that contained Moroccan Jews. The Moroccans expressed their dissatisfaction that the Moroccan Jewish community had never supported them in their nationalist independence movement. We made no commitment on that specific problem, but we noted our anxiety about the security of Jews in an Arab country, emphasizing the tragic experience of Jews in Iraq, Syria, Egypt, and Libya.

In response to these serious concerns, the Moroccans stressed the democratic character of their movement, the fundamental concepts of which were the freedom and equality of all citizens whatever their origins or their religion. The fact remained, however, that advances made by the independence movement meant that ensuring the rights and freedoms of Jews had become an urgent matter for us; all the more so, it should be recalled, because of the increasingly strained relations between Moroccan nationalists and French authorities.

This first meeting with the Moroccan independence leaders took place in a cordial atmosphere, despite criticisms raised by both sides, and we followed it with a series of individual meetings with nationalist leaders. Yet the situation further deteriorated and tension continually mounted.

In this climate the Moroccan nationalists delivered an ultimatum to the French, setting August 20, 1956, as the final date for the removal of the pro-French Sultan Moulay Ben Arafa and the nomination of a Council of Throne Guardians, while awaiting the return of Sultan Mohammed Ben Youssef as King Mohammed V and the installation of a Moroccan government.

While the situation continued to worsen, France nominated Gilbert Grandval as resident general and formulated a plan that foresaw the removal of the sultan then in office, and the establishment of a ruling council and a Moroccan government. Extremely vehement opposition immediately came from French colonists and the powerful right-wing party in Paris. Under these circumstances the date of August 20 was considered the deadline for the acceptance of the so-called Grandval Plan by the French government. The prospect of a huge wave of terrorism rising in Morocco carried the grave danger that Jews might be among its victims.

I traveled to Morocco in the course of the summer to see with my own eyes the enormous tension that had developed between the French and the Moroccan nationalists. One could not ignore the machine-gun-armed French soldiers deployed everywhere on the roofs in Casablanca. I could feel the enveloping nervousness in every fiber of my being, an anxiety capable of provoking explosive acts. I was obsessed with the idea of what might happen in the event of some thoughtless action by a group of Moroccan nationalists who might head in the direction of the Mellah, the old Jewish quarter. The consequences could be catastrophic.

We then decided with all urgency to schedule fresh consultations with the nationalist leaders, and we arranged a luncheon meeting for September 9 in a private room of a large Paris restaurant. The Moroccan side consisted of Si Bekkai, the former pasha of Sefrou, former soldier, and seriously disabled veteran; and two other figures from the independence movement, Abderahman Bouabid, one of the principal leaders of the Istiqlal party and future head of the Moroccan left, and M. Boucetta, secretary-general of the Committee for Moroccan Independence. A. L. Easterman, Dr. Maurice Perlzweig, Armand Kaplan from the Paris bureau, Joseph Golan, and I represented the WJC.

Our principal demand was that our dialogue partners instruct the leaders of the nationalist movements that the physical security of the Jewish population be respected and that their integrity be preserved. The discussion limped laboriously on, going around in circles, and finally bogged down. Those across the table were clearly not prepared for such a request. In order to raise the discussion out of the morass, I made an emotional appeal to Bouabid, who was sitting next to me and whom I knew, and for whom I moreover had a keen appreciation. I said to him in an aside, "For the honor of your struggle, I implore you not to risk fouling your great cause by spilling innocent blood. . . . You will profoundly regret it later." After a few moments of intense reflection, Bouabid turned to Si Bekkai, who was chairing the Moroccan delegation, and simply said, "I believe that we can promise that." Boucetta immediately sided with this stand, to which a clearly impressed Si Bekkai agreed.

We were satisfied with the turn that the discussion had taken, in the course of which we had dealt with our claims for the status of Jews in an independent Morocco. On this occasion, our Moroccan partners announced their desire, and the intention of the nationalist movement, to appoint a Jew to a ministerial position in the future government.

The Moroccan delegation kept their word and communicated the content of our deliberations to the heads of the independence movement. After that, one week later, on August 15, Ahmed Bellafrej, secretary general of the Istiqlal party, issued a lengthy statement in New York. It included this passage in particular:

The fear that Jews might suffer any kind of discrimination in a free Morocco is in no way justified. Moroccan Jews will, *de facto* and *de jure*, be citizens equal to Muslims. They will enjoy the same rights and will have the same responsibilities. Their religious freedom will not be affected. The greatest service that can be rendered Moroccan Jews is to give them our assistance. Morocco is their country, its liberty is their liberty. Anyone who helps Moroccan Jews helps Moroccan independence.

At the same time nationalist leaders issued strict orders to the troops of the liberation movement to respect the Jewish population of the country.

On my various missions to Morocco I noted that the great mass of Moroccan Jews lived completely apart from Moroccans generally and, with rare exceptions, were entirely ignorant of the political movements and parties of the country. It was paradoxical that it fell to me, a foreigner, to explain to them the aspirations of the different political movements. This I did on repeated occasions within the Moroccan section of the WJC. It also proved necessary for me to allay the fears of one group or another and instill them with courage in the face of political uncertainties. The civic sense had been neglected in their education.

We were in fact very well informed about the political spectrum. We had met most of the leaders—including Si Bekkai, Alfassi, Bellafrej, Bouabid, Ben Barka, Benjelloun, Ouazzani, Boucetta, Ben Souda, and others, and, introduced by Joe Golan, we had conducted lengthy conversations with them.

A wave of terrorism broke out on August 20 resulting in many deaths. Although Jews did not succeed in escaping the general upheaval, only a small number of them died, and they were not targeted as such. The immediate result of the tragic events of August 20 was the Aix-les-Bains conference between the French government and the leaders of the Moroccan independence movement. A WJC delegation made up of Alec Easterman and the French deputy, Pierre Dreyfus-Schmidt, chairman of the political commission of the WJC French Section, also attended, as did a delegation from the Moroccan Jewish community. We used the occasion for numerous fruitful discussions with the Moroccan leaders.

These consultations led to an agreement that bore on the principal problems foreseen by Jews in Morocco: full civic equality, rejection of minority status, guarantees for the protection of rights, and in particular an obligation on the part of future governments to respect the universal declaration of human rights. The agreement specifically mentioned the right to emigrate with personal property.

The stand taken by the WJC, in particular that it was in no way opposed to the vision of Moroccan independence, greatly impressed the Moroccan delegation. But not all Jewish circles appreciated our position on Moroccan political aspirations. The president of the Universal Israelite Alliance of France, René Cassin, even called us on the carpet and asked us to defend and justify our position. I have not forgotten the tense atmosphere that Easterman and I confronted. Obviously we could not mention that we had kept the French government informed of our activities, and this made the meeting even more difficult. Much later, when Moroccan matters were well behind us, Jules Braunschvig, who directed the activities of the Alliance in Morocco, admitted to me one day in a private conversation that we had judged the situation better than they, and that he now understood the stand we had taken.

Shortly after Aix-les-Bains, the Throne Council was established and Si Bekkai became a prominent member of it. In this capacity he went to Madagascar to inform Sultan Ben Youssef of the complex of recent political developments. The sultan accepted the program of the nationalists, including the agreement they had just concluded with us. And he expressed a desire to meet us as soon as he arrived in France on his way to Morocco.

During a temporary stay in Saint-Germain-en-Laye, the sultan received Easterman, me, and Golan as WJC representatives. Crown Prince Hassan, later the king of Morocco, acted as official interpreter.

The first independent government established in Rabat in 1956 cordially invited us to meet its leaders in the course of a reception given at the Salé palace. Si Bekkai, now the prime minister, received us warmly surrounded by his colleagues and numerous collaborators, many of whom we already knew.

It is also important to recall that, in its declaration to the Moroccan people, the Council of Throne Guardians had insisted on the absolute equality of all citizens, Muslim and Jewish, a theme that was taken up again in the first address made by the ruler to his people after his return to the country. Two proclamations affirmed the intention of the kingdom to respect the Universal Declaration of Human Rights. The Moroccan government would scrupulously meet its commitment to consider its Jewish nationals free citizens, fully equal under the law.

Six months after the establishment of the new state, when Jewish emigration seemed to be progressing normally, a delicate situation arose as a result of emigration to Israel. On May 13 the national security authorities, on the order of the Ministry of the Interior, suspended departures. Certain improprieties had occurred on the local level, and applicants to emigrate had been interned in a camp in Mazagam, near Casablanca. Over the months that followed, the internees finally numbered some eight thousand persons.

Given the numerous discussions between the WJC and the nationalist Moroccan leaders on freedom of movement, the WJC assumed the task of initiating discussions with the government in Rabat to have the injunction lifted. This intervention, long and difficult as it proved to be, Easterman and I continued with various government leaders on several trips to Rabat. Finally the Moroccan authorities authorized the departure of the internees. They never challenged the principle of emigration but were opposed to organized collective departures.

The multiple difficulties were essentially the result of the often negative attitude of subordinate authorities. I believe it was finally thanks to the inventive spirit of those who were dealing with the problem from the Zionist side, and to the spirit of tolerance of Moroccan authorities, that emigration to Israel was continued. I am personally convinced that the Moroccan authorities, who had been involved in discussions with us from before independence, closed their eyes to this emigration, which turned out to be substantial. This, I believe, offers certain proof of goodwill, which did not always make the situation an easy one for the government in the face of events in the Middle East and of the reaction of Arab public opinion. In general, however, relations with successive Moroccan governments continued to be correct and open, despite the fluctuating, often tense political climate.

On balance our Moroccan policy was quite satisfactory. The evidence of mass emigration without profound upheaval, without any apparent friction (the example above being exceptional), and without victims constituted an unquestionable success. The understanding, even friendly attitude and flexibility of the sultan and Moroccan authorities toward the Jews, often displayed with regard to Israel, were important milestones in our political activity. The small remaining Moroccan Jewish community has for many years taken part in the deliberations of the WJC.

Algeria

Algeria posed for us by far the most complicated problem in the Maghreb region. Some 120,000 Jews, all French citizens by virtue of the famous Crémieux Decree that dated from 1870, lived in Algeria. This law, which clearly benefited the entire Jewish community, did not sit well with the Arab population. The Arabs did not hide their resentment in the face of a situation they judged to be unjust and a status they envied. The Algerian Jews totally identified with the French cause and openly and strongly supported the maintenance of French power. Israel, which was then profiting from French support, shared this attitude.

But who could know whether the Algerian nationalist movement would fail or succeed in its objectives? If successful, would the Algerian partisans not be tempted to take revenge on the Jews who so clearly espoused the French cause?

Given this situation, we believed it our duty to prepare the Jewish community for whatever developments might occur. To the extent possible, the Jews had to be helped to escape the turmoil and especially the possible violence. These political conditions obliged us to promote emigration to Israel as an elementary precaution, and to inform the French authorities of our position. It was obvious they would hardly appreciate an emigration movement that would contribute to a diminution of the French presence in Algeria. It was our task to convince the French government not to oppose an emigration that in no way constituted hostile behavior toward France. As a further precaution, we had to establish contact with the Algerian revolutionary movement, incarnated in the the National Liberation Front (FLN). The WJC leadership entrusted this delicate task to Joseph Golan. Prudence was required because of the consequences any intervention might have for the Jewish community.

We were later able to meet some of the FLN leaders on the occasion of the Mediterranean colloquia on culture. These conferences were organized by Giorgio la Pira, the mayor of Florence and a deeply respected visionary with whom we collaborated closely within the framework of these gatherings.

In early 1961, when the situation in Algeria had reached a critical phase, a WJC delegation went to Algiers, Oran, and Constantine. The principal source of anxiety in the Jewish community was the question of whether French citizenship might be jeopardized.

From the French side, the WJC received a formal assurance of the right of Algerian Jews to retain their French nationality. From the FLN we received no assurance or formal commitment. The public statements of its spokesmen contradicted each other. The Évian cease-fire agreements of March 1962, reached between France and the FLN, did include arrangements intended to protect and guarantee the rights and freedoms of the French citizens of Algeria who could either retain their French citizenship or become full citizens of an independent Algeria. But the prospect of Jewish life in a Muslim state that stood close to the Arab League could only be filled with uncertainties: a climate little suited for confidence in an independent Algeria and in the guarantees specified in the treaty. In this atmosphere, dominated by feelings of insecurity and fear, the Jews en masse joined virtually all non-Jewish French citizens in an exodus to metropolitan France. So ended the rich and vital history of Algerian Jewry.

[SIX]

Other International Activities

IN INTERNATIONAL LIFE since the end of the nineteenth century, voluntary associations have exerted an ever more effective force in influencing governmental decisions that affect their areas of activity. These voluntary movements—all quite independently—serve the most diverse causes: philanthropic, peace-seeking, religious, cultural, educational, scientific, social (we have only to think of the world of labor), and their concerns have been taken more and more seriously by political leaders. These movements, to which those in power are far from indifferent, have a considerable history. A good number of them were already active at the time of the League of Nations and during the disarmament conferences of the 1920s and 1930s. In fact these movements constituted a direct expression of universal public opinion and played a dynamic role in relation to the governments of countries that too often pursued a policy of status quo in international affairs.

Only after World War II did this fact win official recognition when the United Nations charter created consultative status for these organizations. Article 71 of the charter envisages consultation for such organizations in the economic and social spheres, a status that is exercised within the Economic and Social Council and agencies under its authority. In my capacity as WJC representative to the United Nations for some forty years, I maintained close relations with a number of these groups. During these years I envisioned the possibility of enlarging the consultative status of the nongovernmental organizations (NGOs) and of influencing broad segments of society to appreciate our problems.

The WJC was the first Jewish organization to be granted consultative status with the Economic and Social Council. I quickly became aware that to perform a useful function within the particular framework of the UN, rules that favored such action would be required. Thus from the very outset I attentively followed all the discussions that concerned the rules on consultative status and participated in the debates to develop and reinforce them to the greatest extent possible. My goal was to amplify the contribution of the NGOs and enhance their effectiveness.

The first conference of NGOs with consultative status was held in 1948 in Geneva. It gathered all those NGOs that wished to create a base for permanent cooperation, in particular with the goal of obtaining representation on the NGO Committee of the UN Economic and Social Council. Along with my colleagues Easterman and Perlzweig, I represented the WJC on this occasion and took a considerable part in the debate. The WJC was then elected as a member of the permanent committee of the conference. I regularly participated in the meetings of this committee held in New York and Geneva.

At that first conference of NGOs we discussed, among other matters, their international legal status. The NGOs could acquire legal status only in a given country according to the laws of that country. The NGOs consequently became national organizations in legal terms, a status that did not take into account their specifically international character or the particular needs this entailed. In order to resolve this exceptionally complex problem, the NGO conference created a special study committee and appointed me as its secretary. Thus for many years I was concerned with the legal quandary that then existed. This situation lasted until the 1980s when my colleague Daniel Lack finally succeeded in resolving the matter by means of an international convention signed within the framework of the Council of Europe. The 1986 convention took effect with ratification by several member states and was also open to countries that were not members of the Council of Europe.

The principal task of the special committee was to monitor the application of the rules of this convention, which provided for an NGO with consultative status to have the right to participate in meetings (with reserved seats); to receive all the documentation relative to the meeting; to have the right to present written statements regarding the matters on the agenda to be translated and distributed to all participants; and, with the permission of the chair, to have the right to intervene orally in the debate. Some privileged organizations (classified in category A) could even propose items for the agenda.

I worked intensively on the special committee, making it my special concern that the application of consultative status in no way checked the organizations' freedom of expression. I also supported efforts aimed at preventing any arbitrary decisions by the NGO council concerning admission to and the preservation of consultative status. This was the period of the Cold War, whose influence the United Nations could not escape. Under these circumstances and throughout the inevitable tensions, I always maintained a firm line, defending the independence of all the NGOs and in particular their right to express themselves freely—including the right to criticize the actions of governments. It was thus not surprising that I became one of the specialists on the rules of consultative status, constantly called on to clarify, guarantee, and expand them. In 1951 I was appointed deputy secretary-general of the conference committee in Geneva; the secretariat had its seat in New York. Then, in 1953 I was unanimously elected president of the conference, a position I took up in 1955.

I took this task very much to heart and I was pleased to note that my authority was respected by everyone. One aspect of this function has stayed in my memory: the UN had convened a conference of consulting NGOs on the problem of discrimination. Very much at home in this sphere and feeling that as president of the NGOs I was fully responsible for the success of the conference, I wanted to give it some prominence. With this in mind I tried to persuade the various organizations to be present not only via their permanent representatives but also in the persons of their leaders. Drawing in several organizations with the most varied interests, I formed a group to prepare a text that would serve as a basis for discussion. And I persuaded Vincent Auriol, the former president of the French Republic and honorary president of the French Federation of Former Servicemen, to chair the conference. This he did with both authority and good nature. The presence of the former French president among us had the desired considerable effect. It fully guaranteed the success of the conference.

When my term as president expired, I was elected and then reelected treasurer of the conference, thus continuing my activities on the committee for almost thirty years. My colleagues in the WJC secretariat assisted me in the technical aspects of the treasurer's work. The position gave me the opportunity to follow closely the policies of the NGO conference and to suggest many ideas for consideration.

In this spirit I successfully supported efforts aimed at extending consultative status to other organizations of the United Nations as well as to international conferences that it convened. On the other hand there was never any follow-up to our request to expand the NGO consultative status at the General Assembly of the UN.

Within the framework of the NGO conference we formed specialized groups in certain sectors, in particular those of refugees, human rights, and the environment. This stimulated a constructive collaboration among NGOs that faced similar problems while leaving them the advantage of full independence. At important UN conferences, the NGOs created forums on the same topics as were being dealt with, thus exerting a kind of influence on the conferences themselves.

As a specialist on consultative status, I established direct contact with the secretaries general of the United Nations. From time to time they would receive a delegation from the committee of the NGO conference in order to discuss the position of the NGOs within the framework of the UN as well as other topical matters. As I was generally a member of these delegations, I had the personal opportunity to deal with Dag Hammarskjöld, U Thant, Kurt Waldheim, and Javier Perez de Cuellar.

But my role was not limited to strengthening the position and increasing the weight of the NGOs at the UN. It also extended to other institutions in the UN family. Thus, along with the secretary-general of the Federation of Associations for the United Nations, John Ennals, I was a chief protagonist in the creation of consultative status for NGOs at UNESCO, where for the 1956–1958 term I served as president of the UNESCO NGOs.

At the General Assembly of the UN in 1950 I served as the NGO spokesman in our effort to extend such a status to UNICEF. Later I participated in efforts to create consultative status with the International Labor Organization (ILO). Other NGOs expressed interest in certain aspects of the activities of the ILO, and we judged that henceforth they too deserved to be heard. As a consequence, the ILO adopted the notion of consultative status.

All this activity on behalf of the NGOs put me in touch with the representatives of numerous governments. It was not surprising that when I organized the fifth plenary assembly of the WJC in Brussels in 1966, no fewer than twenty-eight governments and eighteen international NGOs were represented. When the NGO Conference celebrated the fortieth anniversary of the UN, three representatives—from the UN secretariat, the member states, and the NGOs with consultative status—were asked to present a review of that period. I was charged with doing this on behalf of the NGO community, an astonishing fact when one remembers the despicable way in which Israel was then being treated in international circles.

In the 1970s, when the NGOs created a special committee for humanitarian questions (on the occasion of the conferences that led to the additional protocols to the Geneva Conventions), I was invited to chair a working group, whose conclusions were approved by some fifty international NGOs of diverse natures and ideologies.

On the whole, my activities in connection with nongovernmental organizations have made the World Jewish Congress known as an organization that is permanent, highly competent, and open-minded.

Cultural Foreign Policy

Of all the organizations in the UN family, the United Nations Educational, Scientific and Cultural Organization (UNESCO) presented a particular challenge for us. We clearly agreed in full with UNESCO philosophy, which found its finest expression in the famous sentence in its charter inspired by Léon Blum: "Since wars begin in the minds of men, it is in the minds of men that the defense of peace must be constructed." But it was not only a question of struggling for peace and of preparing minds for this task; UNESCO also sought to assure every person access to education, to guarantee the right to take part in a free cultural life, to enjoy the arts, and to participate in scientific progress and in the benefits that result from it. UNESCO thus offered an instrument to which all peoples could contribute freely and in a spirit of competitive generosity their own cultural riches, for the common good of humanity.

Aaron Steinberg, who directed the cultural department of the WJC for several decades, originated the idea of employing UNESCO as the vehicle for implementing a cultural foreign policy for the Jewish people, not only to represent their immediate political interests but especially to stand for Jewish civilization in a peaceful rivalry with all the cultures of the world. Steinberg participated on the WJC's behalf in the foundation of UNESCO in London in 1946 and followed its evolution closely for years thereafter, a mission I shared with him. From this long collaboration I arrived at a keen admiration for this man as well as a deep and long-lasting friendship.

Aaron Steinberg had an extraordinarily attractive personality due in large part to his breadth of intellectual vision. Descended from a great Russian Jewish family, he was a man graced with a universalist vision in the true tradition of humanism. Steinberg was a philosopher, historian, jurist, sociologist, writer, and artist. In particular he was a philosopher of history—of what history means and what it can signify, what history can teach and where it can lead us. Thus he passionately questioned the meaning of history and struggled with his reflections all his life.

A true scholar and great thinker, his superior and always alert intelligence did not prevent him from having his two feet planted firmly on the ground. As a man of action, he had remarkable practical sense, which he clearly demonstrated.

Aside from Nahum Goldmann, Aaron Steinberg was doubtless the most eminent and most original of the group of WJC leaders. His thought, originating in the deepest sources of Judaism, greatly influenced me in many respects. The most important and most decisive element of his Jewishness was the concept of a "global Jewish people" (a *Weltvolk*, to use Simon Dubnov's term*), an idea that had brought him to the WJC, and one that I shared. His universalist conception of Judaism encompassed all aspects of life and thought. Steinberg was a deeply religious Jew, very much engaged in the *halakha*, which he considered an obligation. Strictly orthodox, he made an effort to exert his influence through example and shunned any attitude that might be perceived as a means of pressure or a desire to constrain. But he also admitted other movements and other factors as positive contributions to Jewish culture. In fact he accepted the validity of all movements of Judaism, of all forms of expression of Jewish thought, whatever their origins—religious, secular, Zionist, Yiddish, Sephardic, socialist.

His conception of Jewishness was founded on an attitude of positive neutrality toward every creative contribution to Jewish life: all tendencies were important, all must be admitted and recognized. It was the same with what he called the "tribes" of the Jewish people, that is, the different communities that constituted it, communities of Russian, Polish, French, German, British Jews. Each of these communities had its specific characteristics, its own virtues and flaws. Each was a stream of its own, with tributaries, flowing into the great river of Jewish tradition, which assured the creative survival and uninterrupted continuity of the Jewish people.

For Aaron Steinberg, Judaism had a particular mission in the world. It often acted as a catalyst and formed a set of values against which other events and other ideas were to be judged. For him, culture was the true source of human creativity. All the national cultures around the world, including Jewish culture, ran into this river and enriched its future. Together they led to a multifaceted, universal human culture.

We made an effort to base our work in UNESCO on this high conception of culture. Here I will limit myself to relating some particularly significant aspects

---

*Dubnov (1860 Mstislavl, Belorussia–1941 Latvia) was a brilliant Jewish historian, author of many books and essays on Jewish history including the ten-volume *Weltgeschichte des jüdischen Volkes* (Berlin, 1925–1930). In brief, his idea held that despite being scattered in the world-wide Diaspora, the Jews retained and cultivated their identity as members of the Jewish collective no matter where and in what society they lived. They were thus a "world people." Dubnov also revitalized and redirected the writing of Jewish history: the following generation of Jewish historians wrote from the inside, writing a Jewish Jewish history, so to speak.—ED.

of the role we played in the organization, a role that went well beyond our immediate concerns. The defense of culture constituted—one cannot say it often enough—a contribution to all civilization, to the entire spectrum of humanity. This conviction inspired our active collaboration in the struggle for the protection of cultural rights. We particularly affirmed the need to preserve the culture of minority groups including of course their languages, which in the Jewish case meant Yiddish and Hebrew.

We were especially concerned with the revision of history textbooks and with the UNESCO encouragement for editing and publishing them in the years that followed the war.

To what extent was the history of Judaism and the Jews faithfully portrayed in schoolbooks used around the world? To what extent did these books distort and falsify the truth? To what extent did the texts suffer from omissions or suppressions regarding the contribution of Judaism to the progress of world civilization? We were fully justified in asking these fundamental questions, in seeking their answers, and in taking appropriate measures to introduce the necessary revisions.

It was with this perspective that we initiated an inquiry into the major problem posed by the history books in use in numerous countries, a project in which we collaborated with a remarkable West German institution devoted to the subject, the Georg-Eckert-Institut für internationale Schulbuchforschung in Braunschweig.

Quite naturally, too, we involved ourselves in UNESCO's great project to publish a *History of the Cultural and Scientific Development of Mankind*. The objective—doubtless for the first time on such a scale—was to draft a history not conceived from a national or regional or even continental perspective but one that offered a legitimate account of the development of various national cultural features, understanding that all these aspects were to be integrated into a balanced global vision. To use a word I have already emphasized and that expresses our chief concern, this history was to be universalist.

Consequently we were deeply shocked by the presentation of Jewish history in practically all the project's draft texts. These contained chapters on Judaism in antiquity but left the subsequent history of the Jews a blank, in total obscurity from that period until the creation of the State of Israel in 1948. A two-thousand-year-long void, that was how the writers themselves saw the Jewish people over the centuries! It looked as if historians had taken their inspiration from the prejudices of theologians, as if Jewish life during the Diaspora had not existed for twenty centuries, as if—*a fortiori*—it had contributed nothing to the progress of civilization! This was an intolerable situation, for in the end how could the State of Israel rise up out of nothing? But this was the message in the drafts: at best, the Jews had been forgotten for two thousand years; at worst, they had been no more than ghosts for these two millennia. We could not but protest this gross injustice and make recommendations to rectify these brutal falsifications.

Of course we knew that drawing up a cultural and scientific history of humanity with each culture and each nation assigned its due place would be extremely difficult to realize. The member states of UNESCO also understood this and therefore created an independent international commission to revise and complete this history text. Composed of eminent historians, this body faced extremely complex problems since many historical developments were subject to different, divergent, even contradictory interpretations, all of which they had to take into account. The commission dealt in part with this issue by printing various interpretations and commentaries on the page facing the basic text.

In order to ensure a just and balanced treatment of Jewish history we secured the cooperation of a Jewish academic of the first rank, the famous historian Salo Baron of Columbia University in New York. But he was overburdened with work as a result of his own activities, in particular his gigantic *Social and Religious History of the Jews*, and Aaron Steinberg offered to assist him. This led Steinberg to review all the manuscripts of this immense work, volume by volume, and to make a large number of suggestions in order to include in the final draft important components that described the entirety of the Jewish contribution to civilization over the course of centuries. The editors of the project retained and inserted in the definitive text a good number of these proposals.

After lengthy and arduous preparation, spread over almost twenty years, the work was published under the aegis of an international commission chaired by Professor Paul de Berredo Carneira of Brazil. The commission was composed of twenty-two members from eighteen countries and ninety-two corresponding members from forty-two countries.

In his preface to the *History of Mankind: Cultural and Scientific Development of Mankind* (1963), René Maheu, director general of UNESCO, wrote:

> ... this *History of Mankind* parts company with its predecessors on several
> essential points. In the first place, it deliberately confines itself to shedding
> light on one of mankind's many aspects, its *cultural and scientific*
> *development.* In so doing it departs from the traditional approaches to the
> study of history, which, as we know, attach decisive importance to political,

economic and even military factors. It offers itself as a corrective to the ordinary view of man's past.

As time went by, though we continued to share our ideas with our UNESCO partners, we became increasingly disappointed by the deepening politicization of the organization. Gradually all UNESCO's actions with regard to the Jews degenerated into violent resolutions by which the general conference and the executive council condemned various aspects of Israel's policy toward its Arab minority. Much as we could understand certain of these criticisms, we could only be offended by most of these attacks, as arbitrary as they were unjust.

Since I had substantially supported the philosophy that shaped UNESCO's future, these aberrations troubled me deeply. Finally I reached a point at which I had to act, and in 1983 I decided to approach the director general, Amadou-Mahtar M'Bow, for a thoroughgoing discussion of relations between the World Jewish Congress and UNESCO. I explained to him our deep attachment to the organization from its inception and to the ideas it symbolized. I also brought up our serious disappointment in the face of the continuous and sterile drift of the body. I emphasized that far from improving the situation, the resolutions passed with regard to Israel had the opposite effect and reinforced tensions. Was not the true mission of the organization to give Jewish culture and Arab culture the opportunity to affirm themselves freely within the framework of an open competition among different cultures? Was this mission not also to establish a bridge between these two cultures and thereby to fulfill its conciliatory role, with UNESCO contributing to better mutual understanding, a calmer and more peaceful climate? Yet the current UNESCO program showed no trace of this mandate.

This intercession with the director general was not without consequences. Some weeks later the UNESCO secretariat invited me to submit concrete proposals as a follow-up to the claims I had advanced. I believe that afterward I noted a certain moderation in the stand UNESCO took with regard to Israel.

My intervention with the director general occurred on the eve of the 1983 UNESCO General Conference. Since it was impossible for me to attend, I asked my colleague and friend, Professor Jean Halperin, to represent the World Jewish Congress. Jean Halperin was particularly well qualified for this mission since for many years he had chaired the colloquia of French-speaking Jewish intellectuals, one of the WJC's finest creations in the cultural sphere. Concerned to promote an intercultural dialogue, Halperin suggested on behalf of the Congress "that UNESCO take the initiative to promote a Jewish-Muslim or Jewish-Arab dialogue on the reciprocal influence of these two civilizations throughout history."

He went on to say that the WJC had authorized him to make a concrete proposal in this regard: "on the occasion of the eight-hundred-fiftieth anniversary of the birth of the great philosopher, physician, jurist and theologian, the Jew Maimonides, who was strategically situated at the crossroads of Jewish thought, Greek thought, Arab thought and Christian thought, . . . we should appeal to UNESCO and the governments directly interested to organize in the course of 1985, the year dedicated to Maimonides, a great colloquium centered on this prototype of intercultural relations, in the countries where Maimonides had been active."

Professor Halperin asked national governments to support his proposal, in particular those of countries where the life and work of Maimonides took place, that is, Spain, Morocco, and Egypt, without forgetting Israel where he remains an exemplary teacher, as his tomb in Tiberias recalls.

To summarize the consequences of these events, I am pleased to say that UNESCO accepted the World Jewish Congress proposal and implemented it in December 1985. Scholars from West Germany, Egypt, Spain, France, Iran, Israel, Morocco, Senegal, the Soviet Union, the United States, and Turkey participated in the colloquium, conducted in the presence of a large public. It seemed to mark the start of a new policy in the dialogue among civilizations. All the participants were conscious of this new departure and of the symbolic value of the gathering. UNESCO underlined this in the publication of the colloquium's proceedings.*

The Struggle for German Reparations

I did not play a decisive role in negotiations on German reparations, but I did follow them and was at times closely involved, in particular in their first phase, which led to the signing of the famous 1952 Luxembourg Agreements. I was also closely associated with the activities of the Conference on Jewish Material Claims Against Germany, known as the Claims Conference.

I have already noted how at the Atlantic City conference in November 1944 we drew up what would become the postwar reparations program of the Jewish people. In fact that conference proclaimed "the principle according to which the Jewish people has a right to collective reparation for the material and moral losses suffered by the Jewish people, by its institutions or by individual Jews or their heirs."

---

*Maimonide, deliverance at fidélité: Textes du golloque tenu à l'UNESCO en décembre 1985 à l'occasion du 850ᵉ anniversaire du philosophe (Toulouse, 1986).—ED.

But no Jewish action, direct or indirect, was envisaged with regard to Germany. At that time the immense majority of the Jewish people appeared to oppose any formal contact with the Germans and were not even disposed to accept a global reparation payment from Germany. The World Jewish Congress, however, held steadfastly to its argument that a global payment represented the essential element of Germany's obligation to compensate for Jewish losses. It seemed as if many Jews expected a third power to act as intermediary. This expectation did not at all reflect the reality of the situation.

For example, the Allies did not have the same interests as the Jews. The growing tension between the Western Allies and the Soviet Union considerably weakened Jewish hopes of finding unified Allied support. As this tension gradually increased, the Americans and the British became even less disposed to act as spokesmen for Jewish claims. In fact, just the opposite occurred: their distrust and change of policy toward the Soviet Union prompted them increasingly to forget the crimes of Nazi Germany and give the new Federal Republic of Germany a sound political and financial footing.

The WJC and the Jewish Agency held numerous discussions on the question of German reparations, but no one really dared tackle the basic problem. The WJC continued pressing the Allies to include in the peace treaty—or in some quite different instrument that would reestablish German governmental authority—an arrangement that foresaw Germany's obligation to pay. For their part, at least the Western Allies continued to insist that it was for Germany itself to decide whether it would be prepared to act on this claim. This was the situation in 1949.

Within the framework of the World Jewish Congress, Noah Barou, the president of the European executive, made himself the champion of the reparations question. At every meeting he raised the matter of reparations and resolutely pushed us to act. A Russian Jew who had fought his whole life defending Jewish workers, he left the Soviet Union and spent some time in the 1920s in Berlin as the representative of Soviet commercial interests. Thereafter he established himself in London and devoted himself, body and soul, to the Jewish workers' movement in Great Britain.

A faithful member of the Fabian Society, the prestigious institution that gathered the great intellectuals on the British left, Barou was one of the founders and major supporters of the World Jewish Congress in Britain. Noah Barou was extremely personable: generous, always under pressure, in constant movement, and, as his colleagues noted, always doing several things at the same time—which not everyone appreciated! Despite the age difference between us, we became very close.

Barou raised the question of German reparations at the WJC leadership conference in New York in December 1949. Three months earlier the Federal Republic of Germany had been constituted. Its parliament, the Bundestag, had met on September 7 and its president had been elected on the 12th. The new state now prepared to sign an agreement with the Allies. As the president and chancellor had expressed a desire—admittedly in rather vague terms—to compensate for Jewish losses, the WJC Conference addressed the problem of reparations on the basis of these new facts.

But no one yet had a concrete idea of how the problem should best be approached. Having given the matter much thought, I proposed a framework for a procedure as to how things might go forward: it would be necessary that in advance of any negotiations the German government make a formal proclamation before the Bundestag, accepting responsibility for the persecutions and losses suffered by Jews as well as the obligation to right the wrong done to the Jewish people and to effect an equitable reparation that the obligation entailed. Only after such an official government declaration, approved by the Bundestag, could direct negotiation with the German authorities be commenced. My colleagues accepted this idea and incorporated it in a formal declaration that signified to the West German government and parliament what was expected of them: acceptance of the moral and political responsibility for the crimes of the Nazis against the Jews; material indemnification; legislation against anti-Semitism; reeducation of German youth; and a guarantee against nationalist tendencies. The declaration insisted that "Germany can acquit itself of this responsibility through the offer of money only if at the same time it recognizes its full moral and political responsibility."

Following the New York conference on July 25, 1950, Alec Easterman, the WJC political secretary, sent a detailed note about this issue to Lord Henderson, the undersecretary of state at the Foreign Office in London, and in the protocol of a conversation on January 11, 1951, underscored the justification of the claims. Declaring that it was impossible to estimate the totality of the losses suffered, Easterman indicated that he personally believed that a German offer of 500 million pounds sterling could be considered acceptable.

For its part, on March 12, 1951, the Israeli government sent the Allies a note in which it named the sum of $1.5 billion to cover the cost of integrating hundreds of thousands of Jewish refugees into Israel. West Germany would pay two-thirds and East Germany one-third. Israel's calculations were based on the approximately 500,000 Jews it had taken in at an average cost to the state of $3,000. In oral and written communications to the governments in Washington, London, and Paris, the WJC unreservedly supported the Israeli government's demand. The dollar sum proposed by Israel was practically equivalent to that in pounds sterling mentioned by Easterman in his discussions with the British.

Nonetheless, for many long months nothing happened. The Western Allies advised Israel to approach West Germany directly because they could not act as mediators; the Soviet Union never responded to the notes. The crucial matter of Jews negotiating directly with the Germans could no longer be ignored. It was then that Noah Barou decided to act on his own. In London he established personal contact with Herbert Blankenhorn, a senior official in the German Ministry of Foreign Affairs and future ambassador to Rome, Paris, and London, and a close collaborator of Chancellor Adenauer. Barou informed him of the decisions that we had made in New York in December 1949, and Blankenhorn indicated that these could serve as a basis for future negotiations.

In June 1951 Barou told us that he was going to West Germany to see the reaction in financial and industrial circles to the problem of reparations. This trip would be the first in a series of more than forty, all related to this question.

Barou informed us that he would begin his inquiry in his capacity as economic and financial counselor to some large British companies. Only if he met a serious interest on the German side would he disclose his identity as chairman of the World Jewish Congress European executive.

He first met with several bankers and other financial world figures, who showed little interest in the problem of compensation because they were preoccupied with the economic stability of the new state. Barou then approached a number of senior industrialists, who showed a positive curiosity about the matter. Explaining to them that reparations could in part be paid in the form of goods, equipment, and industrial products, he convinced these circles of the justice of our claims and of the interest they would find in cooperating and in thus giving impetus to their own recovery. For example, Barou called the industrialists' attention to the fact that the State of Israel needed a commercial fleet and that German shipyards were in a good position to build passenger and cargo ships.

Encouraged by the reaction of industry leaders, Barou approached Herbert Blankenhorn in Bonn to inform him of his discussions, and proposed that Blankenhorn draft a text for a declaration that Chancellor Adenauer might make before the Bundestag on the question of reparations. Blankenhorn agreed but suggested that Barou draft the statement himself. Barou categorically refused this suggestion, noting that it would be a "historic error." Indeed, the statement on the responsibility for the crimes against the Jews would have to come from a German pen.

Arriving in Zurich the next day, Barou telephoned me at once, asking me to join him as soon as possible in order to take part in a discussion with Nahum Goldmann, to whom he would present a detailed account of his mission to Germany.

The next day the three of us met at the Hôtel Baur-au-Lac. Barou brought us the draft text that Blankenhorn had finally agreed to write for Chancellor Adenauer. He told us that the chancellor was staying at Bürgenstock, a famous resort overlooking Lucerne, where Blankenhorn was to see him in a few days. Before that he would meet Barou in Lucerne in order to learn what we thought of his draft text.

We spent the whole day in Goldmann's sitting room, taking the draft text apart sentence by sentence. This careful examination led us to a concentrated discussion of the serious problem of reparations as such. I believe that a discussion of this topic—and of all the consequences it could have—had never been conducted so profoundly and exhaustively. In fact our discussion and our imaginations anticipated all the problems that subsequent negotiations and the reactions of Jewish public opinion would engender. In a way they constituted a dress rehearsal of all the discussions that would follow.

Joseph Rosensaft, president of the Committee of Liberated Jews in the British Zone, whom his colleagues called the "King of Belsen," joined our deliberations for a few hours. He had been charged by Goldmann with certain unspecified activities in Germany.

Blankenhorn's draft was composed in a humane tone but had serious omissions. The State of Israel, the principal recipient of reparations, was not even mentioned. Similarly, the responsibility of the German state was not clearly formulated, and the text lacked even a mention of the word "responsibility." Today I can still picture Goldmann vigorously correcting the draft by hand.

During our discussions I brought up a question that in my eyes was essential. We knew of the extremely tense relations between the center-right German government and the Social-Democratic opposition party (SPD). We also knew that the SPD harbored a great deal of understanding and support for our cause. We had to avoid letting this adversarial situation in Bonn push them to oppose the chancellor's declaration. I insisted that to preclude this possibility we had to approach the SPD leadership to inform them directly of our initiative and request that they support it. Goldmann immediately accepted my idea, realizing that everything possible had to be done so that the vote in the Bundestag would be as unanimous as possible in support of the government's declaration. There remained the task of contacting the Social-Democratic leadership. Adolph Held, president of the Jewish Labor Committee in New York, made the necessary connection through his German labor counterparts.

Barou insisted at length that I should also be present a few days later at the discussion with Blankenhorn in Lucerne. But I refused, convinced that Jews of German origin should not take center stage in these negotiations between Germany and world Jewry. Others did not share my position on the issue. Prominent German-born Jews, such as Georg Josephsthal and Felix Shinnar, took leading roles in the subsequent negotiations as members of the Israeli delegation.

Since no one was apprised of Barou's initiative and of the consequences it might have, it was absolutely and urgently necessary that we alert the Israelis. To this end Goldmann drafted a long telegram to the attention of Moshe Sharett, the Israeli minister of foreign affairs; we asked the Israeli consul in Zurich to transmit the message.

Barou then left a few days later for Lucerne, where he turned over to Blankenhorn the amendments we had made to his draft. The next day the Foreign Ministry official met with Chancellor Adenauer at Bürgenstock. The chancellor agreed to make a declaration before the Bundestag, but he decided he would write the text himself. This he did. The tone was drier but the text covered all the points we had raised. The definitive wording was brought to Nahum Goldmann in Paris by a Jewish member of the German parliament, Jakob Altmaier, before the declaration was read on September 27, 1951.

Chancellor Adenauer's declaration stated in particular that "unspeakable crimes have been perpetrated . . . which impose on the German people the duty of moral and material redress," and that "the Federal Government is ready, jointly with representatives of Judaism and the State of Israel . . . to advance a solution to the material aspect of the problem of reparations." The German chancellor also spoke of the intention of his government, through the intermediary of the churches and the educational institutions, to see that "the spirit of human and religious tolerance . . . should become a reality for all the German people and in particular for German youth." Last, he proclaimed the will of the Federal Republic "to combat unceasingly all groups that still continue to sustain a hatred of Jews."

Chancellor Adenauer's declaration was approved by a strong majority of the Bundestag. Only a few deputies on the extreme right and extreme left opposed it. The World Jewish Congress received Adenauer's declaration and the vote in the Bundestag with keen satisfaction.

Meanwhile, Israeli Foreign Minister Moshe Sharett urged Goldmann to convene a conference of American, British, and French Jewish organizations in New York. The primary purpose of this meeting was to gather the support of the Diaspora for the creation of an international Jewish organization to support and implement Israeli claims for reparations from West Germany. As a consequence of the declaration by the chancellor, however, this objective was expanded to encompass all Jewish claims, both individual and collective. Thus on October 26 the conference reformed itself into a permanent organization called the Conference on Jewish Material Claims Against Germany and elected Nahum Goldmann, who had initiated it all, president.

The declaration by Chancellor Adenauer and the vote in the Bundestag represented considerable progress toward a solution to the problem. But a large segment of Jewish public opinion in Israel and in the rest of the world remained hostile to any discussion with Germany. Large sectors of Jewish opinion did not believe in the sincerity of German promises and were convinced that the negotiations would lead to nothing.

Even Ben-Gurion—though he, like Nahum Goldmann, hoped for the opening of negotiations with Germany—did not dare pose to the Israeli parliament the question of claims and eventual negotiations. To this point Barou's negotiations with Blankenhorn remained "unofficial" and private. It was under these circumstances that Goldmann took the initiative for a first meeting with Chancellor Adenauer, which took place on December 6, 1951, in London at Claridge's in the presence of Noah Barou and Herbert Blankenhorn. After the terrible tragedy the Germans had perpetrated on the Jewish people during the Nazi era, this meeting was the first to take place between a representative of world Judaism and the State of Israel, and a representative of the German state. Nahum Goldmann had been expressly authorized by Ben-Gurion to speak in the name of Israel but to keep the meeting secret.

As the memoirs of the two protagonists bear witness, both were fully aware of the historic role they assumed at that moment. Goldmann was conscious of his immense responsibility as the Jewish people's spokesman before the German people. An enormous emotional burden weighed on him. The task of Adenauer, perfectly informed as to the immensity of Nazi crimes committed against the Jews, was comparably difficult. He had first to meet the representative of the people that his country had martyred. Adenauer did this with great dignity and a remarkable loftiness of vision.

At the conclusion of a lengthy discussion, Goldmann asked Adenauer to accept Israel's billion-dollar claim against the Federal Republic as a basis for future negotiations and to confirm this in writing. It was only through such a confirmation, he told him, that the Knesset and the Claims Conference could in fact consent to negotiations being initiated. Without consulting his government, the chancellor accepted Goldmann's demand. That same day he sent Goldmann the confirmation letter, based on a draft that Goldmann had dictated to the chancellor's secretary that morning, a gesture that revealed Adenauer's greatness of spirit: he had grasped the fullness of the catastrophe and the necessity of responding to it with an exceptional symbolic act. Goldmann immediately informed Moshe Sharett in Israel, who expressed his and Ben-Gurion's gratitude for this achievement.

Goldmann and Adenauer agreed during their discussion that the negotiations on the details of the reparations agreements would take place in mid-March 1952 in Belgium or the Netherlands, and would be conducted on two parallel tracks: one between the Israelis and the Germans, the other between the Claims Conference and the Germans. The negotiations finally began on March 20, 1952, in Waassenaar near The Hague.

The discussions were lengthy and at times bitter. Nahum Goldmann and Chancellor Adenauer had to intervene personally several times when the situation grew too tense. Fortunately they were able to overcome the crises and clear the way for agreement. The negotiations had to be suspended in June while the Germans met in London with their international creditors to resolve the amount of their debts. Before this problem was resolved, they said they could not agree with the Jews on a specific figure for reparations. Jewish public opinion in Israel and elsewhere generally viewed this as an evasive tactic and believed that Germany's moral and ethical debt to world Jewry took precedence over more mundane commercial debts.

Finally in July the negotiators reached a definitive accord. The Federal Republic undertook to pay Israel the global sum of $715 million, principally in the form of benefits in kind, spread over a period of twelve to fourteen years. The Federal Republic of Germany undertook in parallel fashion to pay the Claims Conference the sum of 450 million German marks against Jewish claims, while 50 million marks were allocated for non-Jewish victims.

A complementary agreement between the Federal Republic and the Claims Conference contained detailed arrangements that Germany undertook to promulgate concerning individual claims for restitution, reparation, and indemnification.

The two agreements reached at Waasenaar were signed on September 10, 1952, in Luxembourg by Konrad Adenauer and Moshe Sharett, and by Nahum Goldmann for the Claims Conference and Chancellor Adenauer.

The Federal Republic of Germany honorably met the obligations of the Luxembourg Agreements. The "German economic miracle" certainly furthered the generous way in which the country faced its responsibilities. In addition, the legislative program concerning individual claims had to be supplemented from time to time with additional, tough negotiations. Germany faced these with good grace. By the end of 1996 it had made total payments of 80 billion marks. Since payments continue in various ways, it is foreseen they will eventually reach 100 billion marks, a sum that is many times higher than that foreseen at the conclusion of the Luxembourg accords.

The indemnification and compensation program not only helped numerous families of Nazi victims recover a decent existence, but through its payments to victims living in Israel, Germany also greatly contributed to the economic health of the State of Israel, which struggled for many years with serious financial difficulties.

The Luxembourg Agreements were remarkable not only by virtue of the extent of the damage they sought to repair, but also by the exceptional legal nature of their arrangements, as is apparent in three extraordinary respects: a state undertakes to pay reparations to another state that did not exist at the time when the wrongs were committed; this same state reaches a valid international agreement with a private organization, the Claims Conference, while in traditional international law only states have an international judicial person; this same state engages itself toward a third party to indemnify some of its own citizens, while the practice of states in general provides such an engagement only toward the citizens of another state.

Few people have taken the full measure of the quite exceptional character of the Luxembourg Agreements, the products of a sequence of complex international negotiations that are among the most successful of those conducted in the postwar era.

On the Edge of a Ditch in No-Man's Land

At the end of World War II the victors and the defeated began a long and laborious process of meetings and discussions to negotiate a series of peace treaties. A 1946 conference in Paris opened the first phase in which the drafting of treaties between the Allied powers, on the one hand, and Bulgaria, Finland, Hungary, Italy, and Romania, on the other, would be carried out by the ministers of foreign affairs of the United States, Great Britain, France, and the Soviet Union.

These treaties were of considerable importance to Jews for two essential reasons. The Jewish populations in these defeated countries (with the exception of

Finland) consisted of survivors of the Nazi extermination policy. In addition, these countries had revised the legal status of the Jewish communities along the lines of the Nazi model. This situation was made the more serious by the hostile attitude of non-Jewish citizens, particularly in Romania and Hungary. Only Bulgaria, under the influence of its Orthodox church, had been able to protect its Jewish population from Nazi deportations. Under the monarchy, Italy had offered Jews a friendly climate until 1938. After the establishment of the Tripartite Axis, the introduction of racial legislation brought a great deal of suffering to Italian Jewish citizens, despite the sympathetic attitude shown them by the vast majority of the Italian population.

The situation of the Jews thus varied considerably from country to country, depending upon the history of the Jews in each. In this regard Romania held the record with eighty years of anti-Jewish legislation, in violation of the 1878 Berlin Treaty and the 1919 treaty on the protection of minorities. This country was notorious for its anti-Jewish attitudes in the period between the world wars. As for Hungary, its anti-Jewish policy began shortly after the 1920 Trianon Treaty and found its culminating point at the moment when German troops entered the country on March 19, 1944. The rapid annihilation of some 550,000 Jews was accomplished with the zealous complicity of Hungarian authorities and a certain portion of the population.

Given this situation, the WJC decided to submit a memorandum on the reparation claims of these communities to the meeting of foreign ministers and to the peace conference that would follow. Since these claims could not be advanced without prior consultation with the communities in question, the WJC decided to invite representatives of all of them to Geneva in May 1946. Deputations of the Jewish communities of Bulgaria, Finland, Italy, and Romania attended and participated. With relative ease we reached an agreement on the claims to be advanced. Only the Hungarian community had no representative at the meeting. Soviet occupation authorities forbade the Hungarian Jews to leave the country. The WJC then charged me with contacting the Jewish communities of Hungary in order to learn where they stood. We were all the more interested as we remembered that after World War I the Hungarian Jews, great patriots that they were, had rejected the protection-of-minorities clauses that had been inserted into the Trianon Treaty on their behalf. During the Nazi period they doubtless had cause to regret that stand. But in this new situation we did not wish to risk another repudiation of this sort.

Since we in Geneva could not gain the least insight into possible communications with Hungary, I took my chances by going without delay to Czechoslovakia, a country bordering Hungary. Once arrived in Prague, I went to find the Hungarian consul to whom I said: "I would like to go to Budapest." "I too," was his reply, which burst out like a despairing denial of such a utopian situation. The consul added that "getting the authorization of the occupying power requires a minimum of three months . . . providing that it is to be granted; as for the risk of a clandestine visit, I strongly advise you against it."

Since my meeting had to take place with all urgency, I had once again to rely on my imagination. Telephone communications between the two countries continued to function, and my Czechoslovak colleagues in Bratislava established contact with Budapest. They arranged a meeting at a fixed hour on the border between Slovakia and Hungary.

Stephen Roth, the secretary of the WJC Hungarian section, drove the president of the Liberal Jewish community, the vice president of the Orthodox community, and a representative of the Zionist movement in Hungary to the border meeting point.

Here is the account of this unusual meeting that Stephen Roth gave forty-five years later on the occasion of my eightieth birthday. His narrative of our "working session" illustrates perfectly the extraordinary conditions under which this meeting took place.

> I set out at 6 A.M. from Budapest to drive up to the Hungarian-Slovakian border, not far from Bratislava, equipped with our documentation, carefully prepared by an expert committee—and several bottles of vodka. Riegner came from Bratislava. After the vodka bottles persuaded the Hungarian and Russian border guards that I merely wanted to meet a long-unseen cousin on the other side, they permitted us to drive, with border-guard escort, through the no-man's land where at the other end the to-me-completely-unknown "cousin" was waiting. We sat down there in the dusty roadside ditch in no-man's land, under the bored eyes of the Russian, Hungarian and now Slovak frontier guards, and went through my documents detailing the historic claims of Hungarian Jewry after their great tragedy, discussed their exact interpretation and feasibility, and after our two to three hours of "cousinly reunion," Riegner flew to Paris where the leaders of the World Jewish Congress were eagerly awaiting our documents—and I returned to Budapest.
>
> How do I remember so exactly the date of this encounter? It was the morning after my wedding. I have long forgiven Riegner.

I should add to this highly colorful but accurate account that my return was rather complicated: the night train from Bratislava to Prague, Prague to Brussels by air, then to Paris again by train, which turned out to be the most rapid itinerary if not the shortest. I arrived in the French capital just as the editorial committee put the finishing touches on the Romanian part of the memorandum before drafting the Hungarian claims. This was a moment of immense relief for all of us.

At last we succeeded in inserting into the peace treaties with Romania and Hungary specific clauses affecting Jewish nationals. But the Communist governments in power consistently ignored them—which led us to resume negotiations with these countries after the collapse of communism in Eastern Europe, this time with much more success.

This adventure on the Slovakian-Hungarian border is a good example of the unusual situations that I encountered in the course of my activities. To quote Stephen Roth again, we had "to have the courage to depart from conservative shibboleths and to embark on as yet untrodden new paths." Such, in fact, has always been my philosophy of action.

Support for the Yugoslavian Jewish Communities

Among the Jewish communities with which I was in contact, I was particularly attached to that of the former Yugoslavia. This community had joined the World Jewish Congress at its founding and then became one of its most faithful members. It impressed me with the high quality of its leaders as well as by the fact that before the war it had succeeded in establishing a remarkable national Jewish cultural center to educate Jews of high intellectual caliber and serve as a source of inspiration for them. Stamped by the powerful personality of Alexander Licht, the center had far-reaching influence. I would come to know Licht well after he took refuge in Switzerland during World War II. He actually ended his days in Geneva.

I was often in touch with this community. I remember having telephoned Simche Spitzer, the secretary-general of the Federation of Jewish Communities of Yugoslavia, on the very evening of the German troops' entry into that country in the summer of 1941. As a result, the situation shifted brutally. The fate of the Jews was catastrophic and was the first act in the process of extermination that would soon spread to all Europe. It occurred long before the January 1942 Wannsee Conference to mobilize all the ministries and agencies of the Third Reich for the purposes of the "Final Solution."

The annihilation policy in Yugoslavia was distinguished from that implemented in other countries by the fact that the Wehrmacht itself carried out the killings, not the infamous security services, and also because senior levels of the German Ministry of Foreign Affairs encouraged and supported it. The pitiless and systematic annihilation of Jews carried out at the camps in Jasen-ovac, Semlin, Stara Gradica, Šabac, and elsewhere ensured that no one who followed those events at the time can efface the name of these horrible sites from his memory. This was a portent of what was to occur later at the exter-mination camps in occupied Poland.

The plan that was intended to make the country free of Jews was executed with such dispatch that it was completed in less than a year. In August 1942 a senior Nazi officer would proclaim proudly to the new commander of Army Group South-East, "Serbia is the only country in which the Jewish question . . . has been resolved."

The result of this appalling policy was that of the seventy to eighty thou-sand persons who made up the Yugoslav Jewish community, scarcely fourteen thousand survived. The survivors were prisoners of war and partisans who succeeded in joining the resistance, operating most often in the mountains.

Throughout the war I remained in contact with the prisoner-of-war camps holding Jewish officers and soldiers. I sent them food parcels, prayer books, and prayer shawls. Shut up together for more than four years, these men experienced a seclusion that bonded their spirits and developed an ex-traordinary solidarity as well as an uncommon intellectual maturity. In fact this long captivity prepared them to assume the leadership of the reconsti-tuted community after the war.

On their return from captivity and the resistance centers in the moun-tains, the survivors found an absolute, terrifying void: fathers, mothers, wives, children, brothers, sisters, friends—all gone. As these men could not or did not wish to live on their own, virtually all married non-Jewish women. With the creation of the State of Israel, somewhat more than half the survivors em-igrated to the new state, the others remaining, perhaps concerned about the problems that mixed marriages might create in Israel.

Entirely made up of former prisoners, the leadership of the small Yugoslav community had a very high notion of its duties. It attempted to maintain co-hesion and at the same time to integrate the community into the new postwar socialist society. It was aided in this task by Moshe Pijade, one of the leaders of the new regime, a close companion of Tito during the resistance years and the president of the new parliament.

I had an opportunity to meet this political fighter, whose deep Commu-nist convictions did not affect his loyalty to his Jewish roots, and I was greatly impressed by his powerful personality. Everything suggested that in playing a prominent role at Tito's side he succeeded in getting the Marshal to compre-hend the scale of the Jewish tragedy.

For the leadership of the reestablished community, it was a matter of utilizing existing religious structures while transforming them into those of a national minority. In this way the Jewish community would de facto be added to the other nationalities that made up the new Yugoslav state. This also meant that, unlike other religious communities, Jews were permitted to be active in the fields of education and culture, to organize summer camps for young people of various ages to whom they were trying to provide a Jewish education. At the same time community leaders brought their parents together in hotels in an effort to strengthen their Jewish identity.

Among the various publications the community produced, I would mention the annual almanac, a newsletter, and especially the celebrated Sarajevo *Haggadah*, a mid-fourteenth-century printed book decorated with superb illuminations. This book was reproduced in a large number of copies. I should also note the particularly moving gesture to erect monuments to the victims of the Shoah in five Yugoslav cities. All these activities bear witness to the impressive vitality and high intellectual level of the leaders of the small Yugoslav Jewish community, scarcely more than 6,500 persons—existing in a Communist country.

I remained in close touch with the Yugoslav community in the postwar years and took part in their congresses that brought the local communities together. For its part, the national Yugoslav community regularly participated in WJC meetings.

One day the president of the Federation of Jewish Communities of Yugoslavia, Professor Albert Vajs, who came to Geneva from time to time to maintain relations with the WJC and the Joint, telephoned me to say that he wanted to meet me "somewhere quiet" to consult with me on a delicate matter. I invited him to my residence for the evening. Professor Vajs, who taught comparative law and political science in Belgrade, shared with me an idea his wife had had, a notion that he himself judged to be rather extravagant but nonetheless close to his heart. It turned out that he was the only Jewish leader in Yugoslavia who had found a Jewish wife after the war. She had miraculously survived the extermination to which her first husband had fallen victim. "My wife," Albert Vajs confided, "plans to create a Jewish kindergarten in Belgrade. What do you think of the idea?" Vajs had no need to explain to me that from a halakhic point of view there no longer were any Jewish children in Belgrade, because from that tradition the Jewishness can be inherited only from the mother. I thought it over and then asked, "How many children do you have?" "About twenty, perhaps a few more in the suburbs." "What would you risk by doing it? Let's see what comes of it. Go ahead and do it!" Such was my reply.

For a long time I heard nothing of the project. Then—and here I jump ahead fifteen years, as in a film—we are in 1967.

The Yugoslav Jewish leadership had, as I have said, a very high conception of its mandate. It knew the difficulty of keeping such a small community alive, spread among the cities of Belgrade, Zagreb, Sarajevo, and more than thirty small communities. How, under such circumstances, could they hope to survive? The Federation of Jewish Communities of Yugoslavia judged that one means of succeeding was to create opportunities to meet other communities from Eastern and Western Europe and the rest of the world, an intention we strongly encouraged. Therefore, taking as pretext the 350th anniversary of the founding of the Jewish communities of Bosnia and Herzegovina, the Federation organized a mass celebration in Sarajevo to which it invited all Jews in the Communist countries, Western Europe, and America. The Federation organized a huge program, which included a historical exhibition in a museum specially created for the event, various concerts—Jewish choirs and a national orchestra under the baton of a Jewish conductor—and many other cultural and social activities. The WJC made a financial contribution to this commemorative event, and I even persuaded Nahum Goldmann to take part knowing that his presence would bestow upon it even more prominence.

On the eve of the festivities I arrived in Sarajevo. In the large reception area of the hotel where I stayed, a young man with a very proud bearing came up to me with the intention of interviewing me "for *Kadima*, the publication of Yugoslavian Jewish youth." I was surprised to learn in this fashion that these young people had received permission to have their own paper, something that was practically impossible in a Communist country. I was in the process of explaining some of the problems of world Judaism to him when I saw Professor Albert Vajs coming up to us. A smile lit up his face. He was clearly happy to see me in discussion with this young man. Pointing to him, Vajs said to me, "Do you remember our conversation in your apartment fifteen years ago in Geneva? Here is the result!" Remembering the first question that I had asked him in the past, I repeated it word for word: "How many children do you have?" "Some fifty boys and about thirty girls, and they are all *like that!*" replied Albert Vajs shaking his fist in his pride and joy. "When the Yugoslav government broke off relations with Israel as a consequence of the Six-Day War, the young people all wanted to hold a rally in the streets. We had all the trouble in the world to talk them out of it!" concluded Vajs, beaming.

I shall never forget that meeting nor having advised that Vajs and his wife undertake the adventure. It had in fact resulted in the rebirth of a dynamic Jewish youth, conscious and proud of its identity. In the mixed marriages, the

exceptional circumstances of which I have mentioned, the Jewish factor
seemed everywhere to have proven itself the stronger.

Among so many others, this Yugoslav experience underlined the importance that should be given to visionary projects when based on statistics. If in
1948 I had been asked how many years of survival I would give the Yugoslav
community, I would doubtless have said twenty at most. Life has taught me
that the predictors of trends and futurologists are often mistaken. Let us take
care not to play prophet but leave to God the task of determining our destinies!

Another Yugoslavian experience is worth recounting. In 1957 when I was
president of the Conference of Non-Governmental Organizations in Consultative Status with UNESCO, I participated in a conference of all the national
committees for that organization in Europe. It was held in the beautiful city
of Dubrovnik during the Jewish high holidays. I had a whole series of claims
to present to the members of the various national committees on behalf of the
NGOs. To get to Dubrovnik I traveled by way of Belgrade, where I met my Yugoslav friends again. Albert Vajs spoke to me of the magnificent synagogue in
Dubrovnik, one of the oldest in Europe, and said I should not fail to visit it.
Reaching the site of the conference on the eve of its opening a few days after
Rosh Hashanah, I took advantage of the free time to go to the old town. Sheltered at its center, opposite the governor's palace, was the famous synagogue
in the narrow street of the Jews. Dating from 1352, the building is in the
Gothic style, and the sanctuary is on the second floor. A Mr. Tolentino received me. With one of his brothers he was the sole surviving male member of
the Jewish community of Dubrovnik. On the eve of Yom Kippur he was obsessed with having a *minyan*, a religious service that gathered at least ten of the
faithful. He implored me to do everything possible to find this quorum, thinking that the forthcoming international conference ought to have a sufficient
number of Jewish participants to reach this goal. The Tolentino brothers had
achieved a *minyan* on only one occasion since the war, when an international
conference of jurists was held in the city. Now they charged me with a formidable mission on the eve of our conference.

I took advantage of the first reception to try to locate in the pool of Jews
some people who could take part in the little service. Happily I discovered a
young attaché from the Israeli embassy in Belgrade; he was in Dubrovnik as
an observer and, in principle, much less busy than I and thus better positioned
to locate people who might attend the *minyan*. I explained the situation to
him, and we went through a list of conference participants to choose those

whom it would be suitable to approach: Julien Cain, the head of the French delegation and director of the Bibliothèque Nationale; Ambassador Werblowsky, the Polish representative, apparently of Jewish origin; Henry Kellerman, the American observer, a diplomat originally from Germany, whose father had been a rabbi; Mr. Zuckerman, a UNESCO official and an Israeli delegate. . . . And there should be a few more Jews among the translators. Two days later I saw my young Israeli friend again, very frustrated by the meager results of his efforts. The head of the French delegation had learned with interest of the existence of one of the oldest synagogues in Europe but had indicated that his "philosophical convictions" prevented his participation in a religious service; the Polish diplomat had not denied his Jewish ancestry, even going on to say that in his youth he had belonged to the Hashomer Hatzair movement and that he knew Moshe Sharett well, but as the official delegate of a Communist country there could be no question of him attending such a service . . . which would not however prevent him from visiting the synagogue. Disappointed, the young Israeli diplomat nonetheless wished to pursue his efforts, and I encouraged him. I also approached Henry Kellerman, who turned out to have been a schoolmate of mine from the Berlin secondary school, one class ahead of me. Thus with the young Israeli attaché, the Israeli official from UNESCO, the American observer, two Jewish interpreters, and me, we numbered only six when we left the conference at the end of the afternoon of Kol Nidrei to go to the synagogue where the Tolentino brothers were waiting for us. We still needed two participants to reach the crucial number of ten. We sat down and we waited . . . waited for a miracle, surrounding the Tolentino brothers, whose tension was almost unbearable. Some women were there, but according to the Jewish rite they could not be counted in the circumstances. After a painful quarter of an hour of waiting, the door opened, pushed by a passing Jewish tourist. That made nine of us! The goal, now so close, still seemed no less distant, unattainable in the tense climate that each passing minute made more burdensome. Finally the door opened again and two men entered, a Yugoslav journalist from the national daily newspaper and Communist organ *Borba*, and a person who appeared to be oriental. A courageous young man, the Yugoslav reporter was Jewish and had learned that we were trying to celebrate a *minyan* the evening of the high holiday. Yet, as he was a Communist official like the Polish diplomat, he too could not take part in a religious service. He then decided to come to the synagogue not as a Jew but as a journalist, knowing very well that from a religious point of view it didn't make any difference. But in order to cover himself in the eyes of the Communist authorities, he had asked an Asian journalist colleague to accompany him to the service. The *minyan* could finally begin, to the indescribable joy of the Tolentino brothers!

Beyond its anecdotal interest, this story constitutes a faithful description of the sociological realities that characterized Judaism in the mid-twentieth century: an assimilated Frenchman who had qualms about participating in a service at the synagogue; a Polish diplomat of Jewish origin who had to hide his religious heritage; an American observer who was in fact a liberal German Jew; two Jewish translators; a Communist Jewish journalist. . . .

I have rarely had such an experience, at one and the same time significant and illustrative of the situation of the Jews of my generation.

Support for Israel

The ongoing World Jewish Congress support of the State of Israel was one of its most consistent concerns. It would be impossible here to offer a full account of these activities; an entire book would scarcely be sufficient. Nevertheless I would like to provide some especially striking examples of my participation in these projects. My first contribution to the cause of Israel was made at a time when the state did not yet exist.

In 1946 the UN established the Anglo-American Committee of Inquiry on Palestine to investigate the conditions there and make recommendations as to the political future of the area, including the question of displaced persons. The Jewish Agency for Palestine, in effect the future Israeli government, strongly supported the establishment of a Jewish state in the region. With this end in view, the Jewish Agency hoped to obtain the support of organized Jewish communities throughout the world. But it happened that while the Jewish Agency and the World Zionist Organization enjoyed close relations with Zionist groups in the various countries, they had scarcely any contact at all with the official Jewish communities.

An influential member of the Jewish Agency executive, Nahum Goldmann, then created a special commission charged with resolving this problem—that is, finding a way to gain the support of these communities. Knowing of my close ties with the representative bodies of Jewish communities around the world, Goldmann appointed me a member of the commission.

I worked closely with Gideon Rafael, who would later have a remarkable career in the Israeli diplomatic service and become director general in the Ministry of Foreign Affairs under Golda Meir. My task was to approach the communities to urge them to submit official memorandums to the Anglo-American Committee of Inquiry in support of the creation of a Jewish state.

I am proud to have succeeded in convincing Jewish organizations in more than thirty countries to adopt this course of solidarity and to come out unreservedly in favor of the establishment of a Jewish state.

We did not limit this effort to the Jewish communities as such. We also extended it to committees representing those displaced persons remaining in the DP camps in the American, British, and French zones of occupied Germany and of Italy. We succeeded in bringing together in Switzerland delegates from all the DP camp committees, which unanimously approved the declaration for the creation of a Jewish state. This vote by elected representatives of some hundreds of thousands of displaced persons, who very keenly felt the need for a new homeland, was under these circumstances of great significance.

When the Anglo-American Committee of Inquiry met in Geneva, I placed a set of offices at the disposal of the Jewish Agency delegation and did whatever I could to further its task. Moshe Sharett, who led the delegation, would not forget the assistance I then provided. Years later, when as prime minister he was scheduled to meet Molotov in Geneva, he rushed into my office without being announced to shake my hand and tell me, "We don't forget our old friends!"

As we know, the work of the Anglo-American Committee was followed by Great Britain's surrender of its mandate over Palestine and by the creation of a UN Special Committee on Palestine (UNSCOP) charged with drafting recommendations on the future of the region. Once again Goldmann's Jewish Agency commission, of which I remained a member, worked to ensure that the Jewish communities throughout the world and the DP camp committees all contributed written support to UNSCOP for the establishment of a Jewish state. And once again we were able to achieve the same degree of success.

UNSCOP finally drew up the proposals that led to the memorable decision of the General Assembly of the United Nations on November 29, 1947: the partition of Palestine, opening the way for the creation of the Jewish state.

Our support for Israel and our deep concern over its security were such an integral part of our activities that I hesitate to list the multitude of ways in which we expressed our solidarity with the new Jewish state. Our efforts on behalf of Israel extended beyond the defense of its rights. We also provided assistance when certain of its officials made blunders, creating prickly and potentially embarrassing situations.

Some people doubtless remember the serious crisis in July 1954 that pitted David Ben-Gurion against Pinchas Lavon, his defense minister. This crisis had its origins in certain activities undertaken by the Israeli secret service in Egypt, in the course of which some Egyptian Jewish boys and girls had undertaken acts of sabotage. The Israeli secret service had foolishly persuaded them to commit these violent acts against British and American property, hoping to blame Egyptian terrorists and thus postpone the British evacuation of the Suez. When the affair blew up in public, Israeli authorities seemed to be at a loss as to what to do. Before too long they turned to us in the WJC to organize the defense of the young people in the Egyptian courts. However much it pains me, I must say that the truth of this lamentable business was hidden from us. One day General G., apparently the official responsible for ordering the young people to act, appeared in my office to ask the WJC to assume the defense of these young Egyptian Jews, whom he represented as victims of anti-Semitic schemes by Egyptians. The general had a thick file in front of him, from which he read out certain extracts. When I asked him to let me read the documents from which he was quoting, or to let me have a copy, he refused. This attitude alerted me at once that there was a deliberate design to keep me, and thus the WJC, ignorant of the facts, and that the Israeli secret service had abused the good faith of militant young Zionists. Nonetheless, of course, I concluded that we had to do everything possible to aid these youngsters who had naively accepted roles in a play they could not possibly have understood.

I immediately turned to the president of the French section of the WJC, the parliamentary deputy Pierre Dreyfus-Schmidt, a lawyer with a solid legal reputation, who was quite willing to take on this formidable task. He persuaded a former president of the Paris bar to work with him in the defense. These honorable men did their best, but there was no possibility of avoiding heavy penalties on the youngsters. Ben-Gurion insisted on a complete investigation, but Lavon's supporters prevented this. Lavon himself resigned in February 1955.

I bring up this sad affair only to show that in certain particularly uncomfortable circumstances the agonized Israeli authorities knew very well where to turn for help to get them out of the mess they had got themselves into!

Until still quite recently, Israel faced not only the constant hostility of a great number of states but also a continuous challenge to the legitimacy of its very existence, particularly in the international organizations connected with the United Nations.

In that august body and in practically all its related agencies such as UNESCO, the International Labor Organization, and the World Health Organization, hostility toward Israel is clearly seen in the repeated adoption of resolutions and frequently arbitrary and unfounded condemnations of the State of Israel. This hostility has motivated refusals to admit Israel to regional bodies to which it had the full right to belong, and the systematic exclusion of its delegates from functions to which member states could lay claim in the various international organizations.

This hostility spewed over into the humanitarian sphere as well: the international community rejected the Israeli symbol of the Red Cross, the Magen David Adom. Similarly the international community tolerated the boycott of Israeli products by Arab states and that of products coming from states that had commercial relations with Israel. In like fashion, the international community far too long tolerated the persecution of Jewish communities in Arab countries and the refusal of numerous states to authorize the emigration of Jewish citizens to Israel and elsewhere. Indeed in all too many ways, UN member states systematically condemned Israel to the role of pariah.

One of the greatest injustices committed against Israel was surely the November 29, 1979, UN General Assembly vote rejecting the Camp David accords signed earlier in the year by Israel and Egypt as a major step toward peace in the region. This was by any measure a scandalous act by an organization created to protect future generations from the scourge of war, one that proclaimed as its principal objective the maintenance of peace and international security!

Let us be honest about this matter: all these devious and hostile acts had but one aim: isolating and banning Israel from the international community. In fact this sequence of systematic negative votes in the UN replicated the earlier historical treatment of the Jew as a pariah among nations.

We believed, and I still believe, that our moral and political imperative lay in the duty to defend the State of Israel, to denounce the gross injustice of challenging the legitimacy of the state (a unique situation in the history of the United Nations), to correct the false and distorted accusations, and to bring to light the inequity of these proceedings.

The role of the World Jewish Congress demonstrated its support of Israel in three major ways: directly through its principal bodies; by encouraging affiliated communities to act on Israel's behalf (generally by interceding with governments, political parties, religious groups, and social institutions); and by displays of support for Israel in international forums such as the various bodies of the UN (in particular the specialized agencies such as UNESCO or the ILO), the Council of Europe, the European Economic Community, the European Parliament, and so on.

I should also emphasize the positive aspects of our initiatives attempting to meliorate the conflict in the Middle East and to promote a climate of understanding, indeed even agreement. An example of this was our support for the visionary activities of Giorgio la Pira, the mayor of Florence from 1951 to 1965, who organized the Mediterranean cultural colloquiums in the hope of effecting some rapprochement among the most antagonistic views in the Middle East. In this same perspective I worked within the International Student Service with groups of intellectuals from around the world.

The hatred and hostility of Arab and Islamic countries toward Israel reached a culmination of sorts when their efforts, implemented in close liaison with the Soviet bloc, succeeded in organizing the adoption by the UN General Assembly on November 10, 1975, of resolution 3379, which defined Zionism as a "form of racism and racial discrimination."

Aimed at deliberately defaming the State of Israel and banning it from the community of nations, the resolution originated in an attack against Israel made in the declaration on the equality of women adopted on the occasion of the International Women's Year celebration held in Mexico in July 1975, and in a resolution of the Organization for African Unity conference held in Kampala at the same time. These aggressive declarations denounced "colonialism, foreign occupation, Zionism and apartheid" as obstacles to the equality of women, and condemned "the racist regime in occupied Palestine."

The UN resolution defining Zionism as a form of racism had first been discussed and adopted on October 17 by the General Assembly's Third Social Committee. Leonard Garment, the American delegate, denounced it at once: "I weigh my words carefully in affirming that this is an obscene act. . . . The language of this resolution constitutes a distortion and a perversion."

Once the Social Committee's vote became public, the World Jewish Congress launched a vigorous protest campaign. Nahum Goldmann, as WJC president, distributed to the major press agencies an indignant statement:

> Not only Jews but fairminded people throughout the world will be shocked to learn that the Third Committee of the United Nations General Assembly, in a resolution adopted on Friday by 70 votes against 29 with 27 abstentions, declared Zionism to be a form of racism and racial discrimination. This resolution is a travesty of historical facts and a defamation of the national liberation movement of a people that for two millennia was deprived of a national existence and the right of self-determination, and was subjected to most cruel persecution. The resolution does more to harm the prestige of the United Nations than it does to Zionism.

In this climate of legitimate outrage and large-scale turmoil, we had to mobilize all the forces of goodwill against the draft resolution as we tried to prevent its adoption by the General Assembly itself. On October 23, as WJC secretary-general, I sent a circular letter to all our affiliates urging them to do everything in their power to convince their governments to oppose the draft and to mobilize public opinion against this ludicrous defamation.

Under the leadership of the WJC, the seven Jewish organizations that had consultative status at the UN addressed a formal protest to the president of the General Assembly, Gaston Thorn, and contacted the greatest possible number of nongovernmental organizations to request their support. Some NGOs raised formal voices against the draft resolution. Additionally—and this is a very impressive example—sixty-five representatives of the most diverse nongovernmental organizations on October 30 signed a declaration in their own names to express their profound disagreement with the resolution on Zionism. The signers of the declaration included the International Federation of Woman Jurists, the World Federation of Veterans, the International Bureau for Catholic Education, the American Baptist churches, the International Association for Esperanto, and even the International Council of Women.

On the same date Niall McDermot, secretary-general of the International Commission of Jurists, declaring his disagreement with the resolution, recalled his "twenty-year-long engagement in the active fight against racism" and emphasized that the Commission of Jurists

> does not believe that this resolution of the Third Committee will further the cause of eliminating racial discrimination. Rather it runs the risk of prejudicing the future of the UN Decade for the Elimination of Racism and Racial Discrimination.

Despite the considerable energy deployed in fighting this dangerous, perverse, and erroneous resolution, despite the largely recognized and supported justice of our struggle, the General Assembly passed the draft without difficulty on November 10, and the struggle continued.

Once more Nahum Goldmann set the tone. "The resolution of the UN General Assembly condemning Zionism is one of the worst and most immoral decisions that the UN has unfortunately indulged in the last few years. To define Zionism as 'racist' is an absurd distortion of the basic facts and a denial of the right of the Jewish people to have its own homeland and its own state, which was established on the basis of an overwhelming decision of the same United Nations." After pointing out that the most civilized states, and in particular the United States and most of the European countries, had voted against this "absurd resolution," he continued: "It is the duty of the Jewish people to react in the most decisive manner against this resolution, by identifying itself with the Zionist ideal and giving its full solidarity to the State of Israel."

Among the reactions to the UN resolution, let me cite that of the World Council of Churches, which expressed its unequivocal opposition "to the equation of Zionism with racism" and pointed out that the resolution "has the seriously damaging effect of exacerbating the already explosive situation in the Middle East." The WCC recognized "the right of the State of Israel to exist peacefully within internationally agreed boundaries. Anything which diverts the attention from these issues or can be utilized to so divert it, will only make the acute risk of new and increasingly broader armed conflicts in the Middle East more and more imminent."

Cardinal Willebrands, chairman of the Holy See's Commission for Religious Relations with Judaism, expressed his astonishment that "phenomena as complex as Zionism and racism should have been treated at the United Nations without precisely defining the way in which these terms are to be understood. This procedure can serve neither the cause of justice nor the peace that we all desire for the Middle East."

On the initiative of 1965 Nobel Prize–winner for medicine André Lwoff, ten Nobel prize–winners signed an appeal inviting "all men of good will to join us in condemning through their moral action this disastrous vote with its serious and unforeseeable consequences," an appeal in which numerous other Nobel Prize–winners would later join.

The World Jewish Congress announced to the NGO Special Committee on Human Rights that for reasons of dignity and self-respect it could not participate in the United Nations Decade Against Racism as long as the resolution identifying Zionism with racism remained an integral part of that program.

To testify to their solidarity with the State of Israel after the infamous UN vote, representatives from throughout the Jewish world met at a great conference in Jerusalem on December 5, 1975, and proclaimed the "historic right of the Jewish people to Eretz Israel." The WJC, of course, sent a large delegation.

The defamation of Zionism continued to prevail for a long time in UN councils and other international bodies and meetings. For example, in 1979 the UN General Assembly, with a large majority, adopted a resolution against political "hegemony." In the fourth paragraph of its preamble, this text repeated the formula identifying Zionism with racism. Consequently we struggled ceaselessly against it.

The Seventh Plenary Assembly of the World Jewish Congress, held in Jerusalem in January 1981, unambiguously condemned the successive resolutions and declarations adopted by the United Nations and conferences held under its auspices that equated Zionism with racism.

The WJC assembly viewed these resolutions and declarations not only as a travesty of the truth, discrediting the United Nations, but also as a gross affront to the dignity of the Jewish people and an effort to disparage its national aspirations. The Eighth Plenary Assembly of the WJC in Jerusalem in January 1986 returned to the same subject. It recalled that since the 1960s the WJC had continued to warn authorities and public opinion that most forms of anti-Zionism could no longer be distinguished from anti-Semitism, and that as a consequence the struggle against anti-Semitism was increasingly becoming one of opposing anti-Zionism.

The assembly particularly condemned the representatives of certain member states, who at the UN and in its special agencies used an anti-Semitic language that incited to racial hatred, transforming UN venues into places for the denigration of the Jewish people. The assembly declared that the defamation and demonization of Zionism—the movement of national liberation and the instrument for the rebirth of the Jewish people—had become one of the most pernicious forms of political anti-Semitism and should be condemned as such.

As a logical consequence, the Eighth Assembly lent its full support to the campaign initiated by the World Zionist Organization, in close cooperation with the WJC and the State of Israel, devoted to combating the defamation of Zionism. It reached its apogee in 1985 in the petition addressed to the UN secretary-general. Signed by eight hundred eminent figures from twenty-eight democratic countries, the appeal invited the United Nations to disavow the abusive resolution and take inspiration from its own charter.

In all, it would take us sixteen years of sustained effort to put an end to the lamentable story of resolution 3379. The changes that occurred in the Middle East situation obviously played a role in this evolution.

It was not until December 16, 1991, on the occasion of the forty-sixth session of the UN General Assembly, that a resolution—to all appearances modest and innocent—was adopted under the rubric "Elimination of Racism and of Racial Discrimination." The text of this resolution limited itself simply to annulling that of November 10, 1975; it gave no indication of the abrogated resolution's subject. I believe it is the only time the United Nations has passed such an annulment.

And that is how we belatedly won our victory.

[SEVEN]

The Jewish Student Movement and International University Organizations

FROM THE BEGINNING and over the long course of my activities with the World Jewish Congress, I interested myself in the Jewish student movement. I recognized the importance of the formation of young intellectuals, in particular so that they might one day assume responsibility for the destiny of the various Jewish communities in the world.

I was fully conscious of the considerable role the Jewish student movements had already played in the history of Zionism. Thus I often thought of prominent personalities such as Chaim Weizmann, Leon Motzkin, Shemaryahu Levin, and Joseph Lurie, to name only a few, whose actions and influence were deployed through Jewish student organizations in Berlin, Bern, and Geneva, and who made such a great contribution to the formulation of the objectives and ideology of the Zionist movement.

I believed that if the World Jewish Congress wished to create a new form for the organization of the Jewish people, it would be essential to look to the future and, more concretely, to prepare a generation of leaders devoted to assuring the destiny of the communities. As a consequence I followed student activity very closely. And it was not pure chance that, when war broke out in 1939, the secretary-general of the World Union of Jewish Students, D. Tecuciano, came to see me in Geneva. Most of the Jewish students had been drafted or had volunteered and were serving in the various armies. It was clear that the secretariat of the Union was no longer in a condition to function effectively, and Tecuciano turned the Union's archives over to me to preserve them for the duration of the conflict.

Geneva was also the seat of the International Student Service. This organization had two major objectives: to establish contact with national university communities to explore how collaboration could be effected in a spirit of peace, and to assist students in need around the world. This meant aid to refugee students before September 1939 and later to students who were prisoners of war.

An annual assembly constituted the supreme body of the International Student Service, and it elected an executive that met at least once a year. Thanks to its vast network of student representatives (and professors) in just about every point on the globe, it remained active during the war and elicited support from Catholic and Protestant student organizations. André de Blonay, a Swiss with a strong personality, was the secretary-general of the organization, and he spared no effort to give it greater and more effective scope. He was aware that Jewish students had to be associated with his work. Since there was no active Jewish student organization at that time, de Blonay turned to Professor Paul Guggenheim, who played a considerable role in Jewish life in Switzerland, and invited him to join the Service in order to represent Jewish interests there.

Professor Guggenheim, who also served as the WJC legal counsel, cooperated with the Service for several years before thinking of finding a successor as his other duties expanded. He began progressively to transfer his function to me. Consequently, during the last year of the war I joined the organization, which by that time was no stranger to me. In fact, during my stay in Paris as a foreign student, the French branch of the Service had granted me a scholarship, which I had been very happy to receive.

By the time the war ended, most Jewish student groups had disappeared. We had to begin all over again by creating a new international Jewish student movement. It fell to me to convene the first conference of the various European Jewish student groups then in the process of re-forming, in order to establish the framework for a new organization. I succeeded in doing this in late 1946 in Paris, and I chose as a venue for the meeting the offices of the International Institute for Intellectual Cooperation (L'Institut International de Coopération Intellectuelle). At the time of the League of Nations, the Institute had played the role that UNESCO would later assume. It counted among its members some prominent and diverse personalities—Thomas Mann, Albert Einstein, Paul Valéry—and thus had enormous prestige. At our 1946 conference, representatives of Jewish student movements came from Britain, Belgium, Germany, France, and Switzerland. I remember a great number of these delegates who would go on to participate in subsequent meetings and then enter upon solid careers and assume senior responsibilities in their respective communities, and I continue to be very proud of this association. Let me name, among many, the Englishmen Israel Finestein and Joseph Jackson, the Frenchmen Adi Steg and Henri Brunschvig, and the Belgian Georges Schneck. I followed the work of the newly created World Union of Jewish Students with keen interest and had the satisfaction of being the first to allocate resources to it in the name of the World Jewish Congress. I am happy I was able to play the role of protector for the resuscitated Union.

Here I should offer an observation that applies beyond the framework of student life. Youth organizations function really well only when they produce (or are capable of attracting) leaders who are full of enthusiasm, launching projects and creating initiatives. But this is not always the case, as each age cohort is not necessarily capable of generating dynamic, competent, responsive leaders. When these are prominent by their absence, the organization is obliged to hibernate and wait for better times. At one point this occurred to us at the World Union, and I withdrew the WJC subsidy, carefully saving it for use by a reconstituted leadership of highly qualified persons. This was a matter of patience, more or less quickly repaid, that only a relatively modest and above all independent organization could permit itself.

The WJC did not limit its assistance to the World Union to finances but also helped it develop and expand its fields of action. For example, I tried for many years to obtain American Jewish students' representation in the World Union, a natural concern when you consider that the United States has the greatest number of Jewish students to be found in any country. However logical this concern might have been, it was difficult to resolve by virtue of the hold exercised on American Jewish students by the B'nai B'rith–created Hillel Foundation. A small, truly independent organization did exist at Columbia University, but it could hardly compete with the Hillel Foundation and its rigorous structure, which directed Jewish students *ex cathedra*. This patriarchal structure did not coincide with the European trends, by and large democratic, that we followed within the World Union. The Hillel Foundation had an educational and philanthropic objective and geared itself to the social life of Jewish students at American universities. It worked effectively for students but in no way involved them in its decisions. On the other hand, as I have noted, students initially ran the World Union. We wanted to establish close contacts with the Hillel Foundation in order to permit European students to collaborate with American students and to help democratize their structures. But this was not easy. And the irony of a European organization attempting to "democratize" an American one was not lost on us.

The World Union would have betrayed its title if it had not also included Latin America, where for all practical purposes I myself set up a branch. At a meeting of Jewish students in Buenos Aires, we began the process of establishing systematic cooperation with the students of other Latin American countries. In a speech I offered them a programmatic approach that would allow them to base their organization on a valid philosophy—that is, the defense of student interests within Jewish organizations and the defense of Jewish interests in national student organizations.

Moreover I attempted to get the World Union of Jewish Students into the Claims Conference and later the Memorial Foundation for the Murdered Jews of Europe (created to oversee the design and construction of the Shoah memorial in Berlin), an idea that other Jewish organizations opposed for ideological reasons. I also tried to obtain subsidies for the World Union from other international Jewish organizations. But these organizations had little notion of the importance of the student movements, in particular the dynamic critical role they were destined to play in their future communities.

I remember how often I fought with Zalman Shazar, then director of the education department of the Jewish Agency, in order to obtain even a modest grant for the students. But Shazar's department opposed any subsidy except those associated with Hechalutz, a pioneer movement of Zionist youth. Not until much later did the Jewish Agency lend its support to the Jewish student organizations without demanding control of their policies and activities. And for its part, the Joint only slowly showed any concern for students. But this reluctance now belongs to the past as these organizations generously support the student cause. As for the World Jewish Congress, today it continues to support the various continental branches of the World Union.

I never tried to impose on students any one political line or any particular action program. I always judged that they had to decide for themselves what they wished to undertake. Of course they might make errors in judgment and action, but they had to take responsibility for what they did and find their own way through the complexities of life, whether I agreed with them or not.

This attitude won me the confidence and respect of several generations of students who often consulted me and followed my advice.

Beginning in the last year of the war, I represented Jewish interests in the International Student Service, and in this organization was able to make a contribution I am pleased to recall. Indeed, I participated in drafting the concepts and principles that would guide the organization in the future. I also insisted on extending its activities to other continents so that the countries of the Third World could profit from our work. I was instrumental in having a secretary of Indian origin for the first time appointed to important functions in the secretariat. This was Malcolm Adishehia, a striking personality who subsequently had an impressive international career, in particular as undersecretary-general of UNESCO.

Furthermore I was one of the first to support the extension of the Service to African universities. I found the quality of the first representatives from that continent, who were professors at the University of Ghana, to be impressive.

Of course the organization could not escape the conflicts that plagued the world at the time. But my experience as diplomat and conciliator helped hold the repercussions of these problems within tolerable if not wholly reasonable limits within the Service. University circles recognized the value of my efforts and insisted I continue the work. The great diversity of the Service's national sections emerged clearly at our meetings in various locales, which were characterized by enormous disparities in standard of living, organization of studies, and ideological points of view. Thus all the conflicts that resonated in the larger world also appeared in our debates. In fact every world tension attended our deliberations, whether it was the antagonism between India and Pakistan, the conflict between Jews and Germans, Israelis and Arabs, or the problems between the old colonial powers and the countries of the Third World—all fed into our discussions and at times created vehement confrontations. How many times did I have to intervene in these debates to calm the opposing parties and find solutions so that we could all work together at our common undertaking! Our efforts hoped to achieve a broader and deeper mutual understanding and closer international collaboration among universities. In the very middle of the Cold War, we hoped to make our contribution to entente among peoples and states and, in short, to world peace.

Lifting the university communities out of the misery in which they were mired was an urgent matter calling for immediate solutions and concrete efforts. How to teach these communities to come to their own rescue, to help themselves, was the great question, one to which our experience could provide some answers if those involved could see the problems in the appropriate perspectives. For example, within the universities we created cooperatives charged with publishing and distributing textbooks that were often otherwise hard to find or difficult to acquire. The Service also set up other cooperatives at the universities training medical doctors, in particular to fight, among other ills, tuberculosis, which affected particularly the poorest and least privileged populations.

The organization was open to all ideological currents. To cite only a single instance, earlier alluded to, Catholic and Protestant students were especially well represented by Bernard Ducret and Philippe Maury, who would go on to become good and faithful friends. I also succeeded in having the World Union of Jewish Students join the International Student Service. An international association of professors and university teachers also joined. And we formed national sections with representatives of national student unions and university presidents and administrators.

From the university world the service attracted numerous figures who displayed an active sympathy and were unstinting in their valuable support. This part of my work was extremely rewarding. As it turned out, my efforts on behalf of students prompted wider support than I had dared hope. Among the personalities who became directly involved—university leaders or people who played a leading role in the intellectual life of their country—I will mention here only a few names such as Reinhold Niebuhr, the American theologian and sociologist, who chaired the American section of the Service; Sir Walter Mobberly and Sir Keith Murray, successive chairmen of the University Grants Committee in Great Britain and heads of the British Service; Gilbert Murray, professor at Oxford and promoter of the idea of the League of Nations in Britain; Sir Maurice Bowra, vice chancellor of Oxford University and a brilliant classicist; J. F. Wolfenden, vice chancellor of the University of Reading; Henri-Irénée Marrou, a French Catholic historian; Jean Baillou, who for many years headed the cultural section of the Ministry of Foreign Affairs in Paris; Zakir Husain, vice chancellor of the great Islamic university of Aligarth in India, who was an intimate of Gandhi and would go on to become president of India; and Mohammad Mujeeb, vice chancellor of the Islamic university Jamia Millia in Bombay.

The national student associations of several countries also included remarkable figures who often attended our conferences. I remember in particular Olaf Palme, who would become prime minister of Sweden. At that time Palme was president of the student association of his country. Thus at these meetings, ties were formed that would prove precious—professionally rewarding, of course, but equally so on the personal level.

My activities with the International Student Service quickly brought me to the position of treasurer, then vice president. Finally I was offered the presidency of the organization. But I initially refused as I had not the benefit of direct and continuous relations with the university world. On the occasion of a visit to the United States with the objective of finding a successor to the presidency, I met Reinhold Niebuhr, whom I would see again at meetings that are among the great moments of my life. An exceptional human being, Niebuhr had—in addition to a profound understanding of international affairs—a penetrating vision of the world based on a religious and ethical consciousness not far distant from my own. My meetings with him opened my eyes to the richness of American intellectual life. This powerful personality possessed a universal perspective on all matters, and his gifts of political analysis were extraordinary. One of the first to have understood Hitlerism and its development in Germany, Niebuhr supported us during the darkest years of the war and similarly supported our efforts to establish the State of Israel. He was the perfect choice to find us a successor to the presidency of the International Student Service. Since an important part of the revenue of the organization came from the United States, it was in fact judicious that an American should chart its future course. Thus, so commissioned, Niebuhr, supported by the American Section, urged that the MIT dean of students and respected Unitarian theologian Everett Moore Baker be elected president—an excellent choice. Baker had a keen understanding of international relations and would do a fine job of making the Service function smoothly. Baker joined us at the next international conference in Bombay in 1950, the first on the Asian continent. This gave us the opportunity for fascinating trips to various Indian intellectual centers. The assembly elected Baker to the presidency, but alas! the new president died on his return flight when his airplane crashed near Cairo. There were no survivors. Still in India when we learned of the disaster, the assembly fell into general consternation. This cruel disappearance obliged me to assume the interim presidency. I performed this function for several years at the insistence of my colleagues and because finding a successor to Everett Moore Baker proved very difficult.

Reelected president despite my reluctance, as one of my first initiatives I contacted the leaders of universities and the National Union of Israeli Students with a view to establishing an Israeli section of the Service. Toward this end I went to Israel on various occasions to take part in several meetings at the residence of the rector of the Hebrew University, the archaeologist Benjamin Mazar. The Israeli Section was born there. Shortly afterward, David Bergman, professor at the Weizmann Institute, became a member of the Service's executive in his capacity as representative of the Israeli section.

During the international conflicts that inevitably broke out within the framework of an institution as vast and dynamic as the Service, I particularly recall the tensions between Jews and Germans, which made my position uncomfortable. For years the World Union of Jewish Students (WUJS) had opposed the admission of a German section to the organization. After the conclusion of the 1952 Luxembourg reparation agreements between Adenauer and Sharett and Goldmann, a new effort to have a German section was made, as might be expected. Since I was officially representing the WUJS, I was not especially happy with this development. The Union again opposed admission of the Germans. The past was not easily forgotten, and the young Jewish student leaders believed they should continue their anti-German stand, at least for the foreseeable future. Clearly this did not make my work easier. Think of my position: on the one hand, I was very close to Nahum Goldmann and his open policy toward the Germans, and I was satisfied with the agreements he had concluded in Luxembourg; on the other hand, as a disciplined member of the WUJS I should align myself with its position and therefore vote against admission. I was happy to observe that one or two members of the Service's assembly were not content that only the Jews should oppose the admission of the Germans. As a consequence and out of solidarity with the WUJS position, they supported a refusal. But the majority voted in favor of admission. In the end, and after having voted against admission, it was my obligation as president to make a welcoming speech to the German delegation. I think I spoke diplomatically and tactfully, expressing the hope of mutually beneficial cooperation that the assembly attached to the presence of the Germans. I made an effort to have them understand that the opposition raised was not directed against them personally but represented the expression of the profound frustration and despair that the Shoah had left in the memory of the immense majority of the Jewish people. I added that their activity within the Service would help in mediating and perhaps overcoming such feelings.

The duties of the presidency entailed another problem for me, just as difficult to resolve. During the war a special organization, World Student Relief (WSR), had been created with the mission of aiding students who had been victims of the war, in particular refugees and prisoners of war. Since most of the funds were raised through the Pax Romana and the World Federation of Christian Students, these two bodies exerted a preponderant influence on the WSR decisions and the distribution of its funds. World Student Relief gave to each of these organizations one-third of the votes. After the war the arrangement lost its rationale, and an effort was made to amalgamate the International Student Service and World Student Relief. This was finally achieved under the name of the World University Service. But the organization retained the French name, Entraide universitaire internationale.

In my opening address at the Oxford conference in 1954 I made a point of laying out the philosophy of the new organization.

> Although WUS subscribes to no set ideology, those who work within it are united by common beliefs in certain human values and fundamental approaches. These are:
>
> First, we believe that the issues and problems facing people of different nations and communities do not exist in isolation but are linked to each other. Consequently, as a university organization, WUS strives to meet university-related problems on a world-wide basis, to engage the interest of all in solving particular problems on a world-wide basis, and to view particular issues in the context and experience of the whole.
>
> Second, we believe in the dignity of man and maintain confidence in his creative and constructive capacities. Through the constructive contribution that is within the power of each of us to make, the responsibility for the future and destiny of the world is inescapably shared by all.
>
> Third, we believe in the equality of nations and races. The variety and diversity of cultures, people, races and nations are essential to the richness of civilization. All have an equal claim and obligation to share in intellectual and economic resources and endeavors.
>
> Fourth, we believe in the principle of academic freedom—the freedom of teaching, study, and independent scientific research.
>
> Finally, we believe in the community of interests and concerns among members of universities and colleges throughout the world. As members of this community, students and teachers have mutual responsibilities to each other and to the society in which they live.

At the Service we were convinced that we had to associate the greatest possible number of groups with our work, be these spiritual or political, as they found expression in university life. From the beginning we were a Western organization but remained open to the rest of the world and conscious of the fact that we had to involve the umbrella organization that represented the Eastern European national student associations as well as those student organizations in countries that had previously been colonized or were on the path to independence. In the former case we had to deal with the International Union of Students, in Prague. We did not harbor pro-Communist sympathies, nor did we have any illusions about the group's political independence. But we very much believed in the idea that contributions to peace—the objective we never lost sight of—could not be made without contacts, even close ties, with the adversary. We hoped to avert the dangers of conflict, doing so through dialogue, even if we had no illusions in that respect. But as long as we talked, we did not fight, a far from negligible consideration.

As early as 1950 the Service's assembly had taken a decision in this direction while still looking for guarantees against abuse of the relationship. After discussing this initiative for several years, at the 1954 Oxford meeting we unanimously decided to plan for cooperation with the International Union of Students, specifying, however, the limits of our collaboration and accompanying them with guarantees against acts that might be prejudicial to the Western countries.

The Western European national student organizations recognized the Communist character of the International Union of Students. Accordingly, they set up a countermovement by creating a Coordinating Secretariat (COSEC) with its seat in Holland. We believed this to be justified, and we also accepted the secretary of COSEC as a member of the Service. Since a decision in principle to accept the International Union of Students had been taken in Oxford, each of us now had to reflect on and accept the rules we had established. To my great surprise, at the next meeting of the executive in May 1955 savage opposition was expressed to the Oxford decisions that had been accepted eight months earlier.

Suddenly the U.S. national student union and some American members representing religious organizations, as well as the COSEC representative, announced their rejection of the Oxford decisions. This coordinated opposition grew in the summer of 1955 at the Helsinki meeting. In order to give representatives of the International Union the right to participate fully in the meeting, the decision on acceptance of the Union—along with its guarantees—had to be voted on as the first order of the day. During the five days of the plenary assembly we discussed nothing *but* the question of admission, and it soon became clear that opposition to admitting the Union was shared by half the assembly and that no room for agreement or even compromise could be found. I vaguely felt "someone" was behind this unexpected opposition—but who?

During the Helsinki assembly, two matters connected with the cultural mandate of the service deeply troubled me. First, the climate of the Cold War jeopardized the organization's politically neutral position: the Service had begun to voice opinions relating to current international conflicts. For me it was essential that it maintain its nonpartisan character, engaged in the ideologies of neither the right nor the left. The organization was intended to be a meeting place for all political tendencies, all religions, all nationalities. Only in this way would we be in a position to examine together how best to face world problems in order to find positions of conciliation and create modes of concrete cooperation.

My second concern was to preserve the excellent team of people who composed the Service's secretariat. I feared that some of the assembly's decisions might prompt them to resign. As we debated the Union's admission for five full days, a strange situation developed. The two opposing parties were of equal strength, and between them there were some who hesitated. This led to surprising votes, intended not to support one side or the other but to prevent either side from carrying the day. Such an unhealthy atmosphere worried me greatly. How could we avoid the dangerous consequences of the situation; how could we resolve it?

I finally succeeded in the following way: I had informed my colleagues several years earlier of my desire to leave the president's post. This, however, I could not do—or could not do yet—for administrative and political reasons. But the secretariat had been formally notified that if I once again agreed to stand for office, it would definitely be for the last time. To general surprise, the "exclusionists" nominated a second candidate at the last minute in the person of the president of the American section of the Service, Professor Buell Gallagher, president of the City College of New York, an institution with some sixteen thousand Jewish students, which meant that he represented as many Jewish students as I did! In the political life of his country he stood as a liberal, so that I could never understand how he could side with the American hard-liners at Helsinki. The group that backed his candidacy did not guarantee, in my eyes, a nonpolitical character to the organization, and so I held to my decision to run for the office. In the end I won the election by a majority of two votes with three abstentions (two of which were those of the candidates themselves).

From this point on my task was to assure the survival of the International Student Service, reeling in a rancorous climate of ideological hostility bordering on mutual hatred. Once again imagination came to my rescue. I realized that I had staked out my own position too sharply, and consequently I found myself unable to achieve the reconciliation necessary to resolve the problem. So I refused to accept the outcome of the election, proposing instead to the assembly that it elect a figure who enjoyed the esteem of all sides, including those who had not been involved in the conflict, and who could achieve unanimity in the university world. This person, who truly stood above the fracas, was the chairman of the Indian Committee, Professor Zakir Husain. I made it clear that I had not even had the time to alert him to this possibility. Thus nothing allowed me to offer assurance that Zakir Husain would reply favorably to my initiative. I was ready, under those conditions, to continue as vice president for one more year, first to assure continuity, second to assist Zakir Husain in the daily work for which he was clearly in no way prepared. Some people have accused me of having chosen a procedure that was scarcely democratic (and in this they were not wrong), but it allowed my plan to succeed. To my keen satisfaction, Zakir Husain consented to accept the office. This permitted me the following year to withdraw from the organization at the assembly in Mysore in India.

The fact remained that I still did not know what lay behind the climate of divisiveness that so seriously threatened the very existence of the International Student Service. I certainly had some suspicions, but I had to wait several years to finally discover the nature of the opposition that had been so underhandedly mounted. It was the Central Intelligence Agency! The Cold War saw a number of reports on the CIA published, revealing how it had funded, among other NGOs, the Coordinating Secretariat (COSEC) of the national student unions and some American university groups.* Among them—in fact, at their head—was the National Student Union, whose representatives had joined the opposition camp at the Helsinki assembly in 1955. I should point out, however, that as far as I was personally concerned, I experienced no negative effects from the CIA's activities.

Looking back, how would I assess my activities within the framework of the World University Service? I am tempted to say that for me it was an uplifting experience, the rewards of which I will never be able to measure completely. I not only learned to chair lively meetings, something that is not taught anywhere, but I also went through a training course in conciliation. All this assisted me enormously later on in the activities undertaken by the World Jewish Congress. Another positive aspect is worth mentioning: I met a number of people who truly belonged to the world's intellectual elite, and these contacts, which were often quite close, broadened my horizons. Such contacts alone would have justified the experience, which was so gratifying in other respects. Assisting the student organizations will remain one of the finest adventures of my life.

---

*For a detailed examination of covert CIA funding of one major liberal anti-Communist organization, see Frances Stonor Saunders's controversial *The Cultural Cold War: The CIA and the World of Arts and Letters* (New York, 2000).

The Weight of Asia

The World University Service held its annual assemblies in a different country each year, generally on the grounds of a university with an international reputation. This custom meant confronting a different academic tradition each time. In particular I remember the assemblies in Grenoble, Oxford, Istanbul, Bombay, and Helsinki, and the passionate encounters that took place there.

The assembly following the 1955 Helsinki meeting was to take place in Indonesia, and we all looked forward to traveling there to discover an ancient Asian civilization. Unfortunately the plan could not be realized. The Indonesian government refused to issue visas to the Israeli participants and, since we could not exclude a national section from the general assembly, at the last moment we transferred the meeting to India. I was pleased that all my colleagues unhesitatingly agreed to the transfer when I proposed it to the executive. The decision to hold the conference in Mysore in India also served as an homage to the new president of the Service, Professor Zakir Husain.

I was profoundly impressed by the experience of meeting the culture of a multimillenary civilization. And the teeming life of the subcontinent, with its numberless crowds, its enormous spaces, the unspeakable poverty, the highly cultivated elites, the peasants scratching out a miserable existence in huts made of scraps, without light, the cruel divisions of the caste system, the millions of refugees from Pakistan literally camping in the streets—all this struck me with particular force.

I also saw the admirable efforts of the government to overcome the terrible problems occasioned by the achievement of independence and the division of the country along religious lines in 1947. Constructing housing for twenty million refugees, founding teachers colleges to train the million necessary schoolteachers, mastering the savage floods of the great rivers, modernizing agriculture, increasing substantially the electricity resources of the country, attempting a bold policy of "affirmative action" to attenuate progressively the discrimination that existed among the different castes—these were some of the gigantic tasks that the government faced.

I learned a further lesson: the inseparable link between national problems and social problems throughout the entire Asian continent. Winning national independence after more than a century of colonial rule and searching for a decent life while trying to come to grips with the unspeakable poverty to which the colonial system had exposed the masses, were two indistinguishable goals.

We understood much of this from conversations we had conducted earlier with some of the country's leaders. I recall in particular the World University Service's meeting with Prime Minister Jawaharlal Nehru in New Delhi, on the occasion of our first meeting in India in 1950. He was an extremely attractive figure, the scion of a family of the most refined Brahmin culture. He had an expressive face of great beauty and possessed extraordinary charm. He received us for several hours and discussed matters with great candor, explaining certain aspects of Indian politics. He also prepared us for our trip to Benares. "Never forget," he told us, "that Benares was already a religious center and a holy city seven thousand years ago, when you Europeans were still climbing around in trees." At that moment I took the measure of the Asian pride expressed through this personality.

With Zakir Husain I had the most interesting exchanges of viewpoint. He impressed me enormously, and I admired him greatly. He had studied in Tübingen, Germany, during the period of the Weimar Republic. He was very well informed about the persecution of the Jews in Nazi Germany and had a deep understanding of our situation. Having acquired great authority as an educator within the Congress party, he was appointed minister of education before becoming the first Muslim president of the country (1967–1969). He maintained good connections with Arab circles and obtained large grants from Saudi Arabia for the Aligarth Muslim University of which he was vice chancellor. We often debated the problems of Asia, educational issues, and the world situation. When he accepted the highest offices in his country's government, I continued to enjoy direct contact with him.

I always hoped that one day he might play the role of mediator with the Arabs and that, as an Indian Muslim of great prestige, he might modify India's negative policy toward the Jewish state, which was principally motivated by its constant competition with Pakistan on the world scene. Unfortunately this hope was not to be realized because he died suddenly during his term as president.

On my visits to India I also had several meetings with the Jewish communities of the country. The community of B'nai Israel in Bombay had at the moment of independence in 1947 some 25,000 souls. In existence for a thousand years before some Jewish officers in the British army stumbled upon it at the beginning of the nineteenth century, the groups had, with some exceptions, preserved Jewish rites and traditions quite well. The miraculous survival of this little community in the midst of the Hindu masses was probably due to the Indian caste system. The Jews, in order to maintain their identity, had almost organized themselves into a caste of their own.

The community arranged a special evening session in which more than five hundred members of B'nai Israel came to hear me speak of the situation of Jews in the world. My speech was soon interrupted by an extremely picturesque personality who did not speak English and who insisted that a translation of my talk be made into Maharati. This was the first and likely the last time in my life that I was interpreted into that language.

In Bombay I also met Jews of Iraqi origin who had succeeded well in business, several of whom served as mayors of their cities. The majority of Bombay Jews today live in Israel. When the office of the chief rabbi of Israel expressed doubt as to the purity of their traditions, the president of the Israeli section of the WJC and I strongly supported the Jews of India, and our cause finally triumphed.

I also visited the small Jewish community in New Delhi, several members of which had important functions in the federal administration, as well as a community of Sephardic origin in Calcutta.

On my second trip to India, in 1956, I also visited the Jews of Cochin, at the extreme southern tip of the country on Cape Comorin. The origins of this community are shrouded in mystery and there are different theories about its origins. Decimated today, the community was then still alive and vigorous and divided between "white" and "black" Jews. I also met the man who led the "revolution" of the "black" Jews against the "white" Jews. One Yom Kippur, in the purest Gandhian tradition of non-violence, the "black" Jews occupied the stairs leading to the "white" synagogue in order to gain admission to the "white" synagogue and put an end to the social discrimination between the two groups. They succeeded with the synagogue but complained that the social separation did not disappear.

All these little communities finally came together as a federation in the Central Jewish Board of India. A Jew of Lithuanian origin living in Bombay, Hersh Cynowicz, worked hard and long to bring this unification to fruition. Brought up in the Zionist tradition, full of energy, he successfully served as a mediator of great skill among the various groups, separated by enormous distances and by quite different traditions.

An Unexpected Problem

I cannot end this chapter without recalling one other experience. It has nothing to do with the problems of students or universities, but it occurred in 1953 on the occasion of an International Student Service general assembly held in Grenoble, France. It is not too much to say that without my presence in the city a subsequent consequential event would never have taken place.

At the end of a meeting of the Service assembly, toward eleven o'clock in the evening, I returned to my hotel in the company of several colleagues from the University of Grenoble. After having chaired the assembly and various committees all day, I was extremely tired. The walk to the hotel took about twenty minutes, and we all appreciated the fresh air after a day of hard work.

After we had been walking for a few minutes we met a group of Grenoble Jews who belonged to the local section of the WJC. They took me to task for being in Grenoble without letting them know, insisting that at least I grant them the time for lunch together.

This we did in the apartment of one of the city's Jewish leaders. We formed a very congenial group of eight around the table. A gentleman whom I did not know, by the name of Moshe Keller, told an extraordinary story about a case of child abduction in Grenoble. The parents of two young Austrian Jews placed them in the care of a Catholic woman, a certain Madame Brun, before the parents were deported to Auschwitz, where the Germans killed them. After the war, two aunts, one living in Israel, the other in New Zealand, demanded the return of the children. Madame Brun refused. She created all kinds of difficulties, and they soon learned that she had had the children baptized and would not let them go.

The aunts asked Keller to bring the matter before the Grenoble courts. Exposed, Madame Brun spirited the children away, and Basque priests hid them in Spain.

I had difficulty believing such a fantastic story. There had been the Mortara Affair in Bologna, where, in 1858, police had removed six-year-old Edgardo Mortara from his family because six years earlier a servant girl had sprinkled water on him believing him near death. The church declared him baptized and had him seized. He never returned to his family. But that had occurred a hundred years earlier. That such events could take place in our own era was hard to accept.

Keller complained bitterly that the Jewish organizations in Paris, in particular those concerned with Jewish children, had shown no interest in the matter and did not react to his urgent requests for help. He earnestly asked me to assist him. I promised that I would and told him that after the summer holidays we would invite him to Paris and also call in representatives of the associations responsible for children as well as some prominent legal professionals to examine together what might be done in the matter. Soon after this luncheon I gave the appropriate instructions to the WJC office in Paris.

The problem of Jewish children hidden by Catholics during the war was not new for me. I had, readers will recall, already discussed it in 1945 with Monsignor Montini in Rome.

The meeting took place in the WJC office in Paris as planned. At the suggestion of David Lambert, a fine jurist and vice president of the French section of the WJC, we decided to ask another eminent lawyer, Maurice Garçon, to attend the next session of the Grenoble court to represent the interests of the Jewish family. And we called the Grenoble trial to the attention of some Parisian newspapers.

Everything proceeded according to plan. Lawyer Garçon intervened in the trial, and his pleading received enormous publicity. Thus the Finaly Affair—for such was the name of the children's family—burst on the scene as a national *cause célèbre*. It had repercussions well beyond France and greatly moved the Jewish community. Various Jewish organizations suddenly woke up. The chief rabbi of France, Jacob Kaplan, intervened personally in the matter and negotiated with the highest authorities of the Catholic church in France. The court ordered the children to their aunt in Israel where today they live as good Israeli citizens. Without my intervention, this story would never have received national attention. The happy conclusion to the Finaly Affair made a considerable contribution to the process of reconciliation between Jews and Catholics.

[EIGHT]

The World Jewish Congress

AT THE SIDE of Dr. Nahum Goldmann and Stephen Wise, I participated in the founding of the World Jewish Congress in 1936. Created under difficult conditions, the organization became enormously successful in achieving its goals over almost seventy years. What did the world look like in 1936?

The Nazis had then been in power for three and a half years and pursued an anti-Jewish policy characterized by discriminatory measures carried out with unheard-of brutality and authoritarian actions based on new legislation affecting civil and judicial authorities. Poland had denounced the League of Nations' protection-of-minorities treaty that guaranteed Jews fundamental rights—an example for other states. In several countries that had been struck by the economic crisis of 1929, economic discrimination left tens of thousands of families without resources. No country in the world was willing to receive the masses of Jews who wished to flee Germany and other European countries that practiced their own brand of anti-Semitism. The Western world seemed paralyzed in the face of the Nazis and their allies. Thus the constitutive assembly of the World Jewish Congress met in a climate of rejection and anguish regarding the future.

Furthermore the founders of the WJC in Geneva represented not the entire Jewish people but only a minority. There were, however, representatives of thirty-two countries from all five continents, including the great majority of the Jews from Poland, Romania, Czechoslovakia, Lithuania, and Latvia, which constituted the living heart of Judaism at that time (unfortunately, there could be no question of counting on a delegation from the Soviet Union). This majority fully supported the formation of the World Jewish

Congress. To be sure, opposing circles included the ultra-Orthodox movement and the Socialist Bund, but on the whole the idea of the Congress was an extremely popular one.

Those who met to confront the mortal danger of Hitlerism—I believe I am the only one of those founders still alive*—understood the urgent necessity of a unified front of all the Jewish communities, with an executive authorized to speak and act in their name. Among the most prominent participants were the writers Sholem Asch and Emil Ludwig, the judge Julian M. Mack, Professors Nathan Isaacs and Horace Kallen, Louis Sturz, Joseph Tenenbaum, Chaim Greenberg, and Marie Syrkin from the United States; Rabbis Ouziel and Fishman, as well as Berl Locker and Itzhak Grünbaum from Palestine; Arieh Tartakower, Anselm Reiss, Chief Rabbi Rubinstein and Emil Sommerstein from Poland; Maurice Eisendrath from Canada, and others. The delegations representing the Jews of Western Europe and North America did not speak for the totality of their communities.

On the international level it was a time of appeasement toward Hitler. At that moment the large Jewish communities of the Western world more or less followed the policies of their respective governments. Thus the World Jewish Congress, at that time a symbol of the active struggle against Nazism, did not find support from those who accepted the policy of appeasement. This was particularly true in France, where there was no central representative Jewish body and where only a minority supported the idea of the Congress. The favorable minority there was above all composed of East European immigrants, grouped for the most part in the Federation of Jewish Societies of France and the Zionist movement.

In Britain the situation was even more complex. The Board of Deputies of British Jews, the national organization, passionately debated the question of whether British Judaism should belong to the World Jewish Congress. An eight-vote majority rejected the proposal. The Board finally joined in 1975, thirty-nine years later.

Still, there has always been strong British support for the WJC. Consequently, after the vote against direct membership, all those who were in favor of the idea of the Congress founded a British WJC Section, which had the good fortune to be served by excellent leaders. During the war they became the intellectual center of European Judaism in a kind of brain trust.

The British section of the WJC attracted a great number of prominent Jews of various leanings who were determined to combat Nazism with all their

*Dr. Riegner died in December 2001, at the age of ninety, in Geneva.—ED.

strength and to make Jewish solidarity a reality. Their leaders included figures as prominent as Lord Melchett, who had been baptized as a child but who under the Nazi threat had returned to Judaism; his sister, the Marchioness of Reading; the young liberal rabbi Maurice Perlzweig; Socialist members of Parliament such as Sydney Silverman, Maurice Orbach, and Ian Mikardo; the founder of the Women's International Zionist Organization (WIZO), Rebecca Sieff; established journalists such as Alec Easterman; the economist and sociologist Noah Barou; and others.

The WJC British section also attracted exiles who had established themselves in England, such as the historian Aaron Steinberg, the jurists Ernst Frankenstein, Franz-Rudolf Bienenfeld, and E. J. Cohn, and others who had escaped from the countries occupied by Nazi Germany.

In the United States the American Jewish Congress (AJC) most strongly promoted the idea of a world congress, but the AJC did not represent the majority of American Jews, especially not the more conservative, older organizations that found a more congenial home in the American Jewish Committee. Small delegations represented the Latin American communities at the founding WJC assembly.

Thus in terms of the proportion of world Jewry represented in it, in 1936 the World Jewish Congress left a great deal to be desired. It would take many long years for the basic idea of the Congress to be more universally accepted, that is, the democratic idea according to which large and small communities would deliberate together on their common problems and act through a permanent executive elected by all concerned. And it took me a long time to understand why this idea—today completely uncontroversial—was so foreign to the mentality of the prewar Jews and why it caused fear. This fear was in fact motivated by two concerns: first, by the anti-Semitic myth of a "world" Judaism aimed at "universal domination"; and, second, by the criticism of double allegiance, that is, the accusation of divided loyalty. As for the myth of a world Jewish conspiracy, the open, public, and transparent organization of the communities in an international world organization proved that they had nothing to hide. As concerns double allegiance, Nahum Goldmann frequently said that no person was without several loyalties: toward a mother, father, child, family, religion, country—these are natural ties. Those who accepted only a sole, unique loyalty were the Nazis; in their extreme mythic nationalism, they did not admit that a person could have responsibilities other than to his people narrowly defined. All this appears rather odd today.

The situation would, in any case, change rapidly after the war. From a conceptual point of view, after the terrible suffering of the Shoah, one viewed these ideological conflicts and the divisions among Jews as tragic shortsightedness. Had the Jews been more united, a great many things could perhaps have been avoided.

It was clear that the communities organized in federations, grouping all the local communities of a country, were better prepared for membership in the WJC than those who were ideologically divided and not entirely representative. Federations existed in most European countries, but not, for example, in France and the United States. There, by reason of the strict separation of church and state, the formation and activities of Jewish organizations remained independent of central control. This led to a great number and great diversity of organizations, so that many years were required to create a basis for their unification in a national body.

This experience taught us that the goal should be the creation of representative bodies gathering all the Jews of a country, either in a federation made up of local communities or in a central organization that united the branches of all religious movements and active ideologies.

We made strenuous efforts in this direction in Latin America during World War II. The First Pan-American Jewish Conference, in Baltimore in 1941, marked an important stage. Along with representatives of American and Canadian Judaism, it brought in a great number of delegates from Latin American organizations. At the same time their presence revealed weaknesses in the Latin American organizational structures.

This fact led the leadership of the Congress to send Dr. Yaacov Hellmann to Latin America. Originally from Riga, Latvia, where for a time he served as a Jewish member of parliament, Hellmann later became a prominent Jewish intellectual and journalist in Poland where from 1933 to 1936 he was editor-in-chief of the large Yiddish newspaper *Dos naye wort.*

After he left Eastern Europe, in late 1939 the WJC appointed him representative for all Latin America with an office in Buenos Aires. Intensely active across the whole continent, he inspired many leaders with his strong personality and succeeded in creating representative central bodies in most of these countries.

These efforts naturally brought the Jewish communities of Latin America into close association with the World Jewish Congress. In 1959 a fourth regional branch of the WJC executive was established, incorporating the Jewish communities of twenty-one Latin American countries, and took its place alongside the branches for North America, Europe, and Israel. This process finally led to the creation, some ten years later, of the Latin American Jewish

Congress, a body representing all the Jews of the continent. Today the Latin American Jewish Congress is a pillar of the WJC.

During the war Hellmann also organized a large fund-raising drive in all the Latin American communities to help the imperiled Jews of Europe. The results allowed the WJC to finance a significant part of the relief action on behalf of the victims of Nazism.

Another initiative taken by the WJC in New York deserves mention. Europe had always been the backbone of the Congress and the principal object of its activities. The expansion of the war and the Nazi conquests gradually reduced the great historic communities to silence. Therefore it was essential that European Jewry's exiled leaders act as de facto representatives until the occupied communities were liberated and could name new spokesmen. Thus in the fall of 1941 the WJC established representative committees for the Jewish communities of eighteen occupied countries, on the model of the governments-in-exile. Together these committees formed a European Jewish affairs council consulting on questions affecting their countries. They also raised funds to come to the assistance of their communities. By these skillful means the Congress allowed the silenced and soon to be destroyed communities a voice in the discussions and actions aimed at saving as many of their brethren as possible.

As the World Jewish Congress evolved, its large extraordinary conference in Atlantic City in November 1944 was, in certain respects, more representative than the founding assembly held eight years earlier.

This War Emergency Conference gathered for the first time since the beginning of the war Jewish representatives from twenty-three countries on five continents, as well as those of the sixteen communities in countries under the Nazi boot. The driving force behind this emergency meeting was the urgent need to formulate a postwar political program for the Jewish people. The declaration and resolutions of the Atlantic City conference would in fact guide us for several decades—a tribute to the conference leaders' lucidity and the vigor of their vision. But in the short term the most pressing problem was to intensify efforts aimed at saving the Jews of Europe. (By virtue of this priority in the final, extremely critical phase of the war, I could not attend the conference: I remained in Geneva precisely to continue our efforts to realize this objective.) The conference appealed to the Jewish people, as a solemn duty to the millions of martyrs of Nazism, "to continue and increase their contribution to the war effort on every front until the total destruction of the Nazi-Fascist system shall have been achieved." The Conference also called for the unfettered support of "the forces which, in the spirit of the Atlantic Charter, are fighting for the triumph of the principles of justice and freedom in human affairs." To this end the conference called for:

> The promulgation of an International Bill of Rights securing full protection of life and liberty for the inhabitants of all countries without distinction of origin, nationality, race, faith, or language, and the enforcement of such a Bill of Rights by an adequate international machinery.
>
> Full and unequivocal equality of rights before the law and in fact for all citizens or subjects in every country and adequate protection of the elementary needs of all the inhabitants, such as the right to a gainful occupation.
>
> The inalienable right of all ethnic and religious groups to maintain and foster their collective identity under the equal protection of the law and with equal assistance of the state, where such system prevails.
>
> The adoption and promulgation of national laws and appropriate international legal instruments providing that antisemitic and anti-racial activities and similar acts of incitement to racial and religious hatred and discrimination are violations of criminal law and public policy.

The conference called for the recognition of specific Jewish needs, for example:

> The declaration as null and void of all measures of discrimination directed against Jews and the full restoration of their rights and status.
>
> Recognition of the particular needs of the Jewish people in the application of relief and rehabilitation measures within the schemes of postwar reconstruction.
>
> Apprehension, trial and punishment of the instigators and perpetrators of the crimes committed against Jews as such and the Jewish people since 1933.
>
> Restitution and reparation for the losses suffered by still existing Jewish communities and the individual Jewish victims of Nazi and Fascist murder and spoliation.
>
> The recognition of the principle that the Jewish people is entitled to a collective reparation for the material and moral losses suffered by the Jewish people, its institutions or individual Jews who or whose heirs are unable to present their individual claims.
>
> The establishment of Palestine as a Jewish Commonwealth.

Excerpts from two speeches—one given by A. Leon Kubowitzki, the other by Nahum Goldmann—seem in my opinion to best situate the enormous responsibility shouldered by the conference.

Concerning efforts made to save the Jews of Europe, Kubowitzki, then WJC secretary-general, declared, "Our task will end with the last Jew to be saved from German barbarity." As for Dr. Goldmann, he concluded with this moving message:

> We are, perhaps, the most tragic generation in Jewish history—one half of which was condemned to see the other half annihilated without being able to help. But this is not yet final. This most tragic of our generations may still become the most blessed if it plays the role which Jewish history calls upon it to play and discharges its responsibilities to lead our unhappy people from the tragic past, through the uncertain present, to a new and better future.

When the war ended, the Jewish communities of Europe met in London in August 1945. The participants were particularly moved when Jewish resistance leaders, including Warsaw Ghetto fighters such as Antek Cukierman and Cyvia Lubetkin, recalled their terrible experiences.

While waiting for a new plenary assembly, the only forum capable of establishing new structures for the Congress, it was decided to create a European secretariat to direct WJC activities in Europe. Several members of the British section, in particular Dr. Noah Barou, Alec Easterman, and I, were chosen to become part of the European secretariat. Shortly thereafter the director of the new Paris office, Sylvain Cahn-Debré, joined us. I was personally charged with the problems of organization and coordination of the European secretariat.

In the immediate postwar years we devoted our principal energies to the reorganization of communities; the elimination of the ravages of the Nazi era; the well-being and future of hundreds of thousands of displaced persons in camps; support for the movement to create a Jewish state; and the first steps in the struggle to draft a charter of human rights at the United Nations. I participated actively in all these efforts as well as in the preparations for the Second Plenary Assembly of the Congress to take place in June 1948 in Montreux, Switzerland. This assembly was one of the most impressive and one of the most important the WJC ever held. I was in charge of technical preparations, and I invited Stephen Roth of the London office to share this responsibility with me.

Because of the tension already growing between East and West, we believed it important that the assembly give us an opportunity to have all the communities of Eastern Europe participate in this vast gathering with the exception of those from the Soviet Union. The great success we achieved in this regard we could not replicate for many long years.

The delegations from Eastern Europe represented communities cruelly diminished by the Shoah. They had been officially "authorized" by the authorities of their countries, of course, and they included a certain number of Jewish Communists. As a result we experienced quite vehement political and ideological debates at the assembly.

We continued to make strenuous efforts to stay in touch with the committees in these countries. For one thing, our attachment to these communities expressed how profoundly we missed those who had disappeared. We also wished to express our attachment to their great traditions and, above all, to support the continuance of Jewish life in those countries where government ideology and practice endangered it.

Another striking feature of the Montreux assembly was the fact that it met six weeks after the proclamation of the State of Israel and that a member of the new Israeli government, David Remez, led a delegation with full participation rights. This was, moreover, the first truly important postwar meeting of Eastern and Western European Jews. It created the foundations for a new cooperation among all communities. To this end the assembly drew up and adopted a new constitution for the organization. It is comforting to note that despite political differences and tensions, the assembly succeeded in agreeing on a program and on clearly defined objectives. We elected a new executive of about fifty persons from sixteen countries on different continents, with Stephen Wise and Nahum Goldmann as directors. We also wanted a representative from Eastern Europe on the executive, and our choice fell on the president of the Federation of Jewish Communities of Yugoslavia, Professor Albert Vajs, whom we greatly admired. Professor Vajs refused, citing the spectacular political changes that precluded him from knowing what conditions he would find upon his return home. Tito's government had just declared its independence from the Soviet Union and withdrawn from the Communist bloc.

In recognition of the services I had rendered during the war and the role I played in the European secretariat, the assembly also elected me as a member of the executive.

Finally, I should note that Montreux was the last WJC meeting that Stephen Wise attended. He was gravely ill at that time; more than once we all feared he might collapse. In his moving final address he did in fact take leave of Congress members. Stephen Wise made a point of recalling two major experiences in his life, and these had marked him deeply.

The first was his meeting with Theodor Herzl on the occasion of the Second Zionist Congress, in 1898. He remembered Herzl saying that he would not live long enough to see the Jewish state but that Wise, much younger, would see it one day. Coming only a few weeks after the foundation of the State of Israel, Wise's recollections provoked strong emotions in us.

Wise told us of the second major experience in his life, namely his visit to Warsaw in 1936, where he had gone before attending the WJC founding assembly in Geneva. His introduction to the Polish communities had enormously impressed him and had shown him the vitality, the spiritual and cultural richness, and the pride of the Jewish populations of Eastern Europe. This was a moving homage to a tragically annihilated Jewish life he describes with great force in his memoirs.*

Israeli Representation in the World Jewish Congress

The creation of the State of Israel posed a problem for our own organization. How were the Jews of the new state to be represented within the WJC? We should recall that the Jews of Palestine (the Yishuv) had already participated in the 1936 founding conference of the Congress. Palestinian Jews were in fact represented by Vaad Leumi, the National Council, the democratically elected representative body of the Jews of Palestine. But this was to disappear with the creation of the Jewish state. It was not easy to find an adequate solution to the problem. Some people were of the opinion that elected members of the Knesset were fully authorized to play this role; others suggested that the municipal governments of the large Jewish towns and cities should choose the Israeli delegates to Congress meetings; and various other solutions were proposed.

In Israel as in the WJC, we devoted long discussions to finding an appropriate means of representation, a matter that was not self-evident. It should be recalled that all Israeli citizens, including Arabs, elected the deputies and municipal officials. As a result they did not specifically represent the Jewish populations in the country. These discussions finally led to a rather hybrid system which satisfied no one completely but which continues to function today.

The solution mandated that the Jewish political parties form an executive in which they are represented in proportion to their number of seats in the Israeli parliament after each general election. This formula has the advantage of assuring representation that corresponds to the political opinions of Israeli Jews but nonetheless has the disadvantage that it faithfully reflects only the political forces of the country and neglects problems of a cultural or social nature. Thus a number of correctives had to be found—national council, commissions, consultative councils—bodies on which those responsible for cultural

*Challenging Years: The Autobiography of Stephen Wise (New York, 1949), pp. 267–273.—ED.

and social life could be associated with WJC programs. In addition, certain rules assured the smaller political parties of minimal representation in Congress proceedings.

In a global sense, from 1959 on we recognized a widespread general desire for decentralization of the World Jewish Congress, solely with a view to furthering our work with a greater degree of independence, especially on the regional level. We envisioned branches for North America, including the United States, Canada, and Mexico; for Latin America, comprising the twenty-two states of the South American continent and Central America; for Europe, and for Israel. Other regional branches would later also achieve suitable representation.

Organizational Changes in the United States

It was, however, during the postwar years in the United States that the World Jewish Congress faced its most difficult organizational problems. The transformation of the American Jewish Congress after 1945, from an organization of associations to one of individual members, came about particularly because younger generations wanted a more expansive democratic basis for membership. At the same time American Jews recognized that because of the weakening of Jewish life in Europe, they would have to play a stronger, more vigorous role in Jewish affairs, especially with regard to Israel.

In addition, the organizations within the American Jewish Congress asserted themselves more and more vigorously in the pursuit of their various goals, independent of the AJC. Thus, under some pressure, the American Jewish Congress adopted a system of individual memberships. Thereafter it scarcely differed from other organizations, which led to a paradoxical situation: while the largest Jewish community in the world now was in the United States, the WJC was least well represented there.

In his occasionally brusque way of making decisions, Nahum Goldmann then tried to replace the WJC with a kind of super-Congress. He envisioned a body that would have greater participation by American organizations, thereafter unaffiliated with the WJC, in addition to the American Jewish Congress. Structurally the new organization would be guided by an executive board empowered to play a role similar to that of the WJC executive. After years of negotiations, in 1963 those who agreed with Goldmann finally established the World Conference of Jewish Organizations, often called COJO in Europe, intended to make possible closer cooperation between the WJC and the other organizations. I must admit that I stood alone in my strenuous opposition to the creation of the new body. In my opinion we had not thus far made sufficient efforts to persuade certain organizations to join us. My voice remained isolated, but subsequent developments proved me right.

Nonetheless COJO sponsored several positive initiatives, including the common memorandum addressed to the Vatican on the occasion of the Second Vatican Council, and the joint organization of the important international conference on the great problems of Jewish education. Yet COJO soon proved more and more superfluous as the organizations that comprised it gradually joined the World Jewish Congress.

In 1963 the WJC created an American section for the United States. Twelve national Jewish organizations and the American Jewish Congress made up the new body.

Another organizational factor of importance affected cooperation among the various American Jewish movements as well as influencing the position of the WJC in the United States. Created on the initiative of Nahum Goldmann, the Conference of Presidents of the Major American Jewish Organizations became transformed, in practical terms, into a conference of the organizations themselves. The Conference of Presidents decided to expand its activities, originally limited to American-Israeli relations, to include all Jewish problems that arose outside the United States. At the same time the Conference envisaged close collaboration with the World Jewish Congress. In particular it sent a large delegation to the Fifth WJC Plenary Assembly in Brussels in 1966. From the date of that assembly on, the influence of the WJC greatly increased in the United States. Two initiatives in particular contributed to this development.

Nahum Goldmann persuaded the leadership of Hadassah, the prestigious organization of more than 350,000 American Jewish women, to join the WJC. Goldmann's Zionist politics were extremely popular in Hadassah circles, which forcefully supported his efforts. When Hadassah wished to change its representation on the executive board of the Jewish Agency (Hadassah's president, Rose Halprin, had for many years and with great talent held various senior offices there), Nahum Goldmann suggested a solution that would lead to Rose Halprin assuming important responsibilities within the WJC itself when Hadassah became a member of the American section.

Second, the Union of Orthodox Jewish Congregations of America became an affiliate. Rabbis Joseph Karasick and Samson Weiss, who, on behalf of the Union, participated as observers in the meeting of the WJC executive board in Strasbourg in 1965 and the following year at the assembly in Brussels, were deeply impressed by the personality of Goldmann and by the seriousness of our work. I pleaded with the two Union representatives during a long private conversation that the most effective way to support Goldmann's policies would be to join the World Jewish Congress. But I observed evident hesitation on their part. Nahum Goldmann was the first to be surprised the next day when in my presence the two American Orthodox leaders announced their decision to join the WJC. The gesture was clearly of great importance in itself, but it also had the signal merit of prompting other large Jewish religious movements in the United States to enter on the path of membership in the Congress. Those that subsequently joined us included the Union of American Hebrew Congregations, the representative body of Reform Jews; the United Synagogue of Conservative Judaism, the central organization of Conservative congregations; and the Reconstructionist Foundation as well as the rabbinical organizations and women's groups of different Jewish religious tendencies. The membership of these organizations amounted to several million persons. The World Jewish Congress thus evolved into a considerable factor on the American scene. In the long run the increased prestige and influence of the Congress affected matters well beyond the United States, in particular in Great Britain (where the Board of Deputies of British Jews joined the WJC) and finally in France where the Representative Council of Jewish Institutions of France (CRIF), after long discussions, joined the WJC European branch. At the same time both sides initiated a pattern of close collaboration between the Congress and the Jewish Agency, which resulted in the inclusion of Agency delegates on the WJC executive board.

The South African Jewish Community and the Congress

Following a policy similar to that of the British Board of Deputies, the large South African Jewish community remained for a long time distanced from the WJC. But when the British organization finally became a member in 1974, the South African Jewish Board of Deputies approached us and expressed a desire to follow that example—and this raised certain difficulties. At that time the international community had assumed an increasingly assertive opposition to the policy of apartheid and had essentially banned South Africa from international society. Even international nongovernmental organizations that had not clearly condemned the policy felt the growing anti-apartheid pressures.

Consequently we found ourselves in a delicate position, for even if a number of eminent individual South African Jews had joined the movement against apartheid in their country, the representative organization of South African Jews had never dared take a stand, explaining that such a position had to be left to individuals. South Africa's official Jewish leaders clearly found themselves in an embarrassing situation: they were face to face with a power that before and during World War II had frequently shown its sympathy for the Nazis. Their comportment and their stand on the racial question were severely limited.

On the other hand, the most representative South African rabbis, both those who belonged to the Orthodox movement and those of the liberal Reform movement, displayed great courage. Many of them, and not the least prominent, categorically condemned apartheid.

Because of the danger of losing various kinds of consultative status in the UN system, there was no cause to show any impatience in bringing the South African Jews into the Congress. Under these circumstances, I chose to temporize the issue. The South African Jews who had come to Congress meetings for some years as observers knew very well that we were in no particular hurry to receive them as full members. Only when the South African Board of Deputies adopted a resolution, proposed by the country's Jewish Student Union, that unequivocally denounced the policy of apartheid did I, as secretary-general of the WJC, drop my opposition to a South African Jewish organization joining the World Jewish Congress.

Repression in Eastern Europe

The Jewish communities of Eastern Europe found their membership in the WJC hindered by the Cold War. As I have already noted, these communities had shown their support in impressive fashion at the Second Plenary Assembly in 1948. Under pressure from their governments, some of them were prevented from remaining WJC members for long periods. Their relations with the WJC varied according to the times and the country. These difficulties prompted us to redouble our efforts on behalf of the Eastern European Jewish communities, efforts that finally reached a successful conclusion.

I have described elsewhere the situation of the Jews in the Soviet Union and our long struggle for equal rights in general and for the exercise of their religious and cultural rights in particular. We never gave up the idea of seeing them join the WJC. But we did have to wait for Gorbachev's assumption of power in 1985 for their liberation to become a reality and for them finally to be in a position to join the World Jewish Congress.

Associated Movements

The World Jewish Congress is comprised of organizations representing the Jewish communities of different countries, therefore their affiliation is based upon geography. Over time a number of international Jewish organizations have sought to be recognized by the Congress and to join it in order to exert their influence there. Some of these included federations established on the basis of the common origin of their members, such as the World Sephardic Federation, the World Federations of Polish Jews, Hungarian Jews, and so on. There were also groups organized on a professional basis, such as the International Association of Jewish Jurists or the World Federation of Jewish Journalists.

Additionally, some international groups had come together in defense of their common interests, such as the World Federation of Former Servicemen, Partisans and Camp Detainees, or the World Union of Jewish Students. There were also important movements that united Jewish women, such as the International Council of Jewish Women and the Women's International Zionist Organization (WIZO). Also, the Zionist ideological movements created international federations that gathered their members in the Diaspora. All these associations played an important role in public opinion, and some exerted a strong influence on the evolution of ideas.

I attempted to integrate these dynamic movements into the activities of the Congress while at the same time respecting the geographical basis of its constitution. In this spirit we created a category for affiliated international organizations; this guaranteed all these groups some representation, particularly at the plenary assemblies. In this way the WJC benefited from the support of the totality of these movements and strengthened the concept of the unity of the Jewish people. In addition, the WJC could not only mobilize their goodwill in support of its political action but also benefit from their special talents and expertise.

In short, all these affiliations and memberships appreciably strengthened the WJC's international position and credibility. And here I should like to recount some aspects of my contribution to the organization's evolution and expansion.

After joining the WJC in 1936, I became the Geneva office director in 1940. At the end of the war I became a member of the secretariat for Europe and was elected to the world executive board in 1948. I was officially appointed coordinator of the Congress in 1959 and went on to be elected secretary-general in 1965, a position I held until 1983. I became secretary-general only relatively late in the Congress's history, out of consideration for senior officials appreciably older than I. But this never prevented me from exercising a strong influence.

I always took my task very seriously, identifying myself deeply with the Congress. I devoted all my energy to its success, both in pursuit of its long-term goals and in its daily activities. Setting our course and maintaining its direction required constant efforts and corrective measures.

In the course of this intense activity, which in fact comprised my entire professional existence and also my private life, I visited Jewish communities everywhere in the world—official visits, of course, but also visits that through their human contacts allowed me to hear the concerns of the communities. It was important that people in these communities feel very directly the ties that bound them to the totality of other communities and to the World Jewish Congress itself. There was a whole web to be woven or renewed.

I have always had a strong desire to be available to all and sundry. To me this seemed an indispensable condition of the mission of the Congress: to be open to everyone, whatever the occasional difficulties and constraints. In this connection I should note the address given by Nahum Goldmann on the occasion when the Congress awarded me its medal. Goldmann called me one of the persons who knew the Jewish communities best, "informed of their problems like no one else." Today I still feel great pride in this, aware that in daily life the communities are the very blood of Judaism. Yet this blood could at times have circulated more forcefully, when for example the rivalry between certain urban communities, reflecting the ambitions of their cities, created problems and endangered harmonious relations, as was the case with the communities of Melbourne and Sidney, or Rio de Janeiro and São Paulo. In order to calm these troubled waters and recover a degree of mutual understanding, I had to use incredible flexibility and tact. This proved to me that it was not enough to be an effective organizer, one also had to be a good diplomat.

I should add that I always tried to arrange direct access to the WJC president when the need arose. The capacity of the Congress at its highest levels to *listen* demanded the availability of its leaders, and circumstances often put this to the test.

It is equally interesting to note our orientation toward modernity, toward progress, which retrospectively seems to have happened on its own, though that was not at all the case. For example, as early as 1953 I introduced a system of simultaneous translation at our large meetings. Making language transparent had always seemed to me a major factor in people understanding one another, a matter of no little consequence. Until 1948 almost all delegates understood Yiddish—our *lingua franca*. Little by little, however, English became the dominant language. (Many thought one day it would be Hebrew.) It was striking to observe the generation gap with regard to the spread of English: the younger generation with English as a first or second language ineluctably swept away the older, Yiddish-speaking generation.

I have always been a capable organizer. My sense of organization has often caused me to suffer when any disorder occurs in my private and professional lives. Apparently this aspect of my personality has often been noticed. In this connection I recall an amusing incident from one of the Congress meetings in Geneva. Israel Sieff, then the head of the famous Marks and Spencer department store in London and an influential, generous figure in the Congress (he was then its vice president), told me that he was so impressed by the organization of the meeting that he would like to have me manage one of his stores somewhere in the world: "It's up to you to pick which of the hundred and twenty branches appeals to you most!" Knowing that every one of them represented fabulous sales figures, I was quite flattered by his offer. I thanked him but said, "If I were interested in money, I would have been a banker, not the secretary-general of the WJC." Nonetheless, however much that proposal surprised me, I consider it the nicest compliment ever paid me by a Congress leader.

I should emphasize another aspect of my work. I had the good fortune to have in Nahum Goldmann an exceptionally open president. The breadth of his vision quickly brought him to the essentials of every question without becoming mired in details. And the confidence he showed in me allowed me to enjoy great independence, without which, as a simple member of staff, I should probably not have remained with the Congress. This independence and the variety of the challenges at the WJC could only stimulate me. These are certainly the decisive factors that led me to devote sixty years of my life to the organization and its mission.

Nahum Goldmann willingly accepted my ideas, often making them his own. All our work aimed at anticipating political developments, foreseeing the future, and preparing Jewish communities for the situations they would eventually face. To achieve such goals we created special structures so that the voice of Jewish youth would be heard in our deliberations, and so that its representatives would learn to become responsible leaders in their own communities. I believe this practical training of the younger generation to be one of the major successes of my life.

After the immediate postwar period, the profound transformations in society and the changes in the situation of Jews around the world required a new examination and analysis of future goals, a reflection on the means to reach them, and a rethinking of the Congress's mandate. The role of the Congress at the heart of Jewish life became a decisive and dynamic factor in its evolution.

The era of the Shoah—during which survival had been the supreme directive for our activities—gradually came to an end. The new era was marked by a renewed will to live and to continue the millenary and highly creative mission of the Jewish people. For us the emergence of the State of Israel and the increasingly central role it played in Jewish life around the world strongly stimulated our thoughts about the future.

It was in this spirit that in 1975, at the Sixth Plenary Assembly, we revised the WJC constitution. Its revised goals took into account this evolution and expressed the priorities that the new situation imposed on us:

> The World Jewish Congress is organized to foster the unity of the Jewish people, to strive for the fulfillment of its aspirations, and to ensure the continuity and development of its religious, spiritual, cultural, and social heritage, and to that end it seeks:
>
> 1. To intensify the bonds of world Jewry, with Israel as the central creative force in Jewish life, and to strengthen the ties of solidarity among Jewish communities everywhere;
>
> 2. To secure the rights, status, and interests of Jews and Jewish communities and to defend them wherever they are denied, violated or imperiled;
>
> 3. To encourage and assist the creative development of Jewish social, religious, and cultural life throughout the world;
>
> 4. To coordinate the efforts of the Jewish communities and organizations with respect to the political, economic, social, religious, and cultural problems of the Jewish people;
>
> 5. To represent and act on behalf of its participating communities and organizations before governmental, intergovernmental, and other international authorities with respect to matters which concern the Jewish people as a whole.
>
> The World Jewish Congress strives to cooperate with all peoples on the basis of universal ideals of peace, freedom and justice.

These principles remain valid. Fundamentally the raison d'être of the World Jewish Congress has not changed in the years that have passed since a new generation succeeded the founding leaders. Its working methods have certainly evolved, but the philosophy of the organization has been steadfast. It is clearly the right and even the duty of each generation to seek to follow the most judicious paths to reach the goals that have been set.

[N I N E]

Into the New Millennium

MY LIFE EXHIBITS an exceptional, perhaps even unique unity and consistency: sixty years devoted without interruption to the same ideal. I have worked during the most dramatic period of our history, characterized by three major developments, one of which shook the international Jewish community to the very foundations of its existence.

The first of these developments, of course, was the Shoah, the gravest crisis in Jewish history since the destruction of the Temple, perhaps even more grave. A mortal enemy deliberately eliminated one-third of our people. The Jewish people are still traumatized by the experience and continue to struggle to understand the significance of this appalling tragedy. The catastrophe touched the Jewish people on the deepest levels of its being. It came close to destroying its confidence in the continuing progress of humanity, as our messianic tradition teaches, reinforced by the ideas of the Enlightenment. This trial raised profound doubts as to the justness of its profession of faith. This wrenching situation demanded a considerable effort to overcome our despair and redefine our true engagement.

I belong to the tragic generation that saw the catastrophe coming and tried to contain its effects, but who, given the lack of foresight, the moral indifference, and the political opportunism of the world that surrounded us, lacked the means to do so.

The second factor of decisive importance for Jewish existence was the rebirth of a Jewish state after two millennia of deprivation, wandering, and persecution. This was our most far-reaching accomplishment, an event that established Jewish sovereignty for the first time in almost two thousand years

434

and at the same time confronted Jews with the dilemmas accompanying empowerment and an active role in the determination of their own history.

The founding of the State of Israel after the profound trauma of the Shoah revealed the indestructible energy inherent in the Jewish people and its unfailing will to reestablish its existence on a new basis in its ancestral land. We took this historic and decisive step not only to liberate us from fear, defamation, and threats to our existence but to create conditions favorable to the development of our own culture in freedom and dignity.

I was an active witness to the developments that led to this miracle, and I participated in many efforts intended to consolidate the new state during its vulnerable first phase, to strengthen it through solidarity and steadfast action by the Jews of the Diaspora, and to defend it against those who questioned its legitimacy.

The third great event of our time was the collapse of the Communist regimes of Eastern Europe and the many consequences that followed. These were particularly apparent on the fiftieth anniversary of the end of World War II and revealed the new situation in which large segments of the Jewish people now found themselves.

By 1995 Jews no longer suffered in captivity. The State of Israel no longer had to fight for its right to exist. The Shoah, the Holocaust, was in the process of being integrated into the main currents of European history. The great religious institutions finally accepted Judaism as a living reality that continues its advance toward the future. Each Jew today is voluntarily a Jew. The fact that a high proportion of Jews have chosen not to disappear into a free society implies solid motivation and above all the desire to redefine their Jewishness in positive terms.

The greatest challenge today facing all religious movements grows out of our living in largely secularized societies. How can these movements withstand the pressures of their societies? There is no doubt that the force of secular influences is profoundly weakening religious movements. The Jewish community is intensely experiencing the consequences of the atmosphere thus created, in which the influences of the secular materialism that surrounds it affect all its members. It is enough to recognize some statistics in order to measure these effects. Traditional Jewish institutions—and in particular the traditional Jewish family, known for its stability—have become extraordinarily difficult to maintain.

At the same time we are witnessing a remarkable resurgence of the Orthodox sector of the community, which reveals the enormous strength and all the fervor of the attachment to traditional forms of the faith. Religious schools and *yeshivot* have developed in extraordinary fashion. The *yeshivot* of Israel, in which tens of thousands of young people receive their education, are today more numerous than in the powerful system of Orthodox education in Eastern Europe, which for centuries constituted the principal center of Jewish religious life and from which most modern Jewish movements issue.

Israel has become a vital center of renewal. A large share of the teachers and educators of the Diaspora have been trained in Israel. Research on Jewish subjects has experienced an astonishing revival. Jewish studies have engaged more minds in Israel during the last decades than during the whole period of the dispersal of the Jews.

In the same way the Conservative and Reform movements—the other principal sectors of Jewish religious life—have devoted immense effort to the maintenance and development of their institutions. Jewish schools, which constitute one of the principal means of transmitting the Jewish spirit to younger generations, have achieved considerable success. The transformation of the synagogue into a center for study and cultural activities of all kinds— from kindergartens to adult education programs, and including the education of young people and athletic associations—attests to a profound attachment to Jewish values and the fervor of efforts devoted to keeping the Jewish community strong and vibrant. Adoption of the principle of paternal descent by the Reform movement, resolutely opposed by other sectors of the community, is another effort to confront the challenges of the times.

Even in the territories that formerly made up the Soviet Union, in which all Jewish activity was virtually proscribed, we see an astonishing awakening of the Jewish spirit and its traditions, and a veritable explosion of initiatives aimed at maintaining and revitalizing Judaism. Who would have thought it possible that only a few years after the fall of the Soviet Union thousands of students in more than fifty state or private universities would be taking courses in Jewish history, Bible study, Jewish philosophy, Hebrew, and many similar subjects, and that some 350 professors and specialists would be engaged in such teaching?

So there is reason for optimism. Yet our statisticians periodically announce an appreciable decline in the numbers of Jews. I do not follow these prophets of doom. It may well be that our numbers are declining. But the intensity of the current engagement of large sectors of the Jewish people seems to me even stronger than during the course of the two last centuries. The Shoah and the creation of the Jewish state have played a great role in this regard. My vision of the assimilation process is that the third generation is seeking to recall its roots, roots that the second generation had tried to forget.

Assimilation is not a modern phenomenon. It has existed throughout our history. Variation in the total number of Jews over the course of the centuries is proof of this.

All the statisticians' speculations tell us nothing about the true meaning of Jewish existence. There is no rational explanation for the fact that, after all the persecutions by secular powers and the powerful challenge to its right to existence from the principal spiritual forces in the world, the Jewish people is still vibrantly and vigorously alive. No one can foresee what God's intentions are for his people, certainly not statisticians.

Throughout the unrelenting, innumerable crises and tensions during the long years of my professional career, I have never lost hope; I never, as you will have seen, gave in, even at the worst moments. I never considered "no" a valid response. When I faced immense difficulties, I looked for ways to overcome them.

I believe that this account of my activities—as this book bears witness—shows that with an absolute faith in the justice of one's cause, unfailing energy, unflinching determination, limitless perseverance, and systematic daily work, one finally achieves results, even when the obstacles initially seem totally insurmountable. Often I have acted on my own. My actions may perhaps serve as an example for others placed in similar situations.

Although throughout my career conditions very often seemed dark indeed, some light did finally appear. The decision of the Rabin-Peres government to renounce all desire to dominate another people and to seek peace with the Palestinians through negotiation, with respect for the essential interests of the other party, completely changed the situation in Israel and provoked an internationally favorable response. This decision, which culminated in the September 1993 signing by Israeli and Palestinian representatives of the Declaration of Principles on Interim Self-Government Arrangements, negotiated in an Oslo suburb, may be considered a return of the Jewish state to the principles that ought to regulate pacific coexistence among nations.* In fact, it was simply in accord with the logic that had motivated Ben-Gurion's and the Israeli authorities' acceptance of the UN decision concerning the division of Palestine in November 1947.

Admittedly, anti-Semitism can still be found in many countries and often rises up, even in unexpected ways. On the whole, however, the situation of the Diaspora has been appreciably strengthened.

---

*Israeli and Palestinian representatives also negotiated and signed an additional agreement in September 1995, the Israeli-Palestinian Interim Agreement on the West Bank and the Gaza Strip. Together they are known as the Oslo Agreements.—ED.

The new position of the Jews found its most striking expression in a series of events proving that we had entered into a historical process that accepts the Shoah as a central, unique fact in the twentieth century and integrates it into European history. This development constitutes a veritable breakthrough for the Jewish position in the contemporary world. It required fifty years for the people among whom we live to recognize the immensity of the catastrophe and take the measure of its transcendental importance. Only gradually did people became conscious of the fact that even though Germany is the principal guilty party in the extermination of one-third of the Jewish people, other peoples were not without blame. All bear a share of the responsibility for what happened. Of the indolence, cowardice, disregard, indifference, frivolousness, inertia, passivity, lack of reaction, and absence of will that characterized the conduct of all, no one may declare himself innocent.

The breakthrough found its most symbolic expression on the occasion of the fiftieth anniversary of the liberation of the camp at Auschwitz. While we had hitherto always been alone in commemorating the Shoah and in our homage to our dead, more than fifty governments took part in this memorable ceremony and with us honored the victims who disappeared on this site.

The address by the president of the Swiss Federation, Kaspar Villiger, on the fiftieth anniversary of the end of the war—in which he apologized to the Jewish people for the wrongs done by Switzerland before and during World War II, in particular for turning away thousands of Jewish refugees and for introducing the "J" stamp on the passports of German Jews—is also part of the new recognition of the wrongs of the past.

Sometime later the president of the International Committee of the Red Cross recognized the "moral failure" of his organization, which can today only regret the omissions and errors it committed in the course of the systematic genocide against the Jewish people.

The declaration of President Jacques Chirac, accepting for the first time the responsibility of the French Republic for the anti-Jewish policy of the Vichy regime, marked another decisive step in the process of reestablishing the truth and recognizing the responsibility that until then had not been admitted, even by his predecessor, the socialist François Mitterrand. This statement, ultimately confirmed by Prime Minister Lionel Jospin, represented a significant moment in this evolution.

The Bishops of France declaration of repentance for their silence with regard to the extermination of the Jews and their responsibility for not having lent aid when protest and protection were necessary and possible is a profoundly moving document and a major act of reparation.

Similar declarations were published by several Episcopal conferences in other countries, deploring the mistakes, failings, and other weaknesses of their churches with respect to Jews during World War II, particularly in Germany, Poland, Holland, Switzerland, the United States, Hungary, and Italy. Finally we must note the text *We Remember: A Reflection on the Shoah*, prepared at the request of John Paul II and published by the Commission for Religious Relations with Judaism on March 16, 1998.

The sometimes passionate discussions and debates on the restitution of Jewish property, on the recovery of Nazi gold that originated in part with the victims, on the failure of various states to respect the obligation to restore confiscated and stolen objects or to indemnify or compensate Jewish survivors for their losses and their sufferings—all this bears witness to an awakening of governments around the world, and of wide sectors of their societies, as well as to a recognition of their past errors and responsibilities. None of this would have occurred—indeed, it would be unthinkable—without the new mentality that today accepts the Shoah as a central event in the history of our past century.

This new situation was severely shaken by the formation of the Netanyahu government in Israel. Its policies not only halted the peace process, in my opinion they deeply undercut the reestablished credibility and prestige of the Israeli state, which once again faced increased isolation. And the same policies everywhere weakened the position of Jews in the Diaspora.

Netanyahu's method consisted of procrastination, and his fallacious and contradictory promises, his inconsistent declarations were deeply resented by a broad spectrum of public opinion. While some regarded this policy, to quote the words of his former minister of foreign affairs, David Levy, as "impenetrable abracadabra," others were persuaded that his true goal was the annulment of the Oslo accords.

Clearly, none of this advanced the cause of peace, but certain positive aspects must also be mentioned. The great majority of Israeli Jews, as all the polls show, are ardently attached to peace and want the peace process to be pursued to its conclusion. The great majority of Jews in the Diaspora share this view.

Similarly, the great majority of Palestinians and governments of Arab states clearly favor the continuation of this process. This is the great difference from the situation at the time of the conclusion of the peace with Egypt, when all the other Arab states and most member states of the UN condemned the peace treaty.

Extremists on both sides are trying to sabotage the politics of peace. They provide mutual aid in this struggle and have until now succeeded in delaying

any constructive solution. I believe, however, that positive forces will ultimately gain the upper hand. Peace is not an idea to trifle with; it is the quin-
tessence of Jewish tradition. The idea that these two peoples, the Jews and the
Palestinians, have a historic and moral right to an independent existence in
this old land, that they both consider it their homeland, is too strong for it to
fail. Let me restate here *my faith in hope*, "without which nothing can be accomplished, with which everything becomes possible."

Another serious problem before us on the threshold of a third millennium
concerns the worsening of religious conflicts and the tensions they cause. The
strengthening and expansion of fundamentalist religious movements that we
see in large parts of the world have led to a growth of fanaticism and intolerance to an extent unknown in the recent past. All these developments have left
their mark on Jewish communities.

The tension between religious groups and nonbelievers in Israeli society
is not a new fact. It has existed since the foundation of the state. This cultural conflict must someday be resolved. Ben-Gurion and the founders of
the state were right to have put it off as long as possible, meanwhile permitting the state to gain strength and cohesion. This tension between two segments of the population has been aggravated since the Orthodox forces of
the country have been considerably strengthened, are increasingly adopting
extremist positions, and are trying by all means possible to shift the country's policies in their direction. Nevertheless Ben-Gurion's policy retains its
raison d'être.

In the United States certain extremist Orthodox groups have gone so far
in their intolerance as to deny the Jewish character of large congregations of
Reform and Conservative Jews! And this in complete contradiction with halakhic teaching, according to which it is almost impossible for a Jew to lose his
Jewish identity.

The strengthening of extremist tendencies in Israel and the rest of the
world is reflected in the immediate serious dangers presented by Orthodoxy.
This found its most dramatic expression in the discussion in Israel on the conversion of non-Jews to Judaism. Orthodox demands in this matter clashed
deeply with the views of representatives of the Conservative and Reform
branches of Judaism, who make up the great majority of American Jews. This
conflict became so sharp and violent that it threatened to explode and cause
an irrevocable split in Judaism. It was only after a great deal of effort at conciliation that the worst was avoided for the moment. Neeman, the Israeli minister of finance, was charged with finding compromise formulas acceptable to
all parties.

The World Jewish Congress, the supreme expression of the principle of unity of the Jewish people, could not stand aloof from this dramatic conflict. As one of its founders and a witness to the creation of the WJC, and the proclamation on that occasion of the unity of the Jewish people as the sole fundamental principle of the new organization, I believe we have a special responsibility: to see that this conflict is resolved and that no effort is spared to find a solution acceptable to all. I am happy to know that President Ezer Weizman also supports this position.*

People are occasionally ironic on the subject of the unity of the Jewish people and its effectiveness. It is true that the Jewish people is highly individualistic and is profoundly committed to the freedom of individual opinion. People sometimes joke that when three Jews discuss something together, they voice four opinions.

But this does not prevent the unity of the Jewish people from being the sole effective framework through which our organizations, our communities, the Diaspora, and the Jews of Israel can be associated and united in the common defense of the rights and interests of all, and in assuring their cohesion.

Since this solidarity and cooperation are based in the free will of all of us, the principle of unity is the sole guarantee of the preservation and perseverance of the Jewish people and its mission in the world.

*Named for then Minister of Finance Yaakov Neeman, the Commission failed to win sufficient support to implement its compromise proposal to establish a joint commission institute when the Israel Chief Rabbinate rejected the plan in February 1998. Ezer Weizman, who left the presidency in July 2000, died in April 2005.—ED.

Index

Abramowicz, Emmanuel, x

Abramowicz, Léon, ix–x

Abyssinia (Ethiopia), 173

Adenauer, Konrad, 25, 378, 380–382, 407

Adishehia, Malcolm, 404

Agagianian, Gregory Peter XV Cardinal, 257

Agudath Israel, 45, 51, 98

Aktion Sühnezeichen (Reconciliation Action), 342

Alchey, Ruthy, x

Alfassi, 361

Alkan, Walter, 13

Altmaier, Jakob, 380

American Jewish Committee, 248, 252, 270, 276,419

American Jewish Congress, 63, 71, 82, 419, 426

American Jewish Joint Distribution Committee (Joint), 73, 140, 218

American Jewish reaction to news of Holocaust, 51

Amit, Rabbi Zeev, 326

Anglican Church and the Jews. See Jews and the Anglican Church, relations between.

Anglican Communion. See World-Wide Anglican Communion.

Anglican Consultative Committee, 335–336

Anglo-American Committee of Inquiry on Palestine (UN), 392–393

Anschluss, 172–173

Anschütz, Gerhard, 19

Anti-Defamation League, 244, 252, 270

anti-Jewish boycott (Germany, April 1, 1933), 21–22, 38

anti-Semitism, 12–13, 18, 20, 25, 120, 238, 297–298, 329; among the Allies (World War II), 58–59, 62; and Catholic church 281; in Eastern Europe and the Soviet Union, 195–197; in Egypt, 256; in Europe, 417; in Hungary, 384; in Romania, 169–172, 384; in Switzerland, 152–157, 162; in the Soviet Union, 212ff., 225; struggle against, 190ff.; wave of 1959–1960, 316–318

Antonescu, Ion, 59

Armenian genocide, 109

Armstrong, Vice Consul, 42

Arndt, Siegfried Theodor, 353

Arnheim, Max, 3

Arnold, Alice, 201

Arrow Cross Party, 95–96

"aryanization," 38

Asch, Sholem, 418

Association of Democratic Students (Berlin University), 20

Auriol, Vincent, 225, 239, 368

Auschwitz, 36, 83, 85, 126, 285, 292, 294, 415, 438; and the Carmelite convent, 195, 293–295; bombing of, 62–64

Auschwitz II (Birkenau), 85–86

Azmi, Mahmud, 179

B'nai B'rith, 243, 252, 254, 258, 270, 276, 338, 402

B'nai Israel (Bombay), 413–414

Babi Yar, 215–217

Bachmann, Hans, 132

Bačkis, Msgr. Audrys J., 192

Baillou, Jean, 405

Baker, Everett Moore, 406

Balfour Declaration (1917), 166

Balzac, Honoré, 24

Baron, Salo, 373

Barou, Noah, 376–381, 419, 423

Barth, Karl, 126, 313

Basdevant, Jean, 356–357

Baum, Gregory, 246–247

Baumann, Johannes, 160

Béa, Augustine Cardinal, 240–249, 251, 253–259, 261–267, 272, 281, 319

Becher, Kurt, 98, 100

Becker, Fritz, 245, 247–248, 272–273

Becker, Myra, x, 83

Bekessy, Janos (a.k.a. Hans Habe), 173–174

Bekkai, Si, 360–362

Bell, Dr. George (Bishop of Chichester), 126

Bellafrej, Ahmed, 360–361

Belzec concentration camp, 66

Ben Arafa, Sultan Moulay, 359, 361

Ben Barka, Ahmed, 361

Ben Youssef, Sultan Mohammed (later King Mohammed V), 359, 362

Benelli, Msgr. Giovanni, 272–274

Beneš, Edvard (Eduard), 25, 52, 173

Ben-Gurion, David, 70, 381, 393–394, 437, 440

Benjelloun, 361

Ben Souda, 361

Berard, Léon, 117

Bergman, David, 406

Berlin University, 20

Bermuda Conference, failure of, 67ff.

Bernadotte, Count Folke, 100, 107

Bernardini, Msgr. Filippe, 40–41, 110–111

Bernhard, Georg, 32–33

Bernheim Petition, 167–168

Berredo Carneira, Paul de, 373

Bertram, Adolf Cardinal, 119–120

Bessis, Albert, 357

Bevan, Aneurin, 53

Bienenfeld, Franz Rudolf, 179–180, 182, 207, 419

Biltmore Conference (1942), 70, 73

Bismarck, Otto von, 166

Blake, Rev. Eugene Carson, 269–270, 320

Blanch, Archbishop Stuart Yarworth, 335

Blankenhorn, Herbert, 378–381

blockade of Germany as hindrance to saving Jews, 60–62

Blonay, André de, 401

Blum, Léon, 78, 370

Blumel, André, 225

Board of Deputies of British Jews, 51, 243, 418, 428

Boetto, Pietro Cardinal, 118

Bonhoeffer, Dietrich, 124

Bonna, Pierre, 136

Born, Friedrich, 95, 97

Bouabid, Abderahman, 360–361
Boucetta, Mohammed, 360–361
Boujour, Edgar, 159, 161–162
Bourguiba, Habib, 357–358
Bourquin, Maurice, 27
Bowra, Sir Maurice, 405
Brandt, Willy, 225
Braunschweig, Saly, 159
Braunsschvig, Jules, 362
British Jewish reaction to news of the
    Shoah, 51
British White Paper on Palestine (1939),
    27
Brockway, Allan, 327
Brodetsky, Selig, 54, 237
Bronfman, Edgar, 231–232, 352–353
Brown, Sydney, 129
Brugioni, Dino, 63
Brunner, Emil, 126
Brunschvig, Henri, 402
Buber, Martin, 223
Buchenwald concentration camp, 83
Bucher, Rudolf, 48
Burckhardt, Carl J., 27, 48–50, 94, 96,
    105–107, 128, 130–132, 135–138,
    141–142, 175
Burzio, Msgr. Guiseppe, 117
Bush, George H. W., 195

Cahn-Debré, Sylvain, 423
Cain, Julien, 391
Camp David Accords, 395
Canadian Jewish Congress, 232
Cantoni, Raffaele, 84, 121, 212
Carli, Msgr. Luigi, 257, 259
Cassidy, Edward Cardinal, 288, 297, 300
Cassin, René, 53, 179, 362
Cassirer, Ernst, 15–16
Cassulo, Msgr. Andrea, 112, 117
Celli, Msgr. Claudio Maria, 304
Central Intelligence Agency (CIA), 411
Central Jewish Board of India, 414

Central Union of German Citizens of
    the Jewish Faith (Centralverein
    deutscher Staatsbürger jüdischen
    Glaubens), 18
Chapuisat, Edouard, 131, 136
Charter for a New Europe, 197
Chenevière, Jacques, 131
Chief Rabbinate of Israel, 271
children: Jewish, murdered, 122; rescue
    of, 89ff.
Chirac, Jacques, 438
Christianity, crisis of, 308ff.
Church of England, 93, 338
Churchill, Winston, 63, 140, 177
Cicognani, Msgr. Amleto, 111
Clinchy, Everet, 237
Cohen, Herrmann, 4–5, 17
Cohen, Martha, 4, 17
Cohn, E. J., 419
Cohn, Oskar, 6
Commission for Relations with Judaism
    (Vatican), 398
Commission for Religious Relations
    with the Jews (Vatican), 267, 288
Commission on Faith and Order (World
    Council of Churches), 319
Commission on Human Rights (Untied
    Nations), 53, 186, 190, 192
Commission on Mandates (League of
    Nations), 26, 28
Committee of Jewish Delegations
    (Comité des délégations juives, CDJ),
    6, 27, 166, 168
Conference of Catholic Bishops in the
    German Democratic Republic, 345
Conference of Non-Governmental
    Organizations (United Nations), 234
Conference of Non-Governmental
    Organizations in Consultative Status
    (UNESCO), 390
Conference of Presidents of Major
    American Jewish Organizations, 427

Conference on Jewish Material Claims Against Germany (Claims Conference), 347, 375, 381–383, 403
Conference on Security and Cooperation in Europe, 229–230
Conference on Soviet Jewry, 227
Congregation for Catholic Education (Vatican), 276, 298, 311
Congregation for Religious Doctrine (Vatican), 276
Congregation for the Oriental Churches (Vatican), 276
Congress of Berlin (1878), 166, 177, 384
Congress of Vienna (1815), 177
Consultation for the Church and the Jewish People (World Council of Churches), 320–323, 325, 327–328
Convention on the Prevention and Punishment of the Crime of Genocide, 194
Coordinating Secretariat (of West European national student organizations, CIA funded), 409, 411
Coughlin, Father Charles E., 58
Council of Europe, 226, 367, 395
Council of European Episcopal Conferences, 299
Cox, Oscar, 87
Cranborne, Lord, 171
Crémieux Decree (1870), 363
Cukierman, Antek (Zuckermann, Itzhak), 423
Culbertson, Paul, 43
Currie, Archbishop (Canterbury) George, 338
Cushing, Richard Cardinal, 246, 258, 262
Cuza, Alexander, 169
Cynowicz, Hersh, 414

d'Holbach, Baron, 224
Dalton, Hugh, 88
Daneels, Cardinal, 294

Darmsteter, Jean-Paul, x
Davy, Mme. M., 237
de Gaulle, Charles, 79, 149
Declaration and Convention of the Elimination of All Forms of Intolerance and Discrimination Based on Religion or Belief, 190ff.
Declaration and Convention of the Elimination of All Forms of Racial Discrimination, 190ff.
Declaration of the Allied Governments (1942), 54ff.
Decourtray, Albert Cardinal, 294
Dehousse, Fernand, 179
DELASEM (Delegation for Assistance to Jewish Emigrants from Italy), 118
Delbos, Yvon, 171
Démann, Father Paul, 236
Democratic Party (Demokratischepartei, DP), 10
Department of State (U. S.) sabotage of relief efforts, 86–87
Deutsch, Bernhard, 71
Dieye, Abdoulaye, 192
Disraeli, Benjamin, 166
Dissemond, Paul, 344, 351
Dobrynin, Anatoly, 232
Doctors' Plot (USSR), 218
Döpfner, Julius Cardinal, 254, 257
Dostoyevsky, Fyodor, 83
Dreyfus, Paul, 153
Dreyfus-Schmidt, Pierre, 361, 394
Dubnov, Simon, 371
DuBois, Josiah, 60
Dubrovnik, minyan in, 390–392
Ducret, Bernard, 405
Dunant, Henri, 127, 137
Duprey, Father Pierre, 259
Dupuy, Father Bernard, 284

East Germany. *See* German Democratic Republic.

Easterman, Alec, 110, 207, 357, 360–363, 367, 377, 419, 423
Eastern Orthodox churches and the Jews, relations between. *See* Jews and the Eastern Orthodox churches.
Eban, Abba, 273
Ebert, Friedrich, 14
Economic and Social Council (United Nations), 190ff., 204–205, 366–367
"Ecumenical Considerations on Jewish-Christian Dialogue," 323–324
Eden, Anthony, 55, 63, 66, 171
Edwards, Mark U. Jr., 332
Ehrenburg, Ilya, 216–217
Ehrlich, Ernst Ludwig, 254, 332, 339
Eichmann, Adolf, 94–95
Einsatzgruppen, 40, 215
Einstein, Albert, 17, 402
Eisendrath, Maurice, 418
Eisenhower, Dwight D., 63
Elchinger, Bishop Léon-Arthur, 246
Elting, Howard Jr., 41–42
Emergency Conference on Anti-Semitism (1947), 237f.
Ennals, John, 369
Erkelenz, Anton, 21
Eshkol, Levi, 273
Etchegaray, Archbishop Roger, 278, 291
Etter, Philippe, 136
European Association of Rabbis, 243
European Economic Community, 395
European Jewish Congress, 294, 300; Commission for Interreligious Relations, 299
Evangelical Academy of Berlin-Brandenburg (GDR), 342, 351
Evangelical Academy of West Berlin, 342–343

failure to save European Jews, 56ff.
Falconi, Carlo, 114
Favez, Jean-Claude, 49, 136, 138, 144, 159

Federation of Associations for the United Nations, 369
Federation of Jewish Communities in the German Democratic Republic, 348
Federation of Jewish Communities of Switzerland (Fédération des communautés juives de Suisse), 35, 157–159
Federation of Jewish Communities of Yugoslavia, 196, 386, 388–389
Federation of Jewish Societies of France, 102, 418
Federation of Protestant Churches of the German Democratic Republic, 342
Federici, Father Tommaso, 290
Fefer, Itzik, 216–217
Feinstein, Dr., 133
Ferrero, Guglielmo, 27
Ferrière, Suzanne, 131
"Final Solution," 45, 48–49, 54, 57, 59, 67, 73, 109, 111–112, 114, 124, 135, 137, 351
Finck, Heinrich, 351
Finestein, Israel, 402
First Pan-American Jewish Conference (1941), 420
Fischer, Maurice, 251–252
Fishman, Rabbi, 418
Flaubert, Gustav, 24
Forck, Bishop Gottfried, 343, 351
Fouché, Christian, 356–357
"Four Freedoms," 177
France, Anatole, 24
Franco, Francisco, 128
Frankenstein, Ernst, 419
Frankfurter, David, 148
Frankfurter, Felix, 44, 66
Freudenberg, Rev. Adolf, 123, 237
Frick-Cramer, Renée-Marguerite, 131
Frings, Joseph Cardinal, 253, 258
Fumagalli, Msgr. Pier, 295

Gadhafi, Muammar, 211–212
Galen, Clemens Cardinal August von, 264
Gallagher, Buell, 410
Garment, Leonard, 396
General Union of Israelites of France (Union Général des Israélites de France, UGIF), 102.
Geneva Conventions, additions to, 200–204
genocide, campaign to prevent and punish, 193ff.
Georg-Eckert-Institut für internationale Schulbuchforschung, 372
Gerbandy, P. S., 66
Gerlier, Pierre-Marie Cardinal, 118
German Democratic Republic: Protestant church role in society, 353; Riegner's relations with churches and government in, 341–353
German reparations, 375–383
German-American Bund (USA), 58
German-Soviet Non-Aggression Pact (1939), 215
Gerson, Walter, 38–39
Gjerding, Rev. Anker, 318
Godfrey, Msgr. William, 111
Goebbels, Joseph, 22, 108, 139
Goga, Octavian, 169, 172
Golan, Joseph, 358, 360–362, 364
Goldmann, Nahum, 6, 16, 26–29, 30–33, 39, 40, 51, 54, 63, 71–75, 79–80, 168–170, 176, 179, 208, 214–215, 217, 219–221, 223, 232–233, 235, 241–242, 249, 251, 261, 264, 272–274, 356, 371, 379–382, 389, 392, 396–397, 407, 417, 419, 422–424, 426–428, 431–432
Gorbachev, Mikhail, 221, 232, 346
Göring, Hermann, 20
Götterdämerung. See Twilight of the Gods.
Graduate Institute of International Studies, Geneva. 25, 27–28, 157

Grandval Plan for Morocco, 359
Grandval, Gilbert, 359
Grass, Günter, 148
Greek Orthodox churches, 339–341
Greenberg, Chaim, 70, 418
Grenoble affair, 415–416. See also Mortara affair.
Gromyko, Andrei, 217, 221
Gronemann, Sammy, 11
Grünbaum, Itzhak, 85, 418
Grüninger, Paul, 163
Guggenheim, Georg, 238
Guggenheim, Paul, 28–29, 41, 48, 50, 94, 144, 157, 159, 401
"Guidelines and Suggestions for Implementing the Conciliar Declaration Nostra Aetate (IV)," 276, 281, 283–286, 302, 312
Guisan, General Henri, 149–150, 155
Gundolf, Friedrich, 19
Gustav V, King of Sweden, 94, 117
Gustloff, Wilhelm, 148
Gysi, Klaus, 343, 345–350

Hadassah, 427
Hahn, Edith, 16
Haller, Edouard de, 136
Halperin, Jean, 374–375
Halprin, Rose 427
Haman, 31
Hamer, Msgr. Jérôme, 267
Hammerskjöld, Dag, 208, 369
Hammerstein, Franz von, 339, 342
Handler, Milton, 87–88
Harnack, Adolf von, 21
Harrison, Leland, 49, 50–51
Hashomer Hatzair, 246, 391
Hassan, Crown Prince, 362
Hay, Michael, 236
Haymann, Erwin, 158
Hebrew law, 165
Hebrew University (Jerusalem), 26, 406

Hechalutz movement, 40
Heenan, John Cardinal, 258
Heidelberg University, 18–19
Held, Adolph, 380
Hellmann, Yaacov, 132, 420–421
Helsinki Conference on European
    Security and Cooperation (1975), 183
Henriod, Henri-Louis, 124–125, 155
Hertling, Ludwig von, 250
Hertzberg, Arthur, 319
Herzl, Theodor, 302, 424–425
Heuss, Theodor, 16
Heydrich, Reinhard, 48
High Commissioner for Refugees
    (League of Nations), 30
High Commissioner for Refugees
    (United Nations), 208
Hildebrandt, Rev. Johannes, 349, 353
Hillel Foundation, 402
Himmler, Heinrich, 57, 98, 100, 103,
    105–107, 141, 313
Hindenburg, Paul von, 14, 20
Hinsley, Arthur Cardinal, 111, 119
Hitler, Adolf, 9, 20, 22, 28–29, 31, 36, 39,
    49, 64, 71, 74, 106, 110, 119, 149, 164,
    172–173
Höfer, Msgr. Joseph, 246, 264–265, 267
Hofmannsthal, Hugo von, 130
Holmes, John Haynes, 44
Holy See. *See* Vatican.
Honecker, Erich, 352
Hopkins, Harry, 108
Höppli, Kurt, 129
Horthy, Miklos, 74, 94–95, 114, 117
Huber, Max, 94, 130–131, 134, 136, 139,
    143–144
Hull, Cordell, 59, 66, 87
human rights: campaign to protect in
    UN Charter, 178; origins and
    conceptions of, 165–166; struggle for,
    164ff.
humanitarian law, 197ff.

Humboldt University (East Berlin),
    351–352
Husain, Zakir, 405, 410–413

immigration to Israel by Soviet Jews,
    220–223
indemnification for Nazi crimes by the
    German Democratic Republic,
    347–348
Independent Social Democratic Party
    (Unabhängige
    Sozialdemokratischepartei), 9
Institute for Industrial Construction
    (Fascist Italian economic
    coordinating agency), 113
Institute for Jewish Policy Research. *See*
    Institute of Jewish Affairs.
Institute of International Studies. *See*
    Graduate Institute of International
    Studies, Geneva. 25, 27–28, 157
Institute of Jewish Affairs, 82, 176–178,
    226, 231
Intergovernmental Committee on
    Refugees, 125
International Association of Jewish
    Jurists, 430
International Catholic-Jewish Liaison
    Committee, 267, 271, 278, 290–292,
    296–298, 304, 308, 311, 345
International Committee of the Red
    Cross, 44, 48–49, 56, 59, 75–78, 89,
    93–97, 103–106, 124–125, 127ff.,
    198–200, 208, 438; controversy
    relating to the Red Cross, the Red
    Crescent and Magen David Adom,
    199–200
International Council of Christians and
    Jews, 238, 350
International Council of Jewish Women,
    430
International Council of Jews and
    Christians, 350

International Covenant on Civil and
Political Rights, 185, 187–189
International Covenant on Economic,
Social and Cultural Rights, 185, 188
International Institute for Intellectual
Cooperation (L'Institut International
de Coopération Intellectuelle), 401
International Jewish Committee for
Interreligious Consultations (IJCIC),
267, 270, 275–276, 278, 294, 319–320,
323–324, 326, 328, 330–331, 335,
339–340
International Labor Organization, 193,
369, 394–395
International Student Service (Entraide
universitaire internationale),
234–235, 312–313, 396, 401, 404–411,
414–415. See also World University
Service.
International Union of Students
(communist), 408
Isaac, Jules 237–240, 307
Isaacs, Nathan, 418
Israel and the German Democratic
Republic, relations between, 347–348
Israel, creation of, 70
Israel-Arab conflicts, 439–440

Jackson, Henry, 228
Jackson, Joseph, 402
Jacobson, Victor, 49
Jacobvits, Chief Rabbi Lord Emmanuel,
335
Jarblum, Marc, 84, 90, 102, 170
Jasenovac concentration camp, 81, 387
Jaspers, Karl, 19
Jewish Agency for Palestine, 27–28, 40,
45, 49, 53, 77, 81, 85–86, 111–112,
217–219, 356, 376, 392–393, 403,
427–428
Jewish Anti-Fascist Committee
(Moscow), 147, 216–217

Jewish Autonomous Region,
Birobidzhan (USSR), 213
Jewish Boy Scouts of France, 102
Jewish communities in the Middle East
in peril, 204ff.
Jewish Community in Switzerland,
156–157
Jewish Council for Interfaith
Consultation (Israel), 276
Jewish Council for Interfaith Relations,
271
Jewish Councils (Judenräte), 100ff.
Jewish National Fund, 7–8
Jewish prisoners of war, 141ff.
Jewish refugees: and Switzerland, 151ff.,
438; in Shanghai, 56
Jewish rescue program, 67ff.
Jewish Yugoslav refugees allowed into
USA, 64
Jewish-Catholic relations, 248–249,
251ff., 272ff., 308ff.
Jewish-Christian relations, 234ff.
Jewish-German symbiosis, 7
Jews: and African Protestant Churches,
relations between, 324–327; and
Jewish emigration in North Africa,
354–365; and the Anglican Church,
relations between, 334–338; and the
Eastern Orthodox churches, relations
between, 338–341; and the Lutheran
Church, relations between, 330–334;
in Cochin, 414; in Danzig, 130–131,
174–176; in Egypt, 208–209; in
Hungary, 73–74, 126; in Hungary,
saving of, 91–97; in Libya, 209–212;
in Poland, 80, 129; in Riga, 45–46; in
Romania, 59; in Syria, 212; in the
Soviet Union, 212ff.; in Transnistria,
89; in Warsaw, 45, 51
Joint Relief Commission (International
Committee of the Red Cross),
133–134, 140

Jong, Louis de, 66
Josephsthal, Georg, 380
Jospin, Lionel, 438
Journet, Abbé Charles, 121, 237
Judaism, German, 6–7
Judenräte. See Jewish Councils.

Kaas, Msgr. Ludwig, 265
Kadelberg, Lavoslav, 196
Kahn, Jean, 299
Kallen Horace, 418
Kaltenbrunner, Ernst, 105–106, 141
Kant, Emmanuel, 7
Kaplan, Armand, 226, 360
Kaplan, Chief Rabbi Jacob, 237, 243,
    278, 416
Karasick, Rabbi Joseph, 427
Karski, Jan, 65–66
Kasztner, Reszo, 98–100
Katyn massacre, 138
Katznelson, Abracha, 199
Katz-Suchy, Juliusz, 205
Keller, Moshe, 415
Kellerman, Henry, 391
Kelsen, Hans, 25–28, 179
Kersten, Felix, 98, 100, 107
Kessel, Albrecht von, 48
Khrushchev, Nikita, 219
Kichko, Trofim, 224
Kielce pogrom, 316
Kimche, John, 357
King, Martin Luther, 225
Kirchner, Peter, 345
Kissinger, Henry, 228
Klein, Theo, 294
Klutznick, Philip, 230
Koechlin, Rev. Alphons, 124, 155
Kohl, Helmut, 196
Kopecky, Jaromir, 85–86, 103–105, 107
Kopppelmann, Isidor, 39–40
Kosygin, Aleksei, 225–226
Krauel, Wolfgang, 147

Kreisauerkreis, 124
Kristallnacht, 38, 348, 351
Kubowitzki, A. Leon, 66–67, 105,
    120–121, 422–423
Kulka, Erich, 86
Küng, Hans, 246
Kurtz, Gertrud, 153

Lack, Daniel, 192, 367
Lambert, David, 416
Lambert, Ernest, 90
Lambeth Conferences, 335–337
language, Nazi euphemistic, 58
Laor, Eran, 218
Laski, Neville, 237
Latin American Jewish Congress,
    420–421
Lavon, Pinchas, 393–394
Lazarus, Jacques, 354
League of Evangelical Churches
    (Switzerland), 155
League of Nations, 26–28, 33, 38, 63, 81,
    166–177, 366, 401; protection of
    minorities treaty, 417
League of Societies of the Red Cross and
    Red Crescent, 127
Lefebvre, Msgr. Marcel, 257
Léger, Paul-Léon Cardinal, 258
Lehmann, Msgr. Karl, 301
Lemkin, Raphael, 193
Lend-Lease program, 108–109
Lercaro, Giacomo Cardinal, 254, 257
Lessing, Gotthold Ephraim, 7
Lester, Sean, 130, 175
Levenberg, Schneier, 53–54
Levin, Shemaryahu, 400
Levy, David, 439
Lewandowski, Alfred, 17
Lewandowski, Jacob, 3
Lewandowski, Louis, 3–4, 17
Licht, Alexander, 386
Lichten, Joseph, 244

Lichtenberg, Father Bernard, 116, 345

Lichtheim, Richard, 40, 45, 49–50, 81, 111–112

Lieber, Isak, 46–47, 50

Liénart, Achille Cardinal, 246, 252–253, 258

Linton, Joseph, 54

Litvinov, Maxim, 214

Livingstone, H. B., 42

Lloyd George, David, 55

Locker, Berl, 53–54, 418

Loeffler, Kurt, 351

Long, Breckenridge, 59

Lopinot, Father Calliste, 237

Lourié, Arthur, 273

Lubetkin, Cyvia (Zivia), 423

Ludwig, Carl, 159, 161

Ludwig, Emil, 418

Lurie, Joseph, 400

Lustiger, Jean-Marie Cardinal, 294

Luther, Martin, anti-Semitism of, 330–333

Lutheran Church and the Jews, relations between. *See* Jews and the Lutheran Church, relations between.

Lutheran European Commission on the Church and the Jewish People, 330, 333

Lutz, Carl, 95

Luxembourg Agreements (1952), 375, 382–383, 407

Lwoff, André, 398

M'Bow, Amadiu-Mahtar, 374

Maccabees, 86

Macharski, Francis Cardinal, 294

Mack, Julian M., 166, 418

Magen David Adom, 395; debate over recognition of, 199–200

Magerius, Friedrich, 353

Maglione, Luigi Cardinal, 112–114, 117, 120

Maheu, René, 373

Maimonides, 375

Maiski, Ivan, 52, 214

Majdanek concentration camp, 83

Malik, Charles, 179

Malines concentration camp, Belgium, 46–47

Malvezzi, Pirello G., 113

mandates (League of Nations), 26–28

Mandel, Georges, 78

Mann, Thomas, 160, 402

Mantoux, Paul, 27

Marchioness of Reading, 419

Margulies, Emile, 168

Maritain, Jacques, 121, 237

Markish, Peretz, 216–217

Marrou, Henri-Irénée, 405

Marshall, George C., 63

Marshall, Louis, 166

Martin du Gard, Roger, 24

Martini, Carlo Maria Cardinal, 299–300

Marx, Wilhelm, 14

Masaryk, Jan, 53

Masur, Norbert, 100, 107

Maury, Philippe, 405

Mayer, Astorre, 254

Mayer, Saly, 98–99, 132, 158–160

Mazar, Benjamin, 406

Mazowiecki, Tadeusz, 237

McBride, Sean, 201

McCarthy, Joseph, 186

McClelland, Roswell, 88, 95, 104

McCloy, John J., 66

McCrae-Cavert, Samuel, 44

McDermot, Niall, 201, 397

McDonald, James G., 30

Mefkur (ship), 61

Mehta, Hansu, 179

Meir, Golda, 217, 392

Mejia, Msgr. Jorge, 288

Melchett, Lord, 419

Memorial Foundation for the Murdered Jews of Europe (Berlin), 403

Menasce, Father Jean de, 237

Mendelsohn, Moses, 346

Mendès-France, Pierre, 78–79, 205, 225, 356

Micescu, Istrate, 170–171

Michelfelt, Father Josef, 345

Mieses, Ludwig von, 27

Mikardo, Ian, 419

Mikhoels, Solomon, 216

Millia, Jamia, 405

Mitterand, François, 438

Mobberly, Sir Walter, 405

Molotov, Vyacheslav, 393

Montgomery, Bernard Law, 138

Montgomery, Ingun, 332

Montini, Msgr. Battista, 113

Montini, Msgr. Giovanni, 120–122. *See also* Pope Paul VI.

Morgenthau, Henry Jr., 60, 87–88, 108–110

Morse, Arthur D., 41, 52

Mortara affair, 263, 415. *See also* Grenoble affair.

Motzkin, Leon, 6, 27–28, 166, 400

Mujeeb, Mohammed, 405

Mulder, Prof., 320

Müller, Heinrich, 57

Muray, Sir Keith, 405

Murray, Father John Courtney, 262

Murray, Gilbert, 405

music in Berlin, 16–17

Mussolini, Benito, 74, 154, 156, 168

Musy, Jean-Marie, 98

Muszynski, Archbishop Henryk, 294

Namier, Lewis, 54

Nasser, Gamal Abdel, 208

National Liberation Front (Algerian), 364

National Union of Israeli Students, 406

Neeman, Yaacov, 441

Nehru, Jahawarlal, 209, 413

Netanyahu, Benjamin, 439

NGO Committee of the UN Economic and Social Council, 201–208

NGO Special Committee on Human Rights, 398

Niebuhr, Reinhold, 405–406

Non-governmental organizations, activities of with the UN, 366ff.

Nostra aetate, 121, 259, 263, 275–277, 279, 282, 285, 288–289, 292, 298, 302, 305, 311

"Notes on the Correct Way to Present Jews and Judaism in Preaching and Teaching in the Roman Catholic Church," 286–288, 303

Nurock, Rabbi Mordechai, 170

Odier, Lucy, 131

Oeri, Albert, 153

Oesterreicher, Msgr. John M., 246–248

Office for Catholic-Jewish Relations (Vatican), 265–267, 276

Oltramare, Georges, 148

Olympic Games in Moscow, boycott of, 231

Opoku, Kofi, 325

Oprecht, Wilhelm, 150

Oranienburg concentration camp, 20

Oranienburgerstrasse Synagogue, 3

Orbach, Maurice, 193, 419

Orsenigo, Archbishop Cesar, 114, 117

Orthodox Center of the Ecumenical Patriarchate (Geneva), 339–340

Oslo Agreements, 437

Ottaviani, Alfredo Cardinal, 251

Oualid, William, 102

Ouazzani, Hassan, 361

Ouziel, Rabbi, 418

Oxford Conference, 238

Palestine Liberation Organization (PLO), 321

Palestine Office (Geneva), 129

Palestine, 8, 23–24, 56, 61, 63, 96, 108–109, 125, 217

Palme, Olaf, 225, 405

Pan-African Conference of Churches, 325–326

Papandreou, Msgr. Damaskinos, 338–340

Pariser Tageblatt, 32

Parkes, James, 235–236

Paul, Randolph, 60

Pax Romana, 407

Pearson, Lester B., 210

Pehle, John, 60

Pekelis, Alexander, 179

Pelt, Adrien, 210

Peres, Shimon, 305, 437

Perez de Cuellar, Javier, 369

Perlzwig, Maurice, 52, 170, 210, 243, 272–274, 360, 367, 419

Pétain, Philippe, 78, 118, 149

Petitpierre, Max, 150

Pijade, Moshe, 387

Pilar, André de (Ritter Piller von Pillersdorf), 132–133

Pira, Giorgio la, 364, 396

Pobiedonosteff, 31

Poirier, Robert, 63

Polish Episcopal Commission for Relations with Judaism, 294

Polish government-in-exile, 52, 115, 138

Polish Home Army, 65

Pontifical Commission for Religious Relations with Jews, 283, 286, 288, 291–292, 294–295, 297, 305

Pontifical Commission on Justice and Peace, 276

Pope John Paul II, 192, 285–286, 288–289, 291–293, 295–298, 304–305

Pope John XXIII, 121, 192, 239–241, 253–255, 262, 286, 309

Pope Paul VI 262, 266–267, 272, 274–275, 278, 281, 285, 302,

Pope Pius X, 302

Pope Pius XII, 52, 94, 112–113, 115–116, 120–121, 237, 240–241

Popular Front government (France) 78

Potemkin, Vladimir, 215

Potter, Philippe, 322, 328

Preuss, Hugo, 8

Preysing, Bishop Konrad von, 116

Prinz, Joachim, 270, 273–274, 319

Protestant Churches and the State of Israel, 321, 324

Proust, Marcel, 24

Rabi, Vladimir, 225

Rabin, Yitzhak, 437

Rackiewicz, Władysław, 52, 116

Raczynski, Edward, 66

Radbruch, Gustav, 19

Rafael, Gideon, 392

Raiser, Konrad, 328

Rapallo, Treaty of, 14

Rappard, William, 25–29

Rathenau, Walter, 14

Ravensbrück concentration camp, inmates of evacuated to Sweden, 106

Reconstructionist Foundation (USA), 428

Red Cross. *See* International Committee of the Red Cross.

Red Cross and the Holocaust, The 49, 136

Rees, Elfan, 316

refugees, Jewish, 30

refuseniks, 228

Reiss, Anselm, 418

Relief Committee for the War-Stricken Jewish Population (Relico), 75

Remez, David, 424

Rendtorff, Rolf, 327

Representative Committee of the Jews in France (Comité représentatif des Juifs de France), 90

Representative Council of Italian Jews (New York), 156

Representative Council of Jewish Institutions in France (Conseil représentatif des institutions juives de France, CRIF), 243, 428

Rhein, Cecile, 46

Ribbentrop, Joachim von, 48, 106

Richter, Eugen, 1

Riegner Telegram, 35ff., 42, 72

Riegner, Agnes (mother of Gerhart), 3, 5, 9–11, 15

Riegner, Heinrich (father of Gerhart), 4, 6–8, 10–11, 14, 21–22

Riegner, Helene (sister of Gerhart), 11

Riegner, Marianne (sister of Gerhart), 5, 11–12

Righteous Among the Nations, 119

Rijk, Father Cornelius, 266–267, 273–275

Ritter, Joseph Cardinal, 258

Robinson, Jacob, 176, 178

Rochet, Waldeck, 225

Röhm, Ernst, 37

Romains, Jules, 24

Roman Catholic Church: and anti-Semitism, 110; and the Shoah, 110–122

Roncalli, Msgr. Angelo, 119, 239. *See also* Pope John XXIII.

Roosevelt, Eleanor, 56, 179, 225

Roosevelt, Franklin D., 42, 58, 60, 62, 66, 70–71, 74, 87, 94, 109, 117, 140, 171, 177

Röpke, Wilhelm, 27

Rosenberg, Alfred, 22

Rosenberg, Marcel, 214

Rosenfeld, Kurt, 9, 15

Rosensaft, Joseph, 379

Rosenstein, Jacques, 39

Rosenstock, Paula, 16

Rosenstock, Theodor, 16

Rosenzweig, Franz, 16

Rossano, Msgr. Pietro, 290

Rossel, Agda, 179

Rosselet (president of the Swiss parliament), 78

rote Fahne, Die, 21

Roth, Stephen, 231, 385–386, 423

Rothenberg, Hugo, 82

Rothmund, Heinrich, 151, 160–161

Rothschild, Edouard de, 90

Rotta, Msgr. Angelo, 114, 117

Rubinstein, Chief Rabbi (Poland), 418

Rudloff, Abbé Leo, 246–247

Ruffini, Ernesto Cardinal, 258

Russell, Bertrand, 225

Russian Orthodox church, 339–340

Saar Plebiscite (1934), 168–169

Šabac concentration camp, 387

Sacerdoti, Chief Rabbi Angelo, 74

Sachs, Chief Rabbi Jonathon, 338

Sachsenhausen concentration camp, 20

Saebø, Magne, 332

Safran, Chief Rabbi Alexandre, 112, 237

Sagalowitz, Benjamin, 35–36, 38–39, 158, 160–161

Saliége, Jules-Gérard Cardinal, 118

Salis, Jean Rudolf von, 139

San Francisco Conference (founding the United Nations), 177

Sandler, Richard, 171

Sandström, Emil, 198

Santa Cruz, Hernan, 179

Savary, Alain, 356

Scavizzi, Father Pirro, 113

Scelle, Georges, 27

Scheps, Samuel, 129

Schiller, Friedrich von, 7

Schindler, Rabbi Alexander, 352

Schirmer, Robert, 95–97

Schleicher, Kurt von, 37

Schmidt, Father Stefan, 245

Schneck, Georges, 402
Schneider, Rev. Peter, 334–335
Schreiner, Stefan, 341–343, 344, 349
Schulte, Eduard, 50
Schulz-Boyson, Harro, 20
Schwartzbard, Ignace (Itzhak), 52–53
Schwartzenberg, Prince Jean-Étienne, 131–132
Second Zionist Congress (1898), 424
Secretariat for the Promotion of Christian Unity (Vatican), 245–246, 248, 256, 265–267, 275, 319
Seelisburg Conference, 238
Semlin concentration camp, 387
Šeper, Franjo Cardinal, 246
Sereni, Enzo, 225
Shakhnovich, Mikhail Iosifovich, 224
Sharett, Moshe, 380–382, 391, 393, 407
Shazar, Zalman, 302, 403
Sheehan, Lawrence Cardinal, 276
Shevardnadze, Edouard, 232
Shinnar, Felix, 380
Shoah, 35ff., 290, 298, 305–307, 314, 342, 407, 419–420, 424, 432, 434–435, 438–439
Shtern, Lina, 217
Sieff, Israel, 53, 235–236, 432
Sieff, Rebecca, 53, 419
Siegman, Henry, 270, 275–276
Silberschein, Adolf, 78–79
Silverman, S. Sidney, 42–43, 53, 55, 92, 419
Simpson, Rev., 237
Singer, Israel, 232
Sisters of Our Lady of Zion, 294
Six-Day War (1967), 226
Smedt, Bishop Xavier Joseph de, 262
Smend, Rudolf, 22–23
Smith, Gerald L. K., 58
Social Democratic Party (Sozialdemokratischepartei, SPD), 9
Socialist Zionists (Poale Zion), 6

Sokolin, Vladimir, 214
Solomon, Rabbi Norman, 335
Soloveitchik, Rabbi Dov, 242, 271
Solvik, Arne, 331
Sommaruga, Cornelio, 144
Sommer, Louise, 27
Sommerstein, Emil, 418
Soviet Union, Jewish communities in, 423, 436
Sovietisch Heimland, 224
Spaak, Paul-Henri, 171
Spanish Civil War, 128
Special Committee on Palestine (United Nations), 198
Spitzer, Simche, 386
Squire, Paul, 41–43, 49–51
Stalin, Josef, 140, 215, 218
Stara Gradica concentration camp, 387
Stasi (*Staatssicherheitspolizei*, GDR), 353
Stauffer, Paul, 138
Steg, Adi, 402
Steiger, Eduard von (de), 124, 153, 160–161
Steiger, Vladimir de, 140
Stein, Boris, 214
Stein, Edith, 296–297
Steinberg, Aaron, 193, 238, 370–371, 373, 419
Stendahl, Krister, 320
Sternbuch, Elie, 98
Sternbuch, Isaac, 45
Stimson, Henry, 66
Stöhr, Martin, 327
Storch, Hillel, 98, 100, 106–107, 133
Stransky, Father, 245
Streicher, Julius, 4, 22
Struck, Hermann, 11
Struma (ship), 61
Sturz, Louis, 418
Sudetenland, 37
Suenens, Léon-Joseph Cardinal, 254, 257
Sugranyes de Franch, Ramon, 245

Suhard, Emmanuel Cardinal, 118
Suritz, Yakov Zakharovitch, 171, 214
survivor guilt, 101
Swiss Federation of Evangelical
Churches, 124
Swiss military mission to Germans on
Eastern Front, 47–48
Switzerland and Jewish refugees. *See*
Jewish refugees and Switzerland.
Switzerland: as neutral viz-à-viz
Germany, 148; military censorship in
wartime, 157–158; political
geography and neutrality of, 148ff.
Symbols, controversy relating to the Red
Cross, the Red Crescent and Magen
David Adom, 199–200
Synagogue Council of America,
270–271, 275–276, 278
Synod of European Bishops (1991),
299–301
Synod of the Evangelical Church of the
Rhineland, 334
Syrkin, Marie, 418
Szálasi, Ferenc, 95, 97
Szmitkowski, Tadeusz, 201

t'Hooft, Willem A. Visser. *See* Visser
t'Hooft, Willem A.
Tal, Uriel, 332
Talmon, Shemaryahu, 271
Tappouni, Ignace Cardinal, 258
Tardini, Msgr. Domenico, 117, 120
Tartakower, Arieh, 418
Taubes, Rabbi Zwi, 237
Tawil, Archbischop Joseph, 258
Taylor, Myron, 111–112
Tecuciano, D., 400–401
Temple, William (Archbishop of
Canterbury), 126
Tenenbaum, Joseph, 418
Terracini, Umberto, 225
Thant, U, 369

Théas, Msgr. Pierre-Marie, 118
Theresienstadt concentration camp-
ghetto, 77, 86, 124
Thieme, Karl, 236
Thorn, Gaston, 397
Tiso, Abbé, 112
Tisserand, Eugène Cardinal, 246–247
Tito, Josip, 209, 387, 424
Tittmann, Harold H., 111–113, 115
Titus, 31
Toaff, Chief Rabbi Elie, 282, 284
Tokyo Draft Convention, 129–130, 135,
143
Tolentino brothers, 390–392
Torrella, Msgr. Ramon, 291
Treaty of Versailles (1919), 149
Treaty of Vienna (1815), 149
Treitschke, Heinrich von, 4
trucks for Jews negotiations, 99
Tsarapkin, Semjon, 217
Tschoerner, Rev. Helmut, 350
Tsoudereos, Virginia, 340
Twilight of the Gods, 103

Ullmann, Fritz, 86
UNESCO. *See* United Nations
Education, Scientific and Cultural
Organization.
UN Resolution 3379 (Zionism as
racism), 396–397
Union of American Hebrew
Congregations, 428
Union of Jewish Communities of Italy,
84, 121, 212, 245, 282, 300
Union of Jewish Societies in France, 102
Union of Orthodox Jewish
Congregations of America, 427
Union of Polish Jews (in America), 65
United Nations, 365ff.; Commission on
Human Rights, 178ff.; Economic and
Social Council, 79; NGO Committee
of, 201–208; Educational, Scientific

and Cultural Organization (UNESCO), 181, 184, 193, 272, 316, 358, 369–375, 391, 395, 401, 404; Relief and Rehabilitation Administration (UNRRA), 73; Special Committee on Palestine (UNSCOP), 393

United States Holocaust Memorial Museum, 145

United Synagogue of Conservative Judaism (USA), 428

Universal Declaration of Human Rights, 358, 362; World Jewish Congress influence on creation of, 180–188

Universal Israelite Alliance of France (Alliance isréalite universelle), 362

Unterstützungsstelle, Cracow (Jewish relief agency), 77

Ury, Lesser, 15

Uth, Illa, 21

Va'ad Hahatzala (Jerusalem), 85

Vaad Leumi, 425

Vadnai, Rabbi, 237

Vajs, Albert, 388–389, 424

Valeri, Msgr. Valerio, 117–118

Valéry, Paul, 402

Vanik, Charles, 228

Vardi affair, 249–251

Vardi, Chaim, 249–251

Vatican, The, 44, 51, 55, 68, 93, 103, 110–114, 116–119, 124, 192, 241, 268, 272–273; Second Council (1965), 121, 234–235, 241, 245ff., 252–254, 268, 272–273, 282, 284, 308, 427; relations with the State of Israel, 301ff.

Veesenmayer, Edmund, 94

Vercors, 225

Veronese, Vittorio, 272–274

Versailles Peace Conference (1919), 6, 166, 177, 384

Vichy France, 41

Visser t'Hooft, Willem A., 122ff., 239, 264, 269, 312–314, 316–317

Visseur, Pierre, 237

Vogt, Pastor Paul, 153

Vossische Zeitung, 32–33

Vrba-Wetzler report, 83, 85–86, 93

Waldheim, Kurt, 25, 293, 295–296, 369

Wallenberg, Raoul, 95

Wannsee Conference, 386

war crimes trials, 83

War Refugee Board, 60, 62, 86ff., 77, 94–95, 97–98, 107–109

Warsaw Ghetto, 65, 80, 293, 295, 423

Wasserstein, Bernard, 60–61

We Remember: A Reflection on the Shoah, 305ff., 439

Weber, Alfred, 19

Weber, Max, 19

Weiss, Rabbi Samson, 427

Weissmandel, Rabbi Michael Dov, 98–99

Weizman, Ezer, 441

Weizmann, Chaim, 26, 30, 63, 166, 400

Weizsächer, Ernst von, 175

Weizsächer, Richard von, 342

Welles, Sumner, 44, 49, 51, 59, 72, 112

Werblowsky, Ambassador, 391

Werblowsky, R. J. Zwi, 271

While Six Million Died: A Chronicle of American Apathy, 41

Whitlam, Hope E., 179

Wigodor, Geoffrey, 271

Wilhelm II, 6

Willebrands, Msgr. Johannes, 259, 267, 276, 278–279, 284, 286, 288, 291, 294, 296–297, 398

Williger, Kaspar, 162

Wilson, Woodrow, 26

Wise, Rabbi Stephen, 27, 31, 42–44, 49, 51, 57, 59–60, 64, 70–72, 80, 92, 109–110, 112, 166, 171, 417, 424–425

Wolfenden, J. F., 405
Women's Zionist Organization, 419, 430
World Conference of Jewish
 Organizations (COJO), 243, 261,
 426–427
World Conference on Human Rights
 (United Nations, 1993), 183–184
World Council of Churches, 93–94,
 122ff., 161, 226, 239, 269, 271, 312ff.,
 348–349, 398; and the Palestinian
 issue, 321–322, 328; Commission on
 International Affairs, 329
World Federation of Christian Students,
 313, 407
World Federation of Former
 Servicemen, Partisans and Camp
 Detainees, 430
World Federation of Hungarian Jews,
 430
World Federation of Jewish Journalists,
 430
World Federation of Polish Jews, 430
World Health Organization (UN), 394
World Jewish Congress, passim; activities
 in Hungary, 384–386; in North Africa,
 354–365; in Yugoslavia, 386–392; and
 American Jewish organizations,
 426–428; and imperiled Jewish
 communities in Middle East,
 204–212; and Soviet Jewry, 212–228;
 and the South African Jewish
 community, 428–429; and the State of
 Israel, 392–399, 425–426; Atlantic
 City conference (1944), 177–178, 375,
 421–423; Geneva Office activities,
 75–86; influence on the creation of
 Universal Declaration of Human
 Rights, 180–188
World Lutheran Federation, 330–334

World Sephardic Federation, 430
World Student Relief, 407. *See also*
 World University Service and
 International Student Service.
World Union of Jewish Students, 400,
 402–403, 405, 407, 430
World University Service (amalgamation
 of International Student Service and
 World Student Relief, founded 1954),
 408–413
World War I, 10–11
World Zionist Organization, 49, 221,
 229, 392, 399
World-Wide Anglican Communion, 330,
 335
Wourgaft, Serge, 201
Wyler, Veit, 158
Wyman, David, 62–63

Yad Vashem, 82, 119
Yakovlev, Alexandr, 232
Yeltsin, Boris, 232
Yevtushenko, Yevgeny, 216
Young Men's Christian Association
 (YMCA), 78, 313

Zahn-Harnack, Agnes von, 21
Zevi, Tullia, 299–300
Zhadanov, Andrei A., 218
Zionism, 32, 396–399; Congress in Basel
 (1946), 160; in the Soviet Union,
 213f.; movments, 430
Zivian, Gabriel, 45–46, 50
Zuckerman, Mr., 391
Zuckermann, Itzhak. *See* Cukierman,
 Antek.
Zweig, Arnold, 11
Zyklon-B, 36, 293